Economic Growth in Theory and Practice

The International Library of Critical Writings in Economics

Series Editor: **Mark Blaug**

        Professor Emeritus, University of London
        Professor Emeritus, University of Buckingham
        Visiting Professor, University of Exeter

This series is an essential reference source for students, researchers and lecturers in economics. It presents by theme an authoritative selection of the most important articles across the entire spectrum of economics. Each volume has been prepared by a leading specialist who has written an authoritative introduction to the literature included.

  A full list of published and future titles in this series is printed at the end of this volume.

Economic Growth in Theory and Practice

A Kaldorian Perspective

Edited by

John E. King

Reader in Economics
La Trobe University, Australia

THE INTERNATIONAL LIBRARY OF CRITICAL WRITINGS IN ECONOMICS

An Elgar Reference Collection

© John E. King 1994. For copyright of individual articles please refer to the Acknowledgements.

All rights reserved. No part of this publication may be reproduced, stored in a retrieval system, or transmitted in any form or by any means, electronic, mechanical, photocopying, recording, or otherwise without the prior permission of the publisher.

Published by
Edward Elgar Publishing Limited
Gower House
Croft Road
Aldershot
Hants GU11 3HR
England

Edward Elgar Publishing Company
Old Post Road
Brookfield
Vermont 05036
USA

British Library Cataloguing in Publication Data
Economic Growth in Theory and Practice:
Kaldorian Perspective. – (International
Library of Critical Writings in
Economics)
  I. King, J. E. II. Series
  339.5

Library of Congress Cataloguing in Publication Data
Economic growth in theory and practice : a Kaldorian perspective /
  edited by John E. King.
      p. cm. — (An Elgar reference collection) (The International
  library of critical writings in economics)
  Includes bibliographical references.
  1. Kaldor, Nicholas, 1908–1986. 2. Economics—History—20th
century. 3. Economic development. I. King, J.E. (John Edward)
II. Series. III. Series: The International library of critical
writings in economics.
HB103.K36E27 1994
338.9′001—dc20   94–5155
                                                                      CIP

ISBN 1 85278 955 7

Printed in Great Britain at the University Press, Cambridge

Contents

Acknowledgements ix
Introduction xiii

PART I   NICHOLAS KALDOR
1. Nicholas Kaldor (1986), 'Recollections of an Economist', *Banca Nazionale del Lavoro Quarterly Review*, **XXXIX**, March, 3–26   3
2. Luigi L. Pasinetti (1983), 'Nicholas Kaldor: A Few Personal Notes', *Journal of Post Keynesian Economics*, **V** (3), Spring, 333–40   27
3. G.C. Harcourt (1988), 'Nicholas Kaldor, 12 May 1908–30 September 1986', *Economica*, **55**, May, 159–70   35
4. Mark Blaug (1990), 'Nicholas Kaldor, 1908–86', *Economic Theories, True or False? Essays in the History and Methodology of Economics*, Aldershot: Edward Elgar, 186–208   47
5. A.P. Thirlwall (1992), 'Talking About Kaldor', conversation with J.E. King, 14 December   70

PART II   THE CAMBRIDGE GROWTH THEORIST
6. Nicholas Kaldor (1954), 'The Relation of Economic Growth and Cyclical Fluctuations', *Economic Journal*, **LXIV** (253), March, 53–71   87
7. Nicholas Kaldor (1957), 'A Model of Economic Growth', *Economic Journal*, **LXVII** (268), December, 591–624   106
8. Nicholas Kaldor and James A. Mirrlees (1962), 'A New Model of Economic Growth', *Review of Economic Studies*, **XXIX**, 174–92   140
9. Kurt W. Rothschild (1959), 'The Limitations of Economic Growth Models: Critical Remarks on Some Aspects of Mr. Kaldor's Model', *Kyklos*, **XII** (4), 567–86   159
10. Ronald Findlay (1960), 'Economic Growth and the Distributive Shares', *Review of Economic Studies*, **XXVII** (3), June, 167–78   179
11. Nicholas Kaldor (1960), 'A Rejoinder to Mr. Findlay', *Review of Economic Studies*, **XXVII**, June, 179–81   191
12. José Encarnación, Jr. (1962), 'Overdeterminateness in Kaldor's Growth Model', *Economic Journal*, **LXXII**, September, 736–8   194
13. N. Kaldor (1962), 'Overdeterminateness in Kaldor's Growth Model: A Comment', *Economic Journal*, **LXXII**, September, 739–40   197

14. G.C. Harcourt (1963), 'A Critique of Mr. Kaldor's Model of Income Distribution and Economic Growth', *Australian Economic Papers*, **2** (1), June, 20–36 — 199
15. K. Kubota (1968), 'A Re-Examination of the Existence and Stability Propositions in Kaldor's Growth Models', *Review of Economic Studies*, **XXXV**, July, 353–60 — 216
16. B.T. McCallum (1969), 'The Instability of Kaldorian Models', *Oxford Economic Papers*, New Series, **21**, March, 56–65 — 224
17. D. Mario Nuti (1969), 'The Degree of Monopoly in the Kaldor–Mirrlees Growth Model', *Review of Economic Studies*, **XXVI**, April, 257–60 — 234
18. Joan Robinson (1969), 'A Further Note', *Review of Economic Studies*, **XXXVI**, April, 260–62 — 238
19. Nicholas Kaldor (1970), 'Some Fallacies in the Interpretation of Kaldor', *Review of Economic Studies*, **XXXVII**, January, 1–7 — 241
20. K. Kubota (1970), 'A Comment on Kaldor's Note', *Review of Economic Studies*, **XXXVII**, January, 9 — 248
21. D.G. Champernowne (1971), 'The Stability of Kaldor's 1957 Model', *Review of Economic Studies*, **38**, January, 47–62 — 249
22. F.H. Hahn (1989), 'Kaldor on Growth', *Cambridge Journal of Economics*, **13**, March, 47–57 — 265

PART III THE ROMANCE WITH VERDOORN

23. Nicholas Kaldor (1966), *Causes of the Slow Rate of Economic Growth of the United Kingdom*, Cambridge: Cambridge University Press, 1–40 — 279
24. J.N. Wolfe (1968), 'Productivity and Growth in Manufacturing Industry: Some Reflections on Professor Kaldor's Inaugural Lecture', *Economica*, New Series, **XXXV**, May, 117–26 — 319
25. Nicholas Kaldor (1968), 'Productivity and Growth in Manufacturing Industry: A Reply', *Economica*, New Series, **XXXV** (140), November, 385–91 — 329
26. Jorge M. Katz (1968), '"Verdoorn Effects", Returns to Scale, and the Elasticity of Factor Substitution', *Oxford Economic Papers*, New Series, **20**, November, 342–52 — 336
27. R.E. Rowthorn (1975), 'What Remains of Kaldor's Law?', *Economic Journal*, **85** (337), March, 10–19 — 347
28. Nicholas Kaldor (1975), 'Economic Growth and the Verdoorn Law: A Comment on Mr. Rowthorn's Article', *Economic Journal*, **85**, December, 891–6 — 357
29. R.E. Rowthorn (1975), 'A Reply to Lord Kaldor's Comment', *Economic Journal*, **85**, December, 897–901 — 363
30. John Cornwall (1976), 'Diffusion, Convergence and Kaldor's Laws', *Economic Journal*, **86**, June, 307–14 — 368

31.	A. Parikh (1978), 'Differences in Growth Rates and Kaldor's Laws', *Economica*, **45**, February, 83–91	376
32.	R.E. Rowthorn (1979), 'A Note on Verdoorn's Law', *Economic Journal*, **89**, March, 131–3	385
33.	P.J. Verdoorn (1980), 'Verdoorn's Law in Retrospect: A Comment', *Economic Journal*, **90**, June, 382–5	388
34.	A.P. Thirlwall (1980), 'Rowthorn's Interpretation of Verdoorn's Law', *Economic Journal*, **90**, June, 386–8	392
35.	P. Stoneman (1979), 'Kaldor's Law and British Economic Growth: 1800–1970', *Applied Economics*, **11** (3), September, 309–19	395
36.	J.S.L. McCombie (1980), 'On the Quantitative Importance of Kaldor's Laws', *Bulletin of Economic Research*, **32**, November, 102–12	406
37.	M. Chatterji and M. Wickens (1981), 'Verdoorn's Law – The Externalities Hypothesis and Economic Growth in the U.K.', in: D. Currie, R. Nobay and D. Peel (eds), *Macroeconomic Analysis: Essays in Macroeconomics and Econometrics*, London: Croom Helm, 405–29	417
38.	N. Kaldor (1981), 'Discussion' [of Chatterji and Wickens], in: D. Currie, R. Nobay and D. Peel (eds), *Macroeconomic Analysis: Essays in Macroeconomics and Econometrics*, London: Croom Helm: 430–33	442
39.	J.S.L. McCombie (1981), 'What Still Remains of Kaldor's Laws?', *Economic Journal*, **91**, March, 206–16	446
40.	A.P. Thirlwall (1983), 'Introduction' [to 'Symposium on Kaldor's Growth Laws'], *Journal of Post Keynesian Economics*, **V** (3), Spring, 341–4	457
41.	A.P. Thirlwall (1983), 'A Plain Man's Guide to Kaldor's Growth Laws', *Journal of Post Keynesian Economics*, **V** (3), Spring, 345–58	461

PART IV INCREASING RETURNS, DECREASING RETURNS AND CUMULATIVE CAUSATION

42.	Nicholas Kaldor (1970), 'The Case for Regional Policies', *Scottish Journal of Political Economy*, **17**, November, 337–48	477
43.	R. Dixon and A.P. Thirlwall (1975), 'A Model of Regional Growth-Rate Differences on Kaldorian Lines', *Oxford Economic Papers*, **27** (2), July, 201–14	489
44.	Nicholas Kaldor (1979), 'Equilibrium Theory and Growth Theory', in: Michael J. Boskin (ed.), *Economics and Human Welfare: Essays in Honor of Tibor Scitovsky*, New York: Academic Press, 273–91	503
45.	Nicholas Kaldor (1986), 'Limits on Growth', *Oxford Economic Papers*, New Series, **38**, July, 187–98	522

46. Ferdinando Targetti (1985), 'Growth and the Terms of Trade: A Kaldorian Two Sector Model', *Metroeconomica*, **XXXVII**, February, 79–96 — 534
47. A.P. Thirlwall (1986), 'A General Model of Growth and Development on Kaldorian Lines', *Oxford Economic Papers*, New Series, **38**, July, 199–219 — 552
48. David Canning (1988), 'Increasing Returns in Industry and the Role of Agriculture in Growth', *Oxford Economic Papers*, New Series, **40**, September, 463–76 — 573
49. H. Molana and D. Vines (1989), 'North–South Growth and the Terms of Trade: A Model on Kaldorian Lines', *Economic Journal*, **99**, June, 443–53 — 587
50. Amitava Krishna Dutt (1992), 'A Kaldorian Model of Growth and Development Revisited: A Comment on Thirlwall', *Oxford Economic Papers*, **44** (1), January, 156–68 — 598
51. A.P. Thirlwall (1992), 'A Kaldorian Model of Growth and Development Revisited: A Rejoinder to Dutt', *Oxford Economic Papers*, **44**, January, 169–72 — 611

Name Index — 615

Acknowledgements

The editor and publishers wish to thank the following who have kindly given permission for the use of copyright material.

Academic Press Ltd. for article: F.H. Hahn (1989), 'Kaldor on Growth', *Cambridge Journal of Economics*, **13**, March, 47–57.

Australian Economic Papers for article: G.C. Harcourt (1963), 'A Critique of Mr. Kaldor's Model of Income Distribution and Economic Growth', *Australian Economic Papers*, **2** (1), June, 20–36.

Banco Nazionale del Lavoro for article: Nicholas Kaldor (1986), 'Recollections of an Economist', *Banca Nazionale del Lavoro Quarterly Review*, **XXXIX**, March, 3–26.

Basil Blackwell Ltd. for articles: Nicholas Kaldor (1954), 'The Relation of Economic Growth and Cyclical Fluctuations', *Economic Journal*, **LXVI**, March, 53–71; Nicolas Kaldor (1957), 'A Model of Economic Growth', *Economic Journal*, **LXVII** (268), December, 591–624; José Encarnación, Jr. (1962), 'Overdeterminateness in Kaldor's Growth Model', *Economic Journal*, **LXXII**, September, 736–8; N. Kaldor (1962), 'Overdeterminateness in Kaldor's Growth Model: A Comment', *Economic Journal*, **LXXII**, September, 739–40; J.N. Wolfe (1968), 'Productivity and Growth in Manufacturing Industry: Some Reflections on Professor Kaldor's Inaugural Lecture', *Economica*, New Series, **XXXV**, May, 117–26; Nicholas Kaldor (1968), 'Productivity and Growth in Manufacturing Industry: A Reply', *Economica*, **XXXV** (140), November, 385–91; Nicholas Kaldor (1970), 'The Case for Regional Policies', *Scottish Journal of Political Economy*, **17**, November, 337–48; R.E. Rowthorn (1975), 'What Remains of Kaldor's Law?', *Economic Journal*, **85** (337), March, 10–19; Nicholas Kaldor (1975), 'Economic Growth and the Verdoorn Law: A Comment on Mr. Rowthorn's Article', *Economic Journal*, **85**, December, 891–6; R.E. Rowthorn (1975), 'A Reply to Lord Kaldor's Comment', *Economic Journal*, **85**, December, 897–901; John Cornwall (1976), 'Diffusion, Convergence and Kaldor's Laws', *Economic Journal*, **86**, June, 307–14; A. Parikh (1978), 'Differences in Growth Rates and Kaldor's Laws', *Economica*, **45**, February, 83–91; R.E. Rowthorn (1979), 'A Note on Verdoorn's Law', *Economic Journal*, **89**, March, 131–3; P.J. Verdoorn (1980), 'Verdoorn's Law in Retrospect: A Comment', *Economic Journal*, **90**, June, 382–5; A.P. Thirlwall (1980), 'Rowthorn's Interpretation of Verdoorn's Law', *Economic Journal*, **90**, June, 386–8; J.S.L. McCombie (1980), 'On the Quantitative Importance of Kaldor's Laws', *Bulletin of Economic Research*, **32**, November, 102–12; J.S.L. McCombie (1981), 'What Still Remains of Kaldor's Laws?', *Economic Journal*, **91**, March, 206–16; G.C. Harcourt (1988), 'Nicholas Kaldor, 12 May 1908–30 September 1986', *Economica*, **55**, May, 159–70; H. Molana and

D. Vines (1989), 'North–South Growth and the Terms of Trade: A Model on Kaldorian Lines', *Economic Journal*, **99**, June, 443–53.

Cambridge University Press for excerpt: Nicholas Kaldor (1966), *Causes of the Slow Rate of Economic Growth of the United Kingdom*, 1–40.

Chapman & Hall for article: P. Stoneman (1979), 'Kaldor's Law and British Economic Growth: 1800–1970', *Applied Economics*, **11** (3), September, 309–19.

Croom Helm for excerpts: M. Chatterji and M. Wickens (1981), 'Verdoorn's Law – The Externalities Hypothesis and Economic Growth in the U.K.', in: D. Currie, R. Nobay and D. Peel (eds), *Macroeconomic Analysis: Essays in Macroeconomics and Econometrics*, 405–29; N. Kaldor (1981), 'Discussion' [of Chatterji and Wickens], in: D. Currie, R. Nobay and D. Peel (eds), *Macroeconomic Analysis: Essays In Macroeconomics and Econometrics*, 430–33.

Helbing & Lichtenhahn Verlag for article: Kurt W. Rothschild (1959), 'The Limitations of Economic Growth Models: Critical Remarks on Some Aspects of Mr. Kaldor's Model', *Kyklos*, **XII** (4), 567–86.

Kaldor Estate for excerpt: Nicholas Kaldor (1979), 'Equilibrium Theory and Growth Theory', in: Michael J. Boskin (ed.), *Economics and Human Welfare: Essays in Honour of Tibor Scitovsky*, 273–91.

M.E. Sharpe, Inc. for articles: Luigi L. Pasinetti (1983), 'Nicholas Kaldor: A Few Personal Notes', *Journal of Post Keynesian Economics*, **V** (3), Spring, 333–40; A.P. Thirlwall (1983), 'Introduction' [to 'Symposium on Kaldor's Growth Laws'], *Journal of Post Keynesian Economics*, **V** (3), Spring, 341–4; A.P. Thirlwall (1983), 'A Plain Man's Guide to Kaldor's Growth Laws', *Journal of Post Keynesian Economics*, **V** (3), Spring, 345–58.

Metroeconomica for article: Ferdinando Targetti (1985), 'Growth and the Terms of Trade: A Kaldorian Two Sector Model', *Metroeconomica*, **XXVII**, February, 79–96.

Oxford University Press for articles: Jorge M. Katz (1968), '"Verdoorn Effects", Returns to Scale, and the Elasticity of Factor Substitution', *Oxford Economic Papers*, New Series, **20**, November, 342–52; B.T. McCallum (1969), 'The Instability of Kaldorian Models', *Oxford Economic Papers*, New Series, **21**, March, 56–65; R. Dixon and A.P. Thirlwall (1975), 'A Model of Regional Growth Rate Differences on Kaldorian Lines', *Oxford Economic Papers*, **27** (2), July, 201–14; Nicholas Kaldor (1986), 'Limits on Growth', *Oxford Economic Papers*, **38**, New Series, July, 187–98; A.P. Thirlwall (1986), 'A General Model of Growth and Development on Kaldorian Lines', *Oxford Economic Papers*, New Series, **38**, July, 199–219; David Canning (1988), 'Increasing Returns in Industry and the Role of Agriculture in Growth', *Oxford Economic Papers*, New Series, **40**, September, 463–76; Amitava Krishna Dutt (1992), 'A Kaldorian Model of Growth and Development Revisited: A Comment on Thirlwall', *Oxford Economic Papers*, **44** (1), January, 156–68;

A.P. Thirlwall (1992), 'A Kaldorian Model of Growth and Development Revisited: A Rejoinder to Dutt', *Oxford Economic Papers*, **44**, January, 169–72.

Review of Economic Studies Ltd. for articles: Ronald Findlay (1960), 'Economic Growth and the Distributive Shares', *Review of Economic Studies*, **XXVII** (3), June, 167–78; Nicholas Kaldor (1960), 'A Rejoinder to Mr. Findlay', *Review of Economic Studies*, **XXVII**, June, 179–81; Nicholas Kaldor and James A. Mirrlees (1962), 'A New Model of Economic Growth', *Review of Economic Studies*, **XXIX**, 174–92; K. Kubota (1968), 'A Re-Examination of the Existence and Stability Propositions in Kaldor's Growth Models', *Review of Economic Studies*, **XXXV**, July, 353–60; D. Mario Nuti (1969), 'The Degree of Monopoly in the Kaldor–Mirrlees Growth Model', *Review of Economic Studies*, **XXXVI**, April, 257–60; Joan Robinson (1969), 'A Further Note', *Review of Economic Studies*, **XXXVI**, April, 260–62; Nicholas Kaldor (1970), 'Some Fallacies in the Interpretation of Kaldor', *Review of Economic Studies*, **XXXVII**, January, 1–7; K. Kubota (1970), 'A Comment on Kaldor's Note', *Review of Economic Studies*, **XXXVII**, January, 9; D.G. Champernowne (1971), 'The Stability of Kaldor's 1957 Model', *Review of Economic Studies*, **38**, January, 47–62.

A.P. Thirlwall for his own article: (1992), 'Talking About Kaldor', conversation with J.E. King, 14 December.

Every effort has been made to trace all the copyright holders but if any have been inadvertently overlooked the publishers will be pleased to make the necessary arrangements at the first opportunity.

In addition the publishers wish to thank the Library of the London School of Economics and Political Science and the Marshall Library of Economics, Cambridge University for their assistance in obtaining these articles.

Introduction

Nicholas Kaldor (1908–86) was one of the most original and inventive economists of the twentieth century, whose contributions to the analysis of economic growth spanned three decades and profoundly influenced the treatment of growth both by Post Keynesians and (less readily acknowledged) by mainstream 'new growth theorists'. This book is in four parts. The first gives an overview of Kaldor's life and work, while the remainder deals with the three phases of his thinking on growth. Intellectually, Kaldor was utterly unable to stand still. He spent the 1950s and early 1960s constructing elaborate formal models of steady-state growth in a one-sector economy. By the mid-1960s he became convinced that this was a mistake, and turned to the relationships between agriculture, manufacturing and the service industries as the key to understanding the process of growth. Then, towards the end of his life, he rejected the single-country, closed economy models of this second phase, and came to emphasize the world economy and the critical importance of export demand. Although his ideas on growth were constantly changing, Kaldor never faltered on some issues: the basic correctness of Keynesian macroeconomics, the irrelevance of perfect competition, the importance of realism and attention to policy objectives in economic theorizing. For him, growth was essentially a practical, not merely a theoretical question.

Nicholas Kaldor

Born in Hungary, Kaldor studied at the London School of Economics in the late 1920s and spent the great majority of his working life in London and Cambridge. In Chapter 1 he admits an early attraction to the ideas of Lionel Robbins, from whom he acquired a (temporary) taste for general equilibrium theory, and the more profound influence of the US economist, Allyn Young. From Young, Kaldor inherited a distrust of abstract systems cut off from reality and an abiding interest in imperfect competition and the implications of increasing returns.

During the Second World War, the LSE was evacuated to Cambridge, bringing Kaldor into much closer contact with Joan Robinson, Richard Kahn, Piero Sraffa and their circle. After four years working for the United Nations in Geneva, Kaldor returned to Cambridge in 1949 as a Fellow of King's College, and remained there for the rest of his life. His involvement in growth theory, he recalls, dates from about this time, with the publication of Roy Harrod's *Towards a Dynamic Economics* and – he might have added – the debates at Cambridge which were to culminate in the publication, in 1956, of Robinson's *Accumulation of Capital*.

In theoretical terms, Harrod's problem was to extend the *General Theory* to the long run, in which investment raises the capital stock as well as aggregate demand, thereby increasing future productive capacity. In assessing the first phase of his own thinking on growth, Kaldor lays claim to two original contributions. One is the notion of 'embodied' technical progress: new techniques cannot normally be grafted onto existing machines but require new investment, making the rate of growth of output per worker a positive function of the rate of growth of capital per worker. (Kaldor is most insistent that this relationship cannot be treated as the first derivative of a static neoclassical production function.) The other is his celebrated macroeconomic theory of income distribution, in which the shares of wages and profits depend upon the investment-income ratio and the savings propensities of workers and capitalists. This latter idea had been foreshadowed, Kaldor admits, by Keynes in the *Treatise*, and by Kalecki, but neither man had fully developed his intuitions. Kaldor distinguishes the 'Mark I', 'Mark II' and 'Mark III' versions of his model of growth, building on these insights; 'Mark I' is reprinted here as Chapter 7 and 'Mark II' as Chapter 8.

Then Kaldor explains his increasing dissatisfaction with these early models, and relates the change of mind which led him to identify four principal weaknesses in them. They lack micro-foundations, specifically for oligopoly, which he had come to regard as the typical market form. They relied on a Harrodian concept of the 'natural' rate of growth, which is valid only for the world, viewed as a whole; for any individual national economy, capacity constraints can be removed by importing labour or capital. One-sector models cannot deal with structural change, above all with the important and complex relations between agriculture and manufacturing industry. Finally, a recognition of the significance of cumulative causation led Kaldor to emphasize the spatial aspects of economic growth and the role of 'growth points'. These ideas dominated the second and third phases of Kaldor's thinking on growth, although he died without being able to set out the comprehensive formal model to which he had aspired.

A personal account of Kaldor and his work is provided by Luigi Pasinetti, a former student and colleague, in Chapter 2. As Pasinetti points out, Kaldor never had very much of a following in the United States, his hostility to both general equilibrium theory and Marxism isolating him from the two rival academic orthodoxies. His 'exuberant, egocentric, and undisciplined character' (reprinted as p. 29) may not have helped, any more than the fluidity of his ideas and his related inability (or unwillingness) to write a systematic treatise. Pasinetti emphasizes the importance of Kaldor's distribution model, which he himself has done much to defend and develop. Here Kaldor reverses the direction of causality in classical political economy: instead of a subsistence wage determining profits as a residual, profits – driven by investment decisions – are now exogenous, and wages become the residual magnitude. Pasinetti also describes Kaldor's support for commodity price stabilization schemes, a subject which constituted a major component of his 'third phase' thinking on economic growth, as will be seen in Part IV.

Chapter 3 is an obituary by Geoffrey Harcourt, briefly (and disastrously) a graduate student of Kaldor's and subsequently a long-term colleague and friend. Harcourt writes appreciatively of the pre-war Kaldor, initially an orthodox economist with interests in the theory of the firm and the stability of equilibrium, and then an enthusiastic Keynesian writing on the trade cycle, the economics of speculation and the Beveridge Plan. After 1945, Harcourt explains, Kaldor became a severe critic not only of mainstream theory but also of Keynes, whom he attacked for treating the money supply as exogenous and neglecting increasing returns. Kaldor's own later work was often disparaged. He became 'less painstaking and careful in his arguments' (reprinted as p. 36), less familiar with the contemporary literature, and less comfortable with the growing mathematization of theoretical economics, while Keynesians also took issue with his 'quixotic conviction' that there must always be full employment (reprinted as p. 41). Accepting the justice of these criticisms, Harcourt also affirms the many virtues of Kaldor's approach, not least his focus on cumulative causation and the relations between primary and secondary industry, and his assertion that models of growth must always try to explain the historically-given 'stylized facts' of actual growth experience.

A rather less sympathetic appraisal is offered by Mark Blaug in Chapter 4. After an early 'critical and polemical' stage, Blaug suggests, Kaldor's career falls into two parts, separated by his break with steady-state growth theory and his discovery of increasing returns. Kaldor began with the 1956 model of income distribution, adding in the following year the technical progress function in response to criticisms that he had wrongly followed Harrod in assuming an arbitrarily-fixed capital-output ratio, and supplementing it with a mark-up pricing rule and an investment function (see Chapter 7). Successive reformulations of the latter led to the final (1962) model, reprinted here as Chapter 8. 'Kaldor', Blaug writes, 'is a post-Keynesian economist in that he rejects many if not all the standard assumptions of the neoclassical approach to economic growth: optimising behaviour, smoothly adjusting competitive markets, continuous factor substitution, aggregate production functions, malleable capital, a single saving function, the dependence of investment on the available flow of savings, and the like' (reprinted as p. 54). Only the postulate of full employment separated him from the Post Keynesian tradition. But equilibrium, in these early Kaldorian models, required that labour productivity grow at the same rate as capital per worker, and Kaldor could never specify the precise mechanism which produced this outcome. Moreover, Blaug objects, most of his supposed 'stylized facts' proved on closer inspection not to be facts at all.

Kaldor's recognition of these difficulties, Blaug continues, led him to abandon steady-state growth theory in the mid-1960s. In his 1966 inaugural lecture (Chapter 23) he enunciated three laws which highlighted structural change in a multi-sector economy as the fundamental determinant of growth. The first law expressed the rate of growth of GNP as a function of the rate of growth of manufacturing output, a relationship attributable either to disguised unemployment in agriculture and services or to dynamic economies of scale in manufacturing. Kaldor's second law, which he owed to the Dutch economist P.J. Verdoorn, made productivity growth in manufacturing a function of manufacturing output growth. Blaug discusses this relationship at some length, pointing to the many problems of interpretation which arise, and in particular to the difficulty of determining the direction of causation. The third law, Blaug explains, expresses the growth of GNP as a function of the rate of labour transference from non-manufacturing to manufacturing, and is again associated with the existence of dynamic economies of scale in secondary industry.

As will be seen in Parts III and IV of this book, Kaldor's growth laws provoked a vigorous controversy, and his own thinking on them underwent considerable change. Blaug comments that Kaldor's eventual repudiation of equilibrium theorizing in economics was a direct result of his reflection on the causes of international differences in growth rates and his related rejection of the standard neoclassical convexity postulates (see also Chapter 44). For Blaug this is going much too far, since it would eliminate Keynesian macro theory along with orthodox microeconomics, leaving Kaldor's analysis of growth as the only intellectually respectable branch of the discipline. Kaldor's, he concludes, was 'essentially a one-man research programme' (reprinted as p. 67). There was no Kaldorian school, and very few disciples.

One economist who has been greatly influenced by Kaldor is his biographer, A.P. Thirlwall, whose views on Kaldorian economics are expressed in a December 1992 interview (Chapter 5). After noting Kaldor's early work in imperfect competition theory, welfare economics and macroeconomic analysis, Thirlwall documents the evolution of his ideas on income distribution, which Kaldor attributed (rather surprisingly) to the neoclassical trade theorist Harry Johnson. His dissatisfaction with steady-state growth theory, Thirlwall explains, stemmed from its excessively abstract and unreal character and from the lack of policy implications following from it. Kaldor turned instead to what Thirlwall terms the 'applied economics of growth', where his thinking was conditioned by two spells as adviser to Labour governments and his increasing concern at the poor growth record of the contemporary British economy. At the analytical level, Kaldor's romance with Verdoorn's law was not a happy one, Thirlwall suggests; he was, apparently, unaware of its neoclassical foundations. As a policy tool, however, the Kaldorian growth laws proved to be very effective, serving as the theoretical basis for the Selective Employment Tax, a measure which might have contributed significantly to the revitalization of British manufacturing if appropriate demand management policies had been adopted at the time.

Thirlwall then shows how the wretched experience of the British economy in the late 1960s led Kaldor to revise his ideas concerning the constraints on economic growth, moving away from his earlier concentration on the supply of labour and focussing on the balance of payments and the growth of export demand (see Chapters 42 and 45). The failure of the 1967 devaluation, and the sombre implications of Britain's impending entry into the European Economic Community, accelerated the shift in his thinking, which by the beginning of the 1970s was complete. Kaldor now argued that exports represented the only genuinely autonomous component of aggregate demand, and that a variant of Harrod's 'supermultiplier' could be devised to demonstrate that it was the rate of growth of export demand which set the real limit to Britain's economic growth. Thirlwall's own models of export-constrained growth owe much to this Kaldorian insight (see Chapters 47 and 51).

The Cambridge Growth Theorist

Kaldor's point of entry into the analysis of economic growth was a 1954 paper dealing with the relationship between growth and cyclical fluctuations (Chapter 6). He begins by surveying the literature on the trade cycle, to which he had made an early contribution in 1940. Contemporary Keynesian models of the cycle were static, generating regular fluctuations but no trend. This could be rectified by introducing population growth and technical change, as Harrod had done in what Kaldor rather dismissively describes as his 'illuminating piece of algebra' (reprinted as p. 98), but the resulting trend was not properly explained. The classical belief that 'thrift' determines the rate of growth could no longer be sustained, given Keynes's demonstration that saving was endogenous, and could in some circumstances actually hinder growth.

Following Schumpeter, Kaldor suggests that entrepreneurship is the critical factor, and closer attention must be paid to the incentives for risk-taking and the pursuit of profit. Prolonged scarcity of labour encourages labour-saving innovations, while shortages of physical capacity provide the impetus for capital accumulation. Thus the trend and the cycle are intimately related, for the volatility of entrepreneurial expectations dictates the amplitude of the cycle, and it is the strength and duration of the boom that determine the longer-term trend rate of growth. This implies, Kaldor argues, that Harrod's 'warranted' and 'natural' rates are interdependent: if the warranted rate exceeds the natural rate of growth for any considerable period, this will lead to an increase in the natural rate by stimulating innovation (and perhaps also faster population growth). 'The same forces therefore which produce violent booms and slumps will also tend to produce a high trend-rate of progress', Kaldor concludes, 'though the connection between the two is far too complex to be reducible (at present) to a single mechanical model' (reprinted as p. 104).

In fact, Kaldor made several attempts during the course of the next decade to set out a formal model of growth in which technical progress occupied centre stage. His first effort – described in Chapter 1 as his 'Mark I model' – appeared in 1957 (Chapter 7). Kaldor begins by asserting that any acceptable theory of growth must be able to explain the 'stylized facts' of long-run capitalist development: constant shares of wages and profits, a constant capital-output ratio and, following from this, a constant rate of profit on capital. His model differs from Harrod's in several ways. The most controversial is Kaldor's assumption of full employment, which he makes not (primarily) on empirical grounds but for theoretical reasons: a Keynesian 'under-employment equilibrium' is not consistent, he argues, with a dynamic equilibrium of steady growth. Kaldor also refuses to make the conventional distinction between increases in productivity resulting from higher capital per worker and those brought about by technical change. The embodied nature of technical progress means that the rate of absorption of new techniques depends on the pace of capital accumulation. Hence Kaldor dismisses as 'arbitrary and artificial' (reprinted as p. 111) the neoclassical distinction between movements along a 'production function' and shifts in the 'production function' (the inverted commas are Kaldor's own, and indicate his profound suspicion of mainstream analysis).

He replaces the neoclassical production function with a technical progress function (reprinted as p. 112, Fig. 1) which incorporates both innovation and the accumulation of capital, and relates the growth of labour productivity to the rate of growth of capital per worker (measured in tons of steel). Its shape and position reflect 'the flow of new ideas'. Equilibrium requires that productivity grows at the same rate as capital per worker, so that the capital-output ratio is constant and technical change is neutral. Kaldor also specifies an investment function, derived from entrepreneurial decisions aimed at bringing the actual capital stock into line with the desired capital stock (the latter maintaining a constant capital-output ratio). He writes investment as a function of the change in output and the change in the profit rate in the previous period. Kaldor assumes that monetary policy plays 'a purely passive role' (reprinted as p. 117), and deliberately ignores the orthodox relationships between the relative prices of capital and labour and the choice of techniques.

The completed model is set out for two cases, with first a constant and then a growing population. On the assumption of zero population growth, Kaldor demonstrates that the long-run equilibrium growth rate depends only upon the parameters of the technical progress function, and not at all on the savings propensities of capitalists and workers or on the characteristics of the investment function. In Harrod's terminology, Kaldor's system tends towards the equality of the warranted and natural rates of growth, getting there partly through the adjustment of the warranted rate and partly because the natural rate changes. He further shows that the equilibrium rate of profit is given by the growth rate divided by the propensity to save out of profits (equation 9.2, reprinted as p. 128). This is one of the fundamental 'Cambridge equations' of economic growth.

Where the population is growing, Kaldor's analysis is essentially Malthusian. He devotes some effort to establishing the stability conditions of the model, which has important implications for the ability of underdeveloped countries to escape from a low-level equilibrium trap. These questions were to reappear in the world economy or 'North-South' models that Kaldor enunciated in the 1970s and early 1980s. In the 1957 paper, however, he uses them as the basis for a very contentious speculation as to the economic history of advanced capitalist nations. In the first stage of their development, which Marx had analysed but not fully understood, technical progress is not powerful enough to offset the effects of rapid population growth, and wages remain at subsistence level. The second stage begins when technical change overtakes population growth, allowing real wages to rise at the same rate as labour productivity. Kaldor concludes on a cautionary note. Although full employment is necessary for stable equilibrium growth, this does not guarantee that it will be achieved. Apparently influenced by Michal Kalecki and Josef Steindl, Kaldor points to the possibility that rigid profit margins will induce over-saving, and thereby cause major breakdowns in the growth process, with heavy unemployment and temporary stagnation.

Such anxieties were less evident in 1962 when Kaldor made his last major incursion into the formal analysis of steady-state growth. In his 'Mark II' model (Chapter 8), Kaldor and his co-author James Mirrlees modify the technical progress and investment functions, introduce obsolescence and the physical depreciation of equipment, and avoid the concept of 'capital' altogether, operating only with the value of current gross investment and its change over time. They assume that entrepreneurial motivation is dominated by the maximization of growth, subject only to a minimum rate of return, and redefine the technical progress function (reprinted as p. 142) as the relationship between the rate of growth of labour productivity and the rate of growth of investment per capita. Accordingly, equilibrium is respecified to require equality between these two rates of growth. Kaldor and Mirrlees report the results of a numerical simulation where 'reasonable' values of the parameters, drawn from the US in the 1950s, are inserted into the model. Policies aimed at increasing the rate of growth, they conclude, must somehow stimulate the technical dynamism of the economy. This requires not only more scientific education and more expenditure on research, but also (and especially) better management which is more receptive to technological change.

A very large critical literature soon grew up around Kaldor's analysis of equilibrium growth. In an early comment Kurt Rothschild (Chapter 9) objects less to the formal properties of the models than to their unreality. Kaldor has restricted his analysis to a very small number of variables, Rothschild observes, and has presented their functional relationships in an over-simplified manner. The savings propensities of capitalists and workers, for example, are not constant but change over time, partly in response to the way in which the existing distribution of income was arrived at; Kaldor's equilibria are therefore path-dependent (though Rothschild does not, of course, use this more modern term). He has also unduly neglected the historical, social and institutional factors which were so prominent in the growth theories of Malthus and Marx, and is seriously mistaken in his full employment assumption. Kaldor's models are nonetheless valuable, Rothschild suggests, because they clearly expose the limitations of steady-state theorizing.

Ronald Findlay's critique of Kaldor (Chapter 10) is quite different. Findlay directs his analysis to Kaldor's 1956 model of income distribution, but the broader implications for the theory of growth emerge very clearly from his article. He proposes a synthesis of the macroeconomic and neoclassical approaches to relative shares, with the relative quantities and prices of labour and capital being fundamental to the argument, and technology now an endogenous variable. Kaldor's is simply a special case of marginal productivity theory, Findlay maintains, and his conclusions do not necessarily hold more generally. In his reply, Kaldor yields nothing (Chapter 11). He lists at the outset the 'unreal assumptions' that are needed for the neoclassical elasticity of substitution to be successfully incorporated into a model of economic growth. Most important is the absence of technical change. Foreshadowing the later shift in his thinking, Kaldor concludes that 'Technical progress is, in fact, the same kind of thing (though more complex) as increasing return[s] to scale' (reprinted as p. 193). This alone is enough, he argues, to render incoherent the very notion of a neoclassical production function.

Kaldor and Findlay were separated by a wide conceptual gulf. Much narrower criticisms could also be made of the logical structure of Kaldor's analysis. Thus José Encarnación, Jr. (Chapter 12) demonstrates that the 1957 model of Chapter 7 is over-determined, with eight supposedly independent equations to determine seven independent variables. The difficulty, he suggests, lies with Kaldor's investment function, which should be reformulated to eliminate the dependence of investment on expectational, as opposed to actual, magnitudes. Kaldor (Chapter 13) accepts the criticism, but points out that it does not apply to the 1962 Kaldor–Mirrlees model (Chapter 8), in which a radically different investment function is employed.

In Chapter 14 Geoffrey Harcourt assesses a number of Kaldor's growth models from the period 1957–62, including the so-called 'Mark II' models which have been omitted, for reasons of space, from the present volume. Harcourt extends Kaldor's analysis to a two-sector model, making an explicit distinction between consumer goods and investment goods and deriving the short-period conditions for the prices of the two goods which must be met if planned investment is to become actual investment by the end of the period. This, he argues, requires significantly differential entrepreneurial behaviour in the two sectors, and it is doubtful whether Kaldor's distributive mechanism could in fact work in the short period. This leads Harcourt to query Kaldor's insistence that full employment is the only possible outcome for a growing economy, and to suggest instead that both an under-employment equilibrium and full employment with inflation are more probable situations. 'Finally', Harcourt objects, 'it is hard to see the logic of using the distributive mechanism which implicitly assumes full employment to ensure that the economy gets to full employment' (reprinted as p. 215). Kaldor never replied to these criticisms in print.

A much more narrow appraisal is provided by K. Kubota (Chapter 15), who demonstrates that in the 1957 model the growth rate is not, as Kaldor had claimed, generally stable. In Chapter 16 B.T. McCallum goes further than this with his claim that 'instability is a pervasive feature of Kaldorian models' (reprinted as p. 224). Capital accumulation will occur at a rate differing progressively from the sustainable rate, and growth equilibria will therefore diverge from the steady-state path. McCallum demonstrates that instability persists even if the investment function is revised and the technical progress function is replaced by a more orthodox production function; it results from Kaldor's fundamental distributive mechanism. Mario Nuti (Chapter 17) identifies a further problem, this time specific to the 1962 model of Chapter 8, where Kaldor and Mirrlees assume both imperfect competition and equality between the real wage and the marginal product of labour. But, Nuti points out, this equality requires perfect competition in the product market. Hence the Kaldor–Mirrlees rule governing the scrapping of old equipment – that quasi-rents must fall to zero – may no longer apply.

Kaldor's Cambridge colleague, Joan Robinson, objects (in Chapter 18) that the level of employment remains unexplained in the Kaldor–Mirrlees model, where a confusion exists between excess capacity relative to labour and excess capacity in relation to demand. The latter phenomenon, she argues, is a normal feature of imperfect competition so long as future demand cannot be precisely predicted. Kaldor responds to these three critics in Chapter 19. Kutoba's stability condition was already present in the 1957 model, he argues (and in Chapter 20, Kubota accepts the substance of this claim). Nuti's formal criticism of the model is correct, but its importance depends upon the actual magnitude of the average degree of monopoly and on its variation between firms in any given market. Turning to Robinson, Kaldor insists that she is mistaken. The motives inducing firms to operate with excess capacity are equally strong in conditions of full employment, so that the existence of surplus capacity cannot be regarded as evidence of deficient demand. Kaldor remains quite unrepentant with respect to his full employment postulate.

In Chapter 19 (reprinted as p. 241), as previously in a very generous footnote to his 1957 paper (reprinted as Chapter 7, p. 106, n. 1), Kaldor thanked D.G. Champernowne for mathematical assistance. The penultimate article reprinted in this section of the book is Champernowne's own investigation of the conditions under which the 1957 model will be stable (Chapter 21). The problem lies with the investment function, Champernowne suggests, and can be solved by reformulating the function to reduce the influence of current profitability on the level of investment. Kaldor, however, had by now lost interest in these highly formal questions, and his own attention was focussed elsewhere.

Soon after Kaldor's death Frank Hahn (Chapter 22) wrote a tribute in which he acknowledged that in this first phase of his thinking on growth Kaldor had been 'more interesting and adventurous than the rest of us who stuck to the straight and narrow of neoclassical theory' (reprinted as p. 265). In both his steady-state analyses and his subsequent, more applied work, he had concentrated upon innovation, learning and dynamic increasing returns, running so far ahead of both theoretical tools and empirical support that a satisfactory appraisal of his ideas was still impossible. Despite its formal defects, Hahn suggests, Kaldor's technical progress function was a real analytical achievement, although there is 'a soft neoclassical underbelly' (reprinted as p. 273) even to his 1962, 'Mark III', model of growth.

The Romance with Verdoorn

In 1966 Kaldor was appointed to a personal chair at Cambridge. His inaugural lecture (Chapter 23) begins by documenting Britain's poor growth performance in comparison with other advanced capitalist countries. He attributes this to the fact that the British economy had been the first to achieve 'maturity', in the sense that output per head was roughly equal in all sectors. Kaldor regresses the growth of GDP on the growth of manufacturing output in twelve countries between 1953–4 and 1963–4, finding a positive relationship. There is also a striking correlation between the overall growth rate and the excess of manufacturing over non-manufacturing growth. This, Kaldor argues, can be explained by the existence of economies of scale. He cites Adam Smith, Marshall and Allyn Young on the significance of increasing returns in manufacturing, which, he claims, underpin Verdoorn's Law. In this context it is significant that Verdoorn's relationship does not apply to agriculture, where diminishing returns prevail, nor to the service industries, where economies of scale (if they exist at all) are much less important than in the secondary sector.

Kaldor claims that the economy is constrained by supply factors, not by demand, and that it is, above all, the supply of labour which imposes an effective limit on the growth rate. Rapid growth, he maintains, depends on the availability of surplus labour – disguised unemployment – in agriculture. Britain's reserves of agricultural labour had already dried up, as could be seen from the very small proportion of the working population still employed in primary production and the approximate equality in output per capita in agriculture and industry. The resulting deceleration of growth is a universal law, Kaldor suggests, which will soon operate in the USA, Belgium and Germany as the structure of these economies approaches that of Britain. He has surprisingly little to say about the policy implications of his analysis, other than to indicate the benefits of increased international specialization, so that resources could be concentrated in fewer branches of industry whose economies of scale could be exploited to the full.

J.N. Wolfe objects, in Chapter 24, that Kaldor's evidence is inconclusive and his policy proposals misguided. Wolfe was the first, but by no means the last, to argue that Kaldor's regression equations are wrongly specified and his interpretation of them questionable. Capital is neglected as a source of growth, Wolfe claims; the cyclical component in productivity movements is ignored; and Kaldor's confidence with respect to increasing returns is not supported by the broader literature on this question. Wolfe denies that labour shortages constrain manufacturing output, pointing to the ability of several industries to expand employment very rapidly in the early 1960s without above-average job vacancy rates. Alternative ways of stimulating manufacturing output, should this be thought desirable, include encouraging saving and restricting government expenditure in order to promote exports and investment demand. 'It seems a curious coincidence', Wolfe concludes rather tartly, 'that these orthodox policy proposals should flow from Kaldor's unorthodox thesis' (reprinted as p. 328). In his reply (Chapter 25), Kaldor insists that the rate of growth of industrial production depends upon the rate at which workers are transferred from the 'labour surplus' sectors, agriculture and services, to manufacturing. He denies that capital is a serious constraint on growth, since an increase in investment spending generates the necessary savings via a rise in the profit share. For Kaldor rapid capital accumulation is a symptom of rapid growth, not the cause.

A neoclassical perspective on Verdoorn's Law is provided by J.M. Katz in Chapter 26. Using a CES production function, Katz demonstrates that the coefficient estimated in the Verdoorn relationship depends upon both the elasticity of substitution and the scale parameter. It follows that the Verdoorn coefficient sheds light on the existence of increasing returns to scale only in special cases. In particular, Katz argues, differences between sectors in the Verdoorn coefficient do not entail corresponding differences in returns to scale, unless the elasticity of substitution is the same in all sectors. In a long footnote (reprinted as p. 337, n. 1) Katz concedes that his empirical evidence, which is drawn from time-series data on Argentinian manufacturing, has little bearing on Kaldor's thesis. But the theoretical considerations, he maintains, are of general validity.

In Chapter 27, R.E. Rowthorn pronounces what was intended as a death sentence on 'Kaldor's Law'. Kaldor's econometric procedures are defective, Rowthorn argues, and his results rely very heavily on one outlying case: productivity growth in Japan exceeded its expected level by several percentage points, and its exclusion would greatly reduce the degree of empirical support for Kaldor's argument. Replying to Rowthorn (Chapter 28), Kaldor reveals very clearly that his ideas are once again, nine years after the inaugural lecture, in a state of flux. He has now abandoned the position that Britain's poor growth performance can be explained by labour shortages resulting from 'economic maturity', recognizing that there are substantial reserves of labour outside agriculture, in the service sector. Much more fundamentally, Kaldor now argues that growth is constrained by demand, not by resources. Where does this leave the Verdoorn relationship? Kaldor is unclear on this question, refusing to repudiate his claim that growth in GDP is strongly correlated with growth in manufacturing output, but apparently undecided as to whether this reflects increasing returns to scale or simply the existence of surplus labour in agriculture or services.

The hornet's nest that he had disturbed continued to buzz noisily for several years. Kaldor had seemed to imply that manufacturing output growth was exogenously determined. For Rowthorn (Chapter 29), this is implausible, since faster productivity growth in manufacturing industry will increase the rate of growth of manufacturing output through its effects on relative prices, both domestically and by stimulating export demand. Rowthorn concludes that the relationships between output, productivity and employment growth are so complex that they must be estimated simultaneously. In John Cornwall's attempt to do so (Chapter 30), manufacturing output growth is regarded as demand-constrained, with manufacturing employment responding passively to increases in the demand for labour. Cornwall suggests that international differences in the rate of growth of manufacturing output can be explained by differential rates of diffusion of best-practice (effectively US) technology in the two postwar decades. His results are broadly confirmed by Parikh (Chapter 31), who is very critical of the procedures adopted by Kaldor and Rowthorn. Strangely, neither Cornwall nor Parikh has an estimating equation for productivity growth, although this variable does appear in the formal structure of Parikh's two models (equations (6) and (10), reprinted as p. 377).

Rowthorn returns to the Verdoorn relationship in Chapter 32, where he argues that since the Verdoorn coefficient is derived from a static Cobb–Douglas production function, and includes the effects of labour supply conditions, it cannot be used to draw any conclusions about returns to scale. There is no technical progress in Verdoorn's original model, Rowthorn claims, and hence its use provides no evidence of dynamic economies of scale. Verdoorn himself (in Chapter 33) puts his original article into its contemporary context, explains how his subsequent work has improved on it, and concludes that the eponymous law is 'much less generally valid than I was led to believe in 1949' (reprinted as p. 391). In Chapter 34, however, A.P. Thirlwall defends Verdoorn against many of Rowthorn's objections, demonstrating that Rowthorn had misspecified the Verdoorn coefficient and maintaining that the law does shed light on the dynamic relations between output, employment and productivity growth. 'Those who have interpreted the Verdoorn coefficient as a dynamic relationship need not repent', Thirlwall concludes (reprinted as p. 394).

Further empirical evidence, for a much longer period, is provided in Chapter 35 by P. Stoneman. Using data for the British economy between 1800 and 1970, Stoneman disposes of a number of econometric problems before arriving at his judgement that the long-run evidence does support Kaldor's claim that there is a close relationship between the rate of growth of GDP and the growth of manufacturing output. It is, however, less clear that GDP growth is unrelated to the growth rate of other sectors. Stoneman's research also points to the existence of a pool of unemployed labour in agriculture over this period, and confirms the operation of Verdoorn's law in manufacturing, on the assumption either that manufacturing output is exogenously-determined or that it is endogenous. In the circumstances his conclusion – that the evidence is not inconsistent with Kaldor's hypotheses, but does not lend strong support to them – seems just a little ungenerous.

In Chapter 36, J.S.L. McCombie focuses on the role of inter-sectoral labour transfers in explaining why productivity growth rates differ. Using data from twelve OECD countries, McCombie finds that Verdoorn's law did operate between 1950 and 1965, but that it seems to have broken down in the period 1965–73, when there is evidence of a 'shake-out' of labour in manufacturing industries. He suggests that Kaldor was correct to emphasize the importance of surplus labour in agriculture, but surplus labour in the service sector is much less significant. McCombie reaffirms Kaldor's analysis in a broader sense, since 'the key to the understanding of the differences in productivity growth lies in explaining the large differences between countries in the growth of the demand for output. This stands in marked contrast to the neoclassical approach with its emphasis on the supply side' (reprinted as p. 415).

A different perspective is adopted by Chatterji and Wickens (Chapter 37), who distinguish Kaldor's use of Verdoorn's law from what they term his 'externalities hypothesis', according to which faster productivity growth in manufacturing induces an acceleration of productivity growth in other sectors, chiefly through improvements in machinery due to technical progress in capital-goods production. Investigating these propositions for the UK between 1961 and 1977, they allow for variations in capacity utilization and for the effects of capital accumulation. Chatterji and Wickens estimate a dynamic model, which provides evidence that Verdoorn's law applies only in the short-run while the externalities hypothesis operates as a long-run phenomenon.

Kaldor's reply (Chapter 38) contains his last published reflections on the Verdoorn controversy and related questions. The importance of manufacturing, he argues, stems from its export-intensity, its ability to produce the capital goods (and generate the savings) required for accumulation, and its capacity to absorb surplus labour from other sectors. Kaldor now stresses his opposition to neoclassical theory, to a much greater degree than in his earlier writings. 'Circular and cumulative causation', he asserts, is central to the understanding of economic development, but is quite incompatible with orthodox analysis. These ideas are explored in much greater detail, by Kaldor and others, in Part IV of this book.

The remaining three chapters in this section are by way of a *post-mortem* on Kaldor's romance with Verdoorn. McCombie (Chapter 39) dismisses what he describes as Kaldor's 'third law', concerning the contribution of labour transfer to the growth process, on the grounds that it has no economic significance, and argues that all previous estimates of the Verdoorn relationship are unreliable. Although Kaldor's insights may indeed be valuable, McCombie concludes, there is little hard evidence to substantiate them. Thirlwall's conclusions are much more positive. In his introduction to the *Journal of Post Keynesian Economics* symposium on 'Kaldor's growth laws' (Chapter 40), he praises Kaldor's recognition of increasing returns, which revived a tradition extending back through Allyn Young to Adam Smith and has far-reaching policy implications. Summarizing Kaldor's laws in Chapter 41, Thirlwall traces the development of Kaldor's thinking from the inaugural lecture in 1966, examines the evidence that he presented at various stages, and assesses the critical literature (full of misunderstandings) that grew up around Kaldor's analysis. Thirlwall ends his appraisal by suggesting that manufacturing industry is indeed the engine of GDP growth, and that manufacturing output is constrained not by labour supplies but by the growth of exogenous – that is, in the last resort, export – demand.

Increasing Returns, Decreasing Returns and Cumulative Causation

The first indication of the change in Kaldor's thinking on growth came in a 1970 paper on regional policy (Chapter 42). Here Kaldor notes that the neoclassical attention paid to resource endowments is relevant only for primary production, since in manufacturing the accumulation of capital is an effect as well as a cause of growth. In the secondary sector, Gunnar Myrdal's notion of circular and cumulative causation must be employed, and 'This is nothing else but the existence of increasing returns to scale – using that term in the broadest sense – in processing activities' (reprinted as p. 480). These result from the development of skill and know-how, from opportunities for the concentration of ideas and experience, and from the growth of specialization. As a consequence of increasing returns, Kaldor argues, trade may widen the gap in comparative costs between countries and regions, injuring the originally less developed areas rather than providing mutual benefits.

Kaldor emphasizes the distinction between 'land-based' and 'processing' activities. The former do not enjoy the benefits of increasing returns, and any increase in demand leads to an increase in price. In the latter, growth in demand causes higher output through the operation of a foreign trade 'supermultiplier'. The exports of any particular country or region depend on the (exogenous) growth of world demand, but also on the (endogenous) movement of real wages relative to productivity, which Kaldor refers to as the trend in 'efficiency wages'. This is where cumulative causation is so important: rapidly-growing areas have above-average productivity growth, declining relative efficiency wages, and in consequence an increasing competitive advantage. Hence, Kaldor argues, there is a permanent need for regional policies. Wage subsidies, in particular, might offer disadvantaged regions the benefits that sovereign nations derive from currency depreciation.

In Chapter 43, Dixon and Thirlwall formalize these ideas in a model of export-led growth. They use the Verdoorn relationship to provide the link between output growth and productivity growth, noting, however, that this produces differences in regional growth rates only if the Verdoorn coefficient varies between regions. Specifying the stability conditions of the model, Dixon and Thirlwall conclude that cumulative divergence in growth rates is no more likely than convergence; stable differences are most probable. Unlike Kaldor, they point to the importance of regional disparities in economic structure, above all in the income-elasticities of demand for the goods in which various areas have come to specialize. They reject wage subsidies as an effective equalizing policy measure, arguing that they tend to ossify economic structures and should be replaced by an industrial policy to promote the development of industries facing high income-elasticities of demand. Dixon and Thirlwall conclude that their 'open economy' version of Kaldor's growth theory offers a plausible explanation of the British experience between 1951 and 1966, but that it could be improved by the addition of an explicit balance of payments constraint.

Kaldor used his new ideas on growth to criticize mainstream equilibrium theory. In a 1973 lecture, not published in English until 1979 (Chapter 44) he argues, like Joan Robinson, that:

... there is nothing in the theory to explain how the system gets into equilibrium and what happens when it is out of equilibrium. The 'production frontier' which is supposed to shift at some exogenous rate in time is meaningful only if the system is actually *on* the frontier and not *within* it. For any movement of the system *toward* the frontier increases capital as well as output, and therefore changes at least one of the parameters which define the 'frontier' (reprinted as p. 507; original stress).

It follows that complementarity between inputs is more important than neoclassical substitution. 'The market is thus not primarily an instrument for *allocating* resources. It is primarily an instrument for transmitting impulses to change' (reprinted as p. 510; original stress). And the stylised facts of economic growth point to the existence of increasing returns in manufacturing industry. The importance of foreign trade, Kaldor argues, suggests the need for a model of the global economic system, since 'There is no such really closed system except the world economy as a whole' (reprinted as p. 516). He sketches the outlines of a two-sector world model in which industrial growth depends on the exogenous components of demand for its products, while the terms of trade for primary production are set by developments in manufacturing.

Once again, these insights were to be formalized by others. Kaldor's final thoughts on growth are contained in another lecture, delivered only months before his death (Chapter 45). Here Kaldor critically assesses J.R. Hicks's interpretation of the breakdown of the postwar boom. The rapid growth after 1945 clearly depended upon adequate supplies of primary products. Hicks had argued that, beginning in the early 1970s, labour- and land-saving technical progress in agriculture and mineral extraction had no longer been sufficient to frustrate the law of diminishing returns. Kaldor disagrees, maintaining that primary production could have adjusted, given a suitable policy regime, to any feasible growth of world industrial output. Commodity price stabilization schemes, supported by buffer stocks, were necessary. Kaldor reasserts the importance of cumulative causation in manufacturing industry, and suggests that the gains from technical progress in both sectors tend to accrue to industry; there is evidence of a long-term deterioration in the terms of trade for primary producers. He distinguishes the 'physical' from the 'actual' limits to growth in manufacturing. For the industrialized world as a whole, the physical barriers to growth are set by labour supplies, while the actual constraint is represented by economic policy, through its effect on aggregate demand.

Targetti's (Chapter 46) is another attempt to tie together the many loose strands in Kaldor's thinking in a single coherent model. He points to a number of weaknesses in Kaldor's arguments, including the lack of any consistent framework for identifying the limits to growth in the world taken as a whole, and the insidious assumption of full employment, which makes it impossible to analyse the stagflationary tendencies of the modern world economy. Targetti's own model follows Kaldor in highlighting the relationship between agriculture and industry, assigning a central role to the terms of trade between the two sectors as the mechanism which regulates the agricultural income which is transformed into demand for manufactures.

Like Kaldor, Targetti assumes a classical savings function, supplemented by a Kaleckian degree of monopoly pricing model for the industrial sector. His Figure 1 (reprinted as p. 539) illustrates the two functional relationships in the model, linking the growth rates of agricultural production and of industrial output to the price of manufactures relatively to primary products. This enables Targetti to specify the conditions under which the terms of trade will show a secular trend in favour of agriculture (the 'classical thesis' of West and Ricardo) or industry (the 'modern' or Prebisch–Singer hypothesis). More likely than either surmise are oscillations in the terms of trade which, combined with faster productivity growth in agriculture, give rise to stagflation. Targetti concludes that Kaldor's original buffer-stock proposals for smoothing commodity price fluctuations may well be essential for uninterrupted growth.

In the same general spirit is Thirlwall's model (Chapter 47), which also rests on the fundamental Kaldorian insight that the long-term growth rate depends upon the expansion of industrial output. Thirlwall shows that, for any individual open economy, the pace of industrial growth is itself determined by agricultural growth in the early stages of development and by export growth thereafter. Kaldor, he argues, had greatly improved on previous theories of growth, both by rejecting the conventional neoclassical assumption that labour and capital were scarce rather than internally generated by the growth process, and by focussing on the demand for industrial output rather than on the supply conditions which had dominated the influential Lewis model.

Thirlwall models the complementarity between industry and agriculture, deriving the equilibrium terms of trade between them and analysing the consequences of disequilibrium. He concentrates initially on the (closed) world economy, setting out a diagrammatic analysis (Figs 1-3, reprinted as pp. 558–60) which is very similar to Targetti's. Agricultural demand for industrial goods varies inversely with the industrial terms of trade, while there is a positive relationship between the rate of growth of industrial output and the relative price of manufactures. Introducing technical change into the model, Thirlwall demonstrates that the industrial growth rate depends in the final analysis only on the pace of land-saving innovation in agriculture, while technical progress in manufacturing affects only the terms of trade. Thus industrial growth is constrained by agricultural technology. The terms of trade depend additionally upon the elasticity of supply of land, and on the rate of innovation and the wage rate in industry. They are thus contingent, not bound by an iron law as both Ricardo and Prebisch, from their opposing viewpoints, had supposed.

Moving from a closed to an open economy, Thirlwall argues that export demand becomes a further source of autonomous demand for industrial output. In the course of time, it comes to dominate the growth of demand from agriculture, so that growth in any individual economy becomes constrained by the balance of payments rather than by the development of agriculture. Thirlwall ends by considering the consequences of cumulative and circular causation, which may benefit industry relative to agriculture and widen the gap between North and South in income and output per head.

Two contrasting criticisms of the Thirlwall model are suggested by David Canning and Amitava Dutt, while H. Molana and David Vines develop another Kaldorian model. In Chapter 48, Canning argues that diminishing returns in agriculture need not constrain growth in the industrial sector, since they may be offset by increasing returns in manufacturing which permit agricultural productivity to grow through the use of bigger and increasingly cheap capital goods. As he himself acknowledges, his model is more neoclassical than Kaldor would have liked, with utility-maximizing workers, profit-maximizing capitalists and a set of Cobb–Douglas production functions. It is, however, Kaldorian in the sense that competition is imperfect and output growth in manufacturing generates productivity growth. The implications of Canning's model are striking: 'The conclusion to be drawn about the role of agriculture in industrial development is almost the opposite of that found in Thirlwall .... by reducing the cost of capital to the agricultural sector .... industry can, by itself, be the driving force behind a sustained process of economic growth' (reprinted as p. 584).

Molana and Vines (Chapter 49) develop their model in a North–South context, allowing for substitution in consumption between primary commodities and industrial goods in the North, and examining the implications of diminishing returns in the South. They assume that output is supply-constrained, and that there are no Keynesian failures of effective demand. Like Canning, their model uses neoclassical production and utility functions. Molana and Vines examine the equilibrium conditions of the model, first when there is surplus land in the South and then when land is scarce and Ricardian diminishing returns apply. They show that technical progress in agricultural production will, in the short run, reduce real incomes in the South, and will generate cyclical instability in the terms of trade. Their tentative conclusion favours Kaldor's proposals for commodity price stabilization.

In Chapter 50, Amitava Dutt takes issue with both Targetti and Thirlwall. He objects that Thirlwall's postulate of mark-up pricing in industry is inconsistent with the rest of his model; in particular, it requires excess capacity in the industrial sector, and this cannot be reconciled with the implicit assumption of full capacity utilization. Dutt analyses the stability properties of the model in some detail. His principal criticism of Thirlwall's specification, however, relates to the treatment of demand. 'Agriculture does not serve as a solution to industry's market problem simply because there *is* no market problem for industry in this model' (reprinted as p. 605; original stress). In this respect, he argues, it is no different from the neoclassical and classical approaches. Dutt concludes by suggesting how demand issues can be introduced into a Kaldorian framework.

Responding to Dutt's criticism, Thirlwall (Chapter 51) denies that his Kaldorian model is effectively identical with the classical Lewis analysis, where industrial growth is supply-constrained. There are, Thirlwall suggests, two senses in which industry has a demand problem: the Keynes or Say's Law question of whether any level of output is self-financing, so that all saving is invested; and the different issue of what determines the level of industrial output itself. Kaldor and Thirlwall assume away the first problem to focus their attention on the second, in which agricultural growth is required to provide growing demand for industrial output. Dutt, on the other hand, is concerned with the first issue. In view of the importance of the subject, and the continuing interest in Kaldorian models of growth and development, it is unlikely that the last word has been said on these matters.

Further Reading

An excellent selection of Kaldor's writings, including some important articles on growth theory which could not be reprinted here, is in F. Targetti and A.P. Thirlwall (eds), *The Essential Kaldor* (Duckworth, 1989). A much larger sample of Kaldor's work is contained in the eight volumes of his *Collected Economic Essays* (Duckworth, 1960–1980), of which Volume I, *Essays on Economic Stability and Growth* (1960, second edition 1980), and Volume V, *Further Essays on Economic Theory* (1978), are most directly relevant to the economics of growth. The definitive biography by A.P. Thirlwall, *Nicholas Kaldor* (Wheatsheaf, 1987) includes a comprehensive bibliography of his writings. A shorter account of Kaldor's life and ideas can be found in Thirlwall's 'Nicholas Kaldor, 1908–1986' in *Proceedings of the British Academy*, **123**, 1987, pp. 517–66. Kaldor was the subject of a special issue of the *Cambridge Journal of Economics* in March 1989, reprinted as T. Lawson, J.G. Palma and J. Sender (eds), *Kaldor's Political Economy* (Academic Press, 1989). A second posthumously-published collection of articles on Kaldor is E. J. Nell and W. Semmler (eds), *Nicholas Kaldor and Mainstream Economics: Confrontation or Convergence* (Macmillan, 1990).

Part I
Nicholas Kaldor

[1]

Recollections of an Economist *

How did I come to be an economist? I was brought up in Budapest, Hungary: my father was a lawyer and my initial expectation was to become a lawyer too — though I had a sneaking desire to become a writer. The experiences during and after the First World War, with its bewildering changes in social régimes from a monarchy to a liberal Republic, then to a Communist dictatorship lasting for four months, followed by a military dictatorship soon moderated by the need to conform to the institutional framework of a Parliamentary system desired by the victorious Western powers, made me interested in the forces which govern the political evolution of society. Then in the summer of 1923, aged 15, I spent a family holiday in the Bavarian Alps, when I had the rare opportunity to observe a state of on-going hyper-inflation and the extraordinary features of behaviour to which it gave rise. At the beginning of the holiday the prices of goods in the shops were raised by large amounts — of the order of 30-40 per cent — at least twice a week. But this process was not stable — it accelerated every week and then day by day. Towards the end everyone queued up outside the offices of banks where the dollar price for the day was posted at midday. Then everyone rushed to go bargain-hunting for goods at "yesterday's price" before the shopkeepers had time to revise their prices in accordance with the rise in the price of the dollar. At the next stage the shopkeepers closed their doors at midday and re-opened an hour later with all prices revised. Even cafes and restaurants refused to accept payments until they worked out what the afternoon price was. At a later stage, which I no longer witnessed, the same process of revising prices occurred several times a day. At the same time I noted that translated into dollars, or other stable currencies, the prices of things, despite their constant revision, were extraordinarily low. There

---

* Contribution to a series of recollections and reflections on professional experiences of distinguished economists. This series opened with the September 1979 issue of this *Review*.

was a yawning and widening gap between the prices of goods in terms of local currency and their prices in foreign currency, which were very much lower.

These extraordinary phenomena aroused all my curiosity. *Why* did these things happen — and if they happened on some occasions how were they avoided in others? No-one could give an intelligible answer to this question, though I soon discovered that there is a branch of knowledge, economics, which should be able to provide a satisfactory answer. It was then that I decided to become an economist.

Apart from a year and a half in which, after finishing school in Budapest, I attended lectures in the University of Berlin (in 1925-26), my chief training in economics was as an undergraduate at the London School of Economics in 1927-30. My first real teacher in economics, albeit for a brief period, was an American, Allyn Abbot Young, who came from Harvard to L.S.E. to succeed Edwin Cannan in 1926. This unfortunately did not last long as in the winter of 1928-29 he died quite unexpectedly of pneumonia. Nonetheless, his lectures and seminars left a lasting impression on my later development, since it was to him that I owe a basic distrust of abstract systems *per se,* and an awareness of the need to adapt the tools of theoretical analysis to the practical problems which they are intended to illuminate. Economics, in Allyn Young's view, is best defined by the particular interests which have prompted its founders — not by its "subject matter" as such.[1]

Young was succeeded at L.S.E. by Lionel Robbins, young, flamboyant and enthusiastic (he was only 30 at the time of his appointment) and extremely devoted both to teaching and to economics as a subject. He lavished his energies and vitality on his pupils and identified himself fully with their success and their attainments. It was inevitable that those of us who were fortunate to have been among his first pupils — and there were a bare dozen of us then specialising at L.S.E. in the subject of "analytical economics" — should fall completely under his spell. Robbins' economics (much influenced by his contacts with Viennese economists, mainly von Mises) was the general equilibrium theory of Walras and the Austrians, rather than of Marshall, and

---

[1] Cf. his classic article on "Economics" in the 14th Edition of the *Encyclopaedia Britannica* (published in 1929). On a recent re-reading this paper gives the impression of being remarkably fresh and up-to-date. However Young is mainly remembered for his famous paper on *Increasing Returns and Economic Progress* (published in the *Economic Journal,* December 1928), which created a considerable stir on its publication, even though its main message was by no means fully understood at the time.

his lectures followed the method of presentation of Wicksell and of Knight, *Risk, Uncertainty and Profit* (a book which contains in its first half an admirably clear and concise account of neo-classical theory). Robbins as a young economist absorbed this theory — the keystone of which is the marginal productivity theory of distribution in its generalised form, as expounded by Wicksell and Wicksteed — with the fervency of a convert and propounded it with the zeal of a missionary. It was thanks to him that I acquired a thorough grasp of that theory without being hampered by doubts and hesitations — which in other circumstances might have inhibited me (as it has inhibited other critics) from mounting the intellectual effort required for mastering its content.

The theory of general economic equilibrium, in Professor Kornai's phrase, is an "intellectual experiment" — a particular method chosen for describing how a market economy works under various simplifying and unreal postulates. These postulates were not intended by its creators to be more than intermediary steps in the process of analysis — they were simplifications which were intended to be removed later when the theory was brought into closer approximation to real life. But it was an inherent consequence of the *a priori* approach of this school that its followers should be pre-occupied with the properties of the notion of "equilibrium" — which meant that progress took the form, not of removing the scaffolding but of constantly *adding* to it. Making the theory more rigorous made the whole construction even more abstract (and hence more distant from its ultimate goal) since it involved the discovery (or recognition) of additional assumptions implied in the results.

As I wrote in a paper some twenty years ago, [2] "it is the hallmark of the neo-classical economist to believe that however severe the abstractions from which he is forced to start, he will win through by the end of the day — bit by bit, if he only carries the analysis far enough, the scaffolding can ben removed, leaving the basic structure intact". I should, perhaps, have added that it is also the hallmark of the neo-classical economist — when he takes off his hat as a pure theorist and puts on his hat as a policy adviser or as an interpreter of current events — to behave as if the scaffolding *had been* removed already, and the basic structure had been *shown* to remain intact. When it comes to judging the effects of particular policy measures — whether it relates to

---

[2] "Marginal Productivity and the Macroeconomic Theories of Distribution", *Review of Economic Studies*, Volume XXXIII, No. 4 (1966).

unemployment, foreign trade, the incidence of taxation, exchange rates, etc. — he applies conclusions derived from the theory of general equilibrium to the real world without hesitation: that is to say, without investigating how far his results are dependent on implied or explicit assumptions that are manifestly contrary to experience.[3]

The economic theory that I was taught is a theory based entirely on the deductive analytical method (though at the time it was not clothed in the language of mathematics, as it is today) and my first effort in exposition is found on the first two pages of one of my earliest published papers.[4]

Such was the almost hypnotic power of Walras' system of equations that it took me a long time to grasp that this method of making an abstract model still more abstract by discovering unsuspected assumptions implied by the results is an unscientific procedure which leads nowhere.

It was a long journey. Most of my early papers were based on the deductive *a priori* method and concentrated on unresolved inconsistencies of general equilibrium theory but without questioning the fundamentals.

For students of the present generation it is difficult to convey the atmosphere of creative tension and excitement which prevailed at L.S.E. in the early years of the 1930s. Much of it was due to the youthful leadership of Robbins; much of it was due to the presence of a number of exceptionally able young graduates who were just beginning their professional careers; much of it arose through the intellectual challenge which the severity of the economic crisis (particularly in 1931-32) presented to all economists. It was a time of endless discussions which went on at all hours of the day and night — during meals, during walks and during weekends. I benefitted enormously from Oxford weekends spent in the company of a brilliant mind, Maurice Allen, who was a year senior to me at L.S.E. and then became a don at

---

[3] A clear example of this is the recent recrudescence of "monetarist" theories and their application (*inter alia*) to the balance of payments which assumes — reverting to pre-Keynesian ideas of the working of the market economy — that the economy is in *continuous* full-employment equilibrium and there is universal perfect competition where all markets "continuously clear" (which means both that buyers buy all that they desire to buy at the ruling price, and that sellers sell all they wish to sell at that price — an assumption which is difficult to reconcile with the facts of modern advertising).

[4] "A Classificatory Note on the Determinateness of Equilibrium, *Review of Economic Studies*, Vol. I, No. 2 (February 1934), pp. 122-36.

Oxford, first in New College and later in Balliol, and who held views which were then to the left of mine on policies concerning unemployment, etc.[5]

The other young economist with whom I spent many hours in discussion in our neighbouring flats, on Sunday walks, or occasionally on a Continental holiday, was John Hicks, then a colleague at L.S.E. Hicks (unlike me) was an indefatigable reader of books in at least three foreign languages, and it was owing to him that I was put on the track (among others) of the younger Swedish economists, particularly Myrdal[6] who first made me realize the shortcomings of the "monetarist" approach of the Austrian school of von Mises and von Hayek[7] and made me such an easy convert to Keynes after the appearance of the *General Theory* three years later.[8]

However, preceding the controversy over Keynes, the problems which interested me most were those concerning the nature of competition between business enterprises. The theory of imperfect competition was 'in the air' long before the books by Joan Robinson and Edward Chamberlin made their near-simultaneous appearance in 1933. Allyn Young devoted a great deal of his lectures to various forms of imperfect competition,[9] his main interest being in exploring the circumstances in which competition had harmful rather than beneficial effects on the workings of the economy. At the same time, there was a prolonged controversy on the theory of costs and returns in the pages of the *Economic Journal*, the most distinguished piece of which was Piero

---

[5] I mention this since we ended up so differently from where we began. In 1932 I was much under the influence of the views not only of Robbins but also of Hayek (the 1930 version of Milton Friedman); whereas Maurice Allen was more under the influence of Dennis Robertson and Roy Harrod. However, he ended up, after an interlude of fighting in Burma, as an Executive Director of the Bank of England noted for his extremely conservative views.

[6] Myrdal's short book on "Monetary Equilibrium" (published in German in 1933) contained many of the features of Keynes' system particularly as regards the role of expectations in investment and the relation of the marginal efficiency of capital to the rate of interest.

[7] My enthusiasm for the doctrines of Professor von Hayek had already suffered a relapse when as a first year research student I undertook to translate his article "Gibt es einen Widersinn des Sparens?" into English, and in the course of struggling with the translation detected various gaps and flaws in the argument. (The paper appeared under the title of "The Paradox of Saving" in *Economica*, May 1931.)

[8] My close friendship with Hicks did not survive his departure from L.S.E., first to Cambridge, then to Manchester and finally to Oxford. Yet on looking back, our intellectual work continued to converge at unexpected points as shown e.g. by HICKS' book on the *Trade Cycle* (1950), or his book on *Capital and Growth* (1965), or his most recent paper on "Monetary Theory and Monetary Experience" (in *Economic Perspectives*, Oxford 1977).

[9] Chamberlin's book (as stated in the Preface) was written originally as a Ph.D. thesis under Young's supervision. (This happened also to be the case with another famous American book of the inter-war period, KNIGHT's *Risk Uncertainty and Profit*.)

Sraffa's famous article on "The Laws of Returns under Competitive Conditions" which appeared in December 1926. This paper anticipated many of the important "discoveries" in economic theory over the next fifty years — though in a somewhat oblique way, so that its true significance was sometimes only appreciated when one arrived at the same conclusions independently after an interval of many years.[10] Sraffa's paper provided the stimulus to a whole series of subsequent papers, many of which assumed, explicitly or implicitly, imperfect competition.[11]

My main contribution to this debate was the paper on "Market Imperfection and Excess Capacity" in the February 1935 issue of *Economica*, the purpose of which was to demonstrate that free competition in the sense of "free and unimpeded entry" into any industry or sector of the economy will only lead to a state of "perfect competition" postulated by equilibrium theory if the law of constant costs applies over the whole range of outputs from the infinitesimal to the indefinitely large. If this cannot be assumed the effect of free entry will necessarily lead to a situation in which the multiplication of "firms" is brought to a halt by the rise in costs per unit as the output of the average firms is reduced in consequence of competition. Hence the typical firm will be operating on too small a scale — near the minimum scale at which his costs are covered (*i.e.*, near its "break-even" point) and not at the optimum scale postulated by the theory of general equilibrium.[12] But the general consequences of postulating decreasing costs at the margin of production — in the short run and not only in the long run — are very far-reaching; since the existence of increasing marginal costs in the neighbourhood of equilibrium (*i.e.*, in the neighbourhood of the actual levels of output of the individual enterprise) is the keystone on which

---

[10] Thus in a lecture at Havard in 1974 on "What is Wrong with Economic Theory" (*Quarterly Journal of Economics*, August 1975) I came to the conclusion that constant costs, or constant returns to scale in terms of transferable resources, was *the* basic axiom underlying the Walrasian theory of general equilibrium. I was quite oblivious at the time that the same assertion was made in Sraffa's article which I had read more than forty years earlier.

[11] The most important contributions, apart from Allyn Young's seminal article, were those of R.F. Harrod in the June 1930 and December 1931 issues, and of G.F. Shove in the March 1933 issue of the *Economic Journal*.

[12] In the absence of perfect divisibility the condition of "perfect competition" will apply only to a limited class of commodities capable of strict standardisation in terms of some universally acceptable system of grading which enable such commodities to be centrally traded in highly organised markets in which "good will" (or the personal element in dealing) is wholly eliminated. (The creation of such markets is in the joint interest of the ultimate buyers and sellers, *i.e.*, of the consumers and the producers, since it serves to minimize the margin absorbed by intermediaries, traders or merchants.)

neo-classical price and distribution theory rests. Its abandonment meant, in the words of Hicks, that "the basis on which economic laws can be constructed is shorn away" thereby causing the "wreckage of the greater part of economic theory".[13]

If economics had been a "science" in the strict sense of the word, the empirical observation that most firms operate in imperfect markets would have forced economists to scrap their existing theories and to start thinking on entirely new lines — in much the same way in which the accidental discovery of an excessive amount of light emitted by pitchblende forced a fundamental reconsideration of the theory of physics. Unfortunately economists do not feel under the same compulsion to maintain a close correspondence between theoretical hypotheses and the facts of experience. When Hicks realised (in 1938) that the contemplation of imperfect markets brought him to the brink of an abyss, he hastily drew back, and his example was eagerly followed by others.[14] In most theoretical work published since World War II (apart from some isolated works on oligopoly), a state of perfect competition is assumed, explicitly or implicitly.

This was even true of Keynes who accepted Marshall's microeconomics in the *General Theory* without realizing that the phenomenon he was dealing with — involuntary underutilisation of *both* productive capacity and of labour — postulates the existence of "excess supply" (*i.e.*, a situation in which the amount actually produced or sold is *less* than the optimal amount individual sellers would prefer to sell at the ruling price), a state of affairs which could not exist under perfect competition. In doing this he made an unfortunate concession to his neo-classical critics, for it meant the acceptance of the traditional postulate of a falling marginal productivity function for labour in the short period which was the main plank of Pigou's *Theory of Unemployment*. That book, which preceded Keynes' by three years, gave the then fashionable explanation of unemployment as being due to the action of trade unions which raised wages above the "equilibrium" level. Keynes' acceptance of this neo-classical postulate made it possible for his conservative critics (from Pigou, Robertson, Viner and Robbins right up

---

[13] *Value and Capital* (Oxford 1939) pp. 83-4. It was already recognized by Marshall (see Appendix H of the *Principles*) that the theory of "normal value" ceases to be applicable in the case of increasing returns.
[14] In fairness to Hicks it should be pointed out that in his most recent publications he completely disowned the attitude he took up in 1939. (See *Economic Perspectives*, Oxford 1977, Preface and Survey); also *Economic Record*, September 1975, pp.365-67.

to Milton Friedman) to reject Keynes on empirical grounds by asserting that there is no evidence that the workers would accept lower real wages, and since a higher level of employment would cause real wages to be lower, there is no reason to suppose that any stimulus to demand could increase employment more than temporarily.

As Keynes said at the end of the Preface to the *General Theory* "the difficulty lies, not in the new ideas, but in escaping from the old ones, which ramify, for those brought up as most of us have been, into every corner of our minds". Keynes' acceptance of increasing marginal cost in the short period (for output as a whole as well as for particular industries) followed from the Marshallian assumption that different pieces of equipment and different workers are not homogeneous in efficiency, and that as a result of the general influence of competition, the more efficient equipment and labour will be used first (and utilized to the full) before any less efficient unit is brought into use. However innocuous or logically compelling this argument may appear to be — it is after all only a simple application of Ricardo's theory of rent — it is contradicted by empirical evidence both as regards the short period elasticity of output with respect to changes in the volume of employment[15] and also as regards the observed association between the movement in real wages and employment.

Though Keynes retracted on his original assertion as a result of various criticisms,[16] his position remained a guarded one, and he never produced a theoretical explanation of *why* his original argument of diminishing returns being a necessary consequence of non-homogeneity was wrong, and what the consequences of its abandonment were. To do so would have required an analysis of monopolistic competition which renders the traditional rules of resource allocation inapplicable. Keynesian unemployment, as distinct from Marxian or classical unemployment, can only subsist under conditions of monopolistic competition.[17-18]

---

[15] This is attested by a large number of statistical studies in the U.S., U.K. and other industrial countries (at least from the late 19th century onwards), the best known of which has come to be called "Okun's Law", according to which a 1 per cent increase in employment is associated with a 3 per cent increase in output. For the U.K., see R.R. NEILD, *Pricing and Employment in the Trade Cycle* (N.I.E.S.R. Occasional Paper, no. XXI, Cambridge University Press, 1963); COUTTS, GODLEY and NORTHAUS, *Industrial Pricing in the U.K.*, (D.A.E. Monograph 26, Cambridge University Press, 1978).

[16] Cf. "Relative Movements of Real Wages and Output", *Economic Journal*, March 1939, pp. 34-51, quoting papers by J.G. DUNLOP *(Economic Journal,* September 1938) and L. TARSHIS *(ibid.* March, 1939, pp. 150-54) and discussions with Mihail Kalecki.

[17] This was perceived at an early stage by Kalecki but not by Keynes, and it is (in my view) the main respect in which Kalecki's original model is intellectually superior to Keynes' *General Theory.*

As it happened, the opportunity to build a new integrated theory based on Keynesian macro-economics combined with micro-economics built on the foundation of imperfect competition and oligopoly was missed. While Keynesian macro-economics opened new avenues for the analysis of the behaviour of the economy, and for the creation of a new theory of economic policy (and was generally triumphant in most industrialised countries for the first twenty five years after World War II), the theories of monopolistic competition atrophied — partly on account of the difficulty of getting beyond the stage of elementary abstract propositions, and partly owing to the sub-conscious desire to resuscitate general equilibrium theories of the Walrasian type which lent themselves to precise formulations in mathematical form. But the cost of this was that no real research was made, and no reliable knowledge acquired, as to how competition operates and how prices and the allocation of sales among competing producers are determined, under conditions of advanced capitalism; and in the absence of such knowledge, all interpretations derived from macro-economic data (which form the basis of policy making) remain surrounded by an aura of doubt and uncertainty.[19]

However, even without such an integrated theory Keynes' macro-economics gave plenty of opportunities for new thought both in the field of theory and policy. It gave an immediate stimulus to new theories of the trade cycle — which meant combining the Keynesian multiplier with some form of the "accelerator" (as was first done in R.F. Harrod's book on *The Trade Cycle* in 1936). My own work in this field consisted of a demostration (in refutation of the contentions of Prof. Pigou) of how Keynes' results can in fact be reached with the aid of a "neo-classical" model employing traditional variables, provided certain

---

However, it is very doubtful, to say the least, whether in the absence of Keynes' genius and personality, his exquisit style and his ability to command attention, the ideas alone would have been sufficient to bring about the intellectual break-through which the 'Keynesian revolution' created.

[18] The full significance of this has not been properly appreciated even now. A world in which marginal costs are below average costs, and are normally constant and not rising (up to the point of full capacity operation) puts 'paid' to all theories which assume a trade-off between real wages and employment. If the productivity of labour is a rising and not a falling function of the level of employment, there is no such thing as a "natural rate of unemployment" and no unique real wage which secures equilibrium in the labour market.

[19] It is only now, after a lapse of forty years, that the necessity for the abandonment of the perfect competition hypothesis and its far-reaching consequences have come to be asserted (or re-asserted) by economists of the "orthodox" school. (Cf. CURT B. EATON AND RICHARD G. LIPSEY "Freedom of Entry and the Existence of Pure Profit" in *Economic Journal*, September 1978.)

critical assumptions are incorporated.[20] This was followed by three papers which have not, I think, been rendered obsolete by subsequent work. The first, "Stability and Full Employment" appeared in the *Economic Journal*, December 1938, the second "A Model of the Trade Cycle" in the *Economic Journal*, March 1940, and the third "Speculation and Economic Stability" in the *Review of Economic Studies*, October 1939. The latter attempted to generalize Keynes' theory of the multiplier by demonstrating that it results from the stabilising influence of speculative expectations on prices which applies in all cases in which the elasticity of speculative stocks is high (in other words, the elasticity of demand for *holding* stocks is distinct from the elasticities of "flow" demand or supply of the ultimate buyers or sellers). One of the purposes of that paper was to show that Keynes' theory of interest contains two separate propositions. The first regards interest as the price to be paid for parting with liquidity, and it arises on account of the *uncertainty* of the future prices of non-liquid assets. The second concerns the dependence of the current rate of interest on the interest rates expected in the future. While the first proposition provides an explanation of why long dated bonds should normally command a higher yield than short-term paper, it is the second which explains why the traditional theory of the working of the capital market was inappropriate — why, in other words, savings and investment are brought into equality by movements in the level of incomes far more than by movements in interest rates. And this second effect will be the more powerful the *less* is the uncertainty concerning the future, or the greater the firmness with which the idea of "a normal price" is embedded in the minds of professional speculators and dealers.[21]

This paper is supplemented by a further paper on Keynes' theory of the own rate of interest which was written about the same time but remained unfinished and was published only after a long delay in

---

[20] "Professor Pigou on Money Wages in Relation to Unemployment", *Economic Journal*, December 1937, pp. 745-53.

[21] This appeared in October 1939. When I met Keynes a few weeks later at a Cambridge tea party I was greatly surprised that he had already read my article and said that I might well be right in my contention that it is the price stabilising influence of the policies of dealers and speculators, rather than the premium which the public requires for parting with liquidity, which explains why the increase in the propensity to save is not in itself capable of generating more investment. Though I met Keynes on a number of occasions later on I never had an opportunity of discussing that point further. But the point of that discussion was, I believe, very much the same as that raised some thirty years later by Leijonhufvud in his book on *"Keynesian Economics and the Economics of Keynes"*.

1960.²² The significance of this latter paper, in the context of present day discussions, lies in its interpretation of the "transmission mechanism" through which changes in the amount of "money" in circulation can affect the level of prices. In Keynes' theory, this presupposes first a fall in the money rates of interest, followed by a corresponding fall in the own rates of *money* interest of assets relatively to their own rates of *own*-interest, which in turn should induce larger stocks to be held of the various assets and thereby stimulate their production; only if production is not elastic, will it raise prices.

All the above refers to papers written and ideas developed before the Second World War. The war caused a change in my surroundings and interests. Physically, it meant the transference of L.S.E. to Cambridge which brought me into much closer contact with the Cambridge economists (some of whom, like Piero Sraffa and Joan Robinson I had already known from pre-war encounters). The immediate effect of this was that I took a much closer interest in current issues of economic policy — primarily stimulated by listening to the lectures on the problems of war finance given by Keynes and to the discussions they gave rise to — I remember particularly the long debates with one of my earliest pupils, Erwin Rothbarth, then Keynes' assistant, in collecting the material for Keynes' pamphlet on *How to Pay for the War*.²³ At Keynes' request I wrote a review article on the White Paper on War Finance in the *Economic Journal* — which later became an annual feature in that Journal and an occasion for reviewing the economic management of the war. I also participated in numerous discussion groups on post-war reconstruction, one of which was organised by William Beveridge and which had as its outcome his book on *Full Employment in a Free Society*, to which I contributed an Appendix on the "quantitative aspects" of the full employment policies.²⁴ This created quite a stir, and became the prototype of far more sophisticated econometric models to serve the purpose both of economic management and forecasting. It also brought me a reputation of being able to combine theory with close factual analysis and led to various invitations — from the U.S. Strategic Bombing Survey for an analysis of the effects of the bombing campaign on the German war economy;²⁵ from the

---

²² In *Essays on Economic Stability and Growth*, London, Duckworth, 1960, pp. 59-74.
²³ He was later killed in action at Arnhem in 1944.
²⁴ Appendix C in BEVERIDGE's *Full Employment in a Free Society*, London Allen and Unwin, 1944.
²⁵ Some of the surprising results of this investigation are summarised in a paper on the "German War Economy", *Review of Economic Studies*, 1945-46, Vol. XIII (1).

Commissariat du Plan Français to examine the requirements of financial stabilization in France, and finally from Gunnar Myrdal, the Executive Secretary of the newly created U.N. Economic Commission for Europe in Geneva, to become the Head of the Research and Planning Division of the Secretariat. I accepted this offer — which entailed my resignation from L.S.E. as I was refused leave of absence — and my first task was to recruit a staff of some twenty five economists and statisticians for the Division which in the circumstances of the immediate post-war period proved to be none too easy. Nevertheless, the work of the Division got sufficiently well organised to complete within nine months — that is, by March 1948 — the first Annual Survey on the Economic Situation and Prospects of Europe. Appearing at the moment when the U.S. Congress was in the throes of debate over the Marshall Plan, its diagnosis of the causes of Europe's difficulties and in particular its huge imbalance of trade with the U.S., attracted instant attention.[26] Though the subsequent annual Surveys improved greatly in the quality and quantity of their information, the basic design — the comparative treatment of the rates of progress of different countries and the conclusion drawn from a commodity analysis of international trade — have remained the same.[27]

My period as a U.N. official involved also some special assignments away from Geneva, two of which deserve mention. One consisted of becoming a kind of 'Counsel' to the Committee of the non-aligned members of the Security Council meeting in Paris in the final months of 1948 on the subject of restoring a common currency for Berlin (which was the Soviet condition for lifting the blockade of Berlin). This involved intricate technical questions which the members of the Committee (mostly diplomats or Civil Servants, under the Chairmanship of Mr. Norman Robertson of Canada) were not in a position to formulate themselves, and to try to hammer out an agreement betwen the Soviet Union (represented by Mr. Malietin, the Soviet Finance Minister) and the Western Powers (represented by Mr. Burke Knapp

---

[26] It had the distinction of being the subject of the first leader on the day of its release in *The Times*, the *New York Times* and the *Guardian*. Its first mimeographed version was printed by the U.S. Government Printing Office for use of members of Congress, months before it appeared in print as a U.N. document; and within a year an unofficial translation appeared in German.

[27] Though the few years spent in Geneva were some of the most stimulating (as well as pleasant) in my life, I would not claim more than that I succeeded in creating a team which worked together with some enthusiasm and produced a unified piece which was both instructive and revealing. Though it is impossible to do justice in a matter of acknowledgements, the members of the team who contributed most to the first Survey included Hal B. Lary, the late Hans Staehle, Mrs. Esther Boserup, Albert Kervyn and Robert Neild.

from the State Department and Mr. Charles Gifford from the Foreign Office). The procedure adopted was to see the Soviet and the Western delegates alternatively, and to put questions to them in the light of each other's pronouncements. The meetings dragged on from October until Christmas, and were chiefly notable for a continued softening of the Soviet attitude, and the continued hardening of the American line, in accordance with the growing success of the airlift in securing adequate supplies for the people of West Berlin. Towards the end the Russians were ready to meet all the essential requirements initially laid down by the Americans but by that time the desire of the Americans to come to a settlement had well-nigh evaporated. Their attitude was justified by subsequent events, for a few weeks after the breakdown of negotiations, Stalin lifted the blockade without any *quid pro quo*.

The other assignment consisted of serving on an Expert Committee appointed by the Secretary General of the U.N. (then Trygve Lie) which was asked to draw up a plan that would enable member States to follow full employment policies. The Committee met in the autumn of 1949, under the shadow of an impending economic recession, and the widespread fear that this would recreate an acute shortage of dollars (due to fall in U.S. purchases) which would force other countries into deflationary measures. The Committee which included two distinguished middle-of-the-road U.S. economists, John Maurice Clark from Columbia and Arthur Smithies from Harvard, in addition to Gilbert Walker from Australia, Pierre Uri from France and myself, managed to hammer out a unanimous report[28] containing a far-reaching proposal for guaranteeing the external supply of currency of any major country against reductions in its foreign disbursements on account of imports, capital exports, etc.

However, the proposals which were well received in some quarters (notably by the British Chancellor of the Exchequer, Hugh Gaitskell) did not find favour in Washington, and this plan, like numerous others which were put forward subsequently by international expert committees of varying kinds, led to some extensive but barren discussions and was then forgotten. Yet on re-reading it one is struck by how well its analysis of the nature of the international propagation of cyclical recession fits the present world situation, once the sea-change in *dramatis personae* is allowed for. However, at the time the expected

---

[28] *National and International Measures for Full Employment*, United Nations, New York, 1949.

world recession did not materialise — the outbreak of the Korean war put a stop to that. The dollar shortage, contrary to everyone's expectation — with the possible exception of Keynes, who foresaw that something of this kind might happen in an article written shortly before his death[29] — gradually gave way to a dollar glut. And America's role as a "chronic surplus country" was gradually taken over by Germany, Japan and Switzerland, joined later by Saudi Arabia and Kuwait. However, owing to the rapid emergence of unregulated international money in the shape of the Euro-currency market, the financial or payments aspects of an international disequilibrium take on a different appearance from what was then expected and they tend to mask the shortfall in effective demand (*in real terms*) which causes the persistence of heavy unemployment combined with inflationary price movements and an almost universal feeling of impotence in dealing with them.

It was during my first year in Geneva that I received an approach from the Provost of King's about a teaching Fellowship in the College. I regarded this as a unique opportunity to return to academic life — in intellectual surroundings that were far more congenial to me than the one I left behind at L.S.E.,[30] or indeed I could have found anywhere outside Cambridge.

I was familiar with the syllabus and the methods of teaching in Cambridge as on Keynes' invitation I gave a special course of lectures on the theory of distribution to the Cambridge Faculty throughout the war and afterwards (until I went to Geneva) and was also an examiner to Part II of the Economics Tripos on several occasions. I accepted, subject to being allowed to postpone my going to Cambridge until October 1949, so as to be able to get the Research Division of the E.C.E. properly going.

The return to academic life brought me back to economic theory again. The focus of interest had in the meantime shifted from the trade

---

[29] "The Balance of Payments of the United States", *Economic Journal*, June 1946, pp. 171-187.

[30] As should be evident to the reader, my later years at L.S.E. in the 1930s were not altogether happy ones. Though the place never lacked intellectual stimulus — and there was plenty of opportunity to expound one's views in Lionel Robbins' weekly seminars — I felt out on a limbo as an early and enthusiastic supporter of Keynes, and out of sympathy with the rigid neo-classicism of Robbins, Hayek and most of the senior members of the Economics Department. Though L.S.E. was always regarded as "left-wing" by outsiders, this was an image largely created by the "media". During the period while I was there 'left-wing' views were confined to Harold Laski and to a few lecturers in law and sociology. The economics department was dominated by those who held orthodox views both on money and the functioning of a free market system — an ideology which I embraced for a brief period, but abandoned well before the appearance of Keynes' *General Theory*.

cycle to economic growth. This was greatly stimulated by the publication of Harrod's *Towards a Dynamic Economics* in 1949 which reintroduced the classical dichotomy in the notion of the 'growth potential', by distinguishing between the growth of its labour-potential, or work-performance potential (defined as the rate of growth of the *effective* labour force, which is the product of productivity per man and the available number of workers) and its capital growth potential (which is identical with the share of savings in income divided by the capital/output ratio). As Harrod (and later Domar) treated these factors as exogenously given, and mutually invariant, the problem of reconciling the two growth potentials — the "warranted" rate of capital accumulation and the "natural" rate of growth in the effective labour force — appeared as the basic "dynamic" problem.

The search for the inter-relationship between the rate of capital accumulation and the rate of growth of labour productivity led me to two important ideas. The first was that technical progress and capital investment are inextricably mixed up — inventions require to be embodied in "machines" or equipment of some kind which did not exist prior to the invention (or not in that form) but the full potentialities of which can only be realized after a long interval as a result of the design improvements that can only be gained from operational experience. It took over a hundred years to get the "best design" in steam locomotives; over fifty years to get the best design (or at least a 'stabilized' design) in sewing machines.[31] It is impossible therefore to isolate the effects of capital accumulation and the effects of "technical progress" on the productivity of labour (or in technical jargon, the "movements along" the production function from "shifts" in that function); all that can be said is that the growth of productivity will be greater the more technological change is "activated" through new investment. Hence all that is legitimate to postulate is a relationship between the rate of productivity growth and the rate of new investment per worker — which I called a "technical progress function" — which

---

[31] Of course we cannot know when (if ever) the 'best design' embodying a particular engineering idea is accomplished. But the universal experience of the last two centuries has been that while there is always a fairly extended period during which important improvements in design take place, well after the first adoption of the new invention, these come to a gradual halt after a further interval of time (which may extend to half a century or more) until a new invention crops up which gradually displaces the original "machine" altogether. (A good example is the steam locomotive, which reached its 'best design' around 1910 while its subsequent total replacement by the diesel engine came in the later 1930s, some thirty five years after the original invention of the latter.)

cannot however be assumed to be the derivative of a production function and of an exogenous rate of technical progress. Once this is accepted it inevitably follows that there is no such thing as a "technological frontier" of substitution between capital and labour, the slope of which (at any one point) would serve to determine the distribution of the product between profits (or "interest") and wages.[32]

Independently of this I felt for a long time that the share of profits in the national income was determined by macro-economic forces which ensure that the expenditures of entrepreneurs themselves generate the profits which serve to finance that expenditure. I was led to this at an early stage through the contemplation of the puzzle of the widow's cruze in Keynes' *Treatise on Money*[33] which was highly suggestive but not properly integrated with the theoretical framework of the *Treatise on Money* nor considered explicitly in the *General Theory*. Kalecki's paper on *A Theory of Profits*[34] carried the story a stage further by clarifying the nature of the assymetry of the position of "capitalists" and "wage-earners" which can be summed up in the well known phrase "capitalists earn what they spend, while wage-earners spend what they earn". But he did not develop this into a theory of distribution, for as regards the determination of distributive shares he continued to rely on the "degree of monopoly" theory of the relation of wages and prices.[35]

It was when I fully grasped the significance of the proposition that the savings of workers and salary earners must have a *negative effect* on the profits of businesses (in the aggregate) because it means a corresponding reduction in the receipts from the sale of goods to the personal sector relatively to the business sector's current outlay, which (in a closed economy and abstracting from the existence of Government expenditure and taxation) is really nothing else than the total wage and salary bill (assuming that all inter-business outlays and receipts arising out of current operations are set off against each other). Therefore for

---

[32] This latter proposition — *i.e.* the marginal productivity theory — continues to dominate the economic text books (and presumably the lecture courses) of most Western Universities, even though it is impossible to endow it with any heuristic value. Apart from postulating the existence of "capital in the abstract" which can be identified (or measured) in reality, it assumes a whole paraphernalia of conditions which do not obtain even approximately in the real world — *e.g.* perfect divisibility, constant returns to scale, perfect competition etc.

[33] *A Treatise on Money*, London, Macmillan, 1939, Vol. 1, p. 39.

[34] *Economic Journal*, June-September 1942, p. 258.

[35] I have never been able to accept that theory for the same reason for which I did not regard the concept of a demand curve applied to the individual firm as a valid one, except in the special case of "polypoly" where each seller decides on his optimal profit margin independently of the prices charged by his competitors.

business receipts to exceed production costs — in other words, for aggregate business profits to be positive and not negative — the capital outlays of businesses must exceed *personal* savings; in order that profits should be a "sizeable" proportion of sales, this excess moreover must be large relative to personal savings. But this implies in turn — since (under the assumption of a closed economy) total savings must always be equal to total investment — that savings out of profits must be large relative both to the total capital outlay and to the total profit. The two basic inequalities of a 'Keynesian' theory of distribution[36]

$$s_p > s_w \geq 0$$
$$s_p > \frac{I}{Y} > s_w$$

are therefore not arbitrarily chosen; they are the necessary conditions for a private enterprise system to function.[37]

The combination of these two ideas — *i.e.*, the technical progress function, and a Keynesian (or classical) savings function — together with a Keynes-Harrod type investment function, led to the formulation of a combined growth and distribution model which I worked out with the help of David Champernowne in the summer of 1957.[38] This has shown that it is possible to construct a model which has a determinate solution in terms of growth rates, the capital/output ratio, the investment coefficient, the profit share and the profit-rate without involving a "production function" or indeed marginal analysis of any kind. It therefore demostrated (if no more) that neo-classical theory is not indispensable — it is possible to build an equilibrium model using entirely different bricks.

---

[36] I put forward this theory in "Alternative Theories of Distribution", *Review of Economic Studies*, Vol. XXIII, No. 2 (February 1956). S_p and S_w stand for the savings co-efficients out of profit and wages respectively, *I* for business investment, *Y* for income.

[37] Consumption expenditure out of profits is itself dependent on profits. It cannot therefore secure any excess of receipts over outlays, unless there is adequate expenditure on capital account to offset the savings (of both individuals and businesses) on income account. (For an individual country, such offsets could take the form of a surplus of exports in foreign trade or loan expenditures by the Government, as well as business investment.) Various economists (J.E. Meade, F.H. Hahn, P.A. Samuelson and F. Modigliani) called into question the universal validity of the second inequality and asserted that on *a priori* grounds there is nothing to prevent the share of investment in output being less than the share of savings in non-profit income. But they overlooked the vital fact that for profits to exist, business expenditure on capital account must exceed non-business savings, and that a capitalist system cannot function unless businesses make a profit.

[38] "A Model of Economic Growth", *Economic Journal*, 1957, pp. 591-624.

However, this model had its shortcomings which neo-classical critics were not slow to point out. It was very much a "Mark I" model (as D.H. Robertson once referred to it) and led to the presentation of improved versions, Mark II and Mark III, in the course of the subsequent five years. These latter models were prepared in 1958[39] and 1962[40] and the Introduction to the volume of Essays[41] published subsequently explains how they arose and the nature of the differences between them. There is no need to go into them here. But as I explained in that Introduction, the development of my theoretical ideas has by no means come to an end with the work on growth models. Since 1965 they have changed fairly drastically, though I have not been able to present the results (though perhaps I might still be able to do so in the future) in the comprehensive form of a "model". The last six Essays in the volume of Essays already referred to[41] — starting with my Inaugural lecture,[42] and covering papers written up to 1976 — illuminate various aspects and implications of my new ways of thought without a systematic presentation of the set of interrelated ideas as a whole.

Not wishing to repeat the account given in the Introduction to the volume of Essays referred to I think I can best explain the nature of this development in terms of the shortcomings gradually perceived in my earlier theoretical work expressed in the growth models published in the years 1956-62. The list presented below follows a logical, not a chronological sequence.

1) A macro-economic model needs to be supplemented by a micro-economic analysis on the level of the single decision making unit, the firm or business, and also of the relations between groups of competing firms [without such a supplementation it is not obvious how the forces isolated in the macro-model actually operate; and it is impossible to say how far (how effectively, or how quickly or slowly) they operate]. In particular we need a theory of how prices are determined in the oligopolistic conditions prevailing in industry, in the "perfectly competitive" conditions prevailing in agriculture and most

---

[39] "Capital Accumulation and Economic Growth", in *The Theory of Capital* (ed. F. Lutz), London, Macmillan, 1961.
[40] "A New Model of Economic Growth" (written in collaboration with J.A. MIRRLEES), *Review of Economic Studies*, Vol. XXIX (1962), No. 3.
[41] *Further Essays on Economic Theory*, London, Duckworth, 1978.
[42] *Causes of the Slow Rate of Growth of the United Kingdom*, Cambridge University Press, 1966.

types of mineral extraction (where the individual producers are price-*takers*, not price-*makers*) and finally under conditions approximating the "pure" imperfect competition or "polypoly" (small-scale businesses combined with free entry, with each seller facing a limited market) which prevails over much of the tertiary sector, such as retail distribution or miscellaneous services. Oligopoly which is typical of modern manufacturing industry invariably involves price-leadership; and the considerations which enter into the determination of the profit margin of the price-leader — governed by the long-run requirements for internal finance on the one hand and the need to preserve the firm's position as price-leader on the other — provide the key to the manner in which manufacturing industry operates under conditions of modern capitalism.[43]

2) The macro-economic growth models leaned heavily on the notion of some kind of exogenous growth potential (which could however be taken to mean a zone rather than a single or a unique rate) which was some variant of Harrod's "natural" rate of growth, and reflected the assumption of an exogenous technical progress function and of population growth. The models showed how the rate of accumulation of capital and the rate of growth of output become 'attuned' to this "natural" growth rate. Such an approach is only valid in a universal context — where it refers to the *whole* productive activity of a closed or self-contained system, which has no "real-world" analogy except when the economy of the world is considered as a whole. It is not a valid assumption for analysing the economy of a single region (and the nation, looked at as a sovereign political entity, is only a particular kind of region) which is dependent on other regions both for satisfying some of its needs and for providing a market for its products; and the "resource-endowment" of which (except for natural resources) cannot be considered as exogenously given. The development of such a region, given its natural endowments (soil and its fertility, and mineral resources) and its past heritage of human and material resources at a given point of time, will depend on the external demand for its products (existing or potential) and the nature of its supply responses which together determine whether the effective demand for its products grows

---

[43] I have never been able to publish my ideas on this subject — which were developed over a run of years as a result of lectures which were annually revised — but my approach was similar to that of Adrian Wood in his book on *A Theory of Profits* (Cambridge University Press, 1975), who however carried the subject much further in some directions than I did.

relatively fast or slowly. This in turn decides whether it will attract resources from outside (through immigration and/or capital imports) or the opposite.[44]

3) The macro-models were in effect "single sector" models; they assumed that the same set of behavioural assumptions could be applied to all sectors of the economy, whereas there are important differences in technology, the type of market structure and the nature of competition as between the primary, secondary and tertiary sectors of the economy, the outputs of which are largely complementary to each other. Even in the first approximation a macro-economic model relating to a closed economy needs to be a two-sector model of Agriculture and Industry. The Keynesian type of analysis in which effective demand plays a leading role is really a theory relating to Industry (which is largely the manufacturing sector). Manufacturing plays a key role in economic development as attested by the strong empirical association between economic growth and the growth of manufacturing activities.[45]

4) Manufacturing activities, on account of economies of scale, internal and external, tend to cluster around particular "growth points" which become areas of vast immigration from more distant areas as well as from surrounding centres. This creates a tendency towards the concentration of industrial development, through a process of cumulative causation, which enhances the growth of the "successful" industrial centres by retarding or inhibiting the industrial development of others.

---

[44] It is usual to assume (for purposes of economic planning or forecasting) that each "individual" country has a potential full-employment growth rate; the purpose of economic policy is considered as one of ensuring that the actual growth-path does not diverge too much from the "full employment potential". Yet over longer periods there is considerable mobility of labour between countries (as it is within countries). Moreover the notion of "full employment output" is itself a question-begging one since it is relative to the (inherited) distribution of the labour force between different sectors. Normally there is considerable scope for increasing output through labour transference from low to high productivity sectors, the effect of which is causally indistinguishable from that due to immigration. In both cases, it is not the limitation of resources, but the limitations on the speed of adaptation or adjustment which set temporary ceilings on production.

[45] All "developed" high income countries have a highly developed manufacturing sector and are important exporters of manufactures. The reasons for this have not perhaps been fully explored; in my view they are connected with the fact that manufacturing industry generates the means for its own "extended reproduction": it generates both the savings required for capital accumulation and also provides the capital goods in which these savings are embodied; it also produces (largely though not entirely) the capital goods for the primary and tertiary sectors. (The exception is agriculture, the savings of which are partly embodied in its own output.) This, together with the existence of static and dynamic economies of scale in manufacturing, is responsible for the fact that both the level and the rate of growth of productivity in the economy as a whole is highly correlated with the level and rate of growth of manufacturing production.

This process of cumulative causation is no doubt mainly responsible for the growing differences, in productivity and real income per head, between rich and poor areas. The spatial aspects of competition under conditions of cumulative causation constitutes a field that has not been explored yet but which may call for radical changes in the prevailing views concerning the effects of freedom of trade between different countries or regions.

And here the matter must rest. I have described at considerable length the evolution of my theoretical "ideas" both before and after the Second World War, simply because throughout my academic life economic theory remained my basic interest. This was true despite increasing pre-occupations with a range of "specialised" matters such as the principles of taxation (as a result of my work on the Royal Commission on Taxation), the international implications of full employment policies, the reform of the international monetary system, commodity policies etc., as well as devoting an increasing amount of time to being an economic or fiscal adviser to various Governments abroad and two successive Labour Governments at home.

Keynes wrote once that few people are able to absorb new ideas after they are twenty-five or thirty years of age. If this did not prove to be so in my case (as it was certainly not in his) I owe it, I think, to the need to give a course of lectures on economic theory to third-year students in Cambridge. This alone gave continuity to my interest in economic theory and forced me to think through afresh each year the reasoning which underlay particular propositions.[46] For that reason I would not recommend to anyone (in the field of social sciences at any rate) that they should concentrate on "research" as against "teaching". It is more fruitful — and in the longer run more creative — to combine both.

* * *

---

[46] I discovered at an early stage that to give a lecture enjoyable to oneself (let alone the audience) it must deal with ideas that are fresh in one's mind. I made it a habit therefore to write out a new set of lecture notes each year, having the previous year's notes in front of me. I found that this annual review of one's ideas caused one to see things in a different light sometimes by slow stages and sometimes by changing one's viewpoint quite unexpectedly as a result of exploring a new line of thought. For the same reason I was loathe to stop lecturing for more than a year or two at most (while I was seconded to the Treasury under the Labour Government) knowing full well that a more prolonged interruption would make it very difficult to get back to lecturing on a subject which required unusual mental concentration.

I have said nothing in the above account about my works in the field of applied economics. These are collected in three volumes of Essays, two of which were published in 1964[47] and the third in 1978[47]. In addition the two further volumes[48] on problems of taxation reproduce, for purposes of record, the *Memorandum of Dissent* of the Royal Commission on Taxation (which I drafted on behalf of two other members of the Commission as well as myself), as well as the Reports submitted to various foreign Governments or Governments agencies (written at their invitation) and a miscellaneous number of papers submitted to various bodies.[49]

There is no need to say much about my "applied" essays since their subject matter and the circumstances in which they were written have already been fully described in the Introduction of the volume of Essays in which they are printed. In the first of these Introductions (to *Essays on Economic Policy*, Vol. I) I describe papers on economic policies as "more ephemeral than the theoretical ideas that form their background". I now find that this was a hasty judgment. At least two of the papers written twenty-eight years ago could have been equally well written now. One of these, a plan for a permanent incomes policy, has recently been described to me by an official dealing with this particular subject as "very good — but rather utopian — the time is not yet ripe for it". Another paper written in 1950 on "Employment Policies and the Problem of International Balance"[50] analyses the various options facing deficit countries confronted by the chronic surpluses of countries who refuse to expand their home demand adequately. This also is very much a live topic, the only difference being that the "chronic surplus countries" of today are not the same as those of thirty years ago.[51]

---

[47] *Essays on Economic Policy*, Vol. I and II, London, Duckworth, 1964. *Further Essays in Applied Economics*, Duckworth, 1978.
[48] *Reports on Taxation*, Vol. I and II, Duckworth, 1980.
[49] These are additional to the five papers on the subject of tax reform which have been included as Part III of *Essays in Economic Policy*, Vol. I.
[50] *Essays on Economic Policy*, Vol. I, pp. 83-94.
[51] That paper prepared for an early Conference of the International Economic Association in Monte Carlo proved to be "very controversial" when it was discussed by the group of academic economists assembled there. If it were put forward today, it would be criticized on much the same grounds by a similar group of establishment economists. The "battle-lines" as they were drawn up then have not really changed in the intervening thirty years; in a sense they have not changed since the debate started between the "Currency School" and the "Banking School" in the 19th century. Recently the adherents of the "currency school" — the monetarists — have become more vocal and more numerous but I feel confident that their influence will fade in much the same way as it did on earlier occasions.

The same is true of other papers written in the 1950s — such as the analysis of the relative merits of fiscal and monetary policies or[52] my memorandum to the Radcliffe Committee on the *modus operandi* of monetary policy submitted in 1958,[53] or the ideas put forward in my review of the Radcliffe Report published in 1960.[54]

I find that on all these matters neither the nature of the problems changed much nor my own views relating to them, though the prospect of reaching an agreed view among economists is no better now than it was twenty-five or thirty years ago. On the contrary, the upholders of the quantity theory of money have become more influential and numerous; it is their opponents, the views represented in the Radcliffe Report, which seem to be on the defensive. Yet I remain convinced that all this recrudescence of pre-Keynesian views, the new monetarism, has nothing to be said for it — I regard it as a symptom of intellectual decadence that so many people should accept it without having the least notion of how the monetary authorities regulate the "money supply" when much the greater part of the money supply consists of transferable-debt certificates of financial institutions, and when the range of institutions prepared to under-write other people's spending is constantly widening.

There is only one important matter on which the events of the 1970s caused me to change my mind. This concerns the relative importance of price (or cost?) competition, as against other "non-price" factors, such as superiority of design or quality, length and reliability of delivery dates, after-sales service, etc. Exchange rate adjustments operate *mainly* on costs and prices, and despite vast changes in relative exchange rates — in real, and not just in nominal terms — there was little effect on the pattern of trade in manufacturing. The trade-gaining surplus countries continued to gain trade, and the trade-losing deficit countries continued to lose it (especially when their own domestic market is taken into account, as well as the foreign markets). It is possible of course that if exchange rate adjustments go far enough, and last long enough, the day will come when they will begin to show results in terms of a trade-loss due to over-valuation and trade-gain due to undervaluation. In the end, if the change in relative prices goes far

---

[52] This is contained in the paper written for the centenary celebration of the Royal Economic Society of Belgium in 1955, reprinted in *Essays on Economic Policy*, Vol. I, pp. 101-08.
[53] *Ibid.*, pp. 128 ff.
[54] *Ibid.*, pp. 154-65.

enough, a point must come when cheapness will compensate the buyer for all non-price disadvantages. But even if that proved to be the case in the next few years, the world would have lost an enormous amount of wealth and well-being — through lost production and mass unemployment — in the intervening years (or decades) of "disequilibrium".

The lesson of the 1970s and the 1980s, to my mind, contradicts the current intellectual trends which seek salvation through a return to a free market system. It shows that instruments which operate through market forces (such as devaluation) are much too slow in their effects to avoid unnecessary (and in the long run, intolerable) hardship caused by reliance on them. If the mainly private-enterprise market economy is to survive (as it must, if even less palatable alternatives are to be avoided) the world needs more planning and more regulation in the matter of income-distribution as well as in the field of international or interregional trade, and not less.

Cambridge,

NICHOLAS KALDOR

[2]

LUIGI L. PASINETTI

Nicholas Kaldor:
a few personal notes

The man

Nicholas Kaldor is one of the most provocative and original economic thinkers of the present century. He belongs to that remarkable group of Central European intellectuals who emigrated from their countries of origin during the interwar period, for various reasons, and came to enrich and strengthen the intellectual standing of the Anglo-Saxon universities. Kaldor settled in England; first at the London School of Economics and then at the University of Cambridge.

He has been to the United States on many occasions. He was there in 1935-36, as a Rockefeller Travelling Fellow, and in 1960-61, as a Visiting Research Professor at Berkeley (University of California). He has also given many lectures on various occasions and in various places. Yet it must be admitted that Kaldor has never been a popular figure in the United States. If it is true that he has many friends, it is also equally true that in the United States, he hardly has any admirers in either academic or government circles. During the whole of his career Kaldor has been a prominent adviser, on matters of taxation, fiscal and monetary policy, and economic development, to a surprisingly high number of governments (India, Ceylon, Turkey, Iran, Ghana, British Guyana, Mexico, Venezuela), to many central banks, to the Economic Commission

---

The author is Professor of Economics, Università Cattolica del Sacro Cuore, Milan. Here and there in these notes he has freely used some excerpts from the biographical essay "Nicholas Kaldor," which he wrote for the *International Encyclopedia of the Social Sciences*, vol. 18, New York, 1979. Thanks are due to The Free Press, a Division of Macmillan Publishing Co., Ltd., New York, for allowing him to do so.

for Europe, to the Economic Commission for Latin America. In Great Britain he held the prestigious post of *Special Adviser* to the Chancellor of the Exchequer of the Labour Governments (1964-68 and 1974-76). But in the United States he has never been asked for any advice by any official institution, whether progressive or conservative, at any time. The only involvement he has had with a U.S. government agency was in 1945, immediately after World War II, in Europe, when he worked as Chief of the Economic Planning Staff for the U.S. Strategic Bombing Survey of Europe.

This may appear rather curious, but it has its logic. American universities are prepared to accept almost infinite variations on the theme of Walrasian general equilibrium analysis and the optimum allocation of given resources. They are also prepared to tolerate, by contrast, a great deal of stuff on the theme of Marx's theories of value and exploitation. Nicholas Kaldor has been a strong critic of both. He is a radical thinker but within the framework of established market institutions. And this is what appears to be so irritating to many of his colleagues, especially American. He is not a revolutionary; but he is a passionate advocate of reforms. His overall view of the working of a market economy is basically an optimistic one, but not in the traditional sense of believing that the market will automatically bring about the best of all positions. Kaldor is convinced that capitalist systems exhibit glaring injustices on income distribution and inherent inefficiencies, leading to involuntary unemployment and international disorder. But he is also convinced that these defects can be corrected by enlightened actions of governments and by international cooperation. He belongs to that generation of Gaitskellite British Socialists, deeply imbued with the Fabian tradition, who are idealists at heart. He is a great believer in the power of reason and intellect, in the ability of intelligent people to develop and apply analytical and practical tools that may help to shape the economic system in the way they want. He has always believed in men and women (and, by the way, in himself) being capable of behaving reasonably and dominating events.

Basic biography

Nicholas Kaldor was born in Budapest, the son of a barrister, on the twelfth of May 1908. His parents—Dr. Julius and Joan Kaldor—must have been expecting the child with some trepidation.

They only had one daughter; and two elder sons had died in infancy. When Nicholas arrived, there can be no doubt of the happiness he brought to his parents, and of the attention and affection he received in return: all this in a rather well-off Jewish family, in one of the major capitals of Central European culture.

The deep mark of this privileged childhood has remained in Kaldor's attitude and demeanor during the whole of his life; it may help to explain his exuberant, egocentric, and undisciplined character.

In Budapest, from 1918 to 1924, he attended a famous "Model Gymnasium," a school for the élite. Incidentally this was the same school which John von Neumann had attended a few years earlier. But Kaldor did not meet him until later on, in the 1930s, in Budapest, when both of them were visiting their respective families. They became friendly, and Kaldor came to know von Neumann's paper on a growing economic system. It was in fact Kaldor who, as editor of the *Review of Economic Studies* immediately after the war, had von Neumann's article translated into English and published.

In 1925-26 Kaldor attended lectures at the University of Berlin but soon moved to London, where he was an undergraduate, in 1927-30, at the London School of Economics (L.S.E.). He graduated with First Class Honours in 1930. The teachers he always mentions as influencing him are Lionel Robbins, Friedrich von Hayek, and most of all, Allyn Young, an American professor who had come to L.S.E. from Harvard University. Among his contemporaries at L.S.E. one must mention John Hicks, Erwin Rothbarth, and Tibor Scitovsky. He was appointed an Assistant Lecturer at L.S.E. in 1932, and in subsequent years he became a Lecturer and then a Reader in Economics.

In 1934 Kaldor married Clarissa Goldschmidt, a charming girl who had brilliantly graduated in History at Sommerville College, Oxford. She gave up a career of her own to give him four daughters and a remarkably happy family life.

During the war the whole L.S.E. (and the Kaldors) moved to Cambridge. But after the war, while the L.S.E. returned to London, the Kaldors remained there. In 1949 Kaldor became a Fellow of King's College (Keynes' college) and a Reader in Economics at the University of Cambridge. He was appointed a Professor in 1966. In 1974, in recognition of his services to the British (Labour) government, he was elevated to the House of Lords as a Life Peer. He retired from teaching in 1976.

Major contributions to economics

The distinct mark of Kaldor's contributions to economic theory and practice is represented by a striking originality of approach and a persistent evolution of his way of thinking.

His early contributions—while he was at the London School of Economics—were in the strict orthodoxy of marginal economics. They mainly refer to the problems under discussion at that time —the theories of imperfect and monopolistic competition and welfare economics. The term "cobweb theorem" is one of his inventions; and the "Kaldor compensation test" is well known to all scholars of welfare economics. He is also the author of a well-known survey of capital theory for *Econometrica* (1937).

But for Kaldor, as for so many economists of his generation, the crucial turning point came with the publication of Keynes' *General Theory* in 1936. Kaldor was 28—an already established economist in the tradition which Keynes put under strong attack. He was struck deeply. One noticed in him, at first, a change of interests, mainly from micro- to macroeconomic problems, and then a complete and radical change of his whole thinking about economic theory and about the practical role of an economist. Around 1939 he wrote a series of articles on macroeconomic problems, the most remarkable of which is "a model of the trade cycle" (1940) which relies on nonlinear investment and savings functions to produce "limit cycles." Later, the break with tradition became wider and final. This coincided with his moving from London to the University of Cambridge, after a spell of two years at the Economic Commission for Europe at Geneva.

At Cambridge Kaldor has done most of his mature work and has finally emerged as one of the major authors—with his friends Richard Kahn, Joan Robinson, and Piero Sraffa—of what has become known as the Post-Keynesian School of economic theory. Kaldor's original contributions to this theory are numerous. They are contained in a long series of polemical papers and in his three different versions of a model of economic growth (1957, 1961, 1962). His major original piece, however, is given in a few pages at the end of an article (1956), where he proposes a "Keynesian" theory of income distribution. The theory is in fact distinctly Kaldor's, and so it has (rightly) been called since.

Kaldor's theory of income distribution is based on the idea that profit recipients have a much higher propensity to save than wage earners. Therefore, in an economic system in which entrepreneurs carry out those investments that correspond to full employment, there exists a distribution of income between profits and wages which—owing to the differentiated propensities to save—will generate precisely that share of profits in the national income that is necessary to sustain the predetermined investments. In this way Kaldor uses Keynes' concepts of saving propensities and inserts them into a macroeconomic theoretical conception of income distribution which is reminiscent of Ricardo's. But Kaldor reverses Ricardo's chain of causation. For, in Ricardo, wages were the exogenous magnitude (determined by the sheer necessity of workers' subsistence), and profits were a residual, or rather a "surplus." In Kaldor, profits take on the character of an exogenous magnitude (determined by the necessity of investments; i.e., of capital accumulation), while wages become a residual. The consequences are far-reaching, both on a theoretical level (for a critique of the marginal theory of income distribution) and also on a practical level (for taxation policy). It can be no surprise that Kaldor's income distribution theory was immediately the target of bitter attacks. There is by now an enormous literature on the subject.

On lines parallel to those on income distribution, Kaldor developed his ideas of an "expenditure tax," proposed in a book (1955) which has by now become a classic. Kaldor's contention is that the present taxation system, basically based on personal *incomes*, is inequitable in many respects. People who inherit private fortunes have an enormous spending and economic power, without contributing in any due proportion to the community's needs and welfare. On the other hand, thrifty people are taxed twice—once on the income they save and a second time on the income they derive from accumulated savings. Kaldor proposes a radical change of the taxation basis so that people may be taxed, no longer on their incomes, but on their actual expenditures.

In the latter part of his career, Kaldor has become more and more interested in empirical work. An example is given by his inaugural lecture as a professor (1966) on "the causes of the slow rate of growth of the United Kingdom." Another interesting example is a paper written in co-authorship with Professors Hart and Tinbergen for the United Nations Conference on Trade and Development, Geneva (1964). The authors propose a scheme for an international currency based on stocks of many physical commodities. They provide computations on the basis of the thirty most traded commodities in the international market, trying to show the actual workability and the advantages of such a commodity-based monetary system. The authors themselves judged the scheme "too radical" to hope it would be accepted under present conditions. Yet, with the present growing chaos in international economic relations and spreading inflation, the proposed scheme may well be rediscussed in the future.

Kaldor has devoted much effort recently to building a theoretical construction based on the idea that the "Keynesian" features of an economy may apply to its industrial sector, while, side by side to it, the primary sector, providing food and raw materials, may be operating with "non-Keynesian" features. This antithetic sectoral analysis may also be applied to the relations between developed and less developed countries. If the "industrial" sector (or country) operates with "increasing returns to scale" (an idea going back to Allyn Young), and the primary sector (or country) operates at decreasing returns to scale (à la Ricardo, only mitigated now and then by "land-saving" innovations), then a whole series of important consequences follow, though it may not be easy to formalize them neatly. Kaldor has written a series of articles along these lines.

The reader may be surprised that I constantly refer to papers and articles in order to present Kaldor's contributions to economics, but this is the way in which he works. Kaldor is not the type of scholar who can sit down and write systematic treatises. He does not have the patience or perseverance to pursue such a task, or—as he himself puts it—he has been too intent on listening to criticisms in order to modify and improve his views. But this process never ends with him. It has clearly been more congenial to his temperament to put his ideas into short papers and then go on to other problems, often changing his mind when going back to the old ones. In this way, he has been able to cover an enormously wide field. Kaldor's ideas are scattered in an incredibly high number of articles, papers, memoranda, and reports, the only exception being the already mentioned short book on an expenditure tax. Fortunately, in the latter part of his career, Kaldor has let himself be convinced—his pride perhaps overcoming his reluctance and laziness—to collect most of his writings into a series of eight volumes (1960-80) which divide neatly into three volumes of theoretical writings, three volumes of applied economics and taxations writings, and two volumes of reports and memoranda to the

United Kingdom and to foreign governments. To read these books is extremely rewarding for any economist, provided one does not get too irritated by the darts he continually fires at traditional economic thinking. Unexpected clever insights, unorthodox remarks, original ideas are disseminated everywhere, even in the most "applied" writings. The introductions to the eight volumes which Kaldor has been compelled to write are illuminating and precious to anybody interested in the evolution of his economic thought. The whole set will remain a rich source of ideas for years to come.

His present whereabouts

Since retirement from teaching, in 1976, Kaldor has increased the number of his visits to the south of France, where he has a house, and has intensified his presence in London, where he has become unusually active at the House of Lords. No major debate on economic policy and very few minor ones can go at present without some speech or intervention or interruption by him. His contributions to the House of Lords form in fact a charming series of speeches. They show Kaldor at his best, as a debater and polemist. The main targets of his attacks have being monetarism ("a terrible curse, a visitation of evil spirits") and more particularly Thatcherism ("a menace to the United Kingdom" and, we may well add, to the world). When these speeches are collected and published, they will provide delightful reading to economists and to the informed general public alike.

The students of Cambridge see him rarely now. To the passer-by his large house in Adams Road looks rather empty, except when one or the other of his daughters arrives with a host of children. But at weekends the old house lightens up and becomes full of life again, especially during those parts of the year (late spring and early autumn) when the Cambridge weather becomes shining and provides insistent invitations to go out in the marvellously green and colorful gardens. And the Kaldors are always responding to the call, with lots of colleagues and friends, mixed with the family and the latest arrivals among King's brightest economics students. Weekends are eventful with the Kaldors, with whom one can always find, as visitors, not only some remarkable British or Hungarian friend, but also some eminent figure in the economic, or political, or financial, or literary circles, from the most remote parts of our little world.

REFERENCES

Kaldor, Nicholas. "The Recent Controversy on the Theory of Capital." *Econometrica*, 1937, *5*, 201-33.

_____. "A Model of the Trade Cycle." *The Economic Journal*, 1940, *50*, 78-95.

_____. *An Expenditure Tax*. London: Allen and Unwin, 1955.

_____. "Alternative Theories of Distribution." *The Review of Economic Studies*, 1955-56, *22*, 82-100.

_____. "A Model of Economic Growth." *The Economic Journal*, 1957, *67*, 591-624.

_____. "Capital Accumulation and Economic Growth." In Douglas C. Hague and Friedrich Lutz, eds. *The Theory of Capital*. London: Macmillan, 1961, 177-222.

_____, and Mirrlees, J. A. "A New Model of Economic Growth." *The Review of Economic Studies*, 1962, *29*, 174-92.

_____, Hart, A. G., and Tinbergen, J. "The Case for an International Commodity Reserve Currency." UNCTAD, Geneva, 1964; reprinted in Kaldor, 1960-80, *4*, 130-77.

_____. *Collected Economic Essays*. 8 vols. London: Duckworth. Volume 1: *Essays on Value and Distribution*, 1960; Volume 2: *Essays on Economic Stability and Growth*, 1960; Volume 3: *Essays on Economic Policy, I*, 1964; Volume 4: *Essays on Economic Policy, II*, 1964; Volume 5: *Further Essays on Economic Theory*, 1978; Volume 6: *Further Essays on Applied Economics*, 1978; Volume 7: *Reports on Taxation, I: Papers Relating to the United Kingdom*, 1980; Volume 8: *Reports on Taxation, II: Reports to Foreign Governments*, 1980.

Nicholas Kaldor, 12 May 1908–30 September 1986

By G. C. Harcourt

Jesus College, Cambridge

Final version received 11 November 1987. Accepted 25 November 1987.

Introduction

Nicholas Kaldor[1] resembled Keynes more than any other twentieth-century economist because of the breadth of his interests, his wide-ranging contributions to theory, his insistence that theory must serve policy, his periods as an adviser to governments, his fellowship at King's and, of course, his membership of the House of Lords. It is impossible in a short article to do full justice to Kaldor's extraordinary achievements, so I shall concentrate on aspects of his theoretical contributions.[2] To put them in perspective at least two things must be remembered. First, while Kaldor was a highly original theorist, full of ideas of his own and making important modifications to and criticisms of the theories of others, he was also fortunate in his mentors, as he generously acknowledged. Second, Kaldor's contributions to theory fall into three distinct stages.

Among Kaldor's mentors were Allyn Young, his teacher at the LSE; John Hicks (as an undergraduate Kaldor came to know John Hicks—JR as he then was—and they became inseparable companions until Hicks went to Cambridge in the mid-1930s, meeting most days and discussing economic theory, often at excellent Italian restaurants near where they lived); von Neumann; and, when he came to Cambridge, Joan Robinson, Richard Kahn and, most especially, Piero Sraffa (with whom he was as likely as not to spend days discussing political issues as well as economic ones). He would also have wished to mention Robbins and Hayek as important influences early on in his career, and through whom (as well as through Hicks) he became familiar with the writings of Walras, Wicksell and Pareto, the British classical economists and Marx, and von Mises and the Austrians generally. He parted company with Robbins and Hayek ideologically and theoretically in the mid- to late-1930s, never to return, mainly because of his absorption of the method and message of *The General Theory* (but also because, again through Hicks and Brinley Thomas, he had come to know the work of Myrdal and the Swedish monetary theorists). Happily, this was not to be his experience with Hicks. For after a separation of ideas in the postwar years, there was a coming together again in the 1980s. One of Kaldor's last publications was his splendid Hicks Lecture, 'Limits on growth' (Kaldor, 1986a), in which he paid an affectionate tribute to his old friend.[3]

There were three stages of Kaldor's career. First, there was the young orthodox theorist at the LSE who made seminal contributions to the theory of the firm, the emerging theory of imperfect competition, welfare economics and capital theory. Second, there was the enthusiastic Keynesian (after a slow start—see Pasinetti, 1979, p. 367), who absorbed Keynes's message very thoroughly indeed and added significantly to the corpus of Keynesian thought in at least two directions: his model of the trade cycle (Kaldor, 1940) and, what is probably his greatest theoretical article (he certainly thought so and so do his most discerning admirers), 'Speculation and economic stability' (Kaldor, 1939b), together with its sequel on 'Keynes's theory of the own-rates of interest' which was written but not published at the time (Kaldor, 1960b, pp. 59-74). Third, there was Kaldor of the postwar period, who painted on increasingly larger canvasses, absorbed with the theory of distribution and accumulation, first for capitalist economies, then for developing ones, and finally for the world as a whole. It was principally during this period that he became increasingly critical of the 'vision' and the methods of mainstream economic theory.

Observers of the Kaldor phenomenon part company at this point. First, there are those who think that Kaldor of the first and possibly the second stage was best, and who regret his transformation into Kaldor of the third stage. They feel that he lost his grip on modern developments and so his influence, at least as a theorist, on the postwar generation. But there are those who, although they admire the cleverness of Kaldor Mark I and certainly would put his early Keynesian articles near the pinnacle of his achievements, also think that the mature Kaldor, who strayed explicitly from the orthodox fold (and explained cogently why), was, in some dimensions at least, the greatest of them all. They admire the maturity of his vision and the extraordinary fertility and ingenuity of his mind, and his 'feel' for economic issues, processes and their outcomes and/or solutions, often set out in conclusions that, as with Keynes, ran ahead of his arguments.

To explain the dichotomy of reactions, it has to be said that after the war Kaldor himself became less painstaking and careful in his arguments and presentations, preferring to sketch outlines and let others fill in the details and provide rigorous concise coherent arguments. (Before the war he was much more careful, revising many times before he submitted papers for publication.) Partly this was because Kaldor was never a good mathematician—he said himself that he was too impatient to learn the techniques. (Nevertheless, few got more mileage than Kaldor from an ability to multiply by 1 in the mathematical expressions of theories.) So, increasingly, he grew to dislike the form in which modern theory is done, as well as its conceptual structure and basic equilibrium methodology which he derisively rejected. (Perhaps the most succinct statement is Kaldor, 1966a, p. 310, in which his characteristic building and scaffolding analogy is set out.) This meant in turn that younger mainstream theorists were impatient with and mystified by both his criticisms and his contributions. Moreover, although Kaldor had a thorough knowledge of the classics in the literature and a keen sense of what the important issues were at any moment of time, he increasingly read less and less contemporary literature. Partly this was because there is so much of it and it is so technical, and he was a slow reader; partly, it was because he preferred to map out his own theoretical structure as he tackled problems, and he did not bother with the facade of most of us, who put the 'scholarship' in afterwards so that the finished products appear as if we had first read the relevant literature and then filled in the niches that emerged. It must also be emphasized, as Ruth Cohen reminded me, that Kaldor was doing a tremendous amount of other things at the same time—for example, political adviser to the British and other governments, teaching, faculty 'politics'. So, even when we allow for his enormous energy, gusto and enthusiasm, there is nevertheless just so much any one person can do. Even Nicky admitted that twenty-four hours *could* be a binding constraint. Kaldor thus paid the price of those who, while they were within the orthodox fold, were acknowledged as potentially one of the greats, and were then dismissed or ignored or ridiculed once they departed from it.

I. First Papers: The LSE Years

I shall now attempt to sketch how Kaldor's theoretical work developed over time, always remembering that this was only part of his output and that he was a busy teacher and often a civil servant at the same time. One of Kaldor's earliest papers (Kaldor, 1934a) still has a very modern ring to it—the determinateness of equilibrium. It concerned existence and stability and dealt principally with the question of whether the ultimate equilibrium in a market (or an economic system) is or is not independent of the path that is taken to it. This eventually was to become in Kaldor's view a conviction that equilibrium itself did not exist (his last book, Kaldor 1985a, was entitled *Economics without Equilibrium*), and that to pose economic questions in the usual way of whether there is an equilibrium (or several) and, if so, whether it is (they are) stable was to place our thinking in a straitjacket. Indeed, it made the world (or at least the theorist's image of it) conform to theory rather than, as he was to argue, the other way around. Ultimately, Kaldor was to proceed from empirical regularities—his famous 'stylized facts'—which are true in the broad majority of observed cases, certainly often enough to warrant explanation, to explanations that themselves should be the most reasonable ways capable 'of accounting for the facts independently of whether they fit into the general framework of received theory or not' (Kaldor, 1985a, p. 8).

In the 1930s, Kaldor also wrote several fine critical articles on the theory of the firm (Kaldor, 1934b), and on imperfect competition (Kaldor, 1934c, 1935), in which he emerged as a sympathetic critic of both Joan Robinson and Chamberlin. In Kaldor (1934b, 1935) he posed the knotty problem as to whether the firm *could* be defined under the conditions of perfect competition; while in his review article of Joan Robinson's *Economics of Imperfect Competition* (Kaldor, 1934c), he was sceptical as to whether any rigorous meaning could be given to the notion of an industry in imperfectly competitive conditions: which set of firms ended up in an industry depended upon the arbitrarily chosen firm and/or product from which the analysis started. Features of Kaldor's early articles were his cleverness and his critical scepticism. For example, in his seminal paper on 'Market imperfection and excess capacity' (Kaldor, 1935), he argued that free entry led to perfect competition only if there are non-decreasing returns to scale. His arguments (1960a, pp. 68-9) as to why the demand curve of a firm is 'indeterminate' in conditions of monopolistic competition are brilliant, especially his demonstration of why the effects of the actions of a single producer will not necessarily spread themselves over a large number of rivals, so that for each the effect is negligible, but rather will ripple along the chain of substitutes. Even when his arguments subsequently were shown to be wrong, or at least incomplete or overstated, as they were in his famous note on the Corn Laws and compensation tests (Kaldor, 1939a), the article itself reads so lucidly that the reader has to be reminded that the reasoning was subsequently shown by Scitovsky (1941) to contain flaws.

His survey of capital theory (Kaldor, 1937) is noteworthy for at least two reasons. First, there was the anticipation of the postwar criticism from Cambridge of the lack of coherence of the notion of a quantity of 'capital' and its marginal product, the germ of which Kaldor subsequently was to argue (Kaldor, 1960a, pp. 6-7) could be found in Knight's criticisms of the Austrians. (In 1937 Kaldor was on the other side—and Solow for one (1963, p. 9) wished he had stayed there.) Second, at the end of the article he independently discovered von Neumann's result (von Neumann, 1945-6) that $r = g$, where r = rate of profits and g = rate of growth—in Kaldor's case in a slave society,[4] though the intuition of both authors was the same. (Kaldor reminded his readers of this result in his 1959 *Economica* papers on growth and inflation, in which he used it in order to provide an economy-wide theory of the rate of profits and to argue for the necessity of continuing inflation in order to keep growth going in a capitalist economy: see Kaldor, 1959a, b.)

II. THE ENTHUSIASTIC KEYNESIAN

Kaldor's contributions to Keynesian economics fall into two distinct periods. First, there is the enthusiastic convert who significantly extended (e.g. in his 1940 article on the trade cycle) and modified the basic structure of *The General Theory* (e.g. in his 1939 article on speculation and stability: 1939b) and who contributed the important empirical Appendix C to Beveridge's *Full Employment in a Free Society* (Kaldor, 1943). In his model of the trade cycle, he showed that the internal rhythms of capitalism are not such as to seek out an equilibrium resting place but, rather, to shuttle backwards and forwards between highs and lows as a result of the interrelationship between overall saving and investment decisions. Kaldor was one of the earliest Keynesians to explore stock and flow relationships and their effects on the desired rate of accumulation, with increases in expected profits and output encouraging accumulation while increasing stocks as a result of past accumulation discouraged it, so that for each short period the position of the relationship between I and Y was affected by the stock of capital goods. In the shape of the corresponding dynamic saving-income relationship there was a hint of the role that the distribution of income was later to play in his work. What was missing was a systematic role for monetary factors, a limitation that was later to be remedied by Hugh Hudson (1957), the editor of the first two volumes of Kaldor's papers (Kaldor, 1960a, b).

Kaldor was attracted to the work of Keynes not only because of his appreciation of its insights but also as a reaction to his increasing dissatisfaction with the parallel work of Hayek. This disillusion first started in the early 1930s when Kaldor (with Honor Croome) translated one of Hayek's books (Hayek, 1929, 1933), into English. In doing so, he came across certain incoherencies which Hayek could never explain satisfactorily. Kaldor was later to criticize the trade cycle theories of Hayek, theories that were built on the foundation of Austrian capital theory—the concepts of the average period of production and roundabout methods of production, and how they responded to changes in the rate of interest. Kaldor was severely critical of a number of versions of the theory, especially of Hayek's inability to distinguish between whether he was discussing what sort of investment or how much investment was being done (see Kaldor, 1939c, 1943). Keynes thought that Kaldor rather overdid it in the end: 'Your attack on poor Hayek is not merely using a sledge hammer to crack a nut, but on a nut which is already decorticated... yours is a brilliant theory, but too much so, perhaps for this subject' (quoted in Thirlwall, 1987, p. 47).[5]

An emphasis that was to run through Kaldor's work for the rest of his life made an early appearance in his speculation and stability paper (Kaldor 1939b), namely, the importance of the existence of established 'norms' for the attainment of stability in economic systems. There, it was applied to Keynesian concerns, especially the theory of interest rates; in the postwar period, it was to be applied to the prices of primary commodities and to the foreign exchanges. Kaldor attributed the great increase in the volatility of fluctuations of these prices in this period, and especially since the 1970s, to the lack of 'norms'. Without them, speculation leads to enhanced rather than to dampened fluctuations. This insight clearly had applications to the liquidity preference explanation of the level of interest rates and for the instability of the function itself, one of Keynes's most prominent conjectures. There are two points to be kept in mind: first, that the story of price formation is fundamentally different in models where stocks dominate flows rather than the other way around, as is more usual; second, in the traditional theories of speculation there is an implicit assumption that there *are* well established 'norms', usually normal prices, which are either known through experience or, at least, are 'out there' to be found. In such circumstances, speculation can be shown to be stablizing. If it is not the case that well established 'norms' exist—here the lack of the link with gold in present exchange rate regimes becomes relevant—the speculative activity is much more likely to feed on itself in a cumulative process of destabilization. These insights allowed Kaldor to show that Keynes's renowned intuition allowed him to make conjectures about the rate of interest (and the operation of the multiplier) that happened to be true only in a special case—but one that was 'a fair approximation to reality' (Kaldor, 1939b, p. 52).

III. THE POSTWAR KEYNESIAN

The second stage of Kaldor's contributions to Keynesian economics concerns Kaldor as the scourge of Friedman's monetarism and Mrs Thatcher's policies, in which he led the fight against the forces of darkness in both the theoretical and the political areas (see, e.g. Kaldor, 1982, 1983a). Balogh and, later, Kaldor were prominent among the few economists who were prepared to see monetarism for what it is—'the incomes policy of Karl Marx', Balogh called it—rather than pussyfoot around at a purely technical level as most of the economics establishment did, even the Keynesian members of it in the United Kingdom (and Australia). In these debates, Kaldor explored what he considered to be the theoretical and tactical weaknesses of *The General Theory* from the point of view of allowing the monetarist attack successfully to occur on both the theoretical and the applied policy fronts. Especially important here are Kaldor's views on the endogeneity of the money supply in a credit economy;

the inappropriateness of Keynes's assumption of perfect competition and the consequent neglect of the role of increasing returns, a neglect that would not have occurred had the microeconomic foundations been imperfectly competitive from the beginning (as Harrod for one urged on Keynes from the 1920s on; see Kregel, 1985); and the limitations of using a closed-economy model so that the sources of both employment and growth contributed by exports, again as Harrod had stressed, were neglected. In making this stand, Kaldor incorporated ideas that stemmed from Allyn Young (on dynamic increasing returns, whereby demand interaction between markets led to accumulation which incorporated technical advances) and Myrdal on cumulative causation, from Harrod's foreign trade multiplier and later from Verdoorn. (The last formed the basis of his Inaugural Lecture at Cambridge in the 1960s, Kaldor 1966b, as well as being the theoretical rationale for the introduction of the Selective Employment Tax (SET) by the Wilson Labour government in the 1960s.)

In the postwar period Kaldor wrote in a number of places about what a weak point in the Keynesian armoury is the assumption of exogeneity of the money supply. Perhaps the fullest statement of his views is his paper (Kaldor, 1983b) in the Keynes Centenary volume edited by Worswick and Trevithick (1983). There, he shows how two rival theories of the general price level are struggling to exist within the quantity theory context in which Keynes was writing. One is the quantity theory of money itself; the other is Pigou's Marshallian mark-up model. Kaldor saw the latter as being elaborated by Keynes in Chapter 21 on prices in *The General Theory*, in which he reinstated those 'homely but intelligible concepts' of marginal cost and short-period elasticity of supply and removed the dichotomy between the 'real' factors of Volume I of the *Principles* and the 'monetary' ones of Volume II, so integrating money, right from the start, into an analysis of a monetary production economy. Kaldor argued that, in a credit-using economy, money *must* be endogenous because the trading banks must within reason meet the 'needs of trade' and the central bank must let them do so because it is the lender of last resort. It is thus no longer possible to specify the tautologies of the quantity theory in such a way that they provide a direct test of the rival predictions of the monetarists and the bastard Keynesians. Previously these tests had always been to the advantage of the former group, if Friedman and Schwartz were to be believed. (Kaldor argued that they were not, quoting both Russell and Friedman and Schwartz themselves to back him up; see Kaldor, 1983b, especially n. 33, pp. 19-20.) His views on the endogeneity of the money supply had earlier been expressed in his evidence to the Radcliffe Committee, whose Report (1959) was much influenced by Kaldor's views.

Because of Kaldor's long sustained emphasis on increasing returns, he was much attracted to Weitzman's influential 1982 *Economic Journal* article on the relationship between increasing returns, imperfect competition and Keynesian unemployment. The argument is that if there is perfect competition there must be constant returns to scale and perfect divisibility. Thus, if anyone were to be dismissed they could immediately set up in business on their own, no doubt obtaining the required capital by borrowing at a given rate of interest on a perfect capital market. How Keynes would have laughed at this gross caricature model of the modern economy that he had in mind in *The General Theory*, even if his microeconomic foundations were Marshallian and out of date (for possible reasons why, see Harcourt, 1987, pp. 12-14). Indeed, I am surprised that Kaldor himself took it on board, for it is at variance with his own postwar methodology (see p. 161 above). Nevertheless, we *can* take on board the implication of Kaldor's criticism that analysis of modern economies should now start with microeconomic foundations that reflect the market structures of the economies concerned.

IV. Distribution and Growth

Coinciding with Kaldor's interest in developing Keynesian theory and policy were his postwar contributions to the theory of distribution and growth for which he is probably best known. Certainly his 1955-6 *Review of Economic Studies* paper, 'Alternative theories of distribution', must be his most referred to (and criticized) paper. With this development went for a decade or so his quixotic conviction that the equilibrium level of activity of a *growing* capitalist economy must be a *full employment* level, certainly of labour if not of capital[6] (see Kaldor, 1970), a conviction that led Samuelson (1964, p. 345) to dub him Jean Baptiste Kaldor. It has always been a mystery as to why he felt he had to make this assumption. Certainly he never satisfactorily established a coherent theory to justify it as an endogenous result, though he tried to do so in several papers, see Kaldor (1955-6, 1957, 1959a, 1959b, 1961, 1962). In the 1955-6 paper the need for such a demonstration stemmed from the argument that the multiplier mechanism could explain *either* the level of income (as a *short-period* phenomenon with prices fixed or at least given) *or* the distribution of income (as a *long-period* phenomenon brought about by price changes in a situation in which $s_\pi > s_w$, where s_π is the marginal propensity to save from profits and s_w, the marginal propensity to save from wages, with income independently determined, i.e. by other forces, at full employment), but not both together.[7] Yet Kalecki before the war and Hahn after the war showed that it was possible simultaneously to determine both income *and* its distribution in the short period in models that embodied something akin to a multiplier process. In Kaldor (1955-6) g_w and g_n, where g_w is Harrod's warranted rate of growth and g_n, his natural rate of growth, were meant to be brought together through the distributive mechanism, while in later papers variants of this process were elaborated on, in some requiring the distributive mechanism to work in the short period despite the initial disclaimer that it was a long-period tendency (see Harcourt, 1963, 1965).

The object of these exercises was to produce integrated models that implied the 'stylized facts' of growth in advanced countries as Kaldor saw them: relatively constant shares of wages, rates of profits and capital-output ratios in a world nevertheless characterized by continuing technical advances in both methods of production and the products themselves. Furthermore, the microeconomic foundations were not competitive but mainly oligopoly-cum-price leadership. A feature of Kaldor's discussion of investment decision-making was the modelling of 'real-world' practices, for example, the pay-off period in the discussions of the choice of technique and the length of life of durable assets (see Kaldor and Mirrlees, 1962). The models include a characteristic Kaldor touch, the technical progress function, which itself went through a variety of forms. It started in Kaldor (1957) as an economy-wide total relationship between accumulation and productivity growth arising from the accompanying embodied technical advances and ended in Kaldor and Mirrlees (1962) in a marginal form, before vanishing altogether. It arose from Kaldor's dissatisfaction with the distinction in orthodox theory between a movement *along* a given production function owing to changing factor prices, and a movement *of* the function itself arising from technical advances, a distinction that he would not accept even in principle. Here, I think he went too far, for Salter's work (1960, 1966; 1965), which was developed at the same time, showed exactly how it could be accepted. All told, although he was to grow increasingly dissatisfied with aspects of this approach, it was a grand attempt to put into practice methods that he, along with Kalecki and Joan Robinson, had developed as their dissatisfaction increased with what they saw to be the orthodox approach.

Eventually, though, Kaldor moved away from the unnecessarily restrictive constraint of requiring full employment. Instead, he emphasized the notion of cumulative causation. He became more and more dissatisfied with equilibrium economics, the notion of balance of forces, the strong tendency of economies to return to former resting places following shocks, or to seek out new ones following changes in underlying conditions. In its place he put the notion that, once economies get a run on (or off), they keep it up rather than return to the pack. His 'fairly drastic' changes in theoretical ideas formed for many years the basis of lectures to undergraduates at Cambridge, although he himself was 'not... able to present the results in the comprehensive form of a "model"' (Kaldor, 1960a, p. xxv). (Others have tried to do so; see Targetti, 1985; Thirlwall, 1986; Molana and Vines, 1987; Canning, 1988.) Had such a model been formulated, it would have taken 'account of the crucial differences, in terms of behavioural assumptions, between the primary, secondary and tertiary sectors of the economy' (Kaldor, 1978a, p. viii). In particular, he was to stress the different production conditions and pricing behaviour of the producers of raw materials on the one hand, and the producers of industrial products on the other, a distinction first used within a modern economy by Kalecki.[8] It is perhaps ironical that the same differences in behaviour with respect to prices are implied in the microeconomic foundations of the models of his full employment phase although there they applied to the respective pricing, employment and investment behaviour of the consumption and investment goods sectors (see Harcourt, 1963).

V. Kaldor and Sraffa

As mentioned above, (see p. 159), Kaldor's best friend at Cambridge was Piero Sraffa. Kaldor's understanding of Ricardo's contributions owes much to Sraffa, not only to the publication of the famous edition of Ricardo's works and correspondence (Sraffa with Dobb, 1951-5; 1973), but also to the access that Sraffa gave Kaldor to his findings before publication when Kaldor gave the lecture on Ricardo to undergraduates in a 'circus' on famous economists during the war. Kaldor's attitude to Sraffa's most important theoretical work, *Production of Commodities by Means of Commodities* (Sraffa 1960), changed over the years—he said 'that it "grows on one" with the passage of time' (Kaldor,

1985b, p. 637). Given Kaldor's own interest in capital theory, his knowledge of von Neumannn's views and article and his independent discovery of the result $r = g$, it is not surprising that he was inclined to interpret Sraffa's basic model as a von Neumann model caught in suspended animation. Moreover, because he was also concerned with distribution and accumulation, he welcomed Sraffa's 'more comprehensive model' in which variations in the division of the product are considered, and especially Sraffa's final move, whereby the rate of profits is made exogenous to the sphere of production, following the initial moves of, first, no explicit subsistence wage, and then a wage that is in principle split into two parts—the ever present element of subsistence, and a variable share of the surplus with profits. Kaldor was also to make accumulation and profits have first claim on the use of the national product, with the wage-earners receiving the residual—exactly the opposite of the procedure in the Physiocratic, Classical and Marxian systems. Finally, Kaldor was to see in Sraffa's writings a rigorous statement of part of his own critique of orthodox theory and of his reasons for breaking with it. He says:

> Whatever view one takes of the importance of Sraffa's book considered as a new theory of value on classical limes, there can be no doubt of his achievement as a critique of existing theory. His demonstration that the solution of the production equations leaves one degree of freedom so that the process of equilibrium reproduction is consistent with differing divisions of the net product between profits and wages for any particular net to gross product ratio is an important result which contradicts the most frequently emphasized implication of existing theories, according to which relative 'factor endowments' determine 'factor prices'. And his demonstration that the system of prices will deviate from those given by the labour theory of value at any particular rate of profit higher than zero in a precise and predictable manner is a considerable advance on Marx's theory of the difference between values and 'production prices' depending on the ratio of fixed to variable capital.   Kaldor (1985b, pp. 636-7)

VI. Conclusion

Kaldor was progressive and humane. He hated stupidity, muddle and injustice. He was immensely clever and confident, an extraordinarily tough arguer, saying exactly what he thought. He was sometimes an intellectual bully, yet generous when he was persuaded that he was wrong and never reluctant to jettison his own intellectual capital. He had the saving grace of an infectious sense of humour. 'He could annoy and irritate, but most people ended by feeling affection for him.' Indeed, he was much loved by those who knew him best—and was sometimes viewed as an ogre by those who did not, and whose policies and vested interests he opposed. With Sraffa, Joan Robinson (his rival as well as his friend), Kahn, Champernowne and later Pasinetti, he was an integral part of a team of outstandingly original and formidable economists.

Many would argue that it is a scandal that Nicholas Kaldor was never awarded the Nobel Prize for economic science. He was another victim of the, perhaps unconscious, boycott by the Electors of those unorthodox creative minds who were too close to Keynes and to England—Kaldor was immensely proud of his adopted country as well as of his Hungarian roots. Of course, he would have loved to have received the prize and his friends would have been delighted for him. But he was far too free a spirit to fret about it, and the insights contained in the extraordinary range of his contributions, published in eight volumes of collected economic essays, will surely allow him the last and lasting word.

ACKNOWLEDGMENTS

I am much indebted to Ruth Cohen, Ken Coutts, Phyllis Deane, Meghnad Desai, Mike Kitson, Peter Kriesler, Bob Rowthorn, Steve Satchell, Robert Skidelsky, Alister Sutherland, Tony Thirlwall, Terry Ward, Adrian Wood and the editors of this Journal for their comments on a draft of this paper. I also wish to thank Tony Thirlwall for allowing me to read part of the manuscript of his biography of Nicholas Kaldor, as well as his British Academy essay, and Adrian Wood for allowing me to read a draft of his Palgrave entry.

NOTES

1. Nicholas Kaldor was born in Budapest on 12 May 1908, the son of Dr Julius Kaldor, a lawyer, and Mrs Joan Kaldor. He attended the famous 'Model Gymnasium' as a boy, studied economics in Berlin in 1925-6 and then moved to London to the LSE in 1927. He graduated with a First in 1930, and was appointed as an Assistant in economics in 1932. This later became an Assistant Lectureship, and he was made a Lecturer in Economics in 1938. During the Second World War the LSE was evacuated to Cambridge and Kaldor taught there until near the end of the war when he served as chief of the economic planning staff of the US Strategic Bombing Survey. After two years in Geneva from 1947 to 1949 as Director of Research at the ECE under Myrdal, Kaldor was elected to a Fellowship at King's College, Cambridge, and was appointed to a University Lectureship in Economics and Politics in 1949. He was appointed to a Readership in the Faculty of Economics and Politics in 1952 and was awarded a Personal Chair in 1966. Kaldor was elected a Fellow of the British Academy in 1963 and he was President of the Royal Economic Society from 1974 to 1976. He had two important spells in government as Special Adviser to the Chancellor of the Exchequer, from 1964 to 1968, and from 1974 to 1976. He was also an adviser to many overseas governments. He was made a Life Peer (Baron Kaldor of Newnham in the City of Cambridge) in 1974. Kaldor retired in 1975. In 1934 Nicholas Kaldor married Clarissa Goldschmidt; they had four daughters and eleven grandchildren.
2. Meghnad Desai and Alister Sutherland have pointed out to me that Kaldor's best known book is *An Expenditure Tax* (Kaldor, 1955), and that his work in the field of taxation had great international influence, indeed notoriety. I can only plead shortage of space and the lack of competence to assess this aspect of his contributions.

   A note on citation: Between 1960 and 1980 Duckworth published eight volumes of economic essays by Nicholas Kaldor. In the references at the end of the article I first give the original places and dates of publication and then in which volumes they are reprinted. The eight volumes are:

   I. *Essays on Value and Distribution* (1960a)
   II. *Essays on Economic Stability and Growth* (1960b)
   III. *Essays on Economic Policy (I)* (1964a)
   IV. *Essays on Economic Policy (II)* (1964b)
   V. *Further Essays on Economic Theory* (1978a)
   VI. *Further Essays on Applied Economics* (1978b)
   VII. *Reports on Taxation (I)* (1980a)
   VIII. *Reports on Taxation (II)* (1980b)

3. Kaldor (1986b, pp. 6-7) also mentions the influence of Maurice Allen, until recently a largely forgotten figure (but see Warren Young, 1987, p. viii), who was one year senior to Kaldor at the LSE.
4. Bob Rowthorn has pointed out to me that the slave society aspect is essentially irrelevant, or possibly misleading, as accumulation may not occur in a slave society.
5. For a full account of the issues involved in these debates, see Thirlwall (1987, pp. 40-7).
6. Bob Rowthorn has pointed out to me that the constraint has to be capital, *not* labour, where a reserve army of labour will keep the wage-earners quiescent, *unless* the wage-earners are farsighted enough to trade-off a low share of income now for the benefits in the future of higher growth overall.
7. It must be remembered that the most controversial part of the article is the last section on a 'Keynesian' theory of distribution; the earlier sections deal with classical theories, mainly Ricardo's, Marx, neoclassical and Kalecki's 'degree of monopoly' theory.

8. Terry Ward has reminded me that Kaldor's interest in international policy and his concern to suggest ways of increasing global stability in order to promote faster economic growth and more rapid, less uncertain, development for Third World countries were based very much on his two-sector model and its implications; see for example Kaldor (1976).

REFERENCES

Works by Kaldor cited

KALDOR, N. (1934a). A classificatory note on the determinateness of equilibrium. *Review of Economic Studies*, 1, 122-36. Reprinted in Vol. I, 13-33.

—— (1934b). The equilibrium of the firm. *Economic Journal*, 44, 60-76. Reprinted in Vol. I, 34-50.

—— (1934c). Mrs Robinson's 'Economics of Imperfect Competition'. *Economica*, 1, 335-41. Reprinted in Vol. I, 53-61.

—— (1935). Market imperfection and excess capacity. *Economica*, 2, 33-50. Reprinted in Vol. I, 62-95.

—— (1937). Annual survey of economic theory: the recent controversy on the theory of capital. *Econometrica*, 5, 201-33. Reprinted in Vol. I, 153-205.

—— (1939a). Welfare propositions of economics and interpersonal comparisons of utility. *Economic Journal*, 49, 549-52. Reprinted in Vol. I, 143-6.

—— (1939b). Speculation and economic stability. *Review of Economic Studies*, 7, 1-27. Reprinted in Vol. II, 17-88.

—— (1939c). Capital intensity and the trade cycle. *Economica*, 6, 40-6. Reprinted in Vol. II, 120-47.

—— (1940). A model of the trade cycle. *Economic Journal*, 50, 78-92. Reprinted in Vol. II, 177-92.

—— (1942). Professor Hayek and the concertina-effect. *Economica*, 9, 359-82. Reprinted in Vol. II, 148-76.

—— (1943). The quantitative aspects of the full employment problem in Britain. Appendix C to *Full Employment in a Free Society* by Sir William Beveridge. London: George Allen & Unwin. Reprinted in Vol. III, 23-82.

—— (1955). *An Expenditure Tax*. London: George Allen & Unwin.

—— (1955-6). Alternative theories of distribution. *Review of Economic Studies*, 23, 83-100. Reprinted in Vol. I, 209-36.

—— (1957). A model of economic growth. *Economic Journal*, 67, 591-624. Reprinted in Vol. II, 259-300.

—— (1959a). Economic growth and the problem of inflation: Part I. *Economica*, 26, 212-26.

—— (1959b). Economic growth and the problem of inflation: Part II. *Economica*, 26, 287-98.

—— (1960a, b; 1964a, b; 1978a, b; 1980a, b). *Economic Essays*. London: Duckworth. (See n.2 above for individual titles.)

—— (1961). Capital accumulation and economic growth. In F. A. Lutz and D. C. Hague (eds), *The Theory of Capital*. London: Macmillan, 177-222. Reprinted in Vol. V, 1-53.

—— (1966a). Marginal productivity and the macroeconomic theories of distribution. *Review of Economic Studies*, 33, 309-19. Reprinted in Vol. V, 81-99.

—— (1966b). Causes of the slow rate of economic growth in the United Kingdom. Inaugural Lecture at the University of Cambridge. Reprinted in Vol. V, 100-38.

—— (1970). Some fallacies in the interpretation of Kaldor. *Review of Economic Studies*, 37, 1-7.

—— (1976). Inflation and recession in the world economy. *Economic Journal*, 86, 703-14. Reprinted in Vol. V, 214-30.

—— (1982). *The Scourge of Monetarism*. Oxford: Oxford University Press.

—— (1983a). *The Economic Consequences of Mrs Thatcher*. London: Duckworth.

—— (1983b). Keynesian economics after fifty years. In Worswick and Trevithick (1983, pp. 1-28).

—— (1985a). *Economics without Equilibrium. The Okun Memorial Lectures at Yale University.* Cardiff: University College Cardiff Press.

—— (1985b). Piero Sraffa 1898-1983. *Proceedings of the British Academy*, London: Vol. LXXI. Cardiff: Oxford University Press.

—— (1986a). Limits on growth. *Oxford Economic Papers*, 38, 187-98.

—— (1986b). Recollections of an economist. *Banca Nazionale del Lavoro Quarterly Review*, no. 156, 3-26.

—— and MIRRLEES, J. A. (1962). A new model of economic growth. *Review of Economic Studies*, 29, 174-92. Reprinted in Vol. V, 54-80.

Other authors

CANNING, D. (1988). Increasing returns in industry and the role of agriculture in growth. *Oxford Economic Papers*, forthcoming.

HARCOURT, G. C. (1963). A critique of Mr Kaldor's model of income distribution and economic growth. *Australian Economic Papers*, 2, 20-36. Reprinted in Harcourt (1982, pp. 67-85).

—— (1965). A two-sector model of the distribution of income and the level of employment in the short run. *Economic Record*, 41, 103-17. Reprinted in Harcourt (1982, pp. 86-103).

—— (1982). *The Social Science Imperialists. Selected Essays.* (ed. Prue Kerr). London: Routledge & Kegan Paul.

—— (ed.) (1985). *Keynes and his Contemporaries. The Sixth and Centennial Keynes Seminar held at the University of Kent at Canterbury 1983.* London: Macmillan.

—— (1987). Theoretical methods and unfinished business. In David A Reese (ed.), *The Legacy of Keynes. Nobel Conference XXII.* San Francisco: Harper and Row, 1-22.

HAYEK, F. A. VON (1929, 1933). *Monetary Theory and the Trade Cycle*, (translated from the German by N. Kaldor and H. M. Croome). London/Toronto: Jonathan Cape.

HUDSON, H. R. (1957). A model of the trade cycle. *Economic Record*, 33, 378-89.

KREGEL, J. A. (1985). Harrod and Keynes: increasing returns, the theory of employment and dynamic economics. In Harcourt (1985, pp. 66-88).

LEKACHMAN, ROBERT (ed.) (1964). *Keynes' General Theory. Reports of Three Decades.* London: Macmillan.

MOLANA, HASSAN and VINES, DAVID (1987). North-South growth and terms of trade: a Kaldorian model. Mimeo, Glasgow.

PASINETTI, L. L. (1979). Kaldor, Nicholas. In David L. Sills (ed.), *International Encyclopedia of the Social Sciences. Biographical Supplement*, Vol. 18. New York: Free Press, 366-9.

RADCLIFFE REPORT (1959). *Report on the Committee on the Working of the Monetary System*, Cmnd. 827. London: HMSO.

SALTER, W. E. G. (1960; 1966). *Productivity and Technical Change.* London: Cambridge University Press. 2nd edn with an Addendum by W. B. Reddaway, 1966.

—— (1965). Productivity growth and accumulation as historical processes. In E. A. G. Robinson (ed.), *Problems in Economic Development.* London: Macmillan.

SAMUELSON, PAUL A. (1964). A brief survey of post-Keynesian developments. In Lekachman (1964, pp. 33-47).

SCITOVSKY, TIBOR (1941). Welfare propositions in economics. *Review of Economic Studies*, 9, 77-88.

SOLOW, ROBERT M. (1963). *Capital Theory and the Rate of Return.* Amsterdam: North-Holland.

SRAFFA, PIERO (1960). *Production of Commodities by Means of Commodities. Prelude to a Critique of Economic Theory.* Cambridge: Cambridge University Press.

—— with DOBB, M. H. (eds.) (1951-5, 1973). *The Works and Correspondence of David Ricardo* (11 vols). Cambridge: Cambridge University Press.

TARGETTI, FERDINANDO (1985). Growth and the terms of trade: a Kaldorian-two sector model. *Metroeconomica*, 37, 79-96.

THIRLWALL, A. P. (1986). A general model of growth and development on Kaldorian lines. *Oxford Economic Papers*, 38, 199-219.

—— (1987). *Nicholas Kaldor. Grand Masters in Economics.* Brighton: Wheatsheaf Books.

VON NEUMANN, J. (1945-6). A model of general economic equilibrium. *Review of Economic Studies*, 13, 1-9.

WEITZMAN, M. L. (1982). Increasing returns and the foundations of unemployment theory. *Economic Journal*, 92, 781-809.

WORSWICK, DAVID and TREVITHICK, JAMES (eds.) (1983). *Keynes and the Modern World.* Cambridge: Cambridge University Press.

YOUNG, WARREN (1987). *Interpreting Mr Keynes. The IS-LM Enigma.* Cambridge: Polity Press in association with Basil Blackwell, Oxford.

[4]

Excerpt from Mark Blaug, *Economic Theories, True or False? Essays in the History and Methodology of Economics*, 186–208.

9 Nicholas Kaldor, 1908–86

Introduction – biographia

Modern economics, like modern physics, is a subject in which reputations are made and unmade by essays rather than books. Nicholas Kaldor is a case in point. Unlike the great economists of the nineteenth century, he has never put his ideas together in a single comprehensive treatise and has instead scattered his ideas over some 90 articles, half a dozen of which have become classics of their kind. He has candidly admitted changing his mind more than once on some vital questions and has explained his own failure to write the 'Great Book' by the belief that he might yet change it again (Kaldor, 1978b, p. xxix). The willingness to rework his pet theories when they are upset by the discovery of some hitherto unsuspected fact is one of the features that give almost all his writings a fresh and lively quality – that and his constant insistence that fruitful economic analysis must be grounded in empirically derived 'laws' or statistical regularities. His own description of his work in the last twenty years perfectly captures this pragmatic element in his approach – to economic questions:

> I tried to find what kind of regularities can be detected in empirically observed phenomena and then tried to discover what particular testable hypotheses would be capable of explaining the association ... It is an approach which is more modest in scope (in not searching for explanations that derive from a comprehensive model of the system) and also more ambitious in that it directly aims at discovering solutions (or remedies) for real problems. (Kaldor, 1978b, p. xviii; also Kaldor, 1985, p. 8)

Kaldor's intellectual career breaks rather neatly into three well-defined phases, as he would be the first to agree (Kaldor, 1986). In the first phase, spanning the 1930s, his efforts were largely critical and polemical. His very first published article (Kaldor, 1934) contained a systematic account of the 'cobweb' theorem and invented its name. In addition, he effectively attacked Chamberlain's excess capacity theorem (Kaldor, 1938) and Hayek's theory of the trade cycle (Kaldor, 1939a, 1942) and traded blows with Frank Knight over the Austrian theory of capital (Kaldor, 1937). In the closing years of that decade, he announced the discovery of the compensation principle in welfare economics (Kaldor, 1939b) and the notion of optimum tariffs in the theory of international trade (Kaldor, 1940b) besides constructing an original model of the trade cycle (Kaldor, 1940a). During the war years and early postwar period, he emerged as one of the most vigorous of Keynes's many disciples and yet by, say, 1950 he had still failed to place a unique stamp of his own on the development of economic theory.

The second phase began in the mid-1950s with a series of papers on the theory of economic growth, embodying the concepts of 'two' saving rates, a mark-up theory of pricing and the 'technical progress function', which formed essential ingredients of what soon came to be known as post-Keynesian economics. Simultaneously, he published a book on *The Expenditure Tax* (Kaldor, 1955), which launched him on a new career as a tax reformer.

His inaugural lecture as Professor of Economics at Cambridge University in 1966, *Causes of the Slow Rate of Economic Growth of the United Kingdom*, marked the onset of the third and final phase of his intellectual development. Convinced that manufacturing industry is characterized by conditions of increasing returns to scale, he broke decisively with the notion of single-sector growth models, including his own, and adopted instead a multi-sector account of the growth process according to which the growth of demand for manufacturing products determines the rate of growth of total output in the economy. The new scheme was designed not merely to explain the differential rates of growth of industrialized countries in recent years, but indeed the entire evolution of the capitalist system. In short, he had at long last arrived at a unique vision of his own of what Adam Smith had called 'the nature and causes of the wealth of nations'.

Kaldor's contributions have ranged so far and wide as to preclude even a summary of them in anything less than a book. We will therefore focus here on the last two phases of his career, labelled for convenience Kaldor II and III, saying little, however, about his views on taxation (Kaldor, 1979a, 1979b) or his writings on international finance (Kaldor, 1963).

Nicholas Kaldor was born in Budapest, Hungary in 1908, the son of a Jewish barrister. As a boy he attended the 'Model Gymnasium' in Budapest, a private school which has produced an almost endless series of famous Hungarians. After a year at the University of Berlin, he moved to Britain in 1927 to study at the LSE, graduating in 1930. Two years later he was appointed an assistant lecturer at the LSE, becoming a lecturer in 1934 and a reader in 1942. He left the LSE in 1947 to become Director of the Research and Planning Division of the Economic Commission for Europe, serving eventually as one of a small group of experts to author the influential UN report *National and International Measures for Full Employment* (1949). He returned to academic life as a fellow at King's College, Cambridge in 1949, becoming a reader in 1952, and a Professor of Economics in 1966. He retired from academic life in 1975.

Throughout this latter period at Cambridge he also served as a tax adviser to the government of India, Sri Lanka, Mexico, British Guyana, Turkey, Iran, Venezuela and Ghana, capped by his appointment as Special Adviser to the Chancellor of the Exchequer of two British Labour governments during the years 1964–68 and 1974–76. Among his many contributions to the economic policies

188   Economic theories, true or false?

of the Labour government were the Selective Employment Tax (1966–72), a payroll tax designed to discriminate against employment in service industries and the Regional Employment Premium (1966–76), designed to subsidize manufacturing employment in depressed areas. But his pleas for an expenditure tax to replace the taxation of income and his opposition to Britain's entry into the Common Market (Kaldor, 1971b, 1971c) fell on deaf ears. He was raised to the peerage in 1974. His speeches to the House of Lords, published under the title of *The Economic Consequences of Mrs Thatcher* (1983) – echoing the title of Keynes's *Economic Consequences of the Peace* (1919) – reveal his brilliance as a political debater with an audience of non-economists. Two lectures to an academic audience, published as *The Scourge of Monetarism* (1982), leave no doubt of his scathing rejection of the policies of the current Conservative government in Britain (see also Kaldor, 1970a).

Kaldor's conviction that manufacturing holds the key to Britain's economic growth rate has been widely disseminated in recent years (John Eatwell's BBC TV series *Whatever Happened to Britain?*, shown in 1984, was pure Kaldor) and indeed were more or less officially adopted by the Labour Party in the run-up to the election. Thus whatever are our ultimate judgements on his views, they clearly merit a considered hearing.

A theory of economic growth
Kaldor's theory of economic growth was propounded in a series of six papers published between the years 1956 and 1962, marking a gradual evolution of the details of the theory without affecting its substantial outlines. It began as a simple Keynesian theory of macrodistribution (Kaldor, 1956), to which was then added a so-called 'technical progress function', a mark-up theory of pricing and a particular investment function (Kaldor, 1957). The investment function was then reformulated (Kaldor, 1958), which produced further changes in the final version of the model (Kaldor, 1962). The original macrodistribution theory is plain sailing; complications only arise when considering the full-blown theory of growth, particularly in its final mature version. We shall not attempt to expound Kaldor's growth theory in all its details[1] but merely to sketch its main outlines, touching upon its peculiar strengths and weaknesses.

A necessary prelude to Kaldor's macrodistribution theory is the growth equation of Roy Harrod. This created the modern conception of the theory of economic growth in the form of a statement of the requirements for steady-state, indefinite expansion:

$$G = s/C$$

where $G = dY/Y$, the actual proportionate rate of growth of national income,
$C = dK/dY$, the marginal capital-output ratio

and $s = S/Y$, the average saving-income ratio (which is assumed to equal the marginal savings-income ratio)

Since planned saving, S, must equal planned investment, I, in equilibrium, we have what Harrod calls the 'warranted' rate of growth, G_w:

$$G_w = \frac{dy}{Y} = \frac{dY}{I}\frac{S}{Y} = \frac{dY}{dK}\frac{S}{Y} = \frac{s}{C}$$

Harrod went on to define G_n as the 'natural' or full employment growth rate resulting from the rate of growth of the labour force and the rate of technical progress as reflected in the average productivity of labour, both of which are taken to be exogenously determined. If we define C_r, as the incremental capital–output ratio required to equip the increasing number of workers at full employment, the Harrod equation for G_n becomes:

$$G_n = s/C_r$$

Kaldor's 'alternative theory of distribution' can now be rendered into the terminology of Harrod. Starting with the identity:

$$Y = W + P \qquad (1)$$

where Y = national income, W = total wages and P = total property income, we postulate constant but different average equals marginal propensities to save out of wages and profits, s_w and s_p, so that total savings, S, is given by:

$$S = s_w W + s_p P \qquad (2)$$

or, substituting for W from (1)

$$S = s_w(Y-P) + s_p p$$

and rearranging

$$S = (s_p - s_w)P + s_w Y \qquad (3)$$

Dynamic equilibrium requires that $I = S$, which implies that:

$$I = (s_p - S_w)P + s_w Y \qquad (4)$$

Equation (4) can be divided by Y and rearranged to obtain the share of profits in national income, P/Y.

190 Economic theories, true or false?

$$I/Y = (s_p - s_w)P/Y + s_w \qquad (5)$$

$$\frac{P}{Y} = \frac{1}{s_p - s_w} \frac{I}{Y} - \frac{Ss_w}{s_p - s_w} = \frac{I/Y - s_w}{s_p - s_w}$$

Thus, a condition for both positive profits and a positive profit share is that:

$$S_w < I/Y < S_p$$

In the special 'classic' case in which the propensity to save out of wage income is assumed to be zero, equation (5) reduces to:

$$\frac{P}{Y} = \frac{I/Y}{s_p} \qquad (6)$$

By the Harrod growth equation, $I/Y = S/Y = s = GC$, and so we have in general:

$$\frac{P}{Y} = \frac{G_w C - s_w}{s_p - s_w}$$

or in the special 'classic' case,

$$\frac{P}{Y} = \frac{G_w C}{s_p} \qquad (7)$$

At full employment, with growth at its 'natural' rate, $G_n C_r = s$, this 'classic' case becomes:

$$\frac{P}{Y} = \frac{G_n C_r}{s_p} \qquad (8)$$

What Kaldor has shown, therefore, is that the share of profits (and also the rate of profit on capital) varies directly with the growth rate of income, the capital–output ratio and workers' saving rate, but it varies inversely with the capitalists' saving rate. At full employment, with growth at the 'natural' rate, the saving propensities determine the profit share, such that the more capitalists consume (the smaller is s_p), the larger is their relative share. Or, to put it differently, with income given at the full employment level and investment given exogenously so as to be consistent with full employment, steady-state growth as defined by Harrod is only possible through changes in the aggregate saving–income ratio; once we follow Kaldor by distinguishing two given saving propensities out of wages and profits and assume $s_w = s_p$, so that total savings is a weighted average of s_p and s_w, the weights being the relative shares of capital and labour, it follows immediately that the shifting of income between workers and capitalists is the only thing that makes steady-state growth possible. This is hardly an earth-shattering conclusion, since everything else but the relative shares of capital and labour is in effect given by the assumption of steady-state growth.[2]

Needless to say, this simple macrodistribution theory was widely criticized, and even ridiculed, on the grounds that it was rested upon two distinctly Harrodian notions: a technically predetermined capital–output ratio unaffected by relative input prices and a 'natural' full employment growth path defined independently of variations in the saving propensities out of wages and profits. It was in reaction to the first of these criticisms that Kaldor (1957) amplified the original version of his model by the addition of a 'technical progress function', which served to determine the capital–output ratio in the steady state.

Rejecting the neoclassical concept of an aggregate production function defined for a given state of technical knowledge and the associated notion of 'disembodied' technical progress taking place independently of capital accumulation, Kaldor begins by making technical progress a function of gross investment. He argues that entrepreneurs always choose that technique which gives the greatest increase in output per worker at the lowest investment per worker, irrespective of the factor-saving nature of the technique. In other words, every economy can be characterized by a 'technical progress function', relating the rate of growth of output per worker to the rate of growth of capital per worker.

In Figure 9.1, the vertical axis shows the percentage rate of growth of labour productivity, y/n, lower case letters denoting (here as elsewhere in this paper), proportionate rates of growth. The horizontal axis shows the percentage rate of growth of investment per worker, i/n. The technical progress function cuts the vertical axis at some positive rate of growth of labour productivity to show that

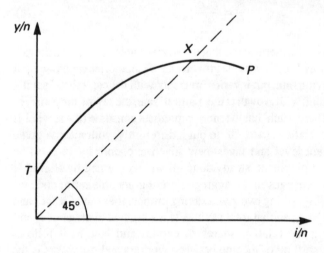

Figure 9.1   The technical progress function

192 Economic theories, true or false?

there will always be some 'disembodied' technical progress, and is concave from below, indicating 'diminishing returns' to ever higher rates of growth of investment per worker. The broken 45°-1ine shows all the points where output per worker and investment per worker grow at the same rate. Hence, an economy in steady-state growth must be somewhere on the 45°-1ine. It must at the same time be somewhere on its technical progress function, from which it follows that the intersection X is the only point where steady-state equilibrium is possible. To the left of X, output per worker is growing faster than the flow of investment per worker, so that the (stock) capital to output ratio is falling; to the right of X, investment per worker is growing faster than output per worker, so that the capital-output ratio is rising; but at X, the capital–output ratio is constant, technical progress is 'neutral' (as measured by the capital–output ratio) and all the critical rates of growth, output, labour, the flow of investment, the stock of capital – as well as the share of wages and profits in output – are likewise constant over time.

The entire argument depends, partly on the position of the technical progress function which expresses what Kaldor calls the 'technical dynamism' of an economy (that is, the willingness of entrepreneurs to invest in new ways of making goods) and partly, and perhaps more critically, on the forces that actually drive an economy towards point X. Kaldor leaves the former unexplained. With regard to the latter he discusses various ways in which an economic system will converge on X, all of which depend on variations in the gap between the actual and expected profit margins of the typical firm in positions of less than, or more than, full employment. It is evident, therefore, that the stability of the position X depends in turn on a theory of pricing that determines profit margins and on a theory of investment.

Kaldor's pricing theory is identical in all three versions of the model (Kaldor, 1957, 1958 and 1962), being a Kalecki-type mark-up theory whereby prices are marked up on labour costs, which are taken to be constant up to the level of full capacity. The investment function, however, is different in each of the three versions of the model. In the first version of 1957, investment is explained as a function of each firms' desired capital–output ratio, which is taken to be an increasing function of the expected rate of profits, thus combining the familiar acceleration principle of investment with Kalecki's 'principle of increasing risk'. This model turned out to have special implications for the stability of steady growth, deriving from the fact that it made investment relatively insensitive to changes in the current rate of profit. Thus, in the second version, Kaldor altered the assumptions about producers' expectations with regard to profit margins; even so, this made steady growth only slightly more stable.

Finally, in the third version, the investment function was radically revised and the old view of a homogeneous capital stock was replaced by the notion of vintage capital, thus implying further changes in the definition of the technical progress function. The new investment function is that firms aim to maximize the growth rate of their sales, subject to the constraint that profitability over a pay-off period of four to five years is sufficient to avoid the risk of bankruptcy or takeover bids. The new technical progress function postulates a relationship between the growth rate of labour productivity and the growth rate of investment per head but now only on newly installed equipment. In consequence, the argument that automatic forces will drive the economy to the position of neutrality on the technical progress function, thus sustaining steady-state growth, is made more plausible but still not perhaps entirely convincing.

Even sympathetic commentators have remained sceptical about Kaldor's arguments with respect to the stability of steady-state growth (Kregel, 1971, pp. 139–40, 203–7; Kregel, 1973, p. 192) if only because it implies that apparently anti-Keynesian conclusion that full employment is the 'natural' condition of capitalism in long-run equilibrium. Kaldor is a post-Keynesian economist in that he rejects many if not all the standard assumptions of the neoclassical approach to economic growth: optimizing behaviour, smoothly adjusting competitive markets, continuous factor substitution, aggregate production functions, malleable capital, a single saving function, the dependence of investment on the available flow of savings, and the like. In one respect, however, he stands alone among post-Keynesians in rejecting the Keynesian concept of 'unemployment equilibrium', at least for purposes of studying growth problems. Joan Robinson, for example, has been primarily concerned (as was Harrod) to emphasize the obstacles which are liable to prevent the attainment of a 'Golden Age' of steady-state growth in an unplanned capitalist economy, whereas Kaldor has always insisted that 'a theory of growth should be based on the hypothesis of full employment' (Kaldor, 1960b, p. 12).

Kaldor supported his assumption of full employment partly by reference to historical experience and partly by references to a theorem which was intended to show that there cannot be unemployment on a balanced growth path in which planned saving equals planned investment (Kaldor, 1958, pp. 24–9). This theorem seems, after due consideration, to depend on the assumption that the marginal propensity to invest exceeds the marginal propensity to save over the range of output below levels of full employment and thus on a static investment function related to the *level* of output and not, as in the acceleration principle underlying his treatment of the investment function, to *changes* in the level of output (Hacche, 1979, pp. 194–6, 206–14). Be that as it may, it raises the perplexing question as to what one may legitimately assume for purposes of growth theory. Growth theory is an intellectual game played according to certain rules, but it is far from clear what governs the rules one may adopt. That is true about the assumption of full employment, but it is also true about rules-of-thumb governing the investment process.

194 Economic theories, true or false?

We may sum up Kaldor's growth theory by saying that it is perhaps the only model of economic growth in which technical progress emerges as the main engine of economic growth, determining the share of investment in income, the share of profits, the average life of equipment, and the rate of growth of productivity of both labour and new capital but, of course, being itself essentially unexplained; it simply determines the level of the technical progress function (the slope being of no particular significance). But that is not the only unique feature of Kaldor's growth theory. Different growth theories have advanced various defences of steady-state growth theory and some have claimed that theories of steady growth have direct empirical relevance in the sense that the broad facts about growth in advanced industrial economies correspond more or less closely to the main results of growth theory (see Hacche, 1979, pp. 26–8). But only Kaldor has consistently adhered to the view that his principal objective is the explanation of 'the characteristic features of the economic process as recorded by experience' (Kaldor, 1958, pp. 177–8). The history of capitalist development over the last century, he contends, testifies to the validity of the following six 'stylized facts':

1. a steady rising trend in the growth of output and output per unit of labour;
2. a steady rise in the amount of capital per worker, however capital is measured;
3. a trendless rate of profit on capital, well in excess of the pure long-term rate of interest as revealed by the yield of gilt-edged bonds;
4. a constant capital–output ratio;
5. a high correlation between the profit share and the investment income ratio and, moreover, the wage and profit shares of income as well as the investment–income ratio are constant in the long run; and
6. wide variations in the growth rate among different economies at any one time. (Kaldor, 1958, pp. 2–3)

Neoclassical growth theory is perfectly capable of accounting for Kaldor's stylized facts with appropriate assumptions about production functions, technical progress, population growth and saving propensities. Indeed, so elastic is the apparatus provided by neoclassical growth theory that it is capable of accounting *ex post* for any facts whatsoever. But only Kaldor's theory seeks to explain these facts in a genuine, causal sense, so that its validity can be said to stand or fall on the occurrence of certain 'stylised facts'.

Unfortunately, many of Kaldor's 'stylised facts' are not facts at all.[3] Facts (1), (2) and (3) are not in dispute; arguments only begin when confronting facts (4) and (5). The capital–output ratio in Britain (that is, the ratio of the constant replacement costs of domestic reproducible fixed capital to the gross domestic product at constant factor costs) declined more or less steadily in the last half of the nineteenth century, from a value of 5 in 1855 to 3.7 in 1900; it then rose and fell back in the period leading up to the First World War and continued in a downward course up to the Second World War; in the 1960s and 1970s it stood at just below 4, only exceeding its mid-nineteenth-century value of 5 in the late 1970s. In the USA the capital–output ratio likewise declined throughout the first half of the twentieth century, recovering most of this fall, however, in the 1950s and 1960s. In a fit of generosity, we might therefore endorse Kaldor's carefully phrased assertion of fact (4): 'Steady capital–output ratios over long periods; at least there are no clear long-term trends either rising or falling, if differences in the degree of utilisation of capacity are allowed for' (Kaldor, 1958, p. 2). But if so, the clock-time implied by the term 'long periods' will have to be stretched to run to 50 years or more. There is actually little evidence in the data to suggest the notion that there is some 'steady trend' or 'normal' relationship between capital and output; which is what Kaldor's stylized fact (4) clearly suggests.

We can be even more categorical about the evidence on relative shares relating to fact (5): the share of wages in aggregate income in both Britain and the USA has increased ever since the nineteenth century and, correspondingly, the share of profits has steadily fallen; and this is true no matter how wages or profits are measured. There never was a law less lawlike than the so-called 'Bowley's Law' of the long-run constancy of the relative shares of wages and profits in total income. Given the lack of a systematic long-term trend in the capital–output ratio and a downwards trend in the profit share, the rate of profit on capital, which is simply the quotient of the profits–income and the capital–output ratios, has shown a downward trend at least in Britain (although less obviously so in the USA).

Fact (5) also suggests that there is a correlation between the profit share and the investment–income ratio. Broadly speaking, such a relationship is indeed found for the last half of the nineteenth century and the interwar period in the twentieth century, but it breaks down completely in the 40 years since the Second World War, which saw a substantial rise in the investment–income ratio without any corresponding rise in the share of profits.

Some commentators (Hacche, 1973, p. 252) add a seventh stylized fact to Kaldor's list, namely, little deviation over the long term from a state of full employment, and as we have seen this is certainly one of the stylized facts to which Kaldor repeatedly appeals. A complete assessment of this claim would take us into the treacherous territory of historical unemployment statistics, which before the 1930s were largely based on members of trade unions rather than all members of the labour force. But even a cursory knowledge of economic history suggests that we will have to explain away the increasing concern with the problem of unemployment in the closing decades of the nineteenth century, probably indicative of rising actual levels of unemployment, the well attested growth of unemployment in Britain all through the 1920s and of course mass

196 Economic theories, true or false?

unemployment throughout the industrialized world during the Great Depression of the 1930s. Against this, we can point to the postwar boom of the 1950s and 1960s as a long period of sustained full or nearly full employment – the very period in which Kaldor was developing his growth theory. But what reason do we have for regarding the postwar boom as typical of long-run growth under capitalism, while rejecting the interwar slump, not to mention the current slump, as atypical? Here, as elsewhere, neither Kaldor nor anyone else has provided us with standards for judging the appropriate length of time for identifying those long-run forces that comprise the staples of modern growth theory.

On balance we must conclude that if Kaldor's growth theory is interpreted as Kaldor would have us interpret it, namely as an explanation of the common experience of the growth process in industrialized countries, the theory has in fact been explaining the wrong things. On the best evidence, even the aggregate features of long-run growth do not correspond to anything that can be described by a steady-state process. It may well be that Kaldor now accepts as much.[4]. At any rate, when in 1966 he turned to explaining Britain's poor postwar growth performance, he drew none of his arguments from his own growth model and instead based his reasonings on yet another 'stylized' fact about long-run economic growth associated with the writings of Colin Clark: the shift of labour in the process of 'industrialization' from primary to secondary and from secondary to tertiary activities (that is, from agriculture and mining to manufacturing and then to the service industries). This involved much more than the replacement of a one-sector model of growth by a multi-sectoral explanation. It represented the rejection of all growth modelling based on the conception of a long-run steady state, adopting instead a 'stage theory' of capitalist development in which the economy is forever in a condition of dynamic disequilibrium.

'Laws of growth'

In the course of his inaugural lecture at the University of Cambridge in 1966 on the causes of Britain's low growth rate, Kaldor (1966b) presented two 'laws' of growth to account for the differences in the growth rates of industrialized countries, to which he subsequently added a third 'law' (Kaldor, 1968), which largely displaces the first two. These three laws have been the subject of a considerable debate, which has left its mark on Kaldor's own interpretation of their significance. The three laws may be baldly stated as:

1. there is a strong positive correlation in all industrialized countries between the rate of growth of manufacturing output and rate of growth of GDP;
2. there is a strong positive correlation in all industrialized countries between the rate of growth of labour productivity in manufacturing and the growth of manufacturing output – this is the so-called Verdoorn Relation, named

after its discoverer, the Belgian economist Paulus Verdoorn (Thirlwall and Thirlwall, 1979); and

3. there is a strong positive correlation in all industrialized countries between employment growth in manufacturing and the rate of growth of GDP, just as there is a strong negative correlation between employment growth outside manufacturing and the rate of growth of GDP.

We need to consider Kaldor's arguments for each of these three laws and then to assess their implications for Kaldor's explanation of international growth differences.[5]

Kaldor's first law
Taking a cross-section of 12 OECD countries over the period 1952–64, Kaldor found a strong positive correlation between the growth rate of manufacturing output, g_M, and the growth rate of GDP, g_{GDP} (9)

$$g_{GDP} = 1.153 + 0.614 \, g_M \qquad r^2 = 0.959$$
$$(0.040)$$
(standard error in parenthesis)

This high correlation between the two variables, he argued, is not the simple result of the fact that manufacturing output constitutes a large proportion of GDP because there is also a significant positive association between the overall rate of growth of GDP and the *excess* of the growth of manufacturing over non-manufacturing output. He found no correlation between the rate of growth of GDP and the growth rate of agriculture or mining, but he did find a significant correlation between GDP growth and the growth of services. He insisted, however, that the growth rate of services should be attributed to the growth of GDP rather than the other way round, on the unconvincing grounds that the demand for most services is in fact derived from the demand for manufacturing output. To this critical argument we will return below. Subsequent research by colleagues of Kaldor essentially confirmed the first law for a larger number of countries and a longer time period

Why should GDP grow faster whenever manufacturing output grows faster than the overall rate of output, that is, when the share of the manufacturing sector in the total economy is increasing? Kaldor offered essentially two answers to this question. The first is that the fast growth of manufacturing draws labour from other sectors which harbour 'disguised unemployment' in the sense that there is no relationship between growth of output and employment growth in these sectors; hence, the transfer of labour to manufacturing causes no decline in the output of these sectors to offset the growth of manufacturing itself. A second answer is that the expansion of manufacturing is peculiarly subject, for reasons

198 Economic theories, true or false?

somehow inherent in the nature of manufacturing itself, to dynamic economies of scale which steadily reduce unit costs as output grows over time. These dynamic economies of scale are brought about by 'induced' technical progress embodied in new capital, by external economies accruing to each firm as a result of the expansion of the whole industry, and by learning-by-doing as a function of cumulative output in the past. They are not to be confused with static increasing returns to scale according to which larger plants, all else being equal, yield lower unit costs, although this probably applies to manufacturing too.

Kaldor's second law

Taking the same cross-section for the same group of countries, Kaldor replicated Verdoorn's Relation, which states that the growth of labour productivity in manufacturing, p_M, is positively correlated with the growth of manufacturing output, g_M:

$$p_M = 1\ 035 + 0.484\ g_M \qquad r^2 = 0.826 \qquad (10)$$
$$(0.070)$$
(standard error in parenthesis)

Since the output of the manufacturing sector is equal to the productivity of labour (value added per worker) multiplied by the volume of employment, it follows that after taking logs of all three variables to express a relationship between growth rates that:

$$g_M = p_M + e_M \qquad (11)$$

where e_M = the rate of growth of employment in manufacturing. Thus, by way of an example, if manufacturing output is growing by 5 per cent per annum and the productivity of labour in manufacturing is rising by 2 per cent per annum, employment in manufacturing must be growing at 3 per cent per annum. Therefore, an alternative way of testing the Verdoorn Relation is to regress e_M on g_M, which results in a similar equation to the previous regression of p_M on g_M:

$$e_M = -1.028 + 0.516\ g_M \qquad r^2 = 0.844 \qquad (12)$$
$$(0.070)$$
(standard error in parenthesis)

In both equations, the Verdoorn coefficient is about 0.5, asserting that a one per cent increase in the growth rate of manufacturing output, g_M, leads to 0.5 per cent increase in the productivity of labour, p_M and equally a 0.5 per cent increase in manufacturing employment, e_M. The effect is not necessarily confined to manufacturing. Kaldor found a similar Verdoorn Relation in public utilities and the construction industry but he found none in agriculture, mining, transport and communication.

Productivity growth in manufacturing is faster, the faster the rate of growth of manufacturing output (Kaldor's second law) and the rate of growth of manufacturing output is faster, the faster the rate of growth of GDP (Kaldor's first law). What, however, determines the growth of manufacturing itself? That question is perhaps best answered in terms of the constraints inhibiting the growth of any sector, such as a low income elasticity of demand for the product of that sector and an inadequate supply of labour or capital or both. Kaldor originally doubted that British manufacturing was in any way constrained on the demand-side and took the view that the effective constraint was on the side of labour arising from the small proportion of the labour force employed in British agriculture. Britain had reached a stage of economic maturity in which there was no low-productive sector outside manufacturing capable of supplying labour to an expanding manufacturing sector. He later withdrew this conclusion of the 1966 lecture (Kaldor, 1968,1978b, p. xx), replacing it with the view that British manufacturing is effectively constrained by a lack of export growth.

Whichever version of the Verdoorn Relation we adopt, that is,

$$p_M = a + bg_M$$

or (employing the identity $p_M = g_M - e_M$)

$$e_M = -a + (1 - b) g_M,$$

(14)

the problem of which is cause and which is effect remains. Kaldor assumed that the growth of labour productivity is entirely 'induced' by the growth of output, in which case it is perfectly correct to regress p_M on g_M. The opposite view is to argue that productivity growth is entirely autonomous and causes output to grow faster, say, by stimulating demand through a reduction in prices rather than being caused by fast output growth. Similarly, Kaldor assumed that employment growth is determined by output growth, in which case it is difficult to see how he could have argued simultaneously that the growth of output in manufacturing is constrained by the shortage of labour. It was precisely this contradiction that led Rowthorn (1975) to attack Kaldor's demonstration of Verdoorn's Relation. The Verdoorn Relation can be specified, not just in two, but in four different ways:

$$p_M = a + bg_M \qquad 0 < b < 1 \qquad (13)$$

$$e_M = -a + (1-b)g_M \qquad (13a)$$

$$g_M = \frac{a}{1-b} + \frac{b}{1-b}e_m \qquad (13b)$$

200 Economic theories, true or false?

and, substituting (3) into (1),

$$p_M = \frac{a}{1-b} + \frac{b}{1-b}e_M \tag{13c}$$

These four versions will only yield identical estimates if the equations are exact without error. Rowthorn criticized Kaldor for estimating the Verdoorn coefficient 'indirectly' using the first two specifications rather than 'directly' using the fourth specification, according to which productivity growth is determined by employment growth as implied by the notion of a labour constraint. In addition, Rowthorn showed that his estimates of equation (13c) were sensitive to the inclusion or exclusion of Japan as an 'outlier' in the relationship between p_M and e_M; excluding Japan yielded an estimate of the Verdoorn coefficient, b, that was not significantly different from unity, thus refuting the notion of increasing returns to scale. In reply, Kaldor discarded the notion of a labour constraint and hence returned to his own formulation of the Verdoorn coefficient in the form of equation (13a), showing that the exclusion of Japan did little to alter its significance, and concluding: 'a sufficient condition for the presence of static or dynamic economies of scale is the existence of a statistically significant relationship between e and g, with a regression .. coefficient which is significantly less than 1' (Kaldor, 1975a, p. 893).

Nevertheless, the problem of possibly spurious correlation has continued to dog the discussion on the Verdoorn Relation. In the first place, it is all too easy to see why changes in the productivity of *labour* in a sector should be positively associated with the growth of output of that sector, if only because labour is a quasi-fixed factor: when output declines, it is difficult to lay off labour rapidly and when output expands, it takes time to recruit new labour. In consequence, output per unit of labour will appear to rise when output growth accelerates. Thus, the Verdoorn Relation has now been confirmed on British time-series data over the period 1900–1977 and US time-series data for the period 1953–78. But the problem with time-series data is that short-run cyclical factors will generate a regression coefficient of about one-half when e_M is regressed on g_M; this is the result of 'Okun's Law', namely that employment fluctuates less than output over the business cycle for reasons that appear to be related to labour market institutions, and which proves nothing one way or the other about static or dynamic returns to scale (McCombie, 1983, p. 421).

In the second place, it is difficult to provide a microeconomic foundation for the Verdoorn Relation, and certainly neither Kaldor nor Verdoorn (1980) himself have ever provided a microeconomic explanation. Employers are motivated to minimize costs per unit of output and that implies maximizing total factor productivity rather than labour productivity – that is, output divided by the weighted sum of labour and fixed capital, the weights being the shares of value added paid to labour and capital respectively. The productivity of labour is frequently taken to be an easily observable proxy for total factor productivity and, in particular, the rate of change of labour productivity is frequently taken to be a very good proxy for the rate of change of total factor productivity. Actually, there is absolutely no reason to believe that the two will vary neatly in tandem over a run of years or even over the duration of a single business cycle. Indeed, the average annual growth of labour productivity in a sector is not even a good proxy for the average annual charge of labour costs per unit of output in that sector, not to mention the average annual change of average costs per unit of output (the inverse of total factor productivity).

Thus, by way of an example, the average annual growth of labour productivity in British manufacturing shows extreme year-to-year variations over the decade of the 1970s and early 1980s, whereas labour costs per unit of output in British manufacturing rose sharply but continuously in the 1970s and less sharply but again more or less continuously in the early 1980s (NEDC, 1985, p. 25). The distinction between the two measures arises partly from variations in hours worked but more fundamentally from variations in the annual rate of growth of nominal earnings. The distinction between labour productivity and total factor productivity on the other hand, arises entirely from variations in the rates of investment per worker.

The notion that the Verdoorn Relation must have something to do with the growth of capital in a sector, an element omitted in the equations estimated by Kaldor, has persuaded a number of investigators to estimate the determinants of productivity growth by including, among other things, capital accumulation on the right-hand side the equation, which generally improves the goodness of fit of the Verdoorn equation (Chatterji and Wickens, 1983; Michl, 1985). Even when we revert to the simple one-variable regression of productivity growth on output growth, there have been signs of a break in the Verdoorn Relation as a result of the universal decline in productivity growth in manufacturing in all industrialized countries since 1973: the statistical fit of the Verdoorn Relation has deteriorated over the 1970s and early 1980s compared with earlier periods (Michl, 1985). One reason for this phenomenon may be that reductions in the growth of output do not affect labour productivity symmetrically with increases in the growth of output: slow or negative growth seems to result in reductions of capacity and a closing down of plants embodying worst-practice technique, thus reducing the association between labour productivity and output.

For this and other reasons, the recent era of productivity slowdown has witnessed the proliferation of 'radical' interpretations of the determinants of labour productivity, resting on a breakdown of the tacit willingness of workers to cooperate with management, a willingness which never is, and never can be, fully specified in a labour contract (see, for example, Kilpatrick and Lawson, 1980; Weisskopf et al., 1984). This view is the precise opposite of Kaldor's because it denies that labour productivity is 'induced' by output growth, insisting instead that it is a prime cause of output growth. The truth probably lies

202 Economic theories, true or false?

somewhere in between these two polar extremes and that suggests immediately that the Verdoorn Relation must be estimated by means of simultaneous equations expressing both the effect of productivity growth on output growth and the effect of output growth on productivity growth.

In principle, either causal sequence is plausible. A rapid growth of output due to rising demand may lead to rapidly rising output per man by allowing firms to reap the advantage of static economies of scale and by permitting the use of the latest, best-practice technique. On the other hand, rapid productivity growth, whether due to endogenous technical progress or a change in industrial relations, reduces costs and prices and thus permits a higher rate of growth of output. But whatever is the initial stimulus, there is every likelihood that the forces set in motion will be mutually self-reinforcing, so that over time output growth stimulates greater productivity, which in turn stimulates greater output growth,[6] all of which is to say that single-equation estimates are unlikely to identify the Verdoorn Relation.

The only attempt to estimate the Verdoorn Relation within a simultaneous equations framework is the study by Parikh (1978). Parikh was fundamentally concerned with establishing the labour-constraint hypothesis, which, as we mentioned before, Kaldor subsequently abandoned. Moreover, the Parikh study suffered from a number of technical deficiencies (McCombie, 1981, pp. 214–15, 1983, pp. 424–6). Thus, the precise significance of the Verdoorn Relation remains an open question to this day.

However, even Kaldor himself no longer attaches any significance to the acceptance or rejection, of the Verdoorn Relation. In his view, the choice is between a neoclassical supply-oriented view of the growth process, according to which the growth of output is essentially cited by the growth of factor inputs, or a Keynesian demand-oriented approach, according to which growth in an economy is essentially limited by the volume of demand and, in an open economy, by the balance of payments: there is enough disguised unemployment in the non-industrial sectors to provide the manufacturing sector with an elastic supply of labour; likewise, capital is automatically provided by the profits generated by the growth process itself and is in no sense a binding constraint. In Kaldor's own words:

> The existence of increasing returns to scale in industry (the Verdoorn Law) is not a necessary or indispensable element in the interpretation of these equations [relating p_{GDP}, q_M, e_M] Even if industrial output obeyed the law of constant returns, it could still be true that the growth of industrial output was the governing factor in the overall rate of economic growth... so long as the growth of industrial output represented a net addition to the effective use of resources and not just a transfer of resources from one use to another. That would be the case if (a) the capital required for industrial production was (largely or wholly) self-generated – the accumulation of capital was an aspect, or a by-product, of the growth of output; and (b) the labour engaged in

industry had no true opportunity-cost outside industry, on account of the prevalence of disguised unemployment both in agriculture and services. There is plenty of direct evidence to substantiate both of these assumptions

The important implications of these assumptions is that economic growth is demand-induced, and not resource-constrained. (Kaldor, 1975a, pp. 894–5)

Nevertheless, despite this repudiation of the assumption of dynamically increasing returns to scale, Kaldor has continued to rely in all his subsequent writings on the notion that growth is inherently cumulative, which necessarily implies some notion as dynamically increasing returns to scale. Be that as it may, Kaldor's second law needs to be replaced by a third law.

Kaldor's third law

Regressing g_{GDP} on e_M and e_{NM} (employment is non-manufacturing), Kaldor found that the faster the growth of manufacturing output in an economy, the faster is the rate of labour transference from non-manufacturing to manufacturing

$$g_{GDP} = 2.899 + 0.821\ e_M\ \ 1.183\ e_{NM}$$
$$(0.169)\ \ \ (0.367) \qquad R^2 = 0.842 \quad (15)$$
(standard errors in parenthesis)

This, the third law, states that the growth of GDP in an economy is positively related to the growth of output and employment in manufacturing and negatively associated with the growth of employment outside manufacturing. In short, manufacture is the engine of growth in GDP and the growth of manufacturing is not constrained by a shortage of labour, being fundamentally export-led.

The evidence for Kaldor's third law is even more difficult to assess than the evidence for the first two laws. The statistical evidence is entirely confined to the proposition that productivity growth in the economy as a whole depends critically on the growth of manufacturing and does not bear on the associated proposition that the growth of manufacturing is export-led. Kaldor's theory of export-led growth is one of a family of such theories (Thirlwall, 1982, 11). His argument is essentially that of Hicks', namely, that the long-run growth rate of an economy depends on the growth of autonomous demand and that export demand is the main component of autonomous demand in an open economy. Thus, differences in the growth performance of Western European countries are due primarily to differences in the rate of growth of exports, which set up a virtuous circle in which higher exports promote investment, which in turn leads to a higher rate of productivity, lower export prices and still higher exports. Whatever the validity of such models of export-led growth, the fact is that they do not require Kaldor's third law, namely, the notion that manufacturing is the engine of GDP growth because the faster the rate of growth of manufacturing

204 Economic theories, true or false?

output, the faster is the rate of growth of labour productivity in manufacturing.

This proposition clearly depends on the hypothesis of dynamic economies of scale in manufacturing. The idea of dynamic economies of scale – costs decreasing over real time in a manner not captured in traditional static theories of returns to scale – is not unique to Kaldor (see Hirschleifer, 1962; Spence, 1981) but what is uniquely Kaldorian is to attach such dynamic economies of scale exclusively to manufacturing. It is difficult to see why the private service industries, such as banking, insurance, communications and wholesale and retail distribution, should not be similarly subject to dynamic economies of scale. The third law of growth, according to which GDP growth is negatively associated with the growth of non-manufacturing employment, is a thin reed on which to hang the denial of dynamic economies of scale outside manufacturing.

Kaldor has little to say about the policy implications of his 'laws' of growth. Presumably what is implied is that demand management must form an integral part of any national policies designed to stimulate growth in stagnating economies like those of Britain. But that conclusion is derivable from any version of neo-Keynesian macroeconomics. A more pointed implication of the Kaldorian growth 'laws' is that what is important is not just a stimulus to overall aggregate demand but a quite specific stimulus to demand for the output of manufacturing, and in particular overseas demand for manufacturers. For example, anything that will improve the competitiveness of manufactured goods, including not just lower prices but also non-price improvements in delivery time, reliability, design, after-sales service, and so on should, according to Kaldor, serve to lift the balance-of-payments constraint on British economic growth. Now, this central element in the Kaldorian position rests on little more than a series of single-equation regressions, which are made to carry far more weight than they are capable of supporting. Apart from these single-equation regressions, no argument is provided to justify the view that manufacturing is absolutely critical to the growth process.

In the case of Britain, for example, it is of course perfectly true that much of the alarming growth of unemployment in the last six to seven years has been the result of an unprecedented contraction in the size of the manufacturing sector. Manufacturing output has been contracting by more than 1 per cent a year on average over the last decade but, on the other hand, the output of the service industries has been expanding by almost 2 per cent a year over the same period. But this fall in the share of employment and output in manufacturing, and the concomitant rise in the share of services, shows up in the figures for all OECD countries and appears to be a common feature of all mature economies. It has been far more pronounced in Britain than elsewhere (with the possible exception of the USA) but it is certainly not unique to Britain and thus provides only slender support for the Kaldorian emphasis on manufacturing as the key to the growth process.

Similarly, approximately two-thirds of Britain's visible exports have traditionally consisted of manufactures. The sharp contraction of British manufacturing could certainly have caused serious balance-of-payments deficits were it not for North Sea oil and, of course, when North Sea oil runs out in the 1990s, there is no guarantee that invisible exports in the form of services will automatically fill the gap created by the decline of manufacturing. On the other hand, they may very well succeed in filling the entire gap – recall that Kaldor's first 'law' found a high correlation between the growth rate of GDP and the growth of output of both manufacturing and services. Once again, the recent change in the composition of British exports cannot itself justify Kaldor's view that manufacturing holds the key to economic growth in Britain as elsewhere.

Similarly, without denying the important role of demand in explaining the disparate growth rates of advanced countries, it is difficult to swallow the Kaldorian notion that, say, rapid growth in Japan and low growth in Britain can be adequately explained without considering supply-side differences in the two countries in attitudes to work, enterprise and innovation, not to mention differences in industrial relations, government policies towards industry, social security provisions, and so on. And yet that is what is implied by Kaldor's studious insistence that demand and demand alone can account for international differences in growth rate.

Conclusion

Kaldor has not been loath to draw the logical conclusions of his recent thinking about international differences in growth rate. The mould of that thinking is essentially different from that of mainstream neoclassical thinking with its reliance on such concepts as general equilibrium, perfect competition, constant returns to scale, marginal productivity payments and allocative efficiency as the central economic problem. In two powerful essays written in the early 1970s (1972, 1975b), he attacked not just static equilibrium analysis but the very concept of equilibrium itself as the nub of what is wrong with standard economic theory.[7] Both of these essays called for more dynamic thinking in economics unrelated to equilibrium relationships between variables, but failed to emphasize that the repudiation of equilibrium economics involves not just abandoning orthodox microeconomics but also Keynesian macroeconomics and all varieties of growth theory, including that of Kaldor II, leaving little else but Kaldor III growth laws as the sum of the content of economics. Needless to say, this is a prospect which will not be welcomed by everyone. Nothing is more difficult than to turn an entire discipline around, asking it in effect to jettison its own history over the last 200 years. It is doubtful whether even so formidable a figure as Kaldor can expect to succeed in so daunting a task.

Kaldor certainly asks Big Questions and attempts to answer them in a Big Way. In this sense, he is a true heir of Adam Smith. The emphasis on difference

206 Economic theories, true or false?

in growth rates as the key problem of economics, the constant appeal to the principle of increasing returns to scale, and even the reliance on stylized facts as furnishing the basis of both the premises of economic theory and the checks on its conclusions, all remind us of Adam Smith. In other respects, however, his analysis lacks the historical and sociological breadth of Adam Smith, being narrowly geared to the growth problems of Britain in recent decades. Moreover, his is essentially a one-man research programme. His ideas link up with the rest of post-Keynesian economics but do not marry very well with the writings of other members of the school, such as Sraffa, Robinson and Kalecki, all of which depend in one degree or another on the concept of equilibrium. Moreover, Kaldor's ideas have developed little since the mid-1970s and have attracted few disciples. There are now any number of schools that have repudiated neoclassical economics and have attempted to move towards a new style of dynamic economics, such as the neo-Austrians, 'evolutionary economics' and the 'new institutional economics' (see Langlois, 1986), none of which have found inspiration in the writings of Kaldor. In short, judged by academic, rather than political, standards, his ideas must be judged as having failed to take off.

Notes

1. For an outstanding exposition of Kaldor's entire growth theory, paying due attention to the successive versions of the model, see Hacche (1979, Chapters 11–13; see also Wan (1971, pp. 82–9).
2. See for example, Bronfenbrenner (1971, pp. 416–21); Pen (1971, pp. 187–90); Johnson (1973, pp. 199–204); and Jones 1975, pp. 146–9). C.E. Ferguson (1969, p. 322) sums up the criticisms:

   the Kaldor model simply determines the profit share that is consistent with full employment, given an exogenous level of investment and the unequal propensities to save. This is far from a theory of distribution. A basic condition of the model is that I must equal S, *ex-ante* and *ex-post*. There is no behavioral equation to explain investment; it simply must equal desired saving. Since P/Y depends on the investment–income ratio, there is also nothing in the model to explain distributive shares. P/Y is what it is because in equilibrium it is related to I/Y, and I/Y is what it is because it can be nothing else. Just as relative shares are technologically determined in neoclassical theory, so they are psychologically determined in Kaldor's theory, being ultimately determined by the propensities to save.

   Note the phrase 'There is no behavioral equation to explain investment', which Kaldor clearly took to heart.
3. Hacche (1979, Chapters 14, 15) provides a superb account of the British–US evidence relating to Kaldor's six stylized facts, on which the subsequent comments in the text are largely based.
4. In 1972, he noted that 'The capital–output ratio in the United States has been falling over the past 50 years whilst the capital/labour ratio has been steadily rising' (Kaldor, 1978b, p. 148) and elsewhere he has conceded that output under capitalism is always constrained by the level of effective demand, so that full employment is far from the typical situation in modern industrialized economy.
5. For an earlier and highly sympathetic account of Kaldor's three laws, to which we are heavily indebted, see McCombie (1981) and Thirlwall (1983)
6. For an attempt to discuss these forces systematically, see Kennedy (1971, chs. 6, 7).
7. 'The powerful attraction of the habits of thought engendered by "equilibrium economics" has become a major obstacle to the development of economics as a *science* – meaning by the term

"science" a body of theorems based on assumptions that are *empirically* derived (from observations) and which embody hypotheses that are capable of verification both in regard to the assumptions and the predictions' (Kaldor, 1975b, p. 176).

References

Bronfenbrenner, M. (1971), *Income Distribution Theory*, London: Macmillan.
Chatterji M. and Wickens M.R. (1983), 'Verdoorn's Law and Kaldor's Law: A Revisionist Interpretation', *Journal of Post-Keynesian Economics*, Spring.
Hacche, G. (1979), *The Theory of Economic Growth: An Introduction*, London: Macmillan.
Hirschleifer, J. (1962), 'The Firm's Cost Function: A Successful Reconstruction, *Journal of Business*, July.
Jones, H. (1975), *An Introduction to Modern Theories of Economic Growth*, London: Thomas Nelson.
Johnson, H.G. (1973), *The Theory of Income Distribution*, London: Gray-Mills.
Kaldor, N. (1934), 'The Determinateness of Static Equilibrium', *Review of Economic Studies*, February, repr in Kaldor (1960a).
Kaldor, N. (1937), 'The Controversy on the Theory of Capital', *Econometrica*, July, repr in Kaldor (1960a).
Kaldor, N. (1938), 'Professor Chamberlin on Monopolistic and Imperfect Competition', *Quarterly Journal of Economics*, May, repr in Kaldor (1960a).
Kaldor, N. (1939a), 'Capital Intensity and the Trade Cycle', *Economica*, February, repr in Kaldor (1960b).
Kaldor, N. (1939b), 'Welfare Propositions in Economics', *Economic Journal*, September, repr in Kaldor (1960a).
Kaldor, N. (1940a), 'A Model of the Trade Cycle', *Economic Journal*, March, repr in Kaldor (1960b).
Kaldor, N. (1940b), 'A Note on Tarrifs and the Terms of Trade', *Economica*, November, repr in Kaldor (1960b).
Kaldor, N. (1942), 'Professor Hayek and the Concertina-effect', *Economica*, November, repr in Kaldor (1960b).
Kaldor, N. (1956), 'Alternative Theories of Distribution', *Review of Economic Studies*, 23 (2), repr in Kaldor (1960a).
Kaldor, N. (1957), 'A Model of Economic Growth', *Economic Journal*, December, repr in Kaldor (1960b).
Kaldor, N. (1958), 'Capital Accumulation and Economic Growth' in F. Lutz (ed.), *The Theory of Capital*, London: Macmillan, repr in Kaldor (1978a).
Kaldor, N. (1960a), *Essays on Value and Distribution*, London: Duckworth.
Kaldor, N. (1960b), *Essays on Economic Stability and Growth*, London: Duckworth.
Kaldor, N. (1962), 'A New Model of Economic Growth' (with J.A. Mirrlees), *Review of Economic Studies*, 24 (3), repr in Kaldor (1978a).
Kaldor, N. (1963), 'The Case for an International Commodity Reserve Currency' (with A.G. Hart and J. Tinbersen) *Essays on Economic Policy*, vol II (London: Duckworth).
Kaldor, N. (1966), *Causes of the Slow Rate of Economic Growth in the United Kingdom*, Cambridge: Cambridge University Press, repr in Kaldor (1978a).
Kaldor, N. (1968), 'Productivity and Growth in Manufacturing Industry: A Reply', *Economica*, November.
Kaldor, N. (1970a), 'The New Monetarism', *Lloyds Bank Review*, July, repr in Kaldor.
Kaldor, N. (1971b), 'The Dynamic Effects of the Common Market', *New Statesman*, 12 March, repr in Kaldor (1978b).
Kaldor, N. (1971c), 'The Common Market - A Final Assessment', *New Statesman*, 22 October, repr in Kaldor (1978b).
Kaldor, N. (1972), 'The Irrelevance of Equilibrium Economics', *Economic Journal*, December, repr in Kaldor (1978b).
Kaldor, N. (1975a), 'Economic Growth and the Verdoorn Law - A Comment of Mr Rowthorn's Article', *Economic Journal*, December.

208 Economic theories, true or false?

Kaldor, N. (1975b), 'What is Wrong with Economic Theory?', *Quarterly Journal of Economics*, August, repr in Kaldor (1978b).
Kaldor, N. (1978a), *Further Essays on Economic Theory*, London: Duckworth.
Kaldor, N. (1978b), *Further Essays on Applied Economics*, London: Duckworth.
Kaldor, N. (1979a), *Reports on Taxation*, vol. I London: Duckworth.
Kaldor, N. (1979b), *Reports on Taxation*, vol. II, London: Duckworth.
Kaldor, N. (1986), 'Recollections of an Economist', *Banco Nazionale del Lavoro Quarterly Review*, March.
Kennedy, K.A. (1971), *Productivity and Industrial Growth, The Irish Experience*, Oxford: Clarendon Press.
Kilpatrick, A. and Lawson, T. (1980), 'On the Nature of Industrial Decline in the UK', *Cambridge Journal of Economics*, March.
Kregel, J.A. (1971), *Rate of Profit, Distribution and Growth: Two Views*, London: Macmillan.
Kregel, J.A. (1973), *The Reconstruction of Political Economy: An Introduction to Post-Keynesian Economics*, London: Macmillan.
Langlois, R.N. (1986), *Economics as a Process: Essays in the New Institutional Economics*, London: Cambridge University Press.
McCombie, J.S.L. (1981), 'What Still Remains of Kaldor's Laws?', *Economic Journal*, March.
McCombie, J.S.L. (1983), 'Kaldor's Laws in Retrospect', *Journal of Post-Keynesian Economics*, Spring.
Michl, T.R. (1985), 'International Comparisons of Productivity Growth: Verdoorn's Law Revisited', *Journal of Political Economy*, Summer.
NEDC (1985), *British Industrial Performance*, London: National Economic Development Council.
Parikh, A. (1978), 'Differences in Growth and Kaldor's Laws', *Economica*, February.
Pen, J. (1971), *Income Distribution*, London: Allen Lane/The Penguin Press.
Rowthorn, R. (1975), 'What Remains of Kaldor's Law', *Economic Journal*, March.
Spence, M. (1981), 'The Learning Curve and Competition', *Bell Journal of Economics*, Spring.
Thirlwall, A.P. and Thirlwall, G. (1979), 'Factors Governing the Growth of Labour Productivity' (translation of P.J. Verdoorn's original article in *L'industria*, 1949), *Research in Population and Economics*, Autumn.
Thirlwall, A.P. (1982), *Balance-of-Payments Theory and the United Kingdom Experience*, London: Macmillan.
Thirlwall, A.P. (1983), 'A Plain Man's Guide to Kaldor's Growth Laws', *Journal of Post-Keynesian Economics*, Spring.
Verdoorn, P.J. (1980), 'Verdoorn's Law in Retrospect: A Comment', *Economic Journal*, June.
Wan, H.Y. (1971), *Economic Growth*, New York: Harcourt Brace Jovanovitch.
Weisskopf, T.E., Bowles, S. and Gordon, D.M. (1984), 'Hearts and Minds: A Social Model of US Productivity Growth', *Brookings Paper on Economic Activity*, 1.

[5]
Talking about Kaldor

A.P. Thirlwall

This conversation took place between J.E. King and A.P. Thirlwall on 15 December 1992.

J.E.K. The first question I'd like to ask is whether there's any connection at all between Kaldor's early 1930's work on the theory of the firm and his later Post Keynesian analyses. Or do they belong to two completely different phases of Kaldor's thought, with very little connection between them?

A.P.T. I don't think there is very much connection, except the concept of excess capacity that he developed in the 1930s[1] he does use in some of his later thinking. It's related to the concept of involuntary unemployment and his attack on the concept of the natural rate of unemployment, because in the case where you have excess capacity, as output and employment increase, marginal product rises and marginal cost falls. So there's actually a positive relationship between employment and real wages, in contrast to the Friedman model of the natural rate, where the assumption is the classical one of an inverse relationship between employment and real wages. Professor Weitzman[2] used this early paper of Kaldor to support the contention that a sufficient condition for involuntary unemployment is imperfect competition and excess capacity, and Kaldor used to cite this article with approval. Kaldor was a very strong critic of the Friedman concept of the natural rate. He didn't feel that it had any operational significance at all, because it is based on classical labour market assumptions of diminishing returns to labour and therefore an inverse relationship between the real wage and employment, whereas, in practice, there are increasing returns to labour and therefore a positive relation between real wages and employment.

J.E.K. Another aspect of Kaldor's earlier views that he seems to have put to the back of his mind altogether is his early writings on welfare economics.

A.P.T. Yes, I talked to him about this when I interviewed him. His 1939 paper on compensation tests generated an enormous secondary literature, but he never contributed to subsequent debates. The way that he put it to me was that he simply thought that the debate was a dead end, because you can't make interpersonal comparisons of utility. Everything boils down to value judgements. Even a social welfare function remains an abstraction. Who specifies the function and who decides the distributional weights?

J.E.K. The whole thing's essentially intractable.

A.P.T. The whole thing was essentially intractable, yes. Having developed the idea of compensation tests, he felt that he'd made his contribution and that was that. The other explanation for leaving the debate, I think, might be that he wrote the paper in 1939 and then, with the onset of the war, he got very much wrapped up in the economics of war finance, and then after the war he got very much involved as a public servant, sitting on all sorts of international Commissions of one sort or another. And then, when other people started getting interested in the late 1940s and 1950s, he was working on other subjects, so he never returned to it. It could also be that all the mathematics became a bit too complicated for him, because, as you know, he wasn't a mathematician by any stretch of the imagination. He had a wonderful intuition, but he wasn't able to formalize things himself mathematically. Virtually all the maths in any of the articles he wrote was done by other people. In the growth models of the 1950s, for example, it was done by Champernowne and Mirrlees.

J.E.K. On the early macroeconomic analysis, as you point out, he almost invented the 'Keynes effect', or at least gave it much more prominence than it might otherwise have had. Do you know his views on the Pigou effect, first, and on the IS–LM formulation of Keynes, second?

A.P.T. Yes, he converted Pigou to the argument that there couldn't be an increase in employment simply through a wage cut alone; it would have to come through a reduction in the rate of interest. Pigou paid Kaldor the compliment of saying that the theory of the relation between money wages and employment, via the rate of interest, was invented by Kaldor – much to the annoyance of Keynes who had discussed all this in Chapter 19 of the *General Theory*. What Kaldor was talking about is what we now call the Keynes effect, essentially a reduction in the rate of interest brought about by an increase in the real money supply. This, of course, is different from the Pigou effect which shifts the savings function through a change in the real value of people's money balances. As far as IS–LM analysis is concerned, I can't think of any of his writing, or any conversation I ever had with him, about the Hicksian synthesis and whether he regarded it as some sort of travesty of Keynesian economics in the way that a lot of fundamentalist Keynesians do. As far as I know, he expressed no opinion on that.

J.E.K. That's very interesting. As you say, a number of the fundamentalist Keynesians regard that as the thing that converted them to being Post Keynesians from being orthodox Keynesians.

A.P.T. Yes, but it is significant that, although we think of Kaldor as a Keynesian and as being very much in the forefront of maintaining Keynesian ideas, and then being one of the architects of Post Keynesian economics, he never wrote anything that one might think of as particularly mainstream Keynesian economics. He never paged through the *General Theory* picking up little bits from here and there and developing them in the way that other Keynesian scholars have done. Perhaps he was never very interested in what one might call comparative static analysis. In that period in the 1950s when he started getting interested in economic theory again, it was all very much a dynamic theory, growth theory and technical progress. The other thing is that he was never really interested in money in a theoretical way, at least after that very famous 1939 article on speculation and economic stability. In my biography, I quote from a letter that Hicks wrote to Kaldor in 1986, saying that he thought Kaldor's 1939 paper was the culmination of Keynesian economics in theory and that Kaldor ought to have had more honour for it. But, following that paper, there was no writing on what one might call theoretical monetary economics. There is his evidence to the Radcliffe Committee, and then his writings on monetarism in the 1970s. But I don't regard that really as monetary theory, in the Tobin sense. It is a much more practical sort of monetary economics.

J.E.K. Perhaps we could come back to that later. I wonder if I could ask you about the 1956 income distribution paper, which, you've written, is derived from the widow's cruse parable in Keynes's *Treatise* and from Kalecki's 1942 article on the theory of profits. What sort of proportions would you assign to the influence of those two sources on Kaldor?

A.P.T. I'm not sure precisely. Kaldor obviously knew of the widow's cruse parable, and he read Kalecki's 1942 paper. Kaldor's own paper has much closer affinities with the widow's cruse. Kaldor told me that he first saw the potential of using multiplier analysis for the purpose of a theory of distribution when, as a member of the Royal Commission on the Taxation of Profits and Income (1951–55), he attempted to analyse the ultimate incidence of profits taxation under full employment. Kalecki didn't explicitly use the widow's cruse concept for a theory of the share of profits in income, relying instead on the concept of the 'degree of monopoly'. Kaldor always attributed his own formulation of the 1955–56 paper to an insight of Harry Johnson, who was then in Cambridge. There was this so-called 'secret seminar' in Cambridge, which wasn't really secret at all. Everybody knew of its existence, but it was called the secret seminar. It was Johnson who recognized that if investment determines savings, and the propensity to save out of profits is higher than the propensity to save out of wages, there must be a unique distribution of income between wages and profits, consistent with full employment and the savings–investment balance. Kaldor developed this article in a very short space of time, coming out of that seminar. There was some very acrimonious correspondence about it between Kahn and Kaldor, because Joan Robinson was also working on this topic at the time. She must have been in the final stages of writing *The Accumulation of Capital*, and Kahn accused Kaldor of stealing ideas and getting into print before Joan Robinson, because her book on the *Accumulation of Capital* didn't come out, I think, until mid-1956. There was the feeling that Kaldor had jumped the gun.

J.E.K. Were there any personal contacts between Kaldor and Kalecki at this point, or any other point, to your knowledge?

A.P.T. Very little. He didn't have very much contact with Kalecki at all, and there is no correspondence either, as far as I know.

J.E.K. That, I suppose, is one of the first cases in which Kaldor displays interest in 'stylized facts' that played a very important part in his thinking for some considerable time. Did he have any deep interest in methodology, or read widely in methodology? What were his influences on methodology?

A.P.T. He didn't read very widely at all. He always used to say to me that he never really read, and that in his later years he only read papers that cited himself! Only a paper that cited himself could be important, he used to joke. He wasn't particularly widely read, and that is also reflected in his library. You might imagine a scholar of his eminence having a large library, but in fact he didn't. I expected, when I first met him, to go into a room that would be full of books, but his library was quite modest. Also he certainly wasn't the sort of person who often went to a library to read. Perhaps he's an example of what is sometimes said, that if you read too much, you think too little, or write too little. If you're going to have original thoughts, it's better not to read at all, otherwise you might find that what you're thinking isn't original after all!

J.E.K. His methodological position, I suppose, would be associated with realism.

A.P.T. Yes, I think so. He would say that you can't describe the world absolutely precisely, you can't model the world absolutely precisely. That's the argument for taking stylized facts; developing models to explain stylized facts. He worked very much in the inductive positive tradition and was generally hostile to abstract theorizing and deductive economics, particularly in his latter years.

J.E.K. This would be one reason why he lost interest in steady-state growth theory?

A.P.T. Probably, yes.

J.E.K. And the other, I suppose, would be a lack of relevance to economic policy of those highly formalized models?

A.P.T. I think so, yes.

J.E.K. And he never really returned to any interest in formal growth models of that sort?

A.P.T. He didn't, no. I would say his last formal growth paper would have been the reply to Samuelson and Modigliani where he develops the so-called 'neo-Pasinetti theorem'.

J.E.K. Which was an act of self-defence rather than aggression?

A.P.T. An act of self-defence, yes. But that would be his last, I think. Interestingly, though, Samuelson and Modigliani never replied, so perhaps Kaldor won!

J.E.K. And so, if you like, that's the first phase of Kaldor's writings on growth. It seems to me there were two other phases: the one-country models based on something like

Verdoorn's law and industry–agriculture relations; and then the world models where north–south relations and foreign trade played a dominant part.

A.P.T. That's right. You get this clutch of theoretical models between 1955 and 1962 – five or six of these theoretical models which try to explain the stylized facts of capitalist economic growth. Then there's a lull, and then you get this interest in the applied economics of growth, stemming largely from the fact that he was a policy adviser in the Labour government from 1964 to 1969, and very much concerned with Britain's poor growth performance.

J.E.K. And the emphasis on manufacturing as the engine of growth, which he seems to have got from Verdoorn to begin with, carries over into the Selective Employment Tax.

A.P.T. Yes, the ideas and policies are all very much interrelated. I never asked him directly why he started to get interested in the applied economics of growth and how the Inaugural Lecture of 1966 came to be written, and how it was that the Verdoorn idea surfaced when it did. Verdoorn's paper was published in Italian in 1949, and Verdoorn was on his staff in Geneva where he was the Research Director of the Economic Commission for Europe between 1947 and 1949, but there's absolutely no evidence that Kaldor had read Verdoorn's paper in the original, or knew very much about what Verdoorn had actually written. All he knew was that there was this relationship between productivity growth in manufacturing on the one hand and output growth on the other, related to increasing returns. But I don't think he ever appreciated that it was actually derived from a static production function of the Cobb–Douglas variety, of which he'd been a critic for many years previously. And Kaldor thought of it as a much more dynamic relationship than simply static increasing returns expressed in the parameters of a production function. But when he was in the Treasury he had other economists working for him on this topic. There were Roger Tarling, Chris Allsop and Francis Cripps, among others. They were all working on this topic of growth-rate differences between countries. And then Kaldor comes up quite suddenly, at the same time, with the idea of a Selective Employment Tax which would tax service employment and give a subsidy to manufacturing. As far as the history of thought is concerned, it's not quite clear whether he had that idea first, and then used his Inaugural Lecture to justify it, or whether he'd really worked out that it was indeed manufacturing growth that was the engine of growth which led him to the idea of the Selective Employment Tax. There's quite clearly an interrelationship, but which actually came first, I honestly don't know.

But Kaldor was one of these people who was very ingenious, who came up with ideas without any sort of warning. There was another example, in 1976, when he came up with the idea of giving tax relief on the value of stocks held by business. When I interviewed Denis Healey, he reckoned that this scheme saved a large section of British manufacturing industry from bankruptcy, because it was a time of depression and it was also a time of rising prices with mounting stocks, and the tax relief on stocks considerably improved the liquidity of companies. That was something that came almost out of the blue, and it seems to be the same with the Selective Employment Tax. The way I describe it in my biography is that Callaghan at the time had promised during the election campaign in 1966 that there would be no increase in taxation, and yet it became increasingly clear that the public finances were under strain. Callaghan then, through this idea of a Selective Employment Tax, was able to raise nearly a billion pounds in extra revenue, while, as he described it, keeping his pledge that *conventional* taxation wouldn't be raised. It was a different form of taxation. It wasn't a tax imposed on individuals, which is what people normally interpret as an increase in taxation. And it seems to have been a very successful tax; it raised a lot of revenue, and hardly led to any increase in prices at all. It was absorbed by the service sector, and productivity in the service sector rose dramatically. What it didn't do was to revitalize manufacturing industry. As Kaldor describes in the paper on the Selective Employment Tax that he wrote many years afterwards, which lays out the theoretical justification for the tax, it was introduced at the wrong time. It was introduced at a time when there was deflation in the economy, and, in a deflated economy, you can't expect manufacturing industry to take on more labour and reap much benefit.

J.E.K. That was essentially a one-country, almost a closed-economy sort of model. The emphasis in what I've described as the third period in Kaldor's interest in growth was very much on exports and the international economy. What moved him in that direction?

A.P.T. Well, I think he did recognize, as a result of thinking about the constraints on growth, that, at the end of the day, it wasn't, as he argued in his Inaugural Lecture, the supply of labour constraining manufacturing growth. It was the overall constraint of the balance of payments. I think there were two things that were going on in his mind: one, that he was reminded by people after the Inaugural Lecture that outside manufacturing there were still substantial reserves of labour, not in agriculture, but in service activities. And that's one thing that changed his mind about labour supply being the major constraint on manufacturing output growth, which he'd argued in the 1966 paper. The other thing was that, having been an advocate of flexible exchange rates for quite some time (he was very much in favour in 1964 of devaluation of the pound, or letting the pound float, rather than trying to maintain its value as we did up to 1967), he then became increasingly disillusioned with the efficacy of exchange rate changes as a balance of payments adjustment mechanism. That being so, he then recognized the balance of payments, and therefore exports and export growth, as the major constraint on Britain's overall growth performance and the growth of the manufacturing sector. So between about 1967, almost immediately after he wrote his Inaugural Lecture, and about 1971–72, you get this fundamental change of view about what drives an open economy.

J.E.K. And it comes very much from his experience with the real world, loosely described?

A.P.T. I think so, yes. He was also at this time concerned with the debate over the Common Market, and that forced him to think much more internationally than he'd been doing up until then: Britain's place in Europe, and the sort of burdens that would be placed on the British economy through the budgetary mechanism in the transfer of funds to Brussels. Also, what's likely to happen as tariff barriers come down? Is Britain likely to benefit from this process? So there were a lot of things going on in his mind at that time which pushed him in that direction. And then you get this famous phrase (I think it was in a *New Statesman* article) that the prewar unemployment problem in the 1930s had transmuted itself into a chronic balance of payments problem in the 1950s and the 1960s. Then there was the paper he wrote as the President of the British Association for the Advancement of Science, 'Conflicts in Policy Objectives', where he first lays out in a formal way this view that exports are different from other components of autonomous demand, because only exports provide the foreign exchange to meet the import requirements that would be necessary for any other expansion in aggregate demand, investment or consumption or whatever it may be. Then, in 1970, you also get the paper, 'The Case for Regional Policies', where he outlines in verbal terms an export-led growth model, drawing on Hicks's concept of the super-multiplier. You get this idea of the growth rate in an economy being fundamentally determined by the major component of autonomous demand, to which other components of demand adapt and, for Kaldor, the only true component of autonomous demand is demand coming from outside the country. In Kaldor's view, the longer the time period taken, the more everything *within* the economy is endogenous.

J.E.K. Including investment?

A.P.T. Including investment, yes. Investment, being a produced means of production, is itself the outcome of the growth process rather than the cause.

J.E.K. It's about this time that he begins to write on money, almost for the first time in his career, as you pointed out earlier. Have you any ideas as to what might have driven him to do this, whom he might have been influenced by in this, or was it a question of almost total originality again?

A.P.T. Again I can't answer what the origin was. The first anti-monetarist attack came in a public lecture at University College, London, which became the 1970 paper published in *Lloyd's Bank Review*. What the origin of that was, I simply don't know. Perhaps there was something welling up inside him as a result of the growing influence of the ideas of Milton Friedman, and monetarist economics in general, emanating from the United States. There was a growing disillusion with Keynesian economics, and monetarism was profoundly anti-Keynesian, so perhaps it was just a reaction against that. He was aware of the work of Friedman and Schwartz and, of course, Friedman's 1968 'natural rate' paper.

J.E.K. Some of the North American Post Keynesians had been tilting at the monetarists for some time before that. I'm thinking about Sidney Weintraub, Paul Davidson, maybe Hyman Minsky. Is there any evidence at all that Kaldor was in contact with these people?

A.P.T. No, there's no evidence at all. I don't think he was, in any productive way.

J.E.K. And it's quite likely that he was totally uninfluenced by them, almost totally unaware of what was going on there?

A.P.T. Yes. I think the clue to that would be if there were any references to these people in the *Lloyd's Bank Review* article, but there are not.

J.E.K. I spent three days in the Weintraub Archives at Duke University on my way here. There's some cursory correspondence between Kaldor and Weintraub, but not very much, and Weintraub seems to have kept almost everything at that period, so I suspect there's probably very little there.

A.P.T. Weintraub and Davidson wrote a paper called 'Money: Cause and Effect' in the *Economic Journal*.

J.E.K. Yes, I think that was later. The notion that the money supply is in fact endogenous almost appears to have originated with Kaldor, which is why I'm interested to know whether he might have picked up this notion somewhere else.

A.P.T. Yes. I got quite interested in this topic myself while I was writing my book. There is reference to endogeneity of money in Chapter 21 of Keynes's *General Theory*. There is a very pertinent phrase where Keynes says that if societies are short of money, they will find ways of overcoming the shortage. You also get hints of the endogeneity argument in Kaldor's 1939 paper, so that's very early.

J.E.K. I was talking to Basil Moore a couple of weeks ago. He obviously gives Kaldor credit for this, but says, as you do, that you can find traces of the idea of endogeneity in the *General Theory*. I wonder if Kaldor would have gone as far as Moore in arguing that the money supply curve is horizontal.

A.P.T. In modern terminology, he would be a horizontalist. I'm sure Moore gets his own inspiration from Kaldor, and not the other way around.

J.E.K. I'm sure that's right.

A.P.T. Yes, Kaldor, on my understanding, is a horizontalist.

J.E.K. Would he perhaps have argued that the notion of independent supply and demand curves was a misleading one?

A.P.T. I think what he would argue would be that, at whatever the rate of interest the monetary authorities want to maintain, the supply of money is elastic with respect to demand, so it's completely horizontal at whatever the rate of interest that is set. The schedule moves up and down at the price at which the monetary authorities want to maintain the rate of interest. In that sense, he's a horizontalist.

J.E.K. Which is almost exactly Basil Moore's position.

A.P.T. Almost exactly, yes.

J.E.K. Moving on chronologically just a little bit, you talk in some places about New Cambridge macroeconomics, which appears to have sunk almost without trace, or did until last week.

A.P.T. I think Nicky was one of the originators of this idea that it is the government budget that determines the balance of payments, but he was embarrassed by it at the end of the day, because (a) it broke down, and (b) it's based on the assumption that the private sector is in balance. But in the theory there's no mechanism by which the private sector gets into balance. And Kaldor was writing at that time as if the budget deficit itself was the *cause* of the balance of payments deficit, and I don't think he would ever have wanted to argue that identities help very much in understanding causal relationships. So from that point of view I think he was embarrassed by the whole thing. And it simply died a death. I think he may have got seduced by some of his Cambridge colleagues. I think he may have got inadvertently mixed up in this but, subsequently, if you talked to him about it, he would blush a bit, I think. I don't think he was committed to the theory.

J.E.K. Towards the end of his life he became a very outspoken critic of equilibrium analysis in economics generally. Do you think his ideas on that question had any great influence?

A.P.T. Well, it certainly forced people to think about the modelling process. Being someone who was interested in the functioning of the real world, like Keynes, I think his point would be that the equilibrium methodology and the assumptions that it has to make in order for it to get definitive results is simply a barren and sterile exercise for understanding real world processes of growth and change. And I think it is another example of what I said earlier, that he wasn't really interested in static analysis at all; what he was interested in was the dynamics of the capitalist system. To understand the dynamics of the capitalist system of growth and change, the sorts of assumptions that neoclassical equilibrium theory makes simply don't help. And so we need alternative models, and although perhaps you can't mathematize these alternative models, you can talk about them in an interesting way, which I think he does. He does, for example, in the Okun Lectures that he gave at Yale University in 1983, entitled 'Economics without Equilibrium'. Although he doesn't have a very strong following in America, certainly there are a lot of distinguished economists who would take note of what he has to say about these sorts of things. If you read the preface, for example, to the Okun Lectures written by Tobin, it's very glowing. Well, I suppose, if someone's giving lectures at your university and you're writing a preface, you have to say glowing things but I think, from Tobin, they were genuine.

J.E.K. His target was clearly, most openly, neoclassical economics. I wonder too if the argument against equilibrium was also directed against the Cambridge neo-Ricardians or Sraffians.

A.P.T. I don't know. This warfare that goes on between these groups within the Post Keynesian camp has passed me by, I'm afraid.

J.E.K. I think it all hinges around the notion of long-run equilibria, prices of production as centres of gravity to which the system eventually moves, which I suppose would have been fairly congenial to Kaldor.

A.P.T. He had a very high regard for Sraffa but he never wrote on this topic.

J.E.K. Not something that would really have concerned him very much? Too abstract and too removed from reality?

A.P.T. Probably, yes. It is quite interesting that Sraffa was his closest friend, both personal and intellectual, and they used to meet very regularly – almost every day when Sraffa was alive. But there's no evidence that they ever discussed *Production of Commodities by Means of Commodities*.

J.E.K. That's amazing. There's certainly no evidence that he ever wrote anything on those questions.

A.P.T. There's no evidence that he wrote anything, or that indeed he really understood Sraffa. Well, he had the broad thrust, but I don't know that he ever read it carefully, or understood the implications.

J.E.K. It's difficult to understand how people could be so close in every sense and yet so completely removed intellectually. Which, I suppose, leads on to another question that I have. You said at the end of your introduction to *The Essential Kaldor*[3] that Kaldor's contribution has been undervalued, and I suspect that's true, not just in the profession more generally but also among Post Keynesians, for whom the neo-Pasinetti theorem seems almost to sum up Kaldor's contribution, and that's clearly a very substantial under-assessment. Have you any thoughts as to why he's been relatively neglected even by people he might think would be sympathetic to him?

A.P.T. Are you sure that he has been neglected by Post Keynesians?

J.E.K. It's certainly true in North America that if you talk about British Post Keynesians, they talk about Joan Robinson and, by extension, Kalecki. I'm inclined to think that's probably true in Britain as well, and in Europe.

A.P.T. Yes, I can see why they perhaps picked out Kalecki, presumably because of the interrelationship between his micro and macro contributions, and the feeling that, if Keynes hadn't written the *General Theory*, then we would be talking about the Kaleckian revolution rather than the Keynesian revolution. I can see that. But I would have thought on the sorts of major issues that Post Keynesian economists are concerned with – if you think of the debates on inflation, for example, and the sources of inflation – then Kaldor would figure much more prominently than Joan Robinson or Kalecki. If you discuss the functional income distribution, you'd certainly refer a great deal to Kaldor. *Kyklos*, for example, celebrated, with a special issue, the 25th anniversary of his 1956 paper. There was a big conference at the New School in New York in 1987, all devoted to Kaldorian themes. If you talk about the applied economics of growth, if you read the *Journal of Post Keynesian Economics*, a lot of papers on the applied economics of growth and Verdoorn's law all refer back to Kaldor's 1966 lecture.

J.E.K. And yet there are a lot of people who would regard themselves as Kaleckian or (a smaller minority) Sraffian, but very few who would describe themselves as Kaldorian.

A.P.T. Well, perhaps it is this theoretical–empirical distinction again. Young, bright people get more captured by theoretical ideas than they do by empirics, and they latch on therefore to Kalecki more than they do to Kaldor for that reason. But I would have thought that Kaldor had as much of a vision of the functioning of capitalist economies in the modern world as did Kalecki and Joan Robinson, although it's not written down in one place. But you can see the vision. One of the things I tried to do in my book was to say there is a Kaldorian economics and an interesting story to tell. Yes, people don't call themselves Kaldorians but do they call themselves Kaleckians. But they don't call themselves Robinsonians either!

J.E.K. No, they don't – that's an interesting point. Another way in which this distinction comes up is in the question of Nobel Prizes or non-Nobel Prizes. There's developing almost a sort of small literature on why Joan Robinson didn't get a Nobel Prize, but very few people, apart from yourself, seem interested in the question of why Kaldor didn't get a Nobel Prize.

A.P.T. Well, I don't think anybody pretends to understand quite how the distribution of Nobel Prizes is decided.

J.E.K. I was talking to Craufurd Goodwin, the editor of *HOPE*, about this, and he thinks it was very largely political, that Joan Robinson was not only closely identified with a particular political line, but was closely identified with a fairly left-wing political line.

A.P.T. Yes. I'm sure personalities are involved as well. We know that there's always been this clash between the Swedish School and the Cambridge School. Remember the Swedes once referred to the unnecessary originality of Cambridge? I mean, the Swedes think they invented it all, in the early 1930s, with Myrdal and others. So I think, yes, there are personalities involved as well as politics. The Nobel Committee seems to do a random survey of economists, because I was asked once for my opinion. I actually nominated Joan Robinson, not Kaldor. But, given that in a random sample you'd pick up probably 70 per cent of Americans or more, if they take any notice of the view of Americans, the decision is going to be largely an American one. And the Cambridge School never went down well in America because it's too nihilistic. It's like taking your lifeline away if you start criticizing neoclassical economics and production functions and these sorts of things. And they were very rude as well.

J.E.K. I haven't met them, but I've met enough people who would confirm that.

A.P.T. They were very rude, even to their own kind. Paul Davidson once mentioned to me how small Joan Robinson had made him feel, for example, in one of the seminars that he had given in Cambridge some years ago. They were rude to each other, let alone the outside world. That sort of thing never went down very well on the conference circuit. It doesn't endear you to members of the Nobel Committee.

J.E.K. However, you'd stand by your judgement that Kaldor was more original than any of the British economists who won the Nobel Prize, like Hicks and Meade?

A.P.T. I think so, yes. My judgement was, and I think still is, that probably he was the third most original British economist this century, in terms of ideas, after Keynes and Harrod. That would be shared by a lot of other people as well. Charles Kennedy, for example, who used to be Professor of Economic Theory here at Kent was a very close friend of Hicks and developed some of Hicks's work, but he never regarded Hicks as particularly original. But I think Meade and Hicks received their prizes for some sort of unified contribution, and Kaldor unfortunately never produced a unified contribution in the form of a treatise. That's what he would have needed, some sort of treatise like *Value and Capital*, or Meade's volumes on international economics.

J.E.K. Perhaps we could talk about your own work, which is in some sense Kaldorian. Can you explain the origins of your interest in Kaldor's ideas and your interest in taking them further?

A.P.T. I got interested in Kaldor first of all because in my early career I was very much interested in regional economics, and I did a lot of work on regional unemployment and regional growth. I think it was his 1970 paper that inspired me, the paper that he gave to the Scottish Economic Society in 1970, entitled 'The Case for Regional Policies', where he laid out for the first time his regional export-led growth model. Then I had here at that time a very bright young PhD student, Robert Dixon, from Australia. We started working on the model and published a joint paper in *Oxford Economic Papers* in 1975, entitled 'A Model of Regional Growth Rate Differences on Kaldorian Lines', where we formalized the model and then derived the stability conditions, to see the conditions under which regional growth rates will diverge, as opposed to converging to some sort of equilibrium. It was after this that I first started corresponding with Kaldor, because he liked the model and he thought it captured his ideas very well. It's a circular model, which is what we wanted to represent. Following on from that, one thing that struck me about the model was that, if it was actually applied to nations, the equilibrium growth rate might be unsustainable because it pulls in more imports than a country is exporting, so balance of payments problems arise. When the model is applied to regions, the balance of payments implications are ignored, because regions don't have balance of payments problems in the sense of having to maintain an exchange rate or to defend an exchange rate. So when Dixon and I applied this model to the United Kingdom, and got what we thought were the best estimates of the variables and parameters to put into the model to predict the actual growth rate over the previous twenty years or so, we found it vastly overestimated the actual growth rate. That's what led me and my own work in the direction of balance of payments constrained growth models. Why not put a balance of payments constraint into the growth model right from the start, and then derive the growth rate consistent with balance of payments equilibrium?

The other interesting thing that happened at this particular time, when all this was going on, was that two economists working in one of the Ministries published a paper trying to indicate that Britain wasn't experiencing a balance of payments problem because, if you looked at the relationship between import and export ratios (that is, as a proportion of GDP), they were both moving together. That led Kaldor to write a letter to *The Times*, saying that these economists would have failed the Cambridge Tripos examination because they didn't realize that, if exports or imports change autonomously, then through the trade multiplier that Harrod had developed in his book *International Economics* in 1933, the level of GDP will so change as to preserve a balance of payments equilibrium between exports and imports. So equality of the ratios says nothing about whether a country has a balance of payments problem, without knowing the level of income at which this balance has settled. And this was quite uncanny, because it also transpired that, out of the end result of my balance of payments constrained growth model, if you assume relative prices remain unchanged, and balance of payments equilibrium is a requirement, the end result will be that the rate of growth of income is equal to the rate of growth of exports divided by the income elasticity of demand for imports, which is the *dynamic* analogue of the Harrod trade multiplier. So Kaldor and I immediately got into correspondence over the Harrod trade multiplier as well. Kaldor had known about the Harrod trade multiplier for a long time because, when he was a student at the LSE in the 1920s, he'd been taught by Barrett Whale, who was one of the only people around at that time who had been questioning the workings of the old Gold Standard, and stressing that it was income that was doing the adjustment of the balance of payments rather than relative price changes as a result of gold flows and money supply changes. So, again, this is something I think Kaldor had stored in the back of his mind and then, quite out of the blue, had released – like all the other things that seem to have just come out of the blue, but had antecedents. So we got into correspondence again over the relationship between growth and the balance of payments, and the link-up with the Harrod trade multiplier. And so, as a result of all this during the middle and latter part of the 1970s, I got very interested in Kaldorian thought. Then in 1979 I went on a sabbatical term to Cambridge with the intention of reading all his work. And that was the start of my intellectual biography.[4]

J.E.K. You don't like to be labelled as a Post Keynesian yourself?

A.P.T. No, I don't like labels too much because in my own professional work I've been much more interested in tackling particular issues and then drawing on what I regard as relevant, rather than drawing exclusively on one scheme of thought or theoretical paradigm. But I think by virtue of the conclusions that you reach, as a result of empirical analysis, if the conclusions that you reach seem to fall within a particular sphere of thought, then I suppose that at the end of the day that does put you in one camp or another.

J.E.K. The policy conclusions in particular, I suppose. You've published work in support of an incomes policy, for example, and I guess the sort of policy conclusions that you draw from your work on the balance of payments would be quite compatible with Post Keynesianism?

A.P.T. Yes, most of the conclusions I reach are interventionist conclusions. In terms of inflation, for example, I don't see any solution to the shifting Phillips curve, or to reconciling full employment with low inflation, without some sort of wages policy. What form it would take, I haven't considered in any detail. I suppose the Post Keynesian position with respect to all theorizing and policy advice is that institutions matter. Economics and economic problems cannot be properly discussed without taking account of institutional arrangements. There's another contemporary example of the argument about an independent central bank and whether it would lead to lower inflation. Now while an independent central bank may suit one country, it doesn't necessarily suit another country, because the institutions differ. And apart from the question of the democratic control of institutions, I don't myself believe that an independent central bank has been the major factor that has enabled Germany to experience low inflation for the last thirty years. I think it's much more institutional. To put it another way, if Germany had the same institutions as the UK and didn't have paranoia about inflation, an independent central bank wouldn't work there. Also I think one has to interpret Kaldor's work on money, for example, as very much rooted in what he regards as the realistic institutional structure that now determines the money supply creation process. It's the contrast between credit money, which is produced by financial institutions, and commodity money, which he argues that Friedman in his model is basically assuming.

J.E.K. And, in terms of international policy, you'd agree presumably with Kaldor that much more intervention is needed than is currently the case?

A.P.T. Yes, I'm persuaded by the view that particularly primary product price instability has a destabilizing effect on the world economy, so there's a strong case for having, as Keynes wanted, a 'commod' control scheme, a buffer stock scheme, for storable commodities, and the use of SDRs to buy up surplus commodities and stop price fluctuations.

Notes

1. 'Market Imperfection and Excess Capacity', *Economica*, February 1935.
2. 'Increasing Returns and the Foundations of Unemployment Theory', *Economic Journal*, December 1982.
3. F. Targetti and A.P. Thirlwall (eds), The Essential Kaldor (Duckworth, 1989).
4. A.P. Thirlwall, *Nicholas Kaldor* (Wheatsheaf, 1987).

Part II
The Cambridge Growth Theorist

[6]

THE RELATION OF ECONOMIC GROWTH AND CYCLICAL FLUCTUATIONS [1]

SINCE the very beginnings of speculation on the problem of the Trade Cycle, the cyclical swings of the economic system have been regarded as being inherently connected with the essentially "dynamic" process of economic growth. For this there were two reasons. In the first place, with relatively unimportant exceptions (such as Jevons's sun spots), even the early writers on the trade cycle (like Marx, Aftalion, Spiethoff or J. A. Hobson) emphasised the key role of the investment process, and of the growth of productive capacity, in the generation of cyclical movements. Secondly, the close connection between the cycle and dynamic change was "visible to the naked eye"—inasmuch as the historical boom periods of the last 150 years were, in many cases, clearly associated with the exploitation of major technical innovations, such as the railways, electricity or the automobile.

At least one distinguished author—Joseph Schumpeter—put forward a trade-cycle theory which makes the cycle itself simply a by-product of economic progress—booms and depressions being "the form which progress takes in a capitalist society." This is because, according to Schumpeter, the realisation of major innovations must await a time when the general economic climate is favourable to them; the adoption of major innovations by the heroic innovating entrepreneurs is followed by a host of imitators, giving rise to an investment boom; when the innovations are thus fully exploited (or over-exploited) the economy once more relapses into a depression, until the accumulation of new ideas creates the favourable climate for a new burst of "innovating" investment.

The trouble with Schumpeter's theory is that it is descriptive rather than analytical. Although it is easy enough to see how one particular part of the story follows from the preceding part, it is not possible to make the story as a whole into a "model" (meaning by a model the sum total of assumptions which are just sufficient —no more and no less—together to provide the necessary and

---

[1] A lecture delivered to the Institut de Science Économique Appliquée in Paris on May 23, 1953.

sufficient conditions for the generation of a recurrent cycle with a clear periodicity) without incorporating into it elements which would suffice by themselves to explain the cycle—without recourse to Schumpeter's own stage army of initiators and imitators, or even the very concept of technical progress. For the necessary " bunching " (in time) of innovating investment, which is essential to Schumpeter's theory, cannot be satisfactorily explained without bringing the Keynesian multiplier, and some variant of the output–investment relationship, to one's aid.

Indeed, the development of trade-cycle theories that followed Keynes's *General Theory* has proved to be positively inimical to the idea that cycle and dynamic growth are inherently connected analytically—to the idea, that is, that the cycle is a mere by-product of, and could not occur in the absence of, " progress." For it has been repeatedly (and in my view, conclusively) [1] shown that a few simple additions to Keynes's own model of a general equilibrium of production in the economy will produce the result that this " equilibrium " will take the form, not of a simple steady rate of production in time, but of a rhythmical movement of constant amplitude and period—in other words, a perpetual oscillation around a stationary equilibrium position. The necessary additions to Keynes's own framework of assumptions to get this result are few and simple. All that is required is to treat the investment demand schedule (Keynes's " marginal efficiency of capital ") not, as Keynes did, as an independent variable, but as a function of both the existing stock of capital and of the current rate of output, or simply of the ratio of output to the stock of capital. This is justified, if future profit-expectations can be regarded as being largely determined by the current rate of profit on capital. For the current rate of profit per unit of capital (or rather per unit of investment) clearly depends on the current relation of output to capital (at any rate if, as a first approximation, profit per unit of output can be taken as given) so that the rate of investment will increase with a rise in output and/or a diminution in the existing stock of capital, and *vice versa*.[2] Since

---

[1] Cf. my own paper " A Model of the Trade Cycle," ECONOMIC JOURNAL, March 1940, which, of course, drew heavily on earlier works of Harrod (*The Trade Cycle*, 1936), Kalecki (*Essays in the Theory of Economic Fluctuations*, 1938) and others. Since that time Richard Goodwin (*Econometrica*, January 1951, pp. 1–17) and Hicks (*A Contribution to Theory of the Trade Cycle*, Oxford, 1950) produced cyclical models which in the essential framework of assumptions, though not necessarily in technique, are identical.

[2] Some writers (notably Harrod and Hicks) prefer to exclude the stock of capital as an explicit variable, and treat instead investment as a function of the

current output depends (via the Keynesian multiplier) on current investment, whereas the current change in the stock of capital depends on past investment (and will be positive or negative according to whether investment in the previous " period " was greater or less than the necessary replacement of the capital goods currently used up in production), the mechanism will in itself produce a periodic fluctuation of constant amplitude (of the output/capital ratio, of the rate of investment and of the level of output), provided two additional conditions are satisfied:

(1) a change in output (income) is associated with a greater change in the rate of investment than of savings, so that the stability conditions of the " Keynesian " equilibrium [1] are not satisfied for levels of output that imply a rate of investment that is higher than the possible minimum and lower than the possible maximum; [2]

(2) the rate of investment at any one time cannot exceed a certain maximum, or fall below a certain minimum, which implies also that the Keynesian stability conditions must be satisfied (partially at any rate) whenever investment is at the maximum or the minimum level.

The second condition must be satisfied by virtue of the fact that gross investment cannot be less than zero, and cannot be greater than the investment corresponding to full employment, or the capacity of the investment-goods industries, whichever is

---

change in the rate of output (the so-called " acceleration principle "). It is important to emphasise that the difference is more a matter of methodological and pedagogic convenience than of substance. It is perfectly easy to translate one technique into another without any difference in the results; though the acceleration method requires far more rigid assumptions as regards production techniques and time lags of adjustment (cf. my review article of Hicks's book in ECONOMIC JOURNAL, December 1951, pp. 837–41).

[1] The Keynesian stability conditions are simply that a rise in production should increase the aggregate demand for output by less than the value of the additional output (*i.e.*, the " aggregate supply price "). Since the marginal propensity to consume is less than 1 (*i.e.*, the additional demand for consumers' goods generated by a rise in income falls short of the rise in income), this condition will be satisfied if: (*a*) the rate of investment is invariant with respect to changes in output; (*b*) the increase in the rate of investment generated by a rise in output is less than the shortfall in marginal consumers' demand over marginal income—*i.e.*, savings out of marginal income.

[2] Actually it is sufficient for the model if this condition is satisfied in the neighbourhood of the hypothetical " long-run equilibrium " position, where investment = current depreciation. It is simpler to assume, however, that it holds for all levels of investment between a certain minimum and maximum.

less.[1] The first condition is likely to be satisfied on account of the fact that in situations in which an increase in output induces the creation of additional capacity, the value of that additional capacity is likely to exceed (perhaps several times) the value of the additional output per unit period; hence the additional rate of investment (per unit period) is also likely to exceed the additional savings generated by that additional output (the length of the critical " period " depends on the time taken to adjust current production to changes in demand).[2]

Properties of the " Static " Model

The above framework of assumptions yields a purely " static " model of the trade cycle—" static " in the sense that it accounts for a regular cyclical movement of constant amplitude and period, in the absence of any " dynamic " change, such as technical innovation, population growth or changes in the political or institutional framework, and in which the whole movement, its duration as well as its amplitude, is fully determined by the parameters of the system. It has strictly four phases—an upward

---

[1] The above statement may be open to criticism on two counts. First, it might be suggested that " full employment " does not set any genuine limit to the rate of investment (in *real* terms), since investment could be increased further at the cost of current consumption, through a process of monetary inflation. Now it is true that by means of inflation it is possible to reduce the proportion of real income consumed. But past experience has repeatedly shown that the extent to which an inflationary process succeeds in augmenting the real rate of savings of the community is very limited; and when, as a result of full employment, the increase in current output slows down, the urge to expand investment further is also reduced. However, there is nothing in the model to prevent an expansionary process from leading to a state of purely monetary inflation (in which case the monetary authorities would be forced to take restrictionist measures sooner or later); the point is rather that it does not make any real difference to the mechanics of the model whether inflation occurs in the course of it or not.

It might also be objected that in the absence of full employment the capacity of the investment-goods industries does not set a limit to the expansionary process either : since in that case there would be an urge to undertake investments to expand the capacity of these industries. That is true; but this second type of reaction might operate far too slowly to be of much consequence in relation to the cyclical process. Thus when the demand for new ships exceeds the capacity of the shipbuilding yards the first result is that order-books and delivery periods are lengthened. If this lengthening of order books went on for several years the shipbuilding industry would be induced to build new shipyards. It is quite possible, however, that before such major extensions get under way the boom is over.

[2] For a fuller explanation of these conditions cf. my paper in Economic Journal, March 1940, cited above, particularly the Appendix, pp. 89–92. As explained there, the advantage of assuming non-linear co-efficients is that it makes it unnecessary to rely on time-lags or to introduce exogeneous stocks of any kind in order to account for a cyclical movement of constant amplitude.

phase, a boom phase, a downward phase and a depression phase, the first and third of which may be relatively short in duration in relation to the second and the fourth. Contrary to the general belief (including my own previous views) that under such " static " conditions the duration of the depression phase would necessarily be very much longer than that of the boom phase (owing to the simple fact that capital goods take much longer to wear out than to build), I now believe that the relative duration of the boom phase and the depression phase is simply a matter of the relationship of the output capacity of the investment-goods industries to the normal annual depreciation of the capital stock. If this output capacity were twice as large as normal depreciation, the duration of boom and depression phases would be identical; if it were more than twice as large, the depression phase would last longer than the boom phase, while if it were less than twice as large, the depression phase would be shorter than the boom. Hence, without introducing any " dynamic " change, it is possible to construct models in which the depression phase is short relative to the boom phase rather than the other way round. The length of the boom phase depends on a complex set of factors : the annual output capacity of the equipment-goods industries, its relation to the capital stock at any one time (which *does* depend both on gestation period and service-life), the " critical " degree of excess capacity which causes entrepreneurs to abstain from adding to capacity further; and finally, the Keynesian multiplier, which determines the extent of utilised capacity at boom and depression levels, respectively. The duration of the depression phase depends on the rate at which existing capacity is reduced by scrapping; and it can be assumed, of course, that it is always the oldest and most obsolete plant which is scrapped. If we suppose that the service-life of equipment produced in any given period is uniquely fixed by technical factors, the equipment which disappears during any given depression phase is the equipment that was created in the earliest of the boom periods which was still extant at the end of the preceding boom phase; and the period required for its disappearance (assuming both a fixed and a constant service-life for equipment) would depend on both the length of that earlier boom phase and the age-distribution of the capital stock at the end of the previous boom. If the lifetime of plant or equipment is not rigidly determined, we cannot take it for granted that the discontinuity in building periods will be reflected in a similar discontinuity of scrapping periods, though in so far as the life-time of equipment can be extended only at a gradually increasing operating cost, there will be an economic motive for keeping obsolete equipment in existence during boom periods and to concentrate the scrapping of equipment on depression periods. Finally, if we suppose that, for purely technical reasons, there is a fairly wide spread in the service-life of the equipment created in any given period (both because equipment is of different kinds and also because equipment of any particular kind has a probability-life-distribution rather than a fixed service-life), the disappearance of old equipment will tend to take place at a more or less steady rate in time, irrespective of the discontinuity in building periods; and it may not show much variation as between boom and depression phases. In each case, however, the length of the boom phase in relation to the length of the cycle as a whole will depend simply on the relationship of the average annual depreciation of the capital stock—during the cycle as a whole—to the annual output of capital goods during the boom. If the latter were twice the former, the boom phase would take up one-half of the full cycle-period and so on.

The inter-relation of the various factors could be made clearer in terms of a simple numerical example. Let us suppose that the capital stock consists of ships, while output consists of shipbuilding (investment) and shipping services (consumption); that ships take one year to build and the capacity of the shipbuilding industry is 1 million tons, so that 1 million tons represents also the maximum output of new ships per annum. Let us further suppose that at the boom-level of income (i.e., when the shipbuilding industry is fully utilised), the demand for shipping services requires a minimum of 12 million tons of capacity and at the depression level of income (when no new ships are built), a minimum of 8 million tons; and finally, that shipowners order new ships whenever the current demand exceeds 80% of their current capacity. On these assumptions the shipping park reaches a maximum of 15 million tons at the end of the boom (125% of 12 million tons) and a minimum of 10 million tons at the end of the depression (125% of 8 million tons): in each case because, at those levels, demand tends to fall below, or rise above, the critical 80% utilisation of capacity. If we now suppose that the service-life of ships is a fixed period of 25 years, the duration of the boom will be 5 years, and the duration of the depression will also be 5 years, since in 5 years the 5 million tons created in the last but three of the building periods (25 years ago) will be scrapped. If we supposed, other things remaining unchanged, the maximum shipbuilding capacity to be 2 million tons, the duration of the boom would be reduced to 2·5 years, but by the same token the duration of the depression would be lengthened to 7·5 years—since, given the size of the shipping park at boom and depression levels, as determined by demand, the age distribution of ships would be such that there would be no ships due for scrapping in the first 5 years of any depression period, and the scrapping would be concentrated in the last 2·5 years of the depression phase, when the 5 million tons of ships built in the boom phase of 25 years before would disappear. Again we could assume that the service-life of ships is 35, 45 or 55 years instead of 25, with similar effects on the relative duration of boom and depression phases; though if the life-time were supposed to be less than 15 years the cyclical mechanism could not go into operation at all unless we also amended some of the other assumptions—*e.g.*, either the minimum demand for shipping services would have to be assumed to be less than the above 8 million tons or the maximum shipbuilding capacity would have to be assumed to be greater than the above 1 million tons per annum.[1]

If we now supposed (again, other things remaining unchanged) that while the *average* service-life of ships is 25 years, there is a fairly wide frequency distribution around that average, ships may be assumed to be scrapped at a (more or less) constant rate of 0·5 million tons per annum both during boom and depression phases (corresponding to $\frac{1}{25}$ of the *average* capital stock of 12·5 million tons). In that case the boom phase will last for 10 years (since, with an annual output of 1 million tons, it will take 10 years to *raise* the shipping park from 10 to 15 million tons), and the depression phase will also last 10 years (since, with a fixed rate of scrapping of 0·5 million tons, it will take 10 years for the shipping park to be reduced from 15 to 10 million tons). The period of each phase, and of the cycle as a whole, would thus be doubled, as compared with the situation in which (for technical or economic

[1] I am conscious, of course, of the fact that in the above numerical examples the figures were so chosen as to avoid the need for any overlapping as between the building periods and the scrapping periods. Assuming that the service-life of ships is rigidly determined by technical factors, this can be the case only when: (*a*) the boom phase takes up one-half or less of the cycle; and (*b*) the service-life of ships is an integral odd-number multiple of the period of the boom. Thus, if in the above example the service life of ships were assumed to be a rigid 20 years, there would necessarily be overlapping between building and scrapping periods, which would cause the boom to be prolonged to 15 years, followed by a depression phase of 10 years; if it were to be assumed to be a rigid 30 years, there would be a boom period of 15 years, followed by a depression phase of 20 years; and there may be other more complicated patterns. On the other hand, if the life-time is not assumed to be *narrowly* determined by technical factors—say, in the above example, ships are scrapped when they are over 20 but less than 25 years old—overlapping would be avoided as a result of the operation of economic factors, since there would be an incentive to keep old capacity in existence during the boom, and thus to concentrate scrapping in times of slump.

reasons) the actual disappearance of equipment is concentrated on depression phases; but otherwise the mechanism would operate in the same way.[1]

The most important factor in the whole mechanism is the capacity of the capital-goods industries, which, given the service-life and gestation period of capital goods, determines the rate of capital accumulation during the boom periods. The greater is this factor, the shorter the duration of the boom phase (both absolutely and relatively to the depression phase) and the greater the amplitude of the cyclical movement. The capacity of the capital-goods industries relative to the consumer-goods industries may in turn be assumed to depend on the proportion of income saved at full-employment income levels—in other words, on the short-run savings function. For supposing that maximum investment, as determined by this capacity, were initially less than full-employment savings, there would be an inducement, in each successive boom, to enlarge this capacity, relatively to the rest of the economy, until the deficiency was eliminated. Similarly, if this capacity in relation to the rest of the economy were initially greater than the proportion of income saved at full employment, some part of the capacity of the capital-goods industries would become permanently redundant—not being utilised even at the peak of the boom—and would thus tend to disappear. If, however, entrepreneurial expectation in the capital-goods industries were more sluggish than in the consumption-goods industries, it is quite possible that the capacity of the capital-goods industries was maintained at too low a level to secure full employment in boom periods, and the cyclical movement itself might be weak in amplitude and the booms relatively long in duration.

Looked at in another way, the mechanism depends on the assumption of a short-run savings function which, though it may be represented as being linear, must contain a negative constant. In other words, it is assumed that while the marginal propensity to save is constant, the average propensity to save is a rising function of

[1] It is important to emphasise therefore that this particular model is in no way dependent on the so-called " echo-effect "—i.e., the bunching of replacement demand in time resulting from past discontinuities in building periods. If there is a wide scatter in the actual service-life of plant and equipment, discontinuities in building periods need not result in corresponding variations in the rate of scrapping—any more than annual fluctuations in the number of births tend to be reflected in corresponding variations in deaths a generation later. But even if the scrapping of equipment is perfectly continuous, there will be a bunching of investment in time as a result of the operation of the multiplier and the " accelerator."

income in the short period. Hence there is a minimum depression level of income at which (gross) savings are zero and a maximum boom level of savings which is attained when income reaches the full-employment level. If we ignore the fact that, for reasons stated above, the maximum rate of investment during a boom (as determined by the actual capacity of the capital-goods industries) may be consistently less than the investment needed for full-employment output, we can simply say that the amplitude and the character of the cyclical movement (*i.e.*, the relative duration of boom and depression phases) is determined simply by the character of the short-run savings function.

Cycle and Trend

The static model outlined above has no trend—which shows that it is not necessary to assume economic growth or dynamic change in order to account for the existence of fluctuations. Each depression phase lasts precisely as long as is required for the capital stock to fall to the same extent as it had risen in the previous boom; the capital stock, as well as the output, in the corresponding phases of successive cycles are identical. As a pure cyclical model it has therefore little resemblance to the cyclical fluctuations in the real world, the most characteristic feature of which has been that successive booms carried production to successively higher levels; while the creation of capital in boom periods has exceeded many times the net capital depletion in depression periods.

The significant point is, however, that a trend can be "incorporated" into the above framework of assumptions without upsetting the mechanism; and thus by this simple device it is possible to produce a model whose features show a far better resemblance to the observed phenomena. The model is capable also of absorbing "random shocks" of all kinds, such as wars, revolutions or revolutionary technical changes caused by major inventions, with no more consequence than of displacing (in time) the operation of the cyclical movement. It strongly suggests therefore that economic growth, as well as other dynamic and erratic changes, should be treated rather as the cause of aberrations from the pure rhythm of the static cycle than as the *sine qua non* without which the basic phenomena could not be accounted for.

The simplest way of introducing a "trend" is to assume a linear percentage growth in population over time. This will mean that the amount of capital created in each successive boom will be higher than in the previous boom (since in each case the expansion would tend to go on until full employment or full capacity in the investment-goods industries is reached; but in this case the capital-goods industries would themselves tend to be enlarged in each successive boom), while the capital used up in the succeeding depression-phases will be consistently smaller than the capital created in the previous boom-phase.[1] It is not certain (because it has not yet been worked out) how the introduction of a logarithmic trend affects the duration of the cycle or the length of the various phases relative to each other. My hunch is that a *logarithmic* trend might leave both these unaffected. While there is more capital created in each succeeding boom, there may also be assumed to be a greater capacity of investment-goods production to create it, so that the length of the boom could remain unchanged; while there is less capital (as a proportion of the total stock) destroyed during the depression, the rate of disappearance of " old " capital is also less (since a greater proportion of the capital stock is of more recent creation), so that the length of the depression phase would also remain unchanged. If this is correct, long booms and short depressions, or *vice versa*, would be promoted by an accelerating or de-celerating trend, rather than by the existence of a trend as such.

It is possible also to make technical progress (in the shape of a linear time-rate of growth in the productivity of labour) the cause of the trend; and so long as this technical progress is assumed to be "neutral"—*i.e.*, leave the ratio of capital and output in production unaffected—its effect on the model is no different from that of population growth. In fact, these two factors are additive—given both "neutral" technical progress and population growth, the trend will be the resultant of the two, since the rate of increase of full-employment output will be the sum of the rate of increase of productivity and of population. It would also be possible to assume that technical innovation is, on balance, capital using (*i.e.*, involving a net substitution of capital for labour) or else capital saving, though the precise consequences of this on the properties of the model are difficult to work out. Finally, it is possible—as Mr. Goodwin had done in one of his " models "[2]—to neglect the

[1] To explain this, it is necessary to assume that savings are a function of income per head, rather than total income—*i.e.*, that the savings function also " shifts to the right " with the rise in full-employment output, so that savings always fall to zero when actual output falls to a certain percentage of full-employment output. Alternatively, it could be assumed (as Hicks assumed) that there is some long-range investment which is autonomous and not responsive to changes in current output, and which is growing at the trend rate.

[2] Cf. " A Model of Cyclical Growth " paper presented to the Oxford meeting of the International Economic Association, September 1952.

replacement of capital altogether, and assume, in effect, that all capital, once created, is permanent. In that case the introduction of a trend would still create a cycle which is basically no different from the other models (though there would be no cycle, of course, in the absence of a trend). The accumulation of new investment opportunities over time would give rise to a periodic boom, in the course of which these opportunities were exploited. The savings-investment mechanism (or shall we call it, the multiplier–accelerator mechanism) would still ensure that investment does not proceed at a steady rate, but is " bunched " in time. The fundamental reason, which is thus common to each variant, is that: (a) the output capacity of the investment-goods industries is greater than the current rate of accrual of new investment opportunities—and it does not make any difference whether these new investment opportunities reflect the using-up and scrapping of old equipment or the growth of population, technical progress or anything else; and (b) that the economic system possesses no short-run stability at levels of investment which are below a certain maximum or above a certain minimum. Further, it is possible to introduce endless complications into the model which would tone down its sharp edges and crudities—as, *e.g.*, that investment is influenced by finance, monetary policy or rising production costs, etc.; that new inventions take the form (in part) of the creation of new industries satisfying new " wants," which would explain why some investments would go on even during a depression, etc.—though it is doubtful whether in our present stage of knowledge the laborious task of working out the consequences on the model of any particular type of complication would be really worth while.

It is thus seen that all the " dynamic " models that were recently presented to the world—such as Kalecki's amended model,[1] Marrama's,[2] Hicks's[3] or Goodwin's[4] (which all contain the same basic assumptions outlined above)—are all variants of the same thing, and, essentially, all consist of the superimposition of a linear trend introduced from the outside on an otherwise trendless model without altering, in any way, its basic character. Some of the authors mentioned deny this. Thus Professor Hicks thinks that " it is on the trend rate of growth that the whole cyclical mechanism depends "[5] and that in the absence of the growth in autonomous investment the cycle could not get off the

[1] *Studies in Economic Dynamics*, London, 1943.
[2] *Review of Economic Studies*, Vol. XIV, p. 34.
[3] *A Contribution to Theory of the Trade Cycle*, Oxford, 1950.
[4] *A Model of Cyclical Growth, op. cit.* [5] *Op. cit.*, p. 108.

floor—or, at any rate, not for an inordinately long time.[1] Similar ideas were expressed also by Mr. Goodwin.[2] This, in my view, is mistaken, and must be due to an insufficient appreciation by the authors of the properties of their own model.

Finally, there is the illuminating piece of algebra produced by Mr. Harrod [3] and Mr. Domar,[4] according to which, given the savings function, there is only one particular rate of growth that can be permanantly maintained—a rate that is entirely determined by the relation of the savings function to the technical relationship between capital and output, and which is thus independent of the trend as given by the assumed rate of growth of population and of productivity. In the present context this need not detain us for long, since—as the two authors would themselves be prepared to admit—this " dynamic equation " is relevant only for determining the trend of a cycle-less economy, and not the trend rate of growth of an economy which does not actually maintain a moving equilibrium of growth, but proceeds by a series of investment booms, interrupted by slumps.[5, 6]

[1] *Op. cit.*, p. 105, note. Hicks's analysis suffers also from a confusion between the idea of "autonomous" investment (*i.e.*, investment which is *not* responsive to changes in current output) and the idea of " new " investment opportunities due to the growth of population and technology. There is no reason whatever why these two should overlap. It is perfectly possible for there to be no autonomous investment in Hicks's sense, and yet be a trend, due to the above factors; equally there could be autonomous investment in a trendless economy. In Mr. Goodwin's recent model, on the other hand, the trend is the direct outcome of the underlying growth in population and productivity, and not of the growth of " autonomous " (in the sense of " non-induced ") investment.

[2] "A Model of Cyclical Growth," *op. cit.*

[3] Harrod, "An Essay in Dynamic Theory," ECONOMIC JOURNAL, March 1939, and *Towards a Dynamic Economics*, 1949.

[4] *American Economic Review*, March 1947.

[5] In other words—to put the matter in Mr. Harrod's own terminology—the *actual* trend resulting from successive booms and slumps reflects the " natural rate " (*i.e.*, the growth of population and productivity) and not the " warranted rate." The " warranted rate " (interproted, as it should be, as the rate of growth at *full-employment savings*) determines, *inter alia*, the duration of the boom, and also the length of the cycle, but not the trend rate of growth. This assumes, of course, that the " warranted rate " is higher than the " natural rate " —but this may be taken as a basic feature of capitalist society. If the " warranted rate " were *less* than the " natural rate," new investment opportunities would accrue faster (in time) than they are exploited through current investment; new investment would thus become steadily more profitable; and it may be supposed that the economic system would gradually evolve the institutional conditions necessary—by raising the profit rate and the amounts set aside out of profits—for a faster rate of exploitation, *t.e.*, for the " warranted rate " to rise. Indeed, the independent role accorded to the savings function in Mr. Harrod's and Mr. Domar's method of approach is one of the criticisms that one can make against their method as a tool for the analysis of *long-run* problems.

[6] Cf. also Joan Robinson, "The Model of an Expanding Economy," ECONOMIC JOURNAL, March 1952, pp. 52–3.

Mr. Harrod makes no claim, in his recent analysis, to put forward a complete model of the cycle; in his view, however, the "dynamic equation" provides the key to the existence of the cycle, since it is the peculiarity of any "equilibrium of steady advance" that it is surrounded, on each side, by "centrifugal forces." If it could be shown that a moving equilibrium of growth is necessarily unstable, while its static counterpart, the stationary equilibrium, is stable, this would indeed provide an inherent connection between the cycle and economic growth. But if our own analysis is correct, this is not so. Exactly the same assumptions which make the moving equilibrium of a growing economy unstable, will produce the same "centrifugal forces" around the stationary equilibrium of a trend-less economy;[1] in fact, the latter can itself be looked upon as a special case of the "dynamic equilibrium" where the equilibrium-rate-of-growth happens to be zero. Hence there is nothing in the assumption of a positive rate of growth as such (such as the assumption of a growing population, or technical progress) that serves as an *explanation* of the tendency to oscillation that could not equally be explained without it.

The Problem of Economic Growth

So far, so good. But is this situation, from an intellectual or analytical point of view, wholly satisfactory? The trend itself is not "explained"; it is introduced as a datum. There can be no pretence, therefore, of these theories providing the basis for a theory of economic growth. Yet the very fact that different human societies experience such very different rates of growth—in fact, differences in rates of growth in different ages or in different parts of the world in the same age are one of the most striking facts of history—in itself provides powerful support for the view that technical invention and population growth, the two factors underlying the trend, are not like the weather or the movement of the seasons, that go on quite independently of human action, but are very much the outcome of social processes. The growth in population, in particular, is as much the consequence of economic growth as the condition of it. This is true both of situations of the Malthusian kind, where it is merely the consequence of a higher rate of survival brought about by an improvement of the means of subsistence, and where population growth is merely the

[1] On this point cf. also my article in Economic Journal, December 1951, pp. 842–3.

passive consequence, or accompaniment, of economic growth; as also of situations where the acute shortage of labour resulting from rapid economic expansion directly stimulates the growth in numbers—as, *e.g.*, in America after the Civil War, or in England in the course of the Industrial Revolution.[1] The same is true of technical invention or innovation. Though new ideas, looked at in isolation, are the spontaneous product of the workings of the human brain, the kind of ideas that come forth, and their frequency, is very much a matter of environment. Few would deny that the greatly accelerated growth of the last 200 years, which is associated with the rise of modern capitalism, was essentially the product of forces endogenous to society; while the vast flow of technical innovation and of population growth, which accompanied this process and which alone made its realisation possible, were themselves the products of these basic social forces and not the initiating causes of it.

Where, then, are we to look for the ultimate factors responsible for the rate of economic growth in human societies? The English classical economists—if one can epitomise their views in a single word—thought they found it in Thrift. The basic factor responsible for growth and progress is the Rate of Capital Accumulation (which in the classical view was responsible for the growth of population as well as material capital); and capital accumulation, on their view, was largely a matter of the habits of thriftiness of the population—its willingness to forsake present enjoyment for future gain. At the present time we are not willing to accord such an important role to the propensity to save. This is not because—or not mainly because—we have learnt, since Keynes, that saving can be a positive impediment of progress, and not always a promoter of it. It is because it is now increasingly realised (perhaps also under the influence of Keynesian ideas) that the proportion of income saved in the community is not so much the result of basic psychological attitudes and propensities, as of the institutional framework of society, which is itself continually (though slowly and gradually) adapted to social requirements. The re-investment of the profits of business enterprise always has been, and still is, the main source of finance of industrial capital accumulation; we are now aware that the rate of accumulation is at the same time one of the main determinants

[1] The fact that in Western European societies in the last fifty to seventy years the increase in population so markedly lagged behind the economic growth potentialities (owing to widespread birth control and the control of immigration) should not blind us to the force of this generalisation as a broad historical tendency.

of the amount of profits that is thus available for financing.¹ Saving and Capital Accumulation therefore are in no different position from Technical Progress and Population Growth, as being one of the features that characterise progressive societies rather than as the ultimate stuff and substance which *makes* societies progressive.

The most plausible answer to the question why some human societies progress so much faster than others is to be sought, in my view, not so much in fortuitous accidents, like major discoveries, or in favourable natural environment (though no doubt all these are important as conditioning factors) but in human attitudes to risk-taking and money-making. The modern business-man or " entrepreneur," as featured in economic textbooks, with his distinctively speculative bent and his interests and energies concentrated on profit making, is clearly a product of capitalist society. But the rise of modern capitalism, in turn, cannot be explained except as the result of the growth of mental attitudes which find in risk-taking and money-making the means of giving expression to the individual's *ego*. Economic speculation here trespasses on the fields of sociology and social history; and the most that an economist can say is that there is nothing in economic analysis as such which would dispute the important connection, emphasised by economic historians and sociologists, between the rise of Protestant ethic and the rise of Capitalism.

An economy, which, over longer periods, shows a relatively high rate of growth is almost certain to be one which keeps " bumping against the full-employment ceiling " fairly regularly, and with reasonable sized bumps. It is an economy which, once set upon the path of rapid expansion, does not stop expanding until it comes up against the physical limitations of capacity or labour; and it is in the strength of the incentives to overcome such limitations that we must look for the main motive force for long-term dynamic growth. Scarcity of labour, as we have argued, directly stimulates population growth—both through immigration into a particular area and through stimulating a higher effective rate of natural growth. But prolonged scarcity

---

[1] That distinguished pupil and critic of English classical economics, Karl Marx, has seen this clearly; and this is perhaps one of the main aspects in which, on a purely analytical level, his doctrine departs from Ricardo's. Marx, however, (as far as I understand him), would regard the continuous growth of knowledge as regards the techniques of production—which goes on, in a sense, independently of society, but which shapes and determines the social relationships between men and the institutional framework of society—as the main " independent variable " of economic growth.

of labour is also the most powerful incentive to the invention and introduction of labour-saving devices,[1] just as shortages of physical capacity provide the incentive to the creation of new capacity.

The conclusion which emerges from this is that so far from the trend rate of growth determining the strength or duration of booms, it is the strength and duration of booms which shapes the trend rate of growth.[2] It is the economy in which business-men are reckless and speculative, where expectations are highly volatile, but with an underlying bias towards optimism, where high and growing profits are projected into the future and lead to the hasty adoption of "unsound" projects involving over-

---

[1] The fact that the productivity of labour in American industry, over the last eighty years appears to have risen at about twice the annual rate as in European industry, could be satisfactorily explained (in my view) only through the fact that the higher expansion-mindedness of American business created prolonged periods of acute labour shortage in the economy, which stimulated both the high rate of immigration prior to 1914 and also the invention of labour-saving devices, such as the belt-line assembly, the single-purpose machine tool, the methods of mass-production generally, and far-reaching standardisation. On the other hand, the sudden slowing down of population growth in the 1920s (largely the result of the immigration laws), by reducing the trend rate of growth, must have been a major cause of the severity of the depression in the 1930s.

[2] It is essential, of course, to suppose for this that the "boom"—implying a state of affairs where production is confined by physical limitations and not by effective demand—is a matter of some duration and not only a fleeting momentary phase in the course of the cycle. I believe that to have been the case with the "strong booms" of history (though not, of course, of all booms); and one reason for my dislike of the use of the "acceleration principle" as a device in trade-cycle theory is that it automatically excludes this possibility. With the acceleration principle, output "bounces back as soon as it hits the full-employment ceiling" in much the same way as a tennis ball when it hits a wall. (This is because in a simple acceleration model the adjustment of the capital stock to the change in output is assumed to take up the same length of time as the adjustment of output to the change in demand. Professor Hicks has attempted to relax this condition in his own model by providing for a *series* of acceleration coefficients, thus allowing for a change in output in a given period to give rise to investment in a whole series of future periods. However, his equations make no allowance for the related fact of a back-log of desired investment accumulating as a result of the investment industries becoming clogged up with the uncompleted investment orders of the past, in which case the rate of investment ceases to have any definite relation to the rate of change in output. It is implicit in Hicks's equations that *all* the investment that is profitable to be undertaken at any given level of output has either been completed or else is in process of building as soon as that level of output is reached. Thus if we applied his equations to our numerical example on p. 58 above, they imply that 5 million tons of new shipping is either completed or in the process of building at the moment when the expansion reaches the full-employment ceiling. But if the capacity of the shipbuilding yards is only 1 million tons, clearly not more than 1 million tons can be in process of building at any one time; and since the maximum expansion of output is reached when shipbuilding attains the rate of 1 million tons, there must be a large back-log of desired investment by the time the "ceiling" is reached, which would prolong the boom well beyond the "two periods" allowed for in his equations.)

expansion, which is likely to show a higher rate of progress over longer periods; while it is an economy of sound and cautious business-men, who are slow at reacting to current events, which is likely to grow at a slow rate. It is true, of course, that it is the very process of over-expansion during the boom which makes the ensuing slump inevitable. But the same cyclical force which causes booms to end after a time and be converted into slumps, also causes slumps to end and be converted into new booms; and the extent of the "over-expansion" in the previous boom influences to a major extent the degree to which the new boom surpasses the peak reached by its predecessor.[1]

This is not to suggest, of course, that the long-term trend of growth is *simply* a matter of the degree of recklessness of society's entrepreneurs. The external "conditioning factors" are still there—in the sense that there probably always is a *maximum* attainable rate of saving, a *maximum* attainable rate of population growth or a *maximum* attainable flow of new ideas. But the point is that the *actual* values of these variables, in any given society and at any given age, are not determined by their theoretical maximum values, but are capable of being slowed down or accelerated in accordance with the push or pull exerted by entrepreneurial behaviour. (Perhaps this idea could best be expressed in Mr. Harrod's terms by saying that while the "warranted rate" of growth and the "natural rate of growth" are two different things, they are not independent of each other, since the more the "warranted rate" tends to exceed the "natural rate," the more it will *bend* the "natural rate" in its own direction.[2])

Here at last we find the inherent link between trend and cycle that we were searching for. For if the above analysis is correct,

[1] This is particularly true of investment in investment-goods industries such as steel capacity, etc. As mentioned earlier, expectations might be responsive to changes in current profits in the consumer-goods industries and yet be sluggish to respond to changes in demand in the investment-goods industries. In that case not only will booms tend to be weak, but the rate of growth in output between successive booms will also be small.

[2] Mr. Harrod seems to me to have drawn the wrong moral from his own analysis in suggesting that an excess of the "warranted rate of growth" over the "natural rate" will make "the economy to be prevailingly depressed," although "at first blush, one would suppose it to be a good thing that the line of entrepreneurial contentment should be one implying an attempt to push forward always at a greater rate than fundamental conditions allow" (*Towards a Dynamic Economics*, p. 38). Our own analysis would suggest that Mr. Harrod's "first blush" was right, and his subsequent analysis was wrong. What he did not allow for was that the "fundamental conditions" determining the natural rate of growth are not determined by Heaven—they are pliable (within wide limits) and can be pushed outwards or pulled inwards by the endogenous forces of the economic system.

both the trade cycle and economic growth are the resultant of particular attitudes of entrepreneurs—more precisely, of the volatility of entrepreneurial expectations. As was stated at the beginning, the basic assumption underlying all recent models of the trade cycle is the dependence of long-term investment decisions on current profits : the speculative frame of mind which causes frequent and far-reaching adjustments of long-term expectations in the light of current experience. Without that no variant of the output–investment relationship, such as the " acceleration principle " or any other assumption, would work, and the system would tend to settle down to a stable long-term equilibrium. If expectations are responsive, but sluggish, we might get a moderate cycle, with weak booms and weak slumps and an equally weak trend. It is when expectations are highly volatile that the expansionary phase of the cycle is likely to be vigorous and sustained; that it will inevitably lead to a strong boom which will burst through the pre-existing " external frame " of the economy and carry it to a new and higher plateau. Once such a higher plateau is reached, the subsequent slump, though severe, will not mean a return to the previous depression-level; it will in time produce a new expansionary process from a higher " floor," leading to a new " ceiling." [1]

The same forces therefore which produce violent booms and, slumps will also tend to produce a high trend-rate of progress; though the connection between the two is far too complex to be reducible (at present) to a simple mechanical model. And

[1] At first sight the proposition that higher volatility of entrepreneurial expectation as such promotes a higher trend rate of progress might appear paradoxical, since the stimulus provided by the greater optimism of the boom would appear to be offset by the greater pessimism of the slump. But my contention is that the effects of the two are not symmetrical. The worst that slump-pessimism can do is to interrupt the investment process altogether. But if the tide of boom optimism carried the economy to a higher plateau of productivity and of the standards of living, the cessation of investment in the subsequent slump will not mean a return to the " floor " of the previous slump—the " floor " will have risen—while the rise in the " full-employment-ceiling " as between successive booms is itself largely conditioned by the tide of optimism in booms. Of course, if entrepreneurial attitudes are in themselves assymetrical—if there is a consistent bias towards optimism—the stimulus to progress will be even stronger than if they are merely volatile.

The above view receives strong support from (and in fact is greatly dependent on) Mr. Duesenberry's analysis of consumption behaviour and saving in *Income, Saving and the Theory of Consumer Behaviour*, according to which once a higher standard of consumption is reached in the boom, the consumption function shifts, and the subsequent fall of consumption in the slump is less than it would have been otherwise. Equally, it supports the view that the maintenance of consumption in slump periods by means of anti-cyclical fiscal devices, unemployment pay, etc., must tend to accelerate the trend rate of growth of the economy.

Schumpeter's hero, the "innovating entrepreneur," whom we dismissed so summarily and rather contemptuously at the beginning, is found, after all, to have an honourable place, or even a key role, in the drama—even though we prefer to endow him with a rather more variegated character. He is a promoter, a speculator, a gambler, the purveyor of economic expansion generally, and not just of the "new" techniques of production.[1]

NICHOLAS KALDOR

King's College,
Cambridge.

---

[1] The conclusion that in a capitalist society—*i.e.*, in a society where investment decisions are made by a multitude of entrepreneurs in the light of profit-expectations—the trend rate of growth is likely to be all the greater the more powerful are the cyclical forces, is not to be taken to imply that progress must necessarily take the form of fits and starts, whatever the institutional arrangements of society. If investment were centrally planned and the consumption function continually adjusted to secure full employment (given the planned rate of investment) there is no reason, in theory, why progress could not take place at an even rate.

A MODEL OF ECONOMIC GROWTH [1]

The purpose of a theory of economic growth is to show the nature of the non-economic variables which ultimately determine the rate at which the general level of production of an economy is growing, and thereby contribute to an understanding of the question of why some societies grow so much faster than others. There is general agreement that the critical factors determining the trend rate of growth are to be sought in the savings propensities of the community (which determine the rate of capital accumulation), the flow of invention or innovation (which determines the rate of growth of productivity) and the growth of population. Until recently, these factors were regarded as the parameters of a growth model—*i.e.*, as non-economic variables which are invariant with respect to changes in the other variables—and theoretical inquiry was confined to the more modest task of showing the particular relationships that must prevail between the values of these different parameters in order that they should be consistent with a steady rate of growth for the economy as a whole. But more recently, there has been an increasing awareness of the fact that neither the proportion of income saved nor the rate of growth of productivity per man (nor, of course, the rate of increase in population) are independent variables with respect to the rate of increase in production; and that the actual rate of progress of a capitalist economy is the outcome of the mutual interaction of forces which can adequately be represented only in the form of simple functional relationships (like supply or demand curves) rather than by constants. The purpose of this paper is to present a simple model of economic growth based on a minimum number of such relationships.[2]

A satisfactory model concerning the nature of the growth process in a capitalist economy must also account for the remarkable historical constancies revealed by recent empirical investigations. It was known for some time that the share of wages and the share of profits in the national income has shown a remarkable constancy in " developed " capitalist economies of

---

[1] This paper owes a great deal to discussions with Professor D. G. Champernowne, both in its general ideas and even more in the detailed presentation of the mathematical parts of the argument. I am particularly indebted for his help in working out the implications of the assumptions in mathematical terms, and for the mathematical proofs of some of the propositions made, though he bears no responsibility for the choice of assumptions underlying the models.

[2] The present paper represents an elaboration and further development of ideas put forward in two earlier papers by the author, " Alternative Theories of Distribution," *Review of Economic Studies*, Vol. XXIII, No. 2 (March 1956), pp. 94–100, and " Capitalist Evolution in the Light of Keynesian Economics," a lecture delivered at the University of Peking in May 1956, and reprinted in *Sankhyā (Journal of the Indian Statistical Institute)*, Vol. 18, Parts 1 and 2, June 1957. Reference may perhaps also be made to two former papers by the author which set out the reasoning underlying some of the arguments and assumptions in more detail, " Mr. Hicks and the Trade Cycle," Economic Journal, December 1951, pp. 833–844, and the " The Relation of Economic Growth and Cyclical Fluctuations," Economic Journal, March 1954, pp. 53–71.

the United States and the United Kingdom since the second half of the nineteenth century.[1] More recent investigations have also revealed that whilst in the course of economic progress the value of the capital equipment per worker (measured at constant prices) and the value of the annual output per worker (also in constant prices) are steadily rising, the trend rates of increase of both of these factors has tended to be the same, so as to leave the capital/output ratio virtually unchanged over longer periods.[2] This means that while progress involved a continuous increase in the amount of capital used per worker—whether capital is measured in terms of an index number of the value of capital goods at constant prices, in terms of horse-power per man or in tons of steel embodied in equipment per operative, etc.—there was no "deepening" of the capital structure in the economist's sense: no increase in the amount of "waiting" per unit of current output, or in the ratio of "embodied" to "current" labour, or in the length of some (arbitrarily measured) "investment period."[3] Constancy in the share of profit and in the capital/output ratio also involves constancy in the rate of profit earned on investments (in the "marginal efficiency" of capital), and this again appears to be confirmed by empirical investigations.[4] Existing theories are unable to account for such constancies except in terms of particular hypotheses (unsupported by any independent evidence), such as the unity-elasticity of substitution between Capital and Labour,[5] or more recently, con-

---

[1] For the United Kingdom the share of wages has shown only small variations around the level of 40% of the national income in the period 1840–1950. (Cf. Phelps Brown and Hart, "The Share of Wages in the National Income," ECONOMIC JOURNAL, June 1952, pp. 253–77.) In the United States the share of wages and salaries remained constant at around 60% of the national income up to about 1929, and has since shown a rising trend, mounting to 69% in the post-war decade, while the share of profits and property income (dividends, interest and rent) declined since 1929 from 38 to around 30%. Some of this change no doubt reflects the rise in wage and salary earners as a proportion of the total population. (Cf. Kuznets, "Long Term Changes in the National Income of the U.S.A. since 1870," *Income and Wealth*, Series II.)

[2] According to Mr. Maiwald's calculations based on fire-insurance figures, the capital/output ratio in Britain remained practically unchanged in the period 1870–1914 (at around 3·3) and fell slightly (to around 3·0) in the period 1914–38 (*Economic History Review*, Part I, 1956, p. 102). The same impression is gained from the study of Phelps Brown and Weber ("Accumulation, Productivity and Distribution in the British Economy, 1870–1938," ECONOMIC JOURNAL, June 1953, pp. 263–88) for the period 1870–1900, though they indicate a rising ratio for the period 1900–14, and a falling ratio for 1924–38. In the United States the capital/output ratio has shown a slightly rising trend from the decade 1879–88 to the decade 1909–18, and a falling trend since, and (ignoring the depression period) is not significantly different now (at around 3·0) than it was sixty years ago. (Cf. Fellner, *Monetary Policies and Full Employment*, Table 3, p. 80, based on Kuznets' estimates.)

[3] The usual explanation for this apparent paradox is, of course, that the productivity of labour increased at the same rate in the capital-goods-making industries (taken as a group) as in the economy as a whole (*i.e.*, in all industries taken together) as a result of the peculiar character of technical progress (the "neutrality" of inventions). As will be shown below however no such assumption is necessary for explaining the constancy of the capital/output ratio.

[4] According to Phelps Brown and Weber (*loc. cit.*) the rate of profit on capital in the United Kingdom (including buildings) remained remarkably steady at around $10\frac{1}{2}\%$ in the period 1870–1914, the annual variations being within the range of $9\frac{1}{4}$–$11\frac{1}{2}\%$. The same steadiness is shown in the United States in the relationship of property income to total capital (cf. Kuznets, *loc. cit.*)

[5] Hicks, *Theory of Wages* (1932) Ch. VI, *passim*.

stancy of the degree of monopoly or the " neutrality " of technical progress.[1] One of the merits of the present model is that it shows that the constancy in the capital/output ratio, in the share of profit and in the rate of profit can be shown to be the consequence of endogeneous forces operating in the system, and not just the result of some coincidence—as, *e.g.*, that " capital saving " and " labour saving " inventions happened (historically) to have precisely offset one another, or that the growth in monopoly happened (historically) to have been counterbalanced by the fall in raw-material prices in terms of finished goods.[2]

Basic Properties of the Model

The present model is based on Keynesian techniques of analysis and follows the well-known " dynamic " approach originally developed by Mr. Harrod[3] in regarding the rates of change of income and of capital as the dependent variables of the system. The properties of our model differ, however, in important respects from those of Mr. Harrod and other writers, and these differences can be traced to the following:

(1) It is assumed here that in a growing economy the general level of output at any one time is limited by available resources, and not by effective demand. The model in other words assumes " full employment " in the strictly Keynesian sense—a state of affairs in which the short-period supply of goods and services in the aggregate is inelastic and irresponsive to further increases in monetary demand. This need not necessarily imply the full employment of labour except in a developed economy where the available capital equipment is sufficient or more than sufficient to employ the whole of the available working force. But it does imply that, excepting for periods in which the process of growth through capital accumulation (for reasons outlined later) is altogether interrupted, the system cannot long operate in a state of (Keynesian) under-employment equilibrium, because at any level of output short of " full employment " the aggregate demand associated with that particular level of output will exceed the aggregate supply price of that output, and thus lead to an expansion in output until a state of full employment is reached. In a state of full employment, on the other hand, aggregate demand and aggregate supply (in real terms) are brought into equality through the movement of prices in relation to prime costs, *i.e.*, the relation of prices to wages. (It is assumed that any rise in prices in relation to wages increases savings relative to investment and thus reduces aggregate

---

[1] Kalecki, *Essays in the Theory of Economic Fluctuations*, Chapter I; Harrod, *Towards a Dynamic Economics*, p. 23; Joan Robinson, *The Rate of Interest and Other Essays*, pp. 90–97, and *The Accumulation Capital*, pp. 73–100.

[2] Kalecki, *op. cit.*, pp. 32–34.

[3] " An Essay in Dynamic Theory," Economic Journal, March 1939, subsequently elaborated in *Towards a Dynamic Economics* (Macmillan, 1949). Substantially the same analysis was put forward in the well known article by Domar (*Econometrica*, 1946).

demand in real terms, and vice versa).[1] The assumption that there can be no under-employment equilibrium in periods in which the rate of growth of capital and income is normal is not arbitrary; it is based on the view that an equilibrium of steady growth is inconsistent with under-employment equilibrium. For in the latter situation the relationship of prices and wages is determined by extraneous factors (such as the " degree of monopoly," full-cost pricing, Marshall's " traditional margin of profit on turnover " or what not) and, as will be shown below, these either yield an insufficient ratio of savings to income (in which case, in a growing economy, the system is not stable *below* full employment) or else an excessive ratio of savings to income (in which case, for reasons described by Mr. Harrod,[2] the process of growth cannot continue, and the system will relapse into stagnation). A state of Keynesian under-employment equilibrium, whilst it is perfectly consistent with a static short-period equilibrium, is therefore inconsistent (except by a fluke) with a dynamic equilibrium of steady growth.[3]

The Keynesian techniques of analysis were originally designed, of course, to explain how an economy can remain indefinitely in a state of under-employment equilibrium; it may seem at first sight paradoxical therefore to label a model " Keynesian " if it is based on the full-employment assumption. However, as I argued in an earlier paper [4] the specifically Keynesian apparatus of thought can be applied to full-employment situations and not only to under-employment situations, and there is some evidence that in an earlier stage in the development of his ideas (in *A Treatise on Money*) Keynes applied the multiplier principle—the idea that is, that expenditure decisions determine income and savings rather than the other way round—for the purpose of a price theory rather than an employment theory, even though in the *General Theory* he explicitly disclaimed that his ideas had any relevance to full-employment conditions.[5] Yet the specifically Keynesian hypothesis that

---

[1] Any sharp and clear-cut distinction between an under-employment equilibrium, where production is limited by effective demand, and a full-employment-equilibrium, where it is limited by available resources, presumes, of course, something like a reverse L-shaped supply function for output as a whole, so that marginal costs are either infinite (or indefinite) or else equal to average prime costs, and thus in neither case exert an important influence on the ruling relationship between prices and wages. In reality there is a twilight zone of semi-full employment in which the supply of goods and services in the aggregate is neither elastic nor inelastic, and in which an increase in money demand will increase both prices and production in roughly equal measure. For the purposes of the present model it will be assumed that this " twilight zone " is sufficiently narrow in range to be left out of consideration altogether. (Its introduction would complicate the exposition without radically altering the basic features of the model.)

[2] "An Essay on Dynamic Theory," *loc. cit.*, pp. 23–26; *Towards a Dynamic Economics*, pp. 77 ff.

[3] I believe it was Mr. Harrod's failure to see the inconsistency between a continuous under-employment equilibrium and a state of steady growth which led him to the belief that a dynamic equilibrium of growth is necessarily unstable. His proposition applies only if the savings coefficient is extraneously determined, and this in turn presumes a state of affairs where short-period output is elastic. It does not apply to full employment or even to the " twilight zone " of semi-full employment.

[4] " Alternative Theories of Distribution," *loc. cit.*, p. 94.

[5] *General Theory*, pp. 3, 26 and 112.

equilibrium between savings and investment is secured through a movement of prices and/or incomes, rather than through changes in the rate of interest, is just as fruitful in the context of a dynamic growth model based on the postulate of full employment as in a (short-period) static model based on the postulate of under-employment; nor does the postulate of full employment appear as unrealistic at the present day (at any rate in the context of a dynamic theory of growth) as it appeared in the 1930s. Although the great depression of the 1930s was both more severe and more prolonged in duration than its predecessors, the gloomy forebodings made at the time that it heralded the approach of an era of long-term economic stagnation have certainly proved premature: since 1945 the momentum of growth in the capitalist economies has been at least as strong as in any comparable period since 1870. It does not therefore seem unrealistic to assume that capitalist economies operate under full-employment conditions in all such periods (and these appear to take up the majority in terms of chronological time) when capital is accumulating and the national income is growing. Similarly, in the case of under-developed economies, whilst there may be vast numbers of unemployed or under-employed the situation is not one of Keynesian under-employment as the supply of goods is in general inelastic in the short period and irresponsive to increases in monetary demand. Here again it certainly appears more correct to assume that output at any one time is limited by the scarcity of resources rather than by effective demand.

(2) The second main respect in which the present model departs from its predecessors is that it eschews any distinction between changes in techniques (and in productivity) which are induced by changes in the supply of capital relative to labour and those induced by technical invention or innovation—*i.e.*, the introduction of new knowledge. The use of more capital per worker (whether measured in terms of the value of capital at constant prices, in terms of tons of weight of the equipment, mechanical power, etc.) inevitably entails the introduction of superior techniques which require " inventiveness " of some kind, though these need not necessarily represent the application of basically new principles or ideas. On the other hand, most, though not all, technical innovations which are capable of raising the productivity of labour require the use of more capital per man—more elaborate equipment and/or more mechanical power. Hence the speed with which a society can " absorb " capital (*i.e.*, it can increase its stock of man-made equipment, relatively to labour) depends on its technical dynamism, its ability to invent and introduce new techniques of production. A society where technical change and adaptation proceed slowly, where producers are reluctant to abandon traditional methods and to adopt new techniques is necessarily one where the rate of capital accumulation is small. The converse of this proposition is also true: the rate at which a society can absorb and exploit new techniques is limited by its ability to accumulate capital.

It follows that any sharp or clear-cut distinction between the movement *along* a " production function " with a given state of knowledge, and a *shift* in the " production function " caused by a change in the state of knowledge is arbitrary and artificial.[1] Hence instead of assuming that some given rate of increase in productivity is attributable to technical progress which is superimposed, so to speak, on the growth of productivity attributable to capital accumulation, we shall postulate a single relationship between the growth of capital and the growth of productivity which incorporates the influence of both factors. The plausible shape of this " technical progress function " is that given by the curve TT' in Fig. 1. Let C_t and O_t represent the capital per worker and the annual output per worker at time t, so that $\frac{1}{C_t}\frac{dC}{dt}$ (measured horizontally) represents the annual percentage growth in capital per worker, and $\frac{1}{O_t}\frac{dO}{dt}$ (measured vertically) the annual percentage growth in output per man. The shape and the position of the curve reflect both the magnitude and the character of technical progress as well as the increasing organisational, etc., difficulties imposed by faster rates of technical change. It may be assumed that *some* increases in productivity would take place even if capital per man remained constant over time, since there are always some innovations—improvements in factory lay-out and organisation, for example—which enable production to be increased without additional investment. But beyond these the growth in productivity will depend on the rate of growth in the capital stock—clearly the more capital is increased, the more labour-saving technical improvements can be adopted, though there is likely to be some maximum beyond which the rate of growth in productivity could not be raised, however fast capital is being accumulated. Hence the TT' curve is likely to be convex upwards and flatten out altogether beyond a certain point. The postulate of the existence of a given curve presumes, of course, a constant flow in the rate of new ideas over time. Variations in the flow of new ideas, and in the readiness with which they are adopted, are likely to be reflected in shifting the height of the curve rather than in altering its general character.[2] In an unprogressive economy, with a low capacity to absorb technical change the height of the TT' curve will be relatively low (as in the dotted line in Fig. 1), whilst important new discoveries (such as the invention of the internal combustion engine or atomic energy) are likely to raise the position of the curve considerably for some time.

P represents the particular point on the TT' curve where it is crossed by

---

[1] The technical possibilities shown by the " production function " of any one period are in fact nothing more than the reflection of the yet unexploited inventions and innovations of the past.

[2] Our TT' curve thus reflects not only " inventiveness " in the strict sense, but the degree of technical dynamism of the economy in a broader sense—which includes not only the capacity to think of new ideas, but the readiness of those in charge of production to adopt new methods of production.

a line drawn from the origin at an angle of 45 degrees—where, in other words, the percentage rate of growth of capital and the percentage rate of growth of output are equal. When the rate of capital accumulation is less than this rate the percentage rate of growth in output will exceed the growth in capital (involving a fall in the capital/output ratio), and vice versa.

The recognition of the existence of a functional relationship between the proportionate growth in capital and the annual proportionate growth in productivity shows the futility of regarding the movements in the capital/

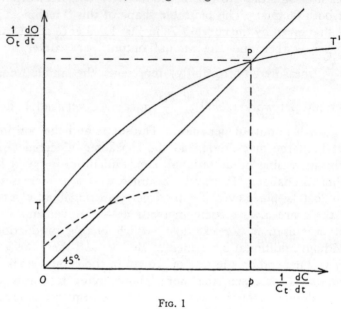

Fig. 1

output ratio as dependent upon the technical character of the stream of inventions—according as they are predominantly " labour-saving " or " capital-saving " in character.[1] For whether the capital/output ratio will be rising or falling will depend not on the technical nature of the inventions, but simply on the relationship between the flow of new ideas (characterised by the shape and position of our TT' curve) and the rate of capital accumulation. If capital accumulation is less than adequate to exploit the current stream of inventions to the point where the growth of capital and the growth in output are equal—if the actual position is to the left of P—the capital/output ratio will be falling, and the character of inventions will appear to be predominantly " capital-saving " in nature; if the position is to the right of P they will appear to be predominantly " labour-saving " in nature.[2] As will be shown below, with a given TT' curve, the system will always tend

[1] Cf. Harrod, *op. cit.*, p. 23; Joan Robinson, *op. cit.*, pp. 164 ff.

[2] New techniques capable of raising the productivity of labour in any given proportion will, of course, be all the more profitable the less additional capital they require for adoption. It is evident, therefore, that relatively labour-saving and capital-using innovations are the more likely to be adopted the higher the rate of capital accumulation.

towards the point where the growth of capital and the growth in productivity are equal—P is therefore the long-run equilibrium point and Op the long-run equilibrium rate of growth. (The basic reason for this is that if the rate of capital accumulation is less than Op, it will tend to be stepped up and the rate of profit on new investment will rise over time; in the converse case, the rate of growth of capital will tend to be slowed down, and the rate of profit will fall. It is only when capital and output grow at the same rate, and the capital/output ratio is constant, that the rate of profit remains constant over time; and then technical progress will appear to take on a "neutral" character.[1]) An upward shift in the TT' curve caused by a burst of new inventions will cause (for a time) a falling capital/output ratio; progress will thus appear to take on a predominantly "capital-saving" character. A drying up in the flow of ideas, represented by a downward shift in the TT' curve will, on the other hand, cause the growth of productivity to lag behind; the capital/output ratio will rise, and innovation will appear to be predominantly "labour-saving."

This is not to deny that *in particular industries* the capital/output ratio may change significantly in an upward or downward direction as a result of the character of new inventions occurring there. If an important capital-saving invention occurs in some industry—due, for example, to some revolutionary improvement in design which raises the productive capacity of capital equipment of a given value—the capital/output ratio in that industry is bound to fall. But precisely because this involves a gradual rise in the rate of profit, and thus in the rate of capital investment, it will induce compensating changes in the capital/output ratio of other industries, so that for the economy as a whole (and in the long run) the overall capital/output ratio will tend to remain constant.

(3) Our model, like other macro-economic models, is based on simple aggregative concepts of income, capital, profits, wages, investment and savings, expressed in real terms—*i.e.*, in terms of values of constant purchasing power. This raises all the familiar difficulties involved in the use of index numbers, as well as the more fundamental questions of the measurement of the quantity of capital. The measurement of the stock of capital in terms of money values corrected for price changes raises peculiar problems of its own on account of: (i) the fact that owing to technical progress, the capital goods produced in any one period are physically non-identical with the capital goods produced in previous periods, and therefore cannot simply be *added* to the latter, even if the proportions of the different capital goods serving different end-uses remained the same;[2] (ii) that the *value* of the stock

---

[1] cf. pp. 609–10 below.

[2] Much the same problem arises, of course, in the measurement of real income, since in a progressive economy new kinds of commodities are constantly being introduced. But whereas in the case of income, the changing character and composition of the constituents could be ignored in the first approximation (by assuming, *e.g.*, a single type of consumption good, such as "bread") in the case of capital goods it cannot, since it is the essence of a change of techniques that the character of the instruments, etc., used in production changes.

of capital existing at any moment is not the sum of the values of the capital goods produced in the past, but is that quantity *less* accrued depreciation.

Whatever may be the situation as regards the "stationary states" of neo-classical theory, there can be no question that in a developing economy with constantly changing knowledge and techniques neither the problem of equating the capital goods produced at different dates and at differing states of knowledge nor the measurement of depreciation admits of any clear-cut theoretical solution: the measurement of the stock of *real* capital must therefore necessarily be based on some (more or less arbitrary) convention. One such convention would measure the stock of real capital in terms of the amount of mechanical power which the outstanding stock of capital goods (or the addition to it in a particular year) represents. Another such convention (which appears rather less arbitrary) measures it in terms of the total weight of steel embodied in the capital equipment.[1] For the purposes of this model we shall adopt the latter convention. We shall also assume that the average price, per ton of steel, of finished capital goods produced in successive periods remains constant in terms of income units so that the rate of growth of capital is the same in "steel" as in terms of real income. (This assumption, while it greatly simplifies the exposition, is not an essential feature of the model.) With regard to depreciation, we shall assume: (*a*) that individual capital goods retain their physical efficiency until they are scrapped; (*b*) that the proportion of the outstanding capital stock which is scrapped in any one year (again measured in tons of steel) is a constant fraction of the total stock of capital. Hence we shall define depreciation as the value of that part of the output of capital goods produced in any one period which is needed to maintain the total weight of steel in the outstanding capital stock constant (and which, in a steadily growing economy, is also a constant fraction of total turnover). We shall define income, savings, investment *net* of depreciation in this special sense of the term "net." The difference between gross and net income and gross and net savings will be assumed to be identically equal to the difference between gross and net investment.[2]

(4) It is evident from the foregoing that the prime mover in the process of economic growth is the readiness to absorb technical change combined with the willingness to invest capital in business ventures. It is through the continued increase in the amount of machinery, etc., used in combination

---

[1] Another variant of this kind of measurement would be the total physical weight of all capital goods produced (of whatever material it consisted).

[2] It would also be possible, of course, to value capital at the original cost of installation of capital goods less accrued depreciation (the latter being spread over the physical life of the assets, either by the straight-line method, the reducing-balance method, etc.) and deflated by an index of capital-goods prices. But the point is that the application of a price index to the historical cost of the capital goods produced at different periods implicitly makes use of some kind of convention of the type introduced here explicitly. (Measuring capital in terms of value deflated by capital-goods-prices is not the same, of course, as valuing capital in real income units; but the complications due to the differences between the two will not be gone into here.)

with labour that the productivity of labour is continuously increased. In a capitalist economy the process of accumulation is the resultant of innumerable investment decisions made by entrepreneurs—using this term in a broad sense, so as to comprise the owners of risk capital generally, as well as the Boards of Directors of companies who take the actual decisions on their behalf. Any act of investment the outcome of which is necessarily uncertain at the time the decisions are taken, implies an act of faith—it involves a favourable judgment concerning the future course of markets, as well as the future relationship of prices and costs. Unless entrepreneurs are willing to revise their estimates of future sales and profits upwards in the light of current experience—unless they are imbued with sufficient optimism to react favourably to favourable events, and to increase the amount of capital invested in response to an increase in current sales and profits—it is difficult to envisage the growth of production and capital as a continuous process. For unless the capacity to produce is continually increased, the increase of production must necessarily come to a halt; a continued growth in output capacity presupposes in turn a belief (which must be grounded, and can only be grounded, in past experience) in the continued growth in markets. In order that there should be continued growth, it is necessary therefore to suppose both that, on the one hand, output increases as a result of capital investment and, on the other hand, investment takes place in response to an increase in output. Hence as a complement to our technical progress function which denotes the former we must postulate a function based on assumptions concerning entrepreneurial psychology to denote the latter. With regard to this second function, which we shall call the investment function, it will be assumed: (i) that given the (expected) rate of profit on capital, entrepreneurs desire to maintain a constant relationship between the amount of capital invested and their turnover; (ii) that this relationship between desired capital and turnover is an increasing function of the expected rate of profit on capital;[1] (iii) that the investment decisions of each " period " are governed by the condition that actual capital is to be brought into line with desired capital, the length of the " period " being so defined as to make it technically feasible to eliminate in one period the backlog of investment (the difference between desired and actual capital) existing at the beginning of the period;[2] (iv) that entrepreneurs expect the same growth in turnover

---

[1] The assumption that for each enterprise there is some *desired* amount of invested capital in relation to turnover which is itself a rising function of the rate of profit can be justified by the greater risk and uncertainty of expectations for the more distant future as against the nearer future and the consequent preference (at equal rates of expected return) for investments with a more rapid turnover of capital as against investments which entail a longer period of inevitable commitment. A high capital/output ratio implies a longer period of commitment because it implies a higher ratio of fixed capital to circulating capital (irrespective of any differences in the durability of fixed capital).

[2] As we shall see later (cf. pp. 619–20 below) this assumption is applicable only to an " advanced " capitalist economy in which, at the ruling rate of profit, the capital stock in the various industries has already been brought into the desired relationship with turnover, so that net investment takes place only in response to a rise in the (expected) turnover or a rise in the rate of profit.

in the coming period as was actually attained in the previous period; (v) that they expect to obtain the same margin of profit on turnover in the coming period as actually obtained in the previous period.

These assumptions imply an investment function which makes investment of any period partly a function of the change in output in the previous period [1] and partly of the change in the rate of profit on capital in that period. They are not, of course, the only possible assumptions that one could choose in this regard. It would be possible to assume, for example, that investment, at any given rate of profit, is a constant percentage addition to the existing stock of capital, rather than a coefficient related to the increase in turnover.[2] But in a model which makes the amount of profits actually generated in the production process dependent on the rate of investment and makes the rate of investment in turn dependent on the growth of profits, it is necessary to postulate a certain minimum " buoyancy " in entrepreneurial behaviour in order to ensure that the investment necessary to generate the profits which call forth a further increase in investment in the next period actually *does* take place, so that productivity, total output, profits and investment continue to grow. Without assuming a certain minimum of " buoyancy," the mere accrual of fresh investment opportunities through technical progress will not alone ensure the continued growth in production [3]—since the latter requires in addition that effective demand and profits should

---

[1] In earlier articles on the trade cycle (cf. ECONOMIC JOURNAL, March 1940, p. 79, and ECONOMIC JOURNAL, December, 1951, p. 837) I strongly criticised the use of the acceleration principle in connection with trade-cycle models, because it assumes a constant relationship between output and capital (or rather between output and output capacity), whereas the recognition of a changing relationship between these two seemed to me essential for an understanding of the cyclical mechanism. I recognised, however, the validity of the principle " as between alternative positions of long period equilibria " (*ibid.*, p. 838). For the purpose of a long-run model of economic growth it is legitimate to divide time into " periods " long enough for the capital stock in any one period to be fully adjusted to the output expected for that period at the beginning of that period; which means that the " acceleration principle " is an appropriate principle to apply to characterise investment behaviour for such " periods."

[2] On the implication of this latter assumption cf. p. 610, note 1 below. The difference between these two kinds of assumptions relating to investment behaviour may be explained as follows. The postulate of an investment function where the rate of increase of the stock of capital (*i.e.*, the rate of investment as a proportion of the existing stock of capital) is treated as an increasing function of the rate of profit on capital implies the assumption that entrepreneurial risk is an increasing function of the rate of capital accumulation, irrespective of the relation between the growth of the capital stock and the growth of turnover. It thus corresponds to Keynes' declining marginal-efficiency-of-capital function, as re-interpreted by Kalecki's principle of increasing marginal risk. The postulate of an investment function where the desired stock of capital in relation to turnover is treated as an increasing function of the rate of profit on capital implies, on the other hand, that the principle of increasing risk is not applicable to the rate of capital accumulation as such, but only to a situation where the (proportionate) rate of capital accumulation exceeds the rate of growth of turnover. This seems a more reasonable supposition for so long as the growth of capital merely keeps pace with the growth of turnover there seems to be little empirical justification for the belief that a faster rate of growth of capital entails a higher subjective marginal risk to the entrepreneur. This latter assumption, moreover, as will be shown below, is consistent with a stable equilibrium of steady growth whereas the former is not.

[3] Cf. ECONOMIC JOURNAL, December 1951 p. 842.

increase sufficiently to match the growth in potential supply, and thus keep the process of accumulation going.

(5) We shall assume that monetary policy plays a purely passive role—which means that interest rates, subject to differences due to borrowers' risks, etc., follow, in the long run, the standard set by the rate of profit obtainable on investments. The operation of our model is consistent with continued price-inflation (with money wages rising faster than productivity) or with a constant price level (money wages rising *pari passu* with productivity). It is in principle also consistent with constant money wages (money prices falling with the rise in productivity), though the latter situation might give rise to additional complications as regards investment behaviour which will not be gone into here. We shall deal with the case of isolated communities only—*i.e.*, we shall ignore the problems arising in connection with trade between regions in differing stages of development.

(6) We shall ignore also the influence of a change in the share of profits and wages and of a change in rate of profit on capital (or of interest rates) on the choice of techniques adopted which has been the focal point of attention of neo-classical theory.[1] At any one time the individual entrepreneur has, of course, a variety of " techniques " to choose from, and he may be assumed to choose the particular technique which secures the lowest cost, or the highest rate of return, on his investment. It seems reasonable to assume, however, that the choice of technique is far more dependent on the prevailing prices of different types of capital goods and on the price of labour in terms of commodities generally (in so far as this reflects the productivity of labour) than on the prevailing rate of profit or the prevailing interest rates. If an entrepreneur in an advanced economy employs bulldozers for making roads, whilst his opposite number in an under-developed country employs only shovels, this is not, to any significant degree, the consequence of differences in the prevailing rates of profit (or of the rates of interest on loans) in the two communities, but simply of the fact that the price of bulldozers in terms of shovels is much lower in the advanced community than in the primitive community. As an economy progresses as the combined result of capital accumulation and technical progress the prices of " superior " capital goods (capable of securing a higher output per unit of work) may be assumed to fall continuously relative to inferior capital goods: the character

[1] The importance attributed in neo-classical theory to the choice between more or less labour-saving and capital-using techniques being dependent on the rate of profit (or the rate of interest) is, of course, inherently connected with the acceptance of the marginal productivity theory as the basic principle in the explanation of the pricing process and the determination of distributive shares: for it is the choice among a range of techniques requiring more or less capital (and less or more labour) per unit of output which alone makes it possible (theoretically) to assign specific marginal productivities to the factors of production, Capital and Labour, in the long run. Our model, however, shows that for the system as a whole the share of wages and of profits, and the rate of profit on capital is determined quite independently of the principle of marginal productivity; the choice of alternative methods of production differing in " capital intensity " at any *given* state of knowledge loses therefore its central importance in the theoretical scheme.

of the most economical type of equipment will continually alter. This alone is sufficient to explain why it becomes profitable to employ bulldozers once a certain level of capital accumulation has been attained which has not been profitable at a lower stage of accumulation.[1] If, in addition, the use of the bulldozer-technique involves a higher investment per unit of output (a higher capital/output ratio) than the shovel-technique (which is by no means necessarily the case!) it will also be true that the rise in wages in terms of commodities, associated with the growth in the productivity of labour, will contribute to making the bulldozer-technique profitable at a certain stage of development.[2] In the latter case it may further be true that the use of bulldozers will be stimulated not only by the rise in wages due to the growth of productivity, but also by a rise in the *share* of wages at any given level of productivity due to a fall in profits. Thus as between two growing communities with equal technical progress functions, but in one of which the rate of profit is lower than in the other (due to a higher propensity to save out of profits and/or wages) the introduction of bulldozers may occur at a somewhat earlier stage of development (at a lower level of productivity and capital accumulation) than in the high-profit community, which in turn may have repercussions on the speed of development—at any rate during an intermediate stage, until an equilibrium of steady growth is attained. But we shall regard these as secondary complications which can safely be neglected in the first approximation; which means that we shall regard the choice of techniques as entirely a matter of the relative prices of different types of capital goods, which can be assumed to alter with the accumulation of capital and the progress of techniques in the capital-goods making industries.

[1] It may be thought that, given international trade, a particular under-developed country, in accordance with the law of comparative costs, would export shovels and import bulldozers and thereby gain the same terms of choice (as between different techniques) as the advanced country. But this pre-supposes a potential market for inferior capital goods in the advanced country (as well as a potential market for superior capital goods in the primitive country) which is non-existent.

[2] The fall in the price of bulldozers in terms of shovels will, of course, reduce the capital/output ratio involved in the bulldozer-technique relatively to the shovel-technique; and it may be supposed that at a certain stage of development the capital/output ratios in the two techniques will become identical. But whether this stage will have been reached or not at the time when the introduction of the bulldozer technique becomes profitable will depend (in part) on the rate of growth of productivity in the bulldozer-making industry relative to the rate of growth in the productivity of labour in the economy in general. The lower the former is relative to the latter, the more its introduction will have been prompted by the rise in wages (in terms of commodities in general) and the less by the fall in the price of bulldozers relative to shovels. If the introduction of the bulldozer technique has in the main been due to the rise in wages, and not to the fall in its price in relation to shovels, its introduction is in the nature of a " compensating " labour-saving innovation prompted by the introduction of capital-saving innovations in other parts of the economy. The fact that in the course of progress the prices of " superior " capital goods fall continually in relation to relatively inferior capital goods is not, of course, inconsistent with our assumption (stated on p. 599 above) that the price of newly produced capital goods per ton of steel embodied remain constant in terms of consumption goods.

The Working of the Model

We are now in a position to set out the essential features of the model. We shall examine its mode of operation in two stages—first, under the hypothesis of a constant working population and second by allowing for population growth. In the former case (constant full employment being assumed) the proportionate rate of growth in total real income, Y_t, will be the same as the proportionate rate of growth in output per head, O_t. In the latter case the proportionate change in total real income will be the sum of the proportionate change in productivity, O_t, and the proportionate change in the working population, L_t.

(a) *Constant Working Population*

We shall postulate: (i) given savings propensities for profit-earners and wage-earners, respectively;[1] (ii) that the investment decisions in any one period are governed by the desire to maintain the capital stock in a given relationship to turnover, modified by any change in the rate of profit on capital; (iii) a given technical relationship between the (proportionate) rate of growth in productivity per man and the (proportionate) rate of growth in capital per man. Writing Y_t, K_t, P_t, S_t, I_t for real income, capital, profits, savings and investment at the time t, we may assume the familiar income identities

$$S_t \equiv I_t \equiv K_{t+1} - K_t$$

To represent our three relationships mentioned above we shall, for expository purposes, adopt linear equations as follows:

(1) *Savings Function*

$$S_t = \alpha P_t + \beta(Y_t - P_t)$$

where $1 > \alpha > \beta \geqslant 0$

(2) *Investment Function*

(2.1) $K_t = \alpha' Y_{t-1} + \beta' \left(\dfrac{P_{t-1}}{K_{t-1}}\right) Y_{t-1}$

(2.2) $I_t = K_{t+1} - K_t = (Y_t - Y_{t-1})\left(\alpha' + \beta' \dfrac{P_{t-1}}{K_{t-1}}\right) + \beta' \left(\dfrac{P_t}{K_t} - \dfrac{P_{t-1}}{K_{t-1}}\right) Y_t$

where $\alpha' > 0$, $\beta' > 0$

(3) *Technical Progress Function*

$$\dfrac{Y_{t+1} - Y_t}{Y_t} = \alpha'' + \beta'' \dfrac{I_t}{K_t}$$

where $\alpha'' > 0$ and $1 > \beta'' > 0$

---

[1] Income is assumed to be divided into two categories, wages and profits, where the wage category comprises salaries as well as the earnings of manual labour; profits comprise not only entrepreneurial incomes but also incomes accruing to property generally.

Equation (1) shows the community's savings as consisting of a proportion α of aggregate profits (P_t) and a proportion β of wages $(Y_t - P_t)$. Equation (2.1) shows that the stock of capital at time t (and which is assumed to be equal to the *desired* stock of capital at time $t-1$) is a coefficient α' of the output of the previous period (Y_{t-1}) and a coefficient β' of the rate of profit on capital of the previous period, multiplied by the output of the previous period. Equation (2.2), derived from (2.1) by difference equation, shows that investment in period t, (I_t), assumed to correspond to the difference between desired and actual capital at t, is equal to the increment in output over the previous period $(Y_t - Y_{t-1})$ multiplied by the relationship between desired capital and output in the previous period $\left(\dfrac{K_t}{Y_{t-1}}\right)$[1] plus a coefficient β' of the change in the rate of profit over that period, multiplied by the output of the current period. Equation (2.2) thus implies that, expressed as a proportion of the existing stock of capital, K_t, the investment of period t is equal to the expected rate of growth of turnover (which in turn is assumed to be equal to the actual rate of growth in turnover for the previous period) if the rate of profit on capital is constant; and it is greater (or smaller) than this if the rate of profit on capital is rising (or falling). Equation (3) shows the rate of growth of labour productivity (and income) as an increasing function of the rate of net investment expressed as a proportion of the stock of capital—i.e., of the (proportionate) rate of growth of the capital stock.

Starting from an arbitrary point of time, $t = 1$, we can regard the existing capital stock, K_1 as a datum, a heritage of the past. We can also take as given the income Y_1 which the fully employed labour force produces with the aid of the capital equipment K_1 and the income and capital in the previous period Y_0 and K_0.[2] Assuming that the capital stock K_1 satisfies the condition

$$(2.1.2) \qquad \frac{K_1}{Y_0} = \alpha' + \beta' \frac{P_0}{K_0}$$

and treating, for the moment, K_1 as well as K_0 and Y_0 as a datum, equation (2.2) can be written in the form

$$(2.3) \qquad \frac{I_1}{Y_1} = \frac{Y_1 - Y_0}{Y_0} \cdot \frac{K_1}{Y_1} + \beta' \left(\frac{P_1}{K_1} - \frac{P_0}{K_0}\right)$$

(bearing in mind that $\dfrac{Y_1 - Y_0}{Y_1} \cdot \dfrac{K_1}{Y_0} = \dfrac{Y_1 - Y_0}{Y_0} \cdot \dfrac{K_1}{Y_1}$), which means that the rate of investment in period 1, as a proportion of the income of that

---

[1] Since it is implicit in equation (2.1) that

$$\alpha' + \beta' \frac{P_{t-1}}{K_{t-1}} = \frac{K_t}{Y_{t-1}}$$

[2] Only three of these magnitudes are independent, since they must satisfy the technical equation (3) above with $t = 0$.

period, equals the rate of growth of income over the previous period multiplied by the capital/output ratio of the current period, plus a term depending on the change of the rate of profit over the previous period. Equation (2.3) can in turn be written in the form

(2.4) $$\frac{I_1}{Y_1} = \left\{\frac{Y_1 - Y_0}{Y_0}\frac{K_1}{Y_1} - \beta'\frac{P_0}{K_0}\right\} + \beta'\frac{Y_1}{K_1}\cdot\frac{P_1}{Y_1}$$

while equation (1) can be written in the form

(1.2) $$\frac{S_1}{Y_1} = \alpha\frac{P_1}{Y_1} + \beta\frac{Y_1 - P_1}{Y_1} = \beta + (\alpha - \beta)\frac{P_1}{Y_1}$$

These two equations, (1.2) and (2.4) then determine both the distribution of income (between profits and wages) and the proportion of income saved

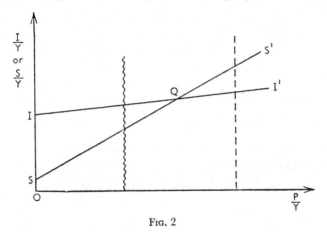

Fig. 2

and invested at $t = 1$. For the level of profits has to be such as to induce a rate of investment that is just equal to the rate of savings forthcoming at that particular distribution of income. This mechanism is illustrated in Fig. 2, where profits as a ratio of income $\left(\frac{P}{Y}\right)$ are measured horizontally and savings and investment as a ratio of income $\left(\frac{S}{Y} \text{ and } \frac{I}{Y}\right)$ vertically. The line SS' represents our equation (1.2) and II' our equation (2.4).[1] The point of intersection Q indicates the short-period equilibrium level of profits and of investment as a proportion of income. If profits are a lower proportion of income the investment plans (although lower than the equilibrium level) will tend to exceed the available savings; prices will rise in relation to costs, until the discrepancy is eliminated through the consequential rise in profits. The equilibrium will be stable if the slope of the SS'

[1] The starting point of SS' on the vertical axis represents β and its slope $\alpha-\beta$. The starting point of II' on the vertical axis depends on the proportional change in income in the previous period and on the rate of profit on capital in the previous period while the slope of II' is $\beta'\frac{Y_1}{K_1}$.

curve exceeds the slope of the II' curve, which implies, that the coefficients of the first two equations satisfy the condition

$$\alpha - \beta > \beta' \frac{Y_t}{K_t}$$

We shall assume that this is so.[1]

The working of the model is subject to two further restrictions, which were explained in an earlier article,[2] and which can be expressed as follows:

(4) $\quad P_t \leqslant Y_t - W_{\min}$

(5) $\quad \dfrac{P_t}{Y_t} \geqslant m$

The first of these restrictions (4) means that the profits determined by equations (1) and (2.2) should not be greater than the surplus available after the labour force has been paid a subsistence wage-bill. If this condition were not satisfied investment would be less than that indicated by equation (2.2) and would be determined by the savings available according to equation (1), when profits are equal to the surplus over subsistence wages. (In Fig. 2 the vertical dotted line represents the maximum permissible level of $\dfrac{P}{Y}$, and this is obtained by deducting the subsistence wage-bill from the full-employment income, determined by this condition. If the dotted line were to fall to the left of Q, as in Fig. 3, the short-period equilibrium would be represented not by Q, but by R. It will be evident that the position of the dotted line in relation to Q depends on the productivity of labour, which in turn depends in our model on the capital stock. In a progressive economy with a growing capital and output per head the dotted line will move steadily to the right, so that *sooner or later* it will pass Q and equation (2) will become operative as in Fig. 2.[3])

The second of these restrictions (equation (5)) means that the profits resulting from equations (1) and (2.2) are higher than the minimum required to secure a margin of profit over turnover below which entrepreneurs would not reduce prices, irrespective of the state of demand. (This minimum

---

[1] The assumption of stability in the savings–investment equilibrium under full employment has quite different implications from the corresponding assumption in a situation of under-employment equilibrium where the short-period output is regarded as variable. In the latter case the stability conditions depend on the effect of the change of income on the proportion of investment to income whereas in the former case only on the corresponding effect of a change in the *distribution* of income. In terms of our equation, a necessary (though not a sufficient) condition for short-period stability in an under-employment equilibrium—irrespective of whether equation (1) holds or not, and provided only that the marginal propensity to consume is higher than zero—is that $K_t < Y_t$ (*i.e.*, the accelerator coefficient in the first term of our second equation is less than unity). In a full-employment model the stability of our equilibrium is not dependent at all on the accelerator coefficient, but only on the change of that coefficient induced by a change in the rate of profit associated with a change in the distribution of income.

[2] Cf. " Alternative Theories of Distribution," *op. cit.*, pp. 97–8.
Cf. also pp. 618–21 below.

margin of profit is that corresponding to the " degree of monopoly," or the traditional profit margin required to cover full costs, etc.) If this condition were not satisfied, full-employment savings indicated by equation (1) would exceed investment (since prices and profits would not fall sufficiently to secure the equality of savings and investment), so that income and employment would be reduced *below* the full-employment level to the point where

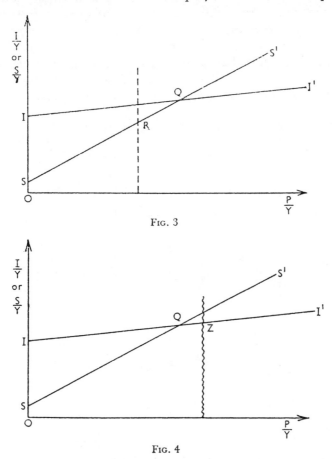

Fig. 3

Fig. 4

the savings generated by that income are no more than sufficient to finance investment. (In Fig. 2 the waved line represents this minimum level of profits. If this minimum were to fall to the right of Q equilibrium would not be at Q, but at Z, as shown in Fig. 4, while income will fall below Y_0 to the point where the savings–income ratio is reduced to the level indicated by Z.)

Our model thus supposes: (i) that the wages $(Y_0 - P_0)$ resulting from equations (1) and (2.2) are higher than the minimum, set by the supply-price of labour; (ii) that the profits resulting from these same equations are higher than the minimum required to satisfy entrepreneurs. The absence of the first condition leads to the Marxian type of model, where profits are determined by the surplus over subsistence wages, and investment is governed by the size of that surplus; the absence of the second condition leads to a Keynesian model of under-employment equilibrium, which, as was indicated above,[1] is inconsistent with the long-run equilibrium of a growing economy. Our model thus relates to a capitalist economy which is sufficiently highly developed for wages to be above subsistence level and sufficiently competitive at the same time to generate adequate demand to secure full employment.

Assuming these conditions are satisfied, our technical progress function (equation (3) above) indicates the growth of income and capital from $t = 1$ onwards, and the gradual movement of the economy from a short-period equilibrium to a long-period equilibrium of steady growth. This is illustrated in Fig. 5, where the proportionate growth of capital is measured

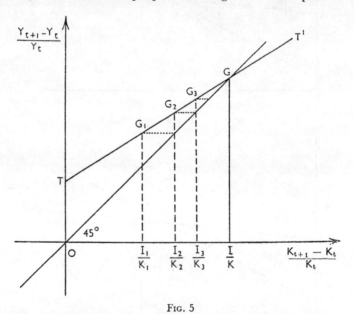

Fig. 5

horizontally and the proportionate growth of income vertically.[2] Suppose that the initial rate of investment, as determined by equations (1) and (2.3), at $t = 1$, $\frac{I_1}{K_1}$ is to the left of $\frac{I}{K}$. This implies that the growth of output, g, in successive units of time will be greater than the growth of capital, $\frac{I_1}{K_1}$,[3] and, in accordance with our equation (2.3), and apart from any changes in the rate of profit on capital, the rate of investment will be stepped up in the

[1] Cf. p. 594 above.

[2] Fig. 5 is identical with Fig. 1 except that in accordance with equation (3), the technical progress function TT' is here represented by a straight line.

[3] We shall denote g_1, g_2, etc., the rates of growth in income corresponding to the points G_1, G_2, etc., in the diagram.

subsequent period so as to make $\frac{I_2}{K_2}$ equal to g_1, which in turn will raise the growth in income in the second period to g_2. By similar reasoning, the growth of output in the third period will rise to g_3 and so on, until G is reached, at which the rates of growth of income and capital are equal.

The indirect effects through changes in the rates of profit on capital will reinforce this process. For since $\frac{Y_t}{K_t}$ is increasing so long as G_t is to the left of G, $\frac{P_t}{K_t}$ will be increasing so long as $\frac{P_t}{Y_t}$ is not decreasing; while, in accordance with equation (1), $\frac{P_t}{Y_t}$ will be non-decreasing provided $\frac{I_t}{Y_t}$ is not decreasing. The change in $\frac{I_t}{Y_t}$ attributable to the first term of (the right-hand side of) equation (2.2) will be positive with any movement of G_t towards G, for the rise in g_t will more than offset the fall in the capital/output ratio, $\frac{K_t}{Y_t}$. It follows that any associated change in the rate of profit on capital $\frac{P_t}{K_t}$ will make the rate of increase in investment even greater. (This means that in Fig. 2 above the point of intersection Q must be moving towards the right, which implies also that the curve II' must be shifting upwards.[1])

[1] A more rigorous proof of the proposition that equation (2) represents a curve in the $\left(\frac{I_t}{Y_t}, \frac{P_t}{Y_t}\right)$ plane which moves upwards when the percentage growth in income exceeds the percentage growth in capital can be given as follows.

Since, according to equation (2.1) and (2.2)

$$K_{t+1} = \left\{\alpha' + \beta' \frac{P_t}{K_t}\right\} Y_t$$

Equation (2.2) can be written in the form

$$I_t = K_{t+1} - K_t = \alpha' Y_t - K_t + Y_t \left\{\beta' \frac{Y_t}{K_t}\right\} \frac{P}{Y}$$

hence

$$\frac{I_t}{Y_t} = \left\{\alpha' - \frac{K_t}{Y_t}\right\} + \left\{\beta' \frac{Y_t}{K_t}\right\} \frac{P_t}{Y_t}$$

This curve must evidently shift upwards with any increase in $\frac{Y_t}{K_t}$, for any fixed value of $\frac{P_t}{Y_t}$.

On the other hand, if instead of equation (2.2) we had chosen an investment function of the form

$$\frac{I_t}{K_t} = \alpha' + \beta' \frac{P_t}{K_t} \quad (\text{where } \alpha' > 0),$$

which makes the proportionate rate of growth of capital depend simply on the rate of profit on capital and without regard to the rate of change of income, the relationship of investment to income will be

$$\frac{I_t}{Y_t} = \alpha' \frac{K_t}{Y_t} + \beta' \frac{P_t}{Y_t}$$

In that case if $\frac{\Delta Y_t}{Y_t} > \frac{I_t}{K_t}$, so that $\frac{K_t}{Y_t}$ is falling, this curve $\frac{I_t}{Y_t}$ in the $\left(\frac{I_t}{Y_t}, \frac{P_t}{Y_t}\right)$ plane will be falling. An investment function of this form therefore, whilst it satisfies the conditions of stability of short-period equilibrium, makes the position of long-period equilibrium at G unstable, since the point G_t in Fig. 5 would be moving away from instead of towards G.

An exactly similar proof could be adduced to show that if G_t were to lie to the right of G, then it must be moving to the left towards G. Long-run equilibrium must therefore be at G, where the rates of growth of income and capital are equal.

It follows from our equations that the long-run equilibrium rate of growth of income and capital is independent of the value of the coefficients of equations (1) and (2.3) (the savings and investment functions), and depends only on the coefficients in equation (3), the technical progress function. It is given by

$$(6) \qquad G = \frac{\alpha''}{1 - \beta''}$$

which is the equilibrium rate of growth in productivity, *i.e.*, that particular rate of growth of productivity which makes the (percentage) rates of growth of capital and income equal, and which (under the hypothesis of a constant population) is itself equal to them both.

Putting

$$\frac{\alpha''}{1 - \beta''} = \gamma'',$$

the equilibrium ratio of investment to income, the equilibrium share of profits to income and the equilibrium rate of profit on capital can all be derived with the aid of equations (1) and (2.3) as follows:

$$(7.1) \qquad \frac{I}{Y} = \gamma'' \frac{K}{Y}$$

Since from equation (1.2)

$$\frac{S}{Y} = \alpha \frac{P}{Y} + \beta \left(1 - \frac{P}{Y}\right)$$

$$\therefore \quad (8.1) \qquad \frac{P}{Y} = \frac{\gamma'' \frac{K}{Y} - \beta}{\alpha - \beta}$$

$$(9.1) \qquad \frac{P}{K} = \frac{\gamma'' - \beta \frac{Y}{K}}{\alpha - \beta}$$

The family resemblance between our set of equations and the Harrod–Domar formula will be evident. Equation (7.1), together with equation (1.2), is a variant of Mr. Harrod's "warranted rate of growth," with the important differences: (i) that the assumption of given savings propensities (for profit-receivers and wage-earners) does not define a unique warranted rate, but is consistent with any number of warranted rates, depending on the distribution of income, which determines the average propensity to save for the community as a whole, the latter in turn being dependent on the ratio of investment to income; (ii) the rate of growth of the system is not determined by the savings function, but by equation (6), which is, in effect, a variant of Mr. Harrod's " natural rate " (under the hypothesis of a constant population) except that the rate of increase in productivity due to technical progress is not treated as a constant here, but as a variable, and our γ'' is that particular rate of increase of productivity which makes the latter equal to the rate of increase in capital per head. In fact, the implications of our model in terms of Mr. Harrod's terminology could be summed up by saying that the system tends towards an equilibrium rate of growth at which the " natural " and the " warranted " rates are equal, since any divergence between the two will set up forces tending to eliminate the difference; and these forces act partly through an adjustment of the " natural " rate, and partly through an adjustment of the " warranted " rate.

So far the expression $\frac{K}{Y}$, though an outcome of the equilibrating process, has not been eliminated from our formulæ. To do so, we must return to our desired capital function (2.1), which, owing to the substitution introduced in (2.1.2), has not so far been made use of. Dividing (2.1) with Y_t, we obtain

(2.1.3) $$\frac{K_t}{Y_t} = \alpha' \frac{Y_{t-1}}{Y_t} + \beta' \left(\frac{P_{t-1}}{K_{t-1}}\right) \frac{Y_{t-1}}{Y_t}$$

Bearing in mind that in long-period equilibrium

$$\frac{P_{t-1}}{K_{t-1}} = \frac{P_t}{K_t} = \frac{P}{K}, \text{ and } \frac{Y_{t-1}}{Y_t} = \frac{1}{1+\gamma''}$$

and putting

$$\frac{K_t}{Y_t} = \frac{K}{Y} = x$$

we obtain the expression

(2.1.4) $$x = \frac{1}{1+\gamma''}\left(\alpha' + \beta' \frac{P}{K}\right)$$

Further, since in long run equilibrium

$$\frac{S_t}{K_t} = \frac{S}{K} = \gamma''$$

equation (1.2), divided by K_t, can be written in the form

(1.3) $$\gamma'' = \frac{\beta}{x} + (\alpha - \beta)\frac{P}{K}$$

Hence $$\frac{P}{K} = \frac{1}{\alpha - \beta}\left\{\gamma'' - \frac{\beta}{x}\right\}$$

and $$x = \frac{1}{1+\gamma''}\left\{\alpha' + \frac{\beta'}{\alpha - \beta}\left(\gamma'' - \frac{\beta}{x}\right)\right\}$$

which can be re-written in the form

$$(\alpha - \beta)(1 + \gamma'')x^2 = \{(\alpha - \beta)\alpha' + \beta'\gamma''\}x - \beta\beta'$$

Hence

(10.1) $$Ax^2 - Bx + C = 0$$

where $A = (\alpha - \beta)(1 + \gamma'')$, $B = (\alpha - \beta)\alpha' + \beta'\gamma''$, and $C = \beta\beta'$

Thus the derivation of the capital/output ratio, $\frac{K}{Y}$, involves a quadratic equation which has two positive roots in $\frac{K}{Y}$, of which normally the greater of the two only would be relevant.[1]

The complication of quadratic solutions is avoided, however (and the formulæ greatly simplified), if we assumed that all savings come out of profits, so that $\beta = 0$. (Since β is in any case likely to be small, the difference introduced by this cannot quantitatively be very significant.) In that case the equilibrium value of the capital/output ratio, derived from (2.1.4) and (1.3), is given by the expression

(10.2) $$\frac{K}{Y} = \frac{\alpha\alpha' + \beta'\gamma''}{\alpha(1 + \gamma'')}$$

while the equilibrium values of the other variables reduce to the formulæ

(7.2) $$\frac{I}{Y} = \frac{\alpha\alpha'\gamma'' + \beta'(\gamma'')^2}{\alpha(1 + \gamma'')}$$

(8.2) $$\frac{P}{Y} = \frac{\alpha\alpha'\gamma'' + \beta'(\gamma'')^2}{(\alpha)^2(1 + \gamma'')}$$

(9.2) $$\frac{P}{K} = \frac{\gamma''}{\alpha}$$

It is interesting to note that the rate of profit on capital depends on the rate of growth, γ'' (and thus ultimately on the coefficients of the technical progress function, α'', and β'' which determine this rate), and on the savings coefficients of profits, α. On the other hand, the investment coefficient and the share of profits in income, just as the capital/output ratio, depend on the coefficients of the investment function, α' and β', as well as on α and α'' and β''.

The result shown by equation (9.2) that the rate of return on capital depends only on the rate of economic growth and the division of capitalists' income between consumption and saving, and is independent of everything else (such as the factors determining the share of profits in income and the capital/output ratio) may sound highly paradoxical at first. Yet a little reflection shows that it must evidently be correct. For if the income accruing to capital were all devoted to accumulation (when that income is

---

[1] Since on any reasonable values o the coefficients, the larger root will be greater than unity and the smaller root less than unity when Y is thought of as annual income, and $\frac{K}{Y}$ is likely to be appreciably larger than 1. (The same holds, of course, with appropriate adjustments in the values of the coefficients, when Y is thought of in terms of some different period.)

the sole source of savings) the rate of profit on capital would evidently be identical with the rate of growth of the capital stock; if capital and output grow at the same rate this rate must be identical with the rate of growth of the economy. If the owners of capital do not save all their income but consume part of it (but profits remain the only source of savings) the rate of profit must exceed the rate of accumulation by the ratio of capitalists' consumption to savings.[1]

(b) *Expanding Population*

According to the Malthusian theory, the rate of population increase is a function of the rate of increase of the " means of subsistence " (which we can assume to be equivalent to the rate of increase in total production.) This doctrine is clearly subject to certain limitations. For any given fertility rate (or gross reproduction rate) in a community the percentage rate of growth in population cannot exceed a certain maximum, however fast real income is rising; and it may be supposed that the rate of population growth will rise only moderately as a function of the rate of growth in income over some interval of the latter before that maximum is reached. The dependence of population growth on the growth of income is best represented therefore in the terms of a curve which is convex upwards, as in Fig. 6 (measuring the proportionate rate of growth of population vertically and that of income horizontally) and whose slope nearly equals unity when the rate of growth of income is relatively low, and which becomes virtually horizontal when the rate of growth of income exceeds a certain critical value.[2] In terms of a linear equation, this relationship can be approximated by two straight lines indicated by the dotted lines in Fig. 6, which can be algebraically expressed as follows. Writing l_t, g_t for the (percentage) rates of growth of population and income, and λ for the maximum rate of growth of population,

(11)
$$l_t = g_t \ (g_t \leqslant \lambda)$$
$$l_t = \lambda \ (g_t > \lambda).$$

---

[1] As (9.1) shows, when profits are not the sole source of savings, the rate of return on capital will also depend on wage-earners' savings, though in no simple fashion, since β (the proportion of wages saved) appears both in the numerator and the denominator of the expression. It follows, however, from (8.1) that $\gamma'' < \alpha \frac{Y}{K}$ when $\frac{P}{Y} < 1$, hence a rise in β must lower the rate of profit on capital (and the share of profits in income). This is the basis of the (seemingly paradoxical) assertion that whereas the capitalists (as a group) can raise their share in the national income by spending *more*, wage-earners as a group can increase their share only by spending *less*.

[2] The maximum rate of population growth is partly a matter of fertility rates (*i.e.*, the gross reproduction rate) and partly of medical knowledge which determines the rate of survival (in particular, the infant-mortality rates) at a given standard of living. The fall in fertility rates in the advanced countries during the last half-century or more lowered the position of their Malthusian population curves considerably. On the other hand, there is a good deal of evidence tending to suggest that the considerable acceleration in the rates of population growth of the under-developed areas which occurred in the last half-century or so was due, in the main, not to an acceleration in the rate of growth of income but to a rise in the survival rate (due to the medical improvements which reduced the incidence of epidemics, etc.) and was attended in some cases by an appreciable fall in the standard of living of the population.

Assuming to start with that the rate of population growth is λ (i.e., $g_t > \lambda$), $\frac{I_t}{K_t}$ in equation (3) is replaced by $\frac{I_t}{K_t} - \lambda$, and $\frac{Y_{t+1} - Y_t}{Y_t}$ by $\left(\frac{Y_{t+1} - Y_t}{Y} - \lambda\right)$. Hence the long-run equilibrium rate of growth of both capital and income becomes

(6.2) $$G = \gamma'' + \lambda$$

The long-run equilibrium values of other ratios are then obtained by substituting $(\gamma'' + \lambda)$ for γ'' in equations (7)–(10).

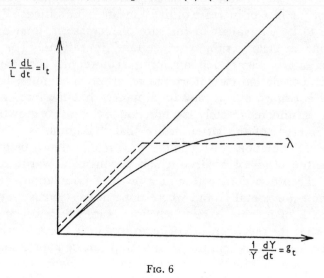

Fig. 6

If to start with, $g_t < \lambda$ (and hence $l_t < \lambda$) the rates of growth of income and population will continually accelerate until the latter approaches λ. In long-run equilibrium population must therefore grow at its maximum rate—i.e., at that indicated by the horizontal section of the curve in Fig. 6.

The above assumes that the shape and position of the technical progress function—i.e., the coefficients α'' and β'' in equation (3) above, and hence γ''—remain unaffected by population changes. This implies in economic terms that there are constant returns to scale to equi-proportionate increases in labour and capital; in other words, that an increase in numbers, given the amount of capital per head, leaves output per head unaffected. This assumption may be valid enough in the case of a young and relatively under-populated country [1]; in the case of over-populated countries, however, the

[1] In general, the density of population in any given area will in itself be conditioned by the availability of natural resources, which means that the density will normally be sufficiently great for the stage of diminishing returns to have been reached. When, however, a new population possessing radically different techniques invades a territory (as in the case of the white settlers in America and other areas in the New World) the point of optimum density, corresponding to the new techniques, may be so radically different that there may occur a manifold increase in population density without encountering diminishing returns.

scarcity of land will cause diminishing returns, which means that, with given techniques and capital per head, an increase in numbers will cause a fall in productivity.[1] Given the rate of the flow of new ideas, the curve denoting our technical progress function will be lowered by an extent depending on the rate of increase in population. It is then possible that instead of the curve intersecting the income-axis in the positive quadrant, as shown in Fig. 1 above, it will cut the capital-axis positively, as in Fig. 7 [2]—which means that it will require a certain percentage growth in capital per head (C_t) even to maintain output per head (O_t) at a constant level. It will be evident that the maintenance of an equilibrium of growth is much more precarious in this case; instead of a single point of intersection of the curve

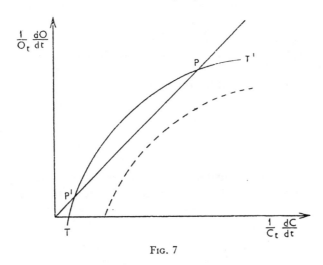

Fig. 7

with the diagonal line, we have two points of intersection, P' and P, of which only the latter is stable, while the former is unstable; if the economy happens to be in a position (or come to a position) which is to the left of P' the rate of growth of income and capital will steadily diminish until—after an intervening period of falling output per head—the growth of capital and income come to a complete standstill. It is even possible in this case that the position of

[1] It is assumed here that diminishing returns due to the scarcity of land are attendant upon an increase in the working population, rather than an increase in the volume of production as such. It is possible, of course, that the scarcity of natural resources would put increasing obstacles to the expansion of output, even when population is constant—in which case, given the rate of invention and innovation, the growth of productivity at any given rate of investment will be slowed down, and our TT' curve will gradually shift downwards over successive periods. Since, however, diminishing returns due to the scarcity of land are peculiarly associated with food supplies, while food requirements vary with the size of the population far more than with income per head, it is more appropriate to treat the problem of diminishing returns in the classical manner and associate it with the " widening " of capital due to an increase in numbers, rather than as restricting the scope of increasing productivity through " deepening."

[2] Since the assumption of a linear function is no longer adequate in this case for exhibiting the various possibilities inherent in the situation, we return to the non-linear mode of representation which was originally employed in Fig. 1.

the TT' curve should be below the diagonal throughout its length (as in the dotted line in Fig. 7), in which case no long-period equilibrium is attainable short of complete stagnation.

Whether an expanding population will be consistent with an equilibrium of growth or not will thus primarily depend on the relative magnitude of two factors: (i) the maximum rate of population increase λ, and (ii) the rate of technical progress, which causes a certain percentage increase in productivity, α'' in equation (3) above, when both population and capital per head are held constant. Since diminishing returns cannot cause the output of a larger working population to be smaller than that of a smaller population, the growth of population cannot lower the position of the TT' curve by more than the rate of population growth itself, so that *if*

$$\alpha'' > \lambda$$

the technical progress function must continue to cut the vertical (income) axis positively, and the possibility of a stable equilibrium of growth will be assured. The long-run equilibrium rate of growth will still be given by the formula

(6.2) $$G = \gamma'' + \lambda$$

bearing in mind, however, that the value of γ'' is not here independently given, but is itself influenced by λ.[1] But when the value of λ is relatively large, and the forces making for technical progress are weak, the formula (6.2) may no longer apply because of the inability of income to grow at a steady rate of λ or above. For example, if we suppose that, as a result of diminishing returns and rapid population growth (made possible by the high value of λ), α'' in equation (3) became negative—which implies that in Fig. 5 the point of intersection G with the diagonal had moved down into the negative quadrant, making γ'' negative—the growth of population would exceed the growth of production when the population grew at the rate λ. In this situation an equilibrium rate of growth is conceivable only when population and income grow at the same rate, and this can be attained only at that particular rate of population growth (lower than λ) which makes γ'' equal to zero. Thus, if we denote by $L(\gamma)$ the rate of population growth which causes γ'' to take the value γ, then in place of equation (6.2) we have

(12)
$$l_t \longrightarrow L(o)$$
$$g_t \longrightarrow l_t$$
$$\therefore \quad g_t \longrightarrow L(o)$$

---

[1] The available data for the more advanced capitalist economies over the last century suggest that the value of γ'' varied between 2 and 4% per annum, for the different countries, which is consistent with a value of β'' of, say, 0·5, and for α'' of 0·01–0·02 or 1–2%. According to Professor Kuznets' investigations (cf. "The Quantitative Aspects of the Economic Growth of Nations," *Economic Development and Cultural Change*, Vol. V, No. 1, October 1956, p. 42), the value of γ'' in the more advanced economies remained relatively unaffected by changes in the rate of population growth. In the under-developed areas, according to the evidence of the same source, the value of γ'' must have been very much lower.

In other words, for economies which are capable of only slow technical progress, and whose potential rate of population growth is relatively large, and which are subject to diminishing returns, the long-run equilibrium rate of growth and income (and capital) is determined by a different set of conditions. It has to be that rate of population growth which allows output per head and capital per head to remain constant over time. (Income and capital per head must be low enough to restrict the rate of population growth to that rate; and the higher the degree of medical knowledge which determines infant mortality, the lower this constant level of income per head will have to be.) This again is a stable position, since there is only one particular rate of population growth which enables the rate of growth of income to be equal to it; at any lesser rate productivity per head will rise, and the growth of income will exceed the growth of population (causing the latter to increase and income per head to cease rising); at any higher rate, productivity will fall and the growth of income will fall short of the growth in population (causing the latter to contract and income per head to cease falling). Long-run growth with a rising standard of living necessarily presupposes that there is some check to the rate of population growth which operates before it reaches the maximum attainable rate of growth of the national income.

The Two Stages of Capitalism

The historical emergence of capitalist enterprise involved a tremendous increase in the " technical dynamism " of the economic system. The most important characteristic of capitalist business enterprise is the continuous change and improvement in the methods of production, as against the relatively unchanging techniques of peasant cultivation and artisan production. In terms of our model, the growth of the capitalist sector in the economy involved a dramatic rise in technical progress function, and hence in the equilibrium rate of growth of productivity, γ''—the increase in savings, investments, both as a proportion of income and of capital, and the great acceleration in the rates of population growth, were consequences of this, and not its initiating causes.[1]

[1] In the same way the important differences in long-period growth rates between different capitalist economies—which manifested themselves, *e.g.*, in the fivefold increase in income per head in the United States in the last 100 years as against a near threefold increase in Britain over the same period—can only be ascribed to the various social factors which cause differences in the degree of " technical dynamism "—in the speed of adaptation to new techniques—rather than to differences in savings propensities, in national environment, etc. Again, the causes of the relatively low rates of progress in the under-developed areas of the world are mainly to be sought in the social and institutional factors which impeded the spread of " technical dynamism," particularly in the agricultural field, and thereby inhibited progress in those sectors of the economy also in which capitalist enterprise could establish itself and where the sociological obstacles to continued technical change were removed. Thus the absence of a progressive agriculture has been the most important factor inhibiting industrialisation in the under-developed areas. (This latter problem is treated in more detail in another paper by the author, " Characteristics of Economic Development," published in *Atti del Congresso Internazionale di Studio sul Problema delle Area Arretrate* (Milan: Giuffre 1955).)

In the early stage of capitalist development the growth in productivity was not attended by a rise in the standard of living of the working classes. The stationary trend in real wages in Britain despite considerable improvement in production per head during the first half of the nineteenth century was the feature of capitalist evolution which so strongly impressed Marx and forms one of the main themes of Volume I of *Das Kapital*. The same has been true of other capitalist countries: in the case of Japan, for instance, real wages increased very little between 1878 and 1917, despite a one-and-a-half-fold increase in real income per head over the period.[1]

This suggests that in the first stage of capitalist evolution, productivity, though rising, is not large enough to allow for a surplus over the subsistence wage which permits the rate of investment to attain the level indicated by equation (2.2); in other words the profits which would result from equations (1) and (2.2) are inconsistent with the restriction indicated by equation (4).

Since equation (2.2) will be replaced by

(4a) $$P_t = Y_t - W_{\min}.$$

this combined with (1) yields

$$S_t = (\alpha - \beta) P_t + \beta Y_t$$

so that

(13) $$S_t = I_t = \alpha Y_t - (\alpha - \beta) W_{\min}.$$

So long as (13) holds $\frac{I_t}{Y_t}$ will be steadily rising with the increase in the productivity of labour so that if, initially, $\frac{Y_t}{K_t}$ is rising (*i.e.*, the situation is to the left of G in Fig. 5) $\frac{I_t}{K_t}$ will be rising also. This movement will not be brought to a halt by approaching G, for while the (current) rate of growth of capital will approach the (current) rate of growth of income (as the rate of investment approaches that corresponding to G), there will be a backlog of investment from previous periods due to the growing divergence between actual capital and desired capital (since the rate of investment at each period was *ex hypothesi* insufficient to bring actual capital into line with desired capital). Hence the increase in the rate of capital accumulation will pass the point G, and the economy will settle down to a steady decrease of $\frac{Y_t}{K_t}$. In this first stage of capitalism therefore the capital/output ratio (at any rate after some initial period) will show a steady increase, in accordance with both the Marxian and the neo-classical models. Since, however, the share of profit in income will also increase continuously, the rise in the

---

[1] Cf. Mataji Umemura. "Real Wages of Industrial Workers" in the volume *An Analysis of the Japanese Economy*, edited by S. Tsuru and K. Ohkava (Tokyo, 1953). In the period 1918–42, on the other hand, the rise in real wages fully kept pace with the growth in output per head.

capital/output ratio will not necessarily imply a falling rate of profit on capital, and may be consistent with a rising rate.

This first stage of capitalism, however, must sooner or later be brought to an end when the capital stock attains the level of "desired capital," indicated by equation (2.1). From that point onwards the rate of investment will no longer be governed by equation (13), but by equation (2.2) and the reaction-mechanism of the system becomes a totally different one. Profits are no longer determined in the Marxian manner, as the surplus of production over subsistence wages; on the contrary, the share of wages becomes a residual, equalling the difference between production and the share of profits as determined in a "Keynesian" manner, by the propensities

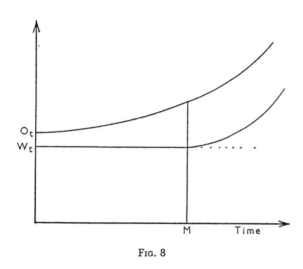

Fig. 8

to invest and to save. From then onwards, and assuming that the parameters in our equations (1)–(3) remain constant, real wages will rise automatically at the same rate as the productivity of labour, so that distributive shares remain constant through time; and since the system will tend to settle down to an equilibrium where the rate of growth of capital is equal to the rate of growth in income, the capital/output ratio, and the rate of profit in capital, will also tend to remain constant over time.

The process of changing-over from Stage I to Stage II is illustrated in Fig. 8 (measuring time horizontally, and productivity, O_t, and wages, W_t, vertically). The dividing line M is at the point of time when the stock of capital attains the "desired" level, indicated by equation (2.1) and the share of profits $(O_t - W_t)$ yields savings that are sufficient to finance a rate of investment corresponding to equation (2.2). Once this stage is reached, any further increase in the "surplus" will not be fully absorbed in increasing investment and/or capitalist consumption; a growing share of the increase in the " surplus " will accrue to labour automatically, through the constellation of prices in relation to wages.

This second and more cheerful stage of capitalism in which production and employment continue to grow, and real wages are steadily rising with the growth in production, was quite unforeseen by Marx. Marxist economists would probably argue that its emergence is prevented by the growth of " monopoly-capitalism," for not only the productivity of labour, but also the degree of concentration of production can be expected to rise steadily with the progress of capitalism. This causes a steady weakening of the forces of competition, as a result of which the share of profit would go on rising beyond the point where it covers investment needs and the consumption of capitalists. Hence, on this argument, by the time the restriction implied in equation (4) is lifted the restriction implied by equation (5) should become operative, and that means that the system will cease to be capable of generating sufficient purchasing power to keep the mechanism of growth in operation.

The plain answer to this is that so far, at any rate, this has not happened. Though the growing concentration of production in the hands of giant firms proceeded in much the same way as Marx predicted, this was not attended by a corresponding growth in the share of profits.[1] On the contrary, all statistical indications suggest that the share of profits in income in leading capitalist economies such as the United States have shown a falling rather than a rising trend over recent decades, and is appreciably below the level of the late nineteenth century; and despite the extraordinary severity and duration of the depression of the 1930s, the problem of " realising surplus value " appears no more chronic to-day than it was in Marx's day.

Trend and Fluctuations

Our model is intended to be a " long-run " model—*i.e.*, a model exhibiting long-run tendencies operating in the economy—and as such it deliberately rules out all kinds of complicating features of the real world which have to be taken into account before the methods of reasoning and the conclusions can be applied to actual situations. In this paper we can do no more than indicate briefly some of these limitations and the influence they are likely to exert, particularly during shorter periods.

(1) One of these is that the theory of distribution underlying this model —which makes the share of profits in income entirely dependent on the ratio of investment to output, and the propensity to save out of profits and wages

---

[1] Moreover—and this is more significant—empirical investigations concerning the ratio of profit to turnover in different industries do not lend any support to the hypothesis that the differences in profit margins are to be explained by differences in the degree of concentration of production. Typically monopolistic industries, where output is largely controlled by a few firms, have in many cases lower profit margins than industries where the degree of concentration is small.

—is only acceptable as a " long-run " theory, since changes in these factors exert only a limited influence in the short period. As was indicated in my earlier paper,[1] in the short period profit margins are likely to be inflexible, in both an upward and a downward direction, around their customary level —which means that they are largely historically determined. What is suggested here is that long-term investment requirements and saving propensities are the underlying factors which set the standard around which these customary levels are formed, and which are responsible for the gradual change of these levels in any particular economy, or for differences as between different economies. This means that in the short period: (i) when investment falls significantly *below* some " normal " level, profit margins will not fall sufficiently to set up a compensating increase in consumption; instead, total income and employment will be reduced, in accordance with the Keynesian multiplier theory; (ii) when investment demand rises significantly *above* some " normal " level profit margins will not rise sufficiently to allow a corresponding increase in real investment; instead, some kind of investment rationing will take place by the lengthening of order books, and/or a tight credit policy, etc., or simply by the rise in the prices of investment goods in relation to consumption goods.[2] The short-period rigidity of profit margins, due to entrepreneurial behaviour, will be reinforced also by another factor: the downward inflexibility of real wages around their customary or attained level. Though over a longer period the *share* of wages is flexible in both an upward and downward direction through *real* wages rising more or less than in proportion to the rise in productivity, in the short period an *absolute* cut in real wages is likely to entail a severe inflationary wage–price spiral; and hence an increase in investment which would entail such a cut is likely to be prevented, if by nothing else, by measures of monetary policy. The speed with which an increase in the proportion of current production devoted to investment can be brought about will therefore be limited by the rate of increase in productivity, as well as by other factors, such as the limited capacity of investment-goods industries.

(2) A second important qualification relates to the hypothesis of a constant flow of invention and innovation over time, which underlies our assumption of a technical-progress function with constant parameters. To the extent that technical progress consists of a great multitude of minor changes and improvements, one may rely on the operation of the law of large numbers

---

[1] Cf. " Alternative Theories of Distribution," *loc. cit.*, pp. 99–100.

[2] This is in any case part of the mechanism through which a rise in investment demand will cause in the long run a rise in the proportion of resources devoted to investment and a corresponding fall in the proportion devoted to consumption. In the short period, investment in real terms is limited by the capacity of the investment-goods industries; a rise in the demand for investment goods must therefore raise first their relative prices, and thereby the relative profitability of investment in these industries; this in turn will entail a gradual rise in the capacity of these industries, relatively to the capacity of the consumption-goods industries.

to ensure that the rate at which improvements are invented and introduced in the economy as a whole remains fairly steady. But in addition there are major innovations due to the discovery of basic new principles; these occur at irregular intervals, and their exploitation opens up vast new avenues of profitable investment. The effects of such major discoveries (such as the invention of electricity, the internal-combustion engine, etc.) are superimposed on the " normal " rate of progress due to minor improvements, and their effect is to raise the TT' curve above its " normal " level during the period of their initial exploitation (which may be spread over several decades). Hence we can expect periods of rising and falling technical progress: periods in which the growth of production and real income runs ahead of the growth of capital, to be followed by other periods when capital investment catches up and the stock of capital increases faster than income.

The effect of the short-period rigidities of profit margins referred to in the earlier paragraph is to slow down the rate at which capital investment is rising in response to an upward shift of the TT' curve; and also to slow down the rate at which actual investment is falling in response to a downward shift of the TT' curve. To a certain extent, therefore, these short-period rigidities act as a stabiliser on the economy; they make it capable of absorbing the shocks created by the unequal incidence of new discoveries without major upheavals—merely by varying the rates at which income and capital are growing.[1] However, these same short-period rigidities may cause " over-saving " (owing to the failure of income distribution to adjust itself promptly enough to the fall in investment) and thus bring about a major breakdown in the process of investment and economic growth, such as occurred during the great depressions of the 1880s or the 1930s. For when rising capital/output ratios and falling profit rates cause the rate of investment to shrink at some critical speed (or below some critical level) the fall in income generated in the investment-goods industries will react unfavourably on the level of demand in the consumption-goods industries, causing a cumulative process of contraction in incomes, investment and employment.

The mechanics of our model are thus consistent both with minor fluctuations in growth rates and with major breakdowns in the process of growth, involving heavy unemployment and temporary stagnation. If the latter occurs, net investment might even become negative, so that eventual revival will be facilitated by the gradual erosion of capital as well as by the rise in

---

[1] On the basis of our model, we should expect an acceleration of the rate of growth of income to be followed by an acceleration in the rate of growth of capital, so that relatively fast and relatively slow rates of growth of income and capital are correlated but the movements in the latter are more sluggish than those in the former. Hence periods of accelerating growth are likely to be periods in which the capital/output ratio is falling, and periods of decelerating growth are those in which the capital/output ratio is rising. Owing to the short-period rigidities, etc., mentioned, there may, moreover, be a rising backlog of investments during periods of accelerating growth which might cause the rate of investment to continue to accelerate for some time after the rate of growth in income had begun to slow down.

the TT' function due to the cumulative effect of unexploited new inventions. The system is liable to such major breakdowns in the wake of exploitation of major discoveries when the economy geared to a higher rate of progress needs to be " switched back " to a more moderate rate of growth; and they should be heralded by a period during which the growth in income lags behind the growth in capital, and the capital/output ratio is rising. But on the assumptions of the model presented here the occurrence of such major breakdowns is neither regular nor inevitable—the most that one can say is that the same forces that are capable of maintaining continued growth at full employment when the underlying factors making for technical change are reasonably stable are liable to break down in their operation when, as a result of instability of these factors, the situation demands a slowdown in the growth of income and capital.

Nicholas Kaldor

King's College,
  Cambridge.

[8]
A New Model of Economic Growth

1. The purpose of this paper is to present a "Keynesian" model of economic growth, which is an amended version of previous attempts put forward by one of the authors in three former publications.[1] This new theory differs from earlier theories mainly in the following respects:

(1) it gives more explicit recognition to the fact that technical progress is infused into the economic system through the creation of new equipment, which depends on current (gross) investment expenditure. Hence the "technical progress function" has been re-defined so as to exhibit a relationship between the rate of change of gross (fixed) investment per operative and the rate of increase in labour productivity on *newly installed* equipment;

(2) it takes explicit account of obsolescence, caused by the fact that the profitability of plant and equipment of any particular "vintage" must continually diminish in time owing to the competition of equipment of superior efficiency installed at subsequent dates; and it assumes that this *continuing obsolescence is broadly foreseen by entrepreneurs* who take it into account in framing their investment decision. The model also assumes that, irrespective of whether plant and equipment has a finite physical life-time or not, its *operative* life-time is determined by a complex of economic factors which govern the rate of obsolescence, and not by physical wear and tear;

(3) in accordance with this, the behavioural assumptions concerning the investors' attitudes to uncertainty in connection with investment decisions and which are set out below, differ in important respects from those made in the earlier models;

(4) account is also taken, in the present model, of the fact that some proportion of the existing stock of equipment disappears each year through physical causes—accidents, fire, explosions, etc.—and this gives rise to some " radioactive " physical depreciation in addition to obsolescence;

(5) since, under continuous technical progress and obsolescence, there is no way of measuring the " stock of capital " (measurement in terms of the historical cost of the surviving capital equipment is irrelevant; in terms of historical cost *less* accrued " obsolescence " is question-begging, since the allowance for obsolescence, unlike the charge for physical wear and tear etc., depends on the share of profits, the rate of growth, etc., and cannot therefore be determined independently of all other relations), the model avoids the notion of a quantity of capital, and its corollary, the rate of capital accumulation, as variables of the system; it operates solely with the value of current gross investment (gross (fixed) capital expenditure per unit of time) and its rate of change in time. The macro-economic notions of income, income per head, etc., on the the other hand are retained.

[1] Cf. N. Kaldor, "Alternative Theories of Distribution," *Review of Economic Studies*, 1955-56, (reprinted in *Essays on Value and Distribution*, pp. 228-236). " A Model of Economic Growth," *Economic Journal*, December 1957 (reprinted in *Essays in Economic Stability and Growth*, pp. 256-300) and " Capital Accumulation and Economic Growth " (presented in Corfu, September 1958 and published in *The Theory of Capital*, Macmillan, 1961, pp. 177-220). N. Kaldor's ideas in connection with the present model were worked out during his tenure as Ford Research Professor in Economics in Berkeley, California.

A NEW MODEL OF ECONOMIC GROWTH

2. The present model is analogous to the earlier models in the following main features:

(1) like all " Keynesian " economic models, it assumes that " savings " are passive—the level of investment is based on the volume of investment decisions made by entrepreneurs, and is independent of the propensities to save; it postulates an economy in which the mechanism of profit and income generation will create sufficient savings (at any rate within certain limits or " boundaries ") to balance the investment which entrepreneurs decide to undertake;

(2) the model relates to an isolated economy with continuous technical progress, and with a steady rate of increase in the working population, determined by exogenous factors;

(3) the model assumes that investment is primarily *induced* by the growth in production itself, and that the underlying conditions are such that growth-equilibrium necessarily carries with it a state of continuous full employment. This will be the case when the purely ' endogeneous ' growth rate (as determined by the combined operation of the accelerator and the multiplier) which is operative under conditions of an unlimited supply of labour, is appreciably higher than the " natural rate of growth," which is the growth of the " labour potential " (i.e., the *sum* of the rate of growth of the labour force and of (average) labour productivity). In that case, starting from any given state of surplus labour and underemployment, continued growth, as determined by these endogenous factors, will necessarily lead to full employment sooner or later; and once full employment rules, continued growth involves that the " accelerator-multiplier " mechanism becomes " tethered " (through variations in the share of profits and through the imposition of a quasi-exogeneous growth rate in demand) to the natural rate of growth.

3. In a situation of continuing full employment the volume of investment decisions for the economy as a whole will be governed by the number of workers who become available, per unit period, to " man " new equipment, and by the amount of investment per operative. It may be assumed that each entrepreneur, operating in imperfectly competitive markets, aims at the maximum attainable growth of his own business (subject as we shall explain below, to the maintenance of a satisfactory rate of return on the capital employed) and for that reason prefers to maintain an appreciable amount of excess capacity so as to be able to exploit any chance increase in his selling power either by increasing his share of the market or by invading other markets. However, when gross investment per period is in excess of the number of workers becoming available to " man " new equipment, the degree of excess capacity must steadily rise; hence whatever the desired relationship between capacity and output, sooner or later a point will be reached when the number of workers available for operating new equipment exerts a dominating influence (via the mechanism of the accelerator) on the volume of investment decisions in the economy.[1]

We shall assume that the equipment of any given vintage is in " limitational " relationship to labour—i.e. that it is not possible to increase the productivity of labour by reducing the number of workers employed in connection with already existing equipment (though it is possible that productivity would, on the contrary, be *reduced* by such a reduction, on account of its being associated with a higher ratio of overhead to prime labour). This does not mean that the equipment of any vintage requires a fixed amount of labour to keep it in operation. The latter would assume the case not only of " fixed coefficients " but of complete indivisibility of the plant and equipment as well.

---

[1] We may assume that for the average, or representative, firm, sales grow at the same rate as production in the economy as a whole. But there will always be of course the exceptional firms who grow at a higher rate, and sub-average firms who grow at a lower rate. Investment in all cases serves the purpose of keeping productive capacity in some desired relationship with expected sales.

Writing n_t for the number of workers available to operate new equipment per unit period and i_t for the amount of investment per operative on machines of vintage t, and I_t for gross investment in fixed capital

$$i_t \equiv \frac{I_t}{n_t} \tag{1}$$

We shall use the symbols Y_t for the gross national product at t, N_t for the working population, and y_t for output per head, so that

$$y_t \equiv \frac{Y_t}{N_t}$$

4. We shall assume that "machines" of each vintage are of constant physical efficiency during their lifetime, so that the growth of productivity in the economy is entirely due to the infusion of new "machines" into the system through (gross) investment.[1] Hence our basic assumption is a technical progress function which makes the annual rate of growth of productivity per worker *operating on new equipment* a function of the rate of growth of investment per worker, i.e., that

$$\dot{p}_t/p_t = f(\dot{i}_t/i_t) \text{ with } f(0) > 0, f' > 0, f'' < 0 \tag{2}$$

This function is illustrated in Figure 1. It is assumed that a constant rate of investment per worker over time will itself increase productivity per worker; but that the rate of growth of productivity will also be an increasing function of the rate of growth of investment per worker, though at a diminishing rate.[2]

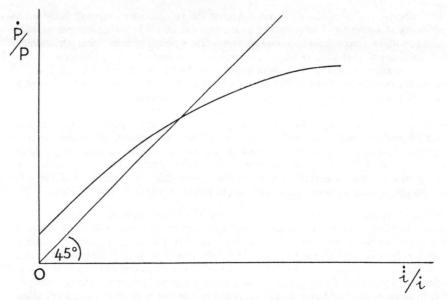

[1] It is probable that in addition to "embodied" technical progress there is some "disembodied" technical progress as well, resulting from increasing know-how in the use of existing machinery. On the other hand it is also probable that the physical efficiency of machinery declines with age (on account of higher repair and maintenance expenditures, etc.); our assumption of constant physical efficiency thus implies that these two factors just balance each other.

[2] It should be noted that the "technical progress function" in this model relates to the rate of growth of output per man-hour of the workers operating newly installed equipment (the equipment resulting from the investment of period t), *not* to the rate of growth of productivity in the economy in general (though in

A NEW MODEL OF ECONOMIC GROWTH

Both output per operative and investment per operative are measured in terms of money values deflated by an index of the prices of " wage goods " (i.e., consumption goods which enter into the wage-earners' budget). This means that changes in the prices of equipment goods in terms of wage-goods (and also of such consumption goods which only enter into consumption out of profits) will in general cause shifts in the f-function. Provided, however, that there is a reasonably stable trend in the prices of these latter goods in terms of wage goods, we can still conceive of the function as stable in time for any particular value of I_t/Y_t in money terms, and the system may still possess a steady growth equilibrium with a constant (equilibrium) value of I_t/Y_t. A full demonstration of this would require, however, a fully fledged 2-sector model in which the technical progress functions of the consumption goods sector and the capital goods sector, the distribution of employment and of savings between the two sectors, etc., are all treated separately. Since this would go far beyond the scope of this paper, it is better to assume, for the present purposes, that the rate of technical progress, as measured by productivity growth, is the same in all sectors, and hence that relative prices remain constant; bearing in mind, however, that the model could probably be extended to cover a wider range of possibilities.

5. With regard to the manner in which entrepreneurs meet risk and uncertainty, we shall make two important assumptions. In the first place we shall assume that entrepreneurs will only invest in their own business in so far as this is consistent with maintaining the earning power of their fixed assets above a certain minimum, a minimum which, in their view, represents the earning power of fixed assets in the economy in general. This is because, if the earnings of a particular firm are low in relation to the capital employed, or if they increase at a lower rate than the book value of the fixed assets, fixed assets will take up an increasing proportion of the total resources of the firm (including its potential borrowing power) at any given rate of growth, with the result that the financial position of the firm will become steadily weaker, with enhanced risks of bankruptcy or take-over bids. Hence we may assume that the sum of the expected profits anticipated from operating the equipment during its anticipated period of operation (or lifetime), T, will earn after full amortisation, a rate of profit that is at least equal to the assumed rate of profit on new investment in the economy generally. Hence for any particular investor

$$i_t \leqslant \int_{t}^{t+T} e^{-(\rho+\delta)(\tau-t)} (p_t - w_\tau^*) d\tau \tag{3}$$

where ρ stands for what the entrepreneur assumes the general rate of profit to be, w_τ^* for the expected rate of wages which is a rising function of future time[1] and δ is the rate of " radioactive " decay of machines (we take it that the investor assumes his machine is an average machine).[2]

full steady growth equilibrium, as we shall see, the two will correspond to each other); and to the rate of growth of gross investment per worker from year to year, not the rate of accumulation of capital (which may not be a meaningful or measurable quantity). It is plausible that, with technical progress, the same investment per operative should yield a higher output per operative in successive years; and that this rate of growth will be enhanced, within limits, when the value of investment per operative is increasing over time.

[1] In a golden age equilibrium, the inequality (3) should be replaced by an equality, and since all the variables will be determined independently by the other equations, (3) can then be taken as determining the rate of profit on investment. Cf. p. 180 below.

[2] Our equation (3) thus postulates conditions under which the amount of " finance " available to the firm is considerably greater than its fixed capital expenditure, so that the firm is free to vary its total investment expenditure per unit of time; and that it will adopt projects which pass the tests of adequacy as indicated by (3) even though it could earn a higher *rate* of profit on projects involving a smaller volume of investment and yielding a smaller *total* profit. (In other words we assume that the firm is guided by the motive of maximising the rate of profit on the shareholders' equity, which involves different decisions from the assumption of maximizing the rate of profit on its fixed investment.)

In the second place, under conditions of continuing technical progress, the expectations concerning the more distant future (whether in regard to money wages or in regard to the prices—or demands—of the particular products produced by a firm, both of which are projected in w^*_τ) are regarded as far more hazardous or uncertain than the expectations for the near future, where the incidence of unforseeable major new inventions or discoveries is less significant. Hence investment projects which qualify for adoption must pass a further test—apart from the test of earning a satisfactory rate of profit—and that is that the cost of the fixed assets must be "recovered" within a certain period—i.e., that the gross profit earned in the first h years of its operation must be sufficient to repay the cost of investment. Hence

$$i_t \leqslant \int_t^{t+h} (p_t - w^*_\tau) \, d\tau \qquad (4)$$

We shall assume, for the purposes of this model, that (3) is satisfied whenever (4) is satisfied—hence in (4) the $=$ sign will apply, i.e., the undiscounted sum of profits over h periods must be equal to i_t. There is plenty of empirical evidence that the assumption underlying (4) is a generally recognised method of meeting the uncertainty due to obsolescence in modern business, though the value of h may vary with the rate of technical progress, and also as between different sectors. (In the U.S. manufacturing industry h is normally taken as 3 years; but in other sectors—e.g., public utilities—it is much higher.)[1]

7. It is assumed, as in the earlier Keynesian growth models, that the savings which finance business investment come out of profits, and that a constant proportion, s, of *gross* profits are saved.[2] Hence (dividing income into two categories, profits and wages, which comprise all forms of non-business income) the share of (gross) profits, π_t, in the gross national product will be given by the equation

$$\pi_t = \frac{1}{s} \frac{I_t}{Y_t} \qquad (5)$$

which, in virtue of equation (1), reduces to

$$\pi_t = \frac{r}{s} \frac{i_t}{y_t} \qquad (5a)$$

[1] The assumptions represented by these two equations should be contrasted with the assumptions made in "Capital Accumulation and Economic Growth," according to which

$$\frac{P}{K} = r + \rho$$

$$\rho = \xi(v) \quad (\xi' > 0)$$

where P/K the rate of profit, r the money rate of interest, ρ the risk premium, v the capital/output ratio. ρ was assumed to be a rising function of v, because v reflects the ratio of fixed to circulating capital, and investment in the former is considered far more risky or "illiquid" than investment in the latter. The present assumptions are not inconsistent with the former hypothesis concerning the higher returns demanded on fixed investments; but they also take into account that the "riskiness" of the investment in fixed capital will be all the greater the longer the period over which the cost of the investment is 'recovered' out of the profits—a matter which depends not only on the capital/output ratio (or rather, the investment/output ratio) but also on the share of gross profits in output. "Gross profits" should for this purpose be calculated net of other charges, including a notional interest charge on the 'liquid' business assets, (i.e., the investment in circulating capital associated with the investment in fixed capital).

[2] Savings out of wages are ignored—i.e., they are assumed to be balanced by non-business (personal) investment (i.e., residential construction). The assumption that business savings are a constant proportion of *gross* profits (after tax) is well supported by data relating to gross corporate savings.

A NEW MODEL OF ECONOMIC GROWTH

where r is defined by

$$r_t = {}^{n_t}/N_t,$$

where N_t is the total labour force at time t and n_t, as earlier defined, is the number of workers available to operate new equipment per unit period.

We shall assume that once equipment is installed the number of workers operating it will only fall in time by the physical wastage of equipment, caused by accidents, fires, etc. —until the whole of the residual equipment is scrapped on account of obsolescence. Writing δ for the rate of (radioactive) depreciation per unit period, and $T(t)$ for the age of the equipment which is retired at t (i.e., the lifetime of equipment as governed by obsolescence), we have the following relationship for the distribution of the labour force:

$$N_t = \int_{t-T}^{t} n_\tau \, e^{-\delta(t-\tau)} \, d\tau \tag{6}$$

and for total output

$$Y_t = \int_{t-T}^{t} p_\tau \, n_\tau \, e^{-\delta(t-\tau)} \, d\tau \tag{7}$$

Since output Y_t is divided into two categories of income only, wages and profits, the residue left after profits is equal to the total wages bill. Writing w_t for the rate of wages at t, we further have

$$Y_t (1 - \pi_t) = N_t \, w_t \tag{8}$$

Finally, since equipment will only be employed so long as its operation more than covers prime costs, the profit on the oldest yet surviving machinery must be zero. Hence

$$p_{t-T} = w_t \tag{9}$$

We shall assume that population grows at the constant rate λ, hence

$$\dot{N}_t = \lambda \, N_t \tag{10}$$

We shall also assume that businessmen anticipate that wages in terms of output units will rise in the foreseeable future at the same rate as they have been rising during the past l periods.

Hence the expected wage rate at a future time T will be

$$w_T^* = w_t \left(\frac{w_t}{w_{t-l}}\right)^{\frac{T-t}{l}} \tag{11}$$

Finally, the model is subject to two constraints (or "boundary conditions") which are known from earlier models:

$$w_t \geqslant w_{min}$$
$$\pi \geqslant m$$

In other words, the wage rate resulting from the model must be above a certain minimum, (determined by conventional subsistence needs) and at the same time the share of profits resulting from the model must be higher than a certain minimum (the so-called " degree of monopoly " or " degree of imperfect competition ").

8. The above system gives 10 independent equations (regarding (3) only as a boundary condition) which are sufficient to determine the 10 unknowns; $I_t, i_t, n_t, p_t, w_t, w^*_t, \pi_t, T, y_t, N_t$, given the parameters, s, h, δ and λ, and the function f.

We shall investigate whether this system yields a solution in terms of a steady growth (or golden age) equilibrium where the rate of growth of output per head is equal to the rate of growth of productivity on new equipment and both are equal to the rate of growth of (fixed) investment per worker, and to the rate of growth of wages ; i.e., where

$$\dot{p}/p = \dot{y}/y = \dot{i}/i = \dot{w}/w ;$$

and where the share of investment in output I/Y, the share of profits in income π, and the period of obsolescence of equipment, T, remain constant. Finally we shall show that there is a unique rate of profit on investment in a steady growth equilibrium.

The assumptions about the technical progress function imply that there is *some* value $\dot{p}/p$ (let us call it γ) at which

$$\dot{p}/p = \dot{i}/i = \gamma$$

Equilibrium is only possible when this holds.

If we integrate equation (4) using (11), we see that

$$i_t = hp_t - w_t \frac{e^{vh} - 1}{v},$$

where v is the expected rate of growth of w. Hence p could only grow faster than i in the long run if w was growing faster than p: that would imply a continuous reduction in T, which would lead to unemployment and stagnation before T fell to h (at which point the rate of profit would be negative). On the other hand, p cannot grow more slowly than i in the long run, since w cannot fall below w_{min} (and there would in fact be a inflation crisis before that point was reached).

It is clear too that, so long as $\dot{w}/w$ does not diverge too far from $\dot{p}/p$, $\dot{i}/i$ would increase if it were less than $\dot{p}/p$, and decrease if it were greater than $\dot{p}/p$. For if $\dot{p}/p$ were less than γ, it would breed, by equation (4), a rate of growth of investment, $\dot{i}/i$ that would require higher $\dot{p}/p$, and so on, until the equilibrium position is reached. A similar mechanism would be at work if $\dot{p}/p$ were greater than γ. Thus the equilibrium would in general be stable; but instability cannot be excluded, and a movement away from equilibrium would be possible in either of the two ways described above. For example a downward drift of the technical progress function might allow the rate of growth of p to fall off, and remain below the rate of growth of w (which reflects the rate of growth of y over the recent past) sufficiently long until with falling investment, unemployment and stagnation set in.[1] Conversely an upward shift in the technical progress function might lead to an inflationary situation at which investment, by one means or another, would be compressed below that indicated by (4) and (13).

---

[1] For example, a slowing down of technical progress in the late 1920's may have been responsible for that " sudden collapse of the marginal efficiency of capital " which led to the crisis and stagnation of the 1930's.

A NEW MODEL OF ECONOMIC GROWTH

Hence, excluding the case where $\dot{p}/p$ is significantly different from $\dot{w}/w$, when

$$\frac{\dot{p}}{p} \gtrless \frac{\dot{i}}{i}$$

there will be a convergent movement until (12) is obtained.

9. It will be convenient to deduce two further relations from the above equations. The first one relates to n_t, the amount of labour available for new equipment: it is obtained by differentiating (6) with respect to t.

$$n_t = \dot{N}_t + \delta N_t + n_{t-T}\left(1 - \frac{dT}{dt}\right) e^{-\delta T} \tag{13}$$

This equation says that n_t will be composed of three elements: (i) the growth in working population, $\dot{N}_t$; (ii) the labour released by physical wastage of equipment all vintages, which is δN_t; (iii) and finally the labour released by the retirement of obsolete equipment.

Differentiating equation (7) in the same way we obtain

$$\dot{Y}_t = p_t\, n_t - p_{t-T}\, n_{t-T}\left(1 - \frac{dT}{dt}\right) e^{-\delta T} - \delta Y_t$$

Substituting w_t for p_{t-T} in accordance with (9) and using (13) this becomes

$$\dot{Y}_t = p_t\, n_t - w_t\,(n_t - \dot{N}_t - \delta N_t) - \delta Y_t$$

Dividing both sides by $Y_t = N_t y_t$ we obtain

$$\frac{\dot{Y}_t}{Y_t} = r\,\frac{p_t}{y_t} - \frac{w_t}{y_t}(r - \lambda - \delta) - \delta$$

Using

$$\frac{\dot{Y}_t}{Y_t} = \frac{\dot{y}_t}{y_t} + \lambda$$

and re-arranging we finally obtain

$$\frac{\dot{y}_t}{y_t} + \lambda + \delta = r\frac{p_t}{y_t} - (r - \lambda - \delta)\frac{w_t}{y_t}. \tag{14}$$

10. In order that entrepreneurial expectations should be fulfilled, it is necessary that wages should grow at constant rate in time, β.

$$\frac{\dot{w}_t}{w_t} = \beta \text{ (constant)} \tag{15}$$

We shall now proceed to demonstrate that when β is constant, T will also be constant, provided that $\gamma < \frac{s}{h} - \lambda - \delta$.

It follows from (9) that

$$\frac{\dot{w}_t}{w_t} = \frac{\dot{p}_{t-T}}{p_{t-T}}\left(1 - \frac{dT}{dt}\right)$$

Hence

$$1 - \frac{dT}{dt} = \frac{\beta}{\gamma}, \text{ a constant.}$$

Integrating with respect to t we obtain

$$T = T_o + \left(1 - \frac{\beta}{\gamma}\right)t \tag{16}$$

where T_0 is the lifetime of equipment at some initial date, $t = 0$.

Substituting (16) into (13) and remembering that $r_t = n_t/N_t$, we obtain

$$r_t = \lambda + \delta + r_{t-T}\, e^{-(\lambda+\delta)T}\, \frac{\beta}{\gamma} \tag{17}$$

In order to show that, in a state of steady growth equilibrium $T = T_0$ and $\beta = \gamma$, we shall first consider the cases where $\beta \neq \gamma$.

(i) When $\gamma < \beta$, clearly steady growth cannot continue since entrepreneurs' profits would become negative sooner or later.

(ii) when $\gamma > \beta$, it follows from equation (16) that T becomes indefinitely large with time (and perhaps this is enough to dispose of this case, since for most goods there may be a maximum physical lifetime, quite apart from obsolescence). In any case this implies, in accordance with (17), that r ultimately tends to $\lambda + \delta$; and since w/y must tend to zero, so that the share of profits, π, tends towards unity,

$$i/y \text{ tends to } \frac{s}{\lambda + \delta}. \tag{18}$$

Also from (4):

i/p tends to h.

Hence from (14):

$$\dot{y}/y \text{ tends to } \frac{s}{h} - \lambda - \delta.$$

(18) shows that y ultimately grows at the same rate as i, which grows at the rate γ.

Therefore

$$\gamma = \frac{s}{h} - \lambda - \delta \tag{19}$$

which implies, in Harrod's terms, that the "natural rate" (here, $\gamma + \lambda + \delta$) is equal to what the "warranted rate" would be if wages were zero and profits absorbed the whole output (since then s would equal the proportion of Y saved, and $h = i/p$).

11. It is easy to see that in fact the rate of growth of output per head cannot in the long run be greater than this quantity $\frac{s}{h} - \lambda - \delta$. By (5), i/y can rise no higher, ultimately, than s/r; hence by (4), even if (as might happen ultimately) the wage rate were negligible in relation to output per head, p/y could not be greater than $s/(rh)$. Turning to equation (14), we see that it implies the inequality

$$\dot{y}_t/y_t + \lambda + \delta \leq r \cdot \frac{s}{rh} = \frac{s}{h}.$$

Hence there can be no steady growth equilibrium unless

$$\gamma \leq \frac{s}{h} - \lambda - \delta.$$

Normally we would not expect to have to worry about this constraint, for the quantity s/h will be large—especially when we remember that h will be small when there is a high rate of growth. If it is asked what would happen if the equilibrium growth rate given by the technical progress function really did fail to satisfy this inequality, the answer must be that the wage rate would be driven down to its minimum level and entrepreneurs would then find themselves unable to invest as much as the prospects would warrant: the equality (4) would become an inequality again. The rest of the discussion will be carried on under the assumption that the equilibrium rate of growth γ does satisfy this inequality.

We can see that, quite apart from the unrealistic value of γ implied by equation (19), equilibrium with $\gamma > \beta$ is a freak case; the slightest shift in γ would either render equilibrium impossible, or make it possible only with $\beta = \gamma$.

12. (iii) It is clear from the above that steady growth equilibrium will involve

$$\beta = \gamma$$

in which case it also involves a constant T.
(17) has now become

$$r_t = \lambda + \delta + r_{t-T}\, e^{-(\lambda+\delta)T},$$

where T is constant, so that r_t will tend to the equilibrium value

$$r = \frac{\lambda + \delta}{1 - e^{-(\lambda+\delta)T}} \tag{20}$$

From equation (5)

$$y_t = w_t + \frac{r}{s}\, i_t,$$

so that, since r is constant in equilibrium, y_t also grows at the equilibrium growth rate γ. It is convenient to write this last equation as

$$\frac{r}{s}\frac{i}{y} + \frac{w}{y} = 1 \tag{21}$$

In equilibrium, expectations are fulfilled, so that $w_t^* = w_t$. Since $w_t = w_0\, e^{\beta t} = w_0\, e^{\gamma t}$ (where w_0 is the wage rate at some initial time), the integral in equation (4) can be evaluated, so that

$$i_t = hp_t - \frac{e^{\gamma h} - 1}{\gamma}\, w_t,$$

which we can write

$$\frac{1}{h}\frac{i}{y} + \frac{e^{\gamma h} - 1}{\gamma h}\frac{w}{y} - \frac{p}{y} = 0 \tag{22}$$

(14) can now be rewritten

$$(r - \lambda - \delta)\frac{w}{y} - r\frac{p}{y} = -(\gamma + \lambda + \delta) \tag{23}$$

Equations (21), (22), (23) can be treated as three simultaneous equations for $\frac{i}{y}$, $\frac{w}{y}$, and $\frac{p}{y}$ (which are all constant in a state of steady growth).

Now equation (9) provides an equation for T:

$$e^{\gamma T} = \frac{p}{w} = \frac{p/y}{w/y}. \tag{24}$$

Using the values of r, $\frac{p}{y}$, $\frac{w}{y}$ found by solving (21), (22) and (23), we obtain:

$$e^{\gamma T} = \frac{1 - \frac{h(\gamma + \lambda + \delta)}{s} \cdot \frac{e^{\gamma h} - 1}{\gamma h} + \frac{\gamma}{r}}{1 - \frac{h(\gamma + \lambda + \delta)}{s}} \tag{25}$$

And from (20), since $e^{\gamma T} = [e^{-(\lambda + \delta)T}]^{-\gamma/(\lambda + \delta)}$

$$e^{\gamma T} = \left[1 - \frac{\lambda + \delta}{r}\right]^{-\frac{\gamma}{\lambda + \delta}} \tag{26}$$

(25) and (26) determine T and r simultaneously in terms of the parameters λ, δ, h, s, and the steady growth rate γ (which was determined by the technical progress function). Equation (20) is not valid when $\lambda + \delta = 0$. In that case we go back to equation (6); integration gives

$$rT = 1, \tag{27}$$

which replaces (26) in this particular case.

13. Although (25) and (26) are rather cumbersome equations, numerical solution for particular values of the parameters presents no particular difficulty. Once T and r are calculated, simultaneous solution of (23) and (24) yields the values of $\frac{p}{y}$ and $\frac{w}{y}$ (the share of wages). Then $\frac{i}{y}$ is found from (22). A demonstration of the existence of a unique meaningful solution to the equations is given in the Appendix.

If capital stock were valued at historic cost, without any allowance for reduction in value through obsolescence, we should have

$$K = \int_{t-T}^{t} i_\tau\, n_\tau\, e^{-\delta(t-\tau)}\, d\tau,$$

and

$$Y = \int_{t-T}^{t} p_\tau\, n_\tau\, e^{-\delta(t-\tau)}\, d\tau, \tag{28}$$

so that the aggregate capital-output ratio,

$$\frac{K}{Y} = \frac{i}{p},$$

since this latter is constant.

However, when obsolescence is *foreseen* the knowledge of the share of profits, π, and of the historical cost of invested capital as shown by (28), does not enable us to calculate either net profits or the rate of profit on capital. The value of capital at any one time will be lower than K_t by the accrued provision made for obsolescence, and the appropriate obsolescence provision — which must take into account the annual reduction in the profits earned on equipment of a given vintage, as well as the retirement of equipment when it becomes T years old—cannot be calculated without knowing the capital on which the profit is earned, which in turn cannot be known without knowing the rate of profit.

14. In a state of fully-fledged golden age equilibrium, where (1) expectations are (in general) fulfilled and the expected profit on new investments is therefore the same as the realised profit, and (2) the rate of profit earned on all investment will be the same, the inequality (3) above can be replaced by an equality and regarded as an additional equation determining ρ (since i_t, p_t, w_t and T are all determined by the other equations of the system.)

$$i_t = \int_0^T e^{-(\rho+\delta)\tau} (p_t - W_{t+\tau}) \cdot d\tau \tag{3a}$$

ρ is constant, so the familiar relation

$$\gamma + \lambda = \rho \sigma, \tag{29}$$

where σ is the proportion of *net* profits saved, holds; for it is easy to check that the value of capital—in terms of output to come—grows at the equilibrium growth rate $\gamma + \lambda$, and that ρ defined by (3a) is equal to the ratio of net profit to the stock of capital. In general, of course, σ depends on ρ, and is best calculated from the relation (29). But when $s = 1$, i.e., when all (gross) profits are invested, σ must also be equal to unity, so that the rate of profit is equal to the rate of growth of output: $\rho = \gamma + \lambda$. On the face of it, it is not clear that this value of ρ satisfies (29): yet it must do. To show that it does, we use the fact that total output,

$$Y_t = \int_0^T p_{t-\tau}\, n_{t-\tau}\, e^{-\delta\tau}\, d\tau,$$

$$= p_t\, n_t \int_0^T e^{-(\gamma+\lambda+\delta)\tau}\, d\tau.$$

Thus, when we put $\rho = \gamma + \lambda$ in the right hand side of (3a), we get:

$$\frac{y_t}{r_t} - w_t \int_0^T e^{-(\lambda+\delta)\tau} d\tau.$$

This last integral $= \dfrac{1 - e^{-(\lambda+\delta)T}}{\lambda + \delta} = \dfrac{1}{r}$, by equation (20). Hence the right hand side of equation (3a) is equal to $(y_t - w_t)/r$, which is equal to i_t when $s = 1$ (by equation (21).)

If $s \neq 1$, we must find ρ from equation (3a). If we perform the integration (which we can do, since p and w are growing exponentially), we get the following relation, which can be solved numerically for $\rho + \delta$:

$$\frac{i}{y} = \frac{1 - e^{-(\rho+\delta)T}}{\rho + \delta} \frac{p}{y} - \frac{1 - e^{-(\rho+\delta-\gamma)T}}{\rho + \delta - \gamma} \frac{w}{y}. \tag{30}$$

Outside a golden age equilibrium a rate of profit on investment does not exist except in the sense of an *assumed* rate of profit, based on a mixture of convention and belief, which enables entrepreneurs to decide whether any particular project passes the test of adequate profitability.

15. Some Numerical Results

The following are the solution of the equations for various arbitrarily selected values of the parameters.[1]

For $s = 0.66$:

h years	$\lambda + \delta\%$	$\gamma\%$	T years	r	$\pi\%$	$I/Y\%$	i/p	$\rho+\delta\%$
3	2	2	8·03	·135	8·0	5·3	·367	21·7
		2·5	8·15	·133	10·1	6·7	·459	22·1
		3	8·27	·131	12·2	8·1	·551	22·4
	4	2	8·68	·136	8·9	5·9	·401	23·0
		2·5	8·82	·135	11·2	7·5	·501	23·4
		3	8·97	·133	13·5	9·0	·601	23·7
4	2	2	11·20	·100	11·2	7·5	·672	17·0
		2·5	11·44	·098	14·1	9·6	·839	17·3
		3	11·68	·096	17·1	11·4	1·006	17·6
	4	2	12·54	·101	12·9	8·6	·759	18·2
		2·5	12·84	·100	16·3	10·9	·948	18·6
		3	13·15	·098	19·8	13·2	1·136	18·9
5	2	2	14·69	·078	14·6	9·7	1·080	14·1
		2·5	15·10	·077	18·5	12·3	1·348	14·4
		3	15·53	·075	22·4	14·9	1·615	14·7
	4	2	17·13	·081	17·8	11·9	1·267	15·4
		2·5	17·71	·079	22·5	15·0	1·579	15·7
		3	18·34	·077	27·4	16·4	1·888	16·0

[1] We are indebted to Mr. D. G. Champernowne for programming these calculations, and to the Director of the Mathematical Laboratory of Cambridge University for making the computer available.

A NEW MODEL OF ECONOMIC GROWTH

Some representative values for different s:

s	h	$\lambda + \delta\%$	$\gamma\%$	T	r	$\pi\%$	$I/Y\%$	i/p	$\rho+\delta\%$
·33	3	2	$\begin{cases}2\\2\cdot5\end{cases}$	20·66 21·26	·059 ·058	20·4 25·6	6·8 8·5	·955 1·169	30·6 30·8
·50	4	4	$\begin{cases}2\\2\cdot5\\3\end{cases}$	19·98 20·66 21·42	·073 ·071 ·070	20·7 26·2 31·8	10·3 13·1 15·9	1·207 1·490 1·765	21·7 22·0 22·3
	5	2	$\begin{cases}2\\2\cdot5\\3\end{cases}$	22·61 23·47 24·41	·055 ·053 ·052	22·2 28·1 34·1	11·1 14·0 17·0	1·655 2·038 2·407	17·0 17·3 17·6
1·00	4	4		$\begin{cases}2\cdot5\\3\end{cases}$	6·08 6·22	·185 ·182	7·7 9·4	7·7 9·4	·387 ·474	6·5 7·0
	5	$\begin{cases}2\\\\4\end{cases}$	$\begin{cases}2\cdot5\\3\end{cases}$ $\begin{cases}2\cdot5\\3\end{cases}$	7·28 7·49 8·20 8·44	·148 ·144 ·143 ·140	9·0 11·1 10·4 12·7	9·0 11·1 10·4 12·7	·561 ·691 ·662 ·812	4·5 5·0 6·5 7·0

For the U.S. in the 1950's, reasonable values of the parameters are $\gamma = 2$ to $2\frac{1}{2}\%$, $\lambda + \delta = 2 - 4\%$, $s = \cdot66$, $h = 4$ to 5 years. The average lifetime of equipment in manufacturing industry has been estimated at 17 years. π as indicated by the ratio of gross corporate profit after tax to the gross income originating in corporations after corporation tax has been 21%, and the ratio of business fixed capital to business gross product around 1·5. These, as the table shows, are close to the results of the model when $s = \cdot66$, $h = 5$, $\lambda + \delta = 4\%$, and when γ is $2 - 2\cdot5\%$.[1]

The rate of profit on investment, on the other hand, appears rather high. However it must be remembered that our equation (3) derives the rate of (net) profit from the stream of gross profit *after* tax, and not (as is usually done) from the gross profit before tax. This involves a smaller provision for obsolescence, and consequently a higher net profit, than in the usual method of calculation. It also implies that in "grossing up" for tax, the relevant rate is the effective tax charge on profits before depreciation, and not the rate of tax on profits net of depreciation. Hence, if the tax on corporation profits is one third of gross profits before tax, a rate of net profit (net of tax) of 12·5 per cent (assuming $\lambda = 1\%$, $\delta = 3\%$) corresponds to a rate of net profit *before* tax of 18·5 per cent.[2]

It can be seen from the figures, too, that π and i/p are quite sensitive to changes in the technical progress function (i.e. in γ), and highly sensitive to changes in s and h, but stable

[1] It should be borne in mind, of course, that no allowance was made in the model for net investment in working capital (inventory accumulation) which would affect the values of T, π, I/Y and i/p, but the effect of which can be subsumed in h. Equally, the model assumes that government savings and investment are equal—i.e., that there is no financial surplus or deficit arising out of government operations, and that personal savings and personal investments (mainly in housing) are equal.

[2] U.S. estimates put the average rate of profit on (business) investment 16 per cent before tax and 8 per cent after tax.

for changes in λ and δ. T is only sensitive to changes in s and h, but *not* to γ. These results may sound surprising at first. One would expect T to be inversely related to γ, and one would also expect r ($= n_t/N_t$) to be positively correlated with $(\lambda + \delta)$. However, a rise in γ leads to a rise in i/p, and hence of π, which more than compensates for the rise in γ in determining the associated change in T; a rise in $(\lambda + \delta)$ reduces (as between one steady growth equilibrium and another) the amount of labour released through obsolescence in relation to the current labour force (since the labour force T years ago was that much smaller, when λ is larger; and of the equipment built T years ago so much less survives to be scrapped when δ is larger) so that it compensates for the increase in $(\lambda + \delta)$, leaving the value of r pretty much the same.

16. *General Conclusions*

The model shows technical progress—in the specific form of the rate of improvement of the design, etc., of newly produced capital equipment—as the main engine of economic growth, determining not only the rate of growth of productivity but—together with other parameters—also the rate of obsolescence, the average lifetime of equipment, the share of investment in income, the share of profits, and the relationship between investment and potential output (*i.e.*, the " capital/output ratio " on new capital).

The model is Keynesian in its mode of operation (entrepreneurial expenditure decisions are primary; incomes, etc., are secondary) and severely *non*-neo-classical in that technological factors (marginal productivities or marginal substitution ratios) play no role in the determination of wages and profits. A " production function " in the sense of a single-valued relationship between *some* measure of capital, K_t, the labour force N_t and of output Y_t (all at time t) clearly does not exist. Everything depends on past history, on how the collection of equipment goods which comprises K_t has been built up. Thus Y_t will be greater for a given K_t (as measured by historical cost) if a greater part of the existing capital stock is of more recent creation; this would be the case, for example, if the rate of growth of population has been accelerating.

Whilst " machines " earn quasi-rents which are all the smaller the older they are (so that, for the oldest surviving machine, the quasi-rents are zero) it would be wrong to say that the position of the marginal " machine " determines the share of quasi-rents (or gross profits) in total income. For the total profit is determined quite independently of the structure of these " quasi-rents " by equation (5), i.e., by the factors determining the share of investment in output and the proportion of profits saved and therefore the position of the " marginal " machine is itself fully determined by the other equations of the system. It is the macro-economic condition specified in (5), and not the age-and-productivity structure of machinery, which will determine what the (aggregate) share of quasi-rents will be.

This technical progress function is quite consistent with a technological " investment function ", i.e., a functional relationship (shifting in time) between investment per worker and output per worker.[1] However, owing to anticipated obsolescence and to uncertainty, it would not be correct to say that the " marginal product " of investment, dp_t/di_t, plays

---

[1] On the relationship of a technical progress function and a production function c.f. John Black, " The Technical Progress Function and The Production Function," *Economica*, May 1962. Whilst it is possible to make assumptions under which a technical progress function is merely one way of representing an (ex-ante) production function of constant elasticity which shifts at some pre-determined rate in time, the postulate of a technical progress function is also consistent with situations in which the rate of technical progress does not proceed at some pre-determined rate (where the shift of the " curve " is bound up with the movement *along* the " curve ") and where therefore one cannot associate a unique production function with a given " state " of knowledge.

a role in determining the amount per man. Since the profitability of operating the equipment is expected to diminish in time, the marginal addition to the stream of profits (which we may call the " marginal value productivity ") will be something quite different from the marginal product in the technological sense, and unlike the latter, it will not be a derivative of a technological function alone but will depend on the whole system of relationships. Further, owing to the prevailing attitude to uncertainty, it would not even be correct to say that " profit-maximising " will involve adding to investment per man until the marginal increment in anticipated profits, discounted at the ruling rate of interest or at some " assumed " rate of profit becomes equal to the marginal addition to investment. Whenever the desire to recover the cost of investment within a certain number of years—owing to the greater uncertainty of the more distant future—becomes the operative restriction (as is assumed in equation (4)), investment per man will be cut short before this marginal condition is satisfied.

The inequality (3) together with equation (4) enables us to specify an investment function in terms of the parameters of the system which determine both n_t and i_t without regard to the relationship between the expected rate of profit on investment and the rate of interest. In previous " Keynesian " models the existence of an independent investment function was closely tied to the postulate of some relationship between the " marginal efficiency " of investment and—an independently determined—rate of interest. This was a source of difficulty, since it either caused such models to be " over-determined "[1] or else it required the postulate that the capital/output ratio (or the amount of investment per worker) itself varied with the excess of the rate of profit over the money rate of interest[2]. The weakness of this latter approach has been that it assigned too much importance to the rate of interest. So long as one could assume that the rate of interest was a constant, determined by some psychological minimum (the " pure " liquidity preference of Keynesian theory), this did not matter very much. But it was unsatisfactory to rely on the *excess* of the rate of profit over the rate of interest as an important element—determining the chosen capital/output ratio and through that, the other variables—considering that this excess is under the control of the monetary authorities; if the authorities were to follow a policy of keeping the money rate of interest in some constant relationship to the rate of profit—which they may be easily tempted to do—this would have endowed them with an importance in the general scheme of things which is quite contrary to common experience.

The present model, by contrast allows the money rate of interest to move up and down, without the slightest effect on investment decisions, provided such movements do not violate certain constraints.[3] This is in much better accord with the oft-repeated assertions of business men (both in the U.K. and the U.S.) that the rate of interest has *no* influence on their investment decisions at least as far as investment in fixed capital is concerned.

Finally there is the question how far the postulate of a " technical progress function " as specified in (2) implies some restraint on the *nature* of technological change. Every change in the rate of investment per worker implies a change in the extent to which new ideas (" innovations ") are actually exploited. Since the " capital saving " innovations—which increase the output/capital ratio as well as the output/labour ratio—are much more profitable to the entrepreneur than the " labour-saving " ones that yield the same rate of

[1] Cf. R. C. O. Matthews, " The Rate of Interest in Growth Models," *Oxford Economic Papers*, October 1960, pp. 249-268.

[2] Cf. Kaldor, " Capital Accumulation and Economic Growth," *op. cit.*, pp. 217.

[3] For it must still remain true, of course, that the expected rate of profit on (fixed) investment must exceed the rate of interest by more than some minimum compensation for the " illiquidity " or other risks.

increase in labour productivity, clearly the former are exploited first and the balance of technological change will appear more "capital-using" (all the less "capital-saving") the greater the rate of increase in investment per man. There is therefore always *some* rate of increase in investment per worker which allows output per man to grow at the same rate as investment per man and in that sense takes on the appearance of "neutral" technical progress; to assume that this rate of increase in investment per man remains unchanged over time implies also assuming that the relative importance of "capital saving" and "capital using" innovations in the total flow of innovations remains unchanged. To assume this is really implied in the assumption that the rate of technical progress is *constant*; since a growing incidence of "capital saving" innovations is the same thing as an upward drift in the technical progress function, and *vice versa*. Therefore the only sense in which the technical progress function postulates some "neutral" technical progress is the sense in which "unneutral" technical progress necessarily involves either a continuous acceleration or deceleration in the rate of increase in productivity for any given value of i/i.

The main "practical" conclusion for economic policy that emerges from this model is that any scheme leading to the accelerated retirement of old equipment (such as a tax on the use of obsolete plant and equipment) is bound to accelerate for a temporary period the rate of increase in output per head $\dot{y}/y$, since it will increase n_t (the number of workers "available" for new machines) and hence I_t; and will thus involve a reduction in p_t/y_t. A more permanent cure, however, requires stimulating the technical dynamism of the economy (*raising* the technical progress function) which is not only (or perhaps mainly) a matter of more scientific education and more expenditure on research, but of higher quality business management which is more alert in searching for technical improvements and less resistant to their introduction.

Cambridge.   NICHOLAS KALDOR.

JAMES A. MIRRLEES.

APPENDIX

We must enquire whether the solution of the equations for a state of steady growth is unique. Equation (25) is a linear equation for $e^{\gamma T}$ in terms of $\frac{1}{r}$; it can be represented on a diagram, with $\frac{1}{r}$ measured along one axis and $e^{\gamma T}$ along the other, by a straight line.

Equation (26), on the other hand, represents a curve of increasing slope (as shown in the diagram). The curve representing equation (26), BB', passes through the point $e^{\gamma T} = 1$, $\frac{1}{r} = 0$; AA', which represents equation (25), has $e^{\gamma T} < 1$ when $\frac{1}{r} = 0$.

A NEW MODEL OF ECONOMIC GROWTH

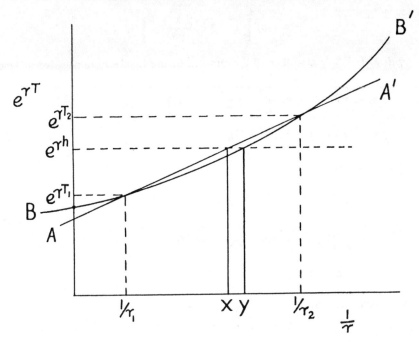

We shall prove that (1) AA', in fact cuts BB', and cuts it in two points, to which correspond the values r_1 and r_2 of r, and T_1 and T_2 of T; (2) $T_1 < h$, so that this case is in fact impossible (for entrepreneurs will make losses). It follows that there is a single possible steady growth state.

(1) To prove that AA' does not fail to cut BB', we show that there are points of BB' lying *below* AA'. Let x be the value of $\dfrac{1}{r}$ corresponding to $T = h$ on the curve AA' (*i.e.*, found by solving equation (25)); and let y be the value of $\dfrac{1}{r}$ corresponding to $T = h$ on the curve BB' (i.e., found by solving equation (26)).

Then

$$\gamma x = e^{\gamma h}\left[1 - \frac{h(\gamma + \lambda + \delta)}{s}\right] + \frac{h(\gamma + \lambda + \delta)}{s}\cdot\frac{e^{\gamma h} - 1}{\gamma h} - 1$$

$$= e^{\gamma h} - 1 - \frac{(\gamma + \lambda + \delta)}{\gamma s}[\gamma h \cdot e^{\gamma h} - e^{\gamma h} + 1]$$

$$= \gamma h + \tfrac{1}{2}(\gamma h)^2 + \tfrac{1}{6}(\gamma h)^3 + \ldots$$

$$\quad - \frac{\gamma + \lambda + \delta}{\gamma s}[\tfrac{1}{2}(\gamma h)^2 + \tfrac{1}{3}(\gamma h)^3 + \tfrac{1}{8}(\gamma h)^4 + \ldots]$$

$$= \gamma h + \tfrac{1}{2}(\gamma h)^2\left[1 - \frac{\gamma + \lambda + \delta}{\gamma s}\right] + \tfrac{1}{6}(\gamma h)^3\left[1 - 2\frac{\gamma + \lambda + \delta}{\gamma s}\right]$$

$$+ \tfrac{1}{24} (\gamma h)^4 \left[1 - 3 \frac{\gamma + \lambda + \delta}{\gamma s} \right] + \ldots$$

Clearly $\gamma + \lambda + \delta > \gamma s$, so that all the terms in square brackets are negative. Hence:

$$\gamma x < \gamma h - \tfrac{1}{2}(\gamma h)^2 \left[\frac{\gamma + \lambda + \delta}{\gamma s} - 1 \right],$$

so that $\quad \gamma x < \gamma h - \tfrac{1}{2} \gamma h^2 . (\lambda + \delta),$ \hfill (28)

since $s \leqq 1$.

Also, $\gamma y \;=\; \dfrac{\gamma}{\lambda + \delta} (\lambda + \delta) y = \dfrac{\gamma}{\lambda + \delta} [1 - e^{-(\lambda + \delta)h}]$

$$> \dfrac{\gamma}{\lambda + \delta} [(\lambda + \delta)h - \tfrac{1}{2}(\lambda + \delta)^2 h^2]$$

$$= \gamma h - \tfrac{1}{2} \gamma h^2 (\lambda + \delta),$$

which, as we have just shown, $> \gamma x$.

Hence $y > x$;

which is to say, that when $T = h$, the curve BB' lies to the right of AA'. Hence AA' meets BB'; for AA' cuts the $e^{\gamma T}$-axis below BB', and BB' eventually rises above AA'.

(2) It also follows from the fact that BB' lies to the right of AA' when $T = h$ that one of the points at which AA' and BB' cut has $t < h$; i.e., $T_1 < h$. Thus only T_2 (which is $> h$) is a possible value for T.

What we have shown is that there exists a single possible solution to our equations for the state of steady growth at rate γ. [The case $\lambda + \delta = 0$ follows in the same way; from (28), $\gamma x < \gamma h$; and $h = y$ in this case.]

[9]

THE LIMITATIONS OF ECONOMIC GROWTH MODELS

CRITICAL REMARKS ON SOME ASPECTS OF MR. KALDOR'S MODEL

Modern growth theory has come of age. When Sir Roy Harrod in 1939 published his famous article, "An Essay in Dynamic Theory"[1], it had a startling (though—because of the —warsomewhat delayed) effect on a professional world which had been completely absorbed by considering the theoretical and practical aspects of a short-run Keynesian model. To be reminded that the successful achievement of full employment of labour and capital in one period has important implications for the full employment problem in the next period (if these periods are taken as longer intervals) was very important indeed. At this stage of economic growth theory it was quite sufficient to work with a few rough aggregates and to show what the logical connections between them have to be, if uninterrupted full employment growth is to be established in a simple model of a competitive capitalist economy.

These early growth models and many of the refinements that were later added did not aim at an explanation of the actual course of capitalist development[2]. This would not have been possible, in any case, since we do not know of any long period of full employment growth in private enterprise economies in times of peace and without massive government intervention. And a development with ups and downs yielding a certain arithmetical average rate of growth may obey rather different rules than a smoothly growing economy with

---

1. *Economic Journal*, March 1939.
2. "These theories (viz. those of Harrod and Domar), though often referred to as theories of growth, are, properly speaking, theories of the requirements of steady growth at full employment. They make no assertions with respect to the likely development of capital formation over time." See MOSES ABRAMOVITZ, "Economics of Growth", in *A Survey of Contemporary Theory*, Vol. II, edited by Bernard F. Haley (Homewood, Ill., 1952), p. 170, footnote.

the same rate of expansion[3]. What the theories did—and that was a very useful achievement indeed—was to draw the attention of economists to certain factors and influences which, while not very important in short-term considerations, must not be neglected when long-term problems are analysed.

As the theory of economic growth has expanded, it has tried more and more to give an account of the *actual* working of the economic system. But the nearer it tries to get towards a description of reality (rather than analysing the requirements for consistency between certain macro-economic aggregates under full employment conditions) the more it is hampered by the restrictions it acquired in the days of its childhood. These restrictions are:

(1) The limited number of the variables taken into account and the simplicity of their functional relationships. This is a perfectly justifiable procedure for the early stages of the theory when the stress is laid on pointing out certain important inter-relationships[4]. Niceties in detail or changes over longer periods do not matter in that context. But when a closer contact with reality is desired it is necessary to consider the influence of a wider circle of factors and to give the functional relationships a more concrete empirical content. That means that the beautiful simplicity and unity of the early growth models will have to be sacrificed.

(2) The neglect of historical, sociological and institutional factors. Modern growth theory is a child of Keynesian theory. It has shown how the fundamental concepts and relationships of Keynes' short-run model are affected by the accumulation of capital, the growth of population, technical progress, etc. But many of the historical and institutional factors which Keynes could neglect in his short-run picture (and which, therefore, do not appear in growth theory) cannot be regarded as invariable when we aim at a realistic theory of economic change stretching over longer periods. Some functions

---

3. People will behave rather differently in a room where temparatures vary between 0 and 40 degrees of Celsius than in a room with a constant temperature of 20 degrees, even if the long-run average is the same in both cases.

4. As Mr. Little puts it: "But growth and distribution theory have only recently again become fashionable with economists, and it may still be worth while to work out the consequences of all sorts of assumptions, even where these are outrageous..." I. M. D. LITTLE, "Classical Growth", *Oxford Economic Papers*, June 1957, p. 175.

which Keynes could take as constants will vary when we deal with longer spans of time. I admit that the introduction of history and sociology as "endogenous variables" will make our functions less simple and less elegant. But it will prevent us from assuming reliable inter-relationships where, in fact, they do not exist.

(3) A serious handicap for a realistic development of growth theory is the starting assumption of an equilibrium growth at full employment level. As I said before, this was a legitimate *analytical* device in order to point out the necessary interrelationships between different economic categories under conditions of growth. When we try to fit growth theory to the task of explaining *actual* growth, the initial assumption of a smoothly growing full employment economy as some sort of "equilibrium" is an impediment which distracts our attention from the actual mechanism of economic expansion and the factors influencing it.

In the following pages I want to illustrate these limitations of modern growth theory by discussing some aspects of Mr. Kaldor's growth model[5]. In choosing Kaldor's essay I do not want to suggest that his model is in any way inferior to other examples in this field. On the contrary; I regard Kaldor's article as a particularly stimulating and well argued piece of research. But just because he pushes the frontiers of growth theory so ambitiously outward, the limitations of the theory become more clearly visible.

I do not intend to discuss Kaldor's theory point by point. I shall deal only with some of its aspects. I must also refrain from summarising all the relevant details of the theory. The reader of this article is expected to have read Kaldor's essay. If he has not, he is strongly recommended to do so.

1. *The Technical Progress Function*

Kaldor's model rests basically on three pillars: a saving function, an investment function, and a technical progress function[6]. I shall deal

---

5. NICHOLAS KALDOR, "A Model of Economic Growth", *Economic Journal*, December 1957, pp. 591–624.

6. The problem of population growth is introduced after the working of the model has been described for a constant population. I shall restrict my remarks to the constant population model.

with the first and third of these functions. This does not mean that no problems of empirical relevancy arise in connection with the investment function. But anything that could be said in this respect would apply to almost any general investment function. Kaldor's solution—he makes long-run investment dependent on turnover and changes in the rate of profit on capital—is certainly not inferior to other assumptions in this field and superior to some of them[7].

Newer ground is broken with the technical progress function. In a short-run Keynesian model technical progress can be safely neglected. Output is simply a function of employment. But when we allow the capital stock to grow significantly, we deal with longer periods in which technical progress will also play its part. Technical progress has often proved as a rather untractable factor in growth theories, since its course seems less amenable to definite abstract formulations than some of the traditional economic relationships. One can, of course, leave it outside the economic framework and regard it as an exogenous variable. This is, however, not very satisfactory from the point of view of both theoretical perfection and practical application.

Kaldor takes the ambitious step of making technical progress an essential element in his theoretical structure. But to keep this structure manageable and determinate within the traditional frame of modern growth theory he has to adopt a very simplified and, it seems to me, rather peculiar technical progress function.

Its main feature is that it establishes a definite link between capital investment and technical progress. There is a steady flow of new ideas, and the rate of investment determines in a unique way how and to what extent these inventions are used. Technical progress, instead of being a separate (endogenous or exogenous) factor influencing the growth of income over and above the application of capital, becomes fused with capital investment into one single re-

---

7. I would, however, take exception to one argument which Kaldor advances in favour of his assumptions. At the end of footnote 2 on p. 601 he points out that his investment function is consistent with a stable equilibrium of steady growth while a certain competing formulation is not. Since the existence of a stable equilibrium of steady growth (in an unregulated market economy) has never been proved, the convenience of a function for such a steady growth model can hardly tell us anything about its realistic quality.

LIMITATIONS OF ECONOMIC GROWTH MODELS

lationship. The form of the relationship is given by Kaldor in Figure 1 of his article, which is reproduced below. C_t and O_t represent the capital per worker and the annual output per worker at time t, so that the abscissa represents the annual percentage growth in capital per worker, and the ordinate the annual percentage growth in output per man. (With a constant population and full employment the diagram also represents the relationship between growth rates in total capital and total output.) The TT' curve represents the link between capital growth and income growth with the technical progress built in uniquely into the investment process. A certain amount of technical progress is assumed to take place independently of new capital investment. That is the reason why the TT' curve starts above the origin. The height of the curve will depend on the inventiveness of a community, but otherwise a certain constancy in the flow of new ideas is assumed.

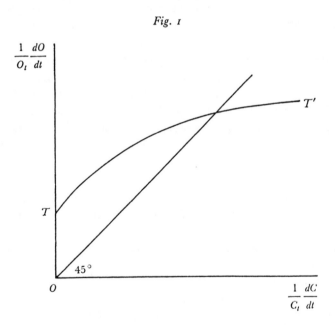

Fig. 1

The relationship between the growth rates of capital and output determines the course of the capital-output ratio. If output grows at a quicker rate than capital, the capital-output ratio will decline and vice versa. Consequently, the capital-output ratio will decline as long as the TT' curve lies above a line drawn from the origin at an angle of 45 degrees (representing equal growth rates for capital and output), and will increase when TT' falls below that line.

To have such a compact theory of technical progress and capital investment is a great boon, if one is on the look-out for a comprehensive theory of economic growth. It permits us to concentrate our attention on the investment process pure and simple without having to worry which different forms it may take and what different consequences it may have with regard to output. As Kaldor puts it: "The recognition of the existence of a functional relationship between the proportionate growth in capital and the annual proportionate growth in productivity shows the futility of regarding the movements in the capital-output ratio as dependent upon the technical character of the stream of inventions—according as they are predominantly 'labour-saving' or 'capital-saving' in character"[8].

The only trouble with this statement is that the existence of the said functional relationship has not yet been "recognised", if we mean by "recognised" empirically tested. This relationship is a very ingenious assumption, but it is at present not more than an assumption, and a highly simplified one at that. Nor does it away with the distinction between "labour-saving" and "capital-saving" inventions. The case is rather that Kaldor has built some very special assumptions about capital-saving and labour-saving innovations into his model which result in his single-valued relationship between the capital-output ratio and net investment.

Kaldor assumes that there are some output-increasing innovations introduced all the time quite independently of any capital investment. That is, he assumes a constant flow and introduction of capital-saving devices. This gives us right from the start (i.e. before any investment takes place) an influence which makes for a fall in the capital-output ratio. As soon as investment sets in it is necessarily of a labour-saving type, since Kaldor assumes continuous full employment so that (with a constant population) there are no reserves of man-power and none must be created. Since, additionally, no spectacular new techniques are introduced, the increasing application of labour-saving devices with growing investment will lead to diminishing returns to capital and a rising capital-output ratio. The

8. *Op. cit.*, p. 597.

LIMITATIONS OF ECONOMIC GROWTH MODELS 573

more investment grows, the more this rising tendency will absorb the initial reduction in the capital-output ratio until—at a certain rate of investment—the ratio begins to surpass the level attained in the previous period[9].

Kaldor has thus not done away with the ticklish problem of labour-saving and capital-saving inventions. He has only assumed a certain definite frame for them by the shape of his TT' function and by stipulating uninterrupted full employment. But is this not a rather artificial picture? Do we not have in reality a considerable pool of technical knowledge and research opportunities on which the capital investor can draw?[10] According to the choice investors make we shall obtain different technical progress functions (TT' curves) and different "points of equilibrium" in Kaldor's system[11]. This does, of course, presume that there are economic factors pulling and pushing investors into different choices. Kaldor's assumptions leave no room for such factors. Two of his assumptions help to escape this problem of varying technical forms of given quantities (or rates) of investment.

The first is the assumption of uninterrupted full employment growth. In such a state (and with a constant population) every given increase in capital yields only one possible capital-labour ratio and therefore a unique degree of "labour-savingness". This leaves (given the known technical methods) only one profitable policy open to the investor[12]: to maximise output *over the given number of workers*. Choices with regard to "capital-saving" and "labour-saving" inventions necessarily lose their meaning, if variations in labour supply are

---

9. For a fuller treatment of this point see the Appendix (pp. 584–586). See also FERDINAND GRÜNIG, "Substitution und technischer Fortschritt im gesamtwirtschaftlichen Wachstumsprozess", *Konjunkturpolitik*, No. 1, 1959, particularly pp. 3–5.

10. "There are many alternative production methods: (1) there are choices among alternative processes; (2) there are choices among variants within processes; (3) there are choices among varieties and grades of a given commodity produced; (4) there are choices among forms of plant or process expansion." H. B. MALMGREN, "What Conclusions are to be Drawn from Empirical Cost Data?", *Journal of Industrial Economics*, March 1959, pp. 136–144.

11. Kaldor admits the possibility of shifts in the TT' curve in times when there is a burst of new inventions or when ideas dry up (p. 598). But for normal times a single and fairly stable TT' curve is assumed.

12. Or rather to the average result of total investment activity.

ruled out and capital accumulation becomes the only variable. As soon as we permit changes in employment and various possible technical combinations between (a given quantity) of capital and labour the uniqueness of the TT' function vanishes. The same amount of capital investment can be combined with different amounts of labour and this will yield different rates of output growth and different capital-output ratios[13].

To this one can, of course, object that it is no use arguing this way, since Kaldor specifically excludes less-than-full-employment situations. But Kaldor quite obviously did not just want to discuss logical relationships within *some* model of full employment; he was out to build a long-term reference model for actual capitalist economies. The aforementioned objection will, therefore, not suffice. If employment variations *do* play a part and investment *can* create or absorb unemployment, then technical development and economic growth may take a different course from that indicated by a model of permanent full employment. If Kaldor excludes unemployment, because "an equilibrium of steady growth is inconsistent with underemployment equilibrium" (p. 594), he argues again in terms of the "traditional" growth models which *presuppose* an equilibrium of steady growth. Experience has, however, shown that such an equilibrium does not exist in free-market economies. Long-term growth is

---

13. Perhaps the gist of the argument can be put this way. (For the sake of simplicity we shall state our argument in terms of absolute quantities rather than in terms of growth rates.)

The capital-output ratio can be expressed as follows:

$$\frac{K}{Y} = \frac{K}{W} \cdot \frac{W}{Y}$$

where K, Y, W are real capital, real output and the number of workers respectively.

Now, if we assume W fixed (at full-employment level) and techniques of production determined by the amount of capital per worker (so that Y is a unique function of K/W), then K/Y is uniquely determined by K/W or simply by K. In other words, a certain amount of *absolute* capital investment will strictly determine the size of the additional output and the capital-output ratio. If we let W vary, Y will still depend on K/W (technical knowledge given) and so will K/Y. But the same *absolute amount* of capital investment will not necessarily be linked with a given amount of W so that Y and K/Y are not uniquely determined by K.

LIMITATIONS OF ECONOMIC GROWTH MODELS 575

the outcome of *un*steady developments which follow rules differing from those of a full employment model.

The objection to Kaldor's unique technical progress (and capital-output) function does, by the way, also hold if we have the kind of full employment we have known since the war. If there is a public sector absorbing and releasing workers in accordance with fluctuations in the private sector, investment in the private sector will still be able to combine capital with a greater or smaller number of workers, to be more "labour-saving" or more "capital-saving"[14]. In this case, too, we can have a multitude of TT' curves rather than a single one.

There is, however, still another point in Kaldor's assumptions by which he tries to get rid of the complexities introduced by the problem of different technical combinations. He regards the choice of "techniques" as independent of changes in the share of profits and wages and of changes in the rate of profit and makes it "entirely a matter of the relative prices of different types of capital goods, which can be assumed to alter with the accumulation of capital and the progress of techniques in the capital-goods making industries" (p. 603). As an illustration Kaldor presents us with the example of a developed and an underdeveloped country, the first one using bulldozers and the second one shovels. The difference in techniques he explains by the relatively lower prices of bulldozers (in terms of shovels) in the developed country. The obvious argument that the underdeveloped country could obtain the same relative prices through international trade he tries to brush aside (in footnote 1 on p. 603) by pointing out that there may be no market for the inferior capital goods in the developed country. But this answer is not very convincing: (1) If it were true that only relative prices of capital goods (and not of labour) count, why should there be no market for relatively cheap shovels in the developed country?[15]. (2) Even if the

14. I assume that Kaldor's technical progress and investment functions apply only to the private sector. A government pledged to full employment will necessarily have to adopt different criteria.

15. If we allow wage and profit levels to enter the picture the preference for bulldozers becomes easily understandable.

Kaldor's assumption also leaves no room for the hypothesis that the development of highly mechanistic methods of production in 19th century America was due to a high supply price of labour (which in turn was closely connected with the availability of free or cheap land).

underdeveloped country imports *all* its capital goods and is thus confronted with exactly the same price relations for capital goods as the developed country, is it not likely—with cheap labour available—to use shovels more often?

Kaldor does not completely deny the influence of wage and profit changes on the choice of techniques, but he tries to belittle this effect and he cuts it out completely when he comes to the construction of his model. In this way the uniqueness of his technical progress function is secured. It depends solely on the rate of investment and establishes an unequivocal link between (full employment) growth rates of investment and growth rates of output. When in the long run the economic forces have established an equilibrium between these two growth rates, the economy (output and capital) will grow at a definite rate which is uniquely determined by the coefficients of the technical progress function. This is Kaldor's equilibrium rate of growth G, where

$$G = \frac{\alpha''}{1-\beta''} = \gamma''$$

(α'' and β'' being the coefficients of the technical progress function).

From what has been said before it will be clear what, in my opinion, the shortcomings of this formulation are. By *assuming* a steady full employment growth and by linking the investment process to one single technical progress function, a basic, technically determined equilibrium rate of growth is established to which other economic variables (e.g. savings) have to adjust. If we, however, admit that over longer periods employment in the private sector can fluctuate and that the form of investment will be influenced by wage-profit relationships, then there will be no unique (technical) relationship between capital growth and output growth but several possibilities (a whole family of TT' curves). The long-term rate of growth emerging from the events in many short-run periods (shall we call it the "equilibrium rate"?) is not a unique technically determined quantity, setting the frame to which other economic variables passively adjust. It will itself be influenced by the way in which this adjustment takes place[16]. Several "equilibrium" rates of growth

16. We can imagine, for instance, that investment and growth will take different forms in a society where the wage share is high and the saving propensity of workers is low, as compared with a society where the wage share is low. In the

become possible. Of course, some technical possibilities are so obvious and some technical limitations so pervasive that the differences between these rates (for a given community) will not be very great. But even small differences in growth rates can have significant repercussions.

2. The Distribution Theory[17]

With the long-term equilibrium rate of growth determined by his technical progress function Kaldor can round off his model by showing how investment and savings adjust to this growth rate. This yields him an interesting distribution theory for a growing economy, the elements of which he had already developed in an earlier paper[18]. As I mentioned before, I shall not deal with the investment function but shall restrict myself mainly to the savings function. This will also

former consumption will be high, investment will be comparatively small and mainly labour-saving (which in turn may influence the level and share of wages), income will grow slowly but perhaps smoothly. In the latter consumption will be low, income and investment will grow at high rates in periods of expansion, but be exposed to greater disturbances and set-backs. These examples are, of course, pretty far removed from Kaldor's assumptions, but they are mentioned in order to indicate how these assumptions are to be relaxed when we try to get nearer to actual growth.

17. Since this was written Professor Bombach has published an interesting article which to a certain extent covers a similar field as Kaldor's essay (GOTTFRIED BOMBACH, "Preisstabilität, wirtschaftliches Wachstum und Einkommensverteilung", *Schweizerische Zeitschrift für Volkswirtschaft und Statistik*, März 1959, S. 1–20). Some of my remarks with regard to Kaldor's theory of distribution could—with certain minor changes—also be applied to some aspects of Bombach's views. His theory is, however, less open to the criticism raised in this article, (1) because his analysis is more short-term than Kaldor's so that the assumption of constancy in the behavioural parameters is more justified, and (2) because Bombach himself stresses that his model is only meant to serve as a "Denkschema" for analysing various possible situations and not as the basis for econometric verification.

18. N. KALDOR, "Alternative Theories of Distribution", *Review of Economic Studies*, Vol. XXIII (1956), No. 2. See particularly pp. 94–100. Much of what is said in the present article is also of relevance in connection with this earlier essay of Kaldor.

Since writing this paper I have come across a short critical appreciation of this article by Kaldor: SIDNEY WEINTRAUB, *An Approach to the Theory of Income Distribution* (Philadelphia 1958), Appendix to Chap. 5 (pp. 104–107). In some points Weintraub's remarks coincide with my own observations.

enable me to say some words about Kaldor's new (or "Keynesian") distribution theory.

In equilibrium "desired" investment will not only be geared to the "equilibrium" rate of growth, savings will also equal "desired" investment. In Keynes' system the adjustment of savings to investment is achieved through changes in income and employment, a certain saving propensity being assumed. This possibility is not open to Kaldor, since he assumes full employment and can therefore not admit adjustments via the employment (and output) mechanism. The place of varying employment with a given average saving propensity is taken in his model by variations in the income distribution and a split of the average saving propensity into a wage-earners' and a profit-earners' propensity. Reduced to linearity, and calling savings S, profits P, and income Y (all in real terms), Kaldor's saving function is of the form

$$S_t = \alpha P_t + \beta (Y_t - P_t) \quad 1 > \alpha > \beta \geqslant 0$$

Here α is the saving propensity of profit earners and β the saving propensity of all other income earners (wage and salary earners). Since α can be assumed to be greater than β, any shift in shares from wages to profits will increase savings and vice versa. We thus get a savings schedule dependent on income *shares* which together with the investment schedule will yield the savings-investment equilibrium together with an equilibrium of income distribution (see Fig. 2)[19].

That Kaldor deals with two separate propensities to save is definitely a step forward in comparison to the simpler notion of a single propensity to save which does not allow for the effects of changes in the distribution of incomes. But let us be clear that the gain in *realism* is small. Kaldor introduces his two propensities mainly for *analytical* reasons. He needs them in order to be able to draw up a savings schedule in a model from which he has banned all lapses from full employment.

When we deal with the (Keynesian) short run where changes in employment are probably of more import than changes in distri-

19. This diagram has to be distinguished from the similar "Keynesian" diagram (see, for instance, L. R. KLEIN, *The Keynesian Revolution*, New York 1947, p. 178, Fig. 11). In the Keynesian diagram we find on the abscissa Y and on the ordinate I and S.

bution, the use of a single saving propensity may be sufficient as a first approach. Similarly, this simplified assumption may be sufficient for a long-term model which wants to show the place of saving in the interplay of forces making for smooth growth. But if we want to grapple more realistically with long-term tendencies (and this is obviously Kaldor's aim) this simple assumption is no longer adequate, not even as a first approach; nor does the mere division of the single propensity into two meet the problem. What now becomes the main question (a question that does not matter in the short run) is the *stability* of the saving propensities.

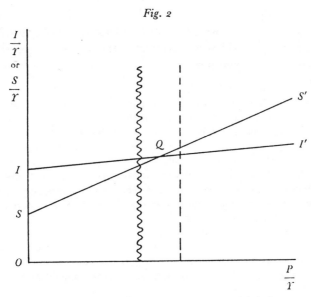

Fig. 2

In Kaldor's system α and β are constants which have a decisive influence on the division of income between profits and wages[20]. This makes the distribution of income the unique result of certain independent psychological and institutional[21] factors. This I regard as inadmissible. α and β, the two saving propensities, cannot be

---

20. "For the level of profits has to be such as to induce a rate of investment that is just equal to the rate of savings forthcoming at that particular distribution of income." "A Model", *op. cit.*, p. 606.

21. KALDOR mentions the importance of company saving. "Alternative Theories", *op. cit.*, p. 95, footnote 1.

580   KURT W. ROTHSCHILD

regarded as constant or even as independent variables in longer-term considerations[22]. They will be influenced by the way in which short-period disequilibria in saving and investment plans (which Kaldor admits into his system) have been resolved, *by the way in which the present income distribution was reached*. Whether in inflationary periods profits or wages push ahead more rapidly, whether prices are "administered" or free, what stratagems the trade unions apply, all this and many things besides will influence what sort of α and β will be combined with a certain income level and income distribution[23]. More than that: the α that has been established (the consumption habits of the capitalists) will have repercussions on β and possibly vice versa. In short, there are a number of historical and sociological factors (bargaining power, militancy of trade unions, government intervention, etc.) which will influence the saving propensities and the distribution of incomes[24]. They must not be neglected when we deal with long periods.

22. KENNETH BOULDING, who about ten years ago constructed a macro-economic model of income distribution which has some points of similarity with Kaldor's theory, recognised this fact. On p. 269 of his *A Reconstruction of Economics* (New York 1950) he writes: "The dynamics of all these models is likely to be complicated by the dynamic instability of the transfer factor, and even of the consumption and investment functions themselves. They are therefore to be taken as illustrative rather than definitive pictures of the economic system, and yield us perhaps more insight than knowledge. They serve to illustrate, however, the complexities of the real world."

23. The idea that the struggle for wages may influence the long-term saving and consumption habits of entrepreneurs was expressed more than thirty years ago by MAURICE DOBB in the chapter on Bargaining-Power in his *Wages* (London and Cambridge, 1928). The following quotation gives a good idea of the views expressed there:

"...it seems logical to conclude that the level of income of yesterday, developing certain customary standards which come to be regarded as 'normal', influences to-day's supply-curve of capital as much as it influences the supply-curve of labour. The one no more than the other can be regarded as an independent variable; and the old theory, formulated as a group of equations, only remains consistent by assuming certain quantities as given (or as 'constants') which can in practice be influenced by custom and hence by arbitrary 'interference' such as that of collective bargaining or legislative action." (p. 103.)

24. Modern consumption theories pay increasing attention to historical and sociological factors. They appear, for instance, in Duesenberry's and Modigliani's models, where income peaks reached in the past and relative status in the income scale influence the propensity to save.

In terms of Kaldor's model this means that there is not a unique S_t/Y_t related to a given P_t/Y_t. Different rates of saving may be compatible with a given share of profits. In Figure 2 there will be not just one but several SS' curves. Which one will apply and what the "equilibrium" point of saving and investment will be, will depend on the path by which this point is reached[25]. The different points will not yield widely differing solutions: in a capitalist economy which is to function, the shares of wages and profits can hardly be dramatically altered. But the differences will be sufficiently important to make the assumption of a singular relationship between savings and the distribution of incomes unpracticable.

The points raised in this and in the previous section help to show the insufficiency of a closed growth model which tries to restrict itself to a few simple economic variables and relationships. Drawing together the equilibrium conditions from his technical progress, investment, and savings functions Kaldor obtains the following formula for the "equilibrium" share of profits to income (giving the equilibrium distribution of income in a steadily growing full employment economy with constant population):

$$\frac{P}{Y} = \frac{\gamma'' \dfrac{K}{Y} - \beta}{\alpha - \beta}$$

(where K is real capital). Here γ'' is given by the technical progress function, K/Y by the investment function, and α and β are the two propensities to save. As I have tried to show, at least γ'', α, and β cannot be regarded as constants in a long-term model, nor can they be regarded as independent of the actual course of the left-hand side of

---

25. A simple artificial example may illustrate this. Let us assume an upper class with a high income share and a high propensity to consume. Their consumption may stimulate prestige spending among the wage and salary earners so that we may have a small α and a negligible β. A more equal distribution of incomes (achieved in one way or other) may *raise* α, if the property-owning classes want to maintain their capital accumulation rather than their consumption *growth*, and the greater equality in consumption may also reduce prestige spending and so raise β. In the end we may have the same amount of saving though the relative shares have changed.

the equation (the distribution side)[26]. To explain the income distribution (and other aspects of the growing economy) one has, therefore, to go beyond the circle of variables and relationships used so far, and to consider how they themselves are changed in the course of economic developement.

3. *The Restricting Conditions*

In this context a further point in Kaldor's model is worth mentioning, because it helps to illustrate the influence of the historical factor.

The working of Kaldor's model is subject to two restrictions, viz. (1) that profits should not be greater than the surplus available after the labour force has been paid a subsistence wage-bill, and (2) that profits are higher than the minimum required to secure a margin of profit over turnover below which entrepreneurs would not reduce prices, irrespective of the state of demand. Now, here again "subsistence wages" and "minimum profit margins" are not absolute but historically grown quantities. What is regarded as a subsistence wage or a minimum profit will largely depend on what level of wages and profits wage and profit earners have been able to cut out for themselves in the past. The room for smooth changes in income distribution (at full employment) will therefore probably be much smaller than Kaldor indicates by the waved and dotted lines in his Figure 2. The frontiers may look more like the lines I have drawn in my Figure 2 (p. 579). This means that a full employment adjustment via a redistribution of incomes will soon come to an end either because of the resistance of workers against a cut in real incomes (or even in real income *growth*) or of profit earners against a fall in profit margins. In the second case the result will be unemployment (through oversaving), in the first case we may also get unemployment, if employers want to break the wage front of the workers, or there will be a shift from investment to consumption (which may actually stabilize the system). These limitations show that the assumption of an equilibrium of steady full employment growth is unlikely to be fulfilled in an unregulated capitalist economy.

26. That some dependence may exist and may disturb the working of his model is—as far as the investment side is concerned—admitted by KALDOR. See his "Alternative Theories", *op. cit.*, p. 98. The notation in this article differs from the one adopted in the "Model" and used here.

LIMITATIONS OF ECONOMIC GROWTH MODELS 583

The historical element in wage and profit levels is fully recognised by Kaldor when he deals in a final section with short-period developments and fluctuations. But he assumes that "long-term investment requirements and saving propensities are the underlying factors which set the standard around which these customary levels are formed, and which are responsible for the gradual change of these levels in any particular economy, or for differences as between different economies"[27]. This view seems to me to be the result of an attempt to find a way back from the modern growth models to reality. But I doubt that this is a realistic approach. The long-term investment requirements and saving propensities are the outcome of the many political and sociological pulls and pushes in the many short periods which make up the long. To be sure, these pulls and pushes take place in an economic environment which gives them only very restricted play. Economic growth models have displayed some of these restricting conditions. But this is no permanent substitute for the inclusion of a larger number of factors and influences which will give us a more realistic though less rounded picture of growth conditions.

4. Conclusion

Economic growth models of the modern type have served an important purpose. They have shown the logical relationships that must exist between different macro-economic aggregates, if an economy is to grow smoothly. In order to do this it was quite sufficient to erect the theory on a few simple assumptions and relationships. Though practical conclusions can be (and were) drawn from that theory, it was from its start not really designed to mirror actual growth in either developed or under-developed countries[28].

The attempt to bring growth theory into closer touch with

---

27. "A Model", *op. cit.*, p. 622.

28. It is typical that the plentiful literature on underdeveloped countries, with its more practical bent, has flowered rather independently of contemporary growth theory. In the view of ALBERT O. HIRSCHMAN "a model based on the propensity to save and on the capital-output ratio is bound to be far less useful in underdeveloped than in advanced economies... It does not really tell us much about the key mechanisms through which economic progress gets under way and is carried forward in a backward environment". *The Strategy of Economic Development*, New Haven 1958, pp. 32/33.

reality soon reveals that the special assumptions on which it builds and which invest it with a rounded completeness are too limited. When we deal with periods stretching over several years or even decades, many of the "given relationships" that were taken over from short-period economics can no longer be regarded as "given". They are moulded by other economic and so-called "extra-economic" influences which are themselves essential parts of the long-term development process. There must be—now that a large part of the important spade work of the young growth theory has been achieved by pioneers like Harrod, Domar, Fellner, Kaldor, Robinson, and others—a greater readiness to admit these "disturbing" factors into the discipline. This does not mean that sensational new developments are the order of the day. Classical growth theory from Malthus to Marx has worked with very definite assumptions with regard to social and sociological influences. Marx, in particular, has shown a mastership in combining economic and sociological development analysis, which has hardly been equalled till to this day. An extension of current growth analysis in these directions will help economic theory to be of more direct use to economic policy[29].

Austrian Institute of Economic Research, Vienna (Austria)　　　　KURT W. ROTHSCHILD

APPENDIX

Kaldor's "Technical Progress Function" takes the following simplified (linear) form in his model (see p. 604/5):

$$\frac{Y_{t+1} - Y_t}{Y_t} = \alpha'' + \beta'' \frac{I_t}{K_t}$$

Y_t, I_t, and K_t are real income, investment and capital in the period t.

It is assumed that $\alpha'' > 0$ and $1 > \beta'' > 0$. But the assumption $\alpha'' > 0$ means that all the time capital-saving inventions are applied (quite independently from capital investment), and the assumption $1 > \beta'' > 0$ means that all the investment (with population constant and employment full) is of the labour-saving type without technical invention preventing diminishing returns to capital. The

---

29. See E. RONALD WALKER, *From Economic Theory to Economic Policy*, Chicago 1943.

LIMITATIONS OF ECONOMIC GROWTH MODELS

result is that a very special course for the capital-output ratio is mapped out. We can see this quite easily by slightly reshaping Kaldor's formula.

$$\frac{Y_{t+1}-Y_t}{Y_t} = \alpha'' + \beta'' \frac{I_t}{K_t}$$

or

$$\frac{\Delta Y}{Y} = \alpha'' + \beta'' \frac{\Delta K}{K} \qquad (1)$$

Taking reciprocals of (1), we get

$$\frac{Y}{\Delta Y} = \frac{K}{\alpha'' K + \beta'' \Delta K}$$

or

$$\alpha'' \frac{K}{\Delta Y} + \beta'' \frac{\Delta K}{\Delta Y} = \frac{K}{Y}$$

Denoting the capital-output ratio K/Y by R, and the marginal capital-output ratio $\Delta K/\Delta Y$ by ΔR, we can write

$$\beta'' \Delta R = R - \alpha'' \frac{K}{\Delta Y}$$

and

$$\Delta R = \frac{1}{\beta''} R - \frac{\alpha''}{\beta''} \frac{K}{\Delta Y}$$

As long as ΔY is small, ΔR will be smaller than R so that the average capital-output ratio will fall. But as ΔY increases (with increasing I) ΔR will approach the first term, and since $\beta'' < 1$, ΔR will become greater than R and the average capital-output ratio will increase.

If we leave Kaldor's special assumptions we easily get a model where the capital-output ratio is more flexible and less uniquely tied to the investment process. Let us, for instance, assume that there is no autonomous supply of capital-saving inventions ($\alpha'' = 0$), and that investment can be accompanied by the invention of capital-saving methods so that (over a certain range) returns to capital can be increasing as well as diminishing (no restrictions on β'' except that it is > 0). In this case Kaldor's technical progress function reduces to

$$\frac{Y_{t+1}-Y_t}{Y_t} = \beta'' \frac{I_t}{K_t}$$

and the capital-output ratio can rise ($\beta'' < 1$) or fall ($\beta'' > 1$) with rising investment *right from the beginning of new investment.*

$$\frac{Y_{t+1}-Y_t}{Y_t} = \beta'' \frac{I_t}{K_t}$$

$$\frac{\Delta Y}{Y} = \beta'' \frac{\Delta K}{K}$$

$$\frac{\Delta Y}{\Delta K} = \beta'' \frac{Y}{K}$$

$$\frac{\Delta K}{\Delta Y} = \frac{1}{\beta''} \frac{K}{Y}$$

$$\Delta R = \frac{1}{\beta''} R$$

If $\beta'' < 1$, the average capital-output ratio increases and vice versa for $\beta'' > 1$.

SUMMARY

In the past twenty years the theory of economic growth has experienced big advances. But the very attempt to push into new and wider regions has shown the limitations set by the assumptions and the framework of modern growth theory.

This theory grew out of the *short-term* Keynesian model as an attempt to find out the logical relationships that must exist between different macro-economic aggregates, if an economy is to grow smoothly in the *long run*. In order to do this it was quite sufficient to erect the theory on a few simple assumptions and relationships.

More recently, however, there has been a growing tendency to build on these foundations theoretical models of actual economic growth. A very advanced example of this type of work is Kaldor's "Model of Economic Growth". This model (and particularly the long-term theory of technical progress and income distribution contained in it) is used as a basis for discussing some of the limitations of current growth theory.

It is shown that with an approach to more realistic problems the special assumptions of the growth models used up till now become too narrow. When we deal with periods stretching over several years or even decades, many of the "given relationships" that were taken over from short-period economics can no longer be regarded as "given". They are moulded by other economic and so-called "extra-economic" influences which are themselves essential parts of the long-term development process. There must be a greater readiness to admit these "disturbing" factors into the discipline. This will give us perhaps a less rounded picture of economic growth, but what is lost in this direction will be gained in realism and relevancy.

[10]
Economic Growth and the Distributive Shares[1]

The analysis of the forces which determine the secular change in the relative shares of the national income distributed to the factors of production has a long history in economic thought, beginning with Ricardo who considered it the "principal problem of political economy." With the marginal revolution interest in the problem seemed to recede and except for such contributions as Rosa Luxemburg's book,[2] which was in the Marxist tradition, little appears to have been written apart from a paper by Cannan[3] and some remarks in Wicksell's *Lectures*.[4]

It was not until the work[5] of Professor J. R. Hicks in the 1930's that a neo-classical approach to the problem was formulated, in terms of the so-called "elasticity of substitution" between factors of production in producing output. A little later Mr. Kalecki presented his analysis[6] based on the concept of the "degree of monopoly." Recently Mr. Kaldor has contributed what he calls a Keynesian approach to the problem[7] since it is related to the "widow's cruse" theory of distribution appearing in the *Treatise on Money*. In this paper I shall attempt to combine the macroeconomic approach of Mr. Kaldor, who emphasizes the investment-income ratio as the major variable affecting the distributive shares with the neo-classical analysis of Professor Hicks, which runs in terms of factor proportions and production functions.

The rest of the paper is in five parts. In Part I the positions of Professor Hicks and Mr. Kaldor are outlined briefly. In Part II a rudimentary general equilibrium growth model is constructed which will serve as the analytical framework for the discussion of the determination of the secular change in the distributive shares in Parts III and IV. In Part V the analysis of Parts III and IV is related to the Hicks and Kaldor formulations and it is shown how the growth model of Part II can be extended by the incorporation of the Kaldor saving function.

---

[1] The author would like to gratefully acknowledge the encouragement and advice given to him in the preparation of this paper by Professor R. M. Solow. He is also grateful to Professor F. M. Westfield and to Messrs. C. F. Diaz and E. M. Foster for reading an earlier draft and suggesting various improvements. The author alone, of course, is responsible for remaining defects and any mistakes. The paper was written at the Massachusetts Institute of Technology, the author's stay there being made possible by a grant from the Ford Foundation for which he is very grateful.

[2] Rosa Luxemburg, *The Accumulation of Capital,* English translation, published by Yale University Press, New Haven, 1951.

[3] Edwin Cannan, "The Division of Income," *Quarterly Journal of Economics*, Vol. XIX, May 1904-05.

[4] Knut Wicksell, *Lectures on Political Economy*, English transaltion published by Routledge and Kegan Paul, London, 1934.

[5] J. R. Hicks, *The Theory of Wages*, MacMillan, London, 1932, Chapter VI ; and "Distribution and Economic Progress : A Revised Version," *Review of Economic Studies*, Vol. IV, No. 1, October, 1936.

[6] M. Kalecki, *Essays in the Theory of Economic Fluctuations*, George Allen and Unwin, London, 1939, Chapter I.

[7] N. Kaldor, "Alternative Theories of Distribution," *Review of Economic Studies*, Vol. XXIII, June, 1955-56.

I

In its original[1] formulation the "elasticity of substitution" approach of Professor Hicks was purely technological. The analysis runs as follows. Suppose that there is only one good, national income, which is produced under conditions of constant returns to scale by two factors of production, Labor and Capital. The factors are assumed to be substitutable for each other in producing any level of output. Diminishing returns are assumed when one factor is increased with the quantity of the other held fixed. Since the production function is homogeneous of the first degree any single isoquant can represent the entire family. A diagrammatic representation of the "elasticity of substitution," due originally to Mr. Lerner,[2] can then be made as follows.

Draw a vector from the origin to the representative isoquant which would indicate a certain Capital-Labor ratio. The slope of the tangent to the isoquant at the point where it is intersected by the ray from the origin represents the factor price ratio prevailing under conditions of perfect competition. As the vector from the origin is rotated the slope of the tangent keeps changing. A diagram can be constructed with the ratio of wages to the return on capital on the vertical axis and the Labor-Capital ratio on the other axis and the relationship between these two variables shown to be represented by a downward sloping curve. The elasticity of this curve is the "Elasticity of substitution." The area of the rectangle under the curve formed by picking any input ratio or factor-price ratio measures the ratio of the wage-bill to total profits. If this area remains constant, as it would if—and only if—the production function were Cobb-Douglas, the "elasticity of substitution" is said to be unity. If it is increased when the Labor-Capital ratio is increased the elasticity is greater than unity and if it is decreased, less than unity.

In terms of this formulation the long-run stability in the ratio of total wages to total profits noted in the industrial countries by several observers[3] can be explained, in view of the fact that the Labor-Capital ratio has been declining secularly, by either of two hypotheses. One is that the aggregate production function has the Cobb-Douglas property of unit-elasticity of substitution and that technological progress has been "neutral," and the other is that the elasticity of substitution has been different from unity but that technological change has been biased in such a way as to preserve constancy in the relative shares.[4]

The explanation in these terms thus seems to be purely technological. In his article cited above, however, Professor Hicks emphasizes that once more than one commodity is assumed to be produced demand conditions will play an important role in determining the relative shares, depending upon the degree to which optimal input ratios differ in the production of the various commodities. His analytical treatment of the matter, however, is more or less confined to a brief and obscure mathematical footnote.[5]

---

[1] *The Theory of Wages.*

[2] A. P. Lerner, "The Diagrammatic Representation of the Elasticity of Substitution," *Review of Economic Studies*, Vol. I, No. 1, 1933-34. For mathematical treatment see *The Theory of Wages*, Appendix II, and R. G. D. Allen, *Mathematical Analysis for Economists*, Macmillan, London.

[3] For references to the relevant literature and a critical analysis of the issues involved, see R. M. Solow, "A Skeptical Note on the Constancy of the Relative Shares," *American Economic Review*, Vol. XLIIII, No. 4, September, 1958.

[4] The latter view is taken by Professor Hicks himself. See *Theory of Wages*.

[5] See the article cited above, p. 8.

ECONOMIC GROWTH AND THE DISTRIBUTIVE SHARES

In Mr. Kaldor's macroeconomic theory the crucial variable affecting the distributive shares is the investment-income ratio. By the manipulation of the Keynesian accounting identities he arrives at the expression

$$\frac{P}{Y} = \frac{1}{(s_p - s_w)} \frac{I}{Y} - \frac{s_w}{s_p - s_w}$$

where P is total profits, Y is national income, I is investment and s_p and s_w are the propensities to save out of profits and wages respectively. The former is taken to be greater than the latter. The model operates at full employment and price level variations are the mechanism through which the profit-income and investment-income ratios are adjusted to each other.

Mr. Kaldor then makes the substitution

$$\frac{I}{Y} = \frac{\Delta Y}{Y} \cdot \frac{\Delta K}{\Delta Y}$$

where $\frac{\Delta Y}{Y}$ is the relative rate of growth of national income and $\frac{\Delta K}{\Delta Y}$ is the incremental capital-output ratio. $\frac{\Delta Y}{Y} \cdot \frac{\Delta K}{\Delta Y}$ is of course the left-hand side of the famous Harrodian equation $GC = S$. Since the Kaldor model operates at full employment $\frac{\Delta Y}{Y}$ in the equation is the "natural rate of growth" in Mr. Harrod's terminology and it is therefore determined exogenously by population growth and technological progress. The capital-output ratio is also an exogenous factor but the savings ratio is not. It is determined in the Kaldor model by the distribution of income between wages and profits and is given by

$$\frac{S}{Y} = (s_p - s_w) \frac{P}{Y} + s_w$$

which is obtained by dividing both sides of $S = s_p P + s_w (Y - P)$ by Y. Permanent maladjustments between GC and S are thus not possible in Mr. Kaldor's system since they are always brought into line by changes in income distribution.

Since $\frac{\Delta Y}{Y}$ is determined exogenously by population growth and technological progress and $\frac{\Delta K}{\Delta Y}$ is also given independently, it follows that the distribution of income can be regarded as the "dependent variable" and $\frac{I}{Y}$ as the "independent variable" since it has to change before the distributive shares can change. The interesting conclusion of Mr. Kaldor's analysis is that a faster rate of population growth or technological progress, since it raises $\frac{\Delta Y}{Y}$ and presumably leaves $\frac{\Delta K}{\Delta Y}$ unchanged, increases the share of profits. This is a much more definite result than would be provided by the marginal productivity theory where the answer would be that "it depends". One suspects that the difference might be due to Mr. Kaldor's assumption that technique is independently given. In the next three sections we shall attempt to construct a simple neo-classical general equilibrium model and hope that by the means of it will we be able to show how the Hicks and Kaldor theories are related to each other and each forms part of a more complete picture.

II

At some initial point of time the economy is assumed to be endowed with certain fixed quantities of Labor and Capital Goods, each of these being a perfectly homogeneous factor of production. We also assume that the services provided by these amounts of Labor and Capital Goods are perfectly inelastic with respect to changes in wages and rentals. Also, only two types of goods are produced in the economy, Consumer Goods and Capital Goods. Both inputs and outputs are assumed to be perfectly divisible.

We also take as given the production functions which relate the outputs of Consumer Goods and Capital Goods to the inputs of Labor and Capital (services of Capital Goods) in each industry. These production functions are taken to admit of substitution between Capital and Labor in the production of either commodity and are assumed to exhibit constant returns to scale and diminishing returns when one factor is increased with the other held constant. We also assume that at any factor-price ratio the Capital-Labor ratio is higher in the production of Capital Goods than in Consumer Goods.

Any change in the output of Capital Goods will affect the available supply of Capital. We assume, however, that the period we consider is sufficiently short so that the output of Capital Goods during the period does not become available for use as an input within the period but becomes fully available in the next period. On this assumption we would be justified in drawing an Edgeworth-Bowley box diagram of production for this initial period and deriving a transformation or production-possibilities curve from it.

Picking any point on such a transformation curve would determine not only the outputs of both goods for the initial period but also the supply of Capital for the next period if we ignore depreciation for the sake of convenience. If the increment in Labor from period to period, due to population growth or other exogenous factors, is given, the choice of a point on the initial period's transformation curve determines both dimensions of the box diagram for the next period. If technology remains unchanged the position and shape of the next period's transformation curve will be fully determined. The greater the current output of Capital Goods the further out will be the transformation curves for subsequent periods. Since Labor growth is given exogenously they will lie unambiguously further out, *i.e.*, will not intersect each other.

The assumption that Labor force growth is completely exogenous can be modified to the extent that we may consider it to be so only down to some minimal level of consumption for the current period, which, if not met, reduces the increment in Labor for the next period. Transformation curves for the next period corresponding to points on the current period transformation curve below the minimal level of consumption will generally intersect each other. For convenience we assume that current consumption and current output of Consumer Goods are identical.

III

For any period of time in the model outlined in Part I the investment-income ratio can be defined as follows

$$\frac{I}{Y} = \frac{kO_k}{cO_c + kO_k} = \frac{1}{\dfrac{c\,O_c}{k\,O_k} + 1} = \frac{1}{r\dfrac{O_c}{O_k} + 1}$$

where O_c and O_k represent the current outputs of Consumer Goods and Capital Goods, c and k their respective money prices (of which either one can be picked arbitrarily) and r

ECONOMIC GROWTH AND THE DISTRIBUTIVE SHARES

is the ratio of the two prices. Since r will generally shift from period to period the same $\frac{I}{Y}$ over time does not imply the same $\frac{O_c}{O_k}$. Notice that our definition of investment is not identical with the change in the value of the Capital stock in terms of Consumer Goods since we ignore the revaluation of the previously existing Capital stock due to the change in r. In Professor T. W. Swan's words[1] we consider only the "value of the change" in the Capital stock and not the "change in the value". We thus shirk the serious difficulties associated with the measurement of Capital that Mrs. Robinson has been concerned with in her recent book.[2]

Let us suppose, initially, that the investment-income ratio is given exogenously. We shall then show how under conditions of perfect competition and full utilization of both factors the secular change in the distributive shares is determined once certain trends in ths investment-income ratio and relative rates of factor growth are specified. Technical progress is ruled out for the present.

The relationships between the variables of the system will first be analyzed for a single period in terms of the model outlined in Part II. Labor and Capital are thus in fixed, inelastic supply within the period. Once the single-period relationships between the variables are determined we shall pass on to a consideration of how these relationships change from period to period with expansion of both factors.

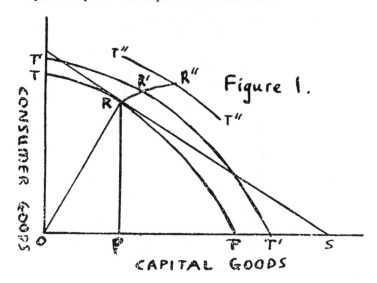

Consider the transformation curve between the two types of goods for an initial period of time as represented by TT in Fig. 1. If a vector is drawn from the origin to any point on TT such as R the slope of OR will measure $\frac{O_c}{O_k}$. The tangent to TT at R, when it intersects the Capital Goods axis, as at S, determines national income measured in terms

---

[1] T. W. Swan, "Economic Growth and Capital Accumulation," *Economic Record*, November, 1956.
[2] Joan Robinson, *The Accumulation of Capital*, Macmillan, London, 1956.

of that commodity. If a perpendicular is drawn from R to the Capital Goods axis intersecting it at P, OP will measure the current output of Capital Goods. $\frac{I}{Y}$ is therefore the ratio of OP to OS. Exactly the same ratio will be determined if we work on the Consumer Goods axis instead, measuring both Capital Goods and national income in terms of Consumer Goods.

If OR is rotated in the direction lowering $\frac{O_c}{O_k}$ the output of Capital Goods rises and national income measured in terms of Capital Goods falls. The investment-income ratio therefore rises as $\frac{O_c}{O_k}$ falls. If all resources are devoted to the production of Capital Goods only, $\frac{I}{Y}$ will be equal to unity and $\frac{O_c}{O_k}$ to zero. If all resources are devoted to Consumer Goods only, $\frac{I}{Y}$ will be equal to zero and $\frac{O_c}{O_k}$ to infinity. The relationship between $\frac{I}{Y}$ and $\frac{O_c}{O_k}$ is shown graphically in the first quadrant of Fig. 2. The curve intersects the $\frac{I}{Y}$ ratio at unity and goes asymptotically to the $\frac{O_c}{O_k}$ axis. The curvature depends upon what may be called the " elasticity of product substitution " between Capital Goods and Consumer Goods, or in plainer language, the curvature of the transformation curve.

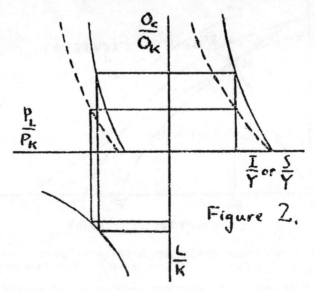

Figure 2.

The next relationship we have to consider is that between $\frac{O_c}{O_k}$ and the ratio of the return to Labor to the return of Capital or $\frac{P_1}{P_k}$. Since we have assumed that both production functions show constant returns to scale and that Capital Goods are always

ECONOMIC GROWTH AND THE DISTRIBUTIVE SHARES

more Capital-intensive than Consumer Goods, it can easily be shown from the box diagram analysis as used, for example, in the famous Stolper-Samuelson article,[1] that the factor price ratio shifts in favor of Labor as $\frac{O_c}{O_k}$ rises.

This relationship is shown in the second quadrant of Fig. 2. The curve goes asymptotically to the value of $\frac{P_1}{P_k}$ which would prevail if all resources were devoted to Consumer Goods production and begins at the value of $\frac{P_1}{P_k}$ at which all resources are used to produce Capital Goods.

The Labor-Capital ratio is measured along the vertical axis of the third quadrant. Given a value for $\frac{I}{Y}$ we can determine corresponding values of $\frac{O_c}{O_k}$ and $\frac{P_1}{P_k}$ which, together with the existing Labor-Capital ratio, will determine the relative shares. The ratio of total wages to total profits $\frac{W}{P}$ will be measured by the area of the rectangle formed by joining the perpendiculars in the third quadrant from the relevant value of $\frac{P_1}{P_k}$ and the existing $\frac{L}{K}$. It is easy to see that within a period $\frac{W}{P}$ is a decreasing function of $\frac{I}{Y}$ since $\frac{L}{K}$ is fixed. The opposite would be the case if we had reversed the factor intensities characterizing the production functions for the two goods.

IV

Our task is now to show how $\frac{W}{P}$ shifts from one period to the next in response changes in $\frac{L}{K}$ and $\frac{I}{Y}$. Population growth is exogenous in our model and, for the present, so is the investment-income ratio. The changes in $\frac{L}{K}$ and $\frac{I}{Y}$ have therefore to be prescribed arbitrarily. Our method of analysis will be quite independent of the particular hypotheses chosen about the behaviour of $\frac{L}{K}$ and $\frac{I}{Y}$, but since it seems to have been more or less the case empirically we shall assume a falling $\frac{L}{K}$ and a constant $\frac{I}{Y}$.

Since $\frac{L}{K}$ is lower in the next period the relationship between $\frac{I}{Y}$, $\frac{O_c}{O_k}$ and $\frac{P_1}{P_k}$ will be altered so that a new pair of curves will have to be drawn in the first and second quadrants of Fig. 2. The problem is to determine the position of the second period's curves as compared to those of the first.

---

[1] W. F. Stolper and P. A. Samuelson, "Protection and Real Wages," *Review of Economic Studies*, Vol. IX, November, 1941.

In order to locate the position of the curve relating $\frac{I}{Y}$ and $\frac{O_c}{O_k}$ we first have to ascertain the relationship between r and $\frac{O_c}{O_k}$ when $\frac{L}{K}$ has fallen. If $\frac{L}{K}$ remained unchanged it is easy to see that the same $\frac{O_c}{O_k}$ would imply the same r since the transformation curves for the two periods will be homothetic (the tangents to them will be parallel at the points where they are intersected by any ray from the origin) and the slope of these tangents is equal to r, since under perfect competition relative prices of commodities are equal to their marginal rates of transformation in production. If Capital increased while Labor remained constant we know from a theorem due to Mr. Rybczynski[1] that the absolute amount of O_c produced would fall if r remained unchanged so that preserving the same r would imply lowering $\frac{O_c}{O_k}$. Therefore increasing Labor relatively less than Capital must lower $\frac{O_c}{O_k}$ with constant r since only if they increased in proportion would the same r imply the same $\frac{O_c}{O_k}$. if $\frac{O_c}{O_k}$ is maintained constant r must rise and the same $\frac{O_c}{O_k}$ therefore means a lower $\frac{I}{Y}$. The curve for the second period relating $\frac{I}{Y}$ and $\frac{O_c}{O_k}$ will therefore be as shown by the broken curve in the first quadrant of Fig. 2.

As we have seen, if Capital increases relatively more than Labor, $\frac{O_c}{O_k}$ would fall at the same product price ratio and hence at the same factor price ratio. If the same $\frac{O_c}{O_k}$ is maintained the Labor-Capital ratio will have to fall in both sectors so that $\frac{P_1}{P_k}$ will rise.

Thus the curve relating $\frac{O_c}{O_k}$ and $\frac{P_1}{P_k}$ for the second period will be to the left of that for the first, as depicted in Fig. 2. Since $\frac{L}{K}$ is known for the second period and $\frac{I}{Y}$ remains constant by hypothesis, $\frac{W}{P}$ is determined. It is at first not possible to determine the direction of change in $\frac{P_1}{P_k}$ between the periods since both the curves in the first two quadrants are shifted to the left.

We know, however, that at the same $\frac{O_c}{O_k}$ for both periods there will be a higher r and therefore a smaller $\frac{I}{Y}$ for the second period. Further, if r remained the same

---

[1] T. M. Rybczynski, "Factor Endowment and Relative Commodity Prices," *Economica*, N. S. Vol. XXII, November, 1955.

$\frac{O_c}{O_k}$ would fall and $\frac{I}{Y}$ would therefore rise. Hence for $\frac{I}{Y}$ to remain unchanged there must be both a fall in $\frac{O_c}{O_k}$ and a rise in r. By a straightforward application of the Rybczynski type box diagram analysis this can be shown to imply that if $\frac{I}{Y}$ remains unchanged $\frac{P_1}{P_k}$ must rise. Since $\frac{L}{K}$ has fallen there are two opposing influences on $\frac{W}{P}$. The rectangle in the third quadrant for the second period may thus have a larger, smaller or the same area as that for the first period. The analysis can be carried on for any desired number of periods. If $\frac{L}{K}$ continues to fall and $\frac{I}{Y}$ to remain constant $\frac{P_1}{P_k}$ will continue to rise. If the south-west corners of the successive rectangles are joined by a smooth curve it will show $\frac{P_1}{P_k}$ varying inversely with $\frac{L}{K}$. It does not seem possible to determine whether the curve falls at a constant, increasing or decreasing rate.

Although technological change has not been introduced it can be done quite easily in terms of the approach for the type of two-factor, two-good model we have been discussing worked out by the author and H. Grubert.[1] Alternative patterns of factor and commodity bias in technological progress can be incorporated into the analysis already undertaken here to show the influence of this additional variable. As would be expected technological progress might benefit either factor, depending upon the composition of output and the original nature of the production functions.

V

The curve generated in the third quadrant of Fig. 2 is superficially identical with the Hicksian " elasticity of substitution curve " since both show an inverse relation between the Labor-Capital and wage-rental ratios. The Hicksian curve, however, is purely technological, depending upon the shape of the production function alone whereas ours depends upon demand conditions as well which determine the allocation of resources between the two industries. The demand factor, as we have shown, is deduced from the investment-income ratio which thus has a dual role in the analysis of distributive shares and economic growth. It not only determines the Labor-Capital ratio, in conjunction with population growth, but also the allocation of both these factors between the Consumer Goods and Capital Goods industries, which has important consequences for the distributive shares. In the well-known neo-classical growth model of Professor Solow[2] the importance of the average propensity to save on investment-income ratio for the distributive shares depends solely upon the nature of the single production function employed. If it is a Cobb-Douglas, for example, the relative shares are quite independent of the propensity to save.

---

[1] R. E. Findlay and H. Grubert, " Factor Intensities, Technological Progress and the Terms of Trade," *Oxford Economic Papers*, Vol. XI, No. 1, February ,1959.

[2] R. M. Solow, " A Contribution to the Theory of Economic Growth," *Quarterly Journal of Economics*, Vol. LXX, February, 1956. In a paper read at a conference of the International Economic Association at Corfu in September, 1958, however, Professor Solow worked out a mathematical model that has the distributive shares dependent upon the rate of growth of the economy, the durability of Capital, the relative importance of Labor in producing Consumer and Capital Goods and other technological factors. The paper is to appear in a volume of the proceedings of the conference.

In the model presented here both production functions might be of the Cobb-Douglas variety but the distributive shares would be a function of the average propensity to save so long as factor-intensities differed between the two industries.

In Mr. Kaldor's model on the other hand, technology, so long as it remains unchanged, appears to have no influence at all upon the secular behavior of the relative shares. One important difference between his model and ours is that a constant $\frac{I}{Y}$ must imply for him a constant $\frac{P}{Y}$ whereas, for us, a constant $\frac{I}{Y}$ is compatible with any type of behavior for the profit share.

This difference can perhaps be explained if we realize that Mr. Kaldor has an explicit function for $\frac{S}{Y}$ in terms of the distribution of income whereas $\frac{S}{Y}$ is an exogenous variable in our model. We shall now, however, show how Mr. Kaldor's savings function can be absorbed into the model we have constructed. This is done in Fig 3.

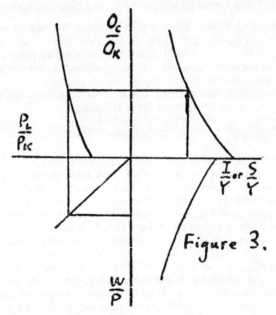

Figure 3.

The first two quadrants of Fig. 3 are identical with Fig. 2. The vertical axis of the third and fourth quadrants, however, now has $\frac{W}{P}$ instead of $\frac{L}{K}$ measured along it. For any single period $\frac{W}{P}$ is obviously proportional to $\frac{P_1}{P_k}$, as depicted in the third quadrant of Fig. 3. In the fourth quadrant the Kaldor savings function is introduced. It is derived from the following expression

$$\frac{S}{Y} = (s_p - s_w)\frac{P}{Y} + s_w.$$

ECONOMIC GROWTH AND THE DISTRIBUTIVE SHARES

If the entire national income is distributed to profits so that $\frac{W}{P}$ is zero, $\frac{S}{Y}$ will obviously be equal to s_p. If the whole national income is abosrobed by wages, $\frac{S}{Y}$ will be equal to s_w. For any intermediate value of $\frac{W}{P}$ the corresponding value of $\frac{P}{Y}$ can easily be found and inserted into the equation to determine $\frac{S}{Y}$. The relationship is shown graphically in the fourth quadrant of Fig. 3. The curve intersects the $\frac{S}{Y}$ axis at s_p and asymptotically becomes parallel to the $\frac{W}{P}$ axis at a value of s_w on the $\frac{S}{Y}$ axis.

It will now be convenient to look at Fig. 3 in conjunction with Fig. 1. Picking a value of $\frac{S}{Y}$ in Fig. 3 determines corresponding values of $\frac{O_c}{O_k}, \frac{P_1}{P_k}$ and $\frac{W}{P}$. In terms of Fig. 1 this amounts to finding a point on TT, such as R, for example, that corresponds to the particular $\frac{S}{Y}$ prevailing for the period. The output-mix represented by R can be located on the efficiency-locus of the box diagram from which TT is derived. Labor-Capital ratios in each industry will then be determined and since the production functions are homogeneous of degree one and factors are in fixed supply for the period the distribution of income is also determined. If we assume no population growth or technological progress, or specify these from outside the system, the position and shape of the next period's transformation curve $T'T'$ will be determined by R. In the absence of further information about demands for the two goods, however, nothing can be said about transformation curves for subsequent periods since production could take place anywhere on $T'T'$.

From Figure 3, however, we see that the Kaldor saving function can be so interpreted as to determine a particular production point for $T'T'$. The interpretation needed is that the $\frac{S}{Y}$ or $\frac{I}{Y}$ ratio for the next period is determined by the $\frac{W}{P}$ ratio of the current period. This of course only differs from Mr. Kaldor's function by assuming a lagged instead of an instaneous relationship between the variables. Since $\frac{W}{P}$ for the current period is determined once an initial $\frac{S}{Y}$ is specified $\frac{S}{Y}$ is determined for the next period by the system itself. In the first three quadrants of Fig. 3 new curves will have to be drawn because of the changed factor endowment of the economy. Proceeding in this way we can generate a growth path as shown by $R\ R'\ R''$ in Fig. 1. Given TT and R not only are successive transformation curves generated by the system itself but the points on each of them at which production takes place as well. In each case, by referring back to the relevant box diagram the distribution of income can be determined. Thus the secular behaviour of the output of both goods, as well as the terms of trade between them and the distribution of income between Labor and Capital are all generated by the model.

If we compare the model of Fig. 2, where the savings function is exogenously given, with that of Fig. 3 we notice that in the former $\frac{I}{Y}$ and $\frac{W}{P}$ can vary in the same or opposite directions and either or both can remain constant. In Fig. 3, however, the Kaldor savings function implies that the secular change in the variables must take place in the opposite direction to each other or both must remain constant. If the savings function were dependent on other variables, such as the level of income for example, this result would not follow.

As we have seen, in Mr. Kaldor's theory a higher rate of population growth always raises the share of profits. In the model presented here there is no reason to expect this, even when the Kaldor savings function is introduced.

The advantage that can be claimed for our model over Mr. Kaldor's is that the optimum technique in each industry in every period of time is determined by the model itself whereas technology appears in his model in the shape of an exogenously given Capital-output ratio which is invariant with respect to changes in the distributive shares and thus of relative factor prices. In our formulation it makes little sense to classify $\frac{I}{Y}$ as "the independent variables" and $\frac{W}{P}$ as "the dependent variable". Both are mutually determined as part of the whole system.

Mr. Kaldor remarks, in discussing his own and the related Marxian and Ricardian macroeconomic theories, that he is "not sure where 'marginal productivity' comes in in all this—except that insofar as it has any importance it does through an extreme sensitivity of V (the Capital-output ratio) to changes in $\frac{P}{Y}$."[1] From our analysis, however, it appears that Mr. Kaldor's system can be regarded as a special case of the neo-classical "marginal productivity" theory (suitably modified to take growth considerations into account in the simplest possible way), its distinguishing features being a particular form of the savings function and an assumed independence between techniques of production and relative factor prices. The Hicksian "elasticity of substitution" theory, on the other hand, has also been somewhat unduly narrow by neglecting the role of the savings function and concentrating too heavily on technology as an explanation of the secular movement in the distributive shares. In any general equilibrium analysis tastes should be an equal partner with technology and the mutual influence of these two forces upon the distribution of income is what, in a very crude and over-simplified way, we have tried to show here.

Rangoon and Massachusetts. RONALD FINDLAY.

---

[1] Kaldor, *op. cit.*, p. 100.

[11]
A Rejoinder to Mr. Findlay

1. I quite agree with Mr. Findlay that if we make a sufficient number of unreal assumptions (such as the absence of technical progress and of subjective uncertainty ; a linear and homogeneous production function in terms of homogeneous units of labour and capital, assuming that, somehow or other, an unambiguous quantitative measure of "capital" can be discovered ; instantaneous adjustment to changes in factor combinations ; perfect competition and the absence of external economies and diseconomies) a place can be found within the framework of a growth model for the "elasticity of substitution" as one of the elements determining distributive shares. Indeed, if Mr. Findlay made the further assumption that the aggregative production function is of the Cobb-Douglas type of constant elasticity, he could have demonstrated that distributive shares are *entirely* determined by the coefficients of that function : for whatever the rate of growth of output capacity, or the propensities to save out of profits and wages, there will always be (on these assumptions) a sufficient compensating variation in the capital/output ratio to maintain the investment coefficient (I/Y) constant in the face of changes in the rate of economic growth or in the parameters of the savings function. I do not think, however, that Mr. Findlay's method of reconciling the neo-classical theory with the "Keynesian" distribution theory, which depends on a special assumption on the relative capital intensity of the capital-goods and the consumption goods trades, is convincing ; and I fully maintain what I wrote at the end of my 1956 article that in a growth-model "marginal productivity" comes only into play through the sensitivity of v (the capital/output ratio) to changes in the P/Y (and, of course, P/K), and its importance as an element in the picture depends entirely on the degree of that sensitivity.

2. Accepting the form of the savings function given in my paper and reproduced by Mr. Findlay, and assuming, for simplicity that $s_w = 0$ (there are no savings out of wages) then in the absence of technical progress the rate of economic growth in a balanced-growth equilibrium is determined by the rate of population increase, λ, and we have the following equilibrium-relationships :—

$$\frac{P}{Y} = \frac{1}{s_p} \frac{I}{Y} \tag{1}$$

$$\frac{I}{Y} = \lambda v \tag{2}$$

From which it follows $\left(\text{since } v \equiv \frac{K}{Y}, \frac{P}{K} \equiv \frac{P}{Y}\frac{Y}{K}\right)$ that

$$\frac{P}{K} = \frac{\lambda}{s_p} \tag{3}$$

and $\quad \dfrac{Y}{P} = \dfrac{\lambda}{s_p} V$

Hence whatever the value of v, the rate of profit on capital (or the rate of interest) is uniquely determined by λ and s_p. The " elasticity of substitution " between the two factors, Capital and Labour, comes in insofar as, in equilibrium, a higher rate of profit on capital, at any given value of v, will be associated with a higher share of profit (P/Y) and a lower wage in terms of commodities (a lower W/P); and that a lower wage in terms of commodities will involve the use of more labour in relation to capital goods, and hence a smaller amount of capital per unit of output (i.e., a smaller v). This means that given a linear and homogeneous production function, and a constant state of " knowledge ", the equilibrium-value of v will be in inverse relationship to the equilibrium rate of profit, a relationship which can be written in the form

$$v = \phi \left(\frac{\lambda}{s_p} \right), \text{ where } \phi' < 0, \phi'' > 0. \qquad (4)$$

Hence, substituting in (1) and (2) we get

$$\frac{I}{Y} = \lambda \phi \left(\frac{\lambda}{s_p} \right) \qquad (2a)$$

$$\frac{P}{Y} = \frac{\lambda}{s_p} \phi \left(\frac{\lambda}{s_p} \right) \qquad (1a)$$

If the ϕ function is one of constant elasticity of minus one, (which means that the capital/output ratio varies in inverse proportion to the rate of profit, doubling the rate of profit involves halving the capital/output ratio, etc.) the equilibrium value of P/Y will remain invariant with respect to changes in λ, s_p and P/K. If on the other hand ϕ' is small, the role of marginal productivity or of the elasticity of substitution will be a subsidiary one, since P/Y will depend predominantly on the " dynamic " determinants, λ and s_p.

As Mr. Findlay has shown, the elasticity of the ϕ function depends not only on the elasticities of substitution between the " factors " in the two industries, but also on the extent to which the production functions in the two " industries " differ from one another, since the latter determines the curvature of his transformation curve (TT) in Fig. 2. This in turn, on the above assumptions as to perfect competition, etc., governs the extent to which a higher rate of production of capital goods raises the prices of capital goods in terms of consumption goods. This effect works in a *contrary* direction to that of the elasticity of substitution between factors—a higher rate of growth, by raising the output of capital goods in terms of consumption goods, will *raise* the capital/output ratio whenever the rate of growth of output capacity is higher, and it is even possible that as a result ϕ' should be zero or positive, even though the elasticities of substitution between the factors are negative in each of the two industries. The assumptions of the aggregative Cobb-Douglas function do not by any means follow from the assumption of constant-elasticity functions for each of the separate " industries ".

The reason why these results do not emerge from Mr. Findlay's diagrams is that the rate of growth does not figure in them as one of the variables, so that a change in I/Y which reflects a change in λ cannot be distinguished from one which reflects a change in v. Moreover to obtain a positive correlation between I/Y and P/Y he relies on an arbitrary assumption, which is contrary to that made in traditional theory, that the capital/labour ratio is higher in the capital-goods using industries, so that an increase in the relative output of capital goods increases the share of profits, and thus of savings. If he assumed instead, with Böhm-Bawerk, Wicksell, etc., that the " capital-intensity " of production is greater in the making of consumption goods (without necessarily going so far as to assume that

A REJOINDER TO MR. FINDLAY

capital goods are made by labour alone !) he would still have obtained his convex transformation curve, but any movement on that curve to the right would have *increased* the relative scarcity of labour, and thus the share of wages on strict marginal productivity lines. In other words, the curve in the second quadrant of his Figs. 2 and 3 would have sloped upwards from left to right, (and not from right to left) and his particular method of showing that a higher I/Y involves a lower W/P would have broken down.[1]

But in order to demonstrate this result we need not assume differences in the two production functions, or even the existence of a convex transformation curve—it is indeed very doubtful that any such result could be reached by making special assumptions about the character or the constellation of the curves in box diagrams. The result follows only from a Keynesian macro-economic model in which a higher level of capital expenditure necessarily increases the aggregate demand function relative to the aggregate supply function, and thereby (under conditions of full employment) raises prices relatively to costs *independently* of any shift along the isoquants of the production functions, or the transformation curve. It is the fall in W/P *caused* by an increase in aggregate demand which may in turn react on the level of capital expenditure through a consequential change in the techniques of production employed.

Thus even within the rigid framework of neo-classical assumptions the change-over from a static equilibrium model to a balanced growth model involves a far more radical change in the determinants of distributive shares than Mr. Findlay realizes. The " elasticity of substitution " between Capital and Labour which loomed so large in the former, becomes, at best, only one of a number of factors which enter into the picture : and its role can be quite a subordinate one.

3. But even that modest role disappears into thin air once we remove the unreal assumptions from which we started. As soon as we allow for a continuous change in technical knowledge, it becomes illegitimate to assume a linear-and-homogeneous production function. Technical progress is in fact, the same kind of thing (though more complex) as increasing return to scale, since (depending on the speed of capital accumulation) an increase in capital *per unit of labour* may yield a proportionate, or even a more-than proportionate, increase in the product ; and it is *not* possible to say that that part of this increase which is due to the change in " knowledge " can somehow be separated off and isolated from that part which would have taken place if knowledge, in some sense, had been " held constant ".[2] The trouble with the neo-classical approach is not that it starts with a lot of unreal abstractions—this is true of any theory, in science just as much as in economics—but that it operates with the kind of abstraction which leads nowhere: which cannot be removed or relaxed without destroying the foundations that were constructed with its aid.

Cambridge. NICHOLAS KALDOR.

---

[1] If Mr. Findlay's hypothesis were correct the profit-share P/Y could only increase, in connection with a higher I/Y, as a result of the shift in the distribution of output from industries with a low profit-share to industries with a high profit-share. The high degree of observed correlation between fluctuations in P/Y and I/Y cannot however be accounted for in this way. As a recent publication of the U.S. Department of Commerce put it, " detailed studies have shown the swing in the profit ratio to be characteristic of a broad range of industries, so that a structural shift toward typically lower-profit industries apparently was not a major factor in it " (*U.S. Income and Output*, Supplement to the *Survey of Current Business*, 1959, p. 15). Cf. also R.M. Solow, " A Skeptical Note on the Constancy of Relative Shares," *American Economic Review*, September 1958, pp. 618-631, particularly Tables 2-4. (Professor Solow would have probably obtained even more striking results if instead of the share of " production workers " he had taken the share of gross profits in value added in the different industries for purposes of comparison.)

[2] These ideas, which are only very briefly sketched here, are developed in more detail in a paper to be published in the proceedings of the Corfu Conference of the International Economic Association.

[12]

NOTES AND MEMORANDA

OVERDETERMINATENESS IN KALDOR'S GROWTH MODEL

THE purpose of this note is to bring out a point of difficulty in the model of economic growth presented by Mr. Kaldor.[1] Although this model has been examined recently and found " internally consistent," [2] it can be shown that the system is overdeterminate and therefore inconsistent. A simplification of the model will, however, remove this formal defect and incidentally make it more plausible without losing its essential properties.

Kaldor employs the following variables: saving S, investment I, income or output Y, profits P and capital stock K. All variables are expressed in real or constant dollar terms. Time is broken into periods long enough " to make it technically feasible to eliminate in one period the backlog of investment (the difference between desired and actual capital) existing at the beginning of the period." [3] It is assumed that

(1) $S_t = \alpha P_t + \beta(Y_t - P_t)$ where $1 > \alpha > \beta \geq 0$

Using asterisks to denote expected magnitudes or desired magnitudes of the corresponding variables—Kaldor does not do so—where the distinction might be useful, Kaldor supposes that

(2) $\dfrac{Y_t^* - Y_{t-1}}{Y_{t-1}} = \dfrac{Y_{t-1} - Y_{t-2}}{Y_{t-2}}$

describes entrepreneurial expectations regarding output during period t.[4] Of course, at the beginning of period t, Y_{t-1} and Y_{t-2} are known. Regarding profits,[5]

(3) $\dfrac{P_t^*}{Y_t^*} = \dfrac{P_{t-1}}{Y_{t-1}}$

Investment decisions are given by [6]

(4) $I_t = K_t^* - K_t$

where K_t is the capital stock at the beginning of t, and

(5) $K_t^* = \alpha' Y_t^* + \beta'\left(\dfrac{P_t^*}{K_t}\right) Y_t^*$ where $\alpha' > 0, \beta' > 0$

---

[1] N. Kaldor, "A Model of Economic Growth," ECONOMIC JOURNAL, December 1957, pp. 591–624.
[2] H. A. J. Green, "Growth Models, Capital and Stability," ECONOMIC JOURNAL, March 1960, p. 67.
[3] Kaldor, *loc. cit.*, p. 600.
[4] *Ibid.*, pp. 600–1.
[5] *Ibid.*, p. 601.
[6] *Ibid.*, p. 604.

Kaldor assumes that

(6) $K_{t+1} = K_t^*$

K_t, which is inherited from the previous period, is given as [1]

(7) $K_t = \alpha' Y_{t-1} + \beta' \left(\dfrac{P_{t-1}}{K_{t-1}}\right) Y_{t-1}$

Writing this for K_{t+1},

(7a) $K_{t+1} = \alpha' Y_t + \beta' \left(\dfrac{P_t}{K_t}\right) Y_t$

Comparison of (7a) with (5), keeping in mind (6), might lead one to suppose that $Y_t = Y_t^*$ and that $P_t = P_t^*$. However, as will be seen, this is false in general.

Combining (4), (5), (7) gives

(4a) $I_t = \left(\dfrac{Y_t^* - Y_{t-1}}{Y_{t-1}}\right) K_t + \beta' \left(\dfrac{P_t^*}{K_t} - \dfrac{P_{t-1}}{K_{t-1}}\right) Y_t^*$

It is seen from this that with Y_t^* and P_t^* determined by (2) and (3), actual investment in period t is determined. Including now the "technical progress function"

(8) $\dfrac{Y_t - Y_{t-1}}{Y_{t-1}} = \alpha'' + \beta'' \dfrac{I_{t-1}}{K_{t-1}}$ where $\alpha'' > 0, 1 > \beta'' > 0$

actual Y_t is determined and, using (1) and

(9) $I_t = S_t$

so is P_t.

Overdeterminateness can be shown most clearly by using (5) and (7a). Subtracting one from the other, in view of (6),

(10) $\alpha'(Y_t - Y_t^*) + \dfrac{\beta'}{K_t}(P_t Y_t - P_t^* Y_t^*) = 0$

The eight independent equations (1)–(3), (4a), (7)–(10) determine seven variables dated t: $Y_t, Y_t^*, P_t, P_t^*, I_t, S_t, K_t$. The other variables are, of course, known from history. Hence, the model involves one too many conditions and is inconsistent.

The source of the difficulty is evidently equation (7) or, which is the same, (7a). In the presence of the assumption (6), that desired capital stock at the beginning of a period is achieved by the end of the period, Kaldor seems to have been led to (7) from (5) via (7a). This wrong identification of realised magnitudes with expected magnitudes was apparently due to the lack of a notational distinction between the two.

---

[1] Kaldor, *loc. cit.*, pp. 604 and 605.

Actually, during the time that the economy is approaching the long-run equilibrium growth position (where $\Delta Y_t/Y_t = I_t/K_t$), I_t/K_t will keep changing with t and, according to (8), so will $\Delta Y_t/Y_t$. Consequently, entrepreneurial expectations regarding output (see equation (2)) will always exceed or fall short of actual output, depending on where we start. Hence, except at long-run equilibrium, $Y_t \neq Y_t^*$. Although not as easily seen, it may also be expected that $P_t \neq P_t^*$ in general.

The simplest way to remove the inconsistency is to drop (7), and therefore also (7a). Then (4a) and (10) will no longer be valid. I_t would have to be expressed simply as

(4b) $I_t = \left(\alpha' + \beta'\dfrac{P_t^*}{K_t}\right)Y_t^* - K_t$

from (4) and (5). For K_t, all that can be said is that

(11) $K_t = K_{t-1} + I_{t-1}$

However, this way out would still retain the property that, except at long-run equilibrium, actual output would always exceed or fall short of expectations in a predictable way. It can hardly be supposed that a fact like this should fail to be noticed by entrepreneurs, and it is likely that the formulæ (2) and (3) will need revision. More important, there is no strong reason for the assumption that investment plans are exactly realised. It is surely preferable to drop this assumption and let I_t be determined in the more usual way as a function of actual rather than expected magnitudes.

Suppose, then, that [1]

(4c) $I_t = \left(\alpha' + \beta'\dfrac{P_t}{K_t}\right)Y_t - K_t$

Dropping all reference to expected or desired magnitudes, the model will now consist of equations (1), (8), (9), (11) and (4c). These five equations determine Y_t, P_t, I_t, S_t, K_t given $Y_{t-1}, K_{t-1}, I_{t-1}$ from the previous period. The essential properties of the system would remain. For, starting from a position of growth rates of capital stock and output lower than the long-run equilibrium ones, $\Delta Y_t/Y_t > I_t/K_t$ and, as Kaldor's discussion will show, P_t/Y_t will increase as t increases. Hence, so would P_t/K_t. Referring to (4c), I_t/K_t will also increase. This leads to a higher percentage increase in output and so on. Similar remarks apply to a starting position from the opposite direction, so that the system is stable. However, the model would be somewhat less interesting perhaps, since expectations will not play a formally explicit role.

José Encarnación, Jr.

University of the Philippines,
   Quezon City.

[1] Cf. Kaldor, *loc. cit.*, p. 610, n. 1.

A COMMENT

Professor Encarnación is quite correct in saying that the system of equations presented in my 1957 article[1] is inconsistent with the assumptions of the model as set out on pp. 600–1 of the paper. Thus the equations for the stock of capital and for current investment assume that the existing capital at the beginning of each " period " is equal to what the " desired " stock of capital would have been at the beginning of the previous period if the income and the profit rate of that period had been correctly foreseen. However, I carefully avoided the assumption of " perfect foresight," and assumed instead " static foresight," as projected in equations (2) and (3) of Professor Encarnación's paper. The purpose of these assumptions was not to introduce expectational magnitudes as separate variables, but rather to allow I_t to be determined as a function of actual, rather than expected, magnitudes—in the same way as Professor Encarnación himself suggests at the end of his paper.

In this case, however, the equation for actual capital, as stated on pp. 604 and 605, and reproduced by Encarnación under (7), is wrong to the extent of suppressing one time-lag; there is one time-lag between the income and profit *realised* in one period and the investment decisions that are based on it (at the beginning of the next period); there is a further time-lag between investment decisions and the resulting change in the capital stock. Thus, if I_t represents the planned investment for the period t, and which results in the capital stock K_{t+1} at the end of the period, the *actual* income and profit experience on which the plans of I_t are based cannot be more recent than Y_{t-1}, P_{t-1} (though it is possible, of course, that the experiences of earlier periods also enter as weights in the determination of the *desired* capital stock of the time t).[2]

The introduction of this additional time-lag means, however, that the investment of any period can no longer be derived from the equations for the *desired* capital in two successive periods; except in a position of long-run growth equilibrium, the " backlog " of investment at any point of time may include investment opportunities resulting from differences between $\dfrac{Y_{t-1} - Y_{t-2}}{Y_{t-2}}$ and $\dfrac{Y_{t-2} - Y_{t-3}}{Y_{t-3}}$, or between P_{t-1}/Y_{t-1} and P_{t-2}/Y_{t-2}, as well as, as Encarnación points out, differences between planned and actually realised investment of the past period. Hence for the investment equation we have simply

$$I_t = \left(\alpha' + \beta' \frac{P_{t-1}}{K_{t-1}}\right) Y_{t-1} - K_t$$

[1] " A Model of Economic Growth," Economic Journal, December 1957, pp. 591–624.

[2] As I emphasised in a later paper, expectations concerning output (or sales) are likely to be more " elastic " than expectations concerning profit margins, simply because sales and output are subject to a trend, whereas there is no clear *trend* in profit margins. (" Capital Accumulation and Economic Growth," in *The Theory of Capital* (Macmillan, 1961), pp. 213–14.)

which differs only by a time-lag from that suggested by Professor Encarnación in equation (4c).

In a new version of the model which has just been published,[1] explicit account is taken both of obsolescence due to " embodied " technological progress, and of the expectation of continuing obsolescence in the future, and any notion of a " desired " capital stock which is in some unique relationship to the rate of profit (or the rate of interest) is abandoned.

N. KALDOR

King's College,
Cambridge.

[14]

A CRITIQUE OF MR. KALDOR'S MODEL OF INCOME DISTRIBUTION AND ECONOMIC GROWTH*

G. C. HARCOURT
University of Adelaide

Since 1956 Mr. Kaldor has been developing a model of income distribution and economic growth in order to explain the observed constancies in the capital-output ratios, the distribution of income, and the rates of profit on capital of the United Kingdom and United States economies.[1] Whether or not the three ratios are in fact constant is in dispute. For example, the participants in the recent conference on capital theory at Corfu, faced with the same empirical evidence concerning the capital-output ratio of the United States, split into two groups—one arguing that it was stable, the other that it was not.[2] However, the dispute is irrelevant to the present discussion which is concerned with the technical features of Kaldor's model. Moreover, his views on the forces which determine the distribution of income and the rate of growth of capitalist economies warrant consideration independently of whether their formal expression in a model implies constancy of the above ratios.

There are three novel features of Kaldor's approach. First, he uses the Keynesian savings-investment relationship to determine the distribution of income instead of the level of output and employment. Secondly, he rejects the traditional idea that it is possible to distinguish between movements on a given production function and movements of the function itself when analysing relationships between growth in productivity, capital accumulation and technical progress. Instead, he uses a technical progress function

---

* This article is a revised version of a paper read to Section G, *Jubilee A.N.Z.A.A.S. Conference*, held in Sydney, August, 1962. The writer is greatly indebted to Mr. Kaldor for his detailed comments on a draft of Section II. He is also indebted to the members of the Departments of Economics and Commerce, University of Adelaide; Professor J. E. Isaac, University of Melbourne; Dr. J. D. Pitchford, Australian National University; and Mrs. Joan Robinson, University of Cambridge; for their comments on drafts of this paper, but is alone responsible for the views expressed.

[1] The latest version of the model is contained in, "A New Model of Economic Growth", *Review of Economic Studies*, June, 1962, pp. 174-92. Other important papers are: "Capital Accumulation and Economic Growth", in F. A. Lutz and D. C. Hague (Eds.), *The Theory of Capital* (London, Macmillan, 1961); "Economic Growth and the Problem of Inflation—Parts I and II", *Economica*, Aug. and Nov., 1959, pp. 212-26 and pp. 287-98; "A Model of Economic Growth", *Economic Journal*, Dec., 1957, pp. 591-624; and "Alternative Theories of Distribution", *Review of Economic Studies*, March, 1956, pp. 83-100. They are referred to below as the *R.E.S.* (2), *Corfu Conference*, *Economica*, *E.J.*, and *R.E.S.* (1) papers, respectively. The *R.E.S.* (2) paper was written jointly with James A. Mirrlees.

[2] See F. A. Lutz and D. C. Hague, *The Theory of Capital*, pp. x-xi.

to describe the relationship between the proportionate rates of growth of output and capital over time. The technical progress function has been modified in the *R.E.S.*(2) paper; it now describes the relationship between the proportionate rate of growth of gross investment per operative and the resulting proportionate rate of growth of productivity of that labour which operates the new machines. Thirdly, Kaldor regards scarcity of resources rather than lack of effective demand as the main obstacle to economic growth; this view implies that full employment is the long-run equilibrium position of a *growing* economy. Each of these features is described more fully below.

The purposes of this paper are, first, to argue that the distributive mechanism (which Kaldor originally described as operative only in the long run) must work in the short period if it is to be included in the model; secondly, to set out the conditions which have to be fulfilled if the distributive mechanism is to work in the short period; thirdly, to argue that Kaldor's demonstration that "it is...impossible to conceive of a *moving* equilibrium of growth to be an under-employment equilibrium",[3] is unsatisfactory. The paper is in four sections. In Section I the distributive mechanism, the technical progress function and the investment function are briefly described. In Section II the criticisms relating to the distributive mechanism and its operation in the short period are developed. It is shown that when the level of planned investment changes as between short periods, the conditions which allow it to work in the short period may imply pricing, and other, behaviour by the entrepreneurs in the investment-goods sector significantly different from the behaviour of entrepreneurs in the consumption-goods sector. Behaviour patterns may differ not only within the bounds of one short period but as between succeeding short periods as well. Section III contains a discussion of the "representative firm" model of the *Economica* and *Corfu Conference* papers. The criticism of this device as a means of justifying the assumption of full employment in the main model is set out in Section IV. The concept of a "representative firm" which is a replica of the whole economy is shown to be untenable when the analysis is extended to a two-sector model. The account in the *Economica* and *Corfu Conference* papers of the movement from an under-employment equilibrium position to a full-employment one is shown to violate the assumptions underlying the construction of the "representative firm" model. Finally, it is shown that there is no position of full-employment equilibrium in the model. Rather, the model implies that over time a capitalist economy will tend, either towards a position of under-employment equilibrium, or towards a position of full employment with inflation.[4]

[3] *Economica* paper, p. 220; *Corfu Conference* paper, p. 201.
[4] Sections III and IV are based on an unpublished paper written jointly with Messrs. R. J. Blandy, J. Y. Henderson and N. Sarah.

I

The Distributive Mechanism

Kaldor developed his theory of distribution because he did not consider marginal productivity to be an adequate explanation of the determination of distributive shares in capitalist society. Briefly, he argues that marginal productivity theory has to assume that it is possible to construct an iso-product curve showing the different proportions of capital and labour which produce a given level of national output. The slope of this curve plays a key part in the determination of the relative prices of capital and labour. However, the curve cannot be constructed and its slope measured until the rates of profit and wages that it is intended to determine are themselves known; for it is only when these rates are known beforehand that capital can be valued. Moreover, the value of the same physical capital and the slope of the iso-product curve vary with the rates chosen—and this makes the construction unacceptable.[5] Kaldor substitutes instead the fruitful idea that the long-run share of profits in national income is likely to be greater, the greater is the enthusiasm, vigour, and (therefore) desire to accumulate capital, of the businessmen in the economy concerned.

A closed two-sector economy with a constant work force is assumed in the analysis below. In Kaldor's argument, if profit margins are flexible; if the savings propensities of profit- and wage-earners are given; if savings out of profits are greater than those out of wages; and if investment expenditure is determined independently of the distribution of income, the share of investment in the national income determines the distribution of income. Initially, investment is taken as given. "The interpretative value of the model... depends on the 'Keynesian' hypothesis that investment, or rather, the ratio of investment to output, can be treated as an independent variable, invariant with respect to changes in the two savings propensities...."[6] The distribution of income (which is assumed to be *full-employment* income) is found by substituting the value of I/Y in the equation,

$$\frac{P}{Y} = \frac{1}{\beta - \alpha} \cdot \frac{I}{Y} - \frac{\alpha}{\beta - \alpha}$$

(which reduces to $P = I/\beta$ if $\alpha = 0$) where I = investment, Y = output or income, P = profits, β = the average and marginal propensity to save out of profits, and α = the average and marginal propensity to save out of wages. It is assumed that the levels of wages and profits are such that the real wage rate exceeds "a certain subsistence minimum" and the rate of profit exceeds "the minimum... necessary to induce capitalists to invest their capital".[7]

---

[5] Detailed accounts of Kaldor's objections to marginal productivity will be found in the R.E.S. (1) paper, pp. 89-91; the E.J. paper, pp. 602-03; and the Economica paper, p. 224.
[6] R.E.S. (1) paper, p. 95.
[7] R.E.S. (1) paper, pp. 97-8.

The model can be illustrated by a simple diagram (see Figure 1).

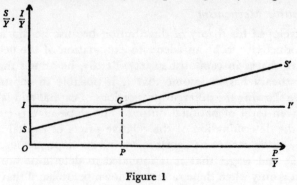

Figure 1

The ratios of long-run planned savings and investment to full-employment national income are measured on the vertical axis, and the share of profits in long-run full-employment national income is measured on the horizontal axis. The I/Y ratio is autonomous, that is, it is drawn as a horizontal straight line, as I/Y is assumed to be independent of P/Y. On the other hand, S/Y is shown as an increasing function of P/Y, which reflects the assumption that the marginal propensity to save out of profits is greater than that out of wages. If profit margins are flexible, prices will so move in relation to money wages that the distribution of income which gives the planned savings required to offset planned investment will be established. In terms of Figure 1, if the ratio of investment to income is OI, the share of profits in income will be OP.

The Technical Progress Function

Kaldor rejects the traditional idea that it is possible to distinguish between movements on a given production function and movements of the production function itself. Instead, he assumes that the flow of new ideas over time occurs at a steady rate, but that their impact on productivity per man depends on the rate at which capital is accumulated. This concept gives the technical progress function, TT', in which the proportionate rate of growth of output $(Y_{t+1} - Y_t)/Y_t$ is an increasing function of the proportionate rate of growth of capital $(K_{t+1} - K_t)/K_t$ (see Figure 2). With no capital accumulation, productivity per man would still grow over time at the proportionate rate, OT. Faster rates, however, require capital accumulation; hence TT' has a positive slope. At E capital and output are growing at the same proportionate rate. The main purpose of Kaldor's papers (from the E.J. paper on) is to show that there are forces at work in a capitalist economy which make E the position of long-run equilibrium. There, the ratio, K/Y, is constant. With capital and output growing at the same pro-

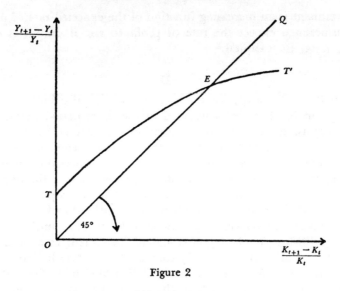

Figure 2

portionate rate, I/Y will be constant also, which implies both constant distributive shares and a constant rate of profit on capital.

The Investment Function

The technical progress function shows how output will change if certain rates of investment are implemented. The rate of investment is determined by the investment function and the distributive mechanism. The investment function determines the *planned* investment of each period; the distributive mechanism determines whether it becomes *actual* investment. The rate of actual investment determines the position of the economy on the technical progress function in each "period". The length of the "period" is such that by its end, actual capital is brought to the level of capital desired at the beginning of the "period". In the investment function in the *E.J.* paper it is assumed that businessmen wish to maintain a constant relationship between capital invested and output; that this relationship is an increasing function of the rate of profit on capital; and that businessmen expect the same rate of growth of output in the current "period" as occurred in the previous "period". These assumptions make current planned investment a function of the previous "period's" rate of growth of output and the change in the current rate of profit. They ensure that if the economy is not at E, there will be forces at work which drive it there. However, it is unrealistic to assume that businessmen desire to maintain a constant relationship between capital invested and output. If they are to the left of E, they could maintain the same rate of increase of output with a falling capital-output ratio. In the *Corfu Conference* paper, this objection is overcome by assuming that investment is an increasing function of the expected rate of profit and that businessmen expect the rate of profit to rise if output is currently growing faster than capital.[8]

II

In the *R.E.S.(1)* paper, Kaldor argued that the distributive mechanism was long run in character, frustrated in the short period by rigidities in profit margins, so that as an explanation (as distinct from an *ex post* identity) it was of relevance only in this long-run sense. But in the later papers he requires the mechanism to work within a period of time which is only long enough to allow the investment plans made at the beginning of the period to be carried out, that is, within the gestation period.[9] Thus, the intersection of the graph of the functional relationship between S/Y and P/Y with that of the relationship between I/Y and P/Y "indicates the *short period* equilibrium level of profits and of investment as a proportion of income".[10] "...all this is perfectly consistent with Marshallian orthodoxy —looking at it as a *short period* theory of distribution."[11] These statements conflict with the position taken in the *R.E.S.(1)* paper and indeed in the *E.J.* paper itself. In the latter paper, he suggests that

> "...the theory of distribution underlying this model—which makes the share of profits in income entirely dependent on the ratio of investment to output, and the propensity to save out of profits and wages—is only acceptable as a 'long run' theory, since changes in these factors exert only a limited influence in the short period. As was indicated in my earlier paper ['Alternative Theories of Distribution', *loc. cit.*, pp. 99-100], in the short period profit margins are likely to be inflexible...around their customary level—which means that they are largely historically determined. What is suggested is that long-term investment requirements and saving propensities are the underlying factors which set the standard around which these customary levels are found..."[12]

For Kaldor's model of economic growth to work, the distributive mechanism must operate in the short period, despite his disclaimer to the contrary. Otherwise, the planned investment of each short period may not become actual investment and the growth of output of each short period then will not be obtained by putting the value of *planned* capital accumulation in the technical progress function. The actual rate of capital accumulation

---

[8] *Corfu Conference* paper, pp. 212-14. The criticism of the investment function in the *E.J.* paper was first made by Mr. H. R. Hudson and Professor J. E. Meade. Their objections may be said to have been overcome in the *Corfu Conference* paper. However, the criticism in this paper (in Section II) concerning the determination of the rate of actual investment applies as much to the later version as to the earlier one.
[9] *E.J.* paper, pp. 604-06.
[10] *E.J.* paper, p. 606, italics not in the original.
[11] *Economica* paper, p. 220.
[12] *E.J.* paper, pp. 621-22.

could always be applied to the technical progress function, but there would then be no guarantee that the economy would move towards E.

What patterns of entrepreneurial behaviour with regard to pricing would allow the Kaldor distributive mechanism to work in the short period (which is taken to be the gestation period of investment)? By "work in the short period" is meant that any change in planned investment at the beginning of a short period is so accompanied by movements of resources, prices and the distribution of income, that the investment planned at the beginning of the period becomes actual investment by the end. In the Kaldor mechanism prices so adjust to changes in demand that the distribution of *full-employment* income changes so as to bring forth the required savings. The purposes of the remainder of this section are, first, to derive the relevant conditions for equilibrium in the short period for a model of a closed two-sector economy, the properties of which are outlined below; secondly, if planned investment is allowed to change from short period to short period, to analyse the process of adjustment, both within each period and as between periods, that allows planned investment to become actual investment in each short period.

Consider the following closed two-sector economy which, initially, is in equilibrium at full employment, that is to say, planned investment equals actual investment, and prices are so related to money-wage costs that the required savings are forthcoming. Suppose that the consumption-goods and investment-goods sectors produce homogeneous commodities, bread and steel respectively. For simplicity, assume that wage-earners spend all their incomes, and profit-earners save all theirs. To avoid the problems associated with the earnings of machines being spread over a number of short periods, assume that the capital stocks of each sector only last for one short period, so that they have to be replaced each period. Assume a constant work force *which is fully employed each period*; that labour will move immediately from one sector to another in response to a rise in money wages; that the amount of labour which moves is a known function of the rise in money wages; and that a definite relative wage structure is associated with each conceivable distribution of the work force between the two sectors (a special case of this relationship is that the same relative wage structure applies, whatever the distribution of the work force). Assume that demands for steel are lodged at the beginning of each short period; that the resulting production plans remain unchanged for each period; and that the final production itself occurs at a point in time, in this case, at the end of the short period concerned.[13] It follows that the production of any short period must be undertaken by labour working with the capital stock in existence at the

---

[13] The writer is indebted to Mr. Kaldor for suggesting the bread and steel model. The assumptions about the nature of the total production process seem a fair interpretation of the period analysis used in his *E.J.* paper (pp. 600-10).

beginning of the period, and that the steel production of the period concerned cannot itself be used to produce steel and bread until the next period. That is to say, the existing stock of steel in each sector is specific, not "Swan-type" meccano sets which can be easily dismantled and moved from one sector to another in the short period. Finally, it is assumed that labour rather than physical capacity is the principal bottleneck, especially in the steel sector. This implies that production will change proportionately with changes in the input of labour.[14] The labour inputs per unit of output of bread and steel in each short period will be determined by the size of the capital stocks in their corresponding sectors, but will be unaffected by changes in the employment of labour itself.

Planned investment will become actual investment and the distributive mechanism will work in the short period, if the following four conditions are fulfilled:

(i) the investment sector has sufficient labour to produce the desired amount of steel and, once the required amount of labour has been secured, the relative wage structure is such that there is no tendency for labour to move from one sector to the other;

(ii) the price of bread is such that, if the level of money demand for bread is known (that is to say, the total wages bill), there is neither unsatisfied demand nor unintended changes in stocks;

(iii) the price of steel is such that the expected rates of profit on the marginal machines in current steel output going to each sector are equal;[15]

(iv) All members of the work force are employed.

The following notation is adopted:

n,N: number of men required to produce one unit of bread and steel respectively;

m,M: the stocks of machines in the bread and steel sectors respectively, measured in steel units;[16]

w,W: the money wage rates per man per short period in the bread and steel sectors respectively;

p,P: the prices of bread and steel respectively;

x,X: employment in the bread and steel sectors respectively;

---

[14] Kaldor explicitly assumes this (see, for example, the *E.J.* paper, p. 593 and the *Economica* paper, pp. 216-17); it reflects his view that the long run equilibrium position of a growing developed economy is a full-employment one. Formally, it involves short run production functions of the form: $O = f(L,K^*)$, where O is output per short period, L is labour, K^* is the constant capital stock in the sector concerned and $\partial f/\partial L$ is constant over the relevant range. See also the prime cost curves in Figure 3 below.

[15] In correspondence Mr. Kaldor has suggested that equality of the overall profit rates as between sectors is the relevant condition. However, this condition seems more appropriate for long period equilibrium. As it happens, the same price of steel is implied, whichever condition is used.

[16] With the special assumptions concerning the lengths of life of machines, m and M are in fact the steel production of the previous period. More generally, they are the stocks of capital in existence at the beginning of each short period in each sector. n and N are functions of m and M respectively such that $\partial n/\partial m$ and $\partial N/\partial M$ are both negative, but they are not related to the employment levels of the two sectors.

The above conditions can be set out formally as follows:

Condition (i)

Suppose that the production of planned investment requires X men working with the existing capital stock in the steel sector. That is to say, planned investment is X/N in physical terms and PX/N in value terms. The employment of X men implies a particular relative wage structure: W/w.

Condition (ii)

The price of bread, p, can be deduced from the following equation:

$$wx + WX = \frac{px}{n}$$

that is

$$p = wn\left(1 + \frac{WX}{wx}\right) \qquad (1)$$

That is to say, the price of bread is its wages cost per unit marked up by the product of the relative wage structure and the ratio of employment in the two sectors (if $w = W$, the mark-up is the ratio of employment alone).

Condition (iii)

The price of steel can be deduced as follows: assume that entrepreneurs in both sectors expect the prices, wages, and the employment and output shares, of the current period to recur in the next period, also.[17] One unit of steel in the steel sector produces PX/MN value units of steel, and one unit of steel in the bread sector produces px/mn value units of bread. Condition (iii) therefore is that

$$\frac{\frac{PX}{MN} - \frac{WNX}{MN}}{P} = \frac{\frac{px}{mn} - \frac{wnx}{mn}}{P}$$

that is

$$P = WN\left(1 + \frac{M}{m}\right) \qquad (2)$$

That is to say, the price of steel is its wages cost per unit marked up by the ratio of the capital stocks of the two sectors in existence at the beginning of the period.[18] With the special assumption concerning the lengths of life of

[17] This assumption is consistent with the assumptions underlying the investment function in the *E.J.* paper (pp. 600-1).
[18] If the alternative condition of equality of profits rates is assumed, the same result can be obtained by solving for P in the following equation:

$$\frac{WX}{Pm} = \frac{\frac{PX}{N} - WX}{PM}$$

(As wage-earners are assumed to consume all their income and profit-earners to save all theirs, profits in the bread sector are equal to the wages bill in the steel sector.)

machines, equation (2) can be written as:

$$P = WN \left(\frac{1}{1-\lambda}\right) \qquad (2a)$$

where λ is the proportion of the *previous* period's production of steel which went to the steel sector itself.

Condition (iv)

All members of the work force will be employed if

$$x + X = \overline{X} \qquad (3)$$

where $\overline{X}$ is the total work force.

These conditions must hold in each short period; otherwise, planned investment will not become actual investment by the end of the period, and the Kaldor distributive mechanism will not have worked.[19]

With the conditions of short-period equilibrium established, it is now necessary to ask, first, how must profit margins and prices change, and labour move, *within a period*, given the level of planned investment of this period relative to that of the period before; secondly, how must profit margins and prices change, and labour move, *as between different periods*, if the pattern of planned investment over time is given? The first question concerns the dynamic process that occurs within a given period. The second question is concerned with comparative statics, the comparison of successive short-period equilibrium situations. Unfortunately, there are no clear cut answers to either question. They depend upon whether or not technical progress is occurring; on the level of investment of the preceding period (in the case of the first question); and on the pattern of change of investment over time (in the case of the second question).

The simplest case is to assume that there is no technical progress; that planned investment each period has long been constant; that money wages in both sectors are the same; that labour moves simply because new jobs are created; and that full employment is maintained. If the analysis is started in period t, the prices ensuring equilibrium will be

$$p_t = wn_t \left(1 + \frac{X_t}{x_t}\right) \; ; \; P_t = wN_t \left(\frac{1}{1-\lambda_{t-1}}\right)$$

Suppose that planned investment increases in period $(t+1)$. This will create additional job opportunities in the steel sector, and as labour moves im-

---

[19] However, for planned investment to become actual investment, only condition (i) need be satisfied. The entrepreneurs in the bread sector could set a price lower than that implied by equation (1), and allow queues to occur so that actual savings would be greater than planned savings. There would then be a situation of suppressed inflation. This would allow the main model to work, but not because the distributive mechanism operated in the short period. The writer is indebted to Dr. K. J. Hancock for this point.

mediately to this sector, entrepreneurs in the bread sector will realise that they can no longer maintain their present level of production. However, provided that they charge a price of

$$p_{t+1} = wn_{t+1}\left(1 + \frac{X_{t+1}}{x_{t+1}}\right)$$

which is greater than p_t, as X_{t+1}/x_{t+1} is greater than X_t/x_t, the lower production of bread will be sold without there being either queues, or an unintended fall in stocks of bread. The steel sector will have gained the additional labour that it needed; the current steel production will sell at a price of

$$P_{t+1} = wN_{t+1}\left(\frac{1}{1-\lambda_t}\right)$$

and planned investment will become actual investment. Now $P_{t+1} = P_t$ (because w is unchanged, N_{t+1} is equal to N_t and λ_t is equal to λ_{t-1}), so that profit margins will remain unchanged in the steel sector though they have lengthened in the bread sector. The share of profits in the national income will have risen, reflecting the rise in investment as a proportion of the national income. Full employment will have been maintained.

It may be supposed that the proportion of steel output which goes to the steel sector at the end of $(t + 1)$ is such that the amount of steel going to the bread sector actually falls.[20] This reflects the expected fall in demand for bread and the expected rise in demand for steel. If, in period $(t + 2)$, planned investment drops back to its original level, equilibrium in this short period requires, first, that *more than the additional labour* of the previous period which moved to the steel sector move to the bread sector; secondly, that profit *margins* on bread fall below their original level; thirdly, that the profit margin in the steel sector lengthen as λ_{t+1} is greater than λ_t. The price of bread may, or may not, rise depending upon whether or not the fall in the profit margin is outweighed by the rise in wages cost per unit due to the lower amount of steel in the sector. Similarly, the price of steel may, or may not, rise because the fall in the wages cost per unit may offset the rise in the profit margin. In period $(t + 3)$, the steel production of $(t + 2)$ having been distributed as in period t, the prices, profit margins, and the compositions of output and employment of period t are all restored. If the rise in planned investment of period $(t + 1)$ is permanent, the story in period $(t + 1)$ is the same, but now the bread profit margin does not fall by as much in period $(t + 2)$ and the price either rises more or falls less. Prices and profit margins take on levels which reflect the fact that the original capital-labour ratio in the steel sector has been restored at the new, higher level of steel production. By period $(t + 3)$ the profit margins and prices of bread and steel

[20] The writer is indebted to Mr. J. R. Hubbard for pointing out an error in a previous version of this paragraph.

will all be at their new, long-period levels. As there is no technical progress the long-period capital-labour ratios of both sectors remain unchanged, and therefore the percentage increases in profit margins in each sector will have been the same. The percentage changes in prices will also have been the same; wage costs per unit in both sectors will have fallen because of the larger amount of steel in both sectors in the new situation. Finally, if investment increases period by period, the story in period $(t+1)$ is the same, but bread profit margins and prices then rise period by period. Whether after period $(t+2)$, the profit margins on steel rise by the same percentage amounts as those on bread depends upon the percentage rate of increase of planned investment.[21] Prices will *never* change by the same percentage amounts because of the rises in wages costs per unit in the bread sector and the falls in wages costs of the steel sector.

The above analysis suggests that the characteristics of the dynamic process within each short period are, first, that entrepreneurs in the steel sector are active: actively bidding for labour (or sacking it), and actively raising (or lowering) production in response to changes in demands. Secondly, and by contrast, the entrepreneurs in the bread sector are passive: passively accepting the loss (or return) of labour and the consequent changes in production. Their only active role is to set the price of bread appropriate to each situation. The analysis also shows that, as between periods, the changes in profit margins and prices over time, and the movement of labour over time, are determined by the corresponding pattern of planned investment. There is no guarantee that the percentage changes in profit margins and prices of the two sectors as between periods will be the same. That is to say, there may be significant differences in the entrepreneurial behaviour of the two sectors *as between the comparative static positions.*

The introduction of technical progress complicates the analysis. Technical progress shows itself by the changes over time in the input coefficients, n and N, the values of these coefficients in any period being determined by the investment of the *previous* period. Consider, first, the case of a once-and-for-all change in the level of planned investment occurring in period $(t+1)$. Suppose that prior to this change, planned investment each period was constant, so that the labour force in steel fell at a rate determined by the fall in the input coefficient, N. The proportion of steel going to the steel sector each period is assumed to fall also, so that the capital-labour ratios in the two sectors remain constant. Profit margins in the bread and steel sectors would then have been falling (whether at the same percentage rate or not will depend upon the percentage fall in N); prices of bread and steel would also have been falling, first, because of the fall in profit margins, secondly,

---

[21] Obviously, this process cannot go on without limit, for there is a level below which real wages cannot be made to fall, so that the transfer of labour to the steel sector will eventually stop.

C

because of the fall in wages costs per unit.[22] When planned investment rises in period $(t+1)$, it is by no means certain that labour will have to move to the steel sector. All that can be said is that the falls in the profit margin and price of bread will now be less than they otherwise would have been. The profit margin and price of steel will be unaffected relative to what they would have been in period $(t+1)$ in the "otherwise" situation, though they will be lower than in period t.

Alternatively, it could be assumed that prior to period $(t+1)$, labour remained constant in the two sectors (so that total steel production each period increased by the same percentage as the increase in productivity per man) and that the proportion of steel going to the steel sector remained constant. Profit margins will have remained constant, and prices will have fallen as between periods by amounts determined by the falls in the input coefficients, n and N. In this case, a rise in planned investment in period $(t+1)$, which is greater than that which can be accommodated by the increase in productivity, will definitely entail a shift of labour to the steel sector and a corresponding rise in the profit margin on bread, though not necessarily in the price of bread. The profit margin on steel (but not the price of steel) will remain unchanged. In period $(t+2)$, if planned investment now reverts to increasing at a rate which can be accommodated by the change in N each period, the profit margin on bread will fall to a level determined by the movement back to this sector of the labour which moved to the steel sector in the previous period. The profit margin on steel will lengthen in period $(t+2)$, but in period $(t+3)$, and subsequently, it will remain constant; both bread and steel prices will resume patterns similar to those followed before the change in planned investment.

Obviously, there are many more variations on this theme. However, enough cases have been analysed to show that it is very doubtful whether entrepreneurial behaviour in the two sectors would be such as to allow the Kaldor distributive mechanism to work in the short period, or over time. The most likely outcome of an increase in investment demand in the short period when there is full employment is inflation, especially when the increased production of investment goods implies a cut in real wages.[23] In summary, there is no guarantee that planned investment will become actual investment, and whether it does or not depends on entrepreneurs in the bread sector following significantly different pricing policies to those in the steel sector. When the assumption of equal money wages is dropped this

[22] Thus, even if profit margins fall at the same percentage rate in both sectors, prices may not move together because the percentage changes in N may differ from those in n. The actual falls in n and N consist of two elements: the falls in the coefficients associated with given levels of steel, and the changes in the levels of steel itself in the two sectors because of the previous period's investment.

[23] This occurs when there is no technical progress, and/or when the rise in planned investment requires such a shift of labour to the steel sector that, even with the rise in productivity per man in the bread sector, total bread producion falls.

conclusion is not altered significantly. Full short-period equilibrium will then require, either that the initial relative wage differential be immediately restored, or that a new one be immediately established. Accordingly, when planned investment increases and if, as a result, the steel sector requires additional labour, steel entrepreneurs will raise money wages in order to attract labour. Bread entrepreneurs must accept passively the resulting loss of labour even though they, at the same time, will be faced with an increased money demand for bread due to the higher money wages in the steel sector and the higher money wages that (under the first alternative) they will have to pay to restore the previous relative wage differential. If a period of time (shorter than the gestation period of investment) elapses before money wages in the bread sector are raised so as to restore the previous relative wage structure, two prices of bread will have to be set within the one short period. The increase in the price of bread within this period will be entirely accounted for by the increase in money wage costs per unit as the profit per unit, WX/x, associated with each price will be the same. With these modifications, the "stories" are the same as before, and what happens to profit margins and prices depends upon the pattern of investment and the rate of technical progress. Furthermore, if the special assumption concerning the lengths of life of machines is dropped once again the analysis is not significantly affected. The profit margin in the steel sector must now be interpreted as $[1 + (M/m)]$; m and M of period t are the capital stocks appropriate for the expected levels of output of period $(t-1)$.

III

The "Representative Firm" Model

In its simplest form Keynesian theory assumes that effective demand has no effect on the price level, but only on the level of output. However, if the level of demand affects the relationship between prices and money wages, a given level of autonomous investment will be associated with different levels of income, depending upon the distribution of that income between wages and profits. Furthermore, once more than normal profits are being earned, so that the current stock of capital is being worked at more than the normal level of capacity, businessmen will be encouraged to add to the capital stock, that is, induced investment will occur. From these ideas Kaldor derives a demand curve for output relating different distributions of income to different levels of output. He uses a "representative firm" which behaves like a small-scale replica of the economy as a whole (so that variations in its output reflect variations in aggregate output). The supply curve, SS', consists of average prime costs, and a minimum margin of profit below which businessmen will not go for fear of spoiling the market (see Figure 3). Average prime costs are wages only as raw material costs cancel for the economy

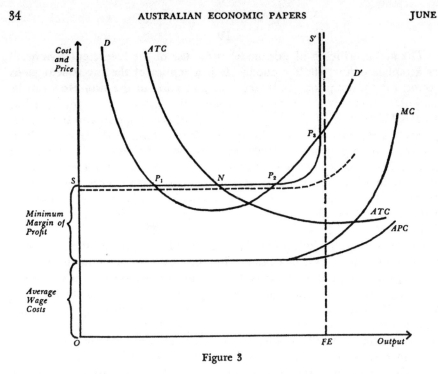

Figure 3

as a whole. The constancy of average prime costs up to near full employment reflects the fact that employment rather than physical capacity is the principal limitation on output.

The corresponding demand curve, DD', is U-shaped showing, first, that the lower are prices relative to wages, the greater is the level of income associated with any given level of autonomous investment; secondly, that once normal profits are being earned (at the point N, where the average *total* cost curve, including normal profits, cuts SS') induced investment will occur. However, there must be a shift to profits in order to bring forth the required planned savings, since in this range of output, the marginal propensity to invest at any *given* distribution of income will exceed the corresponding marginal propensity to save.[24] There are three possible equilibrium positions, namely, P_1, an under-employment one with no induced investment, P_2, an unstable one, and P_3, a full-employment one with positive induced investment. As the national incomes of capitalist economies have, in fact, grown over time, Kaldor argues that only P_3 is consistent with these observations, for only at P_3 does induced investment occur and capacity grow. That is to say, "it...is impossible to conceive of a *moving* equilibrium of growth to be an under-employment equilibrium".[25]

[24] *Economica* paper, p. 219; *Corfu Conference* paper, p. 200.
[25] *Economica* paper, p. 220; *Corfu Conference* paper, p. 201.

IV

The major criticism of this model is the use of the "representative firm" as a replica of the whole economy. Is it a replica of the investment-goods sector, the consumption-goods sector, or a mixture of the two? How can its output, presumably a homogeneous commodity, move at the same speed as national output which (at best) is a mixture of consumption and investment goods, the outputs of which change at different rates at different levels of income and employment? Moreover, as is shown in Section II above, the pricing behaviour of businessmen must differ as between the two sectors, if the Kaldor distributive mechanism is to work in the short period. It is therefore impossible to represent the pricing behaviour of the economy in one diagram. This alone makes it inadequate as a model of the process of inflation, if not of growth.

Unless the equilibrium point, P_1, is the result of applying the multiplier to an autonomous level of consumption, or unless autonomous investment is completely unproductive, it *is* possible for an economy to exhibit both growth in output per head *and* under-employment, that is, for the economy to be at P_1. The fact that the national incomes of capitalist economies have, in fact, grown therefore does not necessarily imply that the long-run equilibrium position is a full-employment one. Indeed, if autonomous investment does increase productivity, average wage costs will fall, lowering the SS' curve, and a given distribution of income and level of autonomous investment will be associated with a higher national product, so that the downward portion of DD' curve will also move to the right. P_1 therefore will move to the right over time, showing that economic growth and under-employment equilibrium are consistent with one another. It is doubtful whether the section of the demand curve between P_1 and P_2 could exist, since the price level needed to establish the output in this range is below the minimum supply price, that is, the price below which businessmen will not cut for fear of spoiling the market. Unless the economy is at an output greater than that associated with P_2, there is no mechanism in the model by which it could reach P_3. Furthermore, it is doubtful whether P_3 could exist, either. The upward sloping portion of the DD' curve shows that there must be a shift to profits to allow planned investment to be offset by planned savings. The DD' curve must rise faster than the money-wages prime-cost curve, APC, and therefore, the supply curve, SS', so that it could never cut SS' from above.[26] That is to say, the "representative firm" model shows that over time capitalist economies tend either towards a position of under-employment equilibrium or towards a position of full employment with inflation. N indicates the level of output where the existing capital stock is worked at normal capacity. As drawn, N occurs at a level well below full employment which is inconsistent with the assumption that labour is the main bottleneck,

[26] The writer is indebted to Mr. E. A. Russell for this point.

and with the constant prime costs associated with it and larger outputs. Finally, it is hard to see the logic of using the distributive mechanism which implicitly assumes full employment to ensure that the economy gets to full employment.

A Re-examination of the Existence and Stability Propositions in Kaldor's Growth Models[1]

The purpose of this paper is to examine whether Professor Kaldor's propositions on the existence and stability of steady growth in his 1957 [1] and 1961 [2] articles are true.

In both articles these propositions may be summarized as follows:

(a) Steady growth of output takes place at the rate of growth

$$G_Y = G_K = \frac{\alpha''}{1-\beta''} + \lambda \qquad \ldots(0.1)$$

where
$\quad G_Y$: rate of growth of output

---

[1] This paper is based on a chapter of my unpublished M.A. thesis submitted to McGill University in Spring 1966. I am indebted to Professors J. C. Weldon and A. Asimakopulos and D. Oke for helpful suggestions.

G_K: rate of growth of capital

α'', β'': parameters in the technical progress function

λ: a constant rate of growth of labour.

(b) This steady rate of growth of output is globally stable.

It will be shown that, in Kaldor's 1957 model, proposition (b) does not in general hold. In his 1961 model, proposition (a) does not hold, hence proposition (b) becomes pointless. I am not going to discuss his specification of the models but his process of reasoning through which the propositions are derived. In the present paper I accept his specifications of the models as they are. When I introduce my own interpretation on the values of parameters in the models, it is done entirely within Kaldor's specifications.

Throughout this paper I shall call propositions (a) and (b), respectively, Kaldor's existence and stability propositions. I shall denote by Kaldor I and II respectively the models presented in [1] and [2].

When I use the term steady growth without qualification I use it to mean that output grows at a constant proportional rate. In my usage of the term, capital or labour may or may not grow at the same rate as output.

1. KALDOR I

1. Kaldor I may be represented as the following set of simultaneous equations: [1]

$$\Delta K(t) = \beta Y(t) + (\alpha - \beta) P(t), \qquad \ldots(1.1)$$

$$K(t+1) = \left(\alpha' + \beta' \frac{P(t)}{K(t)}\right) Y(t), \qquad \ldots(1.2)$$

$$G_Y(t) = \alpha'' + \beta'' G_K(t), \qquad \ldots(1.3)$$

where

Y = output,

K = capital stock,

P = profits,

G_Y = rate of growth of output $\left(\equiv \dfrac{\Delta Y}{Y}\right)$,

G_K = rate of growth of capital $\left(\equiv \dfrac{\Delta K}{K}\right)$,

α, β, α', β', α'', β'': constants and

$1 > \alpha > \beta \geq 0$

$\alpha', \beta' > 0$

$\alpha'' > 0, \; 1 > \beta'' > 0;$

Δ = time difference

t = period t.

In proving his existence and stability propositions in the 1957 article, Kaldor uses a version of Kaldor I in which the supply of labour is constant. Our set of equations

---

[1] (1.1), (1.2) and (1.3) are no more than Kaldor's (1), (2.1) and (3) respectively, on p. 604 of his 1957 article [1]. I have slightly changed the notation and rearranged the terms.

STABILITY PROPOSITIONS IN KALDOR'S GROWTH MODELS

follows this version.[1] Under the assumption of constant supply of labour, λ is zero in Kaldor's existence proposition.

By combining (1.1) and (1.2), $P(t)$ can be immediately eliminated from the set of equations. We then have only two equations in the new set;

$$1 + G_K(t) = \left(\alpha' + \frac{\beta'}{\alpha - \beta}\left(G_K(t) - \beta \frac{Y(t)}{K(t)}\right)\right)\frac{Y(t)}{K(t)}, \qquad \ldots(1.4)$$

$$G_Y(t) = \alpha'' + \beta'' G_K(t). \qquad \ldots(1.3)$$

In this set of simultaneous difference equations time paths of Y and K become completely determinate, once the initial values of Y and K are given. I shall henceforth omit writing time subscripts when all variables in an equation are associated with period t.

2. I first derive Kaldor's existence proposition. By (1.3), when G_Y is constant forever, so is G_K. Therefore, in steady growth, we let

$$G_Y(t) = \eta,$$
$$G_K(t) = \kappa, \qquad \ldots(1.5)$$

where η and κ are constant rates of growth of output and capital, respectively, whose values are to be determined.

On substitution of G_K from the second equation of this set, (1.4) will become

$$\beta\beta'\left(\frac{Y}{K}\right)^2 - (\alpha'(\alpha - \beta) + \beta'\kappa)\frac{Y}{K} + (1 + \kappa)(\alpha - \beta) = 0. \qquad \ldots(1.6)$$

Solving for $\frac{Y}{K}$,

$$\frac{Y}{K} = \frac{\alpha'(\alpha - \beta) + \beta'\kappa \pm \sqrt{(\alpha'(\alpha - \beta) - \beta'\kappa)^2 - 4\beta\beta'(1 + \kappa)(\alpha - \beta)}}{2\beta\beta'}, \qquad \ldots(1.7)$$

provided $\beta \neq 0$. We assume the value of the roots in this solution are real.[2]

Equation (1.7) tells us that both Y and K must grow at the same rate in steady growth. Therefore, using (1.3),

$$\eta = \kappa = \frac{\alpha''}{1 - \beta''}. \qquad \ldots(1.8)$$

This is the explicit solution for the steady rate obtained by Kaldor.

3. Kaldor's own proof for the stability proposition is given in [1], pp. 609-10. He seems to rely on two equations in the main part of the proof: one the technical progress function (our (1.3)), and the other the following equation.[3]

$$G_K(t+1) = G_Y(t) + \frac{\beta'\left[\frac{P(t+1)}{K(t+1)} - \frac{P(t)}{K(t)}\right]}{\alpha' + \beta'\frac{P(t)}{K(t)}} \frac{Y(t+1)}{Y(t)}. \qquad \ldots(1.9)$$

---

[1] With the supply of labour growing at a constant rate, λ, (1.3) is changed. My following treatment in the text, however, will readily apply to this case by always reading α'' as α^* where $\alpha^* = \alpha'' + \lambda(1 - \beta'')$.

[2] This assumption does not violate the restrictions already imposed on α, β, α' and β'. It imposes, however, a new condition that must be satisfied on the values of parameters. The test of the signs shows that the solutions of (1.7) are both positive.

[3] Kaldor does not write out this equation explicitly. It is derived from our (1.2).

For the moment Kaldor takes the second term in the right-hand side of this equation as always zero. The equation, in combination with the technical progress function, then draws a zigzag diagram (Fig. 5 in his article). The steady rate is certainly stable under the neglect of the second term.

He continues, " The indirect effects through changes in the rates of profit on capital will reinforce this process " ([1], p. 610). In the right-hand side of (1.9) the second term is now reviewed. If this term could be shown to be unequivocally positive or negative as the rate of growth of the system is below or above the steady rate, his statement in the quotation would be supported. With positive values of $Y(t)$, $Y(t+1)$, $K(t)$ and $P(t)$, what determines the sign of the second term is the expression inside the square brackets. By the technical progress function, $\dfrac{Y(t)}{K(t)}$ is unequivocally increasing or decreasing over time as the system's rate of growth is below or above the steady rate. Substituting (1.1) into (1.2) through the intermediate of $\Delta K(t)$ and after some arrangement,

$$\frac{P}{K} = \frac{(\alpha'-\beta)\dfrac{Y}{K} - 1}{\alpha - \beta - \beta'\dfrac{Y}{K}}.$$

On differentiation,

$$\frac{d\left(\dfrac{P}{K}\right)}{d\left(\dfrac{Y}{K}\right)} = \frac{(\alpha'-\beta)(\alpha-\beta)-\beta'}{\left(\alpha-\beta-\beta'\dfrac{Y}{K}\right)^2}.$$

The sign of the right-hand side of this equation is ambiguous from Kaldor's specification of the values of parameters only: his proof is illegitimate. It will be valid only when

$$(\alpha'-\beta)(\alpha-\beta)-\beta' > 0.$$

4. The following analysis will show that, if

$$(\alpha'-\beta)(\alpha-\beta)-\beta' < 0, \qquad \ldots(1.10)$$

the steady rate may or may not be stable depending on the initial value of $\dfrac{Y}{K}$.

Solving (1.4) for G_K, substituting G_K from (1.3) and after some arrangement,

$$G_Y = \alpha'' + \frac{\beta''\left\{\left[\alpha'(\alpha-\beta)-\beta\beta'\dfrac{Y}{K}\right]\dfrac{Y}{K} - (\alpha-\beta)\right\}}{\alpha-\beta-\beta'\dfrac{Y}{K}}. \qquad \ldots(1.11)$$

On differentiation,

$$\frac{dG_Y}{d\left(\dfrac{Y}{K}\right)} = \beta'' \frac{\beta\beta'^2\left(\dfrac{Y}{K}\right)^2 - 2(\alpha-\beta)\beta\beta'\dfrac{Y}{K} + (\alpha-\beta)[\alpha'(\alpha-\beta)-\beta']}{\left(\alpha-\beta-\beta'\dfrac{Y}{K}\right)^2}. \qquad \ldots(1.12)$$

Equating the numerator in the right-hand side of this equation to zero, solving for $\dfrac{Y}{K}$, and after simplification,

$$\frac{Y}{K} = \frac{\alpha-\beta}{\beta'} \left[1 \pm \sqrt{\frac{\beta(\alpha-\beta)-\alpha'(\alpha-\beta)+\beta'}{\beta(\alpha-\beta)}} \right]. \qquad \ldots(1.13)$$

We assume that

$$\alpha'(\alpha-\beta)-\beta' < 0. \qquad \ldots(1.14)$$

This assumption constructs a case that satisfies (1.10), makes the value of the roots in (1.13) real and produces only one positive solution for $\frac{Y}{K}^1$.

Equation (1.11) enables us to analyze the behaviour of G_Y over time in relation to $\frac{Y}{K}$. Figure 1 shows (1.11).

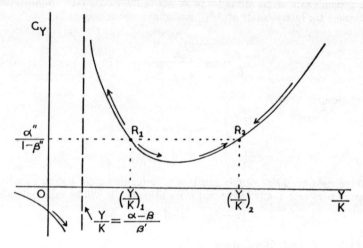

FIGURE 1

The horizontal axis shows $\frac{Y}{K}$ and the vertical axis G_Y. The shape of the curves defined by (1.11) is as follows. There will be a couple of separate curves, one to the right of the vertical line given by $\frac{Y}{K} = \frac{\alpha-\beta}{\beta'}$ (the broken line in the figure) and the other to the left. The curve relevant to our analysis is the one to the right of this line.[2] I shall be concerned with this part only. When $\frac{Y}{K} \to \infty$, (1.11) becomes infinite. When $\frac{Y}{K} \to \frac{\alpha-\beta}{\beta'}$ (when approached from the right-hand side), it will also become infinite. In between these two extremes there must lie a minimum of G_Y at the $\frac{Y}{K}$ indicated by (1.13). The shape of this

---

[1] Since the constant term in the numerator of (1.12) becomes unequivocally negative, the test of the signs will indicate that there is only one positive solution. The assumption (1.14) does not violate any of Kaldor's specifications of parameters. Neither does it contradict the restriction mentioned in footnote 2, page 355. Our main conclusion in this section suffers from no change even when $\alpha'(\alpha-\beta)-\beta'>0$ and (1.10) is satisfied. The stability of the steady rate still depends on the initial $\frac{Y}{K}$.

[2] The other curve to the left of the broken line will never appear to the first quadrant provided $\alpha'' \leq \beta''$.

curve is fixed all the time since all the variables in (1.11) are constants except for G_Y and $\frac{Y}{K}$.

Drawing a line parallel to the horizontal axis showing the steady rate (1.8), a pair of points (such as R_1 and R_2 in the diagram) along the curve (1.11) that correspond to the steady rate will be found. In accordance with the pair, there must be a pair of values of $\frac{Y}{K} \left(\left(\frac{Y}{K}\right)_1 \text{ and } \left(\frac{Y}{K}\right)_2 \text{ in the diagram} \right)$ for steady growth. They are obtained from (1.7).

When G_Y is below the steady rate, $\frac{Y}{K}$ is rising over time and *vice versa*, i.e. in the range

$$\left(\frac{Y}{K}\right)_1 < \frac{Y}{K} < \left(\frac{Y}{K}\right)_2,$$

$\frac{Y}{K}$ is always moving rightwards along the curve with the lapse of time. Outside this range, and unless $\frac{Y}{K} = \left(\frac{Y}{K}\right)_1$ or $\left(\frac{Y}{K}\right)_2$, $\frac{Y}{K}$ is moving leftwards. The directions of movement are shown in the figure by arrows. Thus, the steady rate of growth is stable or unstable, depending on the initial position of $\frac{Y}{K}$. Kaldor's global stability proposition is not in general true.

2. KALDOR II

1. As in the case of Kaldor I, I present Kaldor II as a set of simultaneous equations:[1]

$$\dot{K}(t+\theta) = (G_Y(t)-\lambda-\alpha'')\frac{K(t)}{\beta''} + \lambda K(t) + \mu \frac{d}{dt}\left(\frac{Y(t)}{K(t)}\right), \quad ...(2.1)$$

$$G_Y(t)-\lambda = \alpha'' + \beta''(G_K(t)-\lambda). \quad ...(2.2)$$

Y, K, G_Y, G_K, α'' and β'' are as defined in Section 1.1 except that G_Y and G_K now take differential forms $\left(G_Y \equiv \frac{\dot{Y}}{Y} \text{ and } G_K \equiv \frac{\dot{K}}{K}\right)$. And

$\dot{K}$ = time differential of K,

λ = rate of growth of labour (a constant) and ≥ 0,

μ, θ = constants and μ, $\theta > 0$,

t = point of time t.

(2.2) can be rearranged to solve for $\dot{K}(t)$.

$$\dot{K}(t) = \left(\frac{G_Y(t)-\lambda-\alpha''}{\beta''} + \lambda\right)K(t).$$

The right-hand side of this equation is identical with the first and second terms of the right-hand side of (2.1).[2] Therefore (2.1) can be written as

---

[1] (2.1) is Kaldor's equation (15) on p. 216 of [2]. (2.2) is his (14) on p. 215. In both cases I slightly changed the notation. On p. 220 Kaldor summarizes his model as a set of equations. My primary objection is that in Kaldor II it is impossible for steady growth to occur at such a position. I must use the original equations, from which Kaldor derived his propositions, as the basis of my argument.

[2] Kaldor derived the first and the second terms of the right-hand side of equation (2.1) from (2.2) as the induced part of investment.

STABILITY PROPOSITIONS IN KALDOR'S GROWTH MODELS

$$\dot{K}(t+\theta) = \dot{K}(t) + \mu \frac{d}{dt}\left(\frac{Y(t)}{K(t)}\right),$$

i.e.

$$\dot{K}(t+\theta) = \dot{K}(t) + \mu \frac{Y(t)}{K(t)}(G_Y(t) - G_K(t)). \qquad \text{...(2.3)}$$

2. According to Kaldor's existence proposition steady growth must take place at the rate given by (0.1). But, in view of (2.3), it is impossible at such a rate. Steady growth may take place at a rate other than this but never at this rate.

Suppose steady growth is taking place at the rate given by (0.1). On the one hand, since $G_Y(t) = G_K(t)$ by the present hypothesis, the last term in (2.3) vanishes, i.e.

$$\dot{K}(t+\theta) = \dot{K}(t). \qquad \text{...(2.4)}$$

On the other hand, since by the present hypothesis $G_K(t)$ is positive all the time, $K(t)$ must always be increasing, i.e.

$$K(t+\theta) > K(t).$$

From the hypothesis that $G_K(t)$ is constant,

$$\dot{K}(t+\theta) > \dot{K}(t). \qquad \text{...(2.5)}$$

Inequality (2.5) contradicts equality (2.4). Therefore, the hypothesis, from which we started, that a steady growth takes place at the rate given by (0.1) must be abandoned. Kaldor's existence proposition is wrong.

Since steady growth does not take place at the rate indicated by Kaldor's existence proposition, it becomes pointless to discuss the stability of this rate.

3. The true existence proposition in Kaldor II should be:

Steady growth takes place in the position in which

$$G_Y(t) = 2G_K(t), \qquad \text{...(2.6)}$$

where

$$G_K(t) = \kappa = \frac{\alpha'' + (1-\beta'')\lambda}{2-\beta''}. \qquad \text{...(2.7)}$$

It is further required that the initial values of Y and K satisfy the relationship,

$$\frac{Y(0)}{K(0)^2} = \frac{\exp(\theta\kappa) - 1}{\mu}, \qquad \text{...(2.8)}$$

for the steady growth to take place.

The proof proceeds as follows: we give the following equations as the solution for the set of equations (2.1) and (2.2) in steady growth.

$$\begin{cases} Y(t) = Y(0)\exp(\eta t) \\ K(t) = K(0)\exp(\kappa t). \end{cases} \qquad \text{...(2.9)}$$

η and κ are steady rates of growth of output and capital, respectively, whose values are to be determined. $Y(0)$ and $K(0)$ are initial values of Y and K.

All $Y(t)$, $K(t)$, $\dot{K}(t)$, $\dot{K}(t+\theta)$, $G_Y(t)$ and $G_K(t)$ can then be expressed solely in terms of initial conditions, constants and time. Substitute all the variables in (2.3) by the expressions thus obtained. After rearrangement the result will be

$$\kappa K(0)^2(\exp(\theta\kappa) - 1)\exp(2\kappa t) - \mu(\eta - \kappa)Y(0)\exp(\eta t) = 0.$$

In steady growth this equation must be satisfied regardless of the value of t. This is possible only when [1]

---

[1] The equation may also be satisfied at any value of t if $\eta = \kappa = 0$. But this solution is incompatible with (2.2), with the specified values of parameters there.

$$\begin{cases} \eta = 2\kappa & \quad\ldots(2.10) \\ \dfrac{Y(0)}{K(0)^2} = \dfrac{\exp(\theta\kappa)-1}{\mu}. & \quad\ldots(2.11) \end{cases}$$

Substituting (2.10) into (2.2), we obtain (2.7).

McGill University K. KUBOTA

REFERENCES

[1] Kaldor, N., " A Model of Economic Growth ", *Economic Journal*, **62** (1957), 591-624.

[2] Kaldor, N., " Capital Accumulation and Economic Growth ", in Lutz, F. A., and Hague, D. C. (ed.), *The Theory of Capital* (London, Macmillan, 1961).

[16]

THE INSTABILITY OF KALDORIAN MODELS[1]

By B. T. McCALLUM

DESPITE the vintage of some of the writings, it appears that interest in Nicholas Kaldor's macro-economic models of growth, distribution, and technical change is very much alive.[2] Empirical evidence for this proposition exists in the form of several recent publications: lengthy discussions of Kaldor's models appear in R. G. D. Allen's *Macro-Economic Theory* [1] and in the impressive survey article of Hahn and Matthews [3]; reprints of Kaldor articles appear in two new collections of readings;[3] and even textbooks designed for introductory courses refer to Kaldorian theories [9, 16].

Furthermore, Kaldor's technical progress hypothesis has been pronounced as 'ripe for empirical testing' by Hahn and Matthews [3, p. 889]; Scitovsky has suggested that Kaldor's distribution theory, in conjunction with one of Phelps Brown and Weber, is 'the most, perhaps the only satisfactory macro-economic theory of income distribution' [17]; and Reder has attempted an empirical test [15].

Along with their admirers, however, Kaldor's ideas have attracted their share of critics.[4] Many of these have probably been impressed (as have admirers) by the extent to which Kaldor has departed from neoclassical orthodoxy. Others have criticized the writings on their own grounds, at least two focusing upon the distribution mechanism which is common to all these models.[5]

In this paper it is argued that instability is a pervasive feature of Kaldorian models. While previous writers have questioned the stability of such models in the sense of 'disequilibrium dynamics', we are here concerned only with 'equilibrium dynamics'. The sort of instability in question, then, is such that (assuming forces exist to keep the model economy at full employment of capital and labour) capital accumulation will take place at

---

[1] The author is indebted to J. K. Whitaker, John Conlisk, and Marian Krzyzaniak for important suggestions.

[2] While Kaldor has several more papers in the field, his basic ideas are put forth in [4], [5], and [7].

[3] Kamerschen's collection of *Readings in Microeconomics* [8] contains Kaldor's distribution paper [4]. The Kaldor–Mirrlees article [7] appears in Mueller's *Readings in Macroeconomics* [13].

[4] Modigliani [11], Tobin [18], and Weintraub [19], among others.

[5] Morris finds it significant that Kaldor has devoted only a small fraction of his published words to the topic to 'his account of the *modus operandi* of the distributive mechanism' [10, p. 309], while Moore has found it necessary to 'reformulate the Kaldor effect' [12]. Allen also mentions the possibility that this mechanism will not 'work' [1, p. 310].

a rate differing progressively from that which can be maintained over time.[1] In other words, growth equilibria will diverge from the steady-state path.[2]

Two limitations on what follows should be mentioned. First, only the non-vintage version of Kaldor's technical progress function will be examined. Second, *Kaldor-type* models rather than the precise versions presented by Kaldor will be treated owing to the analytical 'messiness' of the latter. Subject to these limitations, this paper will argue that Kaldorian growth and distribution models are unstable under rather general conditions.

In Section I a streamlined version of Kaldor's basic growth model will be presented; its instability will be demonstrated in II. Sections III and IV will present generalizations on the results of II and a brief conclusion will follow.

I

Kaldor's basic non-vintage growth model, which incorporates his distribution theory, has been well summarized by Allen [1, pp. 305–12].[3] His treatment and notation will be followed rather closely in this section.

The model assumes full employment of capital and labour but, in contrast with neoclassical models, incorporates functions specifying aggregative behaviour of both saving and investment. This is possible because marginal productivity factor pricing is not followed; income distribution adjusts to satisfy these specifications. Aggregate saving S depends upon income distribution since s_p, the marginal and average propensity to save out of 'profits' P,[4] differs from s_w, the propensity to save out of wages $Y-P$:

$$S = s_w Y + (s_p - s_w) P \qquad (0 \leqslant s_w < s_p \leqslant 1). \tag{1}$$

The investment function specifies that the desired capital–output ratio K^*/Y is an increasing linear function of the profit rate P/K:

$$K^*/Y = v + \beta P/K \quad (v, \beta > 0). \tag{2}$$

As usual in growth models labour grows exponentially at the rate n:

$$L = e^{nt}. \tag{3}$$

The usual aggregate production function with labour augmenting technical change is replaced, however, by a 'technical progress function' which suggests that 'the use of more capital per worker inevitably entails the introduction of superior techniques which require inventiveness of some kind', while most 'technical innovations which are capable of raising

---

[1] Hahn and Matthews [3] questioned the stability in this sense of Kaldor's models but did not undertake analysis.

[2] On these concepts and distinctions see Hahn and Matthews [3, pp. 781–2].

[3] One feature of Allen's version which seems to violate the spirit of Kaldor's writings is discussed in Section IV below.

[4] 'Profit' is non-wage income in the Kaldor scheme.

the productivity of labour require the use of more capital per man' [5, p. 595]. If we denote output per man and capital per man by $y = Y/L$ and $k = K/L$ the technical progress function may be written as

$$\dot{y}/y = F(\dot{k}/k), \qquad (4)$$

where a dot designates differentiation with respect to time. The function in (4) is taken to be 'well behaved' so that it will cut a 45° line from the origin and a steady-state growth path (with $\dot{y}/y = \dot{k}/k = m$) can be attained. More precisely the specification is that $F(0) \geqslant 0$, $F' > 0$, $F'(\infty) = 0$, and $F'' < 0$.

These four equations make up the basic model. Equilibrium (full employment of capital and labour) prevails only if $K = K^*$. Using this condition and the $S = I = \dot{K}$ identity with (1) and (2) one can obtain

$$\dot{K} = s_w Y + [(s_p - s_w)/\beta](K^2/Y - vK) \qquad (5')$$

or, dividing by K and subtracting n from each side,

$$\dot{k}/k = s_w \frac{Y}{K} + \left(\frac{s_p - s_w}{\beta}\right)\left(\frac{K}{Y} - v\right) - n. \qquad (5)$$

If we define $R = K/Y$ as the capital–output ratio prevailing at a point in time, then its (proportionate) rate of change is related to *per capita* rates of change in capital and income by the identity

$$\frac{\dot{R}}{R} = \frac{\dot{k}}{k} - \frac{\dot{y}}{y}. \qquad (6)$$

Equations (4), (5), and (6) then yield

$$\frac{\dot{R}}{R} = \frac{s_w}{R} + \left(\frac{s_p - s_w}{\beta}\right)(R - v) - n - F(\dot{k}/k). \qquad (7)$$

In steady-state growth equilibrium $F(\dot{k}/k) = m$ and the capital–output ratio is unchanging so the equation

$$0 = \frac{s_w}{R} + \left(\frac{s_p - s_w}{\beta}\right)(R - v) - n - m \qquad (8)$$

can be solved for the steady-state value of R. (See Allen [1, p. 309].)

Since (8) is a quadratic, it yields two solutions. In his 1957 article Kaldor asserted that for 'any reasonable values of the coefficients, the larger root will be greater than unity and the smaller root less than unity when Y is thought of as annual income' and concluded that 'normally the greater of the two [roots] only would be relevant' [5, p. 613]. Allen finds, under the assumption $v > s_w/(n+m)$, that the smaller root implies a solution with negative profits. He concludes that 'the model has a single steady-state solution' [1, pp. 309–10].

The implausibility of the solution corresponding to the smaller root can be emphasized by using 'reasonable' coefficient values and obtaining solutions to (8), using years as the time unit. For example, the set of values $s_p = 0{\cdot}55$, $s_w = 0{\cdot}05$, $n+m = 0{\cdot}04$, $v = 3$, and $\beta = 2$ gives the two roots 0·06 and 3·1. The smaller value is quite implausible as a steady-state capital–output ratio, when output is in per annum units. Such results are not very sensitive to the choice of values for the coefficients.

The smaller root of (8) therefore yields implausible results and the larger root is supposed to define the steady-state capital–output ratio which can be used in equations (1)–(5) to find steady-state values of the variables for any point in time when initial conditions are specified. In the next section it will be shown, however, that the steady-state equilibrium defined by this root is unstable.

II

Proof of the instability begins by noting that (6) could be rewritten, using the technical progress function, as

$$\frac{\dot{R}}{R} = \frac{\dot{k}}{k} - F(\dot{k}/k) \equiv \phi(\dot{k}/k). \qquad (9)$$

Now the first derivative of ϕ is $\phi' = 1-F'$ and we know that $F' < 1$ in the vicinity of the solution to (8) from the specification of F. Thus we can be sure that $\phi' > 0$ in the vicinity of the steady-state solution. The second derivative of ϕ is $\phi'' = -F''$ and since $F'' < 0$ by assumption, we know that ϕ'' must be positive.

From equation (5) and the $R = K/Y$ definition we see that

$$\frac{\dot{k}}{k} = \frac{s_w}{R} + \left(\frac{s_p - s_w}{\beta}\right)(R-v) - n. \qquad (10)$$

Thus we can write $\dot{k}/k = G(R)$ and can verify that the second derivative of G is $G'' = 2s_w/R^3$. Since $s_w > 0$, G'' is positive for all positive values of R, which are the only ones of interest.

Now using $\dot{R}/R = \phi(\dot{k}/k)$ and $\dot{k}/k = G(R)$, we can write the crucial function (7) as $\dot{R}/R = \phi[G(R)]$. Its second derivative is $\phi'G'' + \phi''(G')^2$ and is positive for positive R since ϕ', ϕ'', and G'' have been found to be positive. The rate of change of R is therefore a convex function of R for positive values of the latter. The function (7) is thus of the general shape indicated by Fig. 1, where the solutions to the quadratic equation (8) are represented by R_L and R_U. We have seen above why Kaldor and Allen view R_L as unacceptable. The graph instantly shows that R_U gives an unstable steady-state growth path, for if $\dot{R}/R$ is positive, R increases with time and vice versa, so if $R > R_U$, R will increase, while if $R < R_U$, the capital–output ratio R will fall.

60 THE INSTABILITY OF KALDORIAN MODELS

Instability is thus established in the basic model.[1] Not only the capital-output ratio is unstable, of course. The investment function implies that movements in R are accompanied by changes in the income shares, as would be expected. In the following section this result will be shown to apply to more general models which retain the essential Kaldorian features.

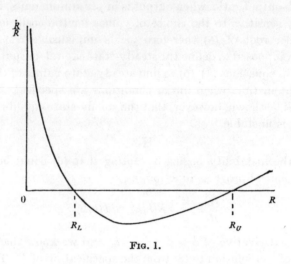

Fig. 1.

III

As a first generalization the linear investment function (2) can be replaced with the more general specification

$$\frac{K^*}{Y} = h(P/K), \tag{11}$$

where h is a continuous, monotonic increasing function with $h'' < 0$. For these conditions imply that the inverse function

$$\frac{P}{K} = h^{-1}(K^*/Y) \equiv H(K^*/Y) \tag{11'}$$

has positive first and second derivatives. The counterpart of (5) then becomes

$$\frac{\dot{k}}{k} = \frac{s_w}{R} + (s_p - s_w)H(R) - n, \tag{12}$$

and accordingly

$$G''(R) = 2s_w/R^3 + (s_p - s_w)H''(R), \tag{13}$$

---

[1] Since Kaldor has stressed the special case in which there is no saving out of wages, it should be noted that if $s_w = 0$ then the first derivative of $\dot{R}/R$ is positive for all $R > 0$ so that there is only one root. The curve then cuts the R axis from below and the single root is therefore unstable.

so $G'' > 0$ and again the plot of $\dot{R}/R$ against R has the shape of Fig. 1 since ϕ is unchanged.[1]

Alteration of the technology specification requires a somewhat more extensive revision of the analysis. But the effect of Kaldor's technical progress function is of considerable interest since it involves a severe

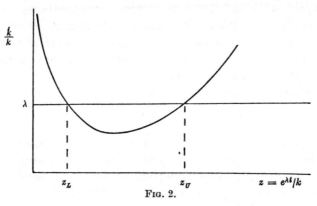

Fig. 2.

departure from the conventional production specification. We thus wish to examine the model when the technical progress function (4) is replaced with a standard neoclassical aggregate production function. Technical change is assumed to be of the labour-augmenting (Harrod neutral) variety so that steady-state growth is possible.

Instead of (4) let us then utilize a well-behaved production function, homogeneous of degree one:

$$Y = f^*(K, e^{\lambda t}L), \qquad (14)$$

where λ is the rate of technical change, or

$$Y/K = 1/R = f^*(1, e^{\lambda t}/k) \equiv f(e^{\lambda t}/k) \qquad (14')$$

with $f(0) = 0$, $f' > 0$, $f'' < 0$. It will be convenient to let $z \equiv e^{\lambda t}/k$ and let $g(z) \equiv 1/f(z) = R$ in which case $g'(z) < 0$ and $g''(z) > 0$. Then substituting into (12) one obtains

$$\dot{k}/k = s_w/g(z) + (s_p - s_w)H[g(z)] - n. \qquad (15)$$

The second derivative with respect to z is

$$s_w f'' + (s_p - s_w)[H'g'' + H''(g')^2], \qquad (16)$$

which is almost certainly positive.[2] Thus we have an equation generally of the form depicted in Fig. 2.[3] In steady-state equilibrium $\dot{k}/k$ must

[1] The graph may not be quite of this shape, but it is apparent from (12) and the properties of ϕ that $\dot{R}/R$ will grow as $R \to \infty$ and as $R \to 0$. It is possible that there will be more (or less) than two roots but such a case seems unlikely. In any case, we see that the largest root will be unstable.

[2] The 'reasonable' values of p. 59, for instance, give a magnitude to the positive second term which is over 200 times that of the negative first term when f^* is Cobb–Douglas with labour elasticity of output equal to 0·65.

[3] Remarks similar to those of n. 1 apply here.

62 THE INSTABILITY OF KALDORIAN MODELS

equal λ, the rate of technical change. But if $z > z_U$, $\dot{k}/k > \lambda$ so k grows faster than $e^{\lambda t}$ and z tends to fall. Conversely, if $z_L < z < z_U$, then $\dot{k}/k < \lambda$ so that z increases. Finally, if $z < z_L$ then $\dot{k}/k > \lambda$ and z falls toward zero. In sum z_U represents a stable solution while z_L represents one which is unstable. But since $z = e^{\lambda t}/k$, the lower root z_L again corresponds to the greater capital stock and the larger capital–output ratio.

As suggested above, this last result is most significant. For it shows that the instability does not derive from the technical progress function[1] and must therefore be due to the distribution scheme which is at the heart of Kaldorian models. The instability result holds, of course, in the special 'stationary state' case in which $n = \lambda = 0$.

IV

There appears to be one important way in which the Allen formulation utilized above is contrary to the spirit of Kaldor's writings. While the investment function (2) makes the capital–output ratio desired by investors a function of the existing profit rate P/K, Kaldor has been explicit about relating the desired K/Y to the *expected* or *prospective* profit rate [5, p. 600] [6, pp. 210–16]. Thus we are led to examine the result of replacing (2) with

$$K^*/Y = v + \beta r, \qquad (17)$$

where r is the expected rate of profit. In order to complete the model we then need some specification of the manner in which expectations are formed. Kaldor has asserted that 'expectations are invariably based on past experience' [6, p. 213], a view which is consistent with our adoption of an expression which can be interpreted as a continuous form of the widely used 'adaptive expectations' model [14] or as a continuously distributed lag with an exponential weighting function [1, pp. 86–93]. Specifically we assume

$$dr/dt = \dot{r} = \alpha[(P/K) - r] \quad (\alpha > 0), \qquad (18)$$

which implies that expectations adjust to wipe out, in a time interval of unit length, the fraction α of the discrepancy $(P/K) - r$ between the actual and expected profit rates. The alternative interpretation of (18) is that expected profit at time t, now denoted $r(t)$, is related to actual past values by the expression

$$r(t) = \int_0^\infty w(\tau) \frac{P}{K}(t-\tau) \, d\tau,$$

where the weighting function $w(\tau)$ is taken to be $w(\tau) = \alpha e^{-\alpha \tau}$.

---

[1] This should come as no surprise as it is well known that a *linear* technical progress function, which was used by Kaldor in [5], can be integrated into a constant-returns Cobb–Douglas production function [1, 2, 3]. Specifically, $\dot{y}/y = a + b\dot{k}/k$ when integrated yields $Y = Ce^{at}K^b L^{1-b}$ where C is a constant of integration with magnitude dependent upon initial conditions.

We now wish to consider how the use of r instead of P/K in the investment function affects the instability conclusions of Section II. There we expressed $\dot{R}/R$ as $\phi[G(R)]$ and showed that the second derivative of the composite function is positive. Our current examination of the model with profit expectations can be limited to the properties of the counterpart of $G(R)$ since ϕ is the same as in II.

First we use equations (17) and (18) with the equilibrium condition $K = K^*$ to obtain

$$\frac{P}{K} = r + \frac{\dot{r}}{\alpha} = \frac{1}{\beta}(R-v) + \frac{1}{\alpha\beta}\dot{R}. \tag{19}$$

Substitution into the saving function leads to

$$\frac{\dot{k}}{k} = \frac{s_w}{R} + \left(\frac{s_p - s_w}{\beta}\right)(R-v) + \left(\frac{s_p - s_w}{\alpha\beta}\right)\dot{R} - n. \tag{20}$$

Except for the presence of $\dot{R}$ this is analogous to equation (10), that is, to $\dot{k}/k = G(R)$. We use equation (9), $\dot{R} = R\phi(\dot{k}/k)$, to eliminate $\dot{R}$ and write the result as an implicit function in R and $\dot{k}/k$:

$$\psi(\dot{k}/k, R) \equiv -\dot{k}/k + \frac{s_w}{R} + \delta(R-v) + \frac{\delta}{\alpha}R\phi(\dot{k}/k) - n = 0. \tag{21}$$

Here δ is used for $(s_p - s_w)/\beta$.

At this point a demonstration that the second derivative of $\dot{k}/k$ with respect to R exceeds zero would again imply instability. The situation, however, is not as clear-cut as before. It is shown in the appendix that the occurrence of instability is related to the speed of adjustment of profit expectations. Specifically the following condition, *sufficient* for instability, is derived:

$$\alpha > \delta R\phi'. \tag{22}$$

The coefficient α represents the speed of adjustment of expectations, so (22) says that instability will prevail if profit expectations adjust rapidly.

We can use the 'reasonable' numerical coefficients of Section I to see what sort of adjustment speed is implied by condition (22). The derivative ϕ' equals $1 - F'$, and the relationship pointed out in p. 62, n. 1 shows that F' should be roughly equal in magnitude to the profit income share. Thus ϕ' is about 0·65 and with values of $\delta = 0·25$ and $R = 3·1$ we see that instability will occur if α exceeds 0·5. This value implies that it would take about 3·2 years for investors to make an 80 per cent correction in erroneous profit expectations, if the 'true' figures became available immediately. While response lags of such length might be typical in the implementation of decisions, it seems unlikely that expectations would be so sticky.

Thus, while suitably sluggish adaptation of profit expectations could lend stability to the Kaldor model, we find yet another version to be quite prone to instability.

THE INSTABILITY OF KALDORIAN MODELS

V

Our conclusions can be summarized briefly. Two steady-state growth paths typically exist in Kaldorian models, corresponding to different capital–output ratios. The path for the smaller ratio has previously been rejected as extremely unrealistic. It is here shown that the other path is unstable. This result holds not only in the basic Kaldorian model summarized by Allen, but also in revised versions incorporating (1) a more general investment function and (2) a production function rather than the unorthodox technical progress function. If investment is made to depend upon expected, rather than current, profitability then instability persists except when expectations adjust slowly.

Thus while some specifications may sidestep the difficulty, it is apparent that there exists a strong tendency toward instability in Kaldor-type models, a result which sits rather uncomfortably with Kaldor's belief that 'one of the merits of ... [his] ... model is that it shows that the constancy in the capital/output ratio, in the share of profits and in the rate of profit can be shown to be the consequence of endogenous forces' [5, p. 593].

APPENDIX

Define $x = \dot{k}/k$. Then the object here is to examine d^2x/dR^2 for equation (21). The first and second partial derivatives are

$$\psi_x = -1 + \frac{\delta}{\alpha} R\phi'$$

$$\psi_R = -\frac{s_w}{R^2} + \delta + \frac{\delta}{\alpha}\phi$$

$$\psi_{xR} = \frac{\delta}{\alpha}\phi'$$

$$\psi_{xx} = \frac{\delta}{\alpha} R\phi''$$

$$\psi_{RR} = 2s_w/R^3.$$

Then d^2x/dR^2 is given by

$$\frac{d^2x}{dR^2} = -(\psi_{RR}\psi_x^2 - 2\psi_{xR}\psi_x\psi_R + \psi_{xx}\psi_R^2)/\psi_x^3. \tag{23}$$

Since ϕ' and ϕ'' are positive, the second partials are all positive so (23) will be positive if (but not only if) $\psi_x < 0$ and $\psi_R > 0$. These two inequalities are not inherent in the *a priori* sign restrictions but we can use the 'reasonable' numerical magnitudes of Section I to see that the second inequality will almost surely hold. For ϕ will be zero on a steady-state path and the value of δ implied by those numbers is about fifty times as great as the implied value of s_w/R^2: $\delta = 0.25$ while $s_w/R^2 = 0.0052$.

The other inequality, $\psi_x < 0$, then yields the condition (22) of Section IV. There is no ambiguity about the number of roots in this case. In steady-state growth $\dot{k}/k$ is a constant and equation (21) is then a quadratic in R, giving two solutions.

REFERENCES

1. R. G. D. Allen, *Macro-Economic Theory* (London: Macmillan, 1967).
2. J. Black, 'The technical progress function and the production function', *Economica*, May 1962, vol. 29, 166–70.
3. F. H. Hahn and R. C. O. Matthews, 'The theory of economic growth: a survey', *Economic Journal*, Dec. 1964, vol. 74, 779–902.
4. N. Kaldor, 'Alternative theories of distribution', *Review of Economic Studies*, 1955–6, vol. 23, 83–100.
5. N. Kaldor, 'A model of economic growth', *Economic Journal*, Dec. 1957, vol. 67, 591–624.
6. N. Kaldor, 'Capital accumulation and economic growth', in F. A. Lutz and D. C. Hague, editors, *The Theory of Capital* (New York: St. Martins Press, 1961).
7. N. Kaldor and J. A. Mirrlees, 'A new model of economic growth', *Review of Economic Studies*, June 1962, vol. 29, 174–92.
8. D. R. Kamerschen, editor, *Readings in Microeconomics* (Cleveland: World Pub. Co., 1967).
9. R. G. Lipsey, *An Introduction to Positive Economics* (London: Weidenfeld and Nicholson, 1963).
10. R. Marris, *The Economic Theory of 'Managerial' Capitalism* (London: Macmillan & Co., 1964).
11. F. Modigliani, 'Comment', in N.B.E.R., *The Behavior of Income Shares*, Studies in Income and Wealth, vol. 27 (Princeton: Princeton Univ. Press, 1964).
12. A. M. Moore, 'A reformulation of the Kaldor effect', *Economic Journal*, Mar. 1967, vol. 77, 84–99.
13. M. G. Mueller, editor, *Readings in Macroeconomics* (New York: Holt, Rinehart and Winston, 1966).
14. M. Nerlove, *Distributed Lags and Demand Analysis for Agricultural and Other Commodities* (Washington: U.S. Dept. of Agriculture, 1958).
15. M. W. Reder, 'Alternative theories of labor's share', in M. Abramowitz, editor, *The Allocation of Economic Resources* (Stanford: Stanford Univ. Press, 1959).
16. P. A. Samuelson, *Economics, An Introductory Analysis*, 7th ed. (New York: McGraw-Hill Book Co., 1967).
17. T. Scitovsky, 'A survey of some theories of income distribution', in N.B.E.R., *The Behavior of Income Shares*, Studies in Income and Wealth, vol. 27 (Princeton: Princeton Univ. Press, 1964).
18. J. Tobin, 'Towards a general Kaldorian theory of distribution', *Review of Economic Studies*, Feb. 1960, vol. 27, 119–20.
19. S. Weintraub, *An Approach to the Theory of Income Distribution* (Philadelphia: Chilton Co., 1958).

University of Virginia

[17]

The Degree of Monopoly in the Kaldor-Mirrlees Growth Model

1. AN INCONSISTENCY

The Kaldor-Mirrlees model of economic growth [4] seems to contain an inconsistency between the assumption of imperfect competition and the relation it postulates between the wage rate and the marginal productivity of labour.

Kaldor-Mirrlees state explicitly that "It may be assumed that each entrepreneur operating in *imperfectly competitive markets*, aims at the maximum attainable growth of his own business (subject as we shall explain below, to the maintenance of a satisfactory rate of return on the capital employed) and for that reason prefers to maintain an appreciable amount of *excess capacity* so as to be able to exploit any chance increase in his *selling power* either by increasing his *share of the market* or by invading other markets. However, when gross investment per period is in excess of the *number of workers becoming available* to "man" new equipment, the degree of excess capacity must steadily rise" [4, p. 188, my italics]. Excess capacity, selling power, share of the market, inelastic factor supply are familiar connotations of imperfect competition. Furthermore, one of the boundary conditions of the model states that "... the share of profits resulting from the model must be higher than a certain minimum (the so-called 'degree of monopoly' or 'degree of imperfect competition')" [4, p. 180] and therefore

$$\pi \geqq m,$$

where π is the share of profits in the national income, and m is the degree of monopoly, very loosely defined as a minimum profit share consistent with the market structure of the economy [4, p. 179].

On the other hand, equation (9) of the model states that

$$p_{t-T} = w_t \qquad \qquad \ldots(9)$$

where p_{t-T} is the product per worker operating equipment of age T at the time t, T is the anticipated (and realized) period of operation of equipment, and w_t is the wage rate at time t. As Kaldor-Mirrlees put it, "... since equipment will only be employed so long as its operation more than covers prime costs, the profit on the oldest yet surviving machinery must be zero" [4, p. 179]. And further on they confirm, in their general conclusions, that "... for the oldest surviving machine, the quasi-rents are zero" [4, p. 188].

But equation (9) holds if and only if there is perfect competition. Let us call o_{t-T} the physical productivity of a worker operating equipment of age T at the time t, and z_t the unit price of the product at the time t. We then have

$$p_{t-T} \equiv o_{t-T} \cdot z_t$$

and from (9):

$$w_t/o_{t-T} = z_t.$$

But w_t/o_{t-T}, the unit operating cost of the plants on the margin of obsolescence, i.e. the plants of age T, is nothing but the marginal cost of the product. If quasi-rents on those plants are zero, i.e. unit wage costs are equal to the price of the product, then marginal cost equals price in all firms operating such plants throughout the economy. This implies conditions of perfect competition. All known species of imperfect competition—monopolistic competition, kinky demand curve, mark-up pricing, oligopolistic competition, etcetera—have one feature in common: firms could produce additional output at a profit, if there was a demand for it at the ruling price. The assumption of excess capacity, explicitly stated by Kaldor-Mirrlees [4, p. 175], automatically ensures that this is the case also in the short run. For all the firms of non-competitive industries, therefore, marginal cost will be lower than selling price:

$$w_t/o_{t-T} < z_t, \text{ from which:}$$

$$w_t < z_t \cdot o_{t-T} \equiv p_{t-T},$$

which contradicts equation (9). This might have puzzled the careful reader, but the contradiction appears to have passed unnoticed in the subsequent literature.[1]

2. A WAY OUT: THE INTRODUCTION OF THE DEGREE OF MONOPOLY

One way out of this striking contradiction could be that of " degrading " the model to describe only perfectly competitive situations, abandoning the more ambitious task of introducing imperfect competition in this growth model. The assumption of perfect competition, however, would clash with the postulated type of investment behaviour, which is based on a fixed pay-off period for investment per worker and is essential to the model and its stability (because it breaks the link between the capital-output ratio and the rate of interest).

A better alternative could be that of introducing the degree of monopoly for the economy as a whole, not as a boundary condition as it was in the model, but as a variable defined as $\mu \equiv (z_t - (w_t/o_{t-T}))/z_t$, i.e. the excess of price over marginal cost, divided by price. But $z_t \equiv p_{t-T}/o_{t-T}$ and therefore $\mu \equiv (p_{t-T} - w_t)/p_{t-T}$. We could now replace (9) by

$$p_{t-T} = w_t/(1-\mu). \qquad \ldots(9')$$

With one more variable and the same number of equations as before, the system would now be underdetermined. Lacking an extra equation for the determination of μ, to make ends meet we have to assume that μ is a constant. The introduction of μ has the following consequences on the other equations of the model and its general conclusions:

(1) The redefined " degree of monopoly " now is no longer a constraint to the value of the share of profit π_t. If before the constraint was not really expected to bite, now by definition the degree of monopoly μ is smaller than π_t, because $p_{t-T} < y_t$, the *average* product per worker at the time t, and hence

$$\mu \equiv \frac{p_{t-T} - w_t}{p_{t-T}} < \frac{y_t - w_t}{y_t} \equiv \pi_t.$$

[1] Hahn and Matthews, for instance, in their authoritative survey of growth theories recognize the importance of the assumption of imperfect competition in the Kaldor-Mirrlees model: " [As a result of] the rejection of perfect competition . . . the profit margin per unit of output at a given capital-labour ratio vecomes a variable. The introduction of this extra variable liberates the distribution of income from the shackles of marginal productivity. It thereby permits the existence of steady-state equilibrium at full employment, notwithstanding element (3) [the investment function], which adds an equation to the standard neo-classical set and would therefore otherwise make the system overdetermined " [1, p. 797]. They take, however, the statements of the model at their face value.

The same contradiction, incidentally, can be found in another paper by Kaldor [3] on the value added tax. On the one hand he says: " Changes in market demand induce variations in the level of activity of *all* firms, and not only the marginal firms. This is evidence that conditions of imperfect competition prevail and the output of the infra-marginal firm is limited by demand, and not by the capacity to produce " [3, p. 273]. On the other hand, he also says: " Old equipment works for what it can get; it will continue to be operated so long as the scrap value of equipment is less than the discounted value of the profits from its operation " [3, p. 275]. This second statement is tantamount to equation (9) of the Kaldor-Mirrlees model. The contradiction undermines Kaldor's analysis of the effects of the value-added tax, but the consequences of this go beyond the scope of this note.

MONOPOLY IN THE KALDOR-MIRRLEES GROWTH MODEL

(2) If μ is a constant, it follows from (9') that

$$\frac{\dot{w}_t}{w_t} = \frac{\dot{p}_{t-T}}{p_{t-T}}\left(1 - \frac{dT}{dt}\right),$$

which is the same result that is derived from the original formulation of equation (9), and is all that is needed in the model to prove that when the rate of growth of the wage rate is constant, T will also remain constant.[1]

(3) A constant μ, however, is only a kind of *deus ex machina*, which does not leave things entirely unchanged. The parameter μ, in fact, enters the equations defining the golden age path. In particular, equation (14) now becomes (14'):

$$\frac{\dot{y}_t}{y_t} + \lambda + \delta = r\frac{p_t}{y_t} - \frac{(r-\lambda-\delta)w_t}{(1-\mu)y_t}, \qquad \ldots(14')$$

where λ is the rate of growth of population, δ the rate of " radioactive " decay of machines, and r the number of workers available to operate new equipment per unit period expressed as a proportion of the working population. Equation (30) now takes the form (30'):

$$\frac{i}{y} = \frac{1-e^{-(\rho+\delta)T}}{\rho+\delta}\frac{p}{y} - \frac{1-e^{-(\rho+\delta-\gamma)T}}{(\rho+\delta-\gamma)(1-\mu)}\frac{w}{y}, \qquad \ldots(30')$$

where i is investment per worker, ρ is the general rate of profit assumed by entrepreneurs, and γ the rate of (neutral) technical progress.

All the numerical values presented in the tables of section 15 of the article [4, pp. 186-187], obtained solving the system for various arbitrarily selected values of the parameters, imply $\mu = 0$. But this is the perfectly competitive case, and is therefore devoid of any interest. Numerical results will have to be reworked anew for alternative values of $\mu > 0$, and it should be an interesting exercise to explore the sensitivity of the solutions to the value of μ. Alternatively, one might take μ as given, and ask what value of π (or s, the proportion of gross profits saved, or T) would be required for the consistency of the model.

The relation between monopoly and distribution was first formulated by Kalecki,[2] in a form which Kaldor dismissed as tautological.[3] Kalecki assumed a reverse L-shaped cost curve, prime costs being constant up to full capacity output and marginal costs equal to average prime costs. The degree of monopoly, defined as the excess of price over marginal cost, divided by price, was hence equal to the share of profits in the output of each firm, and the share of profits in the national income was a weighted average of the degree of monopoly in all the firms of the economy. In a vintage model à la Kaldor-Mirrlees marginal cost (i.e. labour unit cost on the machine on the verge of obsolescence) is higher than average prime cost because of the coexistence of different vintages, and as we have seen $\mu < \pi$, but μ has an effect on π through the solution of the system of equations. By pulling the loose end thus revealed, namely the impact of μ on π, one might well unravel the carefully woven fabric of the Cambridge theory of distribution.

King's College, Cambridge   D. Mario Nuti.

First version received 23.5.68; *final version received* 2.10.68.

[1] [4], pp. 181-182. If μ is not constant in time, the equation becomes

$$\frac{\dot{w}_t}{w_t} = \frac{\dot{p}_{t-T}}{p_{t-T}}\left(1 - \frac{dT}{dt}\right) - \frac{\dot{\mu}_t}{1-\mu_t}.$$

[2] [5], [6, ch. I], [7, 8, 9, 10], [11, ch. I], [12, Part I].
[3] See [2].

REFERENCES

[1] Hahn, F. H. and Matthews, R. C. O. "The Theory of Economic Growth: a Survey", *Economic Journal* (1964), pp. 779-902.

[2] Kaldor, N. "Alternative Theories of Distribution", *The Review of Economic Studies*, **33** (1955).

[3] Kaldor, N. A Memorandum on the Value Added Tax, submitted to the *Committee on Turnover Taxation* in July 1963, reprinted in *Essays on Economic Policy*, vol. I (London, 1964) pp. 266-293.

[4] Kaldor, N. and Mirrlees, J. A. "A New Model of Economic Growth", *The Review of Economic Studies*, **29** (1962), 174-192.

[5] Kalecki, M. "The Determinants of Distribution of National Income", *Econometrica* (1938), pp. 97-112.

[6] Kalecki, M. *Essays in the Theory of Economic Fluctuations* (London, 1939).

[7] Kalecki, M. "The Theory of Long-run Distribution of the Product of Industry", *Oxford Economic Papers* (1941), pp. 31-41.

[8] Kalecki, M. "The Problem of Profit Margins", *Oxford Bulletin of Statistics* (1942), pp. 114-117.

[9] Kalecki, M. "Mr Whitman on the Concept of 'Degree of Monopoly'—A Comment", *Economic Journal* (1942), pp. 111-127.

[10] Kalecki, M. "A Theory of Profits", *Economic Journal* (1942), pp. 258-267.

[11] Kalecki, M. *Studies in Economic Dynamics* (New York, 1943).

[12] Kalecki, M. *Theory of Dynamic Economics* (London, 1954).

[18]

A Further Note

There are two elements in Kalecki's theory of distribution. The first is: " the workers spend what they get and the capitalists get what they spend ". The total gross profit per annum in the economy is the gross investment of the year plus the consumption of profits of the year. The second branch of Kalecki's theory is concerned with prices in the short period. He originally set it out in terms of old-fashioned static marginal and average revenue. It can be more simply (and realistically) expressed in terms of the price policy of firms; profit margins, in each market, settle at the level that yields the expected rate of profit (the best attainable in the given conditions) at an average degree of utilization of plant (permitting super-normal profits in a seller's market and sub-normal profits in a buyer's market to be realised through changes in output at constant prices, instead of through changes in prices, as must be supposed to occur under perfect competition). In terms of the old-fashioned theory, given the policy of all the rest, each finds a kink in his individual demand curve at his actual rate of sales; there is no advantage for anyone in trying to sell more today, but each finds the kink moving outwards through time so that he can plan to increase sales in the future at the same level of profit margins as he is enjoying today.

A FURTHER NOTE

Each firm can invest where it sees profit opportunities. It is not confined to producing a rigidly demarcated single commodity. Thus from the short-period (price policy) point of view the model is monopolistic while from a long-run (investment policy) point of view it is competitive in a broad sense.

There is a missing link in the Mirrlees-Kaldor model as serious as the one pointed out by Mario Nuti—the level of employment is not explained. From a long-period point of view it seems that they assume that the demand for labour (given by the expansion of the capital stock) happens to be growing at the same rate as the supply, but from the short-period point of view they seem to confuse an excess of capacity of capital equipment relatively to the labour force with excess capacity relatively to demand. The first kind of excess capacity is not consistent with equilibrium, because it calls for an increase in the capital-labour ratio by " deepening " or accepting a capital-using bias in technical progress. Surplus capacity in the second sense is a normal and acceptable feature of imperfect competition in a market which (though growing steadily over all) is not exactly foreseeable for the individual seller. (In a world where demand was, and was expected to be, growing perfectly steadily in each market, capacity would be tailored to output and there would be no visible difference between perfect and imperfect competition. There would still be no mechanism to ensure that full capacity and full employment exactly coincided).

With the above amended version of the theory, we must face the paradox proposed by Mario Nuti—under imperfect competition price exceeds marginal prime cost. How then, in a vintage model, can it be true that plant is not discarded until the real wage has risen to the point where its quasi-rent is zero so that price is equal to marginal cost? Let us postulate that accumulation is going on and output growing at a steady rate, the growth of the labour force and the rate of neutral technical progress being sufficient to admit this, and that the overall rate of profit on capital is constant through time. Profit margins are such as to yield the best obtainable rate of profit for each firm.

However imperfect competition may be, the rule still applies that a given output is produced at minimum cost, and total average cost of production is lower the longer a plant can be operated while covering its prime cost. How then can the apparent contradiction be resolved? The answer is that we must distinguish between the short-period and the long-period meaning of marginal cost. Assuming reverse-L marginal cost curves for each plant, short-period marginal cost is given by the foot of the L; long-period marginal cost is the average prime cost of the marginal plant, that is of the oldest plant still in use. Now, it is true that price exceeds the costs shown by the foot of the L at every moment when the plant is being operated. But a reverse L does not mean that average and marginal prime costs are equal. There is always an element of quasi-fixed cost which must be incurred when a plant is kept in running order. Thus average prime cost falls with output up to full capacity. This cost, along with the foot of the L, rises through time as real wages rise. (It may also rise through time because of wear and tear—extra repair costs etc. as the plant grows older).

Taking a firm which is a microcosm of the whole economy, operating plants of each vintage, it may be supposed always to load output onto its lower-cost plants, so that it is the oldest plant which is operated below capacity when demand is at the expected average level. The plant ceases to operate when average prime cost is equal to price, and quasi-rent is zero.

The most important point in Kalecki's analysis is the demonstration that the over-all rate of profit cannot be raised by raising the degree of monopoly. A higher proportion of profit margins leads to lower real wages and lower utilization of plant, not to a higher overall total profit. (Of course, if government guarantees to keep up effective demand by non-productive outlays, the firms, taken as a whole, can extract whatever rate of profit they choose).

The main conclusion holds good when the theory is transposed into long-period terms. In two economies with the same rate of profit and the same technical conditions, that which has higher gross margins has a lower overall output per plant, therefore a higher capital/output ratio and a lower level of real wages.

The speciality of the Mirrlees-Kaldor model concerns the determination of the overall rate of growth through the pay-off principle. This is unaffected by the above amendments.

Cambridge   JOAN ROBINSON

Received 23.5.68

[19]

Some Fallacies in the Interpretation of Kaldor

The Review of Economic Studies has recently published three notes criticizing various aspects of my growth models, by K. Kubota [7], M. Nuti [9] and J. Robinson [10]. As I had no opportunity to comment on these at the time of their publication, the Editors kindly agreed to publish this reply to deal with all three papers together.

I. KUBOTA

Kubota makes two points.

(1) The first relates to my 1957 article [3] and says that the proof of the stability of equilibrium given in pages 609-610 of the paper is illegitimate, and does not follow from the specification of the values of the parameters; to validate the proof requires the further assumption:

$$(\alpha' - \beta)(\alpha - \beta) - \beta' > 0. \qquad ...(1)$$

However his own specification of the assumptions of the model concerning the parameters is incomplete: he overlooked the restriction introduced on p. 607, viz.:

$$\alpha - \beta > \beta' Y_t/K_t. \qquad ...(2)$$

This, together with the assumptions that $\alpha > \beta$ and $P_t/K_t > 0$, *implies* Kubota's condition.

This can be shown in the following way. Subtracting the savings equation (Kubota's equation 1.1) from the investment equation (1.2, remembering that $K_{t+1} = K_t + \Delta K_t$) we get

$$\dot{K}_t = (\alpha' - \beta)Y_t + [\beta'(Y_t/K_t) - \alpha + \beta]P_t,$$

and multiplying each side by $(\alpha - \beta)/Y_t$,

$$(\alpha - \beta)\dot{K}_t/Y_t = (\alpha - \beta)(\alpha' - \beta) + [\beta' - (\alpha - \beta)(K_t/Y_t)](\alpha - \beta)(P_t/K_t). \qquad ...(3)$$

Writing $(\alpha - \beta)K_t/Y_t > \beta'$ for (2) above, equation (3) in the light of (2) ensures that:

$$\beta' < (\alpha - \beta)K_t/Y_t < (\alpha - \beta)(\alpha' - \beta), \qquad ...(4)$$

since the second term of the right-hand side of (3) must be negative if (2) holds and $(\alpha - \beta)$ and P_t/K_t are both positive. Since the assumption given in (2) implies (4), it evidently implies Kubota's condition given under (1) above. (I owe this proof to D. G. Champernowne.)

(2) Kubota's second point concerns my 1961 paper [4] and says that the two equations given there—reproduced as (2.1) and (2.2) on p. 358 of Kubota's paper—rule out a steady growth solution, for the simple reason that they imply

$$\dot{K}(t+0) = \dot{K}(t),$$

whereas steady growth (with $G_k, G_y > 0$) implies

$$\dot{K}(t+0) > \dot{K}(t).$$

This turns out to be a rather trivial point which arises on account of an oversight in the formulation of equation (15) as printed in the paper ([4], p. 216). This has not been spotted earlier; and but for Mr Kubota's careful consideration might not have been spotted at all.

In the context of the model, G_k and G_y are to be interpreted as the rates of growth of capital and output at any *instant* of time; the time lag, θ, is introduced to indicate that investment at any time is induced by output changes which have already taken place. Hence $G_k(t+\theta)$ *reflects* $G_y(t)$; the former should have been denoted as $\dot{K}(t+\theta)/K(t+\theta)$, the latter as $\dot{Y}(t)/Y(t)$; whereas the equation as formulated in the paper implies that

$$G_k(t+\theta) = [K(t+\theta)-K(t)]/K(t).$$

This is clearly wrong, and leads to the absurd results analyzed by Kubota. The proper formalization of the assumptions of the model would have required that equation (15) of my paper be written in the form (expressed in terms of Kubota's own notation, as given in equation (2.1), p. 358)

$$\dot{K}(t+\theta) = [G_y(t)-\lambda-\alpha''][K(t+\theta)/\beta''] + \lambda K(t+\theta) + \mu \frac{d}{dt}[Y(t)/K(t)],$$

in which case the whole of the second part of Kubota's paper becomes irrelevant.

II. NUTI

Nuti's paper relates to the 1962 article [6] and makes a perfectly valid point—i.e. that the model assumes imperfect competition, in which case, equipment by a " typical " profit-maximizing firm will be abandoned before the quasi-rents on that equipment fall to zero. Hence equation (9) of that paper, instead of being as stated (on p. 179)

$$P_{t-T} = w_t$$

should have been written

$$P_{t-T} = w_t/(1-\mu),$$

where μ (" the degree of monopoly ") is the minimum profit required for continued operation of any particular vintage of equipment.

This requires, as Nuti says, the incorporation of a further equation relating to μ which, for want of anything better, could be put in the form

$$\mu = \bar{\mu} \text{ (a constant)}.$$

As a formal criticism of the model this is perfectly correct; how important it is, depends on the actual value of μ in relation to the labour cost per unit of output on the least profitable plant in use. If μ is relatively small, the model probably survives comparatively unscathed (though, as Nuti says, this remains to be demonstrated, by working out the numerical solutions of the equations for particular values of $\mu>0$). It is known, on the other hand, from empirical investigations of F. W. Brechling on the basis of Census of Production data [1] that the share of gross profit in value added shows a very high variation as between different " establishments "; whereas this share is as high as 80 per cent for the top 10 per cent of establishments (i.e. the establishments employing 10 per cent of the labour force with the highest value added per employee) it is only 10-15 per cent for the bottom 10 per cent of " establishments ": which means that for the marginal, say, 1 per cent of establishments it must be lower still.

" Establishments " as statistically defined, are not of course the same thing as individual vintages of " equipment ". We can take it that in so far as any single " establishment " possesses a variety of vintages of " equipment ", the ratio of profit on the output produced with the aid of the least efficient " equipment " must be less, and cannot be greater, than

---

[1] In an as yet unpublished paper.

the share of profit on the output of the establishment as a whole. Similarly, "establishments" are not the same thing as "firms", in that a single firm may control a whole host of establishments. We also know however (from Inland Revenue data, published some time ago [1]) that the share of profits in relation to the value added shows the same kind of scatter among "firms" as it does among "establishments". In a typical "industry" there is generally a fringe of firms operating with near-zero profits; about 10 per cent of output comes from firms operating with a 5-15 per cent ratio of gross profits to value added; and 10 per cent from firms with a profit ratio of 50-60 per cent. It is perfectly possible therefore that the "marginal equipment" of the least efficient firm is one that is considerably older than the "marginal" equipment of a high-profit firm. It is also possible to suppose that equipment of a given vintage will go on being used by *some* firms, long after it has been discarded by its original owner—in the same way as a motor car finds its way to the "marginal car-owner" before it is thrown on the scrap-heap.

Unfortunately we do not possess a fully worked out price-and-competition theory to account for these phenomena. The kind of theory I was working on (which was more fully developed in a subsequent paper [5] on the value-added tax) was a kind of oligopoly-cum-price-leadership theory. The "full cost" on the most efficient "vintages" set prices; the firms possessing older vintages are faced with a kinked demand curve—i.e., they must meet the prices set by the market, but that does *not* imply that they can sell any amount at that price.

This presupposes that differences in the efficiency-ranking (or profit-ranking) of firms are primarily to be explained by factors other than the vintages of equipment which they use: for if these differences were caused by the age of equipment in use and nothing else, competition between firms would tend to eliminate them; it would pay each firm to have its due share of equipment of *all* vintages, and if this is not possible, given the volume of its sales and the degree of indivisibility of equipment, it would pay firms to amalgamate until they achieved this. In that case whilst the profit-profile of different *vintages of plant* would show a wide scatter, the share of profit in output of the different *firms* would be the same.

Since this is clearly not the case, there must be other factors at work (e.g. differences in "selling power", managerial efficiency, etc.) which prevent this from happening; and until we know what these other factors are, it is useless to speculate on the influence of imperfect competition on the length of the working-life of equipment. I have been operating on the "hunch" that the least efficient (i.e. least profitable) firms tend to be also those using the least-efficient equipment: in which case the importance of Nuti's point is not likely to be large. But I confess it is no more than a hunch; it is not an assumption that to my knowledge has yet been tested empirically, nor is there a satisfactory theoretical hypothesis which would show this result as the outcome of the operation of market processes.

The trouble is that existing *theories* of imperfect competition (Chamberlin, Robinson or Kalecki) are largely "micro"-theories: they concern the equilibrium of an individual firm faced with a given market situation. When it comes to considering the equilibrium of a *group* of firms, they all assume (explicitly or implicitly) that all firms are identical with respect to their cost and demand functions—a procedure which assumes away all the interesting (and important) aspects of the competitive process.

III. ROBINSON

Joan Robinson makes two points.

(1) The first is that in the 1962 model "the level of employment is not explained"; since the model assumes that the demand for labour grows at the same rate as the supply,

[1] See [1], Tables 67-81.

despite the fact that excess capacity prevails. Excess capacity in relation to the labour force (as distinct from excess capacity due to insufficiency of demand in times of unemployment) is not, according to Joan Robinson, " consistent with equilibrium because it calls for an increase in the capital-labour ratio by ' deepening ' or accepting a capital-using bias in technical progress." ([10], p. 261).

There is, however, no difference between a state of " unemployment " and a state of " full employment " from the point of view of the prospects and motives of the individual firm operating in imperfect markets. As I argued in a paper published before the war ([2], p. 652) shortages of labour will slow down the expansion of output in the economy as a whole and thereby slow down the growth of effective demand (in real terms); for any particular producer, a slow-down in the growth of demand due to labour-bottlenecks in *some* sector of the economy may appear indistinguishable from a slow-down in the growth of demand due to other causes. And even for producers who experience the labour-shortages directly (by not being able to hire enough labour to prevent their production from lagging behind their inflow of orders) such hold-ups in output will appear as something temporary—a delay in filling vacancies, and not a long-term limitation on the number of workers they can hire.

The motives which cause firms, in a world of imperfect competition, to maintain capacity ahead of output—the motive of being in a position to exploit any chance increase in selling power (cf. [6], para. 3)—operate just as powerfully in times of full employment as at other times. And looking at the empirical side, there is plenty of evidence to show that the amount of excess capacity maintained in a developed economy (such as the U.K. or the U.S.) is considerably greater than the amount that could possibly be activated through a full use of the available labour potential. Whilst " excess capacity " is invariably linked to imperfect competition (in the sense that it would not exist in a world of infinitely elastic demand curves) it would be a mistake to regard it as a symptom of " insufficiency of demand "—something which would disappear if demand were adequate to secure full utilization of " resources ".

For in a period of rising demand and employment, investment activity is accelerated as well; output grows faster, but so does output-capacity. When the expansion of output is slowed down with the approach to full employment, the growth of capacity will also be slowed down, sooner or later—but not sufficiently to eliminate excess capacity in relation to output. It is perfectly consistent to assume that, in long-term equilibrium, both output and output capacity should grow at the same rate, without implying that the one is equal to the other. The assumption moreover that all but the marginal plant will be fully utilized when demand is " at the expected average level ", since " however imperfect competition may be, the rule still applies that a given output is produced at *minimum* cost " (p. 261, my italics) is equally contradicted by empirical evidence. For if it were true, the (short-period) elasticity of output with respect to employment would necessarily be less than 1, and not considerably greater than 1 (such as 3, according to " Okun's Law ").

The view that in a state of (prolonged) full employment excess capacity would disappear would be correct only if full employment of labour combined with excess capacity of plant caused such a rise in wages (in terms of output) and such a shrinkage of profits as to make enough of the less efficient plants unprofitable for the elimination of capital redundancy. This would be true on competitive neo-classical assumptions, under the hypothesis of reverse L-shaped cost curves for each plant: the competition of employers for labour would cause wages to rise, and profits to shrink, until either capital became a " free good ", or the employment capacity of still extant equipment ceased to be excessive in relation to labour. (The same would follow, on somewhat different grounds, under Marxian assumptions, where the existence of unemployment—a "reserve army" of labour—is an essential condition for employers being able to *make* profits.)

Assuming that capital equipment consists of a battery of " vintages " of varying efficiency, this shrinkage of profits would be brought to a halt *before* profits fell to zero—

SOME FALLACIES IN THE INTERPRETATION OF KALDOR

unless one made the extreme assumption that there is more than enough capacity of the most efficient kind (of the "latest vintage") to accommodate the whole of the labour force. On less extreme assumptions there is always some level of profits at which "capacity would be tailored to output"; and profits would go on falling, and capacity shrinking, until this was brought about.

But it is at this point where the "neo-classical" and the "Cambridge" theories of distribution yield opposite predictions. According to the "Cambridge" theory, the labour market does *not* behave in accordance with the postulates of neo-classical theory: with a rise in the demand for labour, there is a rise in the share of profit, and a fall in the share of wages, and not the other way round. (This of course is not inconsistent with a rise in *absolute* wages—in wages per man—if output-per-head also rises with rising employment.) This is because a high demand for labour is associated with a high rate of investment and a high rate of profit on capital. Empirically, the evidence here supports Cambridge, and *not* the implications of neo-classical theory: the share of profit and the level of employment are *positively* correlated, not negatively. To the extent that there is a "choice of techniques" in connection with new investment there would, on neo-classical assumptions, be "enshallowing" rather than "deepening", making "capital-widening" (the rate of growth of capacity) all the greater. At the same time the life of the oldest surviving equipment would also be prolonged—on account of the rise in profits—thereby adding further to surplus capacity. Hence as an investment boom comes up against a labour bottleneck, it is bound to increase capital redundancy still further; and it is through this increase in surplus capacity that the investment boom is ultimately abated.

On the assumptions of my paper the rise in profit would lead to some "capital deepening" rather than "enshallowing" since with a higher share of profit in output, any given pay-off period would breed more investment per unit of capacity. But it could easily be shown that this "deepening effect" could do no more than moderate the strong positive correlation between the ratio of investment to output and the growth of output capacity.

Finally there is the question whether this whole issue (of full employment and labour shortages leading to more "deepening") is relevant to Joan Robinson's main question —i.e. whether a state of steady growth is consistent with full employment, and whether there is a mechanism to ensure that "the demand for labour (given by the expansion of the capital stock) grows at the same rate as the supply". If one assumed that the share of investment in output, I/Y, is exogenously given—either by a neo-classical savings function, or by a Marxian "surplus"—it would clearly follow that the more "deepening" goes on (the higher the amount of investment per unit of output-capacity) the less will be the rate of increase in the demand for labour at any given rate of accumulation, $\dot{K}/K$. Moreover if one takes *both* I/Y and $\dot{K}/K$ as exogenously given, the demand for labour will only grow at the same rate as the supply as a result of a fortunate accident. If the emergence of "full employment" causes extra deepening, and the rate of accumulation remains the same, the demand for labour will rise at a lower rate; if that rate was previously adequate, it will now be inadequate. The "deepening" consequential on full employment clearly played a vital role also in Marx's original crisis theory—it was the increase in the "organic composition of capital" consequent upon a temporary shortage of labour caused by over-investment which restored the reserve army, and enabled exploitation to go ahead again (though only at a lower rate of profit).[1]

But here again, the "Cambridge" theory of distribution (at least the Kaldor-Pasinetti version of it) parts company with both Marx and the neo-classicals. Here I/Y and $\dot{K}/K$

---

[1] There are however passages in Marx's *Kapital* which show that he clearly perceived the regulatory function of changes in the share of wages (of the "degree of exploitation", or the ratio of "paid" to "unpaid" labour) in keeping the growth of (fixed) capital in line with the growth of the labour supply (cf. [8], p. 634). These ideas were not made further use of in his crisis theory (with which they are not consistent); they were developed however, with great force, in our own day, by the German economist, H. J. Rüstow [11] who made it the basis of a dynamic growth model which shows striking similarity with the Kaldor-Mirrlees model [6], but with which we were not familiar at the time.

are *not* exogenously given, but are themselves determined by the condition that the capacity to employ labour should grow at the same rate as the labour supply. If, as a result of more " deepening ", or a capital-using bias in technical progress, more investment is required to secure this, I/Y will rise, and the share of profits will rise sufficiently to generate the extra savings required. If the multiplier-accelerator mechanism is sufficiently powerful to bring effective demand and output up to the full employment ceiling, it will also be powerful enough to keep it there, even when the " ceiling " rises faster owing to a faster, growth of productivity. In other words, the effects of the extra-labour-saving features of new equipment will be balanced by an increase in the rate of growth of both capital and output, and not by a fall in the rate of growth of employment. The " natural rate " of growth will rise. But in a neo-Keynesian model it is the " warranted " rate which adjusts itself to the " natural rate ", and not the other way round.

(2) Joan Robinson's second point concerns Nuti, and deals with the " apparent contradiction " between Nuti's proposition that under imperfect competition price exceeds marginal cost, and the proposition that equipment will not be discarded until its quasi-rent is zero. Her answer is that price can exceed marginal cost, without exceeding *average* labour costs, owing to the existence of overhead labour costs (" quasi-fixed " costs); and the representative firm which is a " micro-cosmos of the whole economy " (possessing a representative battery of vintages) will keep plant in operation until " average prime cost is equal to price, and quasi-rent is zero ".

But in this she is mistaken. Making her own assumptions about profit-maximization and the " micro-cosmos " firm, and assuming imperfect competition with sales limited by demand, it will always pay that firm to abandon plant *before* " quasi-rents fall to zero "; and that means before *average* prime costs, and not just marginal costs, become equal to price. For it would *not* pay a profit-maximizing firm to produce any part of its output on plants on the operation of which it makes no profit, if it is not faced with infinitely elastic demand.

King's College, Cambridge NICHOLAS KALDOR

First version received July, 1969; final version received September, 1969

REFERENCES

[1] *95th Report of the Commissioners of Inland Revenue*, London, H.M.S.O., January 1953, Cmd. 8726.

[2] Kaldor, N. " Stability and Full Employment ", *Economic Journal*, **48** (1938), 642-657.

[3] Kaldor, N. " A Model of Economic Growth ", *Economic Journal*, **62** (1957), 591-624.

[4] Kaldor, N. " Capital Accumulation and Economic Growth ", in Lutz, F. A. and Hague, D. C. (eds.), *The Theory of Capital* (London, Macmillan, 1961).

[5] Kaldor, N. " A Memorandum on the Value Added Tax ", submitted to the Committee on Turnover Taxation in July 1963 and printed in *Essays in Economic Policy*, Vol. I (London, 1964), 266-293.

[6] Kaldor, N. and Mirrlees, J. A. " A New Model of Economic Growth ", *Review of Economic Studies*, **29** (1962), 174-192.

[7] Kubota, K. " A Re-Examination of the Existence and Stability Propositions in Kaldor's Growth Models ", *Review of Economic Studies*, **35** (1968), 353-360.

[8] Marx, K. *Capital: A Critical Analysis of Capitalist Production*, Ed. F. Engels, transl. S. Moore and E. Aveling (London, Swan Sonnenschein, 1887).

[9] Nuti, D. M. " The Degree of Monopoly in the Kaldor-Mirrlees Growth Model ", *Review of Economic Studies*, **36** (1969), 257-260.

[10] Robinson, J. " A Further Note ", *Review of Economic Studies*, **36** (1969), 260-262.

[11] Rustow, H. J. "Akkumulation und Krisen" (doctoral dissertation to the University of Heidelberg, 1926), in *Theorie der Vollbeschäftigung in der freien Marktwirtschaft* (Tübingen, Mohr, 1951).

A COMMENT ON KALDOR'S NOTE [1]

Kaldor's note [1] settles the two problems about his growth models I raised in my earlier note [2]. With respect to the model of 1957, Kaldor points out that my specification of the model was incomplete. This is true and because of the incompleteness I made an invalid charge against Kaldor. I was unaware of the force of Kaldor's assumption:

$$\alpha - \beta > \beta' Y_t / K_t.$$

As Kaldor claims, this assumption in combination with others implies my condition $(\alpha' - \beta)(\alpha - \beta) - \beta' > 0$.

With respect to the model of 1961, Kaldor makes a correction in the specification of the model. The correction eliminates the inconsistency between Kaldor's earlier specification and the existence proposition. Kaldor's existence proposition is now valid.

A new problem arises about the 1961 model: is the steady rate of growth unconditionally stable in the corrected version? As of the present date I have not succeeded in obtaining a definite answer to this question.

New York Office of the K. KUBOTA
United Nations Conference on
Trade and Development

Received October 1969

REFERENCES

[1] Kaldor, N. " Some Fallacies in the Interpretation of Kaldor ", *Review of Economic Studies*, **37** (1970).

[2] Kubota, K. " A Re-examination of the Existence and Stability Propositions in Kaldor's Growth Models ", *Review of Economic Studies*, **35** (1968).

[1] The views expressed in this note are those of the author and do not reflect those of the United Nations Secretariat to which the author belongs.

[21]

The Stability of Kaldor's 1957 Model [1,2]

D. G. CHAMPERNOWNE
Trinity College, Cambridge

1. INTRODUCTION

This article contains a discussion of the conditions which must be satisfied if the growth-path in Kaldor's 1957 model [1] is to be stable. In particular, the upper limit prescribed for the coefficient β' in his second equation, reproduced below as (2.2), will have to be revised downwards in order to rule out the possibility of antidamped cobweb oscillations of period 2. This possibility was overlooked in the original article. It will be shown that if the model is reformulated as a continuous-time model, the limits prescribed in the 1957 article do, as it happens, ensure that steady growth will be stable.

However, the limits on the coefficient β' required for stability indicate considerably less economic influence of the rate of profit upon investment than Kaldor considered realistic. Accordingly he has suggested [2] that the model should be modified to allow investment to be influenced not just by the current rate of profit, but by a moving average of the rate of profit over recent years. This modification is introduced in the latter part of this article, and it enables far higher values of the coefficient β' to be used without destroying the stability of the growth-path.

2. THE BASIC EQUATIONS AND THE RESTRICTIONS

The three equations of the model are given on page 604 of [1] and may be written as

$$K_{t+1} - K_t = \alpha P_t + \beta(Y_t - P_t), \qquad \ldots(2.1)$$

$$K_{t+1} = \left\{\alpha' + \beta' \frac{P_t}{K_t}\right\} Y_t, \qquad \ldots(2.2)$$

$$\frac{Y_{t+1} - Y_t}{Y_t} = \alpha'' + \beta'' \left\{\frac{K_{t+1} - K_t}{K_t}\right\}. \qquad \ldots(2.3)$$

K_t, Y_t and P_t denote capital, income and profits in any period t. A number of restriction were laid down in the article, some for economic reasons, and some to reduce the risk of instability. They included the following:

$$1 > \alpha > \beta \geq 0, \ \alpha' > 0, \ \beta' > 0, \ \alpha'' > 0, \ 1 > \beta'' > 0, \qquad \ldots(2.4)$$

$$\alpha - \beta > \beta' \frac{Y_t}{K_t}, \ \frac{P_t}{Y_t} \geq m > 0, \qquad \ldots(2.5)$$

$$P_t \leq Y_t - W_{\min}. \qquad \ldots(2.6)$$

Denoting the capital-output ratio K_t/Y_t by V_t and its equilibrium value by V^*, the condition (2.5) imposes on β' the restriction

$$\beta' < (\alpha - \beta) V_t. \qquad \ldots(2.7)$$

---

[1] *First version received Jan.* 1970; *final version received April* 1970 (*Eds*).
[2] I am indebted to Dr. P. das Gupta for pointing out some errors in the algebra. He is in no way responsible for any which may remain.

The conditions (2.4-7) suffice to ensure that the step $V_{t+1}-V_t$ is always in the same direction, i.e. has the same sign, as the step V^*-V_t to the equilibrium value.

However, in 1959, a year or two after the publication of [1] I became aware that, under the implicit assumption of (2.2), that investment decisions relating to successive periods are taken at corresponding discrete intervals of time, there is always a possibility that steps generated in the model towards equilibrium might " overshoot the mark " and thus set up antidamped cobweb oscillations of period 2. It became clear that the limit (2.7) imposed on β' was not quite low enough to rule out this case, although it would do so and ensure stability, if the model was reformulated in terms of differential equations instead of difference equations. The economic meaning of this reformulation is that investment plans are now regarded as being *continuously* adjusted to current conditions, and this seems no less interesting an assumption than that of the original model. It was also felt at that time, perhaps wrongly, that the condition of antidamped cobweb oscillations was a freak case, and that the values of β' which would give rise to this case were unrealistic ones. In any case Kaldor had then just produced the model [2] which was designed to allow for the influence of profit-rate on investment more fully without introducing instability. For these various reasons, the possibility of the antidamped cobweb oscillations did not seem sufficiently important to merit publication.

But now that there is an apparent revival of interest in the stability of the 1957 model, see [4] and [6], it is worth setting out the conditions of stability more systematically. In Section 3 the model will be reformulated in terms of differential equations and the claim will be substantiated that the conditions (2.3-7) above, taken from the original article, are sufficient to ensure the global stability of the model. This continuous-time version of the model is easier to analyse than the original version and is, for this reason, analysed first. Having established the global stability of the capital-output ratio, the entire history of V along its path towards the equilibrium V^* is obtained from any feasible initial value V_0: this history is found by obtaining t explicitly as a function of V, and by then regarding V as the inverse function of t.

In Section 4, the original discrete-time model is analysed in the particular case ($\beta = 0$) where there is no saving out of wages, and the necessary conditions for stability are found in the form of a stricter limit on the value of β'. But the general case where $\beta > 0$ is decidedly unwieldy and the analysis of this case is accordingly relegated to an Appendix.

In Section 5 the economic interpretation of the restrictions will be discussed, and it will be considered how the Investment equation (2.2) of the original model or (3.2) of the continuous-time model may be modified in the hope of restoring stability to the model under a wider range of values of β'.

In Sections 6-7 the modified model in the form of differential equations will be analysed and the limits on β' required for local stability of the capital-output ratio equilibrium will be established. The economic meaning of these new results will be briefly discussed.

3. THE DIFFERENTIAL-EQUATION VERSION OF THE MODEL

In this version of the model, we replace K_t, Y_t, P_t and V_t by the continuous variables K, Y, P and V and we denote their time-derivatives by $\dot{K}$, $\dot{Y}$, $\dot{P}$ and $\dot{V}$. For equations (2.1-3) we substitute

$$\dot{K} = \alpha P + \beta(Y-P), \qquad \ldots(3.1)$$

$$K + \dot{K} = \left\{\alpha' + \beta' \frac{P}{K}\right\} Y, \qquad \ldots(3.2)$$

$$\frac{\dot{Y}}{Y} = \alpha'' + \beta'' \frac{\dot{K}}{K}, \qquad \ldots(3.3)$$

and we retain all the restrictions (2.4-7) dropping the suffix t wherever it occurs in them.

We now introduce the further symbols

$$\gamma = \alpha - \beta, \quad \gamma'' = \frac{\alpha''}{1-\beta''}, \quad a = \frac{K+\dot{K}}{K}. \qquad \ldots(3.4)$$

Transforming equations (3.1-3) into terms of V and a, we obtain

$$(a-1)V = \beta + \gamma \frac{P}{Y}, \qquad \ldots(3.1a)$$

$$aV^2 = \alpha'V + \beta' \frac{P}{Y}, \qquad \ldots(3.2a)$$

$$\dot{V} = (1-\beta'')(a-1-\gamma'')V, \qquad \ldots(3.3a)$$

and on elimination of P/Y from (3.1a) and (3.2a),

$$\gamma a V^2 - \{\alpha'\gamma + \beta'(a-1)\}V + \beta\beta' = 0. \qquad \ldots(3.5)$$

Adjusting each side of (3.5) by the same amount, we see that

$$\gamma(1+\gamma'')V^2 - (\alpha'\gamma + \beta'\gamma'')V + \beta\beta' = (1+\gamma''-a)V(\gamma V - \beta'), \qquad \ldots(3.6)$$

so that the expression (3.3a) for $\dot{V}$, using (3.6), becomes

$$\dot{V} = -\frac{(1-\beta'')\{\gamma(1+\gamma'')V^2 - (\alpha'\gamma + \beta'\gamma'')V + \beta\beta'\}}{\gamma V - \beta'}. \qquad \ldots(3.7)$$

(3.7) shows that the equilibrium value, V^*, of V which must allow $\dot{V} = 0$, must satisfy the quadratic equation

$$\gamma(1+\gamma'')V^{*2} - (\alpha'\gamma + \beta'\gamma'')V^* + \beta\beta' = 0, \qquad \ldots(3.8)$$

which, since $\gamma = \alpha - \beta$, checks with Kaldor's equation (10.1) in the original article.

Denoting the two roots of (3.8) by V^* and V^{**}, equation (3.7) may be rewritten in the form

$$\dot{V} = -\frac{\gamma(1-\beta'')(1+\gamma'')(V-V^*)(V-V^{**})}{\gamma V - \beta'}. \qquad \ldots(3.9)$$

It follows from the restrictions (2.4-7) that V cannot equal the lesser root, V^{**} say, since this would entail negative profits. The following further inequalities may also be derived from the restrictions.

$$V^{**} < \frac{\beta'}{\gamma} < V^* < \alpha' - \beta; \quad \beta' < \gamma V < \gamma(\alpha' - \beta). \qquad \ldots(3.10)^1$$

The stability of the equilibrium at $V = V^*$ may now be established, either by consideration of the Phase-diagram I, which illustrates equation (3.9), or more rigorously as follows.

---

[1] From (2.5) we know that initially $\beta' < \gamma V$ and $P > 0$, and from (3.1a) and (3.2a), that

$$V = \alpha' - \beta - (\gamma V - \beta')\frac{K}{P}.$$

Hence

$$\beta' < V < \gamma(\alpha' - \beta). \qquad (I)$$

By definition, V^* and V^{**} are the greater and lesser roots of the quadratic equation

$$Q(V) = \gamma(1+\gamma'')V^2 - (\alpha'\gamma + \beta'\gamma'')V + \beta\beta' = 0.$$

We note that $\frac{\gamma}{\beta'} Q\left(\frac{\beta'}{\gamma}\right) = \beta' - \gamma(\alpha' - \beta) < 0$ by (I) and that $Q(0) = \beta\beta' > 0$. Since $Q(0) > 0$, $Q\left(\frac{\beta'}{\gamma}\right) < 0$ and $Q(+\infty) > 0$, it follows that the two roots of the quadratic $Q(V) = 0$ must be real and satisfy

$$0 < V^{**} < \frac{\beta'}{\gamma} < V^*.$$

The requirement that profits must be positive in equilibrium growth further entails $V^* < \alpha' - \beta$ because of (I) and also entails $\beta < \gamma'' V^*$ because of (3.1a) and (3.3a).

D

Inverting (3.9) and putting

$$X = \gamma(1-\beta'')(1+\gamma'')/(V^*-V^{**}), \qquad \ldots(3.11)$$

we obtain

$$X\frac{dt}{dV} = \frac{\gamma V^* - \beta'}{V^* - V} - \frac{\beta' - \gamma V^{**}}{V - V^{**}}. \qquad \ldots(3.12)$$

Remembering that initially when $t = 0$,

$$\gamma V_0 > \beta', \qquad \ldots(3.13)$$

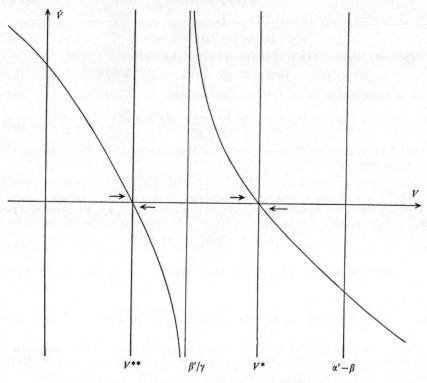

FIGURE 1

we find

$$-Xt = (\gamma V^* - \beta')\log\frac{V-V^*}{V_0-V^*} + (\beta'-\gamma V^{**})\log\frac{V-V^{**}}{V_0-V^{**}}. \qquad \ldots(3.14)$$

Since V is a differentiable function of t, it follows from (3.14) that V remains greater than β'/γ and that $(V-V^*)$ never changes sign. It then follows that as t tends to infinity, $\log[(V-V^*)/(V_0-V^*)] \to -\infty$, so that $V \to V^*$. The exact behaviour of V as t increases can be found from the inverse function of (3.14). Subject to the restrictions (2.4-7) we have established the global stability of the growth path for the model recast in the form of differential equations.

4. THE ORIGINAL MODEL WITH NO SAVINGS OUT OF WAGES, ($\beta = 0$)

In the Appendix, the general case with $\beta > 0$ is examined and an upper limit for β' is established which is *sufficient* to ensure global stability for the steady growth path. In the main text, we shall make the simplifying assumption, also discussed in the original article equations (7.2), (8.2), (9.2) and (10.2), that $\beta = 0$, indicating that there is no saving out of wages. I am particularly indebted to Mr Pesaran for pointing out to me how greatly this simplifying assumption facilitates the task of quickly obtaining quite powerful results.

Putting $a_t = K_{t+1}/K_t$ and setting $\beta = 0$, the three basic equations (2.1-3) may be expressed in terms of V_t, V_{t+1} and a_t as

$$(a_t - 1)V_t = \alpha \frac{P_t}{Y_t}, \qquad \ldots(4.1)$$

$$a_t V_t^2 = \alpha' V_t + \beta' \frac{P_t}{Y_t}, \qquad \ldots(4.2)$$

$$a_t V_t = \{\alpha'' + 1 + \beta''(a_t - 1)\} V_{t+1}. \qquad \ldots(4.3)^1$$

Eliminating P_t/Y_t from (4.1) and (4.2), we obtain

$$\alpha a_t V_t^2 = \alpha \alpha' V_t + \beta'(a_t - 1)V_t, \qquad \ldots(4.4)$$

so that since $V_t \neq 0$,

$$a_t = \frac{\alpha \alpha' - \beta'}{\alpha V_t - \beta'}. \qquad \ldots(4.5)$$

Substituting for a_t in (4.3) we obtain the following expression for V_{t+1} in terms of V_t

$$V_{t+1} = \frac{(\alpha \alpha' - \beta')V_t}{(1 + \alpha'' - \beta'')(\alpha V_t - \beta') + \beta''(\alpha \alpha' - \beta')}. \qquad \ldots(4.6)$$

Let

$$\beta^* = \frac{\beta'}{\alpha}; \qquad \ldots(4.7)$$

then (4.6) simplifies to

$$V_{t+1} = \frac{(\alpha' - \beta^*)V_t}{(1 + \alpha'' - \beta'')V_t + \alpha'\beta'' - (1 + \alpha'')\beta^*}, \qquad \ldots(4.8)$$

namely,

$$V_{t+1} = \frac{V_t}{BV_t + C}, \quad \text{where} \quad C = \frac{\alpha'\beta'' - (1 + \alpha'')\beta^*}{\alpha' - \beta^*}. \qquad \ldots(4.8a)$$

Now let

$$u_t = \frac{1}{V_{t+1}} - \frac{1}{V_t}; \qquad \ldots(4.9)$$

then

$$u_t = B - \frac{1-C}{V_t}, \qquad \ldots(4.10)$$

so that

$$u_{t+1} = B - \frac{1-C}{V_{t+1}} = B - (1-C)\left(B + \frac{C}{V_t}\right) = Cu_t. \qquad \ldots(4.11)$$

---

[1] By definition $a_t = K_{t+1}/K_t$, $V_t = K_t/Y_t$ and $V_{t+1} = K_{t+1}/Y_{t+1}$ so that $\frac{Y_{t+1}}{Y_t} = \frac{a_t V_t}{V_{t+1}}$. Hence, substituting for $\frac{Y_{t+1}}{Y_t}$ in (2.3) we obtain $\frac{a_t V_t}{V_{t+1}} = \alpha'' + 1 + (a_t - 1)\beta''$, and (4.3) follows.

Hence $u_t, u_{t+1}, u_{t+2}, \ldots$, form a geometric progression with common ratio C, given by (4.8a). It follows that where T is any positive integer exceeding t,

$$\frac{1}{V_T} = \frac{1}{V_t} + \sum_{s=t}^{T-1} u_s = \frac{1}{V_t} + u_t \sum_{s=0}^{T-t-1} C^s = \frac{1}{V_t} + u_t \frac{1-C^{T-t}}{1-C}$$

$$= \frac{B - C^{T-t} u_t}{1-C}, \qquad \ldots(4.12)$$

so that a necessary and sufficient condition that $V_t \to \frac{1-C}{B}$ as $t \to \infty$ is

$$|C| < 1, \qquad \ldots(4.13)$$

which condition by (4.8a) becomes

$$|\alpha'\beta'' - (1+\alpha'')\beta^*| < |\alpha' - \beta^*|. \qquad \ldots(4.14)$$

Since (4.14) certainly will be satisfied when $\beta^* \leqslant \frac{\alpha'\beta''}{1+\alpha'}$, and certainly will not be satisfied when $\beta^* > \alpha'$, this condition (4.14) simplifies to the form

$$\beta^*(1+\alpha'') - \alpha'\beta'' < \alpha' - \beta^*, \qquad \ldots(4.15)$$

and then to

$$\beta^* < \frac{(1+\beta'')\alpha'}{2+\alpha''}. \qquad \ldots(4.16)$$

Using the definition (4.7) of β^*, we obtain the corresponding upper limit for β' as

$$\beta' < \frac{1+\beta''}{2+\alpha''} \alpha\alpha', \qquad \ldots(4.17)[1]$$

which is of course rather lower than the limit implied by (2.5), when $\beta = 0$, namely

$$\beta' < \alpha\alpha'. \qquad \ldots(4.18)$$

The use of a diagram is seldom a convincing method of proof, but since we have now established the result analytically, it may be of some interest to consider it in the light of the graph of (4.6) which gives V_{t+1} in terms of V_t. This is always a rectangular hyperbola with asymptotes

$$V_t = \frac{(1+\alpha'')\beta^* - \alpha'\beta''}{1+\alpha'' - \beta''} \quad \text{and} \quad V_{t+1} = \frac{\alpha' - \beta^*}{1+\alpha'' - \beta''}. \qquad \ldots(4.19)$$

Three different cases may be illustrated. They are

$$\beta^* < \frac{\alpha'\beta''}{1+\alpha''}, \qquad \ldots(4.20)$$

$$\frac{\alpha'\beta''}{1+\alpha''} < \beta^* < \frac{\alpha'(1+\beta'')}{2+\alpha''}, \qquad \ldots(4.21)$$

$$\frac{\alpha'(1+\beta'')}{2+\alpha''} < \beta^* < \alpha'. \qquad \ldots(4.22)$$

[1] When the savings-propensity β out of wages is small, a good approximation to the limit on β' is given by

$$\beta' < (1+\beta'')(\alpha-\beta)\left\{\frac{\alpha'-\beta}{2+\alpha''} - \frac{2\beta\beta''^2}{4\beta'' - \alpha'(1+\beta'')}\right\}.$$

For example, when $\alpha = 0.55$, $\beta = 0.05$, $\alpha' = 3.05$, $\alpha'' = 0.01$ and $\beta'' = 0.05$, the above approximation becomes $\beta' < 1.125$ whereas the limit given by the exact equations (A28-30) established in the Appendix is, to the same number of places, $\beta' < 1.122$.

$\beta = 0 \qquad \alpha = \beta'' = 0{\cdot}5 \qquad \alpha' = 2 \qquad \alpha'' = 0{\cdot}01$

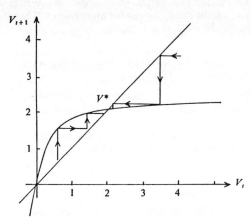

CASE 1. $\beta' = 0{\cdot}4$

STABLE

$$V_{t+1} = \frac{0{\cdot}6V_t}{0{\cdot}255V_t + 0{\cdot}096}$$

FIGURE 2

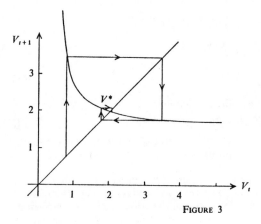

CASE 2. $\beta' = 0{\cdot}6$

STABLE

$$V_{t+1} = \frac{0{\cdot}4V_t}{0{\cdot}255V_t - 0{\cdot}106}$$

FIGURE 3

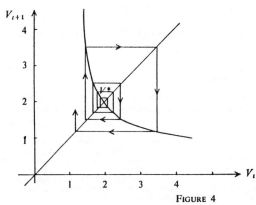

CASE 3. $\beta' = 0{\cdot}8$

UNSTABLE

$$V_{t+1} = \frac{0{\cdot}2V_t}{0{\cdot}255V_t - 0{\cdot}308}$$

FIGURE 4

The three cases are given in Figs. 2, 3 and 4. It should be fairly clear to both mathematical and unmathematical readers that the first two cases entail global convergence towards the equilibrium point V^* but that the third entails antidamped oscillations. A fourth case, corresponding to values of β^* exceeding α', entails steady movement away from V^*, but this is not illustrated: it is the case when the condition (2.7) is violated.

5. AN ECONOMIC INTERPRETATION OF THE RESTRICTIONS AND THE MODIFICATIONS OF THE MODEL

Let us now consider the implications of the results obtained for the continuous-time model of Section 3, and for the discrete-time model discussed in Section 4 and in the appendix.

In the continuous-time model, global stability is guaranteed by the restrictions laid down in the 1957 article [1] and reproduced above as (2.4-7). Consider, in particular the restrictions (2.5), namely,

$$\alpha - \beta > \beta' \frac{Y}{K} \quad \text{and} \quad \frac{P}{Y} \geq m > 0, \qquad \ldots(5.1)$$

where the suffix t has been dropped since we are now discussing the continuous-time model. It is an immediate consequence of (3.1-2) that

$$K - (\alpha' - \beta)Y + \left\{\alpha - \beta - \beta' \frac{Y}{K}\right\} P = 0, \qquad \ldots(5.2)$$

and it follows from (5.1-2) that where $V = K/Y$,

$$\frac{\beta'}{\alpha - \beta} < V < \alpha' - \beta, \qquad \ldots(5.3)$$

and this condition evidently imposes on β' the restriction

$$\beta' < (\alpha - \beta)(\alpha' - \beta), \qquad \ldots(5.4)$$

which lacks the economic intelligibility of the conditions (5.2) but could have been taken instead as a starting point if one had been primarily concerned to construct a neat mathematical toy.[1]

The result (5.4) suggests that the numerical value of β' will have to be fairly small to ensure global stability. The difference $(\alpha - \beta)$ between the savings-propensities of the two classes is unlikely to exceed 0·5, and if we allow a gestation-period of 2 years for investment, so that our time-unit is 2 years, then neither the capital-output ratio V, nor the difference $(\alpha' - \beta)$ are likely seriously to exceed 1·5, so that the condition (5.1) or (5.4) would restrict the value of β' to less than 0·75.

In the discrete-time model with $\beta = 0$, the restriction (4.17) imposed on β' for global stability was

$$\beta' < \frac{1 + \beta''}{2 + \alpha''} \alpha \alpha'. \qquad \ldots(5.5)$$

Still taking 2 years for our time-unit, the values of α and α' are unlikely greatly to exceed 0·5 and 1·5: β'' is harder to estimate; it is the regression coefficient of the growth-rate of income on the growth-rate of capital. It would be an error to attempt to estimate

[1] 'It is obvious that there is no room in economics for long trains of deductive reasoning, no economist, not even Ricardo, attempted them. It may indeed appear at first sight that the contrary is suggested by the frequent use of mathematical formulae in economic studies. But on investigation it will be found that this suggestion is illusory, except perhaps when a pure mathematician uses economic hypotheses for the purposes of mathematical diversions: . . . If we shut our eyes to realities we may construct an edifice of pure crystal by imaginations, that will throw side lights on real problems; and might conceivably be of interest to beings who had no economic problems at all like our own.' Marshall, [7] Appendix D §§ 1-2.

β'' by first estimating the relative share P/Y of profits and then applying some marginalist theory of income-distribution, since Kaldor's model avoids the unrealistic assumption that factor proportions are adjusted so as to equate marginal-value products and marginal costs. Thus β'' may have any value between zero and unity. When β'' is close to unity, the limit on β' will be little different from what it was in the continuous-time model, but if β'' is close to zero, then the limit on β' may almost be halved, for example from 0·75 to about 0·4.

In all these cases, the limits on β' appear low. To interpret them further, we have to consider what are plausible values for the profit-rate (per two years) P/K. We have supposed the capital-output ratio to be 1·5 or less (over 2 years): so if we suppose that profits form 45 per cent of the total income we have $P/Y = 0·45$ and $P/K > 0·3$ (over 2 years).

We have now reached a point where we may consider the influence of the term $\beta'\dfrac{P}{K}$ in equation (3.2a), namely in

$$V + \dot{V} = \alpha' + \beta' \frac{P}{K}. \qquad \ldots(5.6)$$

This equation tells us that if the profit rate were altered from 25 to 35 per cent (per 2 years), then the target ratio of capital (2 years from now) to (present) output would be altered only from $1·5 + 0·25\,\beta'$ to $1·5 + 0·35\,\beta'$: thus, if $\beta' = 0·6$, then the target ratio would be altered only from 1·65 to 1·71. If the change in P/K should happen fairly quickly, the small change in the capital-output ratio admittedly might involve a considerable proportionate change in $\dot{K}$ the rate of net investment: indeed, it is just because of this fact, that β' has to be kept so small, if stability is to be preserved. Yet it is a grave blemish on a theory which places so much emphasis on the effect of high profits in stimulating innovation and growth, that the effect of the term $\beta'\dfrac{P}{K}$ on the target capital output-ratio should be so small in the model.

In the discrete-time version of the model the permissible values for the β' coefficient are even more restricted and the need of some reform of the model is accordingly even more urgent.

In the next section we shall consider a method of reformulating the continuous-time model so as to make anticipated profit-rates depend on an average of past profit rates instead of on the current profit rate. It will be found in the following section that the reformulated model can be stable with considerably higher values of β'.

6. ALLOWANCE FOR SLOW ADJUSTMENT OF PROFIT-RATE EXPECTATIONS

Kaldor has argued that expectations about the rate of profit in the future are likely to be based not only on the current rate of profit but also on the general level of the profit rate for some time back. Steps have already been taken to modify his 1957 model so as to allow for this. Kaldor himself in [2] constructed one such modified model and in [6] McCallum introduced a modified investment equation into a continuous-time version of Kaldor's 1957 model replacing the current rate of profit by a weighted average of past rates of profit. Unfortunately his investment equation ignored the time-lag involved by the gestation period for providing the capital goods required to bring capital up to the level corresponding to the target capital output ratio. This made his unmodified model completely unstable. The modification to the investment equation with respect to the rate of profit still ignored the gestation period for investment but it did restore some measure of stability to the model. In revising our own continuous-time version of Kaldor's model we hit on precisely the same modification as was used by McCallum in [6], but of course we have applied it to our equation (4.2) which does make proper allowance for the gestation lag for investment. There is thus likely to be some difference between the conditions needed for stability in our modified model and those required in the modified model in [6].

The investment equation (3.2) is

$$K + \dot{K} = \left(\alpha' + \beta' \frac{P}{K}\right) Y, \quad \ldots(6.1)$$

and we now modify this to become

$$K + \dot{K} = (\alpha' + \beta' R) Y, \quad \ldots(6.3)$$

where R is a weighted average of the profit-rate over the past. It was clear that a not unreasonable economic definition for R, and one that would be particularly convenient for mathematical handling would be

$$\lambda R = \int_0^\infty e^{-\frac{s}{\lambda}} \frac{P(s)}{K(s)} ds \quad \ldots(6.4)$$

where $P(s)$, $K(s)$ are the values of P and K, s periods previously. (6.4) entails

$$\lambda \dot{R} + R = \frac{P}{K}. \quad \ldots(6.5)$$

This condition will be added to the model as a fourth equation. In the next section, we shall find how the limits on β' are affected in so far as they are required to ensure *local* stability of the model in the neighbourhood of the equilibrium values of the growth rate and of the capital-output ratio. It will be found that they are not so very different from those required in the modified form of McCallum's model in [6].

7. THE CONTINUOUS-TIME MODEL CONTAINING THE MOVING AVERAGE OF PAST PROFIT-RATES

In accordance with the suggestions made in the previous section, we shal now analyse the model:

$$\dot{K} = \beta Y + (\alpha - \beta) P, \quad \ldots(7.1)$$

$$K + \dot{K} = (\alpha' + \beta' R) Y, \quad \ldots(7.2)$$

$$\frac{\dot{Y}}{Y} = \alpha'' + \beta'' \frac{\dot{K}}{K}, \quad \ldots(7.3)$$

$$\lambda \dot{R} = \frac{P}{K} - R, \quad \ldots(7.4)$$

under the restrictions

$$1 > \alpha > \beta \geqq 0, \quad \alpha' > 0, \quad \beta' > 0, \quad \alpha'' > 0, \quad 1 > \beta'' > 0, \quad \ldots(7.5)$$

$$\frac{P}{Y} \geqq m > 0, \quad P \leqq Y - W_{\min}. \quad \ldots(7.6)$$

To the previous notation

$$V = \frac{K}{Y}, \quad a = 1 + \frac{\dot{K}}{K}, \quad \gamma = \alpha - \beta, \quad \gamma'' = \frac{\alpha''}{1 - \beta''}, \quad \ldots(7.7)$$

we now add

$$\Phi = \frac{P}{K}. \quad \ldots(7.8)$$

We denote the equilibrium values[1] of a, V, Φ and R by a^*, V^*, Φ^* and R^* and we

[1] We assume in this section that the parameter values are such as to allow *some* set of real equilibrium values for a, V and R. We then investigate whether growth will be locally stable for values of these variables in the neighbourhood of the equilibrium values.

further define the deviations from them
$$x = a-a^*, \ v = V-V^*, \ \phi = \Phi-\Phi^*, \ r = R-R^*. \qquad ...(7.9)$$
In the notation (7.7-8), equations (7.1-4) may be rewritten as
$$(a-1)V = \beta + \gamma V\Phi, \qquad ...(7.1a)$$
$$aV = \alpha' + \beta' R, \qquad ...(7.2a)$$
$$\dot{V} = (1-\beta'')(a-1-\gamma'')V, \qquad ...(7.3a)$$
$$\Phi = \lambda \dot{R} + R. \qquad ...(7.4a)$$

In the neighbourhood of equilibrium growth, we regard v, x, ϕ, r as small and we will neglect terms of the second and higher orders in them. Neglecting these terms and using the notation (7.9) it follows from (7.1a-4a) that

$$V^*x + \frac{\beta}{V^*} v - \gamma V^* \phi = 0, \qquad ...(7.1b)$$

$$V^*x + (1+\gamma'')v - \beta' r = 0, \qquad ...(7.2b)$$

$$(1-\beta'')V^*x - \dot{v} = 0, \qquad ...(7.3b)$$

$$\phi - \lambda \dot{r} - r = 0. \qquad ...(7.4b)$$

Using the operator D to denote $\dfrac{d}{dt}$ it follows from (7.1-4b) that

$$\begin{vmatrix} 1 & \beta/V^* & -\gamma V^* & 0 \\ 1 & 1+\gamma'' & 0 & -\beta' \\ 1-\beta'' & -D & 0 & 0 \\ 0 & 0 & 1 & -1-\lambda D \end{vmatrix} v = 0. \qquad ...(7.10)$$

When the determinant is expanded it becomes a quadratic in D and we obtain

$$\left[V^*\lambda\gamma D^2 + [\{1+\lambda(1-\beta'')(1+\gamma'')\}V^* - \beta']D + (1-\beta'')\left\{(1+\gamma'')\gamma V^* - \frac{\beta\beta'}{V^*}\right\}\right]v = 0, \quad ...(7.11)$$

The condition for local stability of the capital-output ratio V in the neighbourhood of the equilibrium value V^* is that both roots of this quadratic should have negative real parts. Since the coefficient of D^2 is positive, this condition for local stability is satisfied if and only if the coefficient of D and the constant term in (7.11) are both positive, i.e. if and only if

$$\beta' < \{1+\lambda(1-\beta'')(1+\gamma'')\}\gamma V^* \qquad ...(7.12)$$

and

$$V^* > \frac{\beta\beta'}{(1+\gamma'')\gamma V^*}. \qquad ...(7.13)$$

By definition, V^* and V^{**} are the greater and lesser roots of the quadratic equation (3.8), namely of

$$\gamma(1+\gamma'')V^{*2} - (\alpha'\gamma+\beta'\gamma'')V^* + \beta\beta' = 0. \qquad ...(7.14)$$

Hence condition (7.13) is equivalent to

$$V^* > V^{**}, \qquad ...(7.15)$$

and this obviously is satisfied.

The remaining condition for local stability is (7.12).
From (7.14) we calculate

$$\beta' = \frac{\gamma V^*\{(1+\gamma'')V^* - \alpha'\}}{\gamma'' V^* - \beta}, \qquad \ldots(7.16)$$

and from the footnote to (3.10)

$$\gamma'' V^* - \beta > 0. \qquad \ldots(7.17)$$

Let

$$\mu = (1-\beta'')(1+\gamma''); \qquad \ldots(7.18)$$

then, by means of (7.16), (7.12) may be transformed to

$$(1+\lambda\mu)(\gamma'' V^* - \beta) > (1+\gamma'')V^* - \alpha', \qquad \ldots(7.19)$$

and on rearrangement of this we obtain

$$(1-\lambda\mu\gamma'')V^* < \alpha' - (1+\lambda\mu)\beta. \qquad \ldots(7.20)$$

We now introduce the assumption that

$$\beta < \frac{\alpha'\gamma''}{1+\gamma''}. \qquad \ldots(7.21)$$

In the earlier model with $\lambda = 0$, the condition (7.21) was already implied by the assumptions (2.5), but in this revised model values of the parameters which do not satisfy (7.21) can sometimes allow steady growth when λ is sufficiently large. However these large values of λ are so unrealistic that a detailed examination of the cases where (7.21) is unsatisfied is not worthwhile,[1] and in the rest of this section we shall assume that (7.21) is satisfied.

Granted (7.21), it is easily shown that the inequality (7.20) implies that there will be local stability close to the equilibrium growth-path provided

$$\lambda > \frac{1}{\mu\gamma''}, \qquad \ldots(7.22)$$

and that when $\lambda < \frac{1}{\mu\gamma''}$, the condition for local stability is

$$(1-\lambda\mu\gamma'')\beta' < (1+\lambda\mu)\{\alpha' - \beta - \lambda\mu\beta\}\gamma. \qquad \ldots(7.23)$$

The following numerical example illustrates the operation of these inequalities.

Let $\alpha = 0.52$, $\beta = 0.02$, $\alpha' = 1.52$, $\alpha'' = 0.01$ and $\beta'' = 0.5$, then $\gamma = 0.5$, $\gamma'' = 0.02$ and $\mu = 0.51$.

---

[1] The case where $\beta > \frac{\alpha'\gamma''}{1+\gamma''}$ has strange properties. In this case, unless $\lambda > \frac{1}{\mu\gamma''}$ no equilibrium growth-path, either stable or unstable will be possible: whereas only an *unstable* equilibrium growth-path will be possible if λ lies between the limits $\frac{1}{\mu\gamma''}$ and $\frac{1}{\mu\gamma''} + \frac{(1+\gamma'')\beta - \gamma''\alpha'}{\mu\eta}$ where $\eta^2 = \beta^2 - \frac{\beta\alpha'\gamma''}{1+\gamma''}$.

Finally, where $\beta > \frac{\alpha'\gamma''}{1+\gamma''}$ and $\lambda > \frac{1}{\mu\gamma''} + \frac{(1+\gamma'')\beta - \gamma''\alpha'}{\mu\eta}$ all possible equilibrium growth-paths will be stable, but for any equilibrium growth-path to be possible the value of β' must satisfy

$$\beta' > \frac{\{(\beta+\eta)^2 - \gamma''(\alpha' - \beta - \eta)(\beta+\eta)\}\gamma}{\gamma''^2\eta}$$

so that rather surprisingly a *lower* limit on β' is prescribed as a necessary condition for steady growth to be possible in this case.

For various values of λ the conditions which must be satisfied by β' to allow local stability are shown in the following table.

Values of β' which allow local stability

Values of λ	0	1	2	5	10	20	40
Values of β'	<0·75	<1·13	<1·53	<2·71	<4·75	<9·1	<19·8

Values of λ	60	80	90	>98
Values of β'	<36·2	<77·7	<167	any +ve value

McCallum in [6] analysed a model almost exactly equivalent to that of equations (7.1-4), but instead of (7.2), he used an equation which, when expressed in our notation, is

$$K = \beta Y + (\alpha - \beta)P. \qquad \ldots(7.2a)$$

The stability condition which McCallum obtained, becomes when expressed in our notation

$$\beta' < \lambda(1-\beta'')\gamma V^* \qquad \ldots(7.24)$$

as a necessary condition for stability. In this form the condition is of no immediate use, since V^* is not given. However a little manipulation of his basic equations gives a further equation relating β' and V^*, which enables us to transform (7.24) to the condition,

$$\beta' < \frac{\lambda\gamma(1-\beta'')\{\alpha'\gamma - \lambda(1-\beta'')\beta\}}{\gamma - \lambda\alpha''}. \qquad \ldots(7.25)$$

The following table shows the values of β' permitted under this condition, for the same values of λ as are considered in the above table relating to our own model.

Values of β' needed for stability in McCallum's model

Values of λ	0	1	2	5	10	20
Values of β'	none	<0·38	<0·765	<1·93	<3·94	<8·25

Values of λ	40	60	80	90	98	>100
Values of β'	<18·7	<34·5	<72	<139·5	<666	any +ve value

Thus our model can allow local stability with appreciably larger values of the coefficient β' than can McCallum's model, for those moderate values of λ, say $1 < \lambda < 5$, which seem fairly realistic. For example, a time-unit of two years with $\lambda = 3$ would imply that R was a weighted average of past profit-rates with about half of the weight concentrated on profit-rates during the last four years. In this case, we would find that in the above numerical example the upper limit on β' needed for local stability would be 1·92 in our example as against 1·17 in McCallum's model.

It may be objected that in considering the conditions for stability we have nowhere paid regard to condition (2.6) which places an upper limit on profits. Together with (7.1a) this entails

$$\gamma'' V^* < \alpha, \qquad \ldots(7.26)$$

and hence (7.12) implies
$$\gamma''\beta' < (1+\lambda\mu)\gamma\alpha, \qquad \ldots(7.27)$$
and this may under some circumstances be more restrictive than condition (7.25).

However when one considers numerical examples it appears that those cases when (7.27) is more restrictive than (7.25) allow values of β' which anyhow are far higher than one would regard as realistic. For instance, in the table following (7.23) the only entry requiring revision on this score would be the final one, which would be amended from "β' any +ve value" to "$\beta' < 13 + 6\cdot 63\lambda$" in the case $\lambda > 98$, which is an amendment of no practical interest whatever.

APPENDIX

The discrete-time model with $\beta > 0$

We retain the notation of section 4 and set $\Phi_t = \dfrac{P_t}{K_t}$.

The 3 basic equations may then be written as

$$(a_t - 1)V_t = \beta + \gamma V_t \Phi_t, \qquad \ldots(A1)$$

$$a_t V_t = \alpha' + \beta' \Phi_t, \qquad \ldots(A2)$$

$$a_t V_t = \{1 + \gamma'' + \beta''(a_t - 1 - \gamma'')\} V_{t+1}. \qquad \ldots(A3)$$

Let a^*, V^*, Φ^* denote the equilibrium values of a_t, V_t and Φ_t.
It follows from (A3) that

$$a^* V^* = \{1 + \gamma'' + \beta''(a^* - 1 - \gamma'')\} V^*, \qquad \ldots(A4)$$

and hence that

$$a^* = 1 + \gamma'', \qquad \ldots(A5)$$

and it follows from (A1) that

$$\gamma'' - \gamma \Phi^* = \frac{\beta}{V^*}. \qquad \ldots(A6)$$

Now let the deviations from equilibrium values be

$$x_t = a_t - a^*, \ v_t = V_t - V^* \text{ and } \phi_t = \Phi_t - \Phi^*; \qquad \ldots(A7)$$

then, ignoring terms of the second and higher order in these deviations, we obtain from (A1-7)

$$V^* x_t + \frac{\beta}{V^*} v_t - \gamma V^* \phi_t = 0, \qquad \ldots(A8)$$

$$V^* x_t + (1+\gamma'') v_t - \beta' \phi_t = 0, \qquad \ldots(A9)$$

$$(1-\beta'') V^* x_t + (1+\gamma'')(v_t - v_{t+1}) = 0. \qquad \ldots(A10)$$

Hence where $\Delta v_t = v_{t+1} - v_t$,

$$\begin{vmatrix} 1 & \beta/V^* & \gamma V^* \\ 1 & 1+\gamma'' & \beta' \\ 1-\beta'' & -(1+\gamma'')\Delta & 0 \end{vmatrix} v_t = 0. \qquad \ldots(A11)$$

Expanding the determinant, we find

$$-\frac{\Delta v_t}{v_t} = (1-\beta'')\gamma \frac{V^* - \dfrac{\beta\beta'}{\gamma(1+\gamma'')V^*}}{\gamma V^* - \beta'}. \qquad \ldots(A12)$$

Now since V^* and V^{**} denote as usual the greater and lesser roots of
$$\gamma(1+\gamma'')V^{*2} - \{\alpha'\gamma + \beta'\gamma''\}V^* + \beta\beta' = 0, \qquad \ldots(A13)$$
(A12) becomes
$$-\frac{\Delta v_t}{v_t} = (1-\beta'')\gamma \frac{V^* - V^{**}}{\gamma V^* - \beta'}. \qquad \ldots(A14)$$

Let
$$\beta^* = \frac{\beta'}{\gamma}; \qquad \ldots(A15)$$

then
$$-\frac{\Delta v_t}{v_t} = (1-\beta'') \frac{V^* - V^{**}}{V^* - \beta^*}. \qquad \ldots(A16)$$

For local stability of the value of V_t in the neighbourhood of the equilibrium value V^*, we need
$$0 < -\frac{\Delta v_t}{v_t} < 2. \qquad \ldots(A17)$$

We already know that
$$\beta' < \gamma V^* \quad \text{and} \quad V^* > V^{**}, \qquad \ldots(A18)$$
so that
$$\beta^* < V^* \quad \text{and} \quad 0 < -\frac{\Delta v_t}{v_t}, \qquad \ldots(A19)$$

and we are left with the other condition of local stability, as
$$2(V^* - \beta^*) > (1-\beta'')(V^* - V^{**}), \qquad \ldots(A21)$$
and on rearrangement, this condition is
$$2\beta^* < 2\beta'' V^* + (1-\beta'')(V^* - V^{**}). \qquad \ldots(A22)$$

Since V^* and V^{**} are the roots of (A13),
$$(1+\gamma'')(V^* + V^{**}) = \alpha' + \beta''\beta^*, \qquad \ldots(A23)$$
so that (A22) implies
$$\{2 + (1+\beta'')\gamma''\}\beta^* < \alpha'(1-\beta)'' + 2(1+\gamma'')\beta'' V^*. \qquad \ldots(A24)$$

(A13) and (A24) imply upper limits $\bar{\beta}^*$ and $\bar{V}^*$ for β^* and V^* which satisfy
$$(1+\gamma'')\bar{V}^{*2} - (\alpha' + \gamma''\bar{\beta}^*)\bar{V}^* + \beta\bar{\beta}^* = 0, \qquad \ldots(A25)$$
and
$$2(1+\gamma'')\beta'' \bar{V}^* = \{2 + (1+\beta'')\gamma''\}\bar{\beta}^* + (1-\beta'')\alpha'. \qquad \ldots(A26)$$

We may substitute for $\bar{V}^*$ in (A25) by using (A26). The result after considerable manipulation is a quadratic in $\bar{\beta}^*$, namely
$$Z\bar{\beta}^{*2} - 2S\bar{\beta}^* + T = 0, \qquad \ldots(A27)$$
where
$$Z = (2+\gamma'')^2 - (\beta''\gamma'')^2, \quad S = \{2+(1+\beta''^2)\gamma''\}\alpha' - 2\beta(1+\gamma'')\beta''^2,$$
$$T = (1-\beta''^2)\alpha'^2. \qquad \ldots(A28)$$

Hence
$$\bar{\beta}^* = \frac{S + \sqrt{S^2 - ZT}}{Z} \qquad \ldots(A29)$$

and
$$\beta^* < \bar{\beta}^* \quad \text{and} \quad \beta' < \gamma\bar{\beta}^*. \qquad \ldots(A30)$$

This is the condition for local stability in the discrete-time model.

In the particular case $\beta = 0$, (A30) reduces to

$$\beta' < \frac{(1+\beta'')\alpha'(\alpha-\beta)}{2+\alpha''}, \qquad \ldots(A31)$$

and we have shown in Section 4 that in this case the condition also ensures global stability. In the particular case $\beta'' = 0$, (A30) reduces to

$$\beta' < \frac{\alpha'(\alpha-\beta)}{2+\alpha''}. \qquad \ldots(A32)$$

It seems very plausible that the condition (A30) also ensures global stability in the general case, $\beta > 0$, but the author has not as yet completed a proof of this conjecture. It is hoped that further investigation of this possibility may be the subject of a later paper.

REFERENCES

[1] Kaldor, N. " A Model of Economic Growth ", *Economic Journal* (Dec. 1957), 591-624.

[2] Kaldor, N. " Capital Accumulation and Economic Growth ", in *The Theory of Capital*, F. A. Lutz and D. C. Hague (eds).

[3] Kaldor, N. " Some Fallacies in the Interpretation of Kaldor ", *Review of Economic Studies* (Jan. 1970), 1-8.

[4] Kubota, K. " A Re-examination of the Existence and Stability Propositions in Kaldor's Growth Models ", *Review of Economic Studies* (July 1968), 353-359.

[5] Kubota, K. " A Comment on Kaldor's Note ", *Review of Economic Studies* (Jan. 1970), 9.

[6] McCallum, B. T. " The Instability of Kaldorian Models ", *Oxford Economic Papers* (March 1969), 56-65.

[7] Marshall, A., *Principles of Economics*.

Kaldor on growth

F. H. Hahn*

'... those individuals who are endowed with a special genius for the subject and have a powerful economic intuition will often be more right in their conclusions and implicit presumptions than in their explanation and explicit statements. That is to say, their intuitions will be in advance of their analysis and their terminology. Great respect, therefore, is due to their general scheme of thought, and it is a poor thing to pester their memories with criticism which is really verbal.' [J. M. Keynes (1924) quoted in Kaldor (1972, p. 1249, n. 1)]

What follows is in no way to be taken as an instance of 'Kaldor scholarship'. I knew Kaldor for forty years and before he became disenchanted with my unsound views we saw a great deal of each other and had very many economics arguments. This period coincided with Kaldor's 'growth phase'. Some of the views which I ascribe to him are taken from our discussions. They may or may not have been published and what I report may indeed not always be consistent with what he did publish. One of Kaldor's virtues was the ease with which he allowed new ideas to drive out old. A learned referee of this piece took me to task for not referring to the quite large literature on Kaldorian themes. I do not know that literature. So the reader of this essay is warned: it is a personal reflection on my debates with an economist of a remarkable mental agility and originality.

Kaldor had a vision of the process of capitalist growth. At first he made great efforts to express it in precise models (1957, 1961). But ultimately he found this too constricting and settled for a more literary and narrative style (1972). He always had interesting things to say and often very illuminating things. But he was in advance of both theoretical tools and empirical research and there must be some delay before his contribution can be properly judged. However, even now one must to conclude that he was more interesting and adventurous than the rest of us who stuck to the straight and narrow of neoclassical theory. When and if precise theory and more evidence catch up with him, it may well be that he will be found to have been largely right. Of course, he was sometimes plainly wrong but that is to be expected when striking out in new directions.

I

What Joan Robinson called the 'book of blueprints' most of us call the production set. Robinson and current theory take this set to have a rather straightforward and unambiguous definition. It simply gives a list of activities available for choice by a producer (an activity is a vector whose components are outputs and inputs). A production function (or more generally a transformation function) characterises the set of efficient activities

*University of Cambridge.

contained in the production set. Robinson was interested in the shape of this function (was it smooth, etc.) and in the problem of expressing it in terms of aggregates such as 'capital', 'output', 'labour', etc. As far as I can tell Kaldor was never interested in these problems.

The reason for this, amongst others, is that he did not think that there was anything defined as a production function or for that matter a production set. Alternative activities (techniques) were not to be taken as given but as discovered. No firm had knowledge of the book of blueprints as it could be assembled by pooling all the knowledge and experience there was in the world. In any case, the size of the book was forever changing and indeed its pages grew larger. That is, new goods, especially new producer goods, were continually appearing. Firms and employees 'learned by doing' (Arrow, 1962) which formally is equivalent to discovering new activities. So the pages in the book as known to the firm were not independent of the firm's choices. As a consequence, no outside observer could, on observing, say, an activity with higher output, judge whether the firm had simply turned to a pre-existing page or found one it had not known before. At one time Kaldor made this into a slogan: 'movements along a production function cannot be distinguished from shifts in this function'. Later we shall see that he did not stick rigorously to this view. However, when he did, he believed the notion of a production function to be non-operational—it could, he claimed, not be estimated. It is obvious from the econometric literature that many did not agree.

So Kaldor invented the 'Technical Progress Function' (1957). In its first incarnation he wrote it as follows:

$$\dot{y} = a + \beta \dot{k}$$

where $y = \log$ (output/man), $k = \log$ (capital/man). The idea was to avoid by this dynamic formulation the distinction between movements along and shifts in the production function. However it was soon pointed out to him that this equation could be integrated into

$$Y = A e^{at} K^{\beta}$$

(Y = output/man, K = capital/man, A is a constant of integration). This Cobb–Douglas implication was most unwelcome and Kaldor later insisted that the correct formulation required the Technical Progress Function to be non-linear. The justification for this was not at all detailed.

It was left to Arrow (1962) to give this line of reasoning a more concrete formulation. His paper is justly famous and requires no summary here. However, while the Arrowian formulation did lead to the conclusion that socially too little would be invested and produced (learning at any date depended on the integral of output to that date), it did not lead to a drastic break with neoclassical theory. In particular, if learning was regarded as a kind of externality the neoclassical marginal productivity equations continued to play their usual role. In an important sense, then, Arrow did not capture what Kaldor was looking for or what he said he was looking for.

Yet there is substance in the Kaldorian argument. Atkinson and Stiglitz (1969) have pointed out that a change from one technique to another, even to one which is already known to the firm or to other firms, involves learning. Neoclassical theory takes the production set as an objective entity and that is almost certainly the wrong way in which to take it. General Equilibrium Theory is very silent on new knowledge, new goods and on innovation generally. When attempts to take note of these are successful we may find significant changes in that theory.

Kaldor in his later thinking was much influenced by Allyn Young (1928) who also had a vision and, it must be confessed, also found it hard to give it a precise formulation. He believed that 'every reorganisation of production activities creates the opportunity for further change *which would not have existed otherwise*' (Kaldor, 1972). These reorganisations are facilitated when scale increases and Young held the view that this gave rise to more or less universal 'increasing returns to scale' in manufacturing. However, these are not increasing returns in the sense that a firm is faced with a given non-convex production set. Kaldor calls them dynamic increasing returns and it is these that he wished to capture by means of the technical progress function. In any case, once this picture of an ever expanding production set is accepted, 'the whole view of the economic process as a medium for the "allocation of scarce means between alternative uses" falls apart' (Kaldor, 1972). Indeed, 'except in a purely short-term sense, total output can never be *confined* by resources' (Kaldor, 1972). It is not surprising that these assertions have not found wide acceptance. Such a radical departure from traditional views requires a very great deal of argument and evidence. Kaldor produced neither, which, however, does not mean that his vision was false in its essentials.

The Young–Kaldor view of increasing returns to scale, Kaldor attempted to fashion into a theory of growth. In my view he did not succeed in this, although as usual he made a number of suggestions which strike one as deserving further analysis. Young had worried about the means by which the benefits of increasing returns in his sense could be gathered in one sector and transmitted to another so as to cause expansion there and so lead to a process of 'cumulative causation'—that is endogenous growth. He produced an elasticity condition on an offer curve which modern theory cannot, and Kaldor did not, take seriously. (Apart from other objections, the formulation is obscure.) Kaldor put Young's failure down to the circumstance that he was writing before Keynes. Kaldor's failure, in turn, I put down to his unwillingness to use some of the simplest tools of General Equilibrium analysis. He may be right that General Equilibrium Theory abstracts so much from certain essential phenomena (like increasing returns) as to make it unsuitable as a theory of growth. But he himself distinguishes in this criticism between the short and the long run. Young's puzzle concerns a process and a process is indeed a series of short runs.

This process Kaldor often called 'cumulative causation'. But there is also another interpretation of cumulative causation: it may cause an initial advantage of a firm or of a region over competitors to increase through time until competitors are driven out. Kaldor, I think, believed that this consideration told against the UK joining the Common Market: the advantage, say, of German manufacturing industry would lead to the concentration of production there. (Compare this with a neoclassical story of diminishing returns.) Dasgupta and Stiglitz (1987) have recently provided an interesting analysis of this. I shall be mostly concerned with the first of these two concepts of cumulative causation.

Kaldor's solution to the propagation or 'cumulative causation' problem was to introduce stockholders and merchants of all kinds as essential elements. When Sector A expanded and reaped the benefits of dynamic increasing returns, Sector A's prices might fall a great deal since the income of demanders had not expanded. Merchants, etc. who held expectations of a normal price would buy for stock (really for speculative purposes) and in that way allow Sector A's income to increase. This in turn would lead them to demand more from other sectors whose turn it would now be to reap the benefits of increasing returns. In this way growth based on increasing returns would cumulate. He added that all of this required an adaptive monetary policy. Since there seem to have been periods of rapid growth in the past without such a permissive policy one is rather left

50   F. H. Hahn

wondering about the realism of this proposal. Kaldor elaborates the story somewhat by drawing a distinction between those sectors of the economy which he claimed were subject to increasing returns (manufacturing industry) and those which were not (services).

In this theory Kaldor was building on a splendid early paper of his: 'Speculation and Economic Stability' (1939) which was, however, a careful piece of analysis and which was not concerned with growth. One of its contributions was to provide an explanation for Robertson's (1940, ch. 1) contention that increased investment demand could lead to higher output, that is, could take place without an equivalent increase in savings, if idle balances were dishoarded and goods were dishoarded. Kaldor put such dishoarding down to price (and interest rate) stabilising actions of speculators and others whose price expectations were highly inelastic. A similar argument seems to underlie the growth theory, but here i's are not dotted nor t's crossed.

What is missing in the first instance is the accounting equation of agents which we call budget constraints—one of the tools of the discarded neoclassical analysis. In particular the budget constraints of stockholders are not given or discussed. But they are plainly of considerable importance since to perform the task assigned to stockholders by Kaldor they must either have a rotating stock of idle balances or have access to a more or less perfectly elastic supply of credit. Perhaps that is why Kaldor required a permissive monetary policy. However, it is not clear that, given the dynamic increasing returns assumptions, such a policy would not of its own suffice for 'cumulative causation'. For instance, should the expansion in Sector A be accompanied by a rise in money wages there, then an increasing money stock may transmit demand to other sectors and get the process under way.

But the nuts and bolts of Kaldor's emendation of Allyn–Young are missing. What follows now is a rough outline of what he may have had in mind (see also Thirlwall, 1987).

II

Suppose that there are two sectors in the economy labelled one and two. Households receive at date t the profits and wages from the production of the previous period. All prices are expressed in terms of an (ideal) price index (which is homogeneous of degree one in all prices). Let x_i be household demand for good i, y_i be output of good i, p_i the price, in terms of the index, of good i and m_i^h the stock of money held by households; again measured in terms of the index. Let the operator Δ be defined by $\Delta z(t) = z(t) - z(t-1)$ for any variable $z(t)$. Then the household budget constraint is given by

$$\Sigma p_i(t) x_i(t) + \Delta m_i^h(t) = \Sigma p_i(t-1) y_i(t-1). \tag{1}$$

Suppose now that there are merchants who do not consume, who are capable of issuing money on their own account and who hold stocks $s_i(t)$ of good i. Then

$$\Sigma p_i(t) \Delta s_i(t) + \Delta m'(t) = 0, \tag{2}$$

where $\Delta m'(t) > 0$ is absorption and $\Delta m'(t) < 0$ is new supply of money by merchants. Now make the extreme Kaldorian assumptions that (a) merchants are intent on stabilising prices completely and (b) that this is done by choosing

$$\Delta s_i(t) = y_i(t) - x_i(t). \tag{3}$$

From now on, set $p_i(t) = p_i$ all t. Using (2) and (3) in (1) we obtain

$$\Sigma p_i \Delta y_i(t) + \Delta m^t(t) + \Delta m^h(t) = 0. \tag{4}$$

In all of this the amalgamation of merchants and banks into a single entity, and the neglect of borrowing at interest, cannot matter for the general aim of interpreting Kaldor.

Suppose we start in a situation where $\Delta s_i = 0$, $i = 1, 2$. At date $t = 1$ sector one (perhaps through Schumpeterian animal spirits) decides to expand output by $\Delta y(1)$ while sector two stays at its old output. Since at $t = 1$ households have experienced no change in income and merchants stabilise prices, we obtain

$$\Delta s_i(1) = \Delta y_i(1) + [y_i(0) - x_i(0)] = \Delta y_i(1) \tag{5}$$

and a corresponding increase in the real money stock.

At $t = 2$ receipts of households have increased by $\Delta y_i(1)p_i$. This is assumed to increase their demand for both goods. Hence (a) the amount of good one which merchants have to put to stock at $t = 2$ is less than it was at $t = 1$ and (b) they will have to decumulate some stocks of good two if sector two has not increased its output. At $t = 3$ output of sector two rises, thereby adding to demand for the output of sector one at $t = 3$. Each time output goes up in either sector there are benefits of increasing returns to be reaped. These are made implicit in this account by not putting any physical constraints on output.

The above is not much more satisfactory than is Kaldor's own account. One wants the agents involved to be at least partly governed by rational considerations, and one wants the 'lack of physical constraint on output' spelled out in detail and one surely wants to check that it all leads to a virtuous cumulative process. There is of course also the problem that merchants may either run out of stocks or be continuously accumulating them. Let us try for a little more detail.

Kaldor certainly did not wish us to postulate perfect competition. Let us write the demand for the representative firm in sector i as

$$\log x_i(t) = \varepsilon_{ii} \log p_i + \varepsilon_{ij} \log p_j + \log g_i[y(t-1)] \tag{6}$$

where (a) I continue to suppose $p_i(t) = p_i$ for all t, (b) $y = \Sigma p_i y_i$, (c) $\varepsilon_{ii} < -1$, for $i = 1, 2$. The firm has a cost function $c_i(y_i)$ with $c'_i(y_i) > 0$, $c''_i(y_i) < 0$. In deciding on its output the firm takes the price of the other sector and *total income* as given. If it is profit maximising then for $i = 1, 2$,

$$c'_i(y_i) = p_i \frac{1 + \varepsilon_{ii}}{\varepsilon_{ii}}$$

and also (7)

$$c''_i(y_i) > \frac{p_i}{x_i} \frac{1 + \varepsilon_{ii}}{(\varepsilon_{ii})^2}.$$

Let us start the story with an equilibrium denoted by asterisk superscripts. Choose units such that $p_1^* = p_2^* = 1$. Then

$$y_i^* = g_i(y^*) = x_i^*, i = 1, 2. \tag{8}$$

We do not here worry about the existence of an equilibrium but it should be understood as a stationary state.

Now suppose—say by mistake—that firms in Sector 1 decide that they will produce more at $t = 0$ for sale at $t = 1$. (Recall that households only receive income from period 0 production from the proceeds of sales in period one.) We calculate

$$\frac{\partial x_i(1)}{\partial y_1(0)} = \varepsilon_{iy}\frac{x_i^*}{y^*} \quad i=1,2 \tag{9}$$

where ε_{iy} is the income elasticity of demand for the output of Sector i. If merchants are to meet any shortfall of demand at the equilibrium prices then

$$\left.\begin{aligned}\Delta s_1(1) &= \left[1 - \varepsilon_{1y}\frac{x_1^*}{y^*}\right]\Delta y_1(0) \\ \Delta s_2(1) &= \varepsilon_{2y}\frac{x_2^*}{y^*}\Delta y_1(0).\end{aligned}\right\} \tag{10}$$

Suppose that the desired level of money holdings of households per unit income is a constant k. Then from (1)

$$\Sigma \varepsilon_{iy}\frac{x_i^*}{y^*} = 1 - k. \tag{11}$$

Hence if neither good is inferior:

$$\Delta s_i(1) > 0, i = 1, 2. \tag{12}$$

From (4) we then find that merchants augment the money stock as required:

$$-\Delta m_t^s = k\Delta y_i(0). \tag{13}$$

But now at $t=1$ both kinds of firms perceive that their demand curves have shifted to the right. However, we are at once faced with a problem. If firms realise that speculators will always take up stock to stabilise prices then, as far as they are concerned, they are facing a perfectly elastic demand with dire consequences in view of the postulate of continuing increasing returns. Kaldor is not very explicit although one could read him as arguing that there are limits to the increase in output in any time interval. That is, we are allowed to suppose that in the 'short run' cost curves are U-shaped. But that is not much help since it is then obvious that firms will expand output in every period and one does not have to appeal to 'cumulative causation'.

There are several ways out and I do not know which Kaldor would have favoured. One is that firms never learn the postulated behaviour of merchants so that they always believe themselves to be facing negatively sloped demand curves. Another is that merchants are rational and that they base their actions on expectations of prices and on the level of stocks which they hold. In that case a possible assumption is that firms accurately take account of the actions of merchants. Neither of these routes is simple to follow nor is either particularly attractive. Kaldor left these crucial details out of his account. Certainly it is not obvious that $\Delta y_1(0) > 0$ will start the desired cumulative process.

I find it more reasonable to assume that firms anticipate the actions of merchants. Accordingly I now re-tell the story under this assumption which we know entails that prices are completely stabilised by merchants.

Let aggregate demand for firm i be written as X_i so

$$X_i = x_i + \Delta s_i.$$

Note that Δs_i is not restricted in sign—a supply by merchants leaves firm i with a smaller residual demand to satisfy. Let $h_t = \{p_{t-1}, p_{t-2} \ldots\}$ be the history of prices up to date t, where $p=(p_1, p_2)$. Then using (6) we write

$$x_i(t) = \xi_i[p(t), h_t, y(t-1)] \qquad (14)$$

Define $\sigma_i = \partial\log \Delta s_i(t)/\partial\log p_i(t)$. Kaldor calls σ_i the elasticity of speculation. We are supposing that it is not infinite. Then η_i, the elasticity of aggregate demand is given by

$$\eta_i = \frac{x_i}{X_i}\varepsilon_{ii} + \frac{\Delta s_i}{X_i}\sigma_i. \qquad (15)$$

It is important to note that η_i will in general depend on all the variables in the economy.

Firms choose to produce a profit maximising output on the aggregate demand curve. So for equilibrium we have

$$y_i(t) = \xi_i[p(t), h_t, y(t-1)], \qquad i = 1, 2 \qquad (16)$$

$$c_i'[y_i(t)] = p_i(t)\frac{1+\eta_i(t)}{\eta_i(t)}, \qquad i = 1, 2 \qquad (17)$$

and second order conditions. Since we also have

$$y(t-1) = \sum_i p_i(t-1)y_i(t-1)$$

we should now be able to trace the time paths of outputs from given initial conditions. Notice now that since the elasticity of speculation is finite, prices need not be constant along this path and merchants will not be, say, augmenting the nominal stock in proportion with their purchases. Hence we shall need a further dynamic equation to give us the change in the price index (price level) required to keep the demand for real balances in equality with their supply. Recall however that p_i is expressed in terms of the 'index good' so that relative prices as solved for by (16) and (17) will not be affected. (If demand for goods depended on the real money stock as well as on income this would not be true. The 'money clearing equation' and the appropriate (16) and (17) would need to be solved together.)

It will be seen that it will not be easy to obtain an analytical solution even when we have given all the relevant functions some suitable parametric form. But I shall not try to do this and simply note the obvious point that it will not be true that this economy *must* be characterised by continuous expansion of output. This will 'depend'. To this must be added the caution that the model is highly simplified. For instance, if the government does not properly augment the money stock, the falling price level may have unfortunate consequences for investment and for merchants' willingness to stock.

I have gone through this exercise in order to illustrate a general feature of Kaldor's later work on growth. He painted with a broad brush and often revealed features of an economy which had been unduly neglected—in this case dynamic increasing returns and the role of merchants in transmitting expansion in one sector to another. But he was then inclined to take these neglected matters—and he was right in holding that the neglect was unjustified—as being the whole story. He was impatient of detail and so was in danger of being himself neglected. That is a pity since, possibly by simulation, it may be feasible to analyse a theory of growth which incorporates his main ideas. My guess is that one will find that some economies characterised at some time by certain expectations and dynamic increasing returns will, at least for a stretch, behave as he predicted. Others will not. But it seems unlikely that one will ever be justified in following Kaldor in his belief that there are 'no resource constraints in the long run'. Human ingenuity after all is a resource constraint itself and one can think of others. Kaldor was inclined to claim too much too soon and so his important insights often went unnoticed.

III

Kaldor's more detailed work on growth (1962) is much easier to discuss. I can be brief since that contribution is intimately connected to the distribution theory which he sponsored and that theory is discussed elsewhere in this issue.

Harrod had left no room for any mechanism which could bring equality between the natural and warranted rate of growth. I believe that writers on Harrods' model are mistaken in their claim that he posited fixed coefficients of production. Rather I believe that he had in mind a minimum real interest rate below which accumulation would cease and so a lower bound on the marginal return on investment. (But it must be admitted that Harrod like Kaldor employed a broad brush.) Kaldor, as we have seen, was not prepared to think in terms of a choice of coefficients of production at all. His mechanism for bringing the natural and warranted growth rate into equality was an adaptive change in the distribution of income between profit and wage income which, owing to the difference in the savings propensities of the two groups, would do the trick. I had also hit on this mechanism in my PhD thesis (1951; see Hahn, 1972) but did not argue from this that the steady state real wage of labour was divorced from its marginal product.

Kaldor was adamant in his opposition to marginal productivity playing any role because he was adamant in his objection to the notion of a production function or production set. I could never, and cannot now, understand why his very important insight into dynamic economies of scale should preclude a firm from comparing the cost and advantage of hiring another hour of work. After all, at any moment of time machines, etc. are in place and it makes sense to ask the usual marginal product question. It is true that if labour cannot be hired by the hour, or even the week, benefits can only be calculated on the basis of expectations. But *something* must be compared when labour is hired or fired and Kaldor always lacked one equation. It is paradoxical for a Keynesian that in his growth work Kaldor always *postulated* full employment and never asked what was needed to ensure this.

So Kaldor growth models (unlike Robinson growth models) were always full-employment steady states. Kaldor, no doubt influenced by Kalecki, thought of the equation: warranted equals natural growth, as determining the economy's 'average degree of monopoly', i.e. the Kaleckian distribution of shares. The latter, however, was motivated by a traditional marginal cost equals marginal revenue account which, as far as I can judge, Kaldor did not accept.

In his early formal model Kaldor used the technical progress function which I have already given. In his far more ambitious work with Mirrlees (1962), Kaldor adopted a vintage approach and stipulated

$$\dot{y}_t/y_t = F(\dot{I}_t/I_t)$$

where y_t is output per man on vintage t machines and I_t is gross investment at t. Gross investment was governed by two conditions. Firstly, given the correctly anticipated 'Golden Age' rate of growth in real wages and given the prevailing net rate of profit, the investment must at least earn that rate. Secondly, under the same expectational assumption the undiscounted sum of quasi-rents on the investment of date t must at least cover the cost of the investment at date t in a fixed interval of time.

It is not clear from the paper whether Kaldor realised where Mirrlees's mathematics was leading him. For in the grand finale of the 'Golden Age' both conditions are taken to hold with equality. So the prevailing Golden Age rate of profit has adapted to the payoff period and so in the Golden Age equilibrium will measure what Keynes called the marginal efficiency of investment. Of course, the latter is not straightforward to calculate since it will depend on the endogenous obsolescence date of investment of a given vintage and so really on all the variables. But by adopting the pay-off period approach Kaldor surely hoped to have an alternative means of characterising profits and the rate of profit which did not seem to involve any 'marginal what nots'. But whether Kaldor approved of the step of making both the conditionals on investment binding must, as I have already noted, remain doubtful. Yet without it he would have been one equation short to determine the net rate of profit. So the 'New Model' had a soft neoclassical underbelly.

It is shown that steady state must entail

$$\dot{y}_t/y_t = \dot{I}_t/I_t$$

since otherwise real wages will experience accelerating growth or decline. So the rate of growth of output per man is determined endogenously and not as, say, in Harrod or most neoclassical models, exogenously. Here Kaldor and Arrow reach similar results although Arrow used a different and, as Kaldor conceded, more plausible technical progress function.

The remainder of the model, besides the usual vintage equations for obsolescence and total output, etc., employs the Cambridge saving hypothesis to close the model. The wage at any date t must equal the quasi-rent per worker of the machine scrapped at t and since we know the Golden Age growth rate, wages at all t are determined. However we are not told how to determine the number of workers which will be employed with each vintage. I assume that it is supposed that there is no choice. Had there been choice then indeed both boundary conditions which investment must satisfy would hold with equality, with the consequence which I have already discussed.

In his comments on Arrow's (1962) 'Learning by Doing', Kaldor distinguishes his model from the 'neoclassical Arrow' by supposing that there is an increase in the production of machines. He claims that for Arrow that will entail a rise in the share of wages but for him it will entail a fall. This is 'the broad brush' again. It is not clear from what position the rise in the production of machines is to be taken. What I believe he has in mind is not a 'rise' but a comparison of two economies in steady state, one of which is investing a larger fraction of income than is the other. Given his savings assumption Kaldor properly concludes that the share of profit will be higher in the economy with a larger investment–income ratio. But there is nothing anti-neoclassical in this savings assumption. The model has eleven simultaneous equations (when the rate of profit is determinate) and if two economies differ in their steady state investment–income ratio then they will differ in other respects as well. Kaldor is here committing a sin which Joan Robinson was always condemning: he confused comparison of equilibria with changes in an equilibrium. In any event, it is of course by now well-known that stark neoclassicism (e.g. a Cobb–Douglas production function) combined with a Cambridge savings function yields a perfectly satisfactory growth model—provided one does not ask causality questions of a system of simultaneous equations.

Kaldor's models, as well as all other models of growth, are now out of favour and there is little work on these kinds of problems to be found in the current journals. One of the reasons no doubt is the concentration on steady state equilibria which resulted from the

56   F. H. Hahn

difficulties of studying more general equilibrium paths except in rather simple cases. A more important reason is actually Kaldorian: the formal models do not seem to capture the history of capitalist development as we know it. That is why Kaldor turned to the more speculative and less formal mode of his later work. But while we may have exhausted what we can, or want to, say concerning steady state growth, the theories of the fifties and sixties did teach us some quite important economics and Kaldor's models were no exception.

IV

I have not discussed Kaldor's more empirical work on growth nor his incorporation of growth theory in a theory of development. The reason why I omit this is that I am not really qualified to assess it. For instance, I do not know whether 'Verdoorn's Law' is now regarded as a law (see Kaldor, 1966).

But Kaldor took his own theories seriously when it came to practical economics and for a time he was in a position to induce governments to take the actions which he advocated. The Selective Employment Tax was an example of this. Basically it was justified on the Marshallian-Pigouvian grounds of subsidising increasing returns sectors at the expense of those with decreasing returns. It was not clear why this was best accomplished by the subsiding and taxing of employment. For a thorough analysis the interested reader is referred to Reddaway *et al.* (1973).

For the UK, Kaldor was an advocate of export-led growth (1966, 1971). But I do not know of any formal model of his which studies growth for an open economy. His less formal arguments certainly were not unpersuasive and incorporated his idea of rising productivity in expanding industrial sectors. There is one important criticism which one can make of some of his policy proposals which involved other countries in an essential way. He ignored what for short one can call the 'reaction functions' of other countries. Nowadays, game theory is being applied to these problems of interaction. Kaldor cannot be blamed for not doing so himself. But he is open to criticism for ignoring these matters altogether.

V

It is inevitable that an economist of the originality, verve and devotion to his subject as Kaldor was should invite criticism of some kind. But that should not detract from the judgement that he possessed rare qualities of insight and imagination. It will not be at all surprising if at some future time he will be hailed as an important precursor in the understanding of the processes of growth. At present the scale of his intellectual picture blurred its details and much of this was in any case only loosely sketched. It is too early to make up this deficiency. But when it is done it may turn out to be a very fine and indeed a very reasonable picture.

Bibiography

Arrow, K. J. 1962. The economic implication of learning by doing, *Review of Economic Studies*, XXIX, pp. 155–73

Atkinson, A. B. and Stiglitz, J. E. 1969. A new view of technological change, *Economic Journal*, vol. LXXIV, pp. 573–578

Dasgupta, P. and Stiglitz, J. 1987. 'Learning-by-Doing, Market Structure and Industrial and Trade Policies', mimeo.

Hahn, F. 1972. *The Share of Wages in The National Income*, London, Weidenfeld and Nicholson

Kaldor, N. 1939. Speculation and economic stability, *Review of Economic Studies*, vol. VII

Kaldor, N. 1957. A model of economic growth, *Economic Journal*, vol. LXVII, December
Kaldor, N. 1961. Capital accumulation and economic growth, in Lutz, F. A. and Hague, D. C. (eds) *The Theory of Capital*, London, Macmillan
Kaldor, N. 1966. *Causes of the Slow Rate of Economic Growth in the United Kingdom*, Inaugural Lecture at Cambridge, CUP
Kaldor, N. 1971. Conflict in national economic objectives, *Economic Journal*, vol. LXXXI
Kaldor, N. 1972. The irrelevance of equilibrium economics, *Economic Journal*, no. 328, pp. 1237–1255
Kaldor, N. and Mirrlees, J. 1962. A new model of economic growth, *Review of Economic Studies*, XXIX, pp. 174–92
Reddaway, B. *et al.* 1973. *Effects of the Selective Employment Tax—Final Report*, Department of Applied Economics Occasional Papers 32, Cambridge, CUP
Robertson, D. H. 1940. *Essays in Monetary Theory*, London and New York, Staples Press
Thirlwall, A. P. 1987. *Nicholas Kaldor*, Brighton, Wheatsheaf Books
Young, A. 1928. Increasing returns and economic progress, *Economic Journal*, vol. XXXVIII, December

Part III
The Romance with Verdoorn

Excerpt from Nicholas Kaldor, *Causes of the Slow Rate of Economic Growth of the United Kingdom*, 1–40.

CAUSES OF THE SLOW RATE OF ECONOMIC GROWTH OF THE UNITED KINGDOM

I

ONE of the basic economic facts which has increasingly entered into national consciousness is the relatively slow rate of economic growth of Britain. Thanks to the work of various international organisations, there is now ample material on the comparative growth records of different countries, and in such comparisons Britain appears almost invariably near the bottom of the league-tables. Thus if we take the decade 1953–4 to 1963–4, the rate of growth of our gross domestic product is estimated to have been 2·7 per cent a year, as against 4·9 per cent in France, 5·6 in Italy, 6 per cent in Germany, and no less than 9·6 per cent in Japan. If we take a more recent period, say the five years 1960–5, our rate of economic growth at 3·3 per cent a year looks distinctly better, but our inferiority, in relation to the other advanced countries, appears even more pronounced, since some countries, such as the United States, Canada or Belgium, which previously grew at around 3–3½ per cent a year have all shown much higher growth rates in the more recent period. Indeed every other member of the 'Paris Club' of advanced countries has chalked up a growth rate of at least 4½ per cent in the last five years; Japan remained outstanding with a rate of growth of almost 10 per cent a year.

As these facts became more generally known, the minds of our economists and men of affairs, and the public generally, have become increasingly preoccupied with finding the basic cause, or causes, of this phenomenon. There has been no shortage of explanations. Some put the blame on the inefficiency of our business management; some on the nature of our education giving too little emphasis to science and technology, and too much to the humanities; some on the general social milieu which deprecates aggressive competitiveness and looks down on mere money-making as a career; some on over-manning and other restrictive practices of trade unions; some on the alleged national dislike of hard work; some on the insufficiency of investment, or of the right kind of investment; some on the economic policies of successive governments, being either too inflationary, or too deflationary, or both; and no doubt one could cite many other such 'explanations'.

There may be truth in some, if not all, of these contentions. The difficulty about them is that with one or two possible exceptions, they are not capable of being tested, and there is no way in which their individual role could in any way be quantified. Another basic difficulty with explanations of this kind, is that while they may seem *plausible* in relation to some countries, they look implausible in relation to others, whose relatively poor performance equally calls for explanation. (Thus in the decade 1953–63, though *not* in the five years 1960–5, the rate of economic growth of the United States was almost as low as Britain's. Yet no one suggested that the same kind of factors—inefficiency of business management, slowness in introducing innovations, restrictive labour practices, etc.—were likely to have been the causes of her slow rate of progress.)

However, the purpose of my lecture today is not to dispute the possible validity of such explanations, nor to argue in favour of one or another, but to suggest an alternative approach which seeks to explain the recorded differences in growth rates in terms of the *stage* of economic development attained by different countries rather than in the realm of personal (or rather individual) abilities or incentives. Put briefly, the contention that I intend to examine is that fast rates of economic growth are associated with the fast rate of growth of the 'secondary' sector of the economy—mainly the manufacturing sector—and that this is an attribute of an intermediate stage of economic development: it is the characteristic of the transition from 'immaturity' to 'maturity'; and that the trouble with the British economy is that it has reached a high stage of 'maturity' *earlier* than others, with the result that it has exhausted the potential for fast growth before it had attained particularly high levels of productivity or real income per head. The meaning of the term 'maturity' will, I hope, become evident in the course of this lecture; it is mainly intended to denote a state of affairs where real income per head has reached broadly the same level in the different sectors of the economy.

On this diagnosis the basic trouble with the British

economy is that it suffers from 'premature maturity'. This may sound no less pessimistic a conclusion than the alternative view which attributes our failures to some basic deterioration in the national character—such as working too little, spending too much, too little initiative, vitality or incentive—but at least it has the advantage that if the diagnosis were correct, and if it came to be generally accepted, steps could be taken to ameliorate the situation through instruments more powerful than mere exhortation.

I shall begin by examining the empirical evidence in favour of my contention; I will then discuss the theoretical reasons to justify it; and finally its implication in terms of potential growth rates of Britain and other advanced countries.

II

Let us then begin with the evidence. If we take the twelve industrially advanced countries for which figures are available, as shown in Table 1 (there are a few countries, such as Sweden and Switzerland, which had to be omitted for lack of comparable data), we find that there is a very high correlation between the rate of growth of the gross domestic product and the rate of growth of manufacturing production, and what is more significant, we find that the faster the overall rate of growth, the greater is the *excess* of the rate of growth of manufacturing production over the rate of growth of the economy as a whole.

This is indicated by the regression equation shown at

4

TABLE 1. *Rate of growth of G.D.P. and rate of growth of manufacturing production (twelve industrial countries, average 1953–4 to average 1963–4): exponential growth rates*

	Annual rate of growth of G.D.P.[1]	Annual rate of growth of manufacturing production[1]
Japan	9·6	13·6[2]
Italy	5·6	8·2
West Germany	6·0	7·3
Austria	5·4	6·2
France	4·9	5·6
Netherlands	4·5	5·5[3]
Belgium	3·6	5·1
Denmark	4·1	4·9
Norway	3·9	4·6
Canada	3·6	3·4
U.K.	2·7	3·2
U.S.A.	3·1	2·6

[1] Derived from National Accounts Data of G.D.P., and G.D.P. in manufacturing, at constant prices.
[2] Index of manufacturing production.
[3] G.D.P. in industrial production (including mining).

Sources. National Accounts Statistics, O.E.C.D.; National Accounts Yearbooks, U.N.

Regression. Growth of G.D.P. (Y) on growth of manufacturing output (X), $Y = 1·153 + 0·614X$, $R^2 = 0·959$.
(0·040)

Standard error of residuals as a proportion of mean value of $Y = 0·0825$.

the bottom of the table which, in terms of all the usual tests, shows a highly significant relationship between the rate of growth of the G.D.P. and the rate of growth of manufacturing production. On the basis of this one can predict fairly accurately the rate of growth of an economy—at least over a run of years—if one knows the rate of growth of its manufacturing production.

Of course, the mere fact that the growth of manufacturing output correlates with the growth of the G.D.P. is not in itself surprising, since the manufacturing sector is a fairly large component of the latter—somewhere between 25–40 per cent for the countries considered. But the regression equation asserts more than this. The meaning of the positive constant in the equation and of the regression coefficient which is significantly less than unity is that rates of growth above 3 per cent a year are found only in cases where the rate of growth in manufacturing output is in excess of the overall rate of growth of the economy. In other words, there is a positive correlation between the overall rate of economic growth and the *excess* of the rate of growth of manufacturing output over the rate of growth of the non-manufacturing sectors. I have not investigated how far this has been true of earlier historical periods, but in a study on historical growth rates since the nineteenth century published some years ago, Miss Deborah Paige found the same kind of relationship.[1]

Assuming, for the moment, that this relationship exists, is there some general hypothesis which is capable of explaining it? We must beware of attributing causal significance to a statistical relationship unless it can be shown to be consistent with some general hypo-

[1] Economic growth: the last hundred years, *National Institute Economic Review* (July 1961), p. 41.

thesis, which can be supported by other evidence. Since the differences in growth rates are largely accounted for by differences in the rates of growth of productivity (and not of changes in the working population), the primary explanation must lie in the technological field—it must be related to the behaviour of productivity growth. Is there some general reason which makes the rate of increase of output-per-man, for the economy as a whole, dependent on the rate of growth of manufacturing production? It has been suggested that because the *level* of productivity in manufacturing activities is higher than in the rest of the economy, a faster expansion of the high-productivity manufacturing sectors pulls up the average; and also that the incidence of technical progress—as measured by the *rate of growth* of productivity—is higher in manufacturing activities than in the other fields, so that a greater concentration on manufacturing increases the overall rate of advance.

However, neither of these suppositions seems capable of explaining the facts. The differences in the level of output per head between different sectors, as Beckerman has recently shown,[1] are quite incapable of explaining more than a small part of the observed differences in productivity growth rates, in terms of inter-sectoral shifts. The second proposition, if it were factually correct, would relate the rate of economic growth to the *size* of the manufacturing sector (in relation to the whole economy) rather than to its rate of expansion: it

[1] *The British Economy in 1975* (Cambridge University Press, 1965), pp. 23–5.

would make the rate of economic growth the highest in those countries whose industrial sector, as measured by the proportion of total manpower engaged in it, is the largest. On this test, therefore, Britain ought to come out near the top, not at the bottom of the league-table. But quite apart from this, the proposition is factually incorrect: technological progress and productivity-growth is by no means confined to manufacturing; in many of the countries examined, productivity growth in agriculture and mining has been higher than in manufacturing, or in industrial activities taken as a whole.

There is, however, a third possible explanation—the existence of economies of scale, or increasing returns, which causes productivity to increase in response to, or as a by-product of, the increase in total output. That manufacturing activities are subject to the 'law of increasing returns' was of course a well-known contention of the classical economists. One finds the origin of this doctrine in the first three chapters of the *Wealth of Nations*. Here Adam Smith argued that the *return* per unit of labour—what we now call productivity—depends on the division of labour; on the extent of specialisation and the division of production into so many different processes, as exemplified by his famous example of pin-making. As Smith explained, the division of labour depends on the extent of the market: the greater the market, the greater the extent to which differentiation and specialisation is carried, the higher the productivity. Neo-classical writers, with one or two famous exceptions, like Marshall and Allyn Young, tended to ignore, or to underplay, this phenomenon. As Hahn and Matthews remarked in a recent article 'the reason for the neglect is no doubt the difficulty of fitting increasing returns into the prevailing framework of perfect competition and marginal productivity factor pricing'.[1]

However Adam Smith, like both Marshall and Allyn Young after him, emphasised the interplay of static and dynamic factors in causing returns to increase with an increase in the scale of industrial activities. A greater division of labour is more productive, partly because it generates more skill and know-how; more expertise in turn yields more innovations and design improvements. We cannot isolate the influence of the economies of large-scale production due to indivisibilities of various kinds, and which are in principle reversible, from such changes in technology associated with a process of expansion which are not reversible. Learning is the product of experience—which means, as Arrow has shown,[2] that productivity tends to grow the faster, the faster output expands; it also means that the *level* of productivity is a function of cumulative output (from the beginning) rather than of the rate of production per unit of time.

In addition, as Allyn Young emphasised, increasing returns is a 'macro-phenomenon'—just because so much of the economies of scale emerge as a result of increased

[1] The Theory of Economic Growth: A Survey, *Economic Journal* (December 1964), p. 833.
[2] The Economic Implications of Learning by Doing, *Review of Economic Studies* (June 1962), pp. 155–73.

differentiation, the emergence of new processes and new subsidiary industries, they cannot be 'discerned adequately by observing the effects of variations in the size of an individual firm or of a particular industry'. At any one time, there are industries in which economies of scale may have ceased to be important. They may nevertheless benefit from a general industrial expansion which, as Young said, should be 'seen as an interrelated whole'. With the extension of the division of labour 'the representative firm, like the industry of which it is a part, loses its identity'.[1]

III

This, in my view, is the basic reason for the empirical relationship between the growth of productivity and the growth of production which has recently come to be known as the 'Verdoorn Law', in recognition of P. J. Verdoorn's early investigations, published in 1949.[2] It is a dynamic rather than a static relationship—between the rates of change of productivity and of output, rather than between the *level* of productivity and the *scale* of output—primarily because technological progress enters into it, and is not just a reflection of the economies of large-scale production. Since Verdoorn's work it has been investigated by many others, among them Salter,[3] and more recently by

[1] Increasing Returns and Economic Progress, *Economic Journal* (December 1928), pp. 538–9.
[2] Fattori che regolano lo sviluppo della produttivitá del lavoro, *L'Industria* (1949).
[3] *Productivity and Technical Change* (Cambridge University Press, 1960).

Beckerman,[1] though none of these authors (to my knowledge) has given sufficient emphasis to the fact that it is a phenomenon peculiarly associated with the so-called 'secondary' activities—with industrial production, including public utilities, construction, as well as manufacturing—rather than with the primary or tertiary sectors of the economy.

Its application to the case of the manufacturing industries of the twelve countries in the period 1953–4 to 1963–4 is given in Table 2, which shows for each country the growth rates of production, productivity and employment. The results are summarised in two regression equations, productivity on output, and employment on output—which are two different ways of looking at the same relationship[2]—and which suggest that the growth of output must have played a major role in the determination of productivity growth rates. Again, the relationships by the usual tests are shown to be highly significant and they suggest that apart from an 'autonomous' rate of productivity growth of around 1 per cent a year, the latter is a function of the growth in total output: each percentage addition to the growth of output requires a 0·5 per cent increase in the growth of employment in terms of manhours, and is associated with a 0·5 per cent increase in the growth of productivity. These coefficients are very close to those found by Verdoorn and other investigators.

There are some economists who, whilst admitting

[1] *Op. cit.* pp. 221–8.
[2] One is a mirror-image of the other. The regression coefficients of the two equations add up to unity and the two constants (but for a small discrepancy caused by rounding) add up to zero.

TABLE 2. *Rates of growth of production, employment and productivity in manufacturing industry (twelve countries, average 1953–4 to average 1963–4): annual exponential growth rates*

	Production[1]	Employment[2]	Productivity[3]
Japan	13·6	5·8	7·8
Italy[4]	8·1	3·95	4·2
West Germany	7·4	2·8	4·5
Austria[7]	6·4	2·2	4·2
France[4]	5·7	1·8	3·8
Denmark[6]	5·7	2·55	3·2
Netherlands[8]	5·5	1·4	4·1
Belgium	5·1	1·25	3·9
Norway	4·6	0·2	4·4
Canada	3·4	2·1	1·3
U.K.	3·2	0·4	2·8
U.S.A.[7]	2·6	0·0	2·6

[1] Gross domestic product in manufacturing, at constant prices.
[2] Wage and salary earners adjusted for changes in weekly manhours.
[3] Output per manhour, derived from first two columns.
[4] 1954–5 to 1963–4.
[5] Incorporates estimated change in weekly manhours.
[6] 1955–6 to 1963–4.
[7] 1953–4 to 1962–3.
[8] Industrial production and employment (including mining).

Sources. National Account and Manpower Statistics, O.E.C.D. Statistical Yearbook, U.N.

Regressions.
(1) Rate of growth of productivity (P) on the rate of growth of manufacturing production (X),

$$P = 1{\cdot}035 + 0{\cdot}484X, \quad R^2 = 0{\cdot}826.$$
$$(0{\cdot}070)$$

(2) Rate of growth of employment (E) on rate of growth of manufacturing production (X),

$$E = -1{\cdot}028 + 0{\cdot}516X, \quad R^2 = 0{\cdot}844.$$
$$(0{\cdot}070)$$

the statistical relationship between productivity growth and production growth, argue that it says nothing about cause and effect: the Verdoorn Law, according to this view, may simply reflect the fact that faster growth rates in productivity induce, via their effects on relative costs and prices, a faster rate of growth of demand, and not the other way round.

This alternative hypothesis is not, however, fully specified—if it were, its logical shortcomings would at once be apparent. If the rate of growth of productivity in each industry and in each country was a fully autonomous factor, we need some hypothesis to explain it. The usual hypothesis is that the growth of productivity is mainly to be explained by the progress of knowledge in science and technology. But in that case how is one to explain the large differences in the *same* industry over the *same* period in different countries? How can the progress of knowledge account for the fact, for example, that in the period 1954–60, productivity in the German motor-car industry increased at 7 per cent a year and in Britain only 2·7 per cent a year? Since large segments of the car industry in both countries were controlled by the same American firms, they must have had the same access to the improvements in knowledge and know-how. This alternative hypothesis is tantamount to a denial of the existence of increasing returns which are known to be an important feature of manufacturing industry, quite independently of the Verdoorn Law and one which is frequently emphasised in other contexts—as for example, in analysing the effects of economic integration.

Moreover, to establish this alternative hypothesis, it is not enough to postulate that productivity growth rates are autonomous. It is also necessary to assume that differences in productivity growth rates between different industries and sectors are fully reflected in the movement of relative prices (and not in relative movements of wages and other earnings) and further, that the price-elasticity of demand for the products of any one industry, or for the products of manufacturing industry as a whole, are always greater than unity: none of this, as far as I know, has been submitted to econometric verification.

Once the relationship between productivity growth and production growth is recognised the large differences in the recorded productivity growth rates do not appear so remarkable, and we can take a rather different view of the 'efficiency-ranking' of various countries. We can award marks to each country, not on the usual basis of simple productivity growth, but on a more sophisticated basis of the deviation of its productivity growth from the Verdoorn regression line: in other words, by relating its actual performance to what it could be expected to be, on the basis of the growth rate of total manufacturing production. On this test, we find that there was one outstandingly good performer—Norway—whose recorded productivity growth was one-third higher than could be expected; and there was one outstandingly bad performer—Canada—with a rate of productivity growth which was only one-half as high as the computed figure. There were two moderately poor performers—Italy and Denmark—

with a deficiency of around 15 per cent, and three moderately good performers—Netherlands, Belgium and the United States—whose productivity record was 12-15 per cent above the average. As to the rest, four of them were strictly average—and this group includes Japan, Germany, France and Austria—with deviations of less than 2 per cent from the regression line; and finally there was one *marginally* good performer, with a record that was 7 per cent better than the computed figure—the United Kingdom. If we award, as we must on this test, β to the strictly average performers and $\beta+$ to the moderately good performers, Britain, I think, must be rated $\beta?+$.

All this is subject of course to the statistical uncertainties inherent in all international comparisons, and many of these deviations are too small to be of much significance in judging a country's performance. But the interesting point about them is that with one notable exception—again Canada—they appear to be closely related to investment behaviour. The countries which invested a great deal in relation to their growth rate were the good performers, whilst the countries whose investment was small in relation to their growth rate were poor performers. If we measure investment behaviour by the incremental capital/output ratio (ICOR for short) we find that Norway, the best performer on the Verdoorn test, had the highest ICOR (over 5), all the good performers had over-average ICORs (over 3), all the average performers had average ICORs (around $2\frac{1}{2}$), and the poor performers had low ICORs (below 2).¹ (Canada was the one exception to this rule—a poor performer with a very high ICOR—but I am glad to be able to report that since the dates of this examination Canada has improved her showing quite considerably.) In other words, if we look for the effects of investment behaviour on growth, not in terms of the growth rate itself, but in terms of a country's performance according to the Verdoorn test, the figures make much more sense. But they also indicate that increasing returns is by far the more important cause of differences in productivity growth rates; differences in investment behaviour explain residual differences which are relatively less important.

I am not suggesting that the Verdoorn relationship applies *only* to manufacturing activities or that it applies to every manufacturing industry considered separately. But its application outside the industrial field is clearly far more limited. It certainly does not apply, on the evidence of the statistics, to agriculture and mining, where the growth of productivity has been much greater than the growth in production and where, in so far as any definite relation is shown, productivity growth and employment growth tend to be negatively related, not positively. This supports the classical contention that these are 'diminishing returns' industries: the fact that this is overlaid by technological progress or the adoption of more capital intensive methods may statistically conceal this, but it does not

---

[1] ICOR is defined here as the ratio between gross fixed investment in industry and the level of industrial production, divided by the growth rate of industrial production.

eliminate its significance. In some of the countries the relatively high rate of growth of productivity in agriculture is merely the passive consequence of the absorption of surplus labour in secondary and tertiary occupations, and not necessarily a reflection of true technological progress or of higher capital investment per unit of output.

There remains the tertiary sector, services, comprising such divergent items as transport, distribution, banking and insurance, catering and hotels, laundries and hairdressers, and professional services of the most varied kind, publicly and privately provided—which together account for 40–50 per cent or more of the total output and employment of the advanced countries. Over much of this field learning by experience must clearly play a role but economies of scale are not nearly so prominent and are exhausted more quickly. In the case of activities like research or education, the Adam-Smithian principle of the advantages of specialisation and of the division of labour must operate in the same sort of way as in industrial activities. But precisely in these fields it cannot be directly reflected in the estimates of productivity, since 'output' cannot be measured independently of 'input'. In some fields in which output can be measured independently—as, for example, in transport and communications, statistical evidence shows no correlation between productivity growth and production growth. In yet others such as distribution, productivity—meaning sales per employee—tends to grow the faster the faster the rise in aggregate turnover; but in this case, it is merely a reflection of the changing incidence of excess capacity generated by imperfect competition, and not of true economies of scale. In other words, productivity may rise in automatic response to the rise in consumption caused by the growth of production in the primary or secondary sectors—just as the productivity of the milkman doubles, without any technological change, when he leaves two bottles of milk outside each door instead of one bottle.

It is the rate of growth of manufacturing production (together with the ancillary activities of public utilities and construction) which is likely to exert a dominating influence on the overall rate of economic growth: partly on account of its influence on the rate of growth of productivity in the industrial sector itself, and partly also because it will tend, indirectly, to raise the rate of productivity growth in other sectors. This will happen, or may happen, both in agriculture and in the distributive trades—in the first because it induces a faster rate of absorption of surplus labour; in the second because it secures a faster increase in the through-put of goods into consumption. And of course it is true more generally that industrialisation accelerates the rate of technological change throughout the economy.

IV

It remains to deal with the question of why it is that some countries manage to increase their rate of manufacturing production so much faster than others. The explanation, in my view, lies partly in demand factors and partly in supply factors, and both of these combine to make fast rates of growth the characteristic of an intermediate stage in economic development.

Economic growth is the result of a complex process of interaction between increases of demand induced by increases in supply and of increases in supply generated in response to increases in demand. Since in the market as a whole commodities are exchanged against commodities, the increase in demand for any commodity, or group of commodities, reflects the increase in supply of other commodities, and vice versa. The nature of this chain-reaction will be conditioned by both demand elasticities and supply constraints; by individual preferences or attitudes and by technological factors. The chain-reaction is likely to be the more rapid the more the demand increases are focused on commodities which have a *large* supply response, and the larger the demand response induced by increases in production—the latter is not just a matter of the marginal propensities in consumption but also of induced investment. Viewing this process from a particular angle—what determines the rate of growth of manufacturing output—it will be convenient to consider the problem in two stages: first, from the point of view of the sources of demand, and secondly from the point of view of the factors which govern potential supply.

Looking at the matter from the point of view of demand, this is fed mainly from three sources—from consumption, domestic investment and from net exports—by which I mean the net excess of exports over imports.

The behaviour of consumer demand depends on the changing structure of consumption associated with a rise in real incomes per head. It is well known that a *high* income elasticity for manufactured goods—as reflected in a growing proportion of consumer expenditure spent on manufactured products—is a characteristic of an intermediate zone in the levels of real income per head. At low levels of income a high proportion of both average and marginal incomes is spent on food. At very high levels of real income, the income elasticity of demand for manufactures falls off, both absolutely and relatively to that of services: but for the continued appearance of new commodities, like washing machines or television sets, it would fall off more rapidly. In the middle zone in which this proportion is both large and growing, there is a double interaction making for faster economic growth: the expansion of the industrial sector enhances the rate of growth in real incomes; the rise in real incomes steps up the rate of growth of demand for industrial products.

This, however, is only part of the explanation. A more important source of growth in demand originates in capital investment. It is the peculiarity of a highly developed industrial sector that it largely provides the goods on which capital expenditure is spent, and thereby generates a demand for its own products in the very process of supplying them. Once a country attains the stage of industrialisation at which it largely provides for its own needs in plant and machinery and not just in consumer goods the rate of growth of demand for its products will tend to be stepped up very considerably; since the expansion of capacity in the investment sector by itself raises the rate of growth of demand for the products of its own sector, and thereby provides the incentives, and the means, for further expansion. Provided that entrepreneurial expectations are buoyant, and the process is not hampered by labour shortages, or shortages of basic materials, the very establishment of an investment goods sector makes for a built-in element of acceleration in the rate of growth of manufacturing output that could—theoretically—go on until technological constraints—the input/output relationships *within* the investment goods sector—impose a limit on further acceleration.

The third source of the rate of growth of demand arises from the changing structure of foreign trade. The early stages of industrialisation invariably involve reduced imports of manufactured consumer goods and increased imports of machinery and equipment. During this phase, therefore, the rate of growth of demand for domestic manufactures—which can be supposed to consist mainly of the so-called 'light industries', generally textiles—rises faster than total consumption, on account of the substitution of home production for imports. But as the experience of many countries has shown, this phase of relatively rapid development tends to peter out as the process of import substitution of consumer goods is gradually completed. To maintain the rhythm of development it is necessary for the industrialising country to enter a second stage in which it becomes a growing net exporter of manufactured consumer goods. This is followed (or accompanied) by a third stage, marked by 'import substitution' in capital goods, and for the reasons mentioned, it is likely to be associated with a fast growth rate, as the 'heavy industries' develop out of relation to the growth of the rest of the economy. There is a fourth and final stage, at which a country becomes a growing net exporter of capital goods; it is at this last stage that 'explosive growth' is likely to be encountered—when a fast rate of growth of external demand for the products of the 'heavy industries' is combined with the self-generated growth of demand caused by their own expansion. It has been the passage into this fourth stage which I think mainly explains the phenomenal growth rates of post-war Japan. Fast though her growth of consumption has been, her growth due to the rise in the production of investment goods—both for home use and exports—was very much greater. But this again is a transitional stage: once the investment sector is fully developed, and once a country has acquired a reasonably large share of world trade in investment goods, the growth of demand is bound to slow down, as the broad historical experience of the older industrial countries has shown.

All this is looking at the matter from the demand side alone. The actual course of development may at any stage be slowed down, or interrupted by supply constraints; and as I shall argue presently, it is inevitable that sooner or later the rhythm of development should be slowed down on account of them.

Such supply constraints can take one of two forms: commodities or labour. As the industrial sector expands, it absorbs growing amounts of commodities (and services) produced outside the manufacturing sector: such as food and industrial materials produced by the primary sector (agriculture and mining); manufactured goods which it does not provide itself, or not in sufficient quantities and on which it is dependent on imports—this is probably relatively more important in the earlier stages of industrialisation, but as post-war experience has shown, there is a very large scope, even among the industrially highly developed countries, for trade in manufactured goods for industrial use, both finished goods and components. Finally, industrial growth generates demand for services of numerous kinds—like banking and insurance, lawyers, accountants and so on—and is thus responsible, in part at any rate, for the fast expansion of the 'tertiary' sector. (Also, the growing use of durable consumer goods sets up a growing demand for repair and maintenance services.)

For an *individual* country—though not for the group of industrialised countries together—a commodity constraint generally takes the form of a balance of payments constraint: it arises because a particular rate of growth generates a rate of growth of imports which exceeds the rate of growth of exports. This is certainly true of countries in the early stages of industrialisation when the growth of industry, despite import-substitution, causes a substantial rise in *total* import requirements; at a stage when the industrial development adds little, if anything, to the country's export potential. But it is also suggested that it may slow down the rate of growth of industrially advanced economies; and it is a widely held view that it has been a major constraint on the post-war economic growth of Britain.

It is certainly true that brief periods of relatively high growth during the last twenty years were invariably attended by a rapid growth of imports, resulting in balance of payments deficits; and it was the occurrence of these deficits, as much as the labour shortages and the resulting inflation, which forced the introduction of deflationary measures which brought these periods to an end. It is equally true that if the trend rates of growth in our exports had been higher, we could have sustained higher rates of growth of imports, and that if the rhythm of our development had been more even, imports would not have risen so fast as they did during the recovery phases. But this does not necessarily prove that the balance of payments was the *effective* constraint on our rate of economic growth. This would only follow if it could also be shown that with a faster rate of growth of exports, we could have achieved a higher rate of growth of manufacturing production, or else that we could have increased exports at a faster rate while keeping domestic investment and consumption rising at a lower rate. In the latter context it must be remembered that the volume of our exports has been pretty large in relation to the total volume of our manufacturing production; and while the share of our exports in world trade declined dramatically, the share of exports in our own manufacturing output remained remarkably steady. It is possible to interpret this by saying that it was the trend rate of growth of exports which governed the trend rate of growth of production, since any higher rate of growth of production would not have been compatible with keeping the balance of payments even, over a run of years. It is also possible to interpret this in the opposite way: that over a run of years it was the rate of growth of production of exportable goods which determined the rate of growth of our exports, and not the other way round.

The important question is whether, *apart* from balance of payments constraints, it would have been possible to increase our manufacturing output at a faster rate. Was the growth in production mainly governed by the growth in demand for manufactured products, or was it governed by supply-constraints, which would have frustrated a higher rate of growth of output, irrespective of the growth in demand?

v

And here we come back to the labour situation and to Verdoorn's Law. This as we have seen, suggests that a higher rate of growth of manufacturing output breeds higher rates of productivity growth, but not enough to obviate the need for a faster rate of growth of employment. In post-war Britain periods of faster growth in manufacturing industry invariably led to severe labour shortages which slowed down the growth of output and which continued for some time after production reached its cyclical peak—in fact, on almost every occasion, employment continued to rise after output had begun to fall. All this suggests that a higher rate of growth could not have been maintained unless more manpower had been made available to the manufacturing industry.

Indeed all historical evidence suggests that a fast rate of industrial growth has invariably been associated with a fast rate of growth of employment in both the secondary and the tertiary sectors of the economy. The main source of this labour has not been the growth of the working population, nor even immigration, but the reservoir of surplus labour, or 'disguised unemployment' on the land. In the course of industrialisation there has been a continuous transfer of labour from the countryside to the urban areas in the course of which the percentage of the labour force in agriculture diminishes in a dramatic fashion. But the *longer* this process proceeds, the *smaller* the labour force remaining, the *less* it yields in terms of manpower availabilities in the secondary and tertiary sectors. Moreover, the process of transfer is bound to come to a halt once the gap between agricultural and industrial productivity is eliminated, and this becomes fully reflected in relative earnings. The United Kingdom, almost alone among the advanced countries, has reached the position where net output per head in agriculture is as high as in industry; though there is still a wide gap in relative wages which, I think, is mainly due to the fact that the fall in the demand for agricultural labour, owing to mechanisation, has outrun, over the last ten years, the rate of diminution in the agricultural labour force.

Table 3 shows, for the twelve countries, the rate of growth in the total labour force, and the rate of change in employment in agriculture and mining, industry and the services; Table 4 shows the percentage composition in total employment between the three sectors in 1962-3.

One of the remarkable features of Table 3 is the uniform fall in employment in agriculture and mining in all countries; it varied between 2 per cent and 4½ per cent a year. In countries in which the agricultural labour force was still large, as a percentage of total, this meant a substantial annual addition to the labour force in industry and services—substantial both absolutely and in relation to the growth of the working population, which was relatively modest, in most countries—whilst in the countries where the size of the labour force in primary occupations was small—as in the United Kingdom and the United States—the rate of increase in employment in secondary and tertiary occupations was much smaller. As is shown in Table 3, the United Kingdom had the smallest rate of increase in employment in industry and services taken together, despite the fact that the rate of growth of her total labour force over this period was higher than that of five of the other eleven countries. The explanation is found in Table 4, which shows that Britain had the smallest proportion of the labour force in agriculture and mining.

Table 3 also shows that whilst the absorption of labour in the tertiary sector was substantial in all countries—at least of the same order of magnitude as the increase in industrial employment—it tended to be relatively greater (in relation to the growth of industrial

TABLE 3. *Rates of growth of labour force, and the rate of change of employment in agriculture, mining, industry and services (twelve countries 1954–64): exponential growth rates*

	Rate of growth of labour force	Rate of growth of employment[1] in agriculture and mining	Rate of growth of employment[2] in industry and services		
			Total	Industry[3]	Services[4]
Japan	1·5	−2·6	5·4	5·8	5·1
Italy	−0·1	−4·5	3·9	4·4	3·2
West Germany[5]	1·4	−4·1	2·8	2·7	2·9
Austria	0·2[6]	−3·6[6]	2·3	2·0	2·6
France	0·2	−3·5	2·2	1·9	2·4
Denmark[7]	0·8	−2·8	2·2	2·5	1·9
Netherlands	1·3	−2·0	2·3	1·9	2·7
Belgium	0·3	−4·4	1·9	1·5	2·3
Norway	0·3	−2·5	1·3	0·5	2·0
Canada	2·3	−2·8	3·5	2·3	4·3
U.K.	0·6	−2·3	1·1	0·6	1·6
U.S.A.	1·3	−2·4	1·8	0·8	2·4

[1] Including self-employed and unpaid family workers.
[2] Wage and salary earners.
[3] Manufacturing, construction and public utilities.
[4] Transport, distributive trades, financial and other services, public administration, etc.
[5] 1957–64.
[6] 1951–63.
[7] 1955–64.
Source. O.E.C.D. Manpower Statistics.

employment) in the slow-growing countries than in the fast-growing ones. This may be due to the fact that the growth of labour requirements in services is less sensitive to changes in the rate of economic growth than

TABLE 4. *Percentage composition of total employment between primary, secondary and tertiary occupations (twelve countries, 1962–3 average)*

	Primary (Agriculture and mining)	Secondary (Manufacturing, construction and public utilities)	Tertiary (Services)[1]	Total
Japan	30·0	30·3	39·7	100
Italy	27·8	39·4	32·8	100
Austria[2]	23·8	40·6	35·6	100
France	21·1	37·0	41·9	100
Norway	20·8	33·8	44·5	100
Denmark	19·1	39·5	41·4	100
West Germany	14·3	42·6	39·5	100
Canada	12·9	32·7	54·4	100
Netherlands	12·0	42·3	45·7	100
Belgium	9·4	40·6	48·2	100
U.S.A.	8·9	30·7	60·4	100
U.K.	6·7	44·0	49·3	100

[1] Includes transport, distribution, financial and other services, public administration, etc.
[2] 1961.

Source. O.E.C.D. Manpower Statistics.

the growth of labour requirements in industry. One could certainly think of several reasons why this should be so—for example, the rise in the standard of educational and health services which tends to proceed by its own momentum. It is also possible that the relatively high rate of growth of employment in services is to some extent a consequence of the instability in the demand for labour in manufacturing: in the case of Britain, it may have been a by-product of the stop-and-go cycle. Since employment opportunities in services are less sensitive to short-period variations in demand than manufacturing employment, it is possible that a kind of ratchet effect has been in operation: there may have been a drift of labour into services as a result of a fall in employment in manufacturing in the 'stop' phase, which was not reversed in the subsequent 'go' phase.

However that may be, it is clear that if our basic hypothesis is correct, *all* countries will experience a slow-down in their growth rates as their agricultural labour reserves become exhausted. It is the existence of an elastic supply curve of labour to the secondary and tertiary sectors which is the main pre-condition of a fast rate of development. As Table 4 shows, some of the advanced countries—such as Japan, Italy or France—still possess a large agricultural labour force (of the order of 15–30 per cent) so that they still have a considerable period of potentially fast growth ahead of them. But the United States, Belgium and also Germany are approaching the structural pattern of the United Kingdom. In the case of Germany, the rate of growth of production and employment in industry has already slowed down considerably in the last few years. In the United States—which operated with a high unemployment rate throughout the 'fifties—growth could be accelerated quite considerably by the orthodox techniques of Keynesian economics, but now that unemployment has fallen to lower levels, the rate of growth is likely to slow down again; though the

United States is still far off from a situation of acute labour shortage.

Britain, having started the process of industrialisation earlier than any other country, has reached 'maturity' much earlier—in the sense that it has attained a distribution of the labour force between the primary, secondary and tertiary sectors at which industry can no longer attract the labour it needs by drawing on the labour reserves of other sectors. There are disadvantages of an early start, as well as advantages—as is shown by the fact that some of the latecomers of industrialisation have attained higher levels of industrial efficiency even before they became fully industrialised.

But once it is recognised that manpower shortage is the main handicap from which we are suffering, and once our thinking becomes adjusted to this, we shall, I hope, tend to concentrate our efforts on a more rational use of manpower in *all* fields, and to limit the absorption of labour into those sectors in which—if I may use a Pigovian phrase—the marginal social product is likely to be appreciably below the marginal private product.

It is possible, looking further ahead, that the new technological revolution—electronics and automation—will so radically reduce the labour requirements in industry as to make it possible to combine fast growth with *falling* industrial employment. But there are no signs of this yet. If we take the technologically most advanced country, the United States, we find that her fast growth of manufacturing production over the last few years was associated with large increases in the volume of manufacturing employment—fully in line with what the Verdoorn equation would lead us to expect.[1]

Finally there is the question how far a mature economy could continue to reap the benefits of economies of scale, not through a fast growth in manufacturing industry as a whole, but through greater international specialisation. If the main hypothesis advanced in this lecture is correct, and economies of scale in industry are the main engine of fast growth, at least some of its benefits could continue to be secured by concentrating our resources in fewer fields and abandoning others—in other words, by increasing the degree of interdependence of British industry with the industries of other countries.

[1] In 1962–5 manufacturing output of the United States (as measured by the index of manufacturing production) increased by 6·7 per cent a year; the rate of growth of the volume of man hours of employment was 2·7 per cent. The regression equation at the bottom of Table 2 yields a computed figure of 2·4 per cent.

This inaugural lecture was delivered in the University of Cambridge on 2 November 1966

NOTES

(a) *The role of manufacturing in economic growth*

The significance of the relationship between the growth of manufacturing output and the growth of the G.D.P. shown in Table 1 has been tested (i) by reference to the relation of the growth of non-manufacturing output (i.e. G.D.P. *minus* G.D.P. in manufacturing) to the growth in manufacturing production; (ii) by relating the growth rate of G.D.P. to the *excess* of the growth rate of manufacturing production over the growth rate of the non-manufacturing sectors. The results are summarised in the following regression equations:[1]

(1) Rate of growth of non-manufacturing output (Y) on rate of growth of manufacturing production (X)

$$Y = 1 \cdot 142 + 0 \cdot 550 X, \quad R^2 = 0 \cdot 824.$$
$$(0 \cdot 080)$$

(2) Rate of growth of G.D.P. (Y) on the excess of the rate of growth of manufacturing over the rate of growth of non-manufacturing production (X)

$$Y = 3 \cdot 351 + 0 \cdot 954 X, \quad R^2 = 0 \cdot 562.$$
$$(0 \cdot 267)$$

Both of these are statiscally significant at the 99 per cent level and thus confirm the generalisation derived from Table 1. A comparison of regression (1) above with the

[1] The four regression equations in this section relate to the same group of countries, and the same periods, as indicated in Table 1.

33

regression in Table 1 shows that the exclusion of manufacturing output from G.D.P. makes no appreciable difference to the structural relationship: both the constants and the coefficients in the two equations are very similar.

The significance of these findings has been further tested by examining the relationship between the growth rate of G.D.P. and the growth rate of agricultural production, mining, and the output of services.[1] No correlation was found between the rate of growth of G.D.P. and the rate of growth of either agricultural production or mining. As between G.D.P. and G.D.P. originating in 'services' there is a highly significant relationship but of a different character, as shown by the following equation:

(3) Rate of growth of G.D.P. (Y) on rate of growth of G.D.P. in services (X)

$$Y = -0.188 + 1.060X, \quad R^2 = 0.930.$$
$$(0.092)$$

The fact that the coefficient is so near to unity, and the constant is negligible suggests that the causal relationship here is the other way round—i.e. that it is the rate of G.D.P. which determines the rate of growth of the 'output' of services. It also confirms recent American studies[2] which suggest that, contrary to general belief, the income-elasticity of demand for services is not significantly greater than unity; the fact that most countries (as indicated in Table 3) had a higher rate of employment growth in

[1] The term 'services' comprises transport and communications; wholesale and retail trade; banking, insurance and real estate; ownership of dwellings; public administration and defence; health and educational services and miscellaneous services.

[2] Cf. Victor R. Fuchs, *The Growing Importance of the Service Industries*, New York: National Bureau of Economic Research, Occasional Paper No. 96 (1965).

'services' than in 'industry' is not due to a high income-elasticity of demand, but to a lower rate of productivity growth in services. This latter finding is further confirmed by relating the rate of growth of output in 'services' to the rate of growth of industrial production (manufacturing, construction and public utilities):

(4) Rate of growth of output in services (Y) on the rate of growth of industrial production (X)

$$Y = 1\cdot283 + 0\cdot597X, \quad R^2 = 0\cdot846.$$
$$(0\cdot0805)$$

This shows that the 'real' output of services—as measured in the national accounts of each country at constant prices—grows less than in proportion to industrial output, even though employment grows (in most cases) more than in proportion.[1]

(b) The Verdoorn Law

The 'Verdoorn Law' asserts that with a higher rate of growth of output, both productivity and employment increase at a faster rate, the regression coefficients with respect to each being of the same order of magnitude. This relationship was also investigated with regard to other sectors of the economy for which comparable data could be found in the O.E.C.D. statistics—i.e. public utilities (gas, electricity and water) and construction; agriculture and mining; transport and communications and 'commerce' (the latter term includes the distributive trades,

---

[1] The only exceptions in the period considered (i.e. 1953–4 to 1963–4—though this would not be true of the more recent period, 1960–5) were the U.S.A. and Canada, where the output of services grew at a somewhat higher rate than industrial output.

banking, insurance and real estate).[1] Owing to the lack of data, some countries had to be omitted in some of the estimates, and a somewhat shorter period taken; also, it was not possible to adjust the employment figures for changes in man hours outside the manufacturing sector. The results for each sector (including the manufacturing sector, already shown in Table 2) are summarised in the following set of regression equations:

Annual rates of growth of productivity (P) and of employment (E) on the rates of growth of output (X)[2]

Industry

(1) *Manufacturing*

$$P = 1{\cdot}035 + 0{\cdot}484X, \quad R^2 = 0{\cdot}826,$$
$$(0{\cdot}070)$$

$$E = -1{\cdot}028 + 0{\cdot}516X, \quad R^2 = 0{\cdot}844.$$
$$(0{\cdot}070)$$

[1] It was not possible to separate, on the employment statistics, the distributive trades from banking, insurance, etc. in more than a few cases; but the distributive trades account for much the greater part (around four-fifths or more) of the total output of this sector, and a similar proportion of employment.

[2] Since exponential growth rates have been used throughout, $P + E = X$, and hence the sum of the constants of the two equations should be zero, and the sum of the regression coefficients unity, irrespective of the nature of the correlations involved. However, since estimates of employment growth and of productivity growth have been separately rounded, the sum of these can vary from the total by one decimal point, which explains small deviations from the correct result in some of the pairs of regression equations.

(2) *Public utilities* (11 countries, 1953–63)[1]

$$P = 2 \cdot 707 + 0 \cdot 419 X, \quad R^2 = 0 \cdot 451,$$
$$(0 \cdot 154)$$
$$E = -2 \cdot 690 + 0 \cdot 577 X, \quad R^2 = 0 \cdot 609.$$
$$(0 \cdot 154)$$

(3) *Construction* (11 countries, 1953–63)[1]

$$P = -0 \cdot 543 + 0 \cdot 572 X, \quad R^2 = 0 \cdot 810,$$
$$(0 \cdot 092)$$
$$E = 0 \cdot 552 + 0 \cdot 428 X, \quad R^2 = 0 \cdot 702.$$
$$(0 \cdot 092)$$

Primary sector

(4) *Agriculture* (12 countries, 1953–63)[1]

$$P = 2 \cdot 700 + 1 \cdot 041 X, \quad R^2 = 0 \cdot 812,$$
$$(0 \cdot 155)$$
$$E = -2 \cdot 684 - 0 \cdot 056 X, \quad R^2 = 0 \cdot 013.$$
$$(0 \cdot 155)$$

(5) *Mining* (10 countries, 1955–64)[1]

$$P = 4 \cdot 0714 + 0 \cdot 671 X, \quad R^2 = 0 \cdot 705,$$
$$(0 \cdot 153)$$
$$E = -4 \cdot 0714 + 0 \cdot 329 X, \quad R^2 = 0 \cdot 365.$$
$$(0 \cdot 153)$$

[1] For *public utilities* and *construction*, the equations relate to all countries listed in Table 2, except the Netherlands; the data relate to 1953–63, except for Austria (1951–61), Italy and France (1954–63), Denmark and Canada (1955–63). The same holds for *agriculture*, except that here the Netherlands (1953–63) is also included. The estimates on *mining* exclude Austria and Denmark; they relate to 1955–64, except for Netherlands where they relate to 1955–61.

Tertiary sector

(6) *Transport and communications* (9 countries, 1955–64)[1]

$$P = 2{\cdot}314 + 0{\cdot}224X, \quad R^2 = 0{\cdot}102,$$
$$(0{\cdot}252)$$
$$E = -2{\cdot}314 + 0{\cdot}776X, \quad R^2 = 0{\cdot}576.$$
$$(0{\cdot}252)$$

(7) *Commerce* (9 countries, 1955–64)[2]

$$P = -1{\cdot}751 + 0{\cdot}953X, \quad R^2 = 0{\cdot}932,$$
$$(0{\cdot}098)$$
$$E = 1{\cdot}744 + 0{\cdot}056X, \quad R^2 = 0{\cdot}044.$$
$$(0{\cdot}098)$$

The regressions reveal an interesting pattern. In the case of construction and public utilities, the equations relating to both productivity and employment are similar to those in manufacturing, except that in the case of public utilities the constant term of the equations is much larger, and hence the significance of the relationship is less, than in the case of either manufacturing or construction.[3] One can

---

[1] In the case of *transport and communications*, the estimate excludes Austria, Denmark and Japan; the data relate to 1955–64, except for the U.S.A. (1955–63), France (1956–64) and West Germany (1957–64).

[2] *Commerce* includes G.D.P. originating in wholesale and retail trade, banking, insurance, real estate, at constant prices, and employment relating to the same category, except for Japan where the data on output and employment relate to wholesale and retail trade only. The estimate excludes Austria, Denmark and the Netherlands; it relates to 1955–64, except for Canada (1955–61), U.S.A. (1955–63), West Germany (1957–64) and France (1958–64).

[3] However in the case of the construction sector there is a *negative* constant term of 0·5 per cent a year in the productivity equation, in contrast to manufacturing which shows a positive constant term of 1 per cent a year. The reasons for this are likely to be similar to those given below in the discussion of the equations for commerce.

thus conclude that the effects of economies of scale on the growth of productivity are significant not only for manufacturing industry, but for the industrial sector generally.

Agriculture and mining reveal a different picture. In each case, productivity growth shows a large trend factor which is independent of the growth in total output; the regression coefficient of productivity is not significantly different from unity (except possibly for mining) whilst the regression for employment is not significantly different from zero for agriculture, and barely significant for mining. In both of these cases productivity growth has exceeded the growth of production for every single country; and the growth in productivity has owed nothing to increasing returns to scale.[1]

In the case of transport and communications, there is no correlation whatever between productivity growth and output growth; productivity increased at an independent rate of some 2·3 per cent a year (for the average of the nine countries considered) but beyond this any higher rate of growth of output required a corresponding increase in employment (as shown by the regression coefficient of employment on output which is not significantly different from unity). In this case, therefore, productivity growth appears to have been fully autonomous, and owed nothing to economies of scale.

Finally, in the case of commerce, there is a high correla-

[1] In the case of agriculture the growth of output, for most of the countries considered, has probably been more a reflection of the effects of technological progress and capital investment in raising *yields per acre*, than of the rate of growth of consumer demand. The fact that employment was diminishing in all countries—at a fairly uniform rate of around 2–3½ per cent a year—may have simply been the result of the absorption of disguised unemployment, or the reflection of the fact that technological progress has, on the whole, been more labour-saving than land-saving.

tion between productivity growth and output growth (with a regression coefficient not significantly different from unity) but no relation whatever between the growth of employment and of production. The regressions for commerce are remarkably similar to those of agriculture, except for one very important difference: in the case of agriculture there is a large positive constant, showing a trend-rate of increasing productivity, whereas in the case of commerce the trend-rate of growth of productivity is *negative*. This negative trend-rate has nothing to do with technological factors (which operate in the same sort of way in the distributive trades and banking as elsewhere—as, for example, the development of supermarkets or mechanisation) but is mainly a reflection of the peculiar manner in which competition operates in this field, tending constantly to eliminate abnormal profits through a multiplication of units, rather than through a reduction of prices or distributive margins. These estimates confirm the view that whilst an increase in the total turnover of banking or the distributive trades automatically raises productivity (i.e. turnover per employee) the inflow of labour into these trades is not directly connected with the rise in turnover.

© Cambridge University Press 1966

Productivity and Growth in Manufacturing Industry: Some Reflections on Professor Kaldor's Inaugural Lecture[1]

By J. N. WOLFE

Professor Kaldor's recent inaugural lecture,[2] with its dramatic claims of a new diagnosis of, and recipe for, economic growth, has proved remarkably influential. I propose to demonstrate, however, that his lecture contains logical shortcomings and empirical obscurities of an important sort. It will be argued, too, that his policy recommendations are neither altogether novel nor entirely persuasive.

Kaldor asserts that there are increasing returns to size in manufacturing industry but not in non-manufacturing activities. He asserts that the growth of the productivity of factor inputs in manufacturing will depend largely upon the rate of growth of manufacturing output. The productivity of factor inputs in non-manufacturing activities may also grow, but this growth will not depend on the growth of total output in these occupations.[3] He asserts that the rate of growth of productivity per man in the economy as a whole will be greater, the greater is the rate of growth of manufacturing output. He then suggests that the growth of manufacturing industry in the United Kingdom has been hindered by shortage of labour. This, he says, results from the "maturity" of the UK economy. By "maturity" he seems to mean a situation in which there is a relatively small employment in agriculture. He concludes that the rate of growth of output as a whole may be increased by making labour more plentifully available to manufacturing industry. As an alternative policy he suggests greater international specialization.

We shall, in what follows, examine Kaldor's arguments under three heads: (a) Is there sufficient evidence to support Kaldor's propositions? (b) Are his policy proposals consistent with his propositions? (c) Are any alternative policies implied by his analysis?

---

[1] I am much indebted to Sir Donald MacDougall and Professor A. J. Youngson for their penetrating criticism of an earlier and even less perfect draft of this paper.

[2] N. Kaldor, *Causes of the Slow Rate of Economic Growth of the United Kingdom*, 1966.

[3] This account somewhat over-simplifies Kaldor's position, for he seems in places to wish to argue that there are potential increasing returns in the distributive trades as well as in manufacturing, arising out of the possibility of increasing sales from existing shops without increasing the sales force. We will call this the Distribution Thesis, and revert to it later, p. 125, n. 6.

II

Professor Kaldor offers two sets of statistical regressions as evidence. The first is the regression of the percentage rate of growth of total output on the percentage rate of growth of manufacturing output. The second is the regression of the percentage rate of growth of productivity on the percentage rate of growth of output in manufacturing industry.

The first regression—that of total output growth on manufacturing output growth—is inconclusive. The growth of total output is closely correlated with the growth of manufacturing output. But the growth of total output is also closely correlated with the growth of output of services. Hence it is not possible to tell from the regressions whether the growth of manufacturing output is a more fundamental influence on the growth of total output than is the growth of service output, or vice versa. Kaldor suggests, however, that the size of the constants and regression co-efficients in the two cases supports the view that the growth of manufacturing output is a causal force, while the growth of the output of services is merely induced. This is a slip, for the size of regression co-efficients gives us no evidence of causal connection; and neither does the size of the constant team.

The crux of Kaldor's evidence must therefore be contained in his regression of the rate of growth of productivity per man in manufacturing on the rate of growth of output in manufacturing. This regression is, as Kaldor himself is aware, a somewhat spurious exercise. For the percentage rate of growth of productivity per man, as he defines it, is equal to the percentage rate of growth of output minus the percentage rate of growth of employment. If the percentage rate of growth of employment is small, we would be regressing the growth of output on itself—a thoroughly unsound procedure!

A more reasonable procedure is to regress the percentage growth of output on the percentage growth of employment.[1] For manufacturing industry in the countries which Kaldor has studied this regression gives a reasonably good fit; and this is interpreted as showing that quite large increases in output can be accompanied by relatively small increases in labour input.

Scientific evidence on increasing returns in manufacturing is much more inconclusive than one might suppose. Careful econometric studies of the cost of production of manufacturing firms have usually indicated that, although costs of production of very small firms tend to be higher than those of medium-sized firms, the cost advantage does not continue to increase as firms grow beyond a certain moderate size which varies with the particular industry involved. The evidence is well summarized in Professor J. Johnston's *Statistical Cost Analysis*.[2] Historical studies of particular industries in single countries have also

---

[1] Kaldor confuses things by regressing instead the rate of growth of employment on the rate of growth of output.
[2] J. Johnston, *Statistical Cost Analysis*, New York, 1960.

been attempted; sometimes they support the thesis of increasing returns, and sometimes they do not. A great deal seems to depend upon the importance one attaches to technological change as an independent causal factor in economic growth.

Kaldor's lecture purports to contain new evidence on the subject of increasing returns. He assumes that if there were increasing returns in manufacturing it should show up in the production function—the quantitative relation between input and outputs—for individual industries and for manufacturing industry as a whole. Estimation of the production function has been attempted many times by econometricians for the United States, Australia, India and other countries. Kaldor attempts to determine the production function by using data from a number of countries rather than from any one country.

The use of data drawn from more than one country is a peculiarly hazardous undertaking, partly because relative prices differ from country to country, and partly because the collection of data is never on an exactly similar basis. Moreover, the results of statistical investigation may differ greatly if the underlying theoretical structure differs from study to study. It should not come as a surprise, then, that Kaldor's results differ from those of many previous studies of the production function. Where previous studies have shown little tendency to increasing returns in manufacturing, Kaldor's study seems to show very marked increasing returns in that sector.

To evaluate Kaldor's study we must consider his method of procedure, and compare it with methods used by others. The traditional method of estimating the production function is to assume that there are only two factors of production, labour (L) and capital (C), and that output (O) results from inputs of these two factors. One time-honoured system is to assume that output is related to the inputs in the manner suggested by Professors Cobb and Douglas some 40 years ago, i.e. $O = AC^a L^b$, where A is a constant and a and b are exponents of the inputs. If $a+b=1$, this relationship gives constant returns to scale. This relationship may be treated mathematically to produce $\bar{O} = a\bar{C} + b\bar{L}$, where $\bar{O}$ is the percentage rate of growth of output, $\bar{C}$ the percentage rate of growth of capital, and $\bar{L}$ the percentage rate of growth of employment.

Now Kaldor's estimate seems to be derived from a formula closely related to this, for he is concerned with testing the relationship, $\bar{O} = b\bar{L} + e$, where e is an error term. He finds that b is very large, indeed substantially larger than one.

We should indeed expect that if we measured the effect of L without considering the effect of C we would obtain an exaggerated value for b. This is so because we would be attributing to L alone all the effects of both $\bar{C}$ and $\bar{L}$. Kaldor's results therefore exaggerate the value of b. We shall shortly return to this neglect of capital in Kaldor's model.

There is a further difficulty. The production function is essentially a long-term relationship. It assumes that the level of capital and the employment of labour are properly balanced. This balance does not exist in the short run, in the business cycle. In the upward swing of the business cycle the re-employment of unemployed capital and labour results in a relation between output and measured inputs which is very different from the long-term relationship. In Britain, for example, the relationship during upswings between output growth and employment growth may be about 5:1, and this is known to be far higher than the long-term relationship. It is not impossible to adjust for cyclical changes in a single country. It is more difficult to do so when one is using data from several countries. Even a small unadjusted cyclical element could throw Kaldor's results far from their proper values. Indeed, a study attempted by Professor Frank Brechling and myself several years ago, which used data similar to Kaldor's and which attempted to isolate cyclical influences, seemed to indicate that these cyclical factors are the most important single influence in explaining differences in growth performance among countries.

Throughout his lecture Kaldor gives little prominence to the role of capital formation. This will be surprising to those familiar with the work of Salter, who first made popular in this country what Kaldor calls Verdoorn's Law.[1] Salter explained the tendency for productivity growth to be greatest in industries experiencing the greatest output growth by arguing that growth in output is associated with the introduction of new and more efficient capital equipment, and that there is only limited re-equipment in slow-growing industries. We should, therefore, expect rapid growth in productivity to be associated not just with rapid growth in output, but also with a high level of capital formation. If this were true across industries, it should be true for the whole of manufacturing industry taken across countries. Kaldor does not deny this specifically, but he gives little indication that he regards the supply of capital as a serious limitation to economic growth.[2]

There is finally a curious oversight in Kaldor's reasoning. Even if productivity growth in manufacturing were the main source of growth in output per man in the economy as a whole, and even if productivity growth in manufacturing depended upon the growth in manufacturing output, it would not follow that countries with the greatest rate of growth in manufacturing productivity would have the greatest growth of total output per man. This is so because the growth of total output per man would depend upon the relative size of the manufacturing sector. We should expect that in the stipulated condition the rate of growth of output per man in the economy as a whole would be greater, the greater the share of manufacturing employment in total employment. But this

---

[1] W. E. G. Salter, *Productivity and Technical Change*, 1960 (2nd ed., 1966).
[2] At one point in his lecture (p. 15) Kaldor goes some way towards remedying this deficiency. But he falls into the trap of combining his analysis with analysis by incremental capital/output ratios. Had he followed his analysis consistently and introduced the percentage rate of growth of capital stock as a second explanatory variable, his results might have been quite different.

does not appear to be supported by the evidence. Indeed, if one were to accept the analysis offered by Kaldor, it would appear that in the case of the United Kingdom, with its relatively modest manufacturing sector and its limited access to further increasing returns, the expansion of manufacturing output might be of lesser importance than elsewhere as a source of economic growth.

III

We now turn to a consideration of Professor Kaldor's policy proposals. These include, as already seen, measures to promote greater international specialization. This may be dealt with briefly. A desire for international specialization is not itself remarkable. It is interesting to note, however, that those who, like Kaldor, attach special economic importance to manufacturing are often in practice in favour of high tariffs on such goods. This attitude is particularly notable in North America. Kaldor's proposal may rest upon his (undemonstrated) belief that increasing returns are irreversible, so that a fully-developed country need not fear a decline in productivity in lines adversely affected by imports.

Kaldor's desire to shift labour into manufacturing industries requires more detailed consideration. Marshall was in favour of a subsidy intended to shift demand towards increasing-returns industries. Since a subsidy to one industry has an effect similar to that of a tax on all other industries, Marshall presumably might have approved generally of a tax like the Selective Employment Tax. While the modern theory of welfare economics teaches caution in applying general rules to complex realistic situations, many economists would agree. The difficulty has been to discover the level of tax or subsidy which is appropriate to each industry; and this is still uncertain.

Kaldor's policy proposal appears to be closely related to the present Selective Employment Tax. This may be a coincidence, for this tax may be defended on grounds other than those put forward by Kaldor. It has, in particular, been welcomed in many quarters for the encouragement it is thought to give to exports, and for the shift it allows from direct to indirect taxation.[1] Kaldor's proposal of a labour tax is, however, based upon his belief that a shortage of labour in manufacturing industries has hindered the growth of output in those industries. This contention requires careful analysis. It is certainly true that the growth of total output has been less than it might have been if the labour force had grown faster. But this is a matter of population and immigration

---

[1] The effect of the tax on exports must not be accepted uncritically. If ramifications through the economy via the input-output tables are taken into account, and the import-content of manufactures and of services are given proper weight, it will be found that the net effect on the balance of payments of a shift of labour from services is very small, and perhaps negligible.

policy; a faster growth of total output might have been achieved at the cost of a slower growth in per capita income.

It is true, again, that in so far as productivity in agriculture is lower than that in other occupations, a flow of workers out of agriculture into higher-productivity occupations would allow an expansion of total output and income at a faster rate than would otherwise occur. But the existence of low-productivity sectors is not itself an asset, and the growth available from the elimination of such sectors is merely a reflection of past weakness. In spite of some discussion of the disadvantages of "maturity", Kaldor makes little use of this point in his argument.

Kaldor seems to believe, however, that there has been scarcity of labour in manufacturing in the United Kingdom in a much more direct sense. He seems to feel that the growth of output of manufactured goods has somehow been frustrated by a shortage of labour. This assertion is by no means novel. But the evidence for it is limited. Presumably the shortage is more than that general scarcity of labour which manifests itself in periods of boom. To make sense in the context, the shortage must be relatively greater in manufacturing than in non-manufacturing activities.

Practically the only evidence advanced for the existence of such a shortage is the allegedly slow rate of growth of employment in manufacturing compared with the faster rate of growth of employment in non-manufacturing occupations. But a slow growth of employment in an industry is not usually accepted as conclusive evidence of a shortage of labour in that industry. It may, for example, merely reflect a slow growth of demand for the products of that industry. It is normal in economics to look for one or both of two symptoms when a shortage of labour is suspected in a particular trade. The first is a lower level of unemployment and a higher level of vacancies in the trade than elsewhere. The second is a rise in wages in the trade relative to wages elsewhere.

We may begin, however, by considering the percentages by which employment changed in selected sectors from mid-1960 to mid-1965:[1]

	%
Food, Drink and Tobacco	2·9
Chemicals and Allied Industries	−0·8
Engineering and Electrical Industries	13·7
Textiles	−10·0
Construction	15·6
Transport and Communications	−4·5
Distributive Trades	7·2
Catering, Hotels, etc.	7·3
Public Administration	10·7
All Manufacturing Industries	2·4

[1] Source: *Ministry of Labour Gazette*, December 1967; amended to take account of changes in classification detailed in *Ministry of Labour Gazette*, February 1965, p. 59.

Two points emerge. First, it is clear that growth of employment in manufacturing as a whole lagged behind that in services as a whole over the five year period covered. Equally important, however, is the fact that some manufacturing industries, and particularly the engineering and electrical industries, increased their employment at a very fast rate. Detailed inspection of the services sector reveals, moreover, that it was the public sector which experienced the sharpest rise of employment, and that the growth of employment in the distributive trades was somewhat less marked. These figures alone might give us occasion to question the Kaldor diagnosis. For it is apparent that the scarcity of labour in manufacturing, if it existed, was insufficient to prevent the expansion of those manufacturing industries which were determined to expand. Nor was the alleged preference of workers for the "more stable" service trades sufficient to prevent this happening.

Logically the next step is to examine the pattern of unemployment. If there were a chronic shortage of labour in manufacturing, we might expect to see the fact reflected in a generally lower level of unemployment in manufacturing than in other industries. The data for the period 1960 to 1965 appear, at first glance, to offer some support for Kaldor's contention. The percentage of unemployed was lower in manufacturing industries than in the category "all industries" in each year from 1960 to 1965. A detailed inspection reveals, however, a more complex picture. The figures were high for textiles (an industry of declining employment) but low for chemicals (another industry of declining employment). Even more striking is the fact that unemployment figures were, on the whole, relatively high for two industries, engineering and construction, which were experiencing rapid expansion of total employment.[1]

We may, I think, incline to the view, in any event, that unemployment figures are a relatively poor guide to the labour market situation. A more revealing picture is given when unfilled vacancies are taken into account. Table 1 shows unemployment less unfilled vacancies as a percentage of total employment in various sectors for the period 1962 to 1966. The table shows that the effective level of unemployment (or state of the labour market) was not, in the period, markedly different in the service trades than in manufacturing. The notable exception was the fast-growing public administration sector. It may be surmised that many of the unemployed in this category were in fact seeking positions in clerical occupations in private business. It is well known that clerical and secretarial staff for private firms are often sought privately rather than through the labour exchange; and this seems highly relevant.

[1] The unemployment percentages in selected industries in 1965 were as follows: Food, Drink and Tobacco, 1·3; Chemicals and Allied Industries, 1·1; Engineering and Electrical Industries, 1·7; Textiles, 1·8; Construction, 2·8; Transport and Communications, 1·6; Distributive Trades, 1·2; Catering, Hotels, etc., 2·9; All Industries, 1·4; All Manufacturing Industries, 0·9. (Source: *Monthly Digest of Statistics*. Monthly average of unemployment for year expressed as percentage of employment in June. This procedure gives a rather high percentage for seasonal trades such as hotels and construction.)

TABLE 1
UNEMPLOYMENT LESS UNFILLED VACANCIES AS PERCENTAGE OF EMPLOYMENT, 1962–1966.

	1962	1963	1964	1965	1966
Food, Drink & Tobacco	0·86	0·60	0·04	0·46	0·63
Chemical & Allied Industries	0·50	0·98	0·06	0·06	0·63
Engineering & Electrical Industries	0·01	0·48	−1·03	−1·1	−1·5
Textiles	0·33	1·07	0·76	−0·78	−1·7
Construction	2·57	3·13	1·21	1·66	0·57
Transport & Communications	0·36	0·96	0·13	0·42	0·29
Distributive Trades	0·24	0·82	−0·73	−0·37	−1·24
Catering, Hotels, etc.	0·59	0·16	−1·71	−0·91	−2·5
Public Administration	0·64	1·13	0·54	0·45	0·33
All Manufacturing Industries	1·1	0·47	0·53	0·78	0·49

Source: *Ministry of Labour Gazette*, February 1966.

As a last test, let us examine the rate of growth in wage rates in various trades. We are somewhat handicapped here by the small coverage offered by official statistics of earnings in the service trades. Available data on the percentage increase of average weekly wage rates between 1960–61 and 1964–65 are:[1]

	%
Food, Drink and Tobacco	21·9
Chemicals and Allied Industries	25·2
All Metals (Combined)	17·6
Textiles	19·8
Construction	21·3
Transport and Communications	26·4
Distributive Trades	24·0
Professional and Scientific	26·8
Miscellaneous	22·5
All Industries	22·5
All Manufacturing Industries	20·2

These data show that there was no clear tendency for wage rates to rise more steeply in manufacturing than in other activities between 1960 and 1965; if anything, the reverse was true.[2]

One piece of evidence put forward by Kaldor in support of his thesis

---

[1] Source: *Monthly Digest of Statistics*. The figures refer to averages for all workers.

[2] Available data of increases in average *weekly earnings of male manual workers* indicate a more marked improvement in manufacturing industries, presumably as a result of less short-time working during the period. There is, however, little evidence in the data of a shortage of labour relatively more marked in Manufacturing than in Transport and Communications, "Certain Miscellaneous Services", and Public Administration.

of a shortage of labour in manufacturing is the fact that in recent cyclical upswings employment in manufacturing has generally continued to grow after the peak of manufacturing output has been passed. Other writers, including Professors Ball,[1] Brechling,[2] Kuh[3] and Solow,[4] and Mr. Robert Neild,[5] have been unanimous in ascribing this phenomenon to a lag in the adjustment of actual employment to the level of employment desired for any particular level of output. Extensive econometric work has been done on this point, and there seems little doubt that no "labour shortage" is involved.

We may therefore conclude from all this that the suggestion of a chronic shortage of labour in manufacturing in the United Kingdom is, at best, not proven.[6]

IV

Are there any alternative policy prescriptions which might follow from the acceptance of Professor Kaldor's (admittedly undemonstrated) propositions?

The most important possibility appears to be the desirability of encouraging the growth of demand for those activities which involve a considerable input of manufactures. The chief of these activities are exports, capital formation and the consumption of durable goods. It would seem that Kaldor should, on his own assumptions, be inclined to promote expansion of these activities. It is, however, difficult to increase capital formation or exports without increasing savings. It is widely agreed that, in developed countries at least, the demand for any large class of consumables is markedly inelastic with respect to price

---

[1] R. J. Ball and E. B. A. St Cyr, "Short Term Employment Functions in British Manufacturing Industry", *Review of Economic Studies*, vol. 33 (1966), p. 179.

[2] F. Brechling, "The Relationship between Output and Employment in British Manufacturing Industries", *Review of Economic Studies*, August 1965.

[3] E. Kuh, "Cyclical and Secular Labor Productivity in United States Manufacturing", *Review of Economics and Statistics*, February 1965.

[4] R. M. Solow, Presidential Address to Econometric Society, delivered at the European meeting, Zurich, September 1964.

[5] R. R. Neild, *Pricing and Employment in the Trade Cycle*, 1963.

[6] We must at this point say a word about Kaldor's "Distribution Thesis" (see p. 117, n. 3). Kaldor seems to argue that the possibility of obtaining productivity gains in distribution as total output grows is frustrated by the tendency of distributive traders to multiply the number of service outlets. It is not, however, clear that this could be avoided without seriously reducing the well-being of consumers. There is no evidence that consumers are prepared to face unlimited queues to obtain small price reductions. There is, moreover, the greatest difficulty about the regressions (p. 38) with which the Distribution Thesis is supported. First, there are only nine observations, and five of these are for specially selected years or have differing coverage. Second, the regression of productivity on output is clearly spurious in this case, and the regression of employment on output is so insignificant as to make difficult its interpretation on a production-function sense. It is, finally, difficult to interpret the positive trend in employment as due to the growth of new capacity in response to high profits (as Kaldor does) without some evidence that profit levels are uncorrelated with the growth of demand. Unless it can be given further support I should be inclined to reject categorically Kaldor's interpretation of his results on this point.

changes, so that only very large price changes are likely to have any perceptible effect upon the volume of the goods demanded.

The demand for services is growing partly because the income of the population is growing, and partly because government expenditure is growing. Kaldor does not, one supposes, wish to curb the growth of consumers' income. His analysis seems to suggest some advantage in curbing government expenditure, which has a high services component. We may wonder why Kaldor has not made more explicit this implication of his analysis.

I conclude, then, that the complete acceptance of Kaldor's thesis would imply the need for greater vigour in the pursuit of present policies of export expansion and the promotion of capital formation, and also the need for greater watchfulness in the growth of government expenditure. It seems a curious coincidence that these orthodox policy proposals should flow from Kaldor's unorthodox thesis.

But his thesis cannot, in fact, be accepted as it stands. There is nothing in his evidence to support the tax on employment. The evidence appears, perhaps, to support a sales or turnover tax which should be discriminatory among industries, with the degree of discrimination depending, however, upon a set of measurements which has not yet been made. There is nothing in Professor Kaldor's lecture which should make us alter our view that the main burden of economic growth will continue to fall on technical progress and capital formation, as it does now. None of this, however, is a conclusive argument against a selective employment tax; for such a tax has great administrative convenience and can be made to fit in well with the requirements of regional policy.

University of Edinburgh.

Productivity and Growth in Manufacturing Industry: A Reply

By Nicholas Kaldor

Professor Wolfe attacks me (in the May, 1968 issue of *Economica*) for being obscure and unconvincing in the inaugural lecture which I gave at Cambridge.[1] In this lecture I attempted to put forward a complex thesis concerning the causes of high and low rates of economic growth under capitalism, and this was necessarily somewhat scanty; there is a limit to the material one can pack into a single lecture. Such a treatment could only be successful if received with imagination and some goodwill; Professor Wolfe has picked on a large number of individual points (many of them trivial in substance) without attempting to come to grips with the thesis as a whole. I propose to publish a more comprehensive statement of the theory in due course.[2] Meanwhile rather than follow the negative approach of answering each point in turn—which would be both tedious and unconstructive—I shall concentrate on the main points which have clearly not been understood.

Foremost among these is my notion of "economic maturity". This is not some vague notion which can be defined in terms of "a situation in which there is relatively small employment in agriculture". In my lecture I defined it explicitly "as a state of affairs where real income per head had reached broadly the same level in the different sectors of the economy". I could have added, to convey its significance better, that "economic maturity" could also be defined as "the end of the dual economy"; or a situation in which "surplus labour" is exhausted; or one in which "growth with unlimited supplies of labour" (to use Arthur Lewis' phrase) is no longer possible.

The neo-classical framework of thought cannot accommodate notions like "disguised unemployment", the "dual economy", or the distinction between "capitalist" and "pre-capitalist" enterprise. For neo-classical theory *assumes* that the structure of demand determines the distribution of resources between different uses; that competition and mobility assures that "factor prices" tend to equality in all employments; that profit maximization ensures equality of factor prices with the value of the marginal products of factors; subject only to friction

---

[1] J. N. Wolfe, "Productivity and Growth in Manufacturing Industry: Some Reflections on Professor Kaldor's Inaugural Lecture", *Economica*, vol. XXXV (1968), pp. 117–26; N. Kaldor, *Causes of the Slow Rate of Economic Growth of the United Kingdom*, Cambridge University Press, 1966.

[2] A somewhat more extended exposition was given in three lectures (subsequently published) at Cornell University: cf. *Strategic Factors in Economic Development*, Ithaca, New York, 1967.

etc., each "factor" will tend to be used where is makes the greatest contribution to the national product.

It would be generally agreed that these assumptions are at their most inappropriate in the case of an under-developed country, or a country in the earlier stages of industrialization. In such countries high and low earnings sectors exist side by side; there are vast amounts of "surplus labour" or "disguised unemployment" in the low-productivity sectors, so that labour can be withdrawn from them without adverse effects on the output of those sectors; and the supply of labour in the high-productivity, high-earnings sector is continually in excess of the demand, so that the rate of labour-transference from the low to the high productivity sectors is governed only by the rate of growth of the demand for labour in the latter. In fact the size of the labour force in the non-industrial sector is a residual—entirely determined by the total supply of labour on the one hand and the requirements for labour in the industrial sector on the other hand. The best definition I could suggest for the existence of "labour surplus" in this sense is one which is analogous to Keynes' definition of "involuntary unemployment": a situation of "labour surplus" exists when a faster rate of increase in the demand for labour in the high-productivity sectors induces a faster rate of labour-transference even when it is attended by *a reduction, and not an increase, in the earnings-differential between the different sectors*.

For reasons that I explained in my lecture, the rate of growth of industrialization fundamentally depends on the exogenous components of demand (a set of forces extending far beyond the income elasticities of demand for manufactured goods). The higher the rate of growth of industrial output which these demand conditions permit, the faster will be the rate at which labour is transferred from the surplus-sectors to the high productivity sectors. It is my contention that it is the rate at which this transfer takes place which determines the growth rate of productivity of the economy as a whole. The mechanism by which this happens is only to a minor extent dependent on the *absolute* differences in the levels of output per head between the labour-absorbing sectors and the surplus-labour sectors. The major part of the mechanism consists of the fact that the *growth* of productivity is accelerated as a result of the transfer at both ends—both at the gaining-end and at the losing-end; in the first, because, as a result of increasing returns, productivity in industry will increase faster, the faster output expands; in the second because when the surplus-sectors lose labour, the productivity of the remainder of the working population is bound to rise.[1]

In the literature, the "surplus labour sector" is generally thought of

---

[1] Indeed, the existence of disguised unemployment is by itself capable of explaining these results, even in the absence of increasing returns, since the increase in industrial output, brought about by labour transference, will be a net addition to the GNP—there will be no compensating reduction in output elsewhere. As a matter of historical fact, I am convinced, however, that the growth of productivity resulting from increasing returns (both internal and external) has been a very important part of the picture. (On this see below.)

as agriculture. This is because in the early stages of capitalist development much the greater part of the population draws its living from agriculture. However, disguised unemployment in "services" had been just as prevalent—in Victorian England (as in present-day India or Latin America) there were vast numbers of people who eked out a living in urban areas as hawkers, petty tradesmen, servants, etc. on very low earnings.[1] In the field of services however (unlike in agriculture) there are two contrary processes at work: on the one hand industrialization absorbs labour from services on a large scale; on the other hand, the growth of industry itself gives rise to the growth of services of various kinds which are both complementary and ancillary to industrial activities (by "ancillary" I mean that the demand for these services, e.g. transport, distribution, accountancy, banking services, etc. are derived from, but cannot generate, industrial activities). As a result the total employment in services tends to rise during the process of industrialization though less (in relation to the growth of total output) when the growth in total output is relatively fast.

While it has long been known that labour has no "opportunity cost" in an under-developed country—the absorption of labour through the growth of industry involving no reduction in output elsewhere—it has not been generally recognized that the same applies to most of the so-called "advanced countries" with relatively high incomes per head.

The view that growth rates, even in advanced countries, are dependent on the rate at which labour is transferred into manufacturing from other sectors would find confirmation, in the first place, if over-all growth rates are positively associated with rates of increase in employment in manufacturing.

This is shown for the group of twelve advanced countries given in Table 3 of my lecture for the period 1953/4–1963/4 by the following:[2]

(1) $\quad \dot{G} = 2\cdot665 + 1\cdot066 \dot{E}_M \qquad R^2 = \cdot828$
$\qquad\qquad (0\cdot15)$

where $\dot{G}$ is the rate of growth of GDP and $\dot{E}_M$ is the rate of growth of employment in manufacturing.

This result confirms my general hypothesis unless it could be shown that growth rates in manufacturing employment are themselves closely related to growth rates of total employment so that the former could be regarded as a proxy for the latter. Such positive association seems

---

[1] This relates to both "self-employed" and employees alike. In the population Census of 1891, 15·8 per cent. of the occupied population of Britain were classified as domestic servants. In the Census of 1961 the figure was 1·4 per cent. This reduction cannot be explained in terms of a shift in consumer preferences or by the assumption that domestic service is an "inferior good" with a negative income-elasticity of demand; it can only be explained by the growing absorption of surplus labour in the economy which resulted in a rise in wages in domestic service which was much in excess of the general rise in wages.

[2] The sources for this and the following equations are given in the statistical tables of my lecture.

ruled out, however, by the fact that there is *no association at all* between rates of growth of GDP and rates of growth of *total* employment:

(2) $\quad \dot{G} = 4\cdot 421 + 0\cdot 431 \dot{E}_g \qquad\qquad R^2 = \cdot 018$
$\qquad\qquad (0\cdot 994)$

where $\dot{E}_g$ is the rate of growth of total employment.

The positive correlation in Eq. (1) could only be consistent with the absence of any correlation in Eq. (2) if rates of growth in over-all productivity are *positively* associated with rates of growth of employment in manufacturing and *negatively* associated with rates of growth of employment outside manufacturing. This is duly confirmed by the following three equations:

(3) $\quad \dot{P}_g = 1\cdot 868 + 0\cdot 991\, \dot{E}_M \qquad\qquad R^2 = \cdot 677$
$\qquad\qquad (0\cdot 216)$

(4) $\quad \dot{P}_g = 4\cdot 924 - 1\cdot 800\, \dot{E}_{NM} \qquad\qquad R^2 = \cdot 427$
$\qquad\qquad (0\cdot 660)$

(5) $\quad \dot{P}_g = 2\cdot 899 + 0\cdot 821\, \dot{E}_M - 1\cdot 183\, \dot{E}_{NM} \qquad R^2 = \cdot 842$
$\qquad\qquad (0\cdot 169) \quad\;\; (0\cdot 387)$

where $\dot{P}_g$ denotes growth rates of GDP per person in civilian employment, and $\dot{E}_M$ and $\dot{E}_{NM}$ denote growth rates of employment in manufacturing and non-manufacturing respectively.

It follows from the above also that in a mature economy it would be idle to look for evidence of a labour constraint in manufacturing either in terms of a differential rise in wages in manufacturing or in the relative incidence of unemployment and unfilled vacancies in the different sectors. Since the supply of labour to industry does not become inelastic until wages in the rest of the economy have risen to levels comparable to those in industry, an effective labour constraint in manufacturing would manifest itself in a *general* increase in wages throughout the economy, and in low levels of unemployment in *all* sectors. In a situation of *approaching* labour shortage one would expect the unemployment rate to be falling, and wages to rise faster in the non-manufacturing sectors than in manufacturing.[1]

One would expect, furthermore, that in a "mature" economy constrained by a labour shortage, the average level of unemployment would be *higher* in the manufacturing sector than in the rest of the economy, and not lower. This is because such an economy is almost inevitably

---

[1] This has characterized the recent situation in the United States where, *pari passu* with a large increase in employment in the manufacturing sector (of 2·8 per cent. a year in the last five years), wages rose faster in the low-paid sectors (wholesale and retail distribution and agriculture) than in manufacturing. (Cf. *Annual Report of the Council of Economic Advisers*, Washington, D. C., 1968, pp. 109–10.) It should also be pointed out that in the United States (where the level of unemployment has been much greater than in the United Kingdom throughout the post-war period) earnings in manufacturing are much higher in relation to the national average (and particularly in relation to agriculture and the distributive trades) than in the United Kingdom.

subject to a "stop-and-go" cycle; variations in the pressure of demand induced by fiscal and monetary policies affect demand and employment in industry far more than in the non-industrial sectors.

There is finally the question of the existence of increasing returns to scale in manufacturing industries. I emphasized in my lecture that this is a "macro-phenomenon" which (in the words of Allyn Young) "cannot be discerned adequately by observing the effects of variations in the size of a particular firm or of a particular industry". Studies relating to the cost and size of individual plants are not therefore necessarily relevant; though there is a growing body of empirical evidence relating to individual industries which tends to confirm its importance.[1]

Nor do recent studies which fit production functions by means of linear multiple regressions lead to any confirmation that the parameters of a Cobb-Douglas function conveniently add up to unity. Indeed in all recent studies the Cobb-Douglas function was assumed to be a constantly shifting one, of the form $Ae^{ct}K^aL^b$ and not AK^aL^b, as indicated by Wolfe; and in many of these studies the result $a+b=1$ is a tautological one which gives no indication whatever of the presence or absence of economies of scale.[2]

Wolfe was mistaken in suggesting that the constant in the regression equation of output on employment is an "error term". It is a constant term, which reflects explanatory variables that were excluded, one of which may be an autonomous time trend. It does not follow, therefore, that the introduction of further explanatory variables (such as capital investment) would necessarily reduce the value of the regression coefficient on employment—if the two variables are not inter-correlated, the introduction of a capital term should reduce the constant term, and not the regression coefficient on employment. Since owing to the acceleration principle there is always some inter-correlation between the rate of growth of employment and investment activity, one would expect a multiple regression of output on employment and capital investment to show lower coefficients on employment than a simple regression: but there is no reason to expect that the sum of the two coefficients in the one case should be *lower* than the single coefficient in the other case. I have indeed computed multiple regressions of output on employment and investment, and they show that even when the role of capital is taken into account, the regression coefficient of output on employment remains significantly greater than one.[3]

---

[1] See for example, J. S. Bain, *Barriers to New Competition;* C. Pratten and R. M. Dean, *The Economies of Large Scale Production in British Industry—an Introductory Study;* J. W. Kendrick, *Productivity Trends in the United States;* as well as the sources quoted in E. F. Denison, *Why Growth Rates Differ,* chapter on Economies of Scale.

[2] The existence of a linear-homogeneous production function is derived not from observation but from *a priori* reasoning (i.e. profit maximization under conditions of perfect competition) and the parameters are either "restricted" so as to add up to unity, or else are directly estimated from factor shares which by definition add up to unity.

[3] These multiple regressions were unfortunately not completed in time to be

It would be wrong to suppose that the regression between output and employment showing a coefficient that is significantly greater than unity is a reflection of short-term or "cyclical" influences. The figures in my inter-country studies related to averages of ten-yearly periods, taking two-year averages for both the base-year and the end-year. This virtually eliminates short-period or cyclical influences. The short-period relationship between output and employment—showing in some cases a 5:1 relationship—largely reflects changes in the degree of utilization of capacity. But the fact that there is short period relationship of 5:1 does not exclude a long-period relationship of 1·5:1. It certainly provides no support for assuming that the long-period relationship must be smaller than 1:1.

Nor is it correct to suppose that more than a small part of the "Verdoorn Law" can be explained by "embodied" technical progress coupled with the association of a relatively high level of investment in fast-growing industries, in the absence of increasing returns. Unless one assumes that the rate of technical progress on successive vintages is itself accelerated as a result of a larger volume of investment (as in Arrow's "learning function", which comes to the same thing as increasing returns) the mere postulate of embodied technical progress does not entail that the average rate of growth of productivity should be significantly faster in the faster-growing industries.[1]

Differences in "saving propensities" (as measured by differences in the investment/output ratio) cannot account for more than a small proportion of the observed differences in growth rates. Wolfe is correct in saying that I do not regard "the supply of capital as a serious limitation on economic growth". This is because savings and capital accumulation in a capitalist economy do not represent an independent variable —a faster rate of growth induces a higher rate of investment; it also brings about a higher share of savings to finance that investment, through its effect on the share of profits. It is therefore more correct to say that a fast rate of capital accumulation is a *symptom* of a fast rate of growth than a *cause* of it.

I shall refrain from comment on the last sections of Professor Wolfe's paper concerning "policy recommendations", where he charges me with several sins of both omission and commission. My lecture was concerned with the question why growth rates differ between different countries. The Selective Employment Tax, public sector expenditure, immigration, birth control, etc. were outside its scope and none of these was mentioned.

---

included in the statistical notes appended to my inaugural lecture; they are, however, included in the American version, *Strategic Factors in Economic Development, op. cit.*, pp. 81–3. (In these equations the capital term is measured by the investment/output ratio in industry, which gives—under the assumption that the marginal capital/output ratio is greater than unity—a *lower* limit to the "capital term" of a Cobb-Douglas function. Direct measurement of the rate of growth of the capital stock would have been impossible statistically and pretty meaningless theoretically.)

[1] The reasons for this cannot be gone into here; they are set out in a forthcoming paper by W. A. H. Godley.

Finally, I would commend to Professor Wolfe the following lines from Pope's *Essay on Criticism*:

> "A perfect Judge will read each work of Wit
> With the same spirit that its author writ;
> Survey the WHOLE, nor seek slight faults to find
> Where nature moves, and rapture warms the mind;
> .... In wit, as nature, what effects our hearts
> Is not th'exactness of peculiar parts;
> 'Tis not a lip, or eye, we beauty call,
> But the joint force and full result of all."

King's College, Cambridge.

[26]
'VERDOORN EFFECTS', RETURNS TO SCALE, AND THE ELASTICITY OF FACTOR SUBSTITUTION[1]

By JORGE M. KATZ

1. Introduction

THE statistical relationship between the growth of labour productivity and the growth of output has been recently brought back to the attention of economists.[2] According to J. P. Verdoorn, who first used such statistical relationship in 1949, 'there exists a stable, long-run relation, between labour productivity and the level of output'. This is shown by the fact that the regression coefficient in the logarithmic regression of output per man on output 'is significant, comparatively stable, and varied from industry to industry in different countries between 0·45 and 0·60'.[3]

Different interpretations can be made of the causal mechanism that underlies this statistical relationship. In particular, according to Verdoorn, the expansion of output permits the introduction of more 'roundaboutness' in the production process, this leading to a further division of labour and to a higher labour productivity because there are internal and external economies to be gained with the expansion of output.

This interpretation rules out from the start an alternative line of causation which makes technical progress an autonomous force accounting for labour productivity growth, followed then by falling costs and prices and by the expansion of demand and output.

Whether it is higher output that leads to a higher labour productivity, or whether it is the other way round, is a matter that cannot be settled without some information in addition to Verdoorn's coefficient.

The existence of this identification problem in the interpretation of the regression coefficient of output per man on output has been clearly observed in the literature and is not a subject with which this paper shall be concerned.[4] Instead, we present here an alternative interpretation of Verdoorn's coefficient assuming that it is the level of output that determines the level of the average productivity of labour rather than the opposite.

---

[1] I am very grateful to Professor R. C. O. Matthews, Dr. M. Feldstein, and Mr. J. Flemming, for reading a previous draft of this paper and making several comments and suggestions. Obviously I am solely responsible for the final outcome.

[2] N. Kaldor, *Causes of the Slow Rate of Economic Growth in the UK*. Cambridge University Press, 1967.

[3] J. P. Verdoorn, 'Complementarity and long range projections', *Econometrica*, 1956. Also: 'Fattori che regolano lo sviluppo della produtivita del lavoro', *L'Industria*, 1949.

[4] See on this point W. G. Salter, *Productivity and Technical Change*. Cambridge University Press, 1961. Also: W. Beckerman, *The British Economy in 1975*. Cambridge University Press, 1966.

The plan of the paper is as follows. In section 2 a regression model is derived from the CES (constant elasticity of substitution) production function, containing output as one of the explanatory variables of output per man, i.e. containing Verdoorn's coefficient as one of the regression coefficients of the model. It is then shown that the simple regression of output per man on output does not allow a clear identification of any of the parameters of the production function that underlies the production process, and also that it produces a systematically biased coefficient, the bias being due to the omission of several other terms that properly belong to the model.[1]

Section 3 shows that Verdoorn's coefficient is a function of two different parameters of the production function that underlies the production process, namely the elasticity of factor substitution and the returns to scale parameter. Hence, differences among industries (or among sectors) in Verdoorn's coefficient not necessarily constitute prima facie evidence of interindustry (or intersectoral) differences in returns to scale.

2. CES production functions and the measurement of returns to scale

Two different versions of the CES production function have been discussed in the literature. The best-known version was arrived at by K. Arrow, H. Chenery, B. Minhas, and R. Solow in 1961.[2] Their function assumes constant returns to scale. In so far as it allows for the existence of non-constant returns to scale, the formulation presented by M. Brown and J. de Cani in 1962 is slightly more comprehensive than the original version of Arrow *et al.* The Brown–De Cani version can be written as follows:[3]

$$Y = \gamma[\delta K^{-\rho} + (1-\delta)L^{-\rho}]^{-v/\rho}, \tag{1}$$

where Y, K, and L represent respectively real output, capital, and labour as conventionally measured, and the four parameters γ, δ, ρ, and v stand

---

[1] The empirical evidence presented here corresponds to time series estimates for nine different manufacturing industries of Argentina. There are two major differences between the empirical results reported here and those presented by Professor Kaldor in his analysis of the rate of growth of the British economy, op. cit. First, whereas Kaldor's estimates of Verdoorn's coefficient come from a cross-section study carried out with first difference data of an intercountry population, our own estimates are derived from time series data within given industries. Second, Professor Kaldor's argument centres around the concept of 'stages of economic growth'. The results reported here correspond to the manufacturing sector of Argentina, a country whose industrial sector can be conceived as in transition from the second to the third stage of growth in Kaldor's nomenclature. Thus, our results do not have any particular bearing on the discussion raised by Professor Kaldor regarding the rate of growth of Britain. None the less, the present estimates are relevant for the study of countries in the intermediate stages of industrialization, and they also bring out with clarity a few general remarks we wish to make regarding Verdoorn's coefficient.

[2] K. Arrow *et al.*, 'Capital-labour substitution and economic efficiency', *Review of Economics and Statistics*, 1961.

[3] M. Brown and J. de Cani, 'Technological change and the distribution of income', *International Economic Review*, 1962.

respectively for the 'efficiency' parameter, the 'capital-intensity' or 'distribution' parameter, the 'substitution' parameter, and the degree of homogeneity of the production function, i.e. the degree of returns to scale.

Differentiating (1) with respect to labour, we obtain the following expression for the marginal product of labour:

$$\frac{\partial Y}{\partial L} = v(1-\delta)\gamma^{-\rho/v}(Y/L)^{\rho+1}Y^{\rho(1-v)/v}. \qquad (2)$$

Alternatively, the marginal product of labour can be derived as follows; writing net profit as value added minus the sum of labour and capital costs,

$$\pi = pY - wL - rK. \qquad (3)$$

Differentiating with respect to labour the profit-maximizing condition can be written:

$$\frac{\partial \pi}{\partial L} = p\frac{\partial Y}{\partial L} + Y\frac{\partial p}{\partial L}\frac{\partial Y}{\partial L} - w - \frac{\partial w}{\partial L}L = 0. \qquad (4)$$

Rearranging equation (4) we have:

$$p\frac{\partial Y}{\partial L} + Y\frac{\partial p}{\partial Y}\frac{\partial Y}{\partial L} = w + \frac{\partial w}{\partial L}L. \qquad (5)$$

Therefore:
$$\frac{\partial Y}{\partial L} = \frac{w}{p} + \frac{\partial w/\partial L}{\partial p/\partial Y}\frac{L}{Y} = \frac{w}{p}\left[\frac{1+E_{wL}}{1+E_{pY}}\right]. \qquad (6)$$

Where w/p indicates product wages and salaries, i.e. money wages and salaries deflated by the industry's product price. E_{wL} is the elasticity of wages with respect to labour, and E_{pY} is the elasticity of the industry's product price with respect to the volume of output. Thus, the bracketed term can be regarded as a measure of the degree of imperfection that prevails in factor and commodity markets in each particular industry.

The two expressions for the marginal product of labour can now be equated, obtaining:

$$\frac{w}{p}\left[\frac{1+E_{wL}}{1+E_{pY}}\right] = v(1-\delta)\gamma^{-\rho/v}(Y/L)^{\rho+1}Y^{\rho(1-v)/v}. \qquad (7)$$

Therefore
$$(Y/L)^{1+\rho} = \frac{w}{p}\left[\frac{1+E_{wL}}{1+E_{pY}}\right][v\gamma^{-\rho/v}(1-\delta)]^{-1}Y^{-\rho(1-v)/v}. \qquad (8)$$

Taking logarithms on both sides of equation (8), dividing by $(1+\rho)$, and introducing time as an additional explanatory variable to take into account the existence of (neutral) technical progress due to the mere passage of time, we obtain equation (9) which can be used as a regression model to be estimated by single equation least squares with time series data:

$$\log\frac{Y}{L} = \alpha + \sigma\log\frac{w}{p} + \sigma\log M + b\log Y + \lambda t + u. \qquad (9)$$

where $\alpha = \log[v(1-\delta)\gamma^{-\rho/v}]^{-1}$ is a constant. $M = (1+E_{wL}/1+E_{pY})$ is a measure of the degree of imperfection that prevails in factor and commodity markets in each industry. If perfect competition is assumed on both sides of the market then $\log M = 0$ and this term drops out of the model. $b = (1-\sigma)(v-1)/v$ is the regression coefficient of output per man on output. In other words, this is the 'true' Verdoorn coefficient. $\sigma = 1/1+\rho$ is the elasticity of substitution between capital and labour. w/p refers to wages and salaries deflated by the industry's product price. λ is an estimate of the annual rate of technical change (assumed to be neutral). t indicates time and u is the error term subject to standard assumptions.

Hence, having data on real wage rates, real output per man, and on M we can empirically estimate from equation (9) the elasticity of factor substitution between capital and labour, the 'true' Verdoorn coefficient, and the rate of neutral technical progress.

We have not, as yet, been able to construct reliable time series for M at an industry level and therefore this term has been omitted altogether from the empirical work reported in this paper. Such omission is probably the source of a bias in some of the parameters estimated in the next section. We shall therefore also introduce in the next section a few comments concerning the direction in which some of the results might be biased on account of this omission.

3. The empirical evidence

3.1. *The elasticity of substitution, returns to scale, and 'true' Verdoorn coefficient of nine Argentine industries*

Table I below presents the results obtained from estimating equation (9) by single equation least squares using time series data for nine Argentine industries during the period 1954–61.[1] The level of confidence for the rejection of the two hypotheses $\sigma = 0$ and $\lambda = 0$, the implied value of v—

---

[1] Deflated data at constant prices of 1960 were used throughout the empirical work. The data were obtained from *Distribucion del Ingreso en la Republica Argentina*. Joint publication by ECLA and Argentina's National Development Council. Vol. 2, Buenos Aires, 1965. The reasons for using data for so short a period have been discussed in: J. Katz, 'The application of production function theory to the growth of manufacturing in Argentina'. D.Phil. thesis, mimeographed, Oxford, 1967. Dr. R. Mantel has recently made, in a private communication, a point which is relevant at this stage.

The profit maximization model developed in Section 2 of this paper, is a model derived from the theory of the firm. However, the empirical data to be used corresponds to industry aggregates. Thus, data and model do not seem to correspond to each other.

It is certainly true that it is the firm, and not the industry, that is normally assumed to have a maximizing criteria. However, the less populated an industry is (or, for that matter, the more concentrated it is), the closer will be the association between maximization of the firm and maximization of the industry. Hence, it seems to be true that our present model becomes all the more relevant the closer we are to the noncompetitive extreme of the scale, where 'fewness' and/or business concentration prevail.

'VERDOORN EFFECTS' AND RETURN TO SCALE

returns to scale parameter[1]—the rate of technical progress, and the partial correlation between $\log w/p$ and $\log Y$ are also reported in Table I. Various observations can be made regarding the results of Table I. First, the parameter v—the degree of returns to scale that prevailed in each industry—ranged from 0·80 to 1·60, an interval which appears to be reason-

TABLE I

Returns to scale, 'true' Verdoorn coefficient, technical progress and the elasticity of factor substitution in nine Argentine industries

Industries	Elasticity of substitution	'True' Verdoorn coefficient	Implied value of v	Rate of technical progress annual %	Partial correlation $\log w/p \log Y$
Foodstuffs	0·05 n.s.	0·37	1·50	0·029**	0·67
Textiles	0·03 n.s.	0·29	1·45	n.a.	0·80
Paper	0·43*	0·09	1·12	0·012 n.s.	0·17
Chemicals	0·31*	0·11	1·18	0·054**	0·89
Metals	0·49**	0·24	1·60	0·040**	0·70
Stone, glass	0·47 n.s.	0·12	1·25	0·046**	0·57
Machinery	0·42*	0·25	1·45	0·050**	0·96
Knitting Mills	0·36*	−0·19	0·81	0·025*	0·70
Publishing	0·40 n.s.	−0·18	0·77	0·090*	0·33

n.s. non-significantly different from zero at a 10% or higher level of confidence.

* significantly different from zero at a 10% or higher level of confidence.

** significantly different from zero at a 5% or higher level.

able on the basis of the received theory. Seven industries out of nine exhibit increasing returns to scale, in some cases quite substantial, as for example, Metals, Foodstuffs, Machinery, etc. Second, in almost all cases the rate of neutral technical progress is significantly different from zero at acceptable levels of confidence.[2]

Third, in five industries out of nine the elasticity of factor substitution is significantly different from zero at a 10 per cent or higher levels of confidence. Invariably such parameter came out within the range $0 \leqslant \sigma < 1$.

Fourth, in all industries the partial correlation between $\log w/p$ and $\log Y$ is positive and in the great majority of the cases such correlation is fairly high.

[1] The entries in this column have been obtained by substituting for v and b from the previous columns into the formula $v = (1-\sigma)/(1-\sigma-b)$, or $b = (1-\sigma)(v-1)/v$. Given that b and σ are not known with certainty this procedure is not strictly correct for

$$E[(1-\sigma)/(1-\sigma-b)] \not\equiv 1 - E(\sigma)/1 - E(\sigma) - E(b).$$

[2] The author has shown elsewhere that the joint impact of technical change and increasing returns to scale accounted during the period 1954–61 for nearly 90 per cent of the inter-industry differences in changes in output per man. See J. Katz, op. cit. Mimeographed, Oxford, 1967.

These observations, particularly the last two, provide strong grounds for believing that the way in which Verdoorn's coefficient has been generally estimated by performing the logarithmic regression of changes in output per man on changes in output, introduces a systematic bias in the results, the bias being due to the omission of various explanatory variables that belong to the production function model and that can normally be expected to be different from zero at acceptable levels of confidence.

3.2. *Upwards-biased Verdoorn's coefficient*

Instead of coming from a complete regression model like that of equation (9) Verdoorn's coefficient has normally been estimated from a regression of the following form:

$$\log Y/L = \alpha + \beta \log Y + u \qquad (10)$$

If $\log w/p$ and $\log Y$ are positively correlated—as they were shown to be in Table I—then such a regression will yield a biased estimate of Verdoorn's coefficient, the bias being due to the omission of the second term of the correctly specified model.

Similarly, if $\log M$ and $\log Y$ are positively correlated the omission of the third term of the complete regression model will also introduce a further bias in the estimate of the regression coefficient of output per man on output.

Finally, when working with time series data, the omission of time as an explanatory variable of changes in output per man, would introduce a further bias in the estimated Verdoorn coefficient if $\log Y$ and t are positively correlated as they are certainly likely to be. Obviously this last difficulty disappears in cross sectional studies.

The relationship between the expected value of the estimated Verdoorn coefficient $E(\beta)$ and its 'true' value (b) is given by equation (11):[1]

$$E(\beta) = b + \sigma r_{wY} + \sigma r_{MY} + \lambda r_{tY} \qquad (11)$$

where r_{wY}, r_{MY}, and r_{tY} are respectively the expected values of the regression coefficients of $\log w/p$ on $\log Y$, of $\log M$ on $\log Y$ and of t on $\log Y$, σ is the elasticity of substitution and λ is the rate of neutral technical progress.

Normally all these partial regression coefficients, as well as σ and λ, are expected to be positive. Therefore, equation (10) will normally yield an upwards bias. In other words, the 'true' value of Verdoorn's coefficient (b) will be lower than the value yield by the incomplete equation (10).[2]

---

[1] The criteria for the estimation of the bias has been devised by H. Theil, 'Specification errors and the estimation of economic relationships', *Review of International Statistical Institute*, 1957.

[2] It should be noted that the results reported in Table I for Verdoorn's coefficients cannot be properly considered as the definitely 'true' values of such parameter, since they were obtained with a regression that omitted M as an explanatory variable. Although these values can be regarded as better than those obtained with the incomplete equation (10) we know from formulas (11) that they are still biased upwards by an unknown extent due to the omission of M.

'VERDOORN EFFECTS' AND RETURN TO SCALE

Table II below presents the results obtained from the estimation of equation (10). The level of confidence for the rejection of the hypothesis $(\beta) = 0$ is reported in separate column. We have used exactly the same data as before.

TABLE II

Simple Verdoorn coefficient. Nine Argentine manufacturing industries, 1954–1961

Industries	Simple Verdoorn coefficient	Confidence level θ
Foodstuffs	0·62	10%
Textiles	1·90	10%
Paper	0·32	10%
Chemicals	1·20	1%
Stone, glass	1·20	1%
Metals	1·02	1%
Machinery	0·90	1%
Publishing	1·37	1%
Knitting Mills	1·04	10%

The following observations can be made regarding the results of Tables I and II.

First, in all nine cases the direction of the bias introduced by the incomplete regression is that expected on the basis of *a priori* theory. The 'true' coefficient of Verdoorn is somewhat lower than the coefficient obtained from the incomplete regression model.

Second, given the fact that $0 \leqslant \sigma < 1$, the coefficients of Table II are biased upwards to such an extent that they invariably imply highly unrealistic values for the returns to scale parameter of the production function. (As estimated from $v = 1-\sigma \,/\, 1-\sigma-b$: see p. 346, n. 1.)

4. The meaning to be attached to the (true) Verdoorn coefficient

We turn now to a relatively more interesting question: if a group of industries (or sectors) is ranked with respect to their 'true' Verdoorn coefficient, does this constitute information enough on which to assume that the ranking of such industries (or sectors) with respect to the true returns to scale parameter v will look fairly similar? In other words, what is the precise meaning of Verdoorn's coefficient, when considered in a cross-industry (or cross-sectoral) population?

Verdoorn's coefficient is a function of two different parameters of the production function, namely the elasticity of substitution between capital and labour and the returns-to-scale parameter. It can be written as follows:

$$b = \frac{(1-\sigma)(v-1)}{v}. \tag{12}$$

The relationship between these three variables—'true' Verdoorn coefficient, elasticity of factor substitution, and degree of returns to scale—will be now discussed for the particular case in which there are (a) increasing returns to scale, and (b) elasticities of substitution that take values between $0 \leqslant \sigma < 1$. In Fig. 1 below the coefficient of Verdoorn is measured along the ordinate, and the elasticity of factor substitution is measured along the abscissa.

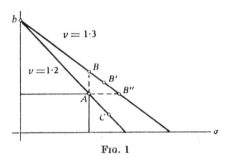

Fig. 1

According to equation (12) for any given value of v greater than unity (increasing returns to scale), b is a linearly decreasing function of the elasticity of substitution σ; as shown in Fig. 1.

The rationale behind this negative association between b and σ is the following: regression equation (6) represents a world in which entrepreneurs behave as prescribed in the neoclassical system. There is profit maximization and factor-proportions are being continuously adjusted on the margin to the ruling ratio of factor prices.

The term in $\log w/p$ in equation (6) takes into account such neoclassical adjustment of factor proportions to factor prices, and therefore brings into the model the incidence of a marginally higher capital–labour ratio as an explanatory variable of part of the observed increases in the average productivity of labour.

Given the cost of capital, an increase in the marginal product of labour (or of the wage rate), calls for marginal changes in capital intensity. How large such changes in the capital–labour ratio will be clearly depends on the actual value of the elasticity of substitution in each particular industry. Large values of this parameter will call for relatively large changes in the K/L ratio, and therefore a relatively larger part of the observed changes in average output per man will be accounted for by changes in factor proportions.

Conversely, small values of this parameter will call for relatively smaller changes in the K/L ratio, and therefore smaller part of the observed changes in average output per man will be accounted for by changes in factor proportions.

350   'VERDOORN EFFECTS' AND RETURN TO SCALE

In the extreme case in which the elasticity of factor substitution is zero, the total change in output per man will be accounted for by the change in output weighted by the 'true' Verdoorn coefficient. There is no marginal adjustment in factor proportions and hence the total change in output per man is thought to derive from the observed change in output.

However, there is no reason *a priori* to assume that the elasticity of substitution should be zero. If we believe that this parameter takes positive values then the marginal adjustment in the capital–labour ratio will partly account for the observed changes in output per man, proportionally reducing the importance of the expansion of output as an explanation of the expansion of labour's average productivity.

All this has an obvious bearing on the formulation of a growth policy. The marginal adjustment of the K/L ratio in response to factor prices clearly constitute an alternative avenue for labour productivity growth, even in the extreme case in which output is not increased. The relative importance of such avenue depends on the actual value of the elasticity of factor substitution, which thus becomes necessary information for policy formulation.

Fig. 1 can now be used to bring out various different points: First, it is only in the very restricted case in which all sectors possess the same elasticity of substitution, that the higher the 'true' Verdoorn coefficient the larger the returns to scale enjoyed by any given industry or sector. The results reported in Table I above approximately correspond to such a case. There is only a very limited interindustry variability with regards to the elasticity of factor substitution. In seven out of nine cases such parameter came out within the range $0 \cdot 31 \leqslant \sigma \leqslant 0 \cdot 49$. Under such conditions we would expect a correlated interindustry movement between the 'true' Verdoorn coefficient and the returns-to-scale parameter. In the present case such correlation is positive and significant at a 5 per cent $[r = 0 \cdot 70]$. This indicates that those industries that exhibit an above-average value of the 'true' Verdoorn coefficient tended also to show an above-average returns-to-scale parameter. And, conversely, lower-than-average 'true' Verdoorn coefficients tended to be associated with lower-than-average returns-to-scale parameters.

The case in which all sectors are assumed to have $\sigma = 0$ is clearly a particular one within the more general case in which all sectors have the same elasticity of factor substitution.

However, there are no *a priori* reasons for assuming that the elasticity of factor substitution will always fluctuate inside so limited a range as the one found in the present empirical application. And a considerable amount of evidence has, in recent years, shown that it almost invariably differs from zero at acceptable levels of confidence.

If we allow the elasticity of substitution to vary among industries then differences in the 'true' Verdoorn coefficient among such industries can no longer be regarded as the necessary indication of differences in returns to scale among such industries.

Consider the cases of industries A, B, and C in Fig. 1.

Two industries may differ in their returns to scale yet having the same 'true' Verdoorn coefficient, as, for example, industries A and B'' in the figure.

Alternatively, two industries may have the same degree of returns to scale yet having different 'true' Verdoorn coefficients, as A and C in the same figure.

Finally, there is yet another interesting case. Industry B' enjoys larger returns to scale than industry A, the difference being due to the joint impact of a higher 'true' Verdoorn coefficient and a higher elasticity of substitution between capital and labour than industry A. In other words, in the general case in which $v > 1$ and $0 \leqslant \sigma < 1$, a higher 'true' Verdoorn coefficient *and* a higher σ imply a higher v.

Just as in the case in which all industries (or sectors) have the same elasticity of factor substitution, also in the case in which there is a positive and significant interindustry correlation between the 'true' coefficient of Verdoorn and the elasticity of factor-substitution, we can expect an associated interindustry movement between the 'true' Verdoorn coefficient and the returns-to-scale parameter, where above average values of the former would tend to be associated across industries (or sectors) with above-average values of the latter, and vice versa. Hence, if one of these two conditions holds true, (*a*) there are not significant interindustry differences in the elasticity of factor substitution, or (*b*) there is a positive and significant interindustry correlation between the 'true' Verdoorn coefficient and the elasticity of factor substitution, then the ranking of industries (or sectors) with respect to the 'true' Verdoorn coefficient will provide a reliable approximation to the ranking of such industries with respect to the true returns-to-scale parameter.

Nuffield College

REFERENCES

ARROW, K. J., et al., 'Capital-labour substitution and economic efficiency', *Review of Economics and Statistics*, 1961.

BECKERMAN, W., *The British Economy in 1975*. Cambridge University Press, 1966.

BROWN, M., and J. DE CANI, 'Technological change and the distribution of income', *International Economic Review*, 1962.

—— —— 'Technological change in the United States 1950–1960', *Productivity Measurement Review*, May 1962.

FELDSTEIN, M., 'Alternative methods of estimating CES production functions for Britain'. Mimeographed, Oxford, 1967. Forthcoming in *Economica*.

352   'VERDOORN EFFECTS' AND RETURN TO SCALE

HIRSCH, W. Z., 'Manufacturing process functions', *Review of Economics and Statistics*, 1952.

KATZ, J., 'The application of production function theory to the growth of manufacturing in Argentina 1946–1961', D.Phil. Thesis. Mimeographed, Oxford, 1967.

KALDOR, N., *Causes of the Slow Rate of Economic Growth in the UK*. Inaugural lecture at Cambridge University. Cambridge University Press, 1966.

NORLOVE, M., 'Statistical production functions. A summary of findings'. Unpublished paper delivered at the 1965 Conference on Income and Wealth.

PITCHFORD, J., 'Growth and the elasticity of factor substitution', *Economic Record*, Dec. 1960.

SALTER, W. E. G., *Productivity and Technical Change*. Cambridge University Press, 1961.

THEIL, H., 'Specification errors and the estimation of economic relationships', *International Statistical Institute Review*, 1957.

VERDOORN, J. P., 'Complementarity and long range projections', *Econometrica*, 1956.

—— 'Fattori che regolano lo sviluppo della produtivita del lavoro', *L'Industria*, 1949.

WHAT REMAINS OF KALDOR'S LAW?

In 1949 P. J. Verdoorn,[1] basing himself on evidence drawn from statistics of industrial production in a number of countries, argued that there is a positive linear relationship between productivity growth p and output growth q. Mathematically, this can be expressed as,

$$p = c + dq \qquad (1)$$

where c and d are constants, and $d > 0$.[2]

In his 1966 Inaugural Lecture Kaldor[3] used a version of this "law" of Verdoorn to explain the relatively poor performance of the British economy. After examining data drawn from twelve countries, he claimed to have confirmed Verdoorn's law for industry by establishing the existence of a strong positive relationship between p and q in manufacturing, public utilities and construction during the period 1953–54 to 1963–64. In each case he estimated d to be in the region of $\frac{1}{2}$. From this Kaldor concluded that the potential growth of industrial productivity is limited by the supply of labour, arguing that when industry suffers from a shortage of labour it is unable to exploit economies of scale and productivity is thereby harmed. Kaldor did not express this proposition in an explicit mathematical form, but implicit in his argument is an equation of the following kind, linking productivity growth p to employment growth e,

$$p = a + be \qquad (2)$$

where a and b are constants and $b > 0$. This equation states that a faster growth of employment is associated with a faster growth of productivity.

For appropriate values of a and b, the two equations are mathematically equivalent and we can view equation (2) as a reformulation of Verdoorn's original law, with employment growth e replacing output growth q as the independent variable.[4] Clearly this substitution is necessary when one is using Verdoorn's law to understand the role of labour supply as a constraint on potential productivity. To avoid confusion let us refer to the alternative formulation given in equation (2) as "Kaldor's Law".

---

[1] P. J. Verdoorn, "Fattori che regolano lo sviluppo della produttivita del lavoro," *L'Industria* (1949).

[2] It is necessary to assume $d < 1$ to obtain economically meaningful results. In Verdoorn's original article the relationship was expressed in a logarithmic form. Provided exponential growth rates are used, however, the version given in the text is both mathematically and economically equivalent to that of Verdoorn. Exponential growth rates are defined as follows. Let P_0, Q_0 and E_0 be respectively productivity, output and employment at the beginning of the period, and P_n, Q_n and E_n be their corresponding values at the end of the period n years later. The exponential growth rates p, q and e are defined as $p = (1/n) \log_e (P_n/P_0)$, $q = (1/n) \log_e (Q_n/Q_0)$ and $e = (1/n) \log_e (E_n/E_0)$. Since $P = Q/E$ it follows that $p \equiv q - e$.

[3] N. Kaldor, *Causes of the Slow Rate of Growth of the United Kingdom; an Inaugural Lecture* (Cambridge University Press, 1966).

[4] If $a = c/(1-d)$ and $b = d/(1-d)$ equations (1) and (2) are equivalent. The condition $b > 0$ is then equivalent to $1 > d > 0$.

Taking his law as established, Kaldor went on to argue that Britain's slow growth of industrial productivity has been caused by a chronic shortage of labour in this sector. Since Britain, unlike its rivals, does not possess a large surplus of agricultural labour available for employment in industry, he concluded that, if potential economies of scale are to be realised, labour must be found elsewhere. One potential source of labour is the service sector and to force labour out of this sector into industry Kaldor devised the Selective Employment Tax (SET).[1] More recently he has argued for export led growth on the grounds that this will concentrate labour in export industries, where substantial economies of scale can be realised.[2] Thus, where SET was based upon the application of Kaldor's law to the entire industrial sector, the drive for export-led growth is based upon its application to the export subsector alone.

Following the publication of Kaldor's lecture, several attempts have been made to examine both the theoretical and empirical foundations of Kaldor's law. In 1971 S. Gomulka,[3] in a study on the diffusion of knowledge, argued that international differences in productivity growth can be best understood by starting from the notion of technological gaps. He provided both theoretical arguments and empirical evidence to suggest that the diffusion of techniques from advanced to backward producers is an important determinant of technical progress, and that the rate of diffusion is itself influenced by social, cultural and political factors which are in principle subject to change. Japan is, in his opinion, the prime example of a country which has effectively geared its economic organisation to the acquisition of knowledge from abroad and has gained massive productivity increases as a result. Gomulka also argued convincingly that in the present epoch the effects of diffusion far outweigh the effects, if any, of Kaldor's law. In the longer run, to be measured in centuries or millennia, he concedes that Kaldor's law may hold, although clearly this conclusion must be seen as highly tentative in view of the underdeveloped state of long-run growth theory.

At the end of his study Gomulka examined the evidence for Kaldor's law using a sample of 39 countries. Productivity growth in industry over the period 1958–68 is plotted against employment growth to give the scatter diagram reproduced here as Fig. 1.[4] In the diagram there is absolutely no relationship between the two variables. It is also clear that Japan is a highly untypical country, with a productivity growth some 4–5 % per annum greater than the average for other countries whose employment has grown by the same amount. The significance of this fact will become clearer below, when the work of Kaldor, Cripps and Tarling is discussed. For convenience

---

[1] SET was introduced by the Chancellor of the Exchequer Callaghan in the 1966 Budget acting on the advice of Kaldor.

[2] N. Kaldor, "Conflicts in National Economic Objectives," ECONOMIC JOURNAL, March 1971.

[3] S. Gomulka, *Inventive Activity, Diffusion, and the Stages of Economic Growth* (Aarhus, 1971).

[4] For western countries other than Finland, Gomulka uses data on manufacturing and for Finland, Eastern Europe and the USSR he uses data on total industrial production.

the countries covered by the latter studies are marked with rings in Gomulka's diagram.

Some two years after the appearance of Gomulka's work Cripps and Tarling[1] published their study, addressed primarily to an examination of Kaldor's "empirical generalisations". Using a cross-section study based on a number of observations from each of twelve advanced capitalist countries over the period 1951–70, they tested Kaldor's law for the basic industrial sectors – construction, public utilities (electricity, gas and water supply) and manufacturing. In construction they found a positive relationship between productivity growth and employment growth, but it was weak and statistically insignificant, having an R^2 of 0·044. In utilities there was a statistically significant relationship, but it was negative, implying that in this sector an inverse Kaldor's law apparently held—faster employment growth being associated with slower productivity growth. Finally, in manufacturing their results were mixed. For the period 1965–70 they found no relationship, the correlation coefficient R^2 being equal to 0·002. For 1951–65, using a sub-sample of 32 observations, roughly three from each country, they found a statistically significant and strongly positive relationship. The value of R^2 was 0·362 and the estimated coefficient b of employment growth in the equation $p_{MF} = a + be_{MF}$, at 0·549, was four times its standard error. Their results for manufacturing are given in Table I and the regression lines are plotted in Figs. 2 and 3, where they are identified by the label "incl. Japan" to indicate that the sample included Japan.

Thus, the study of Cripps and Tarling appears to substantiate Kaldor's law only in the case of manufacturing and only for the period 1951–65. But even this result is open to question on both theoretical and empirical grounds.

Throughout their study Cripps and Tarling follow Kaldor in discounting the view that the level of technical knowledge varied from one country to another within their sample and that its diffusion during the fifties and sixties was uneven. For example, they say "In the groups of advanced countries which provide the evidence in this study it is not unreasonable to supppose that all have access to the same body of technical knowledge".[2] This is a surprising statement in view of the obvious differences at the beginning of the period in both levels and forms of technology amongst the countries of their sample. In the early fifties, for example, Japan cannot properly be described as an advanced country in the sense the term is applied to, say, the United States. Of course, 20 years of growth have ironed out some of the differences between one country and another, as various technological gaps have been closed, but technical knowledge is by no means uniformly possessed or applied even today. More to the point, in analysing the growth process between 1950 and 1970, one must consider the differences between countries at the beginning of the period rather than their similarities at the end: any

---

[1] T. F. Cripps and R. J. Tarling, *Growth in Advanced Capitalist Economies, 1950–70* (Cambridge University Press, 1973).   [2] *Ibid.* p. 3.

closing of gaps will produce an abnormal rise in productivity in the previously backward country.

Underlying the Cripps–Tarling study is the idea that an advanced technology can be acquired simply by taking an existing blue-print out of a drawer, freely and equally accessible to all countries of their sample, and then

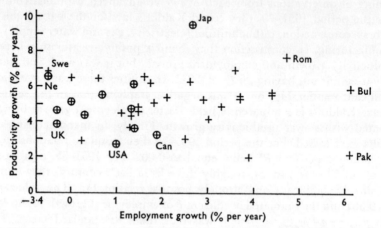

Fig. 1. Relationship between productivity growth and employment growth in industry, 1958–68 (Gomulka). ⊕ = country in the sample of Kaldor, Cripps and Tarling; Bul = Bulgaria, Can = Canada, Jap = Japan, Ne = Netherlands, Pak = Pakistan, Rom = Roumania, Swe = Sweden.

just applying it. In fact this is by no means true. Rapid technical advance requires a massive and determined effort, involving the re-equipment and reorganisation of vast sectors of industry and the training and retraining of personnel, combined with an openness to new ideas, a willingness to copy and adapt foreign technology and an ability to invent new techniques as the scope for "catching-up" diminishes. The institutional basis for such a purposive modernisation is not easy to create and certainly did not exist to the same degree in every country of the Cripps–Tarling sample. Indeed, there are strong reasons for believing that throughout the fifties and sixties Japan possessed an institutional framework far better adapted to the acquisition and application of knowledge than that of most other countries.[1] Moreover, in the early fifties Japan was still a country with a fairly low average level of industrial productivity and its scope for "catching-up" was considerable. There can be no doubt that, within the Cripps–Tarling sample, Japan is a very special case which cannot be treated as just another industrial country.

The presence of Japan in the Cripps–Tarling sample would not have mattered if they had also included, like Gomulka, a large number of other countries with widely differing growth experiences. But they did not. Their sample consists of a small number of countries other than Japan (11) and most of the observations are closely bunched together, with Japan widely

[1] See K. Ohkawa and H. Rosovsky, *Japanese Economic Growth* (Stanford, 1973), esp. pp. 89–95.

separated from the rest. This can be seen quite clearly in Figs. 2 and 3, where Japanese observations have been circled for identification. The deceptive nature of the Cripps–Tarling sample can be seen from Gomulka's scatter diagram (Fig. 1) where their 12 countries are marked with rings. Not only is it clear that the presence of Japan creates a spurious correlation amongst the marked observations, but it is also clear that the effect of restricting attention to these countries is to exclude a number of countries with high rates of employment growth (Bulgaria, Roumania, Pakistan, etc.). If the latter countries had been included, the apparent relationship between productivity growth and employment growth would have disappeared, for most of them had quite normal growth rates of productivity—Japan was a special case even amongst countries with high rates of employment growth.

In order to test how far the results of Cripps and Tarling depend upon the presence of Japan, their regressions were re-calculated using their own data but excluding Japan from the sample. The results are given in Table I and Figs. 2 and 3, where the new regression lines are labelled "excl. Japan".

TABLE I

Regression Results for Manufacturing

$$p_{MF} = a + be_{MF}$$

Sources used	a	b	R^2	No. of observations
Cripps–Tarling, 1951–65				
Incl. Japan	3·179	0·549 (0·133)	0·362	32
Excl. Japan	3·590	0·186 (0·145)	0·057	29
Cripps–Tarling, 1965–70				
Incl. Japan	4·856	0·100 (0·757)	0·002	12
Excl. Japan	5·211	−1·405 (0·556)	0·415	11
Kaldor (1953–54 to 1963–64)				
Incl. Japan	2·632	0·626 (0·220)	0·447	12
Excl. Japan	3·237	0·183 (0·267)	0·050	11

Note: Standard errors in parentheses.

The effect of excluding Japan for the period 1951–65 is striking. The value of R^2 drops to 0·057 and the coefficient b of employment growth drops to the low level of 0·186 and is only marginally greater than its standard error. Thus, without Japan there is no real evidence of any relationship between the two variables, as is in fact obvious from Fig. 2. When Japan is excluded for the period 1965–70 the effect is equally striking. There is now a strongly negative and significant relationship, with higher rates of employment growth being associated with lower rates of productivity growth. Thus, in manufacturing over the later period, there seems to have been an inverse

Kaldor's law operating, although it would obviously be a mistake to put much weight upon this conclusion.

It only remains to explain how Kaldor in 1966 found a strong positive relationship between productivity growth and employment growth in manufacturing over the period 1953–54 to 1963–64. The answer is twofold. Kaldor

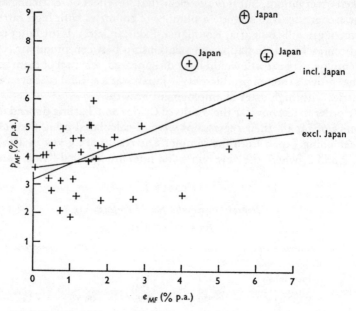

FIG. 2. Relationship between productivity growth and employment growth manufacturing, 1951–65 (Cripps-Tarling).

followed an inappropriate statistical procedure for revealing the relationship between p and e and he used a misleading sample of countries. Let us examine these two questions in turn.

To test the relationship between productivity growth p and employment growth e, as given in equation (2), the obvious procedure is to find the ordinary least squares (OLS) estimator $\hat{b}$ by regressing p on e. As we have seen, this was the method used by Cripps and Tarling. Kaldor, however, did not use this approach but instead proceeded in a more roundabout fashion. First he regressed p against output growth q to get the estimated relationship,

$$p = \hat{c} + \hat{d}q \quad . \quad . \quad . \quad . \quad (3)$$

where $\hat{c}$ and $\hat{d}$ are OLS estimators. Next he made use of the identity $e \equiv q - p$ to derive from equation (3) an estimated relationship between e and q,

$$e = -\hat{c} + (1 - \hat{d})q \quad . \quad . \quad . \quad (4)$$

This new equation, according to Kaldor, expresses the growth of labour requirements in the sector concerned as a function of the growth of output.

When $1 > \hat{d} > 0$ the coefficient of q in each of the estimated relationships (3) and (4) is positive, suggesting a higher growth rate of output will mean an increased growth rate of productivity, but this increase will not be sufficient to obviate the need for additional labour. Reversing the direction of argument, Kaldor concluded that, for $1 > \hat{d} > 0$, a greater supply of labour will

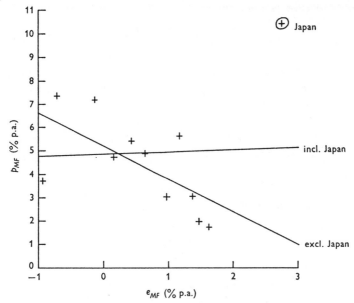

FIG. 3. Relationship between productivity growth and employment growth in manufacturing, 1965–70 (Cripps–Tarling).

allow output and indirectly productivity to grow faster. Although Kaldor did not conduct his reversed argument in explicit mathematical terms, it is easy to do so. All we need do is derive from equations (3) and (4) a set of estimated relations linking p and q to e. When this is done we get

$$q = \frac{\hat{c}}{1-\hat{d}} + \frac{1}{1-\hat{d}} e \quad . \quad . \quad . \quad . \quad (5)$$

and

$$p = \frac{\hat{c}}{1-\hat{d}} + \frac{\hat{d}}{1-\hat{d}} e \quad . \quad . \quad . \quad . \quad (6)$$

Now equation (6) is nothing but an estimated version of the original equation $p = a + be$. Thus, implicit in Kaldor's argument is a quite definite method of estimating the relationship between p and e. Denoting by $\hat{\hat{b}}$ the resulting estimator of b it follows from equation (6) that,

$$\hat{\hat{b}} = \frac{\hat{d}}{1-\hat{d}} \quad . \quad . \quad . \quad . \quad (7)$$

Let us call $\hat{\hat{b}}$ "Kaldor's implicit estimator".

Thus, we have two estimators of b. One of them $\hat{b}$ is derived directly by regressing p on e and the other $\hat{\hat{b}}$ indirectly by regressing p on q. If all the equations held exactly for each country these two estimators would coincide, i.e. $\hat{\hat{b}} = \hat{b}$. If, however, the fit is not perfect (as is naturally the case) then all equations become inexact and the two estimators are no longer identical. In fact their ratio is given by[1]

$$\frac{\hat{\hat{b}}}{\hat{b}} = 1 + \frac{\hat{d}(1 - R_{pq}^2)}{(1-\hat{d})(R_{pq}^2 - \hat{d})} \qquad \qquad (8)$$

If the correlation between p and q is very high, $(1 - R^2)$ is very small, and this ratio is near to unity, indicating that the two methods yield similar results. If, however, the correlation between p and q is not very good (but R^2 is nevertheless greater than $\hat{d}$), then $\hat{\hat{b}}$ will be substantially greater than $\hat{b}$. Table II compares the results obtained by Kaldor's indirect method and those obtained by the conventional direct method for manufacturing. When Japan is

TABLE II

Alternative Estimates of b for Manufacturing in $p = a + be$

	Kaldor's implicit estimate $\hat{\hat{b}}$	OLS estimate $\hat{b}$	R_{pq}^2
Including Japan ...	0·92	0·63	0·82
Excluding Japan ...	0·75	0·18	0·54

Data: Kaldor's figures for manufacturing.

included in the sample the correlation between p and q is quite high, but even so the difference is serious: $\hat{\hat{b}}$ is about one and a half times $\hat{b}$. When Japan is dropped, however, the correlation between p and q falls markedly and $\hat{\hat{b}}$ is no less than four times as large as $\hat{b}$.

The fact that Kaldor used an unusual method of inference does not of itself invalidate his results. There might in principle be a good reason for adopting a roundabout procedure instead of the conventional method of relating productivity growth p directly to employment growth e. But nowhere in his lecture does Kaldor give such a reason and later authors have, correctly in my opinion, preferred the direct method. The advantages of estimating b by OLS regression of p on e are well known. In particular, if the errors are independent of e the estimator will be unbiased. Even if the errors are not independent of e, the OLS estimator may provide a sound basis for predicting the effect of a change in e on p—something which is obviously important when one is considering the effect of various employment policies on productivity. Against these advantages of direct ordinary least squares, Kaldor's roundabout method seems to have nothing to recommend it. We should base our

[1] A simpler expression connecting the two estimators is $(1+\hat{\hat{b}})/(1+\hat{b}) = 1/R_{qe}^2$.

conclusions on the estimates obtained by using the direct method and regressing p on e.

As in the case of Cripps and Tarling, the results with Kaldor's data depend very much upon the inclusion of an extreme special case—Japan—in a small sample of countries. When Japan is dropped the relationship between

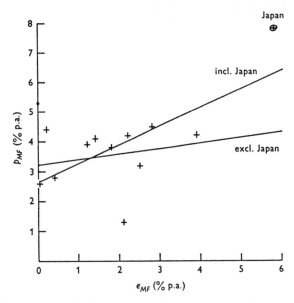

Fig. 4. Relationship between productivity growth and employment growth in manufacturing, 1953–54 to 1963–64 (Kaldor).

p and e virtually disappears. This is hardly surprising as Kaldor uses exactly the same set of 12 countries over much the same time period as Cripps and Tarling. In Table I the regression results obtained when Japan is included and excluded are compared. The regression lines are shown in Fig. 4. The effect of excluding Japan is striking. The value of R^2 drops to 0·050 and the coefficient b of employment growth drops to 0·183—under one third of its original value and considerably smaller than its standard error. Thus, when Japan is excluded, there is no real evidence of any relationship between productivity growth and employment growth. This is, of course, obvious from Fig. 4.

Conclusions

We may conclude from the above discussion that there is no empirical evidence that Kaldor's law has operated during the post-war period in manufacturing. The confirmative results of Cripps and Tarling for 1951 to 1965 and of Kaldor for 1953–54 to 1963–64 simply cannot be accepted. They are based upon a small sample of countries chosen in such a way that the extreme observations of one special case—Japan—account for the bulk of observed correlation between productivity growth and employment growth. Moreover, Kaldor used an unconventional and seriously misleading method of estimation which gave results very different from those obtained by the conventional least squares regression of p on e.

R. E. ROWTHORN

University of Cambridge.

Date of receipt of final typescript: September 1974.

ECONOMIC GROWTH AND THE VERDOORN LAW – A COMMENT ON MR ROWTHORN'S ARTICLE

In an article in the March 1975 issue of this JOURNAL[1] Mr Rowthorn charges me with using "an unusual method" to test the "relationship between productivity growth and employment growth" and asserts that if I had used a more direct method, the results could not have been obtained, except perhaps for a particular period, and for a particular sample of twelve countries which included Japan.

This criticism is based partly on misunderstanding and partly on misrepresentation.

The misunderstanding is perhaps an excusable one for someone who had apparently read my Inaugural Lecture[2] but not the subsequent papers,[3] for the manner of exposition adopted in the lecture left something to be desired. Moreover what Rowthorn (and others) have taken to be the main message of that lecture – that the slow rate of economic growth of the United Kingdom was mainly due to the shortage of labour resulting from "economic maturity" – is one which I have since abandoned as a result of fresh statistical evidence, as well as further historical experience. This answer to Rowthorn's criticism provides an opportunity to state my present views on these issues.

It is best to start by dealing with the misrepresentation first. This lies in his assertion that I derived an "implicit estimator" of the relationship of productivity to employment from a regression of productivity on output, using for the purpose the formula which he gives at the foot of page 16, after having transformed algebraically the regression coefficient of productivity on output into a coefficient of employment on output. This is totally untrue.

From the point of view of my analysis, however, it is also irrelevant. I was not concerned with estimating the regression of p on e as such. I was concerned to find empirical support for the Verdoorn Law, which is usually written in the form

$$p = \alpha + \beta q, \quad \text{with} \quad \beta > 0, \tag{1}$$

but which I preferred to write in the form

$$e = \gamma + \partial q, \quad \text{with} \quad 0 < \partial < 1, \tag{2}$$

because I regarded, and still regard, the existence of a significant relationship between the growth of employment and output as the main test for deciding whether the Verdoorn Law asserts something significant about reality, or whether it is a simple statistical mirage. Clearly, since by definition

$$p \equiv q - e$$

---

[1] "What remains of Kaldor's Law?" ECONOMIC JOURNAL, March 1975, pp. 10–19
[2] *Causes of the Slow Economic Growth of the United Kingdom* (Cambridge University Press, 1966).
[3] Cf. in particular my *Reply* to the criticism of my inaugural lecture by J. N. Wolfe, in *Economica*, November 1968, pp. 385–91.

in any situation in which e is either zero or a constant there *must* be a perfect correlation between p and q – but one which does not assert anything, since it is the automatic consequence of measuring the same thing twice over.[1]

In this way I found that in at least two sectors, Agriculture and Commerce, the Verdoorn equation did not produce meaningful results. In each case the regression coefficient of p on q was around 1, with R^2s between 0·8 and 0·9, and t values of 7–10; but the corresponding relationship of e on q produced R^2s of 0·01–0·04, with t values of $\frac{1}{3}$–$\frac{1}{2}$.

On the other hand in manufacturing, where the regression coefficients for both p on q and e on q were around 0·5, the R^2s were very similar (0·826 in the one case and 0·844 in the other) and the t values of the coefficients were as high as 7 in both cases. These findings were *not* dependent on the inclusion of Japan in the sample. If Japan is excluded from the sample, the results for the remaining 11 countries (based on the data shown in table 2, p. 12, of my Lecture) are as follows:

$$p = 1\cdot359 + 0\cdot417q, \quad R^2 = 0\cdot536,$$
$$(0\cdot129)$$
$$e = -1\cdot331 + 0\cdot574q, \quad R^2 = 0\cdot685.$$
$$(0\cdot130)$$

The exclusion of Japan reduces the closeness of the fit (and also the numerical value of the Verdoorn coefficient, from 0·5 to 0·4) but the results, in terms of t values and R^2s, are still sufficiently good to convey something significant. The coefficient of e on q has a t value of over 4, and is significantly *smaller* than 1, by the test of the t value related to the *difference* of the coefficient from unity.

On the other hand I nowhere suggested in my lecture that a statistically significant positive correlation between p and e is a *necessary* test of the Verdoorn Law. The reason for this was a simple one. Since I regarded output as being in general the exogenous variable (determined by demand) any error or disturbance would be associated with the employment term; and all such "disturbances" would automatically be reflected – with the *opposite* sign – in the productivity series, thereby generating a spurious negative correlation between p and e.

It follows that the existence of statistically significant relationships between p and q and e and q does *not* carry with it that the relationship between p and e is also statistically significant. The latter *may* happen, if the relationship between e and q gives a sufficiently close fit, but it would not hold if the latter relationship is not close enough. There is nothing very surprising therefore in the fact that it is only by including Japan that the regression equation between p and e (as calculated by Rowthorn) is statistically significant; even so, the R^2 in the latter equation is only 0·447 as against 0·844 on the basic equation of e on q, while the t value of the regression coefficient is less than 3 (as against over 7 in the basic equation).

[1] Rowthorn is correct in saying that the coefficients of (2) can be algebraically derived from (1), or vice versa; but whereas a significant relationship between e and q (with $0 < \partial < 1$) automatically ensures that equation (1) (the "Verdoorn equation") is also significant, this is not true the other way round – not unless one also specifies that the coefficient β in that equation is significantly less than 1, which has not hitherto been regarded as an integral property of the Verdoorn Law.

I conclude therefore that a *sufficient* condition for the presence of static or dynamic economies of scale is the existence of a statistically significant relationship between e and q, with a regression coefficient which is significantly less than 1.[1]

If this condition is not satisfied, there are several possibilities. First, that there *is* a significant relationship, but the coefficient of e on q is either not significantly different from unity or is significantly greater than unity. This latter case is sufficient to reject the increasing-returns-to-scale hypothesis.

Second, that there is *no* significant relationship between e and q at all – and this is consistent with all kinds of interpretations. It is in this second sense that the Verdoorn Law can be said to have "broken down" in the period 1965–70.

Rowthorn's equations and scatter diagrams (taken from Gomulka) relate entirely to the relationship between p and e, and we are not told whether the underlying relationships between e and q are of a neo-classical kind (with employment varying in a 1 for 1 relationship with output), or the anarchical or nihilistic kind (with employment being unrelated to output), or of the type described on page 892 above.

One interpretation of the Gomulka–Rowthorn theory is that the rate of growth of employment in manufacturing is exogenously determined, independently of demand.[2] In that case (but only in that case) his strictures concerning "Kaldor's law" would be pertinent.[3] But my whole thesis, originating from the remarkable correlation between the growth of GDP and the growth of manufacturing output,[4] amounted to a denial of this position; I asserted that the labour absorbed in manufacturing in the course of industrialisation does

[1] It was certainly unfortunate that Cripps and Tarling, in dealing with my hypothesis that there is a positive association between productivity and employment in manufacturing, produced a correlation in support of it between p and e, the validity of which depended (apparently without their realising it) on a single extreme observation, Japan, and the significance of which (given the low value of R^2) was in any case dubious. If my above argument is correct this was not *necessary* for supporting the hypothesis that increasing returns prevail in manufacturing. For that they had very much stronger evidence for the 1950–65 period in terms of the nature of the correlation between e and q from which the relationship between p and q automatically follows. For the 1965–70 period, on the other hand, they found no significant relationship between e and q and hence no statistical support for the Verdoorn Law. (Cf. T. F. Cripps and R. J. Tarling, *Growth in Advanced Capitalist Economies, 1950–1970*, D.A.E. Occasional Paper, no. 40, Cambridge University Press, 1973).

[2] This would be the case, for example, if one assumed (*a*) that the total labour force effectively employed grows at an exogenous rate; (*b*) the proportion of the labour force available to the manufacturing sector is given. Both these assumptions are patently untenable, especially if we take into account inter-regional and inter-national migration of labour (which can be shown to have been largely demand-induced) as well as the very large changes (over time) in the inter-sectoral distribution of the labour force of any particular region.

[3] It could be argued that since in the lecture I regarded U.K. manufacturing output as being constrained by labour shortage, this is tantamount to saying that in the case of the United Kingdom I regarded e as exogenous. However this is irrelevant, since the regression equations of e on q and p on q were derived from a sample of countries for which e (i.e. the rate of growth of employment in manufacturing industry) was not exogenously given.

[4] Since readers could hardly be expected to remember this equation, published more than 10 years ago, it is worth reproducing it here (using the notation adopted in the Cripps-Tarling paper):

$$q_{GDP} = 1 \cdot 153 + 0 \cdot 614 q_{MF}, \quad R^2 = 0 \cdot 959.$$
$$(0 \cdot 080)$$

This relationship has since been confirmed by other investigators such as the ECE (*Economic Survey of Europe*... (1969), p. 78), UNCTAD, Cripps and Tarling, etc., and I am sure that it holds equally for Gomulka's sample of 39 countries as for my sample of 12 countries; and that it holds for the 1965–70 period, as well as earlier periods. An important property of the equation is that the regression coefficient is significantly less than unity (implying that for growth rates exceeding 3 % a year, industrial production

not diminish production in the rest of the economy, owing to the existence of surplus labour in agriculture (and also, though I did not say so explicitly, in services) which is only eliminated at a late stage of industrial development, at the stage of "economic maturity".

This view has been strikingly confirmed by Cripps and Tarling's findings in two remarkable correlations (not mentioned by Rowthorn) which explain the overall productivity growth of the economy (the rate of growth of GDP per head) in terms of the rate of growth of industrial output and the (relative) diminution of non-industrial employment. This relationship has in no way been impaired by the failure of the Verdoorn Law in manufacturing in the post-1965 period; indeed the correlation coefficient is even higher for the 1965–70 period than for the 1950–65 period.

The two equations are:

1950–65:
$$P_{GDP} = 1 \cdot 172 + 0 \cdot 534 q_{IND} - 0 \cdot 812 e_{NI}, \quad R^2 = 0 \cdot 805,$$
$$(0 \cdot 058) \quad (0 \cdot 202)$$

1965–70:
$$P_{GDP} = 1 \cdot 153 + 0 \cdot 642 q_{IND} - 0 \cdot 872 e_{NI}, \quad R^2 = 0 \cdot 958,$$
$$(0 \cdot 058) \quad (0 \cdot 125)$$

where P_{GDP}, q_{IND}, e_{NI} stand for the rate of growth of GDP per employed person, the rate of growth of industrial production and the rate of growth of non-industrial employment respectively.[1]

The important thing to note is – and herein lies Rowthorn's misunderstanding – that the existence of increasing returns to scale in industry (the Verdoorn Law) is not a necessary or indispensable element in the interpretation of these equations. Even if industrial output obeyed the law of constant returns, it could still be true that the growth of industrial output was the governing factor in the overall rate of economic growth (both in terms of total output and output per head) so long as the growth of industrial output represented a net addition to the effective use of resources and not just a transfer of resources from one use to another. This would be the case if (a) the capital required for industrial production was (largely or wholly) self-generated – the accumulation of capital was an aspect,

---

invariably rises faster than the GDP as a whole); the standard error is very small—$t = 15$ in the above equation; Cripps and Tarling (p. 22) found that $t = 20$ in a corresponding equation for a bundle of 43 observations—and as I have shown in the Appendix to my lecture, the equation owes nothing to "auto-correlation" since the structure and the coefficient of the equation remain much the same if manufacturing is excluded from the GDP on the LHS of the equation.

[1] Cf. Cripps and Tarling, *op. cit.* p. 30. To see how far (if at all) these equations would be affected by the exclusion of Japan, I asked Roger Tarling to re-compute the two regressions by excluding Japan from the sample. The results are as follows.:

Eleven countries, excluding Japan

1950–65:
$$P_{GDP} = 1 \cdot 768 + 0 \cdot 369 q_{IND} - 0 \cdot 647 e_{NI}, \quad R^2 = 0 \cdot 678,$$
$$(0 \cdot 063) \quad (0 \cdot 171)$$

1965–70:
$$P_{GDP} = 0 \cdot 819 + 0 \cdot 710 q_{IND} - 0 \cdot 848 e_{NI}, \quad R^2 = 0 \cdot 930.$$
$$(0 \cdot 124) \quad (0 \cdot 135)$$

It is interesting to note that whereas the exclusion of Japan somewhat reduces the fit, and the explanatory power of the equation (as measured by R^2 and the size of the constant) for the 1950–65 period, it makes virtually no difference for the 1965–70 period.

or a by-product, of the growth of output; and (*b*) the labour engaged in industry had no true opportunity-cost outside industry, on account of the prevalence of disguised unemployment both in agriculture and services. There is plenty of direct evidence to substantiate both of these assumptions.

The important implication of these assumptions is that economic growth is demand-induced, and not resource-constrained – i.e. that it is to be explained by the growth of demand which is exogenous to the industrial sector[1] and not by the (exogenously given) growth rates of the factors of production, labour and capital, combined with some (exogenously given) technical progress over time.

While in the Lecture I gave the main emphasis to the Verdoorn Law as an explanation for the difference in growth rates, and still believe in its importance, I would now regard the existence of surplus labour, and the critical role of profits and profit expectations in capital accumulation as the more basic cause of the difference of view between the neo-classical and Keynesian (or post-Keynesian) schools of thought: the question, that is, whether one regards economic growth as the resultant of demand (i.e. the growth of markets) or of (exogenously given) changes in resource-endowment.

On the other hand, I now believe that I was wrong in thinking in 1966 that the United Kingdom *had* attained the stage of "economic maturity" (in the sense I defined that term) and that her comparatively poor performance was to be explained by inability to recruit sufficient labour to manufacturing industry rather than by poor market performance due to lack of international competitiveness. Statistical studies that have since come to light[2] make it doubtful whether I was correct in thinking that earnings in the service trades of the United Kingdom had come to be fully competitive with earnings in manufacturing or that the growth of manufacturing industry in the United Kingdom was constrained by labour shortages other than in a purely short-term sense – e.g. of not having sufficient skilled labour in engineering to sustain a rapid expansion of engineering production (which from a long-run point of view is itself a consequence of a low trend rate of growth of demand).[3] But while

---

[1] In saying that growth is explained by the increase in demand which is "exogenous" to the growing sectors I am conscious of the fact that this statement in itself is a simplification but one which does not invalidate the statistical inferences derived from it. The growth of industrial output for any region is governed in part by the growth in productivity which itself influences demand through the change in competitiveness which is induced by it. It is this reverse link which accounts for the cumulative and circular nature of growth processes. There is a two-way relationship from demand growth to productivity growth and from productivity growth to demand growth; but the second relationship is, in my view, far less regular and systematic than the first.

[2] Sleeper, R., "Manpower Redeployment and the Selective Employment Tax," *Bulletin of the Oxford University Institute of Economics and Statistics*, November, 1970.

[3] The belief that the expansion of manufacturing production and thus of exports was hindered by the inelastic supply of labour to manufacturing industry undoubtedly played a role in the introduction of Selective Employment Tax (as was explained in the Government White Paper issued on its introduction). But Rowthorn is wrong in thinking that the existence of increasing returns in manufacturing industry was a necessary part of its justification. Given the fact that over 85% of U.K. exports were manufactured goods, and that the U.K. economy was threatened by a balance-of-payments crisis due to an insufficiency of exports, the existence of a labour shortage would have been a perfectly adequate reason for securing the release of labour from services, irrespective of whether increasing returns or constant returns prevailed in industry. (In the actual case, as events have shown, the improvement of export performance needed a devaluation, however, to improve the competitiveness of British goods in foreign markets.)

I would now modify the story concerning the United Kingdom, such modification would definitely *not* be in the direction of Rowthorn, Gomulka or the neoclassicals. In particular, I would now place more, rather than less, emphasis on the exogenous components of demand, and in particular on the role of exports, in determining the trend rate of productivity growth in the United Kingdom in relation to other industrially advanced countries.[1]

NICHOLAS KALDOR

King's College
Cambridge

Date of receipt of typescript: *April 1975*

---

[1] Gomulka's thesis, favoured by Rowthorn – that the more rapid growth of productivity of latecomers like Japan was to be explained by the diffusion of technical knowledge – could hardly explain how the higher productivity growth rates could have continued after the productivity *levels* of the diffusees came to surpass those of the diffusants.

A REPLY TO LORD KALDOR'S COMMENT[1]

My article has been widely interpreted as a rebuttal of Kaldor's entire writings on economic growth. This it was never intended to be. Indeed, I find many of his ideas very stimulating and agree with his stress on the dynamic and creative aspects of capitalist development: the conquest of new markets, learning by doing, the division of labour and the role of demand in promoting technical progress. The purpose of my article was narrow, being to criticise his view of the importance during the nineteen fifties and early sixties of industrial economies of scale of the type associated with Verdoorn, and his theory that during this period Britain's slow growth of industrial productivity was due to a shortage of labour which prevented her from exploiting such economies of scale.[2]

In his lecture Kaldor attempted to establish the validity of Verdoorn's "law" in manufacturing by means of regression analysis using a sample of twelve countries.[3] He took as independent variable the growth rate q of manufacturing output, against which he regressed the growth rates p of productivity and e of employment, interpreting the results as proof that "each percentage addition to the growth of output requires a 0·5 per cent increase in the growth rate of employment in terms of man-hours and is associated with a 0·5 per cent increase in the growth of productivity".[4] He then applied these results to the British economy, arguing that a greater supply of labour would have allowed a faster growth of manufacturing employment and therefore a faster rise in manufacturing productivity. This argument depends crucially on the existence of a positive relationship between productivity and employment, and I suggested that it is more natural to examine this relationship directly by regressing p on e, rather than indirectly, as Kaldor had done, by regressing p or e on q. Using this direct method I found that there was indeed a strongly positive association between p and e over the period 1953/4 to 1963/4, but I also found that this association depended almost entirely on the presence of one extreme observation. Since the country concerned (Japan) was clearly a special case, I dropped it from the sample, causing almost all trace of an association between p and e to disappear. I concluded that the existence of economies of scale of the Verdoorn type had not been established by Kaldor.

Kaldor now argues that my direct method of regressing p on e is not correct because it assumes the disturbances to be independent of e, whereas according to him they are independent of q, which he considers to be determined exo-

[1] I should like to thank Professor W. B. Reddaway for his constructive comments, which I found most useful during the preparation of this Reply.

[2] Economies of scale of the Verdoorn type require an increase in the total input of labour to the sector concerned. They are to be distinguished from economies of scale and specialisation which come from a more efficient deployment of the existing labour force in larger or more specialised plants. Economies of this latter kind have, I am sure, always been important.

[3] *Causes of the Slow Rate of Growth in the United Kingdom* (Cambridge University Press, 1966). The countries were Japan, Italy, West Germany, Austria, France, the Netherlands, Belgium, Denmark, Norway, Canada, the United Kingdom and the United States.

[4] *Ibid.* p. 11.

genously by "demand".[1] The second part of this claim, that q is exogenous, is most implausible for it implies a unidirectional causality operating from output to productivity and employment, with no significant feedback in the opposite direction. Indeed, I am surprised that Kaldor should resort to such an argument. It hardly squares with his own apparent vision of capitalist development as a process of continuous interaction between supply and demand, in which the separate effects of these two are difficult to disentangle, since they act simultaneously and mutually condition each other so that consumer tastes and productive techniques evolve in a highly interdependent fashion.

Under these circumstances it now seems to me clear that the position can only be represented in mathematical form by a set of simultaneous equations; and, as a corollary, statistical estimates of the parameters of any single equation will be liable to serious error if that equation is considered in isolation.

As an illustration, Kaldor's analysis based on the assumption that q is exogenous would require a specific justification appealing to certain peculiar features of the period in question. Kaldor refers to only one such feature, namely the existence of huge reserves of unemployed and underemployed labour potentially available for employment in the industries of Continental Europe and Japan. The existence of these reserves is not, in my opinion, an adequate reason for regarding either q as exogenous or the positive correlation between p and q as an expression of economies of scale.[2]

Let us first of all consider how productivity may influence output via its effect on demand. At a micro-level a faster-than-average growth of productivity tends to be associated with falling relative costs and thereby with a falling relative price, causing a shift in demand towards the commodity in question: a familiar point, but valid nonetheless. Kaldor tries to counter this argument by saying that the correlation between prices and productivity is not perfect.[3] True enough, but then the correlation between productivity and output is not very high and does not require a very strong correlation between productivity and prices to explain it.

On a macro-level, where one is considering the whole manufacturing or industrial sector of a country, demand depends on productivity in a number of ways. Higher productivity makes exports more competitive on world markets because they are cheaper or of a better quality. This stimulating effect on export demand is most marked when there is a surplus of labour to weaken the bargaining power of workers, so that higher productivity is translated into lower costs rather than higher wages. Bigger exports in turn lead to more industrial output, directly by raising the total demand for the products of export and related industries, and indirectly by financing the purchase of imports necessary

[1] In a later version of his lecture Kaldor himself followed my allegedly incorrect procedure and took e as the independent variable (*Strategic Factors in Economic Development*, New York, 1967, p. 82). Regressing q on e, he found that, for the industrial sector as a whole, a 1% rise in employment was associated with a 1·61% rise in output (and therefore with a 0·61% rise in productivity). Unfortunately Kaldor did not provide the data upon which his estimates were based, and it is not possible to recompute his regression using a sample from which Japan has been dropped. If this were done, I am sure that, as in the case of manufacturing, the result would be an equation indicating little or no association between p and e.

[2] The role of labour supply is discussed below.

[3] *Causes of the Slow Rate of Growth in the United Kingdom* (Cambridge University Press, 1966), p.14.

for a fast growth of domestic output, thereby allowing the state to pursue expansionary economic policies.[1] To the extent that it is not offset by rising wages, higher productivity may also mean higher profits which may in turn raise demand by causing firms to invest more.[2] Finally, higher productivity in industry may stimulate the domestic demand for industrial goods by making them relatively cheaper or because it is accompanied by the introduction of new products. Machinery becomes cheaper relative to labour, encouraging the adoption of more mechanised techniques. Industrial goods become cheaper in relation to a number of services whose productivity has risen slowly, encouraging the replacement of these services by an industrial substitute.[3] Clearly, at a macro-level productivity exercises a powerful influence on output through its effect on demand, and this influence is likely to be most marked precisely under those conditions of surplus labour upon which Kaldor lays so much stress.

This brings me to the question of employment and labour supply. Kaldor says that my criticism of his estimation method is correct only if "the rate of growth of employment in manufacturing is exogenously determined, independently of demand" and that, otherwise, he is justified in taking q as the independent variable because it is exogenous. There are several reasons why this defence is inadequate. To start with, the real question is not whether employment is independent of demand, but whether demand itself depends on factors specifically considered in the model, in which case it cannot be regarded as exogenous, but merely as one variable in an interdependent set.

In examining this question it is useful to distinguish three different situations in the industrial labour market where the supply of labour may be "unlimited", "strictly limited" or "elastic". The supply of industrial labour is "unlimited" if there is a large pool of unemployed or underemployed labour and, at the going wage rate, industrialists can get all the workers they may want. Faced with such a huge surplus of potential workers the government may make no attempt to provide jobs for all of them, but may choose its demand management policies

[1] As always in such cases the historical process is one of interaction: higher productivity means more exports which means greater industrial output which via its effects on investment, innovation and scale of production reacts back on productivity again.

[2] Under depression conditions this mechanism may not work because of the pessimistic state of capitalist expectations and the presence of excess capacity. In the nineteen fifties, however, demand was maintained either by exports or by government policy. Kindleberger has argued that the countries of Continental Europe grew fast precisely because their huge reserves of cheap labour, at the *beginning* of the period, enabled them to hold down wages. As productivity rose so did profits, investment and exports, and their economies moved on to a path of self-sustaining growth. He also argued, however, that this "virtuous circle" would not last and would be broken when labour reserves became exhausted and wages were forced up by the resulting shortage of workers (Charles Kindleberger, *Europe's Post-War Growth – the Role of Labor Supply* (Harvard University Press, 1967).

[3] Note that, although higher industrial productivity leads to greater industrial *output* for the reasons given, it may not always lead to greater industrial *employment*. There are two reasons why this is so. First, there are income effects to be considered – a higher level of industrial productivity will mean a higher level of *per capita* income which, given appropriate income elasticities, may mean a shift towards services and away from manufactures. Secondly, many services are complementary to industrial activities and the demand for them rises almost in line with the demand for industrial products. If productivity in complementary services lags behind industrial productivity, then higher industrial output will mean a relative decline in industrial employment as compared to employment in such services. Under certain circumstances this could actually mean an absolute decline in industrial employment.

to achieve some aim such as a sound balance of payments or a stable price level.[1] When this is the case, moderate or even large variations in the potential supply of industrial labour may produce no change in government policy and therefore in the level of demand, and as a result there may be no feedback from labour supply to output.[2] Employment will then respond passively to demand – industrial wages will not be bid up in an attempt to attract new workers, although they may rise for other reasons such as trade-union pressure, and output will not be limited by a shortage of labour. This is the situation assumed by Kaldor in his discussion of post-war growth.

At the opposite end of the spectrum is a situation of "strictly limited" labour supply where industrial employment is growing at or near the maximum rate allowed by an exogenously given supply of labour. This situation may have been caused by the spontaneous forces of economic expansion or it may be the result of deliberate government policy designed to bring the employment of labour into some preconceived relation with its supply. Provided that these economic forces are sufficiently expansionary or government objectives do not alter, any variation in the quantity of available labour will lead to a change in the level of employment. In the former case the government will raise or lower the overall level of demand to make sure that the requisite number of workers are employed, and in the latter case the adjustment will come about automatically. When employment is adapted to a given supply of labour in this way it must be taken as exogenous for the purposes of regression analysis and therefore used as the independent variable. Moreover, the regression of p or q on e will then provide estimates of the *productive* relations between these three variables and not of demand relations in the goods market.

An intermediate case occurs when, over the relevant range, the supply of labour is "elastic" with respect to the level of industrial wages, so that the industrial sector in the country concerned can attract more labour by paying higher wages.[3] This complicates the analysis by introducing a labour supply equation into the model.

These theoretical objections to Kaldor's procedure can be summed up as follows. His method of estimating the productive relations between p, e and q is appropriate only when (1) there is an "unlimited" supply of labour in virtually every country in his sample and (2) demand is not significantly affected by the movement of productivity or employment. Under these conditions it is formally correct to take q as the independent variable and to interpret the results as evidence about technology. If these stringent conditions are not met, however, Kaldor's method is incorrect and, depending on the circumstances, one may be estimating instead a demand relationship in the goods market, a labour supply relationship or else some hybrid combination of possible relationships.

[1] This situation is most likely to arise when the unemployed or underemployed are located abroad and lack the political power to influence government policies which are decided primarily by domestic considerations.

[2] It is assumed here that the government is powerful enough to ensure the achievement of its targets.

[3] In his celebrated article "Fattori che regolano lo sviluppo della produttività del lavoro" (*L'Industria*, 1949) Verdoorn himself assumed that employers would attract additional labour only by paying higher wages.

The above is clearly a formidable list of objections. In practice, of course, their force depends upon the actual labour-market situation in the countries concerned and upon the actual effect of productivity upon demand. Kaldor clearly believes that, in general, there was an "unlimited" supply of labour in the countries of his sample. This belief does not, in my opinion stand up to serious examination. It is true that at the beginning of his period, in the early fifties, there were massive *internal* reserves of unemployed or underemployed labour in countries such as West Germany, Italy and Japan. Under the impact of sustained economic growth, however, these reserves were quickly run down and by the late fifties or early sixties there were widespread labour shortages.[1] Labour was still leaving agriculture but no longer at a fast enough rate to provide for industrial requirements.[2]

To overcome these shortages of labour, the advanced countries of Europe imported millions of workers from the Mediterranean Area and, in the case of Britain, from the Black Commonwealth. Even so, the rate at which they could be brought in was actually or potentially limited by a number of political and economic factors: hostility of the local population, an inadequate recruiting system, cultural barriers, costs of absorption, inappropriate skills and so on. The relative importance of these various factors is open to dispute and has since changed, but there can be no doubt that collectively they had a significant limiting effect on the rate of immigration. It seems to me unreasonable to assume that Government policies on demand management were uninfluenced by the changing state of the labour market.

To conclude may I thank Professor Kaldor for his comment. It has made me realise, as I did not before, the importance of interaction and simultaneity in the economic processes concerned.

R. E. ROWTHORN

University of Cambridge

Date of receipt of final typescript: July 1975

---

[1] See G. C. Allen, *Japan's Industrial Expansion* (Oxford University Press, 1965), chapter 11, and Charles Kindleberger, *Europe's Post-War Growth – the Role of Labor Supply* (Harvard University Press, 1967). There remained a large amount of labour in agriculture which, from a strictly technical point of view, was redundant. To get these remaining peasants off the land, however, was a slow job, for they were deeply attached to their holdings and stubbornly resisted the economic forces undermining their position. Moreover, the conservative regimes in power needed peasant support which they bought with subsidies, guaranteed prices and other measures designed to cushion the impact of market forces and retard the decline of peasant farming.

[2] In theory employers could have encouraged peasants to leave the land by offering higher wages, but this would probably have been self-defeating as the peasantry would have responded by demanding more economic aid, designed to restore the previous income differential between industry and agriculture.

DIFFUSION, CONVERGENCE AND KALDOR'S LAWS[1]

I. INTRODUCTION

The notion that the manufacturing sector plays a key role in the process of economic development and growth has been a popular one among economists and has been supported by casual empiricism, statistical studies, and theoretical considerations.[2] For example, the notion of the manufacturing sector as the "engine of growth" plays a critical role in Kaldor's view as to why growth rates differ as well as in Cripps and Tarling's recent efforts to further substantiate "Kaldor's laws".[3] In addition, in the Kaldor approach to growth, high rates of growth in manufacturing output are very much contingent upon high rates of growth of employment in manufacturing which in turn require high rates of growth of the non-agricultural labour force. Thus, Kaldor's model can be summarised in the form of three equations. First, an engine of growth equation can be written

$$\dot{Q} = a_0 + a_1 \dot{Q}_m, \tag{1}$$

where $\dot{Q}$ and $\dot{Q}_m$ represent the rates of growth of total output and manufacturing output, respectively. Secondly, a kind of production function is added with $\dot{Q}_m$ the dependent variable and the rate of growth of employment in manufacturing, $\dot{E}_m$, the independent variable or

$$\dot{Q}_m = b_0 + b_1 \dot{E}_m. \tag{2}$$

The model is then completed with

$$\dot{E}_m = c_0 + c_1 \dot{E}, \tag{3}$$

where equation (3) denotes the dependence of labour supply in manufacturing upon the growth of total labour supply, $\dot{E}$, which may include surplus labour from agriculture, foreign labour and growth in the indigenous labour force.[4]

It is important to notice the "supply-determined" nature of growth in this type of model. Total labour supply determines manufacturing labour supply, manufacturing labour supply determines manufacturing output and the latter determines total output. In particular, it is not the rate of growth of demand for manufacturing output that determines the rate of growth of

---

[1] The author wishes specially to thank Professors Charles Stalon and Ronald Tracy for comments. This study was financed by PHS Research Grant No. 1-R01-Hd059890-01A1 for NIH.
[2] See, for example, N. Kaldor, *Strategic Factors in Economic Development* (Cornell University, Ithaca, 1967), C. P. Kindleberger, *Europe's Postwar Growth: The Role of Labor Supply* (Harvard University, Cambridge, 1967), A. C. Kelley, J. G. William and R. J. Cheetham, *Dualistic Economic Development, Theory and History* (University of Chicago, Chicago, 1972), T. F. Cripps and R. J. Tarling, *Growth in Advanced Capitalist Economies, 1950–1970* (University of Cambridge, Cambridge, 1973) and Alfred Maizels, *Growth and Trade* (Cambridge University Press, Cambridge, 1970).
[3] *Ibid.*
[4] Cripps and Tarling, *ibid.*, consider alternative measures of the supply of labour available to manufacturing.

the employment in manufacturing since no demand variables enter into equation (2), only a variable depicting a supply constraint.

It is the pivotal role of labour supply in the Kaldor explanation of why growth rates differ that has come under critical review in this JOURNAL and others.[1] For example, Rowthorn has correctly pointed out that the statistical basis for a modified version of equation (2) disappears when Japan, which provides an "extreme value" in Cripps and Tarling's study as well as Kaldor's, is omitted from the sample. This lack of an even moderate association between employment and output in manufacturing when one country is dropped from the sample, certainly casts doubt on the notion of explaining differences in growth rates in terms of differences in labour supply.

In this paper a model is proposed that dispenses with the view that rates of growth of output in manufacturing have been constrained by labour supplies and instead assumes that when the demand for labour in manufacturing is strong, supply is forthcoming. The justification for this radical respecification of the Kaldor model is a belief that throughout the period in question, 1950–70, "pools" of labour were found in the agriculture and service sectors of the various developed capitalist economies, in neighbouring countries, in growth of the indigenous labour force or some combination of these that allowed an expansion of employment in manufacturing, provided the demand for labour was forthcoming. As a corollary to this change in viewpoint, it is hypothesised that the rate of growth of manufacturing output during this period can be explained in terms of demand variables and the influence of an international diffusion process arising from a technological gap between countries at the beginning of the 1950s. The model is tested against the behaviour of the twelve OECD countries chosen by Cripps and Tarling, utilising their method of eliminating cyclical influences. Among other things, the model will allow for a more detailed discussion of the possibilities of convergence of growth rates of the various developed capitalist economies.

One final point: it should be stressed, that even if Kaldor and others are quite wrong in incorporating something like equation (2) in their models, this does not mean that rapid growth of manufacturing output is not the key to rapid growth of total output. The importance of the expansion of the manufacturing sector for the overall growth of the economy is a question quite distinct from that of the existence or absence of a labour supply constraint in manufacturing.[2]

II. THE SUPPLY OF LABOUR FOR MANUFACTURING

During the period from the early 1950s until the end of the 1960s, the rate of growth of employment in manufacturing was less than or approximately equal to the overall rate of growth of employment in five countries in the

---

[1] See R. E. Rowthorn, "What Remains of Kaldor's Law?", this JOURNAL, March 1975, and J. N. Wolfe, "Productivity and Growth in Manufacturing Industry: Some reflections on Professor Kaldor's Inaugural Lecture", *Economica*, May 1968.

[2] Using Cripps and Tarling's terminology, Kaldor's "alternative approach" may still be preferred to the "traditional approach". See Cripps and Tarling, *op. cit.*

sample: Belgium, Canada, the Netherlands, the United Kingdom and the United States. In six of the seven other countries, the annual average rate of growth of employment in manufacturing was at least double the growth rate of total employment.[1] In specifying a model to explain the rate of growth of manufacturing output, the issue is whether or not these differences in employment patterns resulted from a supply constraint, a lack of demand for labour in manufacturing or both.

The chief sources of labour for manufacturing in the post-war period were the agricultural sector, new entrants to the labour force (mostly school leavers) and workers in poor countries adjacent to the countries under discussion. Of the five countries just cited, only Belgium and the United Kingdom had less than 10% of their labour forces employed in agriculture at the beginning of the period. And while civilian employment in agriculture fell below 10% in 1963 in the Netherlands, in 1955 in the United States and in 1966 in Canada, all three countries experienced annual rates of growth of the indigenous population that were greater than 1% throughout the period. If, for the moment, it can be somewhat arbitrarily assumed that a rate of growth of the indigenous population greater than 1% and/or an agricultural labour force that is initially 10% or greater was adequate as a source of labour supply for manufacturing during this period, then only in Belgium and the United Kingdom might it be argued that the expansion of manufacturing output was somehow constrained by supply factors. Since there exist scant data on Belgium, any attempt to resolve the issue will have to be confined to the United Kingdom.

The case for those who wish to argue that British manufacturing suffered from a shortage of labour is strengthened by the realisation that migration to Britain from the New Commonwealth countries was severely curtailed after 1962 and by the fact that the expansion of the Irish economy in the 1960s acted to curtail this source of "surplus labour" to British manufacturers. To set against this are two studies by Sleeper indicating that in Britain during this period some of the service sectors provided "pools" of labour for manufacturing, when demand was strong in the latter, allowing these service sectors to function in a manner similar to the agricultural sector in other countries.[2] However, trying to determine the net impact of these influences on the supply of labour would not answer the question of whether or not output in British manufacturing was actually constrained by a labour shortage. What is involved here is an identification problem since the employment data do not allow us to determine whether the small growth of employment in British manufacturing was due to a supply shortage, a lack of strong demand for labour

---

[1] The annual average rates of growth of overall employment and of employment in manufacturing are: Belgium, 0·52 and 0·49%; Canada, 2·33 and 2·16%; the Netherlands, 1·19 and 1·19%; the U.K. 0·38 and 0·39%; the U.S.A. 1·42 and 1·15%. In contrast in Germany and Japan the same rates were: 1·18 and 2·84% and 1·59 and 4·62%, respectively. Data taken from Cripps and Tarling, *op. cit.*

[2] See R. D. Sleeper, "Manpower Redeployment and the Selective Employment Tax", *Bulletin of the Oxford University Institute of Economics and Statistics*, November 1970, and "SET and the Shake-out: A Note on the Productivity Effect of the Selective Employment Tax", *Oxford Economic Papers*, July 1972.

or both. Short of constructing and estimating the parameters of a simultaneous equation model, the answer must be found by indirect means.

The relevant data are meagre in this regard, but what are available do suggest that the slow growth of employment in manufacturing in Britain was due to a lack of strong demand by manufacturing firms for labour. There is, for example, Wolfe's analysis of employment and vacancy patterns in Britain from the early 1960s to the mid-1960s, the latter date corresponding to a time of high employment by British standards.[1] Vacancy–unemployment patterns were not found to be significantly different between the high-paying sectors of manufacturing and the low wage sectors of the service group. Unemployment fell and vacancies rose as a percentage of employment for both groups but not in any noticeably different way, suggesting that while demand for labour in manufacturing rose during this boom, this measure of the "state of the labour market" did not indicate undue shortages of labour for manufacturers. In addition, other events in the labour market do not support the contention that demand for labour was strong but manufacturers were constrained by a lack of labour. Thus, studies by Reder and Wachter indicate that when labour markets tighten, the industrial dispersion of wage rates narrows.[2] Yet, an empirical study by Papola and Bharadwaj showed that comparing successive cyclical peaks in Britain during the 1950s and 1960s the dispersion of wages across manufacturing industries actually widened over time.[3] None of this is conclusive, to be sure, but taking into account Rowthorn's results as well, at the very least a statistical test of a model which assumes that when demand for labour in manufacturing is strong labour supply is forthcoming is certainly in order.

III. AN ALTERNATIVE EXPLANATION OF THE GROWTH OF MANUFACTURING OUTPUT

When Kaldor's labour constraint in manufacturing is rejected, the chain of causation of the growth process alters dramatically. For one thing, it is the rate of growth of manufacturing output that determines the rate of growth of labour in manufacturing. Instead of equation (2), the model developed would include a relationship such as

$$\dot{E}_m = d_0 + d_1 \dot{Q}_m \tag{4}$$

or some more complicated model that "inverts" equation (2). Then, a radically different explanation of $\dot{Q}_m$ would be specified. It is only the second relationship that will be explored here.

Rowthorn, following Gomulka and others, has suggested that the rate of growth of manufacturing output and productivity for any country is very much dependent on the size of the technological gap between an industrial

---

[1] See Wolfe, *op. cit.*
[2] M. W. Reder, "The Theory of Occupational Wage Differentials", *American Economic Review*, March 1970.
[3] T. S. Papola and V. P. Bharadwaj, "Dynamics of Industrial Wage Structure: An Inter-country Analysis", ECONOMIC JOURNAL, 1970.

leader and the country in question.[1] A recent UN study also adopted this view, utilising *per capita* income as a measure of the level of industrial development.[2] Using the period 1953–67, this cross-section study of most of the advanced capitalist economies expressed the rate of growth of manufacturing output as a function of *per capita* incomes in various forms. The most successful form of the relationship was

$$\dot{Q}_m = e_0 + e_1/Y \tag{5}$$

or

$$\dot{Q}_m = 2\cdot 82 + 2888/Y, \tag{5a}$$

where Y is *per capita* income. Equation (5a) states quite simply that if the growth patterns over time of the countries in the sample are correctly reflected in the cross-section estimates, then as *per capita* incomes rise, $\dot{Q}_m$ converges asymptotically to a growth rate a little less than 3%.

However, while it may be true that the ability to realise rapid rates of growth of manufacturing output is greatest, other things being equal, when *per capita* incomes are low, because there is so much technology to be borrowed, equations (5) and (5a) are unsatisfactory on *a priori* grounds. There are no variables included in the equations to measure the extent to which countries attempt to take advantage of a technological gap or other factors that might be expected to influence the growth of manufacturing output. For this reason, it was hypothesised that manufacturing investment as a share of value added in manufacturing (I), the rate of growth of exports of manufactured goods ($\dot{E}_x$), and the rate of growth of total population ($\dot{P}$), should be included as explanatory variables. Thus, the higher is I the greater should be demand pressures and the lower will be the "macro risks" of investment.[3] In addition, the higher is the investment ratio, the greater should be the proportion of a country's capital stock that embodies the latest techniques. High rates of growth of exports act to sustain and increase the initial levels of demand through their multiplier effect. Related to this, high rates of growth of exports free an economy from deflationary measures that may be required if exports grow slowly and a balance of payments constraint is encountered.[4] Finally, Chenery and Taylor have suggested that population size, P, will have a positive influence on the level of manufacturing output because it allows for economies of scale which shift the comparative advantage of large countries toward manufacturing at an earlier stage in their development.[5] Hence, in explaining differences in rates of growth of manufacturing output, the rate of population growth may also be a factor.

---

[1] See Rowthorn, *op. cit.*; S. Gomulka, *Inventive Activity, Diffusion, and the Stages of Economic Growth* (Institute of Economics, Aarhus, 1971), and L. Nabseth and G. F. Ray (eds.), *The Diffusion of New Industrial Processes* (Cambridge University Press, Cambridge, 1974).

[2] See *Economic Survey of Europe 1969*, Part I (United Nations, New York, 1970), chapter 3.

[3] See A. Lamfalussy, *Investment and Growth in Mature Economies* (Macmillan, New York, 1961).

[4] Kaldor has himself emphasised the importance of "export-led growth". See his "Conflicts in National Economic Objectives" in *Conflicts in Policy Objectives*, ed. N. Kaldor (Augustus M. Kelley, New York, 1971).

[5] See H. B. Chenery and L. Taylor, "Development Patterns: Among Countries and Over Time", *The Review of Economics and Statistics*, November 1968.

The rate of growth of total output was not included as an independent variable. It is certainly true that manufacturing output contains a large final output component and, therefore, Q_m should be related to Q in accordance with most standard versions of the consumption function. From this it follows that the rate of growth of total output will also influence the rate of growth of manufacturing output. However, to stress the importance of the manufacturing sector in growth, the model was estimated in such a way as to emphasise a causal chain. The process entailed the specification of a "structural" equation of the form $\dot{Q}_m = f(I, 1/Y, \dot{E}_x, \dot{P}, \dot{Q})$, with all symbols having their previous meaning. Then, an engine of growth equation, such as equation (1) was substituted into this equation and $\dot{Q}$ eliminated, giving $\dot{Q}_m = F(I, 1/Y, \dot{E}_x, \dot{P})$. This last equation was then viewed as a reduced form equation whereby a set of exogenous variables determined the rate of growth of manufacturing output which, in turn, determined the rate of growth of total output as given by equation (1), $\dot{Q} = a_0 + a_1 \dot{Q}_m$. Using this form of the model for estimating purposes made explicit the recursive structure of an economy envisaged by economists who stress the key role of the manufacturing sector in the growth process.

Various regressions were run using Cripps and Tarling's pooled cross-section time-series data that incorporated these variables. In keeping with the findings of Cripps and Tarling as well as Rowthorn, regressions were run that included as well as excluded Japan, that included and excluded the last period for each country, that omitted Austria, Denmark and Norway in some regressions as well as Italy in others (in the interests of comparability of data), and which limited the analysis to the five or six larger OECD countries – France, Germany, Japan, the United Kingdom, the United States and sometimes Italy. The rate of growth of manufacturing output was initially treated as a function of the reciprocal of *per capita* income, $1/Y$, the investment ratio in manufacturing, I, the rate of growth of manufacturing exports, $\dot{E}_x$, and the rate of growth of the population, $\dot{P}$. Early regressions showed that the population variable was never significant and the model was re-estimated without this variable. Preliminary regressions also showed that the elimination of the last period for each country improved the fit slightly but not enough to justify the finding of an important structural change after the mid-1960s that Cripps and Tarling found.[1] This should not be surprising since Cripps and Tarling were estimating a production function whereas the model tested here stresses the demand for manufacturing output. In discussing the regression results that follow, the period of analysis is extended to include roughly the second half of the 1960s.

Table 1 summarises the regression results for different groups of countries. The results are sensitive to the inclusion or exclusion of Japan but not nearly to the extent that they were found to be by Rowthorn. The R^2 is lower when

---

[1] The variable Y^{us}/Y, where Y^{us} represents *per capita* income in the United States, was also tried but gave slightly less favourable results than simply using $1/Y$. For Italy it was necessary to use industrial investment relative to value added in industry instead of manufacturing investment relative to value added in manufacturing. Data on the volume of manufacturing exports was not available for Austria, Denmark and Norway. Hence, in the regressions using these three countries, it was necessary to use the rates of growth of total exports.

Table 1

Regression Results for Various Groups of Countries

All countries $\quad \dot{Q}_m = 0{\cdot}240 + 1909/Y + 0{\cdot}175\dot{E}_x + 0{\cdot}117I \quad R^2 = 0{\cdot}76 \quad (5b)$
$\quad\quad\quad\quad\quad\quad\quad\quad (401) \quad\quad (0{\cdot}059) \quad\;\; (0{\cdot}050)$

All countries except Japan $\quad \dot{Q}_m = 1{\cdot}83 + 1664/Y + 0{\cdot}206\dot{E}_x \quad R^2 = 0{\cdot}55 \quad (5c)$
$\quad\quad\quad\quad\quad\quad\quad\quad\quad\quad\;\; (447) \quad\quad (0{\cdot}051)$

All countries except Austria, $\quad \dot{Q}_m = -0{\cdot}055 + 1872/Y + 0{\cdot}132\dot{E}_x + 0{\cdot}167I \quad R^2 = 0{\cdot}78 \quad (5d)$
Denmark and Norway $\quad\quad\quad\quad\quad\quad\quad (455) \quad\quad (0{\cdot}068) \quad\;\; (0{\cdot}064)$

All countries except Italy $\quad \dot{Q}_m = 0{\cdot}036 + 2163/Y + 0{\cdot}181\dot{E}_x + 0{\cdot}177I \quad R^2 = 0{\cdot}79 \quad (5e)$
$\quad\quad\quad\quad\quad\quad\quad\quad\quad (441) \quad\quad (0{\cdot}069) \quad\;\; (0{\cdot}049)$

All big countries $\quad \dot{Q}_m = 0{\cdot}156 + 1625/Y + 0{\cdot}173\dot{E}_x + 0{\cdot}163I \quad R^2 = 0{\cdot}82 \quad (5f)$
$\quad\quad\quad\quad\quad\quad\quad\quad (575) \quad\quad (0{\cdot}081) \quad\;\; (0{\cdot}073)$

All big countries except Japan $\quad \dot{Q}_m = 1{\cdot}80 + 1781/Y + 0{\cdot}225\dot{E}_x \quad R^2 = 0{\cdot}67 \quad (5g)$
$\quad\quad\quad\quad\quad\quad\quad\quad\quad\quad\quad\; (644) \quad\quad (0{\cdot}076)$

Figures in parentheses are standard errors of the coefficients: all coefficients are statistically significant at the 5% level or less.

Data

Rates of growth of output in manufacturing and the investment ratio are taken from Cripps and Tarling, *op. cit.*, and K. Allen and A. Stevenson, *An Introduction to the Italian Economy* (Martin Robertson and Co., Ltd., London, 1974), table 2-3, p. 51. Cripps and Tarling divide the time period covered for each country into subperiods, each subperiod beginning and ending at a cyclical peak. Growth rates of output are then computed on a peak to peak basis giving rise to several observations for each country. The total period covered for each county in the regressions above are:

Japan (1953-1969)   Canada (1951-1969)   United States (1951-1969)
Austria (1957-1970)   France (1960-1969)   Germany (1951-1970)
Belgium (1951-1970)   Denmark (1957-1969)   Norway (1951-1970)
Netherlands (1951-1970)   Italy (1951-1970)   United Kingdom (1951-1969)

Figures for the investment ratio are averages of annual values in each subperiod so defined.

Per capita income figures are derived from data in *Labour Force Statistics* (OECD, Paris), *International Financial Statistics* (International Monetary Fund, Washington, D.C.), *Demographic Yearbook* (United Nations, Geneva), and *Statistical Yearbook of Japan* (Bureau of Statistics, Tokyo). *Per capita* income figures were first calculated in constant 1963 prices and then converted to dollars by use of official exchange rates. The *per capita* figure for any country during the first year of any subperiod was used in the regressions.

Figures for the volume of exports are from *International Financial Statistics* (International Monetary Fund, Washington, D.C.) and *Monthly Bulletin of Statistics* (United Nations, New York). Figures for the growth rates of exports are for the same subperiods as those used to derive growth rates of output.

Japan is excluded and the investment ratio, I, becomes non-significant, but nevertheless the statistical results have some claim to respectability even when Japan is excluded from the sample.

The exclusion of Austria, Denmark and Norway gives more importance to I and less to $\dot{E}_x$. When the sample is limited to five of the six biggest countries or the six biggest (Italy included) the fit is improved. These latter results would be expected *a priori* because the growth patterns of small countries are liable to be dominated by special considerations.[1] All things considered, the results seem to indicate that the model is not particularly sensitive to what countries are included or excluded in the sample with the one exception. Thus, the existence of a technological gap (to the extent that it is adequately

[1] See A. Maizels, *op. cit.*, pp. 69-71.

measured by Y), a strong propensity of manufacturers to invest, and a successful export performance appear to be important factors leading to a rapid rate of growth of manufacturing output.

IV. CONCLUSIONS

In this paper, a model for explaining why growth rates differ was developed that is essentially a "demand-determined" model of growth. In particular, Kaldor's view that differences in growth rates can be explained by differences in the supply of labour available to the manufacturing sector during the period 1950–70 was rejected. Instead, a model was specified whereby the amount of labour available to the manufacturing sector was always sufficient to meet the demand for labour which was, in turn, derived from the demand for manufacturing output.

This model was then applied to the post-war period and the parameters of an equation explaining the rate of growth of manufacturing output were estimated. The explanatory variables in the equation included a variable depicting the size of the technological gap faced by each country and therefore a measure of the amount of technology that could be borrowed by each country from the industrial leaders. In addition, it was felt necessary to include variables that measured the efforts actually made by a country in "catching up" with the industrial leaders.

The results were successful, judged by the usual statistical criteria. While they were somewhat sensitive to the inclusion of Japan in the sample, this sensitivity was not nearly as acute as in earlier studies. Moreover, the model showed a great deal of insensitivity to the inclusion or exclusion of countries other than Japan.

While the model in no sense gives the final word on why growth rates differ, it is, hopefully, highly suggestive for formulating a strategy to explore this interesting question in macrodynamics in more depth and detail.

Finally, while it can be argued that no strong labour constraint was operative in the period up to the beginning of the 1970s, this assumption would be harder to maintain in the period after 1969. Agricultural workers were being constantly pulled from the agricultural sector in every country during the 1950–70 period, so that by the end of the period in seven of the twelve countries in the sample, the agricultural sector employed less than 10 % of the labour force (compared with only two at the beginnings of the 1950s). To this must be added a factor of possibly greater importance; the political intervention in several countries to stop or restrict the flow of foreign labour. This suggests that in any attempt to explain the rate of growth of manufacturing output in the period after 1970 one would be well advised to work with a simultaneous equation model that specifies the structure of both demand and supply side of the market.

JOHN CORNWALL

Southern Illinois University

Date of receipt of typescript: September 1975

Differences in Growth Rates and Kaldor's Laws

By A. PARIKH

University of East Anglia

Kaldor (1966) asserted that the slow rate of economic growth of the United Kingdom was due mainly to the shortage of labour resulting from "economic maturity". Kaldor (1975), in a subsequent comment on Rowthorn's (1975a) article, abandoned this reasoning and presented the strict Verdoorn law as

(1) $\quad p = \alpha + \beta q \quad \text{with} \quad \beta > 0$

and his own presentation of Verdoorn's law as

(2) $\quad e = \gamma + \delta q \quad \text{with} \quad 0 < \delta < 1 \quad \text{and} \quad e = q - p$

where p is the rate of growth of productivity, q is the rate of growth of output, e is the rate of growth of employment, and α, β, γ and δ are parameters.

Kaldor regressed e on q to support his conclusion that the slow growth of industrial productivity was due to a shortage of labour which prevented exploitation of economies of scale. He took the growth rate q of manufacturing output as an independent variable and regressed the growth rate of productivity p and of employment e on q, concluding that each percentage addition to the growth of output requires a 0.5 per cent increase in the growth rate of employment, in terms of man-hours, and is associated with a 0.5 per cent increase in the growth of productivity. The argument depends on a positive relationship between productivity and employment, and Rowthorn (1975a) examined this by regressing p directly on e rather than indirectly by regressing p or e on q as shown in (1) and (2). He concluded that the positive association depended entirely on the presence of one extreme observation, and that if Japan were excluded from the sample the association between p and e disappeared.

The main purpose of this paper is to argue that both sets of results are subject to simultaneous equations bias and that mis-specification of estimated equations leads to incorrect estimates and wrong conclusions.

I. Alternative Models

In this section two models are presented and estimated. In Model 1 the rate of growth of employment is determined by the growth of output and of the workforce. The rate of growth of manufacturing output in turn is determined by the rate of growth of exports, the rate of growth of employment and the investment-output ratio in the manufacturing sector. There are two identities: (a) the growth rate of the workforce is a weighted average of the growth rates of manufacturing employment and of others (non-manufacturing and unemployment); (b) the productivity relation is a definitional relationship and it is equal to output growth less growth in employment in the manufacturing sector.

The model uses demand and supply factors in the determination of output, employment and productivity growth. The explicit demand factors are the rate of growth in exports and investment–output ratio. The supply factor is the rate of growth of employment in the manufacturing sector. If employment growth is constrained by the slow growth in output in the manufacturing sector, the coefficient of $\mathring{Q}_m$ will be statistically significant in equation (3). The specification of $\mathring{Q}_m$ in Model 1 is similar to Cornwall's demand-oriented model. Cornwall (1976), however, did not use the equation for $\mathring{E}_m$ explicitly in his study.

Model 1

(3) $\quad \mathring{E}_m = a + b\mathring{Q}_m + c\mathring{G}_w + U_1$

(4) $\quad \mathring{Q}_m = d + e\mathring{E}_m + f\mathring{X} + gI + U_2$

(5) $\quad \mathring{G}_w = \lambda \mathring{E}_m + (1-\lambda)NM\mathring{E}_s$

(6) $\quad \mathring{P}_m = \mathring{Q}_m - \mathring{E}_m$

Model 2

(7) $\quad \mathring{E}_m = a + b\mathring{Q}_m + c\mathring{G}_w + dI + U_1$

(8) $\quad \mathring{Q}_m = e + f\mathring{E}_m + g\mathring{X} + U_2$

(9) $\quad \mathring{G}_w = \lambda \mathring{E}_m + (1-\lambda)NM\mathring{E}_s$

(10) $\quad \mathring{P}_m = \mathring{Q}_m - \mathring{E}_m$

Endogenous variables

$\mathring{E}_m$ = rate of growth of manufacturing employment

$\mathring{Q}_m$ = rate of growth of manufacturing output

$\mathring{G}_w$ = rate of growth of the workforce

$\mathring{P}_m$ = rate of growth of productivity in the manufacturing sector

Exogenous variables

I = investment–output ratio in manufacturing sector

$\mathring{X}$ = rate of growth in exports

$\mathring{G}_w - \lambda \mathring{E}_m = NM\mathring{E}_m$ = rate of growth in non-manufacturing workforce

λ = manufacturing employment as a proportion of labour force in the first year of the sub-period

U_1 and U_2 are stochastic variables.

The difference between Models 1 and 2 lies in the specification of equations for $\mathring{Q}_m$ and $\mathring{E}_m$. In Model 1 the rate of growth in manufacturing employment does not depend upon investment–output ratios in that sector, while in Model 2 it does.

Data for this study come from Cripps and Tarling's (1973) pooled cross-section time-series data. Data on exports and growth rates of manufactured exports are derived for the same sub-periods as those used to derive the growth rates of manufacturing output, and the growth rate of the labour force is used instead of a population growth variable. Both models have behavioural equations and two identities. Equation (3) is over-identified and equation (4) is just-identified in Model 1.

The productivity growth equation is a definitional relationship, and similarly the growth in the workforce is a weighted average of the growth in manufacturing and others, including growth in unemployment. The weights are respectively the proportion of the labour force in the manufacturing sector to the total in the base year of each of the sub-periods. We can substitute the identity (5) in equations (3) and (4), and the estimated equations (3) and (4) may be used to derive productivity growth. In a simultaneous equation framework, the productivity relationship is derived from solved reduced forms of structural equations.

We thus estimate for Model 1:

(11)
$$\mathring{E}_m = \frac{a}{1-\lambda c} + \frac{b}{1-\lambda c} \mathring{Q}_m + \frac{c}{1-\lambda c} N\mathring{M}E_m + \frac{U_1}{1-\lambda c}$$

$$\mathring{Q}_m = d + e\mathring{E}_m + f\mathring{X} + gI + U_2.$$

λ is known for each sub-period and for each of the 12 countries, $\mathring{E}_m$ and $\mathring{Q}_m$ are simultaneously determined, and $(1-\lambda)N\mathring{M}E_s = N\mathring{M}E_m$ is treated as an exogenous variable. The estimated equations for Model 1 are (including Japan):

$$\mathring{E}_m = -0{\cdot}7287 + 0{\cdot}3826\mathring{Q}_m + 0{\cdot}2638 N\mathring{M}E_m$$
$$(1{\cdot}4980) \quad (5{\cdot}3030) \quad\quad (1{\cdot}3230)$$

$$R^2 = 0{\cdot}2826 \quad SEE = 1{\cdot}078$$

(12)
$$\mathring{Q}_m = -0{\cdot}7658 + 0{\cdot}3543\mathring{X} + 0{\cdot}2233I - 0{\cdot}0451\mathring{E}_m$$
$$(0{\cdot}5110) \quad (1{\cdot}7750) \quad (1{\cdot}7350) \quad (0{\cdot}0330)$$

$$R^2 = 0{\cdot}6443 \quad SEE = 1{\cdot}9144 \quad R^2 = (\mathring{P}, \hat{\mathring{P}}) = 0{\cdot}6220.$$

Both the equations are estimated by the method of two-stage-least squares (TSLS). The R^2 statistic in TSLS does not have the properties of the R^2 statistic of the OLS but it is computed to show goodness-of-fit from the solved TSLS structural form equations. The F-test for significance cannot be applied. All the bracketed figures under the coefficients are asymptotic t-ratios obtained from the asymptotic variance–covariance matrix of the TSLS estimates. The lower the standard error of the estimate, the better is the fit. The standard error of the estimate refers to the structural form equations, while R^2 refers to the reduced forms of estimated structural form equations in which over-identifying restrictions are explicitly used. The TSLS estimates of the structural form equations of Model (11) excluding

Japan are shown below:

$$\mathring{E}_m = -0.4850 + 0.3342\, \mathring{Q}_m + 0.2402\, N\mathring{M}E_m$$
$$(0.5010)\quad (1.9580)\quad\quad (1.0300)$$
$$R^2 = 0.0679 \quad SEE = 1.0903$$

(13)
$$\mathring{Q}_m = 4.0425 + 0.5539\mathring{X} - 0.0131 I - 2.2573\mathring{E}_m$$
$$(0.7010)\,(0.8020)\quad (0.0530)\quad (0.3590)$$

$$R^2 = 0.4352 \quad SEE = 4.5764 \quad R^2 = (\mathring{P}, \hat{\mathring{P}}) = 0.4691$$

The estimated equations reveal R^2 to be lower without Japan. The coefficient of the $\mathring{Q}_m$ variable is statistically significant in both sets of equations. These results reveal that growth in employment in the manufacturing sector is determined by the growth in manufacturing output while the growth in output in the manufacturing sector is determined by the growth in exports in that sector (in equation (12)). It can be easily seen that it is the rate of growth in industrial output that seems to be constraining the growth in employment, and low growth in manufacturing output may be attributed to demand factors.

For Model 2 we have obtained similar estimates with and without Japan.

$$\mathring{E}_m = -0.6921 + 0.4003\mathring{Q}_m + 0.2659 N\mathring{M}E_m - 0.0086 I$$
$$(1.2540)\,(2.7670)\quad (1.3270)\quad\quad (0.1410)$$

$$R^2 = 0.1238 \quad SEE = 1.0806$$

(14)
$$\mathring{Q}_m = 1.5364 + 0.1322\mathring{X} + 1.9907\mathring{E}_m$$
$$(1.9370)\,(0.7840)\quad (2.5870)$$

$$R^2 = 0.2135 \quad SEE = 2.0910 \quad R^2(\mathring{P}, \hat{\mathring{P}}) = 0.1864$$

Equation (7) was just-identified while equation (8) was over-identified, and both of them are estimated by the method of TSLS. There were 41 observations in both models which included Japan. Once again, the coefficient of the $\mathring{Q}_m$ variable is significant. Moreover, the coefficient of the $\mathring{E}_m$ variable in the second equation of (14) is significant. This system of equations will remain under-identified if the non-zero restrictions on the structural form coefficients are not fulfilled. None of the other coefficients is statistically significant and, therefore, we may conclude that non-zero restrictions on the coefficients are not true and the model remains under-identified. This is the case where identifiability criteria are satisfied through mis-specification which is borne out in the estimated coefficients. In Model 2 we dropped Japan from the sample to see whether the estimates differed.

$$\mathring{E}_m = -0.3468 + 0.3739\mathring{Q}_m + 0.2518 N\mathring{M}E_m - 0.0228 I$$
$$(0.3410)\,(1.9070)\quad (1.0850)\quad\quad (0.3960)$$

(15)
$$R^2 = 0.0687 \quad SEE = 1.076$$
$$\mathring{Q}_m = 3.8139 + 0.5346\mathring{X} - 2.1226\mathring{E}_m$$
$$(1.0570)\,(0.9670)\quad (0.3910)$$

$$R^2 = 0.4376 \quad SEE = 4.1448 \quad R^2(\mathring{P}, \hat{\mathring{P}}) = 0.4789$$

The estimated regression coefficients differ markedly, and only the coefficient with respect to the $\mathring{Q}_m$ variable is statistically significant. The growth in employment is constrained by the manufacturing sector's output growth. The standard error of the estimate for the second equation of (15) is very high and it can be firmly established that both models are highly sensitive to the exclusion of Japan from the sample data.

II. Revised Model and Estimation

Here we try to test Gomulka's (1971) hypothesis that the rate of growth of manufacturing output and productivity for any country is dependent on the size of technological gap between an industrial leader and the country in question. Cornwall (1976) uses the demand-oriented equation

(16) $\quad \mathring{Q}_m = e_0 + e_1\left(\dfrac{1}{Y}\right) + e_2\mathring{X} + e_3 I$

where e_0, e_1, e_2 and e_3 are constants, Y is *per capita* income, and the other variables are as before. It is expected that the sign of coefficient associated with $(1/Y)$ will be positive. This is because when *per capita* incomes are low there is so much technology to be borrowed, and with its diffusion the ability to realize rapid rates of growth in manufacturing output is increased. We tried Cornwall's model, which turns out to be a modified version of Model 1, here called Model 3. The uneven diffusion of technology among OECD countries is considered explictly by the *per capita* income variable as a proxy for development. It is expected that the standard error of the estimate will decline and the goodness-of-fit will improve with the inclusion of this variable. We used a consistent set of data on *per capita* income in US dollars at current prices and current exchange rates from the OECD national accounts. Obviously, *per capita* income is an unsatisfactory proxy for technological diffusion. Cornwall's data come from two or three different sources, and the compiled data on *per capita* income were reduced to 1963 prices and then converted to dollars by the use of official exchange rates. As data on GDP and GNP differ from one source to another, we have followed one source, and the problem is that we would not reduce such data to constant prices. We estimated Model 1 with the inclusion of *per capita* income variable as the proxy for the state of technology, and the estimated equations are presented below.

Model 3 with Japan (*TSLS estimates*)

$\mathring{E}_m = -1 \cdot 1666 + 0 \cdot 4527 \mathring{Q}_m + 0 \cdot 2855 N\mathring{M}E_m$
$\quad\quad\quad (2 \cdot 6560)\ (7 \cdot 0430)\quad\quad (1 \cdot 4730)$

(17) $\quad SEE = 1 \cdot 0494 \quad R^2 = 0 \cdot 4818$

$\mathring{Q}_m = -0 \cdot 5050 + 0 \cdot 2816\mathring{X} + 0 \cdot 1413 I + 1876 \cdot 38\left(\dfrac{1}{Y}\right) - 0 \cdot 1497 \mathring{E}_m$
$\quad\quad\quad (0 \cdot 4500)\ (2 \cdot 4020)\quad (2 \cdot 2440)\quad (1 \cdot 0510)\quad\quad (0 \cdot 1180)$
$\quad\quad SEE = 1 \cdot 6496 \quad R^2 = 0 \cdot 7669 \quad R^2(\hat{P}, \hat{P}) = 0 \cdot 5780$

Model 3 without Japan (TSLS estimates)

(18)
$$\overset{\circ}{E}_m = -1 \cdot 5101 + 0 \cdot 5187 \overset{\circ}{Q}_m + 0 \cdot 3615 N\overset{\circ}{M}E_m \quad SEE = 1 \cdot 0029 \quad R^2$$
$$(2 \cdot 0430) \quad (4 \cdot 0130) \quad (1 \cdot 7510)$$

$$R^2 = 0 \cdot 2486 \quad SEE = 1 \cdot 0029$$

$$\overset{\circ}{Q}_m = 1 \cdot 6483 + 0 \cdot 3536 \overset{\circ}{X} - 0 \cdot 0627 I + 2353 \cdot 26 \left(\frac{1}{Y}\right) - 0 \cdot 2447 \overset{\circ}{E}_m$$
$$(1 \cdot 4880) \ (2 \cdot 8800) \quad (0 \cdot 6270) \quad (1 \cdot 5710) \quad (0 \cdot 2800)$$

$$SEE = 1 \cdot 4719 \quad R^2 = 0 \cdot 5956 \quad R^2(\overset{\circ}{P}, \overset{\circ}{P}) = 0 \cdot 3976$$

It can be seen that the Gomulka hypothesis of technological diffusion has some support from these estimates. It is not conclusive because the coefficient on the income variable with Japan included does not have statistical significance at the conventional 5 per cent level, but when Japan is excluded the *t*-statistic indicates significance at the 10 per cent level. The estimates below give strong support to the technological diffusion hypothesis, and the reason why the *per capita* income coefficient is not significant seems to be due to some collinearity between the *per capita* income variable and growth in employment. The inclusion of the *per capita* income variable reduces the standard error of the estimate, improves the fit and raises the importance of demand factors in the explanation of growth in manufacturing output. The exclusion of Japan reduces the standard error of the estimate, but, at the same time, none of the other estimates change substantially except the coefficient associated with investment–output ratios, and here again the greater variability in the dependent variable produced by the inclusion of Japan in the sample is largely explained by the investment–output ratio variable. Cornwall (1976) obtained a similar result with respect to the investment–output ratio variable.

III. Recursive Model

Since the coefficient of the $\overset{\circ}{E}_m$ variable in the second equation of most of the models is insignificant (after excluding Japan), we decided to drop this variable from the second equation of (17) and reestimate the set of equations by ordinary least squares sequentially. When the $\overset{\circ}{E}_m$ variable is dropped from the equation, the simultaneous nature of the model is lost and the system of equations follows a recursive framework. The growth in manufacturing output is determined by the growth in exports, investment–output ratios in the manufacturing sector and the technolical diffusion variable. The results of this model including Japan are given below:

(19)
$$\overset{\circ}{Q}_m = -0 \cdot 4177 + 0 \cdot 2713 \overset{\circ}{X} + 0 \cdot 1392 I + 1671 \cdot 22 \left(\frac{1}{Y}\right)$$
$$(0 \cdot 5410) \ (3 \cdot 7710) \quad (2 \cdot 5230) \quad (4 \cdot 3570)$$

$$\bar{R}^2 = 0 \cdot 7478 \quad F(3, 36) = 39 \cdot 54 \quad SEE = 1 \cdot 5071$$

$$\overset{\circ}{E}_m = -1 \cdot 1575 + 0 \cdot 4521 \overset{\circ}{Q}_m + 0 \cdot 2693 N\overset{\circ}{M}E_m$$
$$(2 \cdot 1550) \ (5 \cdot 7460) \quad (1 \cdot 1350)$$

$$\bar{R}^2 = 0 \cdot 4495 \quad F(2, 37) = 16 \cdot 69 \quad SEE = 1 \cdot 2861 \quad R^2(\overset{\circ}{P}, \overset{\circ}{P}) = 0 \cdot 5689$$

The OLS estimates are best linear unbiased estimates and the variance–covariance matrix of the estimators is the minimum one in finite samples for the first equation of (19). The demand-determined explanation of the growth in manufacturing output is clearly supported. The diffusion of techniques among the OECD countries is measured by a proxy such as *per capita* income, and this explains the variation in growth rates in manufacturing output better in this model. The adjusted multiple coefficient of determination ($\bar{R}^2$) and the F-statistic have the usual interpretation. When Japan is excluded from the sample the following results are obtained:

(20)
$$\mathring{Q}_m = 1\cdot6008 + 0\cdot3271\mathring{X} - 0\cdot0456I + 1971\cdot28\left(\frac{1}{Y}\right)$$
$$(1\cdot7400)\ (4\cdot9720)\quad (0\cdot6850)\quad (3\cdot7650)$$
$$\bar{R}^2 = 0\cdot5583 \quad F(3, 32) = 15\cdot75 \quad SEE = 1\cdot2369$$
$$\mathring{E}_m = -1\cdot4444 + 0\cdot5089\mathring{Q}_m + 0\cdot3189 N\mathring{M}E_m$$
$$(1\cdot5830)\ (3\cdot1830)\qquad (1\cdot2490)$$
$$\bar{R}^2 = 0\cdot1887 \quad F(2, 33) = 5\cdot07 \quad SEE = 1\cdot2654 \quad R^2(\mathring{P}, \mathring{\hat{P}}) = 0\cdot4102$$

The estimates of the second equation in both the sets of equations are consistent, and the asymptotic t-ratios are shown in parentheses for the second equation.

The $\bar{R}^2$ is much lower without Japan than with Japan. However, most of the regression coefficients are statistically significant in both the sets of regressions. The inclusion of Japan produces a higher variability, and the investment–output ratio variable explains a significant part of this variation in the data. In this recursive system OLS estimates of the second equation are obtained after substituting the predicted rate of growth of output from the first equation into the second equation.

The slow rate of growth in exports has strong effects on the rate of growth of output in the manufacturing sector. When we introduce demand and supply factors in the explanation of differences in growth rates in manufacturing sector in 12 OECD countries, we find that the lower growth of employment in the manufacturing sector is explained by the lower rate of growth in output in the manufacturing sector, which itself is due to the slow rate of growth in exports owing to lack of demand and the slow rate of growth in investment in the economy. Kaldor's law as formulated by Rowthorn and Cripps–Tarling thus does not turn out to be tenable with the empirical data of 12 OECD countries, and demand factors seem to be relevant in explaining the slow growth in the manufacturing sector.

IV. Conclusion

Three conclusions emerge from this study. (a) Kaldor's supply determined version or Rowthorn's version of Verdoorn's law are not supported, and the rate of growth of manufacturing output is constrained by the rate of growth in demand for exports and the rate of investment. Kaldor has stressed exports, investment, goverment policy and other demand side factors in explaining manufacturing growth in his demand-determined framework, and this hypothesis is supported by the study. (b) The rate of growth of employment in the manufacturing sector seems to be determined by the rate of growth of manufacturing output. It is confirmed that every 1 per cent growth in output leads to about 1/2 per cent growth in employment. It is, however, the ambiguity and mixed character of Kaldor's formulation that confuses the issue, and it is the supply-determined hypothesis that is refuted by the present study. (c) The technological diffusion hypothesis is broadly supported by the empirical study on cross-section data of 12 OECD countries.

In the United Kingdom in 1974 the agricultural labour force was 3 per cent of the total labour force compared with 33–36 per cent in industry; and, although the release of labour from agriculture to the manufacturing sector may not be feasible (since 3 per cent is probably the absolute minimum), it is not true to say that the growth in manufacturing output is constrained by the non-availability of labour to the manufacturing sector. It is plausible that this conclusion is dominated by the data of the 11 other OECD countries where, broadly, the labour force in the agricultural sector was about 9–10 per cent and the percentage of the workforce in the industrial sector was between 24 per cent (Japan) and 39 per cent (Austria) in the mid-1960s. In this case there is a danger of drawing a misleading conclusion for the United Kingdom. Instead of a pooled cross-section time-series data of 12 OECD countries, data on the United Kingdom alone on a time-series basis may be used. The standard production function approach in a simultaneous equation framework is a possibility if data on capital stock and user cost of capital are available for the entire period. The output, labour and capital growth equations can be derived from such a model.

Moreover, the model uses the rate of growth in the non-manufacturing workforce as an exogenous variable, and what is required is an endogenous workforce variable. This implies that all sectors of the economy should be considered together, and output and employment relations for all sectors must be estimated as a complete system of demand equations.

It must be borne in mind that the positive association between $\mathring{Q}_m$ (output growth) and $\mathring{X}$ (exports growth) and $\mathring{Q}_m$ and I (investment–output ratio) does have a precise implication about the direction of causation. It is plausible that the drive for technolgical diffusion (especially imitation) could lead to higher labour productivity and higher competitiveness in world markets, which in turn could yield higher $\mathring{Q}_m$ and $\mathring{X}$. Higher $\mathring{Q}_m$ creates in turn higher derived demand for capital investment, and this will raise the issues on the observed association between variables versus ultimate causes of differences in growth.

ACKNOWLEDGMENTS

The author wishes to thank Mr F. Allen, Mr David Bailey, Dr T. R. Gourvish and the referee for their helpful comments and criticisms, and Mrs S. Bailey for providing valuable computational assistance. Data for the 12 OECD countries, (Austria, Canada, Norway, Belgium, USA, UK, Japan, West Germany, Italy, France, Netherlands and Denmark) can be obtained from the author.

REFERENCES

CRIPPS, T. F. and TARLING, R. J. (1973). *Growth in Advanced Capitalis. Economies,* 1950–1970. Cambridge: University Press, Department of Applied Economics Occasional Paper 40.

CORNWALL, J. (1976). Diffusions, convergence and Kaldor's laws. *Economic Journal,* **86,** 307–314.

GOMULKA, S. (1971). *Inventive Activity and the Stages of Economic Growth.* Aarhus: Institute of Economics.

KALDOR, N. (1966). *Causes of the Slow Rate of Growth of the United Kingdom, An Inaugural Lecture.* Cambridge: University Press.

—— (1975. Economic growth and Verdoorn's law: a comment on Mr Rowthorn's article. *Economic Journal,* **85,** 891–896.

ROWTHORN, R. E. (1975a). What remains of Kaldor's law? *Economic Journal,* **85,** 10–19.

—— (1975b). A reply to Lord Kaldor's comment. *Economic Journal,* **85,** 897–901.

A NOTE ON VERDOORN'S LAW

In a celebrated article, *Fattori che regolano lo sviluppo della produttività del lavoro* (L'Industria 1949), P. J. Verdoorn investigated the relationship between labour productivity and output, using data drawn from a number of different countries. His article is frequently cited in British and American literature, yet, as far as I am aware, has never been published in English, and does not seem to have been read very carefully by those who cite it. The present brief note describes, in a simple fashion, the mathematical model used by Verdoorn and points out some of the limitations of his approach.

Verdoorn makes the following assumptions about employment: (1) industry employs all the labour available at the going wage rate, (2) the supply of labour to industry is influenced by the industrial wage rate, and (3) the wage rate is proportional to industrial productivity. With these assumptions, a rise in industrial productivity causes wages to rise, which attracts new workers from other sectors, notably agriculture, and industrial employment increases. Thus the growth rate e of industrial employment depends on the growth rate p of industrial productivity. Although Verdoorn himself never spelled out this link, his own equations imply the following linear relationship:

$$e = -\frac{\mu}{\rho} + \frac{1}{\rho} p, \tag{1}$$

where μ and ρ are constant, and $1/\rho$ is the elasticity of labour supply with respect to the industrial wage. Since output growth q equals $p+e$, the above equation can be written as,

$$p = \frac{\mu}{1+\rho} + \frac{\rho}{1+\rho} q. \tag{2}$$

Thus, implicit in Verdoorn's model is a linear relationship between p and q which is determined by the conditions of labour supply and is independent of the technology of production.

To complete the model one must specify the technology of production and an investment function. Verdoorn assumes that output Q is related to employment E and capital K by means of a *static* Cobb–Douglas production function of the form

$$Q = E^\alpha K^\beta. \tag{3}$$

After rearrangement this can be written as follows:

$$p = \frac{\beta}{\alpha+\beta} k + \frac{\alpha+\beta-1}{\alpha+\beta} q, \tag{4}$$

where k is the rate of growth of capital *per worker*.[1] It is clear that *in itself* equation (4) does not establish a one to one relationship between p and q, since k is

---

[1] Equation (3) may be written $q = (\alpha+\beta)e+\beta k$. Substituting $e = q-p$ and rearranging gives equation (4).

as yet unspecified. This difficulty does not, however, arise in Verdoorn's own model because of the peculiar nature of his investment function. He assumes that each country invests the same proportion γ of its industrial output and that the capital-output ratio in each country is equal to zero. With these assumptions the stock of industrial capital grows at the same rate γ and therefore capital per worker grows at a rate $k = \gamma - e$. Substituting in equation (4) gives the following productive relationship between p and q,

$$p = \frac{\beta}{\alpha}\gamma + \frac{\alpha - 1}{\alpha}q. \tag{5}$$

Thus, implicit in Verdoorn's model are two distinct equations, (2) and (5), linking productivity growth to output growth, the former equation reflecting labour supply conditions and the latter reflecting investment and technology. Between them they establish *unique* values of p and q given by

$$p = \frac{(1-\alpha)\mu + \rho\beta\gamma}{\omega} \quad \text{and} \quad q = \frac{-\alpha\mu + (1+\rho)\beta\gamma}{\omega}, \tag{6}$$

where $\omega = 1 + \rho - \alpha$.

Verdoorn's article also contains some statistical analysis. He examines the ratio of p to q, which he calls the "elasticity" of productivity with respect to output, and finds that a 10 % increase in output is on average associated with a 4·5 % increase in labour productivity. He also regresses p on q, using data from a number of different countries, and gets a coefficient of q equal to 0·573. This suggests a somewhat stronger relationship in which a 10 % increase in output is associated with a 5·7 % rise in productivity.

These results can be interpreted in a variety of ways, and Verdoorn's own opinions are not entirely clear. However, the thrust of his argument suggests that he sees the association between p and q as evidence about the technology of production and for the existence of increasing returns to scale. The difficulties with this interpretation, and the circumstances under which it is justified, are by now well known, and there is no need to repeat them here. What is more interesting, however, is that Verdoorn interprets his empirical results in a way which is not consistent with his own model. In the first place, the supply of labour to the industrial sector is endogenous in his model, and depends on the level of productivity in the sector. This in itself creates an identification problem which makes it impossible to interpret the observed association between p and q as evidence about the technology of production. Secondly, even if one were able to estimate correctly the productive relationship (5), the coefficient of q would not give an accurate indication of returns to scale. This coefficient is equal to $1 - 1/\alpha$, whereas returns to scale are measured by the sum $\alpha + \beta$.[1]

To conclude, it is interesting to note that there is no technical progress in

---

[1] If one assumes that Verdoorn's regression provides a correct estimate of equation (5) the economic implications are extraordinary. The value of α is then 2·3, which implies that, *with no additional investment*, an extra 10 % in employment leads to an extra 23 % in output! This bizarre result is due to the fact that no allowance is made for differences in the rate of growth of capital stock when estimating the relation between p and q.

Verdoorn's model. There are, it is true, increasing returns to scale, but these are of a purely static kind, and there is no "learning by doing" or any of the other "dynamic economies of scale" upon which later authors have laid so much stress. Each country is assumed to have the same given production function, and changes in output, employment and productivity are caused entirely by shifts along this function. This is clearly a major weakness, as technical progress is an obvious feature of economic development. Moreover, any observed returns to scale are more likely to be the result of a dynamic learning process than of a purely static choice between already known techniques.[1]

Faculty of Economics and Politics, Cambridge R. E. ROWTHORN

Date of receipt of final typescript: June, 1978

[1] My own views on this matter have changed since I criticised Kaldor for his emphasis on dynamic economics, and I now think they are of great practical importance. See "What Remains of Kaldor's Law", ECONOMIC JOURNAL March 1975.

VERDOORN'S LAW IN RETROSPECT: A COMMENT

1. It was gratifying to find Mr Rowthorn's note[1] devoted exclusively to a critical discussion of the theoretical appendix of my 1949 article in *L'Industria*, whereas most authors simply discard it when discussing my so-called 'law'. This gives me the opportunity for some comments on this note as well as on my own conclusions thirty years ago.

2. The model in the appendix aimed to explain the alleged invariance of the long-term elasticity between the growth rates of productivity and output in manufacturing. For this purpose I used Tinbergen's (1942) neoclassical model.[2] Apart from this, the appendix is based on what, at that time, I called the 'normal assumptions of long-period analysis' (section 3 of the main text), namely that the growth-rates of the variables concerned are approximately constant, and hence that their period-averages are roughly representative of what is currently called the steady-state of the system.

To simplify the formulae, the initial values (at $t = 0$) of the variables, also that of capital (b) and output (y), have been put at unity. The investment function $b_t = \gamma y_t$ then leads to $\dot{b}_0/b_0 = \gamma y_0/b_0 = \gamma$. Mr Rowthorn rightly points at this formula being an anomaly in the context of the appendix. In itself, however, it is quite all right if one remembers that by this choice of units γ represents not the ratio of net investments to output but $\gamma = \gamma'/\kappa_0'$ (γ' being the true value of this ratio and κ_0' that of the capital–output ratio at $t = 0$).

It is relevant, however, that following this approach the rate of capital accumulation is constant.[3,4] At the same time I overlooked that the steady-state requires the model to be solved for the asymptotic growth rates, at $t \to \infty$, of capital and output as did, for example, Domar (1946). As a consequence, my final formula for the productivity–output elasticity is burdened by quite a few terms that vanish in the asymptotic case.

3. A correct and at the same time more elegant and readily interpretable form for the elasticity is obtained, as the present author did (1959, with a follow-up in the 1960 report by a group of experts of the European Community), following Domar and Solow by studying the asymptotic growth rates, and replacing the labour demand and supply equations by one single relation for effective labour demand. Denoting labour by a, the system then reduces to:

$$y_t = a_t^\lambda b_t^\mu e^{vt}, \qquad (1)$$

[1] See the March 1979 issue of this JOURNAL, pp. 131–3.
[2] This is, I think, the first example of a model of this kind. Written as it was in German, it has remained little known. An English translation, however, is to be found in his *Selected Papers* (1959).
[3] Since γ' is assumed constant, γ is uniquely determined by the value of κ_t at $t = 0$.
[4] Tinbergen avoided this pitfall and solved the system for $b(t)$, anticipating one of Solow's results (1956, p. 76) by 14 years. Primarily interested in differences in the time-shape of the trends, unlike Domar and Solow, Tinbergen did not analyse the asymptotic case. One wonders whether this foreshadows the misgivings voiced by some later authors as to the *actual* significance of the steady-state.

$$b_t = \gamma y_t, \qquad (2)$$

$$a_t = a_0 e^{\pi t}, \qquad (3)$$

where the production function (1) allows for both economies of scale,[1]

$$\xi = \lambda + \mu > 1,$$

and technical progress.

The time-path of $\dot{y}_t/y_t$ then takes the form

$$\dot{y}_t/y_t = \frac{(\pi\lambda + \nu)}{1-\mu} A_t, \qquad (4)$$

where A_t is given by:

$$A_t = 1 + \mu \frac{\gamma(1-\mu) - \kappa_0(\pi\lambda+\nu)}{\gamma(1-\mu)[e^{(\pi\lambda+\nu)t}-1] + \kappa_0(\pi\lambda+\nu)}, \qquad (5)$$

κ_0 being the initial capital–output ratio.[2]

As is easily verified, $A_t \to 1$ if $t \to \infty$, yielding as the steady-state values of the system:

$$\lim_{t\to\infty} \frac{\dot{y}}{y} = \lim_{t\to\infty} \frac{\dot{b}}{b} = \frac{\pi\lambda+\nu}{1-\mu}, \qquad (6)$$

$$\lim_{t\to\infty} \kappa = \frac{\gamma(1-\mu)}{\pi\lambda+\nu}, \qquad (7)$$

whereas the growth-rates of productivity and the productivity-output elasticity, η, are:

$$\lim_{t\to\infty} d\ln(y/a) = \frac{\pi(\xi-1)+\nu}{1-\mu}, \qquad (8)$$

$$\lim_{t\to\infty} \frac{d\ln(y/a)}{d\ln y} = \lim_{t\to\infty} \eta = \frac{\pi(\xi-1)+\nu}{\pi\lambda+\nu}. \qquad (9)$$

One inference from (7) and (8) is that in the steady-state the neoclassical model degenerates into quasi-complementarity, a fact hinted at by Mr Rowthorn when he states that in my 1949 model the growth-rates of productivity and output are constant (his equation 16).

4. As stated in the footnote on the first page of the 1949 article, the latter is not more than a progress report. With the hindsight of my 1959 publication its main shortcoming, from the operational point of view, was that it insufficiently emphasised that rigid constancy *over time* of the productivity-output elasticity is only to be expected in the steady-state. As a matter of fact, considerable changes in $d\ln(y/a)$ and η_t are to be expected if in the case of disequilibrium growth A_t in (4) differs appreciably from unity. To demonstrate this: let in the case of an

---

[1] See, for a macro-economic justification of economies of scale and their long-run impact on inflation, Verdoorn (1973).

[2] Equations (4) and (5) are obtained by solving the system for b_t in terms of $\dot{b}_t$ and the initial values of the variables. Upon integration and substitution of the resulting expression for b_t in the production function and logarithmic differentiation of the latter (4) and (5) follow.

originally steady-state development, a sudden and permanent change of the investment–output ratio, from γ_0 to γ_1, set in. The value of A_t then becomes

$$A_t = 1 + \mu \frac{\gamma_1 - \gamma_0}{\gamma_1[e^{(\pi\lambda+\nu)t} - 1] + \gamma_0}, \qquad (10)$$

and

$$\eta_t = 1 - \frac{\pi(1-\mu)}{(\pi\lambda + \nu)A_t}, \quad t = 0, ..., \infty. \qquad (11)$$

Table 1. *Effects of Doubling of Net Investment–Output ratio*

($\gamma_1 = 2\gamma_0$; $\xi = 1\cdot1$; $\lambda = 0\cdot734$; $\mu = 0\cdot366$; $\pi = 0\cdot0174$; $\nu = 0\cdot00785$)

	Ratios to asymptotic values		
t	$d \ln (y/a)$	$d \ln y$	η_t
0	1·776	1·361	1·305
1	1·761	1·345	1·301
5	1·647	1·301	1·266
10	1·540	1·251	1·231
15	1·456	1·212	1·201
20	1·357	1·166	1·164
30	1·290	1·135	1·137
40	1·220	1·102	1·107
50	1·170	1·079	1·085
60	1·134	1·062	1·067
80	1·084	1·039	1·043
100	1·054	1·025	1·028
∞	1·000	1·000	1·000
Corresponding absolute steady-state values:			
∞	0·0151	0·0325	0·465

Quantitatively, the effects of a doubling of the investment–output ratio are shown in Table 1 for an arbitrary case. Analogous effects occur if the initial value of the capital–output ratio is too low, i.e. if

$$\kappa_0 < \frac{\gamma(1-\mu)}{\pi\lambda + \nu}. \qquad (12)$$

It is probable that the superposition of these two effects goes far in explaining the boisterous post-war growth in Western continental European countries (an initially too low value of κ_0 followed by a large increase in the rate of saving).

5. Conversely, it should be clear that η's derived from periods subject to disequilibrium growth cannot but yield unreliable values if used for extrapolation under conditions that differ appreciably from those of the period of observation. Nor can they be taken as representative for the steady-state, if A_t – taken as a period average – differs non-negligibly from unity. As suggested by Mr de Vries of Erasmus University a simple test on the existence of the steady-state in the period observed is the equality of $\dot{b}/b$ and $\dot{y}/y$, as required by (6). The condition implied is a necessary but not sufficient one: compensating gradual changes of π and of γ or one or more of the technical coefficients are possible.

A moot point, finally, that also affects *inter-country comparisons*, is that even given steady-state and identical values for the technical coefficients λ, μ and ν, differences in π may lead to quite different values of η. As is seen at a first glance from (9):

$$\lim_{\pi \to 0} \eta = 1 \quad (\nu \neq 0), \tag{13}$$

a situation in manufacturing we have gradually learned to live with.

6. The 'law' that has been given my name appears therefore to be much less generally valid than I was led to believe in 1949.

Erasmus University, Rotterdam   P. J. VERDOORN

Date of receipt of final typescript: October 1979

References

Domar, E. (1946). 'Capital expansion, rate of growth and employment.' *Econometrica*, vol. 14 (April), pp. 137–47.
Office Statistique des Communautés Européennes (1960). 'Méthodes de prévision du développement à long terme.' *Informations Statistiques*, vol. 6 (November/December), pp. 566–70.
Solow, R. M. (1956). 'A contribution to the theory of economic growth.' *The Quarterly Journal of Economics*, vol. 70 (February), pp. 76–7.
Tinbergen, J. (1942). 'Zur Theorie der langfristigen Wirtschaftsentwicklung.' *Weltwirtschaftliches Archiv*, vol. 55.3 (May), pp. 511–49.
——, (1959). 'On the theory of trend movements.' In *J. Tinbergen, Selected Papers*, pp. 182–221. Amsterdam.
Verdoorn, P. J. (1949). 'Fattori che regolano lo sviluppo della produttivitá del lavoro.' *L'Industria*, 1, pp. 3–10.
——, (1959). 'The role of capital in long-range projections.' *Cahiers Économiques de Bruxelles*, vol. 5 (October), pp. 59–69.
——, (1973). 'Some long-run dynamic elements of factor price inflation.' In *Economic Structure and Development; Essays in honour of J. Tinbergen*, pp. 111–37. Amsterdam.

ROWTHORN'S INTERPRETATION OF VERDOORN'S LAW*

Rowthorn (1979) is probably right that many who cite Verdoorn's Law have never read the original article in Italian. I translated the article into English several years ago and circulated copies privately.[1] I find it difficult to agree with Rowthorn's interpretation of the law; in particular, his implied suggestion that the two distinct relationships between productivity growth and output growth, which can be derived from Verdoorn's system of equations, can themselves be interpreted as 'Verdoorn' coefficients. Rowthorn discusses the production relationship derived from the Cobb–Douglas production function (his equation 5) as if $(\alpha - 1)/\alpha$ was a measure of the Verdoorn relationship. This would mean that the Verdoorn coefficient depends only on the *partial* elasticity of output with respect to labour (α), whereas it is clear in Verdoorn's derivation that the coefficient depends on the *total* elasticity of output with respect to labour which includes the effect of scale economies (static and dynamic) and capital deepening. No wonder the 'bizarre' results that Rowthorn refers to in his footnote 1 on page 132. Let us concentrate on the production relationship.

Rowthorn takes the static Cobb–Douglas production function $Q = E^{\alpha} K^{\beta}$ and after a number of unnecessary manipulations derives the equation

$$p = \frac{\beta}{\alpha}\gamma + \frac{\alpha - 1}{\alpha} q, \qquad (1)$$

where p is the rate of growth of labour productivity; q is the rate of growth of output; α is the partial elasticity of output with respect to labour; β is the partial elasticity of output with respect to capital, and γ is the investment ratio which is equal to the rate of growth of capital on the assumption that the capital–output ratio is unity.[2]

The manipulations are unnecessary because the relationship in equation (1) can be derived quite straightforwardly by putting the Cobb–Douglas Function into a rate of growth form, and then using the identity that the rate of change of employment is equal to the rate of change of output minus the rate of change of labour productivity, which yields

$$p = \frac{\beta}{\alpha}\frac{dK}{K} + \frac{\alpha - 1}{\alpha} q. \qquad (2)$$

This is a more general form making no special assumptions about the capital–output ratio. But $(\alpha - 1)/\alpha$ is not Verdoorn's coefficient.[3] Likewise, the coefficient in the labour supply function (Rowthorn's equation 2) is not an independent estimate of Verdoorn's coefficient. It is clear in Verdoorn's paper that the

---

* I am grateful for discussion with my colleague, Dr R. Dixon.
[1] Available on request.
[2] Rowthorn says that Verdoorn assumes that the capital–output ratio is zero but this must be a slip.
[3] If the capital–output ratio is constant, dK/K and q would be perfectly correlated and $(\alpha - 1)/\alpha$ would be picking up the direct and indirect effects of capital accumulation.

two relations together determine jointly the elasticity of labour productivity with respect to output growth, which is the ratio of p to q in Rowthorn's equation (6). This ratio incorporates the *total* elasticity of output with respect to labour.

It may be helpful to describe what Verdoorn does. First, he derives the elasticity of labour productivity with respect to output and then uses the Cobb–Douglas production function to obtain an expression for the total elasticity of output with respect to labour. The elasticity of labour productivity with respect to output is defined as:

$$V = \frac{\frac{d\,(Q/E)}{dt} \Big/ \frac{Q}{E}}{\dot{Q}/Q} = \left(\frac{E}{Q}\right) \frac{E\dot{Q} - Q\dot{E}}{E^2}, \tag{3}$$

where a dot denotes the first derivative with respect to time.

Therefore
$$V = 1 - \frac{\dot{E}/E}{\dot{Q}/Q}. \tag{4)^1}$$

An expression for $(\dot{Q}/Q)/(\dot{E}/E)$ is then derived from the Cobb–Douglas production function by totally differentiating with respect to time and dividing through by $\dot{E}/E$ which gives

$$\frac{\dot{Q}/Q}{\dot{E}/E} = \alpha + \beta \frac{\dot{K}/K}{\dot{E}/E}. \tag{5}$$

Substituting (5) into (4) gives Verdoorn's coefficient as

$$V = 1 - \frac{1}{\alpha + \beta \frac{\dot{K}/K}{\dot{E}/E}}. \tag{6}$$

V is obtained by Verdoorn from the reduced form expressions of the model as a whole. Thus Verdoorn's (own) coefficient explicitly depends on returns to scale and the rate at which capital is growing relative to labour. This specification is very different from Rowthorn's interpretation of Verdoorn where in equation (1) (his equation (5)) the Verdoorn coefficient simply depends on α. The economic implications would indeed be extraordinary! As he says a Verdoorn coefficient of 0·57 would imply $\alpha = 2·3$ and that a 10 % increase in employment would lead to a 23 % increase in output.[2] By contrast using Verdoorn's own coefficient gives much more sensible empirical results. For example, assuming an elasticity of output with respect to capital of 0·3 and a rate of growth of the capital stock four times faster than the rate of growth of employment (which is about the average for developed countries) a Verdoorn coefficient of 0·57 would imply $\alpha = 1·16$, or slightly increasing returns to labour which is what the empirical evidence suggests. It is true that there is not an explicit technical progress term in the production function, but there is no reason to suppose that the elasticity parameters do

---

[1] Equation (4) would be the same as the coefficient on q in equation (1) if the reciprocal of $(\dot{E}/E)/(\dot{Q}/Q)$ were defined as the *partial* elasticity of output with respect to labour, but it is not.
[2] 0·57 was Verdoorn's estimate across countries for the interwar period. Kaldor (1966), who revived Verdoorn's Law, estimated a coefficient of 0·484 for a different set of countries in the post-war period.

not include 'dynamic' effects as well as static returns;[1] and the rate at which capital is growing relative to labour will partly be dependent on the rate of technical progress.

Thus Rowthorn is wrong to conclude that while Verdoorn 'sees the association between p and q as evidence about the technology of production and for the existence of increasing returns to scale' – he 'interprets his empirical results in a way which is not consistent with his own model' because 'the coefficient of q would not give an accurate indication of returns to scale'. Taking Rowthorn's interpretation of Verdoorn in equation (1) this is correct, but is not correct taking Verdoorn's own coefficient. Those who have interpreted the Verdoorn coefficient as a dynamic relationship need not repent.[2] Verdoorn himself says 'one could have expected *a priori* to find a correlation between labour productivity and output, given that the division of labour only comes about through increases in the volume of production; therefore the expansion of production creates the possibility of further rationalisation which has the same effects as mechanisation'. It is precisely because the production function is shifting that Verdoorn rejects its use to estimate future levels of productivity and employment and wants to rely on what he regards to be a fairly constant relationship within countries and over time between productivity growth and output growth.

The stability of the Verdoorn coefficient depends partly on the constancy of $(\dot{K}/K)/(\dot{E}/E)$. Most of the mathematical appendix of Verdoorn's paper is designed to prove that the growth of the capital–labour ratio will be constant, using a system of equations similar to those used by Tinbergen. A realistic estimate of V from Verdoorn's theoretical model is 0·5. One of the reasons why the Verdoorn relation may have broken down in the turbulent years since 1966 (if it has broken down)[3] is the instability of the relationship between capital and labour.

University of Kent at Canterbury   A. P. THIRLWALL

Date of receipt of final typescript: November 1979

References

Dixon, R. and Thirlwall, A. P. (1975). 'A model of regional growth rate differences on Kaldorian lines.' *Oxford Economic Papers*, July.

Kaldor, N. (1966). *Causes of the Slow Rate of Economic Growth of the United Kingdom.* Cambridge University Press.

Rowthorn, R. E. (1979). 'A note on Verdoorn's Law.' Economic Journal, March.

---

[1] If technical progress is embodied in labour and capital and therefore correlated with $\dot{E}/E$ and $\dot{K}/K$, its effect will be included in the estimates of α and β.

[2] There are, of course, other ways in which a relationship between labour productivity growth and output growth can be derived without recourse to the Cobb–Douglas production function. Dixon and Thirlwall (1975) used Kaldor's technical progress function in which the Verdoorn coefficient depends on the rate of induced disembodied technical progress; the degree to which capital accumulation is induced by growth and the extent to which technical progress is embodied in capital. The relationship here is clearly dynamic.

[3] Time series evidence for O.E.C.D. countries prepared by Mr G. Holtham of the O.E.C.D. suggests that it has not broken down.

Kaldor's law and British economic growth: 1800–1970

P. STONEMAN

University of Warwick, Coventry, U.K.

I. SUMMARY

This paper considers the validity of Kaldor's Law when applied to time series data on British economic growth since 1800. The results lead us to the view that the Kaldor hypothesis is not inconsistent with British growth performance over this period, but neither does it merit strong support.

II. KALDOR'S LAW AND BRITISH ECONOMIC GROWTH 1800–1970[1]

In his inaugural lecture Kaldor (1966) hypothesised that Britain's growth performance was closely tied to the principles of Verdoorn's Law. He tested his hypothesis on cross section data for a number of countries post World War II. Here we make an attempt to apply the hypothesis to U.K. economic growth since 1800. Cripps and Tarling (1973) followed Kaldor's application to a cross section sample but their estimation method has led to an interchange between Rowthorn (1975a and b) and Kaldor (1975). In this piece it is also hoped to throw some further light on this controversy.

To attempt such an application of Kaldor's hypothesis is, of course, economic history on the grand scale, and as such ignores much detail. The main reason for pursuing the time series analysis is that apart from generating new results, there are well known econometric problems in mixing time series and cross section data in the manner of the three above authors (see Kmenta, 1971, pp. 508–517) which we are able to overcome. It is felt therefore that the time series approach can yield some useful insights, despite the lack of detail.

---

[1] I would like to thank Peter Law, Keith Cowling, Dennis Leech and others for their helpful comments on earlier drafts.

The major points of Kaldor's argument are:

(1) The growth of gross domestic product is closely related to the growth of manufacturing output but not to the growth of output in other sectors.

(2) In manufacturing, the growth of productivity is closely related to the growth of output (Verdoorn's Law) but in other sectors the growth of productivity is not so related.

(3) The growth of manufacturing output requires increases in the manufacturing labour force, and this increase is at least partly met by running down a pool of under-employed labourers in agriculture.

In what follows we let

P_i = rate of growth of productivity in sector i
e_i = rate of growth of employment in sector i
q_i = rate of growth of output in sector i

where $i = M$ for manufacturing, A for agriculture, G for G.D.P., S for services and NM for the whole non-manufacturing sector.

III. DATA

To test these hypotheses we have collected data on British growth performance since 1800. The main source is Feinstein (1972) with data from 1856, supplemented from Deane and Cole (1969) prior to this, and using Cripps and Tarling's (1973) data for 1965–1970. Care has been taken to standardize for the removal of Southern Ireland for post 1920 data.

All series are defined as logarithimic growth rates, i.e. if we have two observations for t and $t + n$, the growth rate of x is defined as

$$g x = \frac{1}{n} (\log_e x_{t+n} - \log_e x_t)$$

Not surprisingly in certain cases the data are incompatible across sources. We have thus always used Feinstein's data where it exists, in preference to any other, except in the case of employment data. We derived two series on employment, one using Deane and Cole's data to 1920, supplemented by Feinstein, the other using Deane and Cole's data to 1860 supplemented by Feinstein. As both series behaved similarly only results using the first series are presented.[2]

Because of data difficulties we have in general made comparisons of only two sectors, agriculture and manufacturing, in generating our results. This is not felt to be too serious a problem. It should be noted however that in Deane and Cole's data (used for observations to 1860) manufacturing output includes mining and building. Their estimates of output have also been corrected, using the Rousseaux price index (separating manufacturing and agriculture) to generate real output series.

The data on growth rates are presented in the Appendix. As will be seen the time periods over which the growth rates are calculated vary. In an ideal world we would wish to

---

[2] The series refer only to numbers employed. In an ideal world hours worked ought also to be considered but such data is, not surprisingly, unavailable.

compare across cyclical peaks. This we have done for post 1920 data, with peaks 1920, 1925, 1929, 1937; 1951, 1955, 1960, 1969. (There is no comparison pre- and post-second world war). For earlier years, data on all variables only exist for benchmark years (1801, 1811, ... 1911), so we have had to make the calculations across these years. This must introduce some error, but there is no obvious way out of this problem. Unfortunately this procedure does lead to some outlying observations. We must tread warily in using these to derive our estimates (see Rowthorn's (1975a) comment on Cripps and Tarling). Thus, in the estimates presented below, we take care to present results which exclude the years of the Napoleonic wars (1801–1811, 1811–1821), and 1920–1925, which are the main outlying observations. In fact one would not expect war years to fit the general pattern of observations and the 1920–1925 observation is something of an anomaly, as it must be heavily influenced by the ramifications of World War I.

IV. ESTIMATION

We begin by following Kaldor and Cripps and Tarling by estimating Equations 1 and 2 below as tests of Kaldor's first hypothesis relating sectoral growth rates to G.D.P. growth.

$$q_G = \alpha_1 + \beta_1 q_M + \mu_1 \tag{1}$$

$$q_G = \alpha_2 + \beta_2 q_A + \mu_2 \tag{2}$$

The results are presented in Table 1. In Equations a and b the sample is all of Feinstein's data 1856–1965 using annual growth rates. In Equations c and d the sample is all of the data in the Appendix, Equations e–h covering sub-periods. Bracketed figures are t statistics. These

Table 1. *Regression results for Equations 1 and 2*

Variable	Sample							
	1856–1965	1856–1965	1800–1969	1800–1969	1821–1969	1821–1969	1821–1911 1925–1969	1821–1911 1925–1969
N	97	97	18	18	16	16	15	15
name	(a)	(b)	(c)	(d)	(e)	(f)	(g)	(h)
constant	0.010	0.019	0.016	0.021	0.010	0.019	0.010	0.019
	(6.63)	(7.46)	(7.55)	(11.51)	(4.14)	(10.18)	(3.88)	(10.30)
q_M	0.386		0.189		0.446		0.442	
	(15.43)		(2.91)		(5.106)		(4.78)	
q_A		0.135		0.069		0.203		0.218
		(2.62)		(0.87)		(1.851)		(1.99)
R^2	0.715	0.067	0.346	0.045	0.651	0.196	0.637	0.234
D.W.	2.13	1.80	1.993	1.595	1.771	1.670	1.796	1.670
F	238.35	6.66	8.47	0.752	26.07	3.425	22.86	3.96

Dep. variable = q_G.

estimates illustrate:

(a) whereas q_M always has a coefficient significantly different from zero, q_A has so only in one sample and

(b) whereas estimates of Equation 1 yield high R^2 those of Equation 2 are always low.

(c) the removal of outliers and war years does not affect these conclusions.

Such estimates have been taken to support Kaldor's first hypothesis. The problem that arises is essentially that there seems no reason to estimate 1 and 2 as two equations. If it is the case that all sectors could influence the rate of growth of G.D.P., then it would seem appropriate to estimate an equation such as

$$q_G = \alpha_3 + \beta_3 \, q_M + \gamma q_A + \delta q_S + u \tag{3}$$

(where u is an error term assumed to have the properties required for a classical linear regression). However there is also a definitional relationship between all these growth rates:

$$q_G \equiv q_M \frac{M}{G} + q_A \frac{A}{G} + q_S \frac{S}{G} \tag{4}$$

where M/G, A/G, and S/G are sectoral shares in G.D.P. As we do not have data on services and the pure form of the Kaldor hypothesis is that $\gamma = \delta = 0$, we aggregate agriculture and services into a non-manufacturing sector, yielding Equations 5 and 6.

$$q_G = \alpha + \beta_3 q_M + \gamma q_{NM} + u \tag{5}$$

$$q_G = q_M \frac{M}{G} + q_{NM} \frac{NM}{G} \tag{6}$$

Realising that $G = M + NM$ we substitute from Equation 6 into 5 for q_{NM}, and obtain 7.

$$q_G = -\gamma q_M \frac{\frac{M}{G}}{1 - \gamma - \frac{M}{G}} + \alpha_3 \frac{1 - \frac{M}{G}}{1 - \gamma - \frac{M}{G}} + \frac{\beta_3 q_M \left(1 - \frac{M}{G}\right)}{1 - \gamma - \frac{M}{G}} + \frac{u \left(1 - \frac{M}{G}\right)}{1 - \gamma - \frac{M}{G}} \tag{7}$$

If $\gamma = 0$ then Equation 7 reduces to Equation 1. Thus Equation 1 only yields reasonable estimates of the effect of a change in q_M on q_G if a change in q_{NM} has *no* effect on q_G. In all other cases i.e. in general, Equation 1 will yield biased estimates of β_1 using O.L.S. techniques. Similarly only if there is no relationship from q_M to q_G will Equation 2 yield unbiased estimates of the relationship between the rate of growth of G.D.P. and the rate of growth of the non-manufacturing sector. We suggest that one ought to fit Equation 7 to the data to estimate γ and β_3 and thus the relationship between q_G and the rate of growth of the constituent parts of G.D.P.

Equation 7 is non-linear. We use non-linear least squares to estimate the coefficients.[3] Initial estimates yielded very unlikely values of α_3, β_3 and γ and thus we generated two further sets of estimates. First we allowed γ to vary between -1 and $+1$ in steps of 0.1 and estimated α_3 and β_3, secondly we let β_3 vary between -1 and $+1$ in steps of 0.1 and estimated α_3 and γ (note in the former case that Equation 7 is linear for any given γ). As

---

[3] Note that in Equation 6 M/G is in fact the share of manufacturing in the base year and is thus predetermined in Equation 7. Data on M/G are derived from the same sources as the other data.

Kaldor's law and British economic growth 1800–1970

Table 2. *Estimates of Equation 7*

(a) 1800–1969

γ	−1.0	−0.5	−0.1	0.0	0.1	0.2	0.9	1.0
α_3	0.037	0.027	0.018	0.016	0.014	0.012	−0.002	−0.004
	(7.28)	(8.199)	(7.807)	(7.555)	(7.154)	(6.50)	(−2.37)	(−3.62)
β_3	−0.059	0.119	0.173	0.189	0.209	0.236	0.219	0.236
	(−0.47)	(1.238)	(2.480)	(2.910)	(3.394)	(3.897)	(14.666)	(10.86)
10^3 × R.S.S.	0.262	0.288	0.364	0.413	0.503	0.703	0.618	0.424
D.W.	1.914	1.986	2.021	1.993	1.914	1.726	1.689	1.526

(b) 1821–1969

γ	−1.0	−0.5	−0.1	0.0	0.1	0.2	0.9	1.0
α_3	0.026	0.018	0.018	0.010	0.008	0.006	−0.004	−0.006
	(4.191)	(4.224)	(4.199)	(4.139)	(3.99)	(3.64)	(−3.04)	(−3.26)
β_3	0.472	0.455	0.446	0.446	0.449	0.459	0.366	0.364
	(2.073)	(2.911)	(4.438)	(5.106)	(5.96)	(6.99)	(7.30)	(5.60)
10^3 × R.S.S.	0.198	0.198	0.206	0.214	0.233	0.288	0.283	0.262
D.W.	1.72	1.753	1.782	1.771	1.726	1.592	1.16	1.23

Equation 7 does not contain a constant and thus R^2 means very little, we use the residual sum of squares as a measure of goodness of fit. When we assume a value of β_3 the R.S.S. is much higher than if we assume a value of γ. Thus we present only a sample of the preferred results where γ is assumed. These are in Table 2.

Prior to discussing these results it is clear from Equation 7 that the error term does not fulfil the classical requirements for least squares regression. In fact heteroscedasticity is present. This will not lead to biased estimates of the coefficients but will mean that the least squares estimators are not efficient. (Kmenta (1971), pp. 254–256). One can avoid this by transforming all the variables so that the error term is homoscedastic. The reason we have not done this is that for each γ the dependent variable will be different, and thus comparisons of residual sums of squares could not be performed. Holding in mind that our estimated standard errors and t statistics are thus liable to be biased, what can we say of our estimates?

Consider first the results for 1800–1969. The poorest results (in that setting q_G equal to the mean of q_G is preferred) occurred for values of γ between 0.2 and 0.9, i.e. most of the positive quadrant. For values of $\gamma > -0.2$, β_3 attained significance at the 95 per cent level. These results lend reasonable support to β_3 being positive, for a large negative value of γ seems unrealistic. When we remove some of the outliers (Table 2b, the results excluding the 1921–1925 period are similar) the worst results occur for values of γ between 0.5 and 0.7. For all other values of γ, β_3 is estimated as positive and significant, with an approximate value of 0.45 which seems to vary little with γ. There would thus seem some support for considering that the growth of manufacturing output has a positive effect

($\beta_3 > 0$) on the growth of G.D.P. The evidence on the effect of the growth of the non-manufacturing sector is unclear. In the whole sample (Table 2a) the lowest R.S.S. is achieved by large negative values of γ (i.e. $\gamma < -1$), for the restricted sample the lowest R.S.S. is found for $\gamma = -0.7$, although as γ tends to unity the R.S.S. improves (but the $D.W.$ statistic indicates autocorrelation). As we do not expect γ to be a large negative we have reached an impasse. We may say that there is some support for the relationship between q_G and q_M but we cannot draw any conclusion on the relationship between q_G and q_{NM}.

The next step is to test for the existence of Verdoorn's Law in manufacturing. We state the law as that if p is defined as in Equation 8 then in manufacturing, at least, Equation 9 holds, i.e. as the rate of growth of output increases, the rate of growth of productivity increases.

$$p \equiv q - e \tag{8}$$

$$p \equiv \alpha_4 + \beta_4 q, \; \beta_4 > 0 \tag{9}$$

We thus have three relevant variables for each sector, p, q, and e. Kaldor (1975) argues that p_M is endogenous and determined in the manufacturing sector, and e_M is endogenous to the manufacturing sector but q_M is exogenous to the sector. This exogeneity follows from,

(1) the growth of manufacturing output is demand determined, possibly by export demand, which is itself exogenous to the economic system and

(2) there are no supply constraints on q_M, (a) because of Kaldor's third proposition that labour can always be taken from the agricultural sector where there is a pool of under-employed labour and (b) because one can also argue that capital is not a constraint for it is a produced input like any other intermediate input. Thus for the manufacturing sector we propose that the hypothesis can be tested by using ordinary least squares on Equation 9.

In the agricultural sector, obviously e_A is not endogenous because of the pull from the manufacturing sector. Moreover, if there is a pool of unemployed labour in agriculture there will be no relationship between q_A and e_A. Thus if we were to fit Equation 9 to the agricultural sector we would expect to estimate a coefficient on the rate of growth of output equal to unity.[4]

We present in Table 3 O.L.S. estimates of Equation 9 for the manufacturing and agricultural sector. The t statistics in brackets refer to a test of the hypothesis that $\beta_4 = 0$ for manufacturing but that the corresponding coefficient in agriculture is unity.

We have corrected for autocorrelation using a first order auto regressive scheme in those results where a value of ϕ is indicated.

As can be seen from Table 3, the results for manufacturing support the Kaldor hypothesis ($\beta_4 > 0$). In agriculture, our hypothesis of a unitary coefficient is supported by the first two sets of estimates but not the third. The third however requires such a large correction for autocorrelation as to be not considered reliable.

This is not however a complete test of Kaldor's hypothesis for there is a counter proposal (see Rowthorn (1975a)) that the appropriate test of Verdoorn's Law in manufacturing should be one where e_M is considered exogenous and q_M endogenous (to which of course

---

[4] If $p_A = q_A - e_A = \alpha + \beta_4 q_A$ and e_A and q_A are not related we expect to estimate $\beta_4 = 1$.

Kaldor's law and British economic growth 1800–1970

Table 3. Regression results for $p = \alpha_4 + \beta_4 q + u$ (O.L.S. estimates)

	Manufacturing		Agriculture		
	1800–1969	1821–1911 1925–1969	1800–1969	1800–1969	1821–1911 1925–1969
α_4	0.0013	−0.0020	0.0094	0.0230	0.126
	(0.246)	(−0.3712)	(2.379)	(1.507)	(0.694)
β_4^a	0.655	0.759	0.953	0.902	0.772
	(4.112)	(3.987)	(−0.2708)	(−0.917)	(−2.301)
R^2	0.5139	0.5501	0.6533	0.8170	0.9166
D.W.	1.7548	1.4417	0.4765	2.564	1.731
F	16.913	15.896	30.143	66.96	120.83
ϕ	—	—	—	0.859	0.991
N	18	15	18	17	13

[a] t statistics are in brackets. For agriculture the hypothesis that $\beta_4 = 1$ is being tested.

one could add the possibility that p_M is exogenous[5]). If we consider e_M exogenous and q_M endogenous the estimating equation derived from Equation 9 is 10

$$p = \frac{\alpha_4}{1-\beta_4} + \frac{\beta_4}{1-\beta_4} e + u. \qquad (10)$$

From arguments presented previously we expect for agriculture that the coefficient on e_A would be equal to minus unity. In manufacturing, if Verdoorn's Law holds we expect $\beta_4 > 0$ i.e. the coefficient on e_M to be greater than zero. The results of fitting Equation 10 are presented in Table 4 (again the results were corrected for autocorrelation using a first order autogressive scheme but these are not presented). The overall picture from Table 4 is that we still observe the predicted result for agriculture but the estimates for manufacturing no longer support the existence of Verdoorn's Law as a deterministic relationship.

In response to the suggestion that our results may suffer from errors in variables we re-estimated the above relationships using instrumental variables with the lagged independent variable as the instrument. The results are detailed below for Equation 10 applied to agriculture.

$$p_A = 0.0759 - 1.3126\, e_A \qquad R^2 = 0.5598$$
$$(1.541) \quad (0.839) \qquad D.W. = 1.8295$$
$$F = 19.07$$
$$N = 17$$

[5] This possibility belongs to the rival neoclassical or 'sources of growth school' where if one assumes a constant return to scale Cobb–Douglas production function one may write

$$q = t + \alpha \frac{dk}{dt} \times \frac{1}{k} + (1-\alpha)\frac{dL}{dt} \times \frac{1}{L}$$

Here q is endogenous, the rate of growth of factor productivity, t, and the rate growth of labour and capital inputs are exogenous.

Table 4. *Regression results* [a] *(O.L.S. estimates)* $\quad p = \dfrac{\alpha_4}{1-\beta_4} + \dfrac{\beta_4}{1-\beta_4} e + u$

	Manufacturing		Agriculture	
	1800–1969	1800–1911 1925–1969	1800–1969	1800–1911 1925–1969
$\alpha_4/1-\beta_4$	0.022	0.023	0.014	0.0092
	(4.72)	(5.355)	(2.63)	(1.95)
$\beta_4/1-\beta_4$	−0.342	−0.546	−0.903	−1.140
	(−1.128)	(−1.517)	(−0.271)	(−0.477)
R^2	0.074	0.1505	0.2838	0.5371
F	1.273	2.303	6.342	15.0834
ϕ	—	—	—	—
N	18	15	18	15

[a] t statistics are in brackets. The t statistic for the coefficient of e_A tests the hypothesis that the coefficient equals minus unity.

This result showing a t statistic testing the difference of the coefficient on e_A from minus unity, does not lead us to change our view of the agricultural sector i.e. that q_A and e_A are not related, and thus the existence of a pool of unemployed labour (for whatever reason) is not an unfair assumption. As other tests of the Verdoorn relationship using instrumental variables yielded poor results (in terms of R^2), we do not present them. As we have no way of knowing exactly what errors in variables are present however and thus how we ought to compensate for them, we ought not to put too strong an interpretation on these results.

We are thus in the position where we are willing to accept the pool of unemployed labour in agriculture but before accepting or rejecting the existence of Verdoorn's Law in manufacturing we have to decide whether q_M or e_M is exogenous. The best approach would seem to be to postulate a simultaneous relationship.

Kaldor (1975) has suggested that exports, through demand pressures, determine the rate of growth of output, and thus exports are the true exogenous variable. Rowthorn has disputed this by arguing that export growth may well depend on productivity growth. If we postulate a lag in the relationship between exports and output, then this simultaneity may be removed. Thus we can represent the Verdoorn relationship as Equation 11 and the relationship between output growth and export growth (lagged one period) as Equation 12. From the reduced forms, Equations 13 and 14, one can get an estimate of β_4 allowing for possible simultaneity.[6]

Thus if

$$e_M = -\alpha_4 + (1-\beta_4)q_M \qquad (11)$$

[6] Although Equation 12 is not identified, so we cannot estimate its coefficients, the important variable is β_4 and that is identified.

Kaldor's law and British economic growth 1800–1970

and
$$q_M = a + be_M + cX_{MLAG} \tag{12}$$

then
$$q_M = \frac{a - \alpha_4 b}{1 - (1 - \beta_4)b} + \frac{c}{1 - (1 - \beta_4)b} X_{MLAG} \tag{13}$$

and
$$e_M = \frac{(1 - \beta_4)a - \alpha_4}{1 - (1 - \beta_4)b} + \frac{(1 - \beta_4)c}{1 - (1 - \beta_4)b} X_{MLAG} \tag{14}$$

Using the full data set possible[7], we estimated

$$q_M = 0.039 - 0.417 X_{MLAG}$$
$$(6.7709) \quad (-2.296)$$
$$R^2 = 0.26, D.W. = 1.202, F = 5.27, N = 17$$

and

$$e_M = 0.013 - 0.245 X_{MLAG}$$
$$(2.883) \quad (-1.675)$$
$$R^2 = 0.157, D.W. = 1.922, F = 2.81, N = 17$$

These results are not very spectacular,[8] especially the F statistics, but we can estimate

$$1 - \beta_4 = \frac{-0.245}{-0.417} = 0.58580$$

i.e. $\beta_4 = 0.4142$, which is as our hypothesis predicts.

V. CONCLUSIONS

In this paper we have attemped to apply Kaldor's Law, as exemplified by its three propositions above, to data on British economic growth since 1800. Initial investigation of the relationship between the rate of growth of G.D.P. and the rate of growth in its constituent sectors using ordinary least squares regression was extended to allow for a definitional simultaneity. This work led us to accept the first of Kaldor's hypotheses of a deterministic relationship between the rates of growth of G.D.P. and the manufacturing sector but the results with respect to the non-manufacturing sector were inconclusive.

Extending into testing the Verdoorn hypothesis we found that the implications for the relationship between growth rates of the existence of a pool of underemployed labour in agriculture were borne out by a number of estimates, even if we used methods to cater for possible errors in variables.

[7] If we change the data set, the results worsen in that the coefficients on X_{MLAG} are no longer significantly different from zero.
[8] We attribute the negative coefficients on X_{MLAG} to a large value for b.

This pool of labour allows one to argue that labour has not constrained the growth of manufacturing output, which with further discussion leads one to consider the rate of growth of manufacturing output as an exogenous variable. On this basis we find that the Verdoorn hypothesis has support in the manufacturing sector. If however one cannot accept output as exogenous and thus consider employment growth as endogenous, one must move to estimating other relationships. We show that even if both output and employment growth are endogenous we can find some support for the Verdoorn hypothesis in manufacturing.

We conclude therefore that the data on British economic growth over the last 175 years are not inconsistent with Kaldor's hypothesis, but neither are they such as to give strong support to it.

APPENDIX

Data	q_G	q_M	e_{M1}	e_{M2}	q_A	e_{A1}	e_{A2}	X_M
1801–1811	.019	.003	.019	.019	.067	.005	.005	−.0137
1811–1821	.025	.086	.034	.034	.003	.000	.000	.0223
1821–1831	.035	.054	.022	.022	.008	.000	.000	.0151
1831–1841	.023	.015	−.010	−.010	.017	.005	.005	.0287
1841–1851	.022	.031	.016	.016	.037	.010	.010	.0425
1851–1861	.010	.005	.011	.011	−.009	−.004	−.004	.0468
1861–1871	.023	.032	.008	.009	.002	−.009	−.012	.0612
1871–1881	.017	.018	.007	.005	−.004	−.005	−.008	.0239
1881–1891	.019	.021	.013	.001	.006	−.006	−.008	.0142
1891–1901	.021	.017	.014	.008	−.009	−.006	−.007	.0137
1901–1911	.014	.016	.012	.008	.004	.006	−.001	.0409
1920–1925	.017	.017	−.029	−.029	.018	−.019	−.019	.0326
1925–1929	.020	.029	.011	.011	.022	−.011	−.011	.0064
1929–1937	.019	.035	.010	.010	.002	−.018	−.018	−.0331
1950–1955	.028	.037	.012	.012	.013	−.018	−.014	.0292
1955–1960	.024	.028	.006	.006	.031	−.018	−.015	.0235
1960–1965	.033	.031	.003	.003	.030	−.034	−.034	.0362
1965–1969	.023	.028	−.009	.009	−.009	−.036	−.036	.0638

Sources: Growth rates derived from data as follows.

q_G: 1801–1861   Dean and Cole (1969), Table 3.7, p. 166, price deflator from Mitchell and Deane (1962).
      1861–1965   Feinstein (1972), Table 6.
      1965–1969   Cripps and Tarling (1973), p. 56.
q_M 1801–1861   as for q_G.
      1861–1965   Feinstein (1972), Table 51.
      1965–1969   as for q_G.
e_{M1} 1801–1920   Deane and Cole (1969), Table 31, p. 143.
      1920–1968   Feinstein (1972), Table 59.
      1965–1969   as for q_G.

e_{M2}	1801–1861	Deane and Cole (1969), Table 31, p. 143.
	1861–1965	Feinstein (1972), Tables 59 and 60.
	1965–1969	as for q_G.
q_A	1801–1861	as for q_G.
	1861–1965	Feinstein (1972), Table 8.
	1965–1969	as for q_G.
e_{A1}	1801–1920	Deane and Cole (1969), Table 31, p. 143.
	1920–1965	Feinstein (1972), Table 59.
	1965–1969	as for q_G.
e_{A2}	1801–1861	Deane and Cole (1969), Table 31, p. 143.
	1861–1965	Feinstein (1972), Tables 59 and 60.
	1965–1969	as for q_G.
X_M	1801–1871	Mitchell (1971), pp. 62–65.
	1871–1965	Feinstein (1972), Table 15.
	1965–1969	Monthly digest of Statistics, Table 138, price deflators for 1801–1861, implicit national income deflator of Deane and Cole (1969), 1861–1965 Feinstein (1972), Table 61.

Definitions

q_G = rate of growth of gross domestic product
q_M = rate of growth of manufacturing output
e_{M1}, e_{M2} = rate of growth of employment in manufacturing
e_{A1}, e_{A2} = rate of growth of employment in agriculture
q_A = rate of growth of agricultural output
X_M = rate of growth of exports

REFERENCES

Cripps, F. and Tarling R. J. (1973), *Growth in Advanced Capitalist Economies*, Cambridge University Press.
Deane, P. and Cole, W. (1969), *British Economic Growth 1688–1959*, Cambridge University Press.
Feinstein, C. H. (1972), *National Income, Expenditure and Output of the U.K. 1855–1965*, Cambridge University Press.
Kaldor, N. (1966), *Causes of the Slow Rate of Economic Growth of the United Kingdom*, Cambridge University Press.
Kaldor, N. (1975), Economic Growth and the Verdoorn Law, *Economic Journal*, 85, 891–96.
Kmenta J. (1971), *Elements of Econometrics*, Macmillan.
Rowthorn, R. (1975a), What remains of Kaldor's Law?, *Economic Journal*, 85, 10–20.
Rowthorn, R. (1975b), A reply to Lord Kaldor's Comment, *Economic Journal*, 85, 897–901.
Mitchell, B. R. (1971), *The Fontana Economic History of Europe Statistical Appendix 1700–1914*, Fontana.
Mitchell, B. R. and Deane, P. (1962), *Abstract of British Historical Statistics*, Cambridge University Press.

ON THE QUANTITATIVE IMPORTANCE OF KALDOR'S LAWS

Over the past fifteen years or so, the usefulness of the neoclassical paradigm in explaining the persistent disparities in the long term growth rates of the advanced countries has been increasingly questioned. To a large extent, these criticisms stem from two important papers by Lord Kaldor (1966, 1968) where it was argued that the empirical evidence is at variance with two of the fundamental assumptions of the neoclassical approach, namely the prevalence of constant returns to scale, and the equality of the marginal product of labour in all sectors of the economy.

Kaldor argued that for industry as a whole there exist substantial increasing returns to scale. In support of this contention, he cited the famous Verdoorn Law as demonstrating that the marginal product of labour in industry is nearly twice its average product. The Verdoorn Law is an empirical generalization based on the regression of the growth of industrial productivity on that of output, namely

$$p_{IND} = \alpha_1 + \beta_1 q_{IND} \tag{1}$$

where p_{IND} and q_{IND} are the growth rates of industrial productivity (output per man) and output, respectively.

When equation (1) is estimated on the basis of cross-country data for both the inter-war period and the years 1950 to 1965, it is found that the estimate of β_1 is significantly different from zero and takes a value of approximately one half. In other words, an increase in the growth of output by one percentage point induces an increase in the productivity growth rate by half a percentage point and economic growth is seen as progressing in a cumulative manner. In his inaugural lecture, Kaldor (1966) attributed the slow post-war rate of productivity growth of the United Kingdom to the fact that, alone of all the advanced countries, this nation experienced a labour shortage which constrained the growth of industrial output. This prevented the United Kingdom from benefiting from the gain in productivity growth due to increasing returns to such an extent as the faster growing countries.

On the basis of subsequent evidence, Kaldor (1975) later revised this view, believing now that even in the case of the United Kingdom, the growth of output was demand, rather than supply, constrained. Related to this is Kaldor's second tenet, namely that an economy is not 'resource constrained' merely because it is at 'full employment'. Kaldor argues that there is surplus labour in much of the non-industrial sector with a consequence that a reduction in the level of employment would not result in a concomitant reduction in output. The advanced countries are in fact 'dual economies'. The implications of this are far reaching since the fundamental determinant of the growth of total productivity is the growth of the exogenous components of demand. Furthermore, Kaldor argues that (omitting a footnote)

(the) higher the rate of growth of industrial output which these demand conditions permit, the faster will be the rate at which labour is transferred from the surplus-sectors to the high-productivity sectors. It is my contention that it is the rate at which this transfer takes place which determines the growth rate of productivity as a whole. The mechanism by which this happens is only to a minor extent dependent on the *absolute* differences in the levels of output per head between the labour-absorbing sectors and the surplus-labour sectors. The major part of the mechanism consists of the fact that the *growth* of productivity is accelerated as a result of the transfer at both ends — both at the gaining-end and the losing-end; in the first, because, as a result of increasing returns, productivity in industry will increase faster, the faster output expands; in the second because when the surplus-sectors lose labour, the productivity of the remainder of the working population is bound to rise. (1968, p. 386)[1]

In support of this contention, Kaldor (1975) later adduced the 'Third Law' which is inferred from the regression of the equation

$$p_{GPD} = \alpha_2 + \beta_2 q_{IND} + \beta_3 e_{NI} \qquad (2)$$

where p_{GDP}, q_{IND} and e_{NI} are the growth rates of Gross Domestic Product per man, industrial output and non-industrial employment, respectively. The estimation of equation (2) using cross-country data yields a good fit with estimates for β_2 and β_3 of approximately 0.35 and −0.65. Consequently, Kaldor argues that this confirms his thesis of the importance of the growth of industrial output and the transfer of labour from the non-industrial sector (the latter being evidenced by the statistical significance of the coefficient of the growth of non-industrial employment) in determining the growth of total productivity. However, recently, McCombie (1979) has argued that an underlying identity vitiates any attempt to give the Third Law any behavioural explanation.

Moreover, the specification of the Verdoorn Law has been subject to a number of well-known criticisms (Rowthorn, 1975a, 1975b, 1979, Kaldor, 1975). The most notable objection to Kaldor's procedure arises from the fact that if employment is taken to be the independent variable and if Japan is omitted from the sample, the regression results provide no support for the hypothesis of increasing returns to scale (although, of course, Kaldor maintains that such a procedure is mis-specified since output, not employment, growth is the exogenous variable). It is not the purpose of this article to pursue any further these controversies (although we shall have occasion to return briefly to the Rowthorn–Kaldor debate), but rather to attempt to quantify the extent to which Kaldor's thesis of the reallocation of labour may explain the international differences in total productivity growth.[2] To accomplish this, use is made of a standardization technique which enables us to calculate the contribution to total productivity growth of the inter-sectoral transfer of labour on the basis of a number of assumptions concerning the degree of returns to scale and whether or not surplus labour exists in a particular sector of the economy.

---

[1] The neoclassical 'growth accounting approach' of Denison (1967) also stresses the importance of economies of scale and under-employment of agricultural labour, but the attempt to reconcile this with the explicit use of the neoclassical marginal productivity theory of distribution is not convincing.

[2] For a discussion of the evidence concerning the existence of dual economies in the advanced countries, see Cornwall (1977).

The Growth of Total Productivity and Its Standardized and Structural Components

The level of total labour productivity at time t may be defined as

$$P_{WE}(t) \equiv \frac{Q_{WE}(t)}{E_{WE}(t)} \tag{3}$$

where Q and E are the levels of output and employment, respectively, and the subscript WE denotes the whole economy. Equation (3) may be written as the weighted average of each sector's productivity,

$$P_{WE}(t) \equiv \sum_i \frac{Q_i(t)}{E_i(t)} \cdot \frac{E_i(t)}{E_{WE}(t)} \equiv \sum_i P_i(t) a_i(t) \tag{4}$$

where i denotes the three sectors that are considered, namely, agriculture (AG) industry (IND) and the rest of the economy (ROE). Hence, a_i is the sectoral share of total employment.

The exponential growth rate per annum of total productivity is given by

$$p_{WE} \equiv \frac{100}{T} \left\{ ln\left(\sum_i P_i(t) a_i(t)\right) - ln\left(\sum_i P_i(o) a_i(o)\right) \right\} \% \tag{5}$$

where (o) and (t) denote the initial and terminal years of the period lasting T years.

Following the approach of an early United Nations' study (1964), this may be disaggregated to give

$$p_{WE} \equiv \frac{100}{T} \left\{ \left[ln\left(\sum_i P_i(t) a_i(o)\right) - ln\left(\sum_i P_i(o) a_i(o)\right) \right] \right.$$
$$\left. - \left[ln\left(\sum_i P_i(t) a_i(t)\right) - ln\left(\sum_i P_i(t) a_i(o)\right) \right] \right\} \% \tag{6}$$

The expression in the first square bracket on the right-hand side of equation (6) may be termed the standardized productivity growth and is the increase in productivity that would have occurred if employment in all sectors had grown at the same rate. In other words, the standardized level of total productivity at time t is given by

$$\sum_i P_i(t) a_i(o) \equiv \sum_i \frac{P_i(t) E_i(o) e^{\phi T}}{E_{WE}(t)} \equiv \sum_i \frac{Q_i^*(t)}{E_{WE}(t)} \tag{7}$$

where 100ϕ is the percentage growth rate per annum of total employment.

$Q_i^*(t)$ may be termed the standardized level of output of sector i at time t. This is the hypothetical level of output that would have occurred if the sector had experienced its observed level of productivity at time t but if its employment had grown at the rate of the total labour force.

The terms in the second square bracket of equation (6) (the structural component) provide a measure of the increase in total productivity due to variations in the sectoral employment growth rates being associated with the differences in the sectoral levels of productivity. This procedure is equivalent to assuming that constant returns to scale prevail in all sectors and that sectoral productivity increases at an exogenously determined rate which is independent of the transfer of labour. Employment is thus assumed to be limitative throughout the economy. These are, of course, the usual neoclassical assumptions which are so severely criticized by Kaldor, and it is convenient to term them collectively *Assumption A*.

In the light of Kaldor's strictures, a more interesting exercise is to relax these postulates. Under *Assumption B* we assume that surplus labour exists in agriculture, but, for the moment, the assumption of constant returns in the other sectors is retained. The assumption of surplus labour means that the marginal productivity of labour is zero and the growth of agricultural output is unaffected by the growth of employment in this sector. It follows that the standardized level of output in agriculture at time t is identical to that which is actually observed, since the fact that we assume that employment only grows at the rate of the total labour force will not alter the growth of output. In other words, $Q^*_{AG}(t) = Q_{AG}(t)$. Therefore, the contribution that the agricultural sector makes to the standardized level of productivity is $Q_{AG}(t)/E_{WE}(t)$ or, equivalently $P_{AG}(t)a_{AG}(t)$. The standardized growth of total productivity is given by

$$P_{WE} \equiv \frac{100}{T} \left\{ ln\left(P_{AG}(t)a_{AG}(t) + P_{IND}(t)a_{IND}(0) + P_{ROE}(t)a_{ROE}(0)\right) - ln\left(\sum_i P_i(0)a_i(0)\right)\right\} \% \qquad (8)$$

The growth of the structural component is again the difference between the observed and the standardized productivity growth.

Under *Assumption C*, the hypothesis of surplus labour is extended to the whole of the non-industrial sector. (In the limit, if surplus labour exists in all sectors of the economy, the observed and standardized productivity growth rates would be identical since, of course, with total output growth independent of that of employment, the inter-sectoral reallocation of labour would have no influence on the growth of total productivity.)

We turn next to Kaldor's contention of the importance of economies of scale in industry in conjunction with the transfer of labour as a determinant of total productivity growth.

If increasing returns exist in industry, the growth of productivity in this sector will no longer be independent of the growth of employment and, hence, of the transfer of labour. The relationship between the growth of productivity and employment may be derived from the Verdoorn Law (equation (1). Since $p_{IND} \equiv q_{IND} - e_{IND}$, the former is given by

$$p_{IND} = \alpha_3 + \beta_4 e_{IND} \qquad (9)$$

where β_4 takes a value of unity since the Verdoorn coefficient (β_1) is one half. The Rowthorn–Kaldor debate is germane to the way the value of β_4 is derived. If equation (5) were to be estimated directly, Rowthorn (1975a) has shown that the estimate of β_4 would not differ significantly from zero (when Japan is omitted from the sample as an outlier). However, following Kaldor, we are now assuming that surplus labour exists within the non-industrial sector with the consequence that output growth is demand, and not supply, constrained.

Hence, the correct procedure is to derive the value of β_4 from the estimate of β_1 using the identity mentioned above.

Since, in calculating the standardized growth of productivity, we assume that all sectors grow at the rate of growth of total employment, the growth of standardized industrial productivity is given by

$$p^*_{IND} = p_{IND} - e_{IND} + e_{WE} \qquad (10)^1$$

Under *Assumption D*, where increasing returns in industry and surplus labour in agriculture are present, the growth of standardized total productivity is given by

$$p^*_{WE} \equiv \frac{100}{T} \left\{ ln\left(P_{AG}(t)a_{AG}(t) + P_{IND}(0)e^{\rho T}a_{IND}(0) + P_{ROE}(t)a_{ROE}(0)\right) - ln\left(\sum_i P_i(0)a_i(0)\right) \right\} \% \qquad (11)$$

where $\rho = p^*_{IND}/100$.

Finally, we assume increasing returns in industry and surplus labour in both agriculture and the rest of the economy (*Assumption E*).

It must be emphasized that the standardization technique can only be regarded as yielding an indication of the likely order of magnitude of the gains in total productivity growth induced by the transfer of labour. Like many standardization techniques, the method used here is dependent upon the level of aggregation chosen and ignores any possible gains derived from the intra-sectoral reallocation of labour. Of course, if there is surplus labour in a sector, there can be no gains due to intra-sectoral transfer of labour. Moreover, the United Nations' study (1964) found negligible gains due to the reallocation of labour within industry. The technique also neglects the undoubtably important relationship between the transfer of labour and the accumulation of capital. Furthermore, as the Verdoorn Law is a statistical rather than an exact relationship, taking β_4 to be equal to unity for all countries may introduce a further error into the calculations.

The Results

Before discussing the results of the standardization, it is worth briefly mentioning the well known reservations that arise concerning the reliability of the statistics for the growth of service real output. Data for the sectoral levels of output (measures at constant prices) and numbers employed are taken from the O.E.C.D. National Accounts and Labour Force Statistics, respectively. A problem arises because the indicator of real output growth in much of the tertiary sector consists simply of employment changes with either no allowance imputed for productivity growth or only an arbitrary adjustment made. (See, for example, Hill and McGibbon (1966)). This measurement problem, of course, affects all studies (including the neoclassical growth accounting

---

[1] An alternative procedure would be to ascribe the *total* gain in industrial productivity due to increasing returns to the structural component. In this case equation (10) becomes

$$p^*_{IND} = p_{IND} - e_{IND} \qquad (10a)$$

TABLE I

TOTAL PRODUCTIVITY GROWTH AND THE STANDARDIZED AND STRUCTURAL COMPONENTS

Country	PERIOD 1950–65				PERIOD 1965–73			
	(1) Productivity growth	(2) Standardized productivity growth	(3) Structural productivity growth	(4) Column (3) as a percentage of column (1)	(1) Productivity growth	(2) Standardized productivity growth	(3) Structural productivity growth	(4) Column (3) as a percentage of column (1)
Assumption A. (*The contribution of the transfer of labour on the assumption of constant returns in all sectors*)								
Japan	7.64	6.44	1.20	15.7	8.64	7.64	1.00	11.5
West Germany	4.95	4.32	0.63	12.7	4.59	4.36	0.23	4.9
Italy	4.20	3.64	0.56	13.3	5.21	4.61	0.60	11.6
France	4.91	4.35	0.56	11.4	4.51	4.21	0.31	6.9
Netherlands	3.71	3.73	−0.02	−0.5	4.55	4.58	−0.03	−0.7
Denmark	3.65	3.39	0.26	7.1	3.42	3.18	0.24	7.0
Austria	4.79	4.16	0.63	13.2	6.04	5.53	0.51	8.4
Canada	2.41	2.21	0.20	8.3	2.14	2.14	0.00	0.0
Norway	3.83	3.36	0.47	12.3	3.54	3.10	0.44	12.4
Belgium	3.06	3.06	0.00	0.0	4.15	4.17	−0.02	−0.4
United States	2.34	2.20	0.14	6.0	1.78	1.80	−0.02	−1.1
United Kingdom	2.05	2.03	0.02	1.0	2.75	2.68	0.07	2.5
Assumption B. (*The contribution of the transfer of labour on the assumption of surplus labour in agriculture, constant returns in the other two sectors*)								
Japan	7.64	5.83	1.81	23.7	8.64	7.18	1.46	16.9
West Germany	4.95	3.98	0.97	19.6	4.59	4.19	0.40	8.7
Italy	4.20	2.87	1.33	31.7	5.21	4.04	1.17	22.4
France	4.91	4.00	0.91	18.5	4.51	4.83	0.68	15.0
Netherlands	3.71	3.23	0.48	12.9	4.55	4.35	0.20	4.4
Denmark	3.65	2.66	0.99	27.1	3.42	2.62	0.70	20.5
Austria	4.79	3.77	1.02	21.2	6.04	5.27	0.77	12.7
Canada	2.41	1.56	0.85	35.3	2.14	1.91	0.23	10.9
Norway	3.83	2.97	0.86	22.4	3.54	2.75	0.79	22.2
Belgium	3.06	2.79	0.27	8.8	4.15	3.89	0.26	6.3
United States	2.34	1.97	0.37	15.8	1.78	1.67	0.11	6.4
United Kingdom	2.05	1.89	0.16	7.8	2.75	2.58	0.17	6.2

Continued overleaf

TABLE I

TOTAL PRODUCTIVITY GROWTH AND THE STANDARDIZED AND STRUCTURAL COMPONENTS

Country	PERIOD 1950–65				PERIOD 1965–73			
	(1) Productivity growth	(2) Standardized productivity growth	(3) Structural productivity growth	(4) Column (3) as a percentage of column (1)	(1) Productivity growth	(2) Standardized productivity growth	(3) Structural productivity growth	(4) Column (3) as a percentage of column (1)

Assumption C. (The contribution of the transfer of labour on the assumption of constant returns in industry, surplus labour in the other two sectors)

Japan	7.64	6.58	1.06	13.9	8.64	7.74	0.90	10.4
West Germany	4.95	4.18	0.77	15.6	4.59	4.54	0.05	1.1
Italy	4.20	3.61	0.59	14.0	5.21	4.95	0.26	5.0
France	4.91	4.34	0.57	11.6	4.51	4.51	0.00	0.0
Netherlands	3.71	3.60	0.11	3.0	4.55	5.03	−0.48	−10.5
Denmark	3.65	2.85	0.80	21.9	3.42	3.43	−0.01	−0.3
Austria	4.79	4.66	0.13	2.7	6.04	5.83	0.21	3.5
Canada	2.41	2.42	−0.01	−0.4	2.14	2.54	−0.40	−18.7
Norway	3.83	3.69	0.14	3.6	3.54	3.56	−0.02	−0.6
Belgium	3.06	2.92	0.14	4.6	4.15	4.41	−0.26	−6.2
United States	2.34	2.39	−0.05	−2.1	1.78	2.11	−0.33	−18.5
United Kingdom	2.05	1.94	0.11	5.4	2.75	3.07	−0.32	−11.6

Assumption D. (The contribution of the transfer of labour on the assumption of increasing returns in industry, surplus labour in agriculture and constant returns in the rest of the economy)

Japan	7.64	4.88	2.76	36.1	8.64	6.31	2.33	27.0
West Germany	4.95	3.26	1.69	34.1	4.59	4.13	0.46	10.0
Italy	4.20	2.31	1.89	45.0	5.21	3.77	1.44	27.6
France	4.91	3.44	1.47	29.9	4.51	3.84	0.67	14.9
Netherlands	3.71	3.11	0.60	16.2	4.55	4.89	−0.34	−7.5
Denmark	3.65	1.91	1.74	47.7	3.42	2.64	0.78	22.8
Austria	4.79	3.63	1.16	24.2	6.04	5.06	0.98	16.2
Canada	2.41	1.58	0.83	34.4	2.14	2.34	−0.20	−9.3
Norway	3.83	2.81	1.02	26.6	3.54	2.57	0.97	27.4
Belgium	3.06	2.65	0.41	13.4	4.15	4.17	−0.02	−0.5
United States	2.34	2.03	0.31	13.2	1.78	2.02	−0.24	−13.5
United Kingdom	2.04	1.79	0.25	12.2	2.75	2.93	−0.18	−6.5

TABLE 1 — continued

Assumption E. *(The contribution of the transfer of labour on the assumption of increasing returns in industry, surplus labour in the other two sectors)*

Japan	7.64	5.72	1.92	25.1	8.64	6.90	1.74	20.1
West Germany	4.95	3.49	1.46	29.5	8.59	4.49	0.10	2.2
Italy	4.20	3.10	1.10	26.2	5.21	4.70	0.51	9.8
France	4.91	3.81	1.10	22.4	4.51	4.51	0.00	0.0
Netherlands	3.71	3.48	0.23	6.2	4.55	5.56	−1.01	−22.2
Denmark	3.65	2.12	1.53	41.9	3.42	3.45	−0.03	−0.9
Austria	4.79	4.53	0.26	5.4	6.04	5.62	0.42	−7.0
Canada	2.41	2.43	−0.02	−0.8	2.14	2.96	−0.82	−38.3
Norway	3.83	3.54	0.29	7.6	3.54	3.17	−0.37	−10.5
Belgium	3.06	2.78	0.28	9.2	4.15	4.68	−0.53	−12.8
United States	2.34	2.45	−0.11	−4.7	1.78	2.45	−0.67	−37.6
United Kingdom	2.04	1.83	0.21	10.3	2.75	3.42	−0.67	−24.4

Note: Periods covered

Country	1950–65	1965–73
Japan	1953–64	1964–69
West Germany	1951–65	1965–73
Italy	1951–63	1963–73
France	1957–64	1964–73
Netherlands	1951–65	1965–73
Denmark	1957–65	1965–69
Austria	1957–66	1966–73
Canada	1951–66	1966–73
Norway	1951–65	1965–70
Belgium	1951–64	1964–73
United States	1951–66	1966–73
United Kingdom	1951–65	1965–73

Sources: OECD National Accounts (various years)
OECD Labour Force Statistics (various years)

approach) that are concerned with service, and hence total, output growth rates. This also provides another reason why the results must be regarded with a certain amount of caution.

The two components of productivity growth were calculated for the twelve advanced countries for two post-war sub-periods and the results are reported in Table 1. The first time span covers the years approximately from 1950 to 1965, while the second is from 1965 to 1973. During the latter period there is evidence of a 'shake-out' of labour in the industrial sectors of the advanced countries. It is not coincidental that the Verdoorn Law breaks down in a statistical sense during this time. 1973 was chosen as the terminal year as it is the last peak year of the post-war growth cycles. (For three countries statistical discontinuities meant that either 1969 or 1970 had to be chosen as the last year.)

The results under *Assumption A* confirms both the United Nations' findings and Kaldor's contention that differences in the sectoral levels of productivity by themselves explain only a small proportion of the growth of total productivity. In absolute terms, the greatest contribution which the structural component makes occurs in the case of Japan where it accounts for a growth rate of about one percentage point per annum in both sub-periods. Nevertheless, even here this comprises less than 16% of the total growth rate. For seven of the countries (nine in 1965–73), the gain is less than half of one percentage point per year.

Once surplus labour in agriculture is postulated, the transfer of labour makes a considerably greater contribution even though constant returns are still assumed to prevail in industry (*Assumption B*). Not surprisingly, the greatest effect is found once again in Japan where the growth of the structural component is 1.81% and 1.46% per annum in the first and second periods, respectively. This is closely followed by Italy (1.33% and 1.17% per annum). It may be objected that the assumption of surplus labour is unrealistic in the case of those countries with a high level of observed agricultural productivity (e.g. the United Kingdom and the United States). However, the numbers transferred in these countries are sufficiently small that, even under this assumption, they make little contribution to the overall productivity growth. In the second sub-period, the gains from the reallocation of labour are diminished as the size of the transfer becomes smaller.

At first sight, it may seem somewhat paradoxical that the gains become smaller (and negative in the case of two countries in the first period and seven in the second period) when we introduce Kaldor's more controversial assumption of surplus labour in the whole of the non-industrial sector (*Assumption C*). The reason is quite straight forward. Unlike the case of agriculture, the observed rate of growth of employment in the rest of the non-industrial sector in all countries exceeded the growth of the total labour force, regardless of the period under consideration. Thus, the standardized rate of growth of employment is less than that which actually occurred and this in conjunction with the assumption of surplus labour (which, as has been mentioned, means that the standardized growth of output is the same as the observed) means that the standardized growth of productivity in the rest of the economy exceeds the observed growth rate. As may be seen from the table, this reduces the contribution that the structural component makes, so that in 1950–65 it is not much greater than under *Assumption A*. In the second period, for several countries, it is, in fact, smaller.

QUANTITATIVE IMPORTANCE OF KALDOR'S LAW

The greatest contribution that is made by the transfer of labour occurs when we combine the postulate of increasing returns in industry with surplus labour in agriculture alone (*Assumption D*). During 1950–65, the structural component accounts for over 30% of total productivity growth in five of the countries.[1] For the period 1965–73, we retain the assumption that β_4 is unity, even though the Verdoorn Law has broken down. As the slower growth of industrial employment has not been associated with a commensurate reduction in the growth of industrial productivity, this reduces the effect of the interaction of the transfer of labour and increasing returns. Consequently, as there are also fewer workers transferred during this latter period, the structural component is reduced for all countries. It is interesting to note that the reduction in the component was not accompanied by a reduction in total productivity but that rather there was a concomitant rise in the standardized productivity growth. In both periods, there is a tendency for the growth of the structural component to be greatest for those countries which had the greatest growth rates of productivity: the Spearman rank correlation coefficients of 0.804 (1950–65) and 0.664 (1965–73) being significant at the 0.05 confidence level.

Introducing the asumption of surplus labour in the rest of the economy (*Assumption E*) once again reduces the contribution of the reallocation of labour. While the structural component still accounts for over 20% of the total productivity growth in five of the countries in 1950–65, in the period 1965–73 it makes a negative contribution in the case of eight countries. Nevertheless the Spearman rank correlation coefficient of 0.757 which is found in both sub-periods between the growth of productivity and that of the structural component is still significant at the 0.05 confidence level.

To conclude; the results suggest that Kaldor is correct, at least for the period 1950–65, in his emphasis on the importance of the transfer of labour if surplus labour exists in agriculture. On the other hand, the influence of the re-allocation of labour is much weaker once it is hypothesized that surplus labour exists in the whole of the non-industrial sector. Nevertheless, in spite of the stress Kaldor has placed on the effect of the transfer of labour, this is by no means an indispensable element in his explanation of 'why growth rates differ'. International differences in the growth of productivity are, by definition, the result of variations in both the growth of employment and output. Under the assumption of surplus labour, the growth of employment in the non-industrial sector is due to the difference in demand for industrial employment and the growth of the labour force. Since the former was not large enough relative to the latter to cause a substantial net transfer of labour, the key to the understanding of the differences in productivity growth lies in explaining the large differences between countries in the growth of the demand for output. This stands in marked contrast to the neoclassical approach with its emphasis on the supply side.

J. S. L. McCOMBIE

UNIVERSITY OF HULL

Date of receipt of final typescript: July 1980

---

[1] If we adopt the alternative procedure for calculating the standardized productivity growth outlined in footnote 3, the structural component explains an even greater proportion of total productivity growth ranging from Canada where it accounts for 70.1% to Belgium (19.6%).

REFERENCES

Cornwall, J. (1977), *Modern Capitalism. Its Growth and Transformation*. Martin Robertson.

Denison, E. (1967), *Why Growth Rates Differ. Postwar Experience in Nine Western Countries* The Brookings Institution, Washington, Mass.

Hill, A. T. P. and McGibbon, J. (1966), 'Growth of Sector Real Product: Measure and Methods in Selected O.E.C.D. Countries'. *Review of Income and Wealth*, series 12, pp. 35–55.

Kaldor, N. (1966), *Causes of the Slow Rate of Growth in the United Kingdom, An Inaugural Lecture*. Cambridge University Press.

Kaldor, N. (1968), 'Productivity and Growth in Manufacturing Industry: A Reply', *Economica*, Vol. 35, pp. 385–91.

Kaldor, N. (1975), 'Economic Growth and the Verdoorn Law: A Comment on Mr Rowthorn's Article', *Economic Journal*, Vol. 85, pp. 891–96.

McCombie, J. S. L. (1979), 'What Still Remains of Kaldor's Laws?', forthcoming, *Economic Journal*, March 1981.

Rowthorn, R. E. (1975a), 'What Remains of Kaldor's Law?', *Economic Journal*, Vol. 85, pp. 10–19.

Rowthorn, R. E. (1975b), 'A Reply to Lord Kaldor's Comment', *Economic Journal*, Vol. 85, pp. 897–901.

Rowthorn, R. E. (1979), 'A Note on Verdoorn's Law', *Economic Journal*, Vol. 89, pp. 131–33.

United Nations Economic Commission for Europe (1964), *Economic Survey of Europe in 1961, Part 2; Some Factors in Economic Growth in Europe during the 1950s*. Geneva.

Excerpt from D. Currie, R. Nobay and D. Peel (eds), *Macroeconomic Analysis: Essays in Macroeconomics and Econometrics*, 405–29.

14. VERDOORN'S LAW - THE EXTERNALITIES HYPOTHESIS AND ECONOMIC GROWTH IN THE U.K.

M. Chatterji and M. Wickens

Introduction

In a pioneering paper Kaldor (1966) put forward the view that in order for an economy to achieve a higher rate of economic growth it is necessary to raise the rate of growth of manufacturing output and this could be achieved by transfers of labour from the non-manufacturing to the manufacturing sector. Kaldor argued that the main engine of this growth is the presence of Verdoorn's Law in manufacturing. Using cross-section data from twelve countries, Kaldor tested Verdoorn's Law and found it to be broadly supported.

Our purpose in this paper is to re-assess Kaldor's views using quarterly time series data for the U.K. for the period 1961-1977. First, we wish to test Verdoorn's Law with these data. Secondly, we wish to analyse the effects on economic growth of factors other than Verdoorn's Law and in particular we wish to analyse the effect of the Externalities Hypothesis. Finally, we wish to reconsider Kaldor's proposition about the effects of a labour transfer on the growth of output in the U.K.

In Section 1 we discuss Verdoorn's Law, the Externalities Hypothesis and Kaldor's Proposition regarding the transfer of labour. A simple two sector growth model is constructed to analyse the relationship between these hypotheses. In Section 2 we briefly review the literature on Verdoorn's Law and discuss some of the issues raised by the debate. In Section 3, we report estimates of some simple models suggested by Kaldor in order to test Verdoorn's Law, the Externalities Hypothesis and Kaldor's Proposition. These simple static specifications are found to be inadequate. Accordingly in Section 4, we generalise these simple models by the addition of further explanatory variables and a dynamic structure. In Section 5 we report estimates of these more general models which are shown to be much more satisfactory than the simple models of Section 3. Section 6 contains an evaluation of the quantitative importance of Kaldor's Proposition and Section 7 contains our conclusions.

Section 1 : Verdoorn's Law, the Externalities Hypothesis, and Kaldor's Proposition

In his Inaugural Lecture, Kaldor (1966) put forward the proposition that a transfer of labour from agriculture and services to manufacturing thereby increasing the rate of employment growth in manufacturing and reducing the rate of employment growth in agriculture and services, will permit faster growth of the economy as a whole. This proposition we shall refer to throughout as Kaldor's Proposition. Kaldor viewed his proposition as being a direct consequence of the presence of Verdoorn's Law in manufacturing.[1] Verdoorn's Law states quite simply that there is a positive relationship between the rate of productivity growth and employment growth, viz:

$$p_m = \alpha + \beta e_m , \quad \beta > 0 \qquad (1)$$

where p_m is the proportional rate of productivity growth in manufacturing and e_m is the proportional rate of employment growth in manufacturing. Thus the greater is employment growth in manufacturing industries the larger will be output growth in manufacturing and, as a result, in the whole economy.

In addition to this direct effect on total output of employment growth in manufacturing, Kaldor also suggested that there would be a secondary effect operating through induced productivity growth in non-manufacturing. Thus Kaldor says "...the rate of growth of manufacturing production...will tend, indirectly, to raise the rate of productivity growth in other sectors". Kaldor (1966 p.18). We shall call this proposition the Externalities Hypothesis, as it suggests that the manufacturing sector generates external economies in which the growth of manufacturing output is positively related to productivity growth in non-manufacturing industries. Presumably part of these external economies is technical progress which is embodied in new machines.

According to our interpretation, therefore, Kaldor's Proposition is about the effect of employment growth in manufacturing on the total growth of output and rests on two hypotheses. The first, and the most important, is the presence of Verdoorn's Law in manufacturing, and the second is the Externalities Hypothesis.

Cripps and Tarling have put forward an even stronger proposition: "The suggestion is that even in the absence of increases in the labour force, transfers of labour from agriculture and services to manufacturing employment will permit faster growth of the economy as a whole, and *this transfer does not impede the growth of output in the sectors which give up labour*". (Cripps and Tarling (1973) italics added). The main difference between the Cripps-Tarling Proposition and Kaldor's Proposition is that Kaldor does not require the labour transfer to increase the rates of output growth in both sectors, but only that the overall growth rate should increase. On the other hand, Cripps and Tarling require in addition that the labour transfer be a Paretian improvement in the sense that both sectors' output growth rates should increase.[2] Clearly Kaldor's Proposition is subsumed in the Cripps-Tarling Proposition. In other words, the Cripps-Tarling Proposition is sufficient but not necessary for Kaldor's Proposition to be valid.

In order to examine these propositions in greater detail, we construct the following simple model. The economy is conceived of as consisting of two sectors: a manufacturing sector denoted by "m" and a non-manufacturing sector denoted by "n". The following notation is used:

(i) Q_m, Q_n denote output in manufacturing and non-manufacturing respectively.

(ii) E_m, E_n denote employment in the two sectors.

(iii) P_m, P_n denote productivity (output per man) in the two sectors, i.e. $P_m = Q_m/E_m$ and $P_n = Q_n/E_n$.

(iv) Y denotes aggregate output measured in non-manufacturing output units.

(v)   p denotes the price of manufacturing output in terms of non-manufacturing output and is assumed constant.

(vi) lower case letters denote proportional rates of growth; for example

$$q_m \equiv \frac{1}{Q_m} \frac{dQ_m}{dt}$$

The main variable which the model seeks to explain is y, the growth rate of total output. By definition

$$Y = Q_n + pQ_m \tag{2}$$

and hence by differentiation,

$$y = \theta q_n + (1-\theta)q_m \tag{3}$$

where θ is the share of non-manufacturing in total output.

Kaldor's view that Verdoorn's Law applied to manufacturing yields the "productivity function" for manufacturing:[3]

$$p_m = \beta e_m, \quad \beta > 0 \tag{4}$$

The "productivity function" for non-manufacturing is obtained by combining two elements. The first of these is the assumption (accepted by Kaldor) that non-manufacturing is characterised by decreasing returns to employment so that productivity growth and employment growth are inversely related. The second is the assumption (discussed earlier) that the growth of the manufacturing sector yields externalities which increase productivity growth in non-manufacturing. These two assumptions together imply that:

$$p_n = \lambda e_n + \mu q_m, \quad \lambda \leq 0, \; \mu \geq 0 \tag{5}$$

where μ measures the strength of the external effect.[4,5] Since for both sectors $q \equiv p + e$, it follows from (4) that

$$q_m = (\beta + 1)e_m \tag{6}$$

and from (5) that

$$q_n = (\lambda + 1)e_n + \mu(\beta + 1)e_m \tag{7}$$

Hence,

$$y = \theta(\lambda + 1)e_n + (\beta + 1)\left[\theta\mu + (1 - \theta)\right]e_m \tag{8}$$

Assuming an overall labour constraint and an initial static position, the transfer of labour from non-manufacturing to manufacturing implies an increase in e_m and a

Verdoorn's Law etc.

simultaneous decrease in e_n i.e. $de_m > 0$ and $de_n < 0$. Kaldor's Proposition may be interpreted as implying that the consequence of a transfer of labour such that $de_m > 0$ and $de_n < 0$ is an increase in y, i.e. $dy > 0$. The Cripps-Tarling Proposition may be interpreted as implying that the consequence of $de_m > 0$ and $de_n < 0$ is that dq_m is positive whilst dq_n is non-negative. We shall examine the Cripps-Tarling Proposition first.

From (6) and (7) it is clear that

$$dq_m = (\beta + 1)de_m \tag{9}$$

and

$$dq_n = (\lambda + 1)de_n + \mu(\beta + 1)de_m \tag{10}$$

Since $(\beta + 1) > 0$ and $de_m > 0$, it follows that $dq_m > 0$. The sign of dq_n depends crucially on the value of λ. If $\lambda + 1 = 0$, then this is sufficient to guarantee $dq_n \geq 0$, if however $\lambda + 1 > 0$, then $\mu > 0$ is a necessary but not sufficient condition for $dq_n \geq 0$. In either event, Verdoorn's Law ($\beta > 0$) is obviously not critical. Thus, so long as the marginal productivity of labour in non-manufacturing is positive ($\lambda + 1 > 0$), the Externalities Hypothesis and not Verdoorn's Law is the critical element for the validity of the Cripps-Tarling Proposition.

Turning to Kaldor's Proposition, we obtain from (8) that

$$dy = \theta(\lambda + 1)de_n + (\beta + 1)\left[\theta\mu + (1 - \theta)\right]de_m \tag{11}$$

It should be clear from (11) that neither Verdoorn's Law nor the Externalities Hypothesis is critical for this proposition. The restrictions $\beta > 0$ and $\mu > 0$ are not (either separately or jointly) necessary or sufficient.

This simple model has shown therefore that if the marginal productivity of labour in non-manufacturing is zero so that $\lambda + 1 = 0$, then the Cripps-Tarling Proposition is valid independently of the Externalities Hypothesis or Verdoorn's Law. *A fortiori*, the same is true of Kaldor's Proposition. However, in the possibly more plausible case when the marginal product of labour in non-manufacturing is positive, so that $\lambda + 1 > 0$, the Externalities Hypothesis is critical for the Cripps-Tarling Proposition though not for Kaldor's Proposition.[6] More importantly the model suggests that Verdoorn's Law is not critical for either proposition.[7] Hence it would appear that the emphasis placed on Verdoorn's Law by Kaldor and subsequent authors, and their relative neglect of the Externalities Hypothesis has not been warranted.[8] Accordingly in Section 8 we attempt to empirically investigate the Externalities Hypothesis as well as Verdoorn's Law using time series data for the U.K. Before presenting our own estimates in Section 3, we briefly review the issues raised by the empirical work of Kaldor and other authors in Section 2.

Section 2 : Empirical Tests of Verdoorn's Law

In order to test his theory Kaldor did not estimate (1) but rather the equivalent relationship

$$p_m = a + bq_m \tag{12}$$

where q_m is the rate of output growth in manufacturing.

Using data for the rates of growth of twelve countries over the period 1953-54 to 1963-64, Kaldor estimated (12) on a cross-section basis and obtained a well determined estimate of b in the neighbourhood of $\frac{1}{2}$. As $p_m \equiv q_m - e_m$, it follows that $\beta = \frac{b}{1-b}$ and hence $\beta > 0$ is equivalent to $0 < b < 1$. Given the precision of his estimate of b, Kaldor had no difficulty in accepting the hypothesis $0 < b < 1$. Hence he inferred that the equivalent hypothesis $\beta > 0$ was also acceptable. In other words, Kaldor verified his hypothesis of interest by an indirect method.

In a critique of Kaldor's methodology, Rowthorn (1975), argued that the appropriate method would be to estimate (1) directly and then test the hypothesis $\beta > 0$. This was indeed the method employed in a detailed study by Cripps and Tarling which basically confirmed Kaldor's findings.[9] However, Rowthorn demonstrated fairly convincingly that the Cripps-Tarling results are crucially affected by the removal of Japan from their sample. The omission of Japan makes it impossible to reject the hypothesis $\beta = 0$. This led Rowthorn to reject Kaldor's assertion that manufacturing is characterised by Verdoorn's Law, and hence also to reject Kaldor's Proposition.

In reply to Rowthorn, Kaldor (1975) argued that the

choice of estimating (1) or (12) really depends on whether one regards e_m or q_m as being exogenous (i.e. independent of the error term); and he asserted that q_m being demand determined is exogenous.[10] He further shows that dropping Japan from the sample does not seriously affect the robustness of his results providing that (2) is the equation estimated.

Parikh (1978) tested Verdoorn's Law with the Cripps-Tarling data in a simultaneous equation framework using Two Stage Least Squares (2SLS). He concluded that there was no evidence in support of Verdoorn's Law. Stoneman adopted a procedure similar to Parikh but used a long historical annual time series for the U.K. alone. His conclusion was similar to Parikh's that "Verdoorn's Law does not apply to manufacturing".

All of the above studies define growth rates over a long period, usually peak to peak. Hence, they can be thought of as testing the long-run validity of Verdoorn's Law and Kaldor's Proposition. One of our points of departure from this framework is to use quarterly growth rates for the U.K. and hence to analyse the dynamics of Verdoorn's Law, the Externalities Hypothesis, and Kaldor's Proposition. This is surely relevant to any study of growth. However, we begin by estimating the simplest static formulations largely with a view to throwing further light on whether employment growth or output growth is the appropriate exogenous variable. The results are reported in the next section.

Section 3 : Verdoorn's Law and the Externalities Hypothesis - Preliminary Estimates

In this section we report estimates of the simple models discussed in sections 1 and 2 paying equal attention to Verdoorn's Law and to the Externalities Hypothesis. The data used is for U.K. manufacturing and non-manufacturing including agriculture and services for the period 1961(2) to 1977(2) and is seasonally adjusted. We would prefer to use unadjusted data but this is not available for all the series.[11] We begin by examining Verdoorn's Law for manufacturing industries.

Verdoorn's Law

The basic estimating equations are obtained by adding disturbance terms to equations (1) and (12). It will be recalled that Rowthorn favoured using (1) as the estimating equation and Kaldor preferred (12). The OLS estimates obtained are

$$\hat{p}_m = 0.008 + 0.187 e_m, \quad \bar{R}^2 = -0.014, \quad \hat{\sigma} = 0.0172,$$
$$\quad\quad\quad (3.27) \quad (0.50)$$

$$T = 64, \quad Q_{20} = 24 \quad\quad\quad\quad\quad\quad\quad\quad\quad\quad (13)$$

and

$$\hat{p}_m = 0.003 + 0.869 q_m, \quad \bar{R}^2 = 0.897, \quad \hat{\sigma} = 0.00059,$$
$$\quad\quad\quad (3.35) \quad (20.94)$$

$$T = 64, \quad Q_{20} = 302 \quad\quad\quad\quad\quad\quad\quad\quad\quad (14)$$

where the numbers in parentheses are t statistics, T is the sample size, and Q_{20} the Box-Pierce residual correlogram statistic which will be assumed to have a limiting χ^2 distribution with 20 degrees of freedom under the null hypothesis of serially uncorrelated errors.[12] The critical value of a χ^2_{20} variable with a significance level of 5% is 32 indicating that Q_{20} is insignificant in equation (13) but highly significant in equation (14). Seasonal dummies are not included in these equations as they are insignificant, no doubt due to the fact that seasonally adjusted data has been used.

According to Verdoorn's Law, β, the coefficient of e_m, is positive. The estimate of β obtained from equation (13) is 0.187 and is not significantly different from zero whilst the estimate from (14) is $0.869/(1-0.869) = 6.63$ with an asymptotic t value of 2.74[13] which strongly supports Verdoorn's Law. However, given the massive residual serial correlation in (14), estimates obtained from (14) are not reliable. Furthermore, it is possible that both sets of estimates suffer from asymptotic bias due to the endogeneity of the regressors. As indicated earlier, this can be removed by using an appropriate instrumental variable estimator.[14]

Verdoorn's Law etc.

Using the first four lags of e_m as instrumental variables for e_m and q_m, the following results were obtained:

$$\hat{p}_m = 0.007 - 0.115 e_m, \quad \bar{R}^2 = -0.026, \quad \hat{\sigma} = 0.017,$$
$$(2.75) \quad (0.27)$$

$$T = 60, \quad Q_{20} = 23, \quad K_3 = 9.4 \tag{15}$$

and

$$\hat{p}_m = 0.004 + 0.673 q_m, \quad \bar{R}^2 = 0.842, \quad \hat{\sigma} = 0.0070,$$
$$(3.48) \quad (6.53)$$

$$T = 60, \quad Q_{20} = 95, \quad K_3 = 25.2 \tag{16}$$

Once again the estimate of β obtained from the employment equation (15) is not significantly different from zero and the estimate of β obtained from the output equation (16) which is 2.06 supports Verdoorn's Law but is implausibly large. Furthermore, the Box-Pierce statistic indicates serially correlated disturbances in equation (16) but not in equation (15). The statistic K_3 provides a test for the validity of the instruments. If the instruments are valid, then K_3 is distributed as a χ_3^2 variable.[15] Since $\chi_3^2(.05) = 7.8$ and $\chi_3^2(.025) = 9.4$, the instruments are clearly unacceptable for equation (16) and barely adequate for equation (15). However, the instrument test is only valid when the model is not misspecified. A significant test statistic could also occur when the model is misspecified due, say to omitted variables if these latter are correlated with the instruments. Thus equations (13) to (16) may well be misspecified. Further investigation into this possibility will be made in Section 4.

In the meantime, these results suggest that Rowthorn's version of Verdoorn's Law is to be preferred to Kaldor's which (i) produced implausibly large estimates of β, and (ii) given the massive residual serial correlation in equations (14) and (16) and the significance of the instruments, seems to indicate some misspecification. The main problem with Rowthorn's model is that the estimates of β are not significantly different from zero; in fact the estimate from equation (15) is negative. This, taken together with the fairly high value of the instrument test statistic in equation (15), cannot be regarded as providing any serious evidence in support of Verdoorn's Law in manufacturing.

The Externalities Hypothesis and the Cripps-Tarling Proposition

Both of these hypotheses can be tested by adding a constant and a disturbance term to the "productivity function" for non-manufacturing (equation (5)) to yield

$$p_n = \mu + \lambda e_n + \mu q_m + u \qquad (17)$$

The Externalities Hypothesis requires $\mu > 0$ whilst a sufficient condition for the Cripps-Tarling Proposition is $\lambda = -1$. OLS estimation of (17) yields:

$$p_n = 0.003 - 0.887 e_n + 0.301 q_m, \quad \bar{R}^2 = 0.388$$
$$(3.23) \quad (3.84) \quad (5.42)$$

$$\hat{\sigma} = 0.0077, \; T = 64, \; Q_{20} = 111 \qquad (18)$$

These results appear to offer strong support for the Externalities Hypothesis and the Cripps-Tarling Proposition as the hypothesis $\mu = 0$ can be rejected in favour of $\mu > 0$ and the hypothesis $\lambda = -1$ cannot be rejected. However equation (18) is not satisfactory as it possesses highly serially correlated residuals which may reflect misspecification. It may also exhibit simultaneous equation bias. In an attempt to remove this bias, equation (17) was re-estimated using instrumental variables. Using the first four lags of e_m and e_n as instruments for e_n and q_m, the following results were obtained:

$$\hat{p}_n = 0.004 - 1.322 e_n + 0.284 q_m, \quad \bar{R}^2 = .334,$$
$$(3.06) \quad (1.98) \quad (2.50)$$

$$\hat{\sigma} = 0.0080, \; T = 60, \; Q_{20} = 95, \; K_6 = 6.1 \qquad (19)$$

Once again these results suggest that $\mu > 0$ and that $\lambda = -1$ cannot be rejected, thus corroborating the Externalities Hypothesis and the Cripps-Tarling Proposition. The statistic K_6 is not significant and hence indicates that that the instruments appear to be valid. However, the

Verdoorn's Law etc.

statistic Q_{20} is highly significant and reflects the presence of serially correlated residuals. These results suggest that both the Externalities Hypothesis and the Cripps-Tarling Proposition may well be correct, but like the results on the productivity function for manufacturing, there is a strong possibility that the productivity function for non-manufacturing is misspecified. Further investigation into this possibility is carried out in Section 4.

Section 4 : A General Model

The models estimated in the previous section were very much basic models and, as we showed, need considerable respecification in order to fit the data more closely. The re-specification could take the form of adding further explanatory variables and/or adding dynamic structure to the models. In re-specifying the "productivity functions" of manufacturing and of non-manufacturing industries we shall focus attention on both possibilities. In particular, we shall concentrate on (i) the effect on productivity of operating at less than full capacity, (ii) the role of capital accumulation, and (iii) dynamic specification.

(i) Capacity Utilisation

Productivity changes can be thought of as resulting from short-run movement to capacity output with more or less fixed factor inputs (i.e. movements *to* the production frontier) and long-run movements due to changes in factor inputs (i.e. movements *along* and *of* the frontier). A possible explanation for the results of equations (13) to (16) which indicate that variations in productivity growth in manufacturing are largely due to variations in output growth and not employment growth, is that most short-run variation in productivity is caused by changes in capacity utilisation which, not surprisingly, is being picked up by output changes. A comparison of the standard deviation of productivity, output, and employment over the sample, which are 0.018, 0.019 and 0.006 respectively support this view. In the light of this, the residual correlograms of equations (14) and (16) and the very high implied returns to scale of these equations, it is probable that in effect these equations are using q_m to explain itself. Much of the short run variation in output and therefore of movements to the production frontier is due to variations in the utilisation rate of factor inputs. This suggests that the growth rate in average hours worked in manufacturing (h_m) may capture movements in capacity utilisation and should be included as an additional explanatory variable.

(ii) Capital Accumulation

Verdoorn's Law focuses attention on the relationship between productivity growth and employment growth, ignoring the role of capital growth.[16] It would seem more sensible, however, to allow capital growth to have an independent influence on productivity growth since capital accumulation often embodies technical progress and may be expected to raise output per man. In contrast to the growth of hours whose effect on productivity has been interpreted as measuring movements to the production frontier, capital growth reflects movements of the frontier. In order to capture the effects of capital accumulation, the rate of growth of capital stock in manufacturing and non-manufacturing industries should be included in the productivity functions.

At this point it is necessary to consider whether it is sensible to include the growth of average hours and capital stock into both the employment and output versions of the manufacturing productivity function. Kaldor's argument for favouring the output version of Verdoorn's Law in manufacturing is that q_m is an exogenous variable. But the results of Section 3 have raised severe doubts about the validity of this assumption. A further consideration is that output growth will almost certainly be correlated with hours growth and capital stock growth. Indeed a possible reason why the coefficient of q_m is so large in equations (14) and (16) is that it contains omitted variable bias due to the correlation between q_m and the omitted variables (hours and capital growth). On the other hand, employment growth is much less likely to be dependent on growth of capital or hours. In view of these arguments it was decided not to use the output version of Verdoorn's Law (equation 12) any further but to generalise the employment version of Verdoorn's Law by including capital and hours growth as additional variables.

Accordingly, we may write the productivity functions for manufacturing and non-manufacturing as:

Verdoorn's Law etc. 417

$$p_n = \alpha + \beta e_m + \gamma h_m + \delta k_m \qquad (20)$$

and

$$p_n = \pi + \lambda e_n + \mu q_m + \eta h_n + \phi k_n \qquad (21)$$

where k_m, k_n are the rates of growth of the capital stock in manufacturing and non-manufacturing respectively whilst h_m and h_n are the respective growth rates of average hours.[17]

(iii) Dynamic Specification

Equations (20) and (21) though considerably more general than their earlier counterparts (equations (1) and (5) respectively) are still completely static. They imply that any adjustment takes place instantaneously. In the empirical work of Kaldor, Cripps and Tarling, Rowthorn and Parikh, the data used were cross-section and the interpretation of their results and those of Stoneman who used growth rates measured peak to peak from 1800, concerned the long-run. One advantage of our use of quarterly time series data is that it is possible to examine the dynamic response of productivity growth to changes in the growth of employment, hours and capital and thus distinguish between short-run and long-run effects. Fairly general formulations which incorporate the idea that the response of productivity growth to changes in the growth of employment, hours and capital is distributed through time are:

$$p_m(t) = \alpha + \sum_{s=0}^{5} \beta_s e_m(t-s) + \sum_{s=0}^{5} \gamma_s h_m(t-s)$$

$$+ \sum_{s=0}^{5} \delta_s k_m(t-s) + \sum_{s=1}^{5} \epsilon_s p_m(t-s) + u(t) \qquad (22)$$

and

$$p_n(t) = \pi + \sum_{s=0}^{5} \lambda_s e_n(t-s) + \sum_{s=0}^{5} \mu_s q_m(t-s)$$
$$+ \sum_{s=0}^{5} \eta_s h_n(t-s) + \sum_{s=0}^{5} \phi_s k_n(t-s)$$
$$+ \sum_{s=1}^{5} \psi_s p_n(t-s) + v(t) \qquad (23)$$

where $u(t)$ and $v(t)$ are assumed to be random disturbance terms each with zero mean and constant variance.

Equations (22) and (23) can be related to the literature. First, they can be regarded as transformed production functions in which the lagged variables can be interpreted as capturing the short-run behaviour of the frontier, of factor efficiency or, in the case of the externality terms, embodied technical progress. Second, they are similar in some respects to Hazledine's (1974) productivity function in which output per man hour is thought to be a quadratic function of employment; productivity falls as employment either exceeds or drops below a certain optimal level. Finally, they can be related to Okun's Law which postulates that *short-run* deviations in output from its capacity level are related to short-run deviations of the unemployment rate from the natural rate. Since changes in the unemployment rate are inversely related to changes in the employment rate, a fall in the unemployment rate will cause a short-run increase in employment and hence in productivity. Thus Okun's Law can be viewed as a short-run version of Verdoorn's Law. For further details of these various interpretations see Chatterji and Wickens.

Section 5 : Estimates of the Dynamic Model

Before reporting the estimates of our general dynamic models, we note a number of difficulties associated with the estimation. The first of these concerns the construction of a capital stock series for both manufacturing and non-manufacturing from which k_m and k_n can be derived. The capital stock series is calculated from total invest-

Verdoorn's Law etc.

ment using a constant depreciation rate which was chosen on the basis of a rough grid search to be 0.02 per quarter.[18] Another difficulty was the absence of a quarterly series for average hours worked in non-manufacturing. Hence we were forced to use average hours in manufacturing as a proxy for average hours in non-manufacturing on the presumption that the two are closely correlated. Accordingly we used h_m instead of h_n in equation (23). Having obtained unrestricted estimates of (22) and (23), we attempted to find a more parsimonious dynamic specification which would capture the essential short and long run features of the unrestricted estimates of (22) and (23). Besides the appeal of simplicity such formulations may well provide more efficient estimates. It is these restricted estimates which are reported here.

Our preferred estimates were obtained using OLS and are:

manufacturing:

$$p_m(t) = -0.011 + 0.742\ h_m(t) + 0.705\ \Delta_3\ e_m(t-1)$$
$$(2.25)\quad (6.57)\qquad\qquad (3.26)$$

$$-0.241 \sum_{s=1}^{4} e_m(t-s) - 2.043\ \Delta_3\ k_m(t-1)$$
$$(2.00)\qquad\qquad\qquad (2.40)$$

$$+0.249 \sum_{s=1}^{4} k_m(t-s) - 0.19\ \Delta_4\ p_m(t-1) \qquad (24)$$
$$(9.39)\qquad\qquad\qquad (13.15)$$

$\bar{R}^2 = 0.649$, $T = 56$, $\hat{\sigma} = .0105$, $Q_8 = 4.93$,

where $\Delta_s x_t \equiv x_t - x_{t-s}$.

non-manufacturing:

$$\hat{p}_n(t) = 0.0055 + 0.325\ h_m(t) - 0.500\ e_n(t)$$
$$(2.33)\quad (5.18)\qquad\qquad (2.36)$$

$$- 0.231 \sum_{s=0}^{5} e_n(t-s) + 0.064 \sum_{s=0}^{4} q_m(t-s)$$
$$(3.31) \qquad\qquad\qquad (3.04)$$

$$+ 3.099\, k_n(t) - 2.886\, k_n(t-1) - 0.352 \sum_{s=1}^{2} p_n(t-s) \qquad (25)$$
$$(4.08) \qquad\qquad (3.75) \qquad\qquad\qquad (4.65)$$

$$\bar{R}^2 = 0.654,\ T = 56,\ \hat{\sigma} = 0.0058,\ Q_8 = 6.0.$$

The corresponding long-run steady growth solutions are:

$$p_m = -0.011 + 0.742\, h_m - 0.96\, e_m + 1.00\, k_m \qquad (26)$$

$$p_n = 0.0032 + 0.191\, h_m - 1.107\, e_n + 0.188\, q_m$$
$$+ 0.125\, k_n \qquad (27)$$

From equations (24) and (26) it can be seen that productivity growth in manufacturing has a significant and quite large transitory response to employment growth in manufacturing but that in the long-run, the cumulative effect of employment growth on productivity growth is significantly negative. This implies that manufacturing is characterised by a strong but short-lived Verdoorn's Law and that this effect is more than offset in later periods leaving no Verdoorn's Law effect in the long-run. This phenomenon, which is in contrast to some of the earlier results can best be explained by means of the simple diagram on the next page. The diagram shows a production function relating output to employment. The function is drawn for a given level of capital stock and for a given socio-legally determined maximum level of hours. The slope of any ray through the origin measures productivity. In the short-run, the economy is assumed to be operating inside the frontier at some point A with employment of E_A and hours less than the maximum. The increases in demand lead to simultaneous increases in employment (to E_B) and hours to their maximum level, i.e. to point B where productivity is higher. The move from A to B is a manifestation of Verdoorn's Law. In the longer run, however, increased output demand can only be met by increased employment and the economy moves from B to C accompanied by a fall in productivity. This is a manifestation of the inverse relationship between employment growth and productivity growth.

Diagram 1.   Output, Employment and Productivity

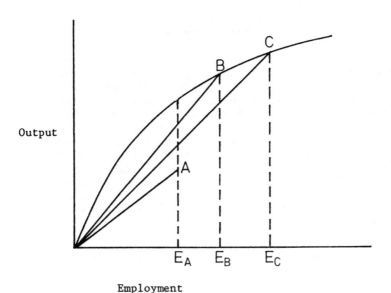

Turning to other variables, equations (24) and (26) show that the growth of average hours and capital have significant positive effects on productivity growth in the long-run, thus confirming once more our earlier conjectures. In addition, however, there is a large negative transitory response to new investment and a negative transitory feedback. The constant term implies a significant negative rate of disembodied technical progress but, since capital will embody technical progress, the total effect of technical progress would not be expected to be negative.

Turning to non-manufacturing productivity, equation (25) indicates that employment growth has a fairly strong and negative instantaneous effect on productivity growth and a much larger long-run effect.

As with manufacturing industry, these results show that changes in capacity utilisation, as proxied by the growth rate of hours in manufacturing, as well as changes in the growth rate of capital have a significant influence. Capital growth has a strong instantaneous effect which is largely but not entirely offset in the following period. The distributed lag function on the lagged dependent variable shows that there is marked negative feed-back for about six months which attenuates the sum of the distributed lag coefficients to produce reduced long-run multipliers.

The estimates of the distributed lag function for employment growth in non-manufacturing indicates a fairly strong and negative instantaneous effect of employment growth on productivity growth and a much stronger total effect with a long-run multiplier of 1.107 which is not significantly different from − 1, and suggests that the Cripps-Tarling Proposition receives support in the long-run.[19] The estimates of the distributed lag function for output growth of manufacturing industries indicate a weak short-run impact but a significant and moderately strong long-run influence. This confirms the Externalities Hypothesis but suggests that it is primarily a long-run phenomenon.

Section 6 :   *Kaldor's Proposition Reconsidered*

The central issue of concern to Kaldor and to Cripps and Tarling is whether or not a transfer of labour from non-manufacturing to manufacturing industries will raise the rate of growth of total output. We have argued that Kaldor's Proposition rests on two hypotheses, Verdoorn's Law and the Externalities Hypothesis, but we have found evidence to support the existence of only the latter. Nevertheless, we have shown that this is a sufficient condition for Kaldor's Proposition to hold. It remains to estimate from our results the quantitative importance of this transfer. We shall consider below only the long-run implications.

From equations (26) and (27) we obtain the long-run output growth equations for manufacturing and non-manufacturing:

Verdoorn's Law etc.

$$q_m = -0.01 + 0.74\, h_m + 0.04\, e_m + 1.00\, k_m \qquad (28)$$

$$q_n = 0.19\, h_m - 0.11\, e_n + 0.19\, q_m + 0.13\, k_n \qquad (29)$$

Using the CSO estimate of the share of non-manufacturing in total output computed for the index of industrial production we have $\theta = 0.745$ when equation (3) becomes:

$$y = 0.745\, q_n + 0.255\, q_m$$

and hence the long-run reduced form equation for total output growth is:

$$y = 0.00 + 0.48\, h_m + 0.02\, e_m - 0.08\, e_n$$
$$+ 0.40\, k_m + 0.10\, k_n \qquad (31)$$

Since the purpose of the exercise is to analyse the effects of *reallocating* labour, we shall assume that total employment is unchanged.[20] Hence a transfer of one per cent of non-manufacturing employment raises manufacturing employment by 2.112 per cent. This transfer implies a one percentage point fall in the growth rate of non-manufacturing employment (e_n) and an increase of 2.112 percentage points in the growth rate of manufacturing employment (e_m).[21] Substituting into (31) that a *sustained* transfer of $e_n = -1$ implies $e_m = 2.112$ we find that $y = 0.12$, implying that the growth rate of total output increases by only 0.12 percentage point.

As sustained transfers are not feasible in the long-run due to the existence of constraints on labour, it is perhaps of more interest to examine the effect of a *once-for-all* transfer of labour. These calculations are made in Chatterji and Wickens using a dynamic simulation of the original model, equations (24) and (25) together with (30). It is found that there are no significant gains in output growth beyond the first two quarters and these are completely offset in later periods reaching the long-run value of zero in about two years.

Although this is true if one considers the *growth rate* of output (as Kaldor and Cripps and Tarling did), it may be the case that even a once-for-all transfer could have permanent effects on the *level* of output. These calculations suggest that the gains in cumulative output from the once-for-all transfer increase during the first year and then decline steadily. But after five years output is only approximately 0.28 percent higher than it would have been without the transfer.

Section 7 : Conclusions

The main conclusions to be drawn from our results are as follows. First, Verdoorn's Law does not hold for the U.K. manufacturing industry in the long-run. This result is consistent with the results obtained by Rowthorn, Parikh and Stoneman. Secondly, U.K. manufacturing industry is characterised by a short-run Verdoorn's Law which is analagous to Okun's Law. This result cannot be compared with previous empirical work because the earlier literature cited concentrated exclusively on long-run tests. Thirdly, the Cripps-Tarling Proposition and, *a fortiori*, Kaldor's Proposition regarding the possibility of increased output growth by a transfer of labour do hold but are due almost entirely to the Externalities Hypothesis rather than Verdoorn's Law. Again this result is not easily comparable with the previous literature as earlier researchers did not attempt to test these propositions directly. Fourthly, the impact of the labour transfer on economic growth, though positive, is of little quantitative significance. The long-term pay-off of the labour transfer in terms of an increased growth rate of output is only 0.12 percentage points and if the labour transfer is applied only once, then the pay-off in terms of an increased growth rate of output is highly transitory but very small in the long-run. Finally, it is possible to conduct a similar analysis considering an investment transfer instead of a labour transfer. The results of this exercise, which are reported in Chatterji and Wickens, are found to be much larger.

APPENDIX

A Test for the validity of the Instruments

The test statistic is obtained by multiplying the sample size by the R^2 obtained from an OLS regression of the residuals obtained from the instrumental variables estimation against the instrumental variables. The asymptotic distribution of this test statistic is obtained as follows:

Consider the linear model

(A.1) $\quad y = X\beta + u$

where y is a T×1 vector of observations on the dependent variable, X is a T×k matrix of observations on k explanatory variables, u is a T×1 vector of disturbances which are assumed to be distributed $N(0,\sigma^2 I_T)$ and β is a k×1 vector of coefficients. It is assumed that X is stochastic such that plim $(X'u/T) \neq 0$ and plim $(X'X/T) = M_{xx}$ is finite non-singular.

Let Z be a T×p matrix of observations of $p > k$ linearly independent instrumental variables for which lim $(Z'Z/T) = M_{zz}$ is finite non-singular and plim $(Z'X/T) = M_{zx}$ has full column rank. On the null hypothesis that the instruments are valid for X it is assumed that the limiting distribution of $Z'u/\sqrt{T}$ is $N(0,\sigma^2 M_{zz})$ and, on the alternative hypothesis that the instruments are not valid, plim$(Z'u/T) \neq 0$.

In order to derive a test statistic suitable for H_0 we shall consider the distribution of the explained sum of squares of a regression of the instrumental variables residuals of (A.1), namely $\hat{u}$, on the instruments Z, i.e. we consider the distribution of $\hat{u}'Z(Z'Z)^{-1}Z'\hat{u}$. Now

$$\hat{u} = y - Xb = -X(b-\beta) + u$$
$$= \left[I_T - X(X'P_z X)^{-1}X'P_z\right] u$$

where $b = (X'P_zX)^{-1}X'P_zy$ is the IV estimator of β and $P_z = Z(Z'Z)^{-1}Z'$. It follows that

$$\hat{u}'P_z\hat{u} = u'\left[P_z - P_zX(X'P_zX)^{-1}X'P_z\right]u$$

$$= u'Au$$

where $A = P_z - P_zX(X'P_zX)^{-1}X'P_z$ is an idempotent matrix with rank $p - k$. On H_0, the limiting distribution of $u'P_zu/\sigma^2$ is the same as that of $u'Au/\sigma^2$ which converges to that of

$$u'Z\left[M_{zz}^{-1} - M_{zz}^{-1}M_{zx}(M_{xz}M_{zz}^{-1}M_{zx})^{-1}M_{xz}M_{zz}^{-1}\right]Z'u/\sigma^2$$

which is a χ^2_{p-k}. If σ^2 is consistently estimated by $\hat{u}'\hat{u}/T$, the required test statistic is given by

$$K = T\frac{\hat{u}'P_z\hat{u}}{\hat{u}'\hat{u}} = T.R^2_{\hat{u}.z}$$

where $R^2_{\hat{u}.z}$ is the squared multiple correlation coefficient from the regression of $\hat{u}$ on Z. In view of the above results, the distribution of K on H_0 can be approximated by a χ^2_{p-k} with large values leading to a rejection of H_0. Note that unless $p > k$ the test cannot be used.

ACKNOWLEDGEMENTS

This paper is part of a larger project on dynamic macro-econometric model building. We wish to acknowledge, with sincere thanks, the SSRC for providing financial support for the project. We also wish to thank Hassan Molana for his invaluable assistance and Pravin Trivedi for his comments on an earlier draft.

REFERENCES

Chatterji, M. and M.R. Wickens (1980). Productivity, Factor Transfers and Economic Growth in the U.K. *Economica*. (forthcoming).

Cripps, T.F. and R.J. Tarling (1973). *Growth in Advanced Capitalist Economies, 1950-1970*. Cambridge University Press.

Hazledine, T. (1974). Employment and Output Functions for New Zealand Manufacturing Industries. *Journal of Industrial Economics*, 22, 161-198.

Kaldor, N., (1966). *Causes of the Slow Rate of Economic Growth of the United Kingdom*. Cambridge University Press.

Kaldor, N., (1975). Economic Growth and the Verdoorn Law - A Comment on Mr. Rowthorn's Article. *Economic Journal*, 85.

Parikh, A., (1978). Differences in Growth Rates and Kaldor's Laws, *Economica*, 45, 83-91.

Rowthorn, R. (1975). What Remains of Kaldor's Law? *Economic Journal*, 85, 10-19.

Stoneman, P., (1979). Kaldor's Law and British Economic Growth: 1800-1970. *Applied Economics*, 11, 309-319.

FOOTNOTES

1. Certainly this interpretation is also imputed by Stoneman (1979).
2. It may be the case that the Cripps-Tarling Proposition can be implicitly inferred from Kaldor's Inaugural Lecture. However, Kaldor has not explicitly stated the Cripps-Tarling Proposition.
3. Throughout this paper we are interpreting Verdoorn's Law as a *partial* effect in a structural equation. It is possible to interpret Verdoorn's Law as the *total* effect of e_m (or q_m) in a reduced form equation for p_m. This however implies that other factors which may have an influence on productivity growth, for example, capital accumulation, can be represented as functions of e_m and possibly p_m (or q_m) alone which is surely unreasonable. Furthermore, if one takes this view that the effects of capital accumulation etc. are included in the formulation of Verdoorn's Law, it is difficult

to argue that the validity of Verdoorn's Law implies a reallocation of labour. Accordingly, we interpret Verdoorn's Law as the partial effect of employment growth and allow explicitly for the separate influence of other variables such as capital accumulation etc. in Section 4.

4. As with Verdoorn's Law, we are interpreting the Externalities Hypothesis as a partial effect in a structural equation. This approach is also implicitly adopted by Stoneman who has also tested a version of the Externalities Hypothesis. However, it is possible to view the Externalities Hypothesis as the *total* effect of q_m in a reduced form equation for p_n. In this case the Externalities Hypothesis is trivially true and not of much interest.

5. The "productivity functions" (4) and (5) can be integrated to yield the production functions:

$$Q_m = A_m E_m^{\beta+1}, \quad \beta + 1 \geq 1 \text{ and}$$

$$Q_n = A_n E_n^{\lambda+1}, \quad E_m^{\mu(\beta+1)}, \quad \theta \leq \lambda + 1 \leq 1, \quad \mu > 0,$$

where A_m, A_n are constants. Thus $\beta = -1$ and $\lambda = -1$ represent the limiting case of zero marginal productivity of labour in the two sectors.

6. Kaldor has hinted that the marginal productivity of labour in agriculture may well be zero. Whilst this may be plausible for *agriculture*, it is improbable for *non-manufacturing* as a whole.

7. Of course, if Verdoorn's Law is true so that $(\beta + 1) > 1$, then the *likelihood* of $dq_n \geq 0$ and $dy > 0$ is increased. This is also true of the Externalities Hypothesis.

8. Exceptions are Stoneman and Cripps and Tarling. But the latters' main emphasis is still on Verdoorn's Law whilst Stoneman's specification of the Externality Hypothesis is somewhat strange.

9. There are, however, some qualifications for the later periods of study.

10. In fact the choice between using (1) or (2) as the estimating equation is important if OLS is to be used but if a suitable consistent estimator is used, either (1) or (2) can be chosen.

11. For a detailed account of the data sources see Chatterji and Wickens (1980).

12. Strictly the Box-Pierce statistic applies to the original disturbances and not to the residuals.
13. See Phillips and Wickens (1979), Chapter 2, for details of this calculation.
14. This is similar to the approach adopted by Parikh and Stoneman.
15. For details of this test, see the Appendix.
16. See footnote number 3.
17. We have deliberately not worked in a production function framework, but if we assume a simple Cobb-Douglas production function, then we can write:

$$q_m = (\beta + 1) e_m + \gamma h_m + \delta k_m$$

The dependence of q_m on h_m and k_m is now clear and the corresponding productivity function is $p_m = \beta e_m + \gamma h_m + \delta k_m$ which is of the preferred form.

18. Unrestricted estimates of (22) and (23) as well as the methodology underlying our choice of preferred restricted specifications is fully described in Chatterji and Wickens.
19. For details of this test and other statistical calculations in this section, see Chatterji and Wickens.
20. We do not discuss the method whereby this transfer of labour is to be achieved. Kaldor's suggestion was S.E.T.
21. For details of these calculations see Chatterji and Wickens.

[38]

Excerpt from D. Currie, R. Nobay and D. Peel (eds), *Macroeconomic Analysis: Essays in Macroeconomics and Econometrics*, 430–33.

DISCUSSION: N. KALDOR

Messrs. Chatterji and Wickens' paper is a further addition to the increasing literature on the 'Verdoorn Law' which seems to be in vogue at present. I am not sure that I succeeded in understanding just what they are after, but I think there are a number of statements which I regard as false or misleading and which need to be pointed out.

(1) I never intended to put forward the view that 'the main engine of economic growth was the presence of Verdoorn's Law in manufacturing', though I can see that superficial readers of my inaugural lecture may have formed that impression.

I did suggest that the main engine of economic growth for industrially developed countries was the manufacturing sector, and that this is due to (a) the importance of exports from the point of view of growth; (b) the manufacturing sector has the peculiarity that it accumulates its own resources, i.e. it manufactures the capital goods which it uses and provides the savings for it through the profits which its own investment activities generate; (c) in its expansion, it absorbs labour from the agricultural and/or the services sector of the economy, where labour, in the relevant sense of the word, is in surplus. As a result of that, the growth of output of the manufacturing sector does not cause a diminution of output of these other sectors, but on the contrary, it stimulates their growth.

(2) I also disagree with their exposition of the Verdoorn Law. They use Rowthorn's formulation which can be put as

$$P_m = f(e_m), \quad f' > 0$$

This is not a *necessary* condition of the law (though it may be a *sufficient* one) for the simple reason that if output, and not employment, is regarded as the exogenous variable, any statistical error which occurs in the endogenous variable e_m sets up a change of the opposite sign in P_m and thus generates a spurious negative correlation which has the effect of making the relationship appear a great deal weaker than it is if set in the form which I prefer:-

$$e_m = f(q_m), \quad f' > 0 < 1 \qquad (ii)$$

The usual formulation

$$P_m = f(q_m), \quad f' > 0 \qquad (iii)$$

I regard as unsatisfactory since, in view of t identity $P_m \equiv q_m - e_m$, it may be no more than a tautology unless equation (ii) holds; whereas if (ii) holds, (iii) is automatically satisfied.

(3) I disagree with their statement that manufacturing output cannot be regarded as "exogenous" for any number of countries. Of course the export demand for any one country depends on the growth of output of all other countries, but this no more invalidates the exogeneity condition than the fact that the demand for, say, matches in a particular country or region depends on the total output of that country or region from which its consumers are drawn. I cannot, therefore, accept their criticism of the use of cross-section data which I still feel avoids some of the pitfalls of time-series data. Assuming, however, that these pitfalls do not matter, the time series data should serve to confirm the findings of cross-section data.

(4) So, far from saying that I regard the exogeneity of the growth of q_m as being grounded on the Verdoorn Law, I repeatedly expressed the opposite view. I did so explicitly both in my paper in *Economica*, August 1958, and in my reply to Rowthorn in the *Economic Journal*, December 1975, where I said that:

> 'The important thing to note is – and herein lies Rowthorn's misunderstanding – that the existence of increasing returns to scale in industry (the Verdoorn Law) is not a necessary or indispensable element in the interpretation of these equations. Even if industrial output obeyed the law of constant returns, it could still be true that the growth of industrial output was the governing factor in the overall rate of economic growth (both in terms of total output and output per head) so long as the growth of industrial output represented a *net*

> *addition* to the effective use of resources, and not just a transfer of resources from one use to another.'
>
> (p. 894)

(5) My assumption that labour is not a constraint on output as a whole or on the output of any particular sector such as manufacturing is basic to my whole approach in economics. It is, of course, a denial of the basic neo-classical hypothesis according to which in a market economy there is both full employment and a "pareto-optimal" allocation of the labour force. As against that I assert that in agriculture and services the marginal social product is normally zero (or could even be negative for all kinds of reasons, such as that too much labour prevents the optimum organisation of the individual production unit, such as the optimum sized farm in agriculture) or else leads to excess capacity (as in the case of distribution) and the division of sales among too many selling units. The reason why a 'pareto-optimal' full employment equilibrium does not exist in these cases is partly because the land constraint may be binding, and the fact that there are limits to the range within which labour and land are effective substitutes for one another at the margin; partly because of imperfect competition and the absence of homogeneous and linear production function in services, which means that there is always a minimum scale of production (higher than zero) below which unit costs are rising with a further fall in sales. Given these facts, the marginal (social) product of labour is normally in excess of the average product of labour in manufacturing industry and is very much below it in both agriculture and services. This is the basic reason for my rejection of neo-classical economics. As far as I understand, all these points are subsumed by Messrs. Chatterji and Wickens under the notion of the "externalities hypothesis", but calling it by that name is not just a matter of semantics - it concedes the general validity of the neo-classical approach to economics (which I deny).

(6) The Verdoorn Law is however essential for the existence of "circular and cumulative causation" which I regard as critical for understanding the nature of the process of economic development, but the assumption of which is incompatible with neo-classical economic theory (i.e. the theory of general equilibrium). The latter regards the essence of the economic problem as the allocation of scarce resources

between different uses; but it is the *rate of creation* of resources (and the factors that promote it or inhibit it) rather than their allocation which are the really important issues to be considered.

I agree that the main difference between economists like myself and those who believe in neo-classical theory, is essentially a difference in empirical assumptions. It is not always easy to isolate an aspect of reality the observation of which is capable of rejecting the one hypothesis and not the other. For example, if we were to find that the rate of growth of agricultural production is fairly close to two per cent per annum among a large number of countries differing in other respects, whereas the rate of growth of labour productivity in agriculture can be either much higher or much lower than this, depending on both fertility and the growth in numbers engaged outside agriculture (which in turn is a reflection of the growth of demand in the other sectors of the economy which draw their additional labour requirements from agriculture), this would be sufficient, in my view, to reject the neo-classical hypothesis and to support the opposite hypothesis, that of surplus labour. Such examples could be multiplied.

WHAT STILL REMAINS OF KALDOR'S LAWS?*

Lord Kaldor has long maintained that an important explanation of the persistent differences in the growth of the advanced countries is the prevalence of both dynamic and static economies of scale in the manufacturing sector. In support of this contention, he has cited the famous Verdoorn Law which asserts that every increase in the growth of output by one percentage point will induce an increase in productivity growth of half a percentage point. The Law is inferred from the fact that when manufacturing productivity growth is regressed on that of output on the basis of cross country data, the regression coefficient takes a value of one half. Nearly ten years after Kaldor first developed this thesis in his inaugural lecture (1966), Rowthorn (1975a) questioned the specification of the Law. If the slow rate of growth of the United Kingdom is due to the relative inelasticity of the labour supply to manufacturing, then the correct statistical procedure is to regress productivity growth directly on employment and this estimation provides no justification for rejecting the hypothesis of constant returns to scale.

The subsequent exchange in this JOURNAL between Kaldor (1975) and Rowthorn (1975b) clearly demonstrated the importance of the assumption that is made as to whether output or employment growth should be treated as exogenous. Kaldor by no means accepted Rowthorn's strictures but argued that the growth of demand for industrial output is the important factor in determining the long term growth of the advanced countries. In support of this argument he adduced a further empirical generalisation which may, for convenience, be termed the 'Third Law' and which was 'not mentioned by Rowthorn'.[1] In this paper we examine the statistical and conceptual foundations of the multiple regression which forms the basis of this Law, which is seen by Kaldor as being important for two related reasons. In the first place, it provides in its own right an explanation for international differences in the growth of total productivity. Secondly, by confirming the existence of surplus labour and, hence, the absence of any supply constraint, it justifies the traditional use of output growth as the regressor in the specification of the Verdoorn Law. We shall show that, notwithstanding Kaldor's recent reaffirmation of his belief in the importance of this law (1978, pp. xx–xxi), an underlying identity vitiates any attempt to give the regression result any behavioural interpretation.

We also examine the contention that the existence of surplus labour in a large sector of the economy may be inferred from the lack of any relationship between employment and output growth in non-industry. It appears that this failure of the Verdoorn Law may be entirely attributable to the well-known

---

* I am grateful to Lord Kaldor, John de Ridder, John Treble and two anonymous referees for helpful comments. Of course, this should not be taken to imply they necessarily agree with the arguments advanced in this paper nor that they are responsible for any remaining errors.

[1] Kaldor's first two laws are (a) the relationship between the growth of total output and industry and (b) the Verdoorn Law (together with Rowthorn's specification).

inadequacies inherent in the measurement of the growth of service output. A similar, though less serious problem occurs with regard to industrial output. This leads to the interesting suggestion with which we conclude the paper that the Verdoorn Law may well be spurious and solely the result of bias induced by measurement errors.

We commence with an assessment of Kaldor's Third Law.

I. THE THIRD LAW – LAW OR IDENTITY?

Kaldor has succinctly stated his interpretation of the Law in his rejoinder to Rowthorn and it is difficult to do better than to quote the relevant passage, (with a small change in notation and omitting a footnote).

> This view [of the existence of surplus labour in the non-industrial sector of the economy] has been strikingly confirmed by Cripps and Tarling's findings in two remarkable correlations (not mentioned by Rowthorn) which explain the overall productivity growth of the economy (the rate of growth of GDP per head) in terms of the rate of growth of industrial output and the (relative) diminution of non-industrial employment. This relationship has in no way been impaired by the failure of the Verdoorn Law in manufacturing in the post-1965 period; indeed the correlation coefficient is even higher for the 1965–70 period than for the 1950–65 period.
>
> The two equations are:
>
> 1950–65:
> $$p_{GDP} = 1\cdot172 + 0\cdot534\ q_{IND} - 0\cdot812\ e_{NI} \qquad R^2 = 0\cdot805.$$
> $$\phantom{p_{GDP} = 1\cdot172 + }(0\cdot058)\phantom{\ q_{IND}\ }(0\cdot202)$$
>
> 1965–70:
> $$p_{GDP} = 1\cdot153 + 0\cdot642\ q_{IND} - 0\cdot872\ e_{NI} \qquad R^2 = 0\cdot958.$$
> $$\phantom{p_{GDP} = 1\cdot153 + }(0\cdot058)\phantom{\ q_{IND}\ }(0\cdot125)$$

Where p_{GDP}, q_{IND}, e_{NI} stand for the rate of growth of GDP per employed person, the rate of growth of industrial production and the rate of growth of non-industrial employment respectively.

The important thing to note is – and herein lies Rowthorn's misunderstanding – that the existence of increasing returns to scale in industry (the Verdoorn Law) is not a necessary or indispensable element in the interpretation of these equations. Even if industrial output obeyed the law of constant returns, it could still be true that the growth of industrial output was the governing factor in the overall rate of economic growth (both in terms of total output and output per head) so long as the growth of industrial output represented a net addition to the effective use of resources and not just a transfer of resources from one use to another. This would be the case if (*a*) the capital required for industrial production was (largely or wholly) self-generated – the accumulation of capital was an aspect, or a by-product, of the growth of output; and (*b*) the labour engaged in industry had no true opportunity cost outside industry, on account of the prevalence of disguised unemployment both in agriculture and services. There is plenty of direct evidence to substantiate both of these assumptions [1975, pp. 894–5].

It is apparent that Kaldor has shifted the emphasis of his argument as set out in his inaugural lecture (1966) so that it no longer rests solely on the Verdoorn Law, but also includes the dual sector nature of the advanced economies. Given that surplus labour exists in the non-industrial sector, then the faster is the rate of growth of industry, the faster, *ceteris paribus*, will be the transfer of labour out of the rest of the economy and the greater will be the induced productivity growth in this sector. The presence of increasing returns in industry will merely reinforce this acceleration of total productivity growth to the extent that an increase in the growth of industrial output will also increase the growth of industrial productivity. The Verdoorn Law, although important, is no longer the *sine qua non* of Kaldor's thesis, and its breakdown subsequent to 1965, as well as Rowthorn's argument, are no longer so damaging.

This reasoning would be most persuasive were it not for the fact that p_{GDP} is *definitionally* related to q_{IND} and e_{NI}. It transpires that the underlying identity precludes any behavioural interpretation of the regression results as the estimated coefficients simply reflect the shares of industrial output in total output and non-industrial employment in total employment, respectively, albeit that the estimates are biased.

To show this, total productivity may be defined as

$$P_{GDP} \equiv \frac{Q_{IND} + Q_{NI}}{E_{IND} + E_{NI}} \tag{1}$$

where P, Q and E are the levels of productivity, output and employment and GDP, IND and NI denote, as before, Gross Domestic Product, industry and non-industry, respectively.

Hence, the growth of total productivity is given by

$$p_{GDP} \equiv aq_{IND} - be_{IND} + (1-a)q_{NI} - (1-b)e_{NI}, \tag{2}$$

where a is the share of industrial output in total output and b is the share of industrial employment in total employment.

If equation (2) were to be estimated, the coefficients could be unambiguously interpreted as the relevant sector shares and the goodness of fit would simply be a function of the inter-country variation of these values. In practice, a and b do not greatly vary between countries. Moreover, since the average ratio of sectoral to total productivity does not differ greatly from unity (in 1970, the ratio of industrial to total productivity ranged from 1·26 (Austria) to 0·87 (the United Kingdom)), a and b are approximately equal and they take a value of about 0·35. If we omit e_{IND} and q_{NI} to obtain the specification of the Third Law, a bias will be induced in the estimates of the two remaining coefficients. A standard result of Ordinary Least Squares states that the bias will be equal to the true value of the coefficient of the omitted variable multiplied by the appropriate regression coefficient obtained when the excluded variable is regressed on the included variables. Since the two 'auxiliary' regressions are already known, being none other than Kaldor's first two laws, it is possible to predict the coefficients of the Third Law.[1] For the period 1950–1965, the first two laws take the form:

$$q_{NI} = 2\cdot0 + 0\cdot3 q_{IND} \quad \text{(The First Law)},[2] \tag{3}$$

$$e_{IND} = -1\cdot5 + 0\cdot5 q_{IND} \quad \text{(The Verdoorn Law)}. \tag{4}$$

Equations (3) and (4) imply that we should expect the regression of total productivity growth on industrial output and non-industrial employment to yield the following result;

$$p_{GDP} = 1\cdot83 + 0\cdot37 q_{IND} - 0\cdot65 e_{NI}. \tag{5}$$

This argument also holds for the later period, 1965–70, except that there has now ceased to be any statistical association between industrial employment and output growth. It is therefore to be expected that the estimated value of the coefficient of q_{IND} will increase to about 0·55 with the removal of the element of downward bias formerly caused by the Verdoorn Law. It is somewhat ironical that the fact that the Third Law does not depend solely upon the existence of economies of scale in industry may be inferred (under Kaldor's interpretation) from the increase in the value of the coefficient of q_{IND}, and, by implication, the importance of this variable at a time when the Verdoorn Law breaks down in a statistical sense. This anomaly is explained once it is realised that this occurs precisely because of, and not in spite of, the collapse of the Verdoorn Law.

Table 1 reports the results of the estimation of the various equations, and the estimates strikingly confirm the above arguments. The estimation of the complete identity for both periods yields, not surprisingly, a very good fit, with the value of the coefficients reflecting the magnitude of the appropriate sectoral shares.[3] For the period 1950–65, the regression of the relationships between the excluded and included variables confirm the First and Verdoorn Laws.

Turning next to the period 1965–70, the breakdown of the Verdoorn Law is confirmed but the First Law also gives a poor fit. It should be noted, however, that there is an unexpectedly significant coefficient of e_{NI} in the 'auxiliary' regression of e_{IND} on q_{IND} and e_{NI}. This seems to be spurious and without any economic meaning and does not occur in the earlier period. It comes as no surprise to learn that the Third Law still retains its high $\bar{R}^2$ and low standard errors and the estimated coefficients are again close to what is expected. It is difficult to see any justification for the conclusion of Cripps and Tarling that the Third Law provides 'a striking indication of the significance and stability of Kaldor's generalisations.' (1973, p. 30). The goodness of fit conceals the fact

---

[1] Strictly speaking, the 'auxiliary' regression should also include e_{NI} as a regressor but this does not seriously affect the argument.

[2] This is a preferable specification of the First Law since it avoids the spurious correlation due to the inclusion of q_{IND} in both sides of the equation that occurs in Kaldor's original procedure of regressing q_{GDP} on q_{IND}.

[3] The reported results exclude Japan, although use of the full sample of twelve countries does not produce markedly different estimates. The results for the period 1970–3 (not reported here) are similar to those for 1965–70 and the Verdoorn Law also failed to re-establish itself.

Table 1

The Third Law: Regression Results

Dependent variable	Constant	q_{IND}	e_{IND}	q_{NI}	e_{NI}	R^2
Period 1950–65						
(1) p_{GDP}	−0·105 (−1·04)	0·410 (15·99)	−0·380 (−11·90)	0·628 (19·36)	−0·689 (−21·50)	0·987
(2) p_{GDP}	1·670 (5·08)	0·388 (7·05)	—	—	−0·625 (−4·20)	0·625
Relationship between excluded and included variables.						
(3) e_{IND}	−1·637 (−3·83)	0·608 (8·49)	—	—	0·219 (1·13)	0·741
(4) q_{NI}	1·835 (4·36)	0·334 (4·73)	—	—	0·234 (1·22)	0·474
Period 1965–70						
(1) p_{GDP}	−0·002 (−0·02)	0·439 (19·81)	−0·349 (−7·43)	0·558 (13·09)	−0·660 (−31·71)	0·998
(2) p_{GDP}	1·168 (2·68)	0·623 (7·77)	—	—	−0·751 (11·22)	0·954
Relationship between excluded and included variables.						
(3) e_{IND}	0·476 (0·55)	−0·030 (−0·18)	—	—	0·353 (2·66)	0·350
(4) q_{NI}	2·394 (2·51)	0·312 (1·78)	—	—	0·058 (0·40)	0·107

Sources: National Accounts and Labour Force Statistics, (O.E.C.D., various years), Cripps and Tarling, (1973).
Note: t statistics in parentheses.

that both Kaldor's other laws have broken down and the Third Law, *per se*, has no economic significance. The underlying identity vitiates any attempt to give the estimated coefficients any behavoural interpretation and the Third Law is nothing more than the estimation of an identity, although mis-specified.[1]

II. THE VERDOORN LAW AND MEASUREMENT ERRORS.[2]

Although no support is provided by the Third Law for the hypothesis that surplus labour exists in a substantial part of the economies of the advanced countries, it has also been suggested that this contention may be substantiated

---

[1] The Third Law was originally specified by Kaldor (1968) in a slightly different form. The rate of growth of total productivity was taken to be a function of industrial *employment* growth (rather than output), together with the decline of non-industrial employment. Although this version of the Law holds for 1950–1965, Cripps and Tarling (1973) found the coefficient of e_{IND} was no longer significant when the period 1965–1970 was considered. This seems to have led Kaldor to abandon his original specification in favour of the formulation discussed above, which was first reported in Cripps and Tarling's study. The initial approach adopted by Kaldor is also subject to the same criticisms outlined above, and the poor fit found for the later period is merely the result of the small variance in both employment growth rates, rather than due to any economic cause.

[2] I am especially indebted to an anonymous referee for his suggestions concerning the following section.

by the failure to find a Verdoorn relationship for the non-industrial sector. (For example, Cripps and Tarling (1973, p. 27) found that the coefficient of determination between output and employment growth was only 0·003.) The force of this argument is considerably reduced not only by the mis-specification problem due to the omission of the growth of the non-labour inputs,[1] but also by reservations that arise concerning the accuracy of the non-industrial output growth statistics. This measurement problem also affects the confidence we can place on the reliability of the estimates of the growth of industrial output, although in this case the position is not quite so serious. Nevertheless, it is worth pursuing the implications further, since it suggests an alternative explanation of the discrepancy found between Kaldor's and Rowthorn's specification of the industrial Verdoorn Law.

The methodology involved in the construction of the O.E.C.D. National Accounts Statistics have been examined in detail by Hill and McGibbon (1966). They came to the conclusion that the slow rate of growth of the service sector output compared with that of industry cannot be attributed to either variations in income elasticities of demand or differential growth rates of technical progress. 'In practice, the main reason for the comparatively slow rate of growth of services in all countries seems to be that a substantial proportion of the real output indicators used in this sector consists simply of employment changes. Whereas substantial increases in labour productivity may be recorded in other sectors, including agriculture, the output indicators in use over a wide range of general services permit little or no increase in output per person' (p. 38). The method of deriving the statistics for service output growth also varies considerably between countries and this, together with the practice of often *assuming* service productivity growth is either negligible, or making an arbitrary allowance for it, renders the estimates totally devoid of economic or any other significance. It is thus dangerous to draw any conclusions from the failure of the Verdoorn Law in the non-industrial sector.

In the case of industry, measurement errors are less serious, being imparted by, for example, the method of deflation employed (whether single indicator or double deflation), the treatment of quality change and the usual sampling errors (see, for example, Hill, 1971, especially chapter IV). In order to discuss the implications of these errors, it is useful to commence by assuming Kaldor is correct in specifying the Verdoorn Law as

$$p' = a'_1 + b_1'q' + w_1, \qquad (6)$$

where w_1 is the 'true' error term. We further postulate that, given that there

---

[1] Since the Verdoorn Law is a production relationship and the focus of attention is on the degree of returns to scale, it is meaningless simply to regress productivity on output growth unless allowance is made, either explicitly or implicitly, for the growth of the capital stock. As Rowthorn (1979) has pointed out, under the assumptions of Verdoorn's original model, the estimated value of the returns to scale are most implausible, being 2·3 for the labour input alone. On the other hand, Kaldor's procedure may be defended from this criticism. There is strong evidence that there has been little, if any, growth in the postwar capital-output ratios of the advanced countries. Consequently, if the growth of output and that of the capital-output ratio are orthogonal, the Verdoorn coefficient obtained by regressing p on q may be interpreted as an estimate of $(\alpha + \beta - 1)/\beta$, where α and β are the output elasticities of capital and labour, respectively. If we further assume that α does not exceed β, then a Verdoorn coefficient of one half implies that the returns to scale will not be less than 1·33.

are errors of measurement in both output and employment, the true growth rates are given by $q' = q - u$ and $e' = e - v$, where q and e are the observed values and u and v are the measurement errors. It seems plausible to assume that u and v are uncorrelated both with each other and with the systematic components of the equation. Given that $p' \equiv q' - e'$ and $p \equiv q - e$, it follows that

$$p = a'_1 + b'_1 q + [(1-b'_1)u + w_1 - v]. \tag{7}$$

In the probability limit, the estimate of the Verdoorn coefficient (b_1) and its true value (b'_1) will be related by the expression

$$b_1 = b'_1 + \frac{(1-b'_1)}{1+k} k, \tag{8}$$

where $k = \sigma_u^2/\sigma_{q'}^2$ and σ_u^2 and $\sigma_{q'}^2$ are the variance of u and q', respectively. It is readily apparent that the estimation of the Verdoon Law using data subject to measurement errors will yield a regression coefficient that is biased upwards and in favour of accepting the hypothesis of increasing returns to scale, so long as b'_1 and b_1 are less than unity, which proves to be true of the case under consideration here. On the other hand, the estimation of Rowthorn's specification

$$p = a_2 + b_2 e + w_2 \tag{9}$$

will produce an understatement of the true coefficient, b'_2, given that b'_2 and b_2 exceed minus one. Asymptotically, the following inequality holds; $b_1 \geqslant b'_1 \geqslant b_2/(1 + b_2)$. Unfortunately, in the absence of any further evidence about the size of the measurement errors, this inequality proves to be inconclusive as it is no longer possible unambiguously to reject or to accept the hypothesis of constant returns to scale.

Indeed, it is possible to argue that measurement errors *alone* are responsible for generating the Verdoorn Law. If b'_1 is zero then equation (8) shows that b_1 will converge to $k/(1 + k)$. A necessary assumption for measurement errors to generate a Verdoorn coefficient of one half is for the variance of u to be equal to that of q' which is, perhaps, rather implausible. On the other hand, if we are prepared to treat the Verdoorn Law as a deterministic relationship with no error in the equation and to assume that employment growth is free of measurement errors, then Rowthorn's specification may be interpreted as being, in effect, an inverse regression and b_2 will hence be consistent. This would, of course, entail a rejection of Kaldor's thesis of the importance of increasing returns.

An alternative procedure is to retain the assumption that the Verdoorn Law is a functional relationship but to postulate that there are measurement errors in employment as well as in output and that the ratio of the variances of the errors is proportional to the ratio of the observed variances of employment and output growth. Generally, in the absence of any other prior information, it has been common practice, in such circumstances, to assume that the two ratios are equal although, of course, this is a rather arbitrary assumption. In this case, the consistent estimate of the Verdoorn coefficient is given by

$$b_3 = 1 - \sqrt{\left(\frac{1-b_1}{1+b_2}\right)}, \qquad (10)$$

where b_1 and b_2 are the regression coefficients of the Verdoorn Law and Rowthorn's specification, respectively.

The variance of b_3 is somewhat more complicated to determine but may be approximated by an expression derived by Madansky (1959). The result of this weighted regression is reported in Table 2, where for completeness, we also include the estimates of Kaldor's and Rowthorn's specifications. It is perhaps worth emphasising that these results are not strictly comparable because the various specifications are based on differing underlying assumptions about the error structure, especially the errors introduced by measurement deficiencies. Thus, for at least two of the procedures, the regression coefficients and standard errors must be biased.

Table 2

Alternative Estimates of the Verdoorn Coefficient, 1950–1965

Method	Estimated coefficient		t statistic
Kaldor's direct procedure	b_1	0·396	5·40
Weighted regression	b_3	0·286	3·43
Rowthorn's specification	$b_2/(1+b_2)$	0·156	1·28

Note: Japan is excluded from the sample.

The results of the weighted regression tend to support Kaldor since the Verdoorn coefficient is significantly greater than zero, but the value is considerably less than the traditional value of 0·5.

Various instrumental variable methods have been suggested as a means of obviating the errors in variables problem and Table 3 reports the results obtained using the approaches suggested by Wald, Bartlett and Durbin.

These results, if anything, merely serve to emphasise the divergence of results obtained by Kaldor and Rowthorn. It may be that the errors are of

Table 3

Instrumental Variable Estimates of the Verdoorn Coefficient, 1950–1965

	Regressor			
	Output growth		Employment growth	
Method	b_1	t statistic	$b_2/(1+b_2)$	t statistic
Wald's two group method	0·506	(5·04)	0·288	(1·28)
Bartlett's three group method	0·462	(5·09)	0·185	(1·00)
Durbin's ranking method	0·455	(5·74)	0·196	(1·18)

Note: Japan is excluded from the sample.

sufficient magnitude to disturb the groupings or rankings and that the instrumental method approaches that are used here are not appropriate.

At this juncture, it is necessary to consider the additional complication introduced by the possibility of simultaneous equation bias. Once this possibility is admitted, it is no longer possible to determine the direction of bias without explicitly estimating the relevant system of equations. The possibility of simultaneity arises from the fact that the growth of output is likely to be a function of the growth of prices. The growth of prices is, in its turn, likely to be determined by the growth of 'efficiency wages', (the growth of money wages minus that of productivity). Thus a faster rate of growth of productivity will induce, *ceteris paribus*, a faster growth of output. On the other hand, if the supply of labour to manufacturing becomes increasingly inelastic, so manufacturing wages may be bid up, capital accumulation may be decreased and there may be a curtailment in the output growth rate. In either case, output growth should not be treated as exogenous. The difficulty in specifying such a simultaneous system is that it is by no means clear which variables can be deemed exogenous in the context of long run growth and hence used to identify the model. To argue that the rate of growth of exports, the gross investment–output ratio and the growth of non-manufacturing employment may be treated as exogenous as does Parikh (1978), in his attempt to estimate a simultaneous equation model to test the labour surplus hypothesis, entirely begs the question.

It is true that the rate of growth of exports is an important factor determining total output growth under the Kaldorian assumptions but if manufacturing output is affected by the conditions of the labour supply, it would be most implausible to assume that exports (of which a large proportion are manufactured goods) are not similarly constrained. As far as the gross investment–output ratio is concerned, it is one of Kaldor's central tenets that capital accumulation is as much a result of, as a cause of, output growth. Finally, if Kaldor is correct, we should expect that the observed rate of growth of non-manufacturing employment will be partially determined by the growth of demand for labour emanating from the industrial sector rather than being exogenously determined. It would thus be premature to accept Parikh's conclusion that the issue has been settled in favour of Kaldor.

The issue of simultaneity also occurs in the estimation of orthodox (neoclassical) production functions where the discussion usually has been in terms of the well-known Marshak-Andrews problem – namely, the simultaneity engendered by the input demand equations drived from the marginal productivity conditions. In practice, it is commonly found that when the production function is estimated as a single equation model, the ratio of the variance of the error term to the systematic component is sufficiently small that Wold's (1957) 'proximity theorem' suggests that the asymptotic bias may be negligible. An interesting corollary of this occurs in the case of the Verdoorn Law. An alternative method of obtaining an estimate of the Verdoorn coefficient is to regress the logarithmic value of the *level* of productivity on that of output, since differentiating this relationship with respect to time will yield the Verdoorn Law. (There are, of course, other underlying structures of the Law depending upon the assumption made about the constant of integration.) When the 'static' Verdoorn Law is estimated a very good fit is obtained with the coefficient of determination exceeding 0·9, and both Kaldor's and Rowthorn's specifications suggest constant returns to scale. This returns us to the errors in variables problem since one explanation of this 'dynamic-static' paradox is based on the observation that it is commonly found empirically that the relative error in a macrovariable, especially, is often considerably less than the relative error in the first differences. This occurs because if two variables x_t and x_{t+1} are subject to measurement errors which have variances v_t and v_{t+1} respectively, then the measurement error associated with $x_{t+1} - x_t$ will have a variance of $v_t + v_{t+1}$, so long as the measurement errors are independent of each other. The implication is that the 'static' Verdoorn Law may provide a more reliable estimate of the Verdoorn coefficient and that the estimate of the 'dynamic' Law may be subject to a greater degree of measurement bias. This conclusion, though, must be regarded as tentative since it is possible that the use of growth rates may reduce the relative error as in the case of, for example, constant omitted factors. (There are also other explanations of this paradox and these are discussed in McCombie (1980a).)

To summarise, while it is not possible categorically to attribute the value of the Verdoorn coefficient to measurement errors, it may help explain why the estimated size of the returns to scale in the traditional specification of the Verdoorn Law are so large, (notwithstanding the results of the instrumental variable procedures). The errors in variables problem will also affect the estimation of the Third Law but in a rather more complicated manner, especially as the errors in the non-industrial employment and output will be correlated with each other and with the systematic component. However, this is very much of a secondary issue in view of the criticisms raised above, and will not be pursued here.

III. CONCLUDING COMMENTS

Lord Kaldor's disquiet over the use of the neoclassical paradigm to explain both the allocation of resources within the advanced countries and their growth stems from what he considers to be the untenable assumption of constant returns and the postulate that employment is the limiting factor in all sectors of the economy. Yet, in spite of Kaldor's insistence that for economic analysis to be fruitful it must be firmly grounded in empirical generalisations or 'laws', we have shown that the so-called Third Law cannot be taken as providing any support for the surplus labour hypothesis. Further reservations were raised, in addition to those of Rowthorn, concerning the specification of the Verdoorn Law.

On the other hand, it should not necessarily be inferred from these findings that Kaldor is mistaken in his arguments as to the determinants of economic growth, but, rather, little or no support is provided at this stage by the empirical evidence he adduces. The use of the dual sector model of growth in the case of the advanced countries has also been advocated by Kindleberger (1967) and, more recently, Cornwall (1976, 1977). They both substantiate their arguments by recourse either to indirect evidence or to descriptive statistics, although these must be viewed as suggestive rather than conclusive. The potential importance of Kaldor's thesis has also been confirmed by McCombie (1980b) who attempted to quantify the contribution to total productivity growth of increasing returns in manufacturing and of surplus labour in conjunction with the intersectoral transfer of labour, on the assumption that Kaldor is correct. It was found that these two phenomena can account for between 20 and 70% of total productivity growth, depending upon the country under consideration. Consequently, it may well be that Lord Kaldor's stress on the overriding importance of demand rather than supply factors will still prove to be of the utmost importance for the understanding of the long run growth of the advanced countries.

University of Hull J. S. L. MCCOMBIE
Date of receipt of final typescript: May 1980

REFERENCES

Cornwall, J. (1976). 'Diffusion, convergence and Kaldor's Laws.' ECONOMIC JOURNAL, vol. 86, pp. 307–14.
—— (1977). *Modern Capitalism: Its Growth and Transformation.* London: Martin Robertson.
Cripps, T. F. and Tarling, R. J. (1973). *Growth in Advanced Capitalist Economies, 1950–1970.* Cambridge University Press, Department of Applied Economics, Occasional Paper, 40.
Hill, A. T. P. and McGibbon, J. (1966). 'Growth of sector real product: measures and methods in selected O.E.C.D. countries.' *Review of Income and Wealth*, series 12, pp. 35–55.
Hill, T. P. (1971). *The Measurement of Real Product: A Theoretical and Empirical Analysis of the Growth Rates for Different Industries and Countries.* Paris: O.E.C.D.
Kaldor, N. (1966). *Causes of the Slow Rate of Growth of the United Kingdom, An Inaugural Lecture.* Cambridge University Press.
—— (1968). 'Productivity and growth in manufacturing industry: a reply.' *Economica*, vol. 35, pp. 385–91.
—— (1975). 'Economic growth and the Verdoorn Law – a comment on Mr Rowthorn's article.' ECONOMIC JOURNAL, vol. 85, pp. 891–6.
—— (1978). *Further Essays on Economic Theory.* Duckworth.
Kindleberger, C. P. (1967). *Europe's Post-war Growth: The Role of the Labour Supply.* Cambridge (Mass.): Harvard University Press.
McCombie, J. S. L. (1980a). 'Economic growth and Kaldor's Laws.' *Mimeo*, University of Hull.
—— (1980b). 'On the quantitative importance of Kaldor's Laws.' *Bulletin of Economic Research*, vol. 32.
Madansky, A. (1959). 'The fitting of straight lines when both variables are subject to error.' *Journal of the American Statistical Association*, vol. 54, pp. 173–205.
Parikh, A. (1978). 'Differences in growth rates and Kaldor's Laws.' *Economica*, vol. 45, pp. 83–91.
Rowthorn, R. E. (1975a). 'What remains of Kaldor's Law?' ECONOMIC JOURNAL, vol. 85, pp. 10–9.
—— (1975b). 'A reply to Lord Kaldor's comment.' ECONOMIC JOURNAL, vol. 85, pp. 897–901.
—— (1979). 'A note on Verdoorn's Law.' ECONOMIC JOURNAL, vol. 89, pp. 131–3.
Wold, H. O. A. and Faxer, P. (1957). 'On the specification error in regression analysis.' *Annals of Mathematical Statistics*, vol. 28, pp. 265–7.

Symposium: Kaldor's growth laws

Introduction

A. P. THIRLWALL

This symposium celebrates Nicholas Kaldor's seventy-fifth birthday. There are three main types of economist: those who theorize without measuring; those who measure without theorizing; and those who observe what is around them and attempt to model the behavior they see. Kaldor is a master craftsman in the latter category. His various attempts to explain the "stylized facts" of dynamic capitalist economies are well known. His attempts to explain differences in the growth performance of nations outside the neoclassical paradigm are perhaps less well known, but they can be reduced to three generalizations or "laws." First, the faster the rate of growth of manufacturing industry, the faster the growth of total national output; second, the faster the growth of manufacturing, the faster the growth of labor productivity in manufacturing; and third, the faster the growth of manufacturing, the faster the growth of productivity outside manufacturing. This symposium in Kaldor's honor outlines some of the theory and the latest evidence.

Kaldor has been a long-standing critic of neoclassical equilibrium theory as a basis for understanding how economic processes work in growing capitalist economies. Equilibrium theory is static and cannot easily cope with change. To overcome this problem by introducing time as a dimension or to assume exogenous trends is not satisfactory because development and change cannot be foreseen, and things do not change at constant exogenous rates. Second, equilibrium theory is obsessed with substitution and ignores the complementarity between factors of production and between activities. If factors of production and activities are complementary, there can be no such thing as a full employment equilibrium

The author is Professor of Applied Economics at the University of Kent at Canterbury.

because in the process of resource allocation and production, the productive possibilities of the community increase. The productivity of resources is not the same in all activities, and increased production and capital accumulation are part and parcel of the same process. Production augments resources as well as using them up. Third, the production possibility curve itself is not concave (or linear for that matter) but convex to the origin in the Allyn Young sense that increases in the output of one product can be had at the sacrifice or displacement of *proportionately smaller* quantities of other products.

The assumption of constant returns, of course, pervades the whole of equilibrium theory, and yet we know that industrial activities are subject to increasing returns, both static and dynamic, and land-based activities are subject to diminishing returns. Adam Smith recognized the importance of increasing returns over 200 years ago. Productivity depends on the division of labor, which in turn depends on the size of the market. As the market expands, productivity expands; but the increase in productivity resulting from a larger market in turn enlarges the market for other things, and this causes productivity in other industries to rise. As Young (1928) observed

> Adam Smith's famous theorem amounts to saying that the division of labour depends in large part on the division of labour. [But] this is more than mere tautology. It means that the counter forces which are continually defeating the forces which make for equilibrium are more pervasive and more deep rooted than we commonly realise.... Change becomes progressive and propogates itself in a cumulative way.

The difference between industrial and land-based activities has profound implications for the growth and development process in the world economy, where some countries concentrate on activities primarily subject to diminishing returns while others produce goods subject to increasing returns. The existence of increasing returns not only undermines the concept of a competitive equilibrium but makes the whole growth and development process a cumulative one in favored "regions" relative to others. Trade and factor mobility between "regions" become disequilibriating rather than equilibriating as far as income, employment opportunity, and other indices of welfare are concerned.

The policy implications are far-reaching. A country neglects its manufacturing sector and foreign trade sector at its peril. The long-run growth of output cannot be regarded, as in neoclassical theory, as determined by an *exogenously* given long-run rate of growth of the total labor force and technical progress. Firstly, the sector where the growth takes place is important; and secondly, the growth of the labor force, capital accumulation, and technical progress must be regarded as largely *endogenous* to an economic system, dependent on the strength of demand for a country's products, which in an open economy depends on export demand relative to the propensity to import. In the long run, which means considering an economy over a period of time as opposed to a point in time, the concept of a full-employment level of resources loses meaning, and production cannot be said to be supply constrained because if demand is effective, there will be an augmentation of resources, both labor and investable resources, as the postwar economies of Germany, Switzerland, and France demonstrate, not to mention buoyant regions within countries. Supply-side policies to revive lagging national or regional economies will by themselves be abortive unless at the same time they relieve constraints on overall effective demand. It is left to the reader of the symposium to decide on whether the Kaldorian or neoclassical approach to an understanding of growth rate differences is the more relevant, and what policy implications are more pertinent.

In the first paper I give a Plain Man's Guide to Kaldor's Growth Laws, with a brief discussion of tests of some of the Laws and criticisms of the Kaldor model. Kaldor owes a strong intellectual debt to his early teacher, Allyn Young, and in the second paper Charles Blitch exposits Young's pioneering paper on increasing returns, which in turn derives its inspiration from Adam Smith. But as Kaldor has bemoaned, it is from Chapter 4 of Book One of the *Wealth of Nations* that economics went wrong. In the third and fourth papers McCombie and de Ridder and Gomulka use state data for the United States and Eastern European data, respectively, to examine some of Kaldor's propositions relating to manufacturing as the engine of growth and Verdoorn's Law. Chatterji and Wickens in a further paper examine productivity differences between six European countries and suggest that generalized versions of both Verdoorn's Law and Kaldor's Law have a role to play in understanding the growth process, though not quite in the manner originally suggested by Verdoorn and Kaldor. Finally, McCombie provides a lucid summary of the existing state of knowledge relating to Kaldor's Laws. Bon appetit!

REFERENCE

Young, A. "Increasing Returns and Economic Progress." *Economic Journal*, December 1928.

[41]

Kaldor's growth laws

A plain man's guide to Kaldor's growth laws

A. P. THIRLWALL

In the course of his Inaugural Lecture at Cambridge in 1966 on the causes of the U.K's slow growth rate, Kaldor (1966) presented a series of "laws" to account for growth rate differences between advanced capitalist countries; he later elaborated these laws in a lecture at Cornell University (1967). These laws, and their interpretation and validity, have been the subject of considerable scrutiny and debate, and Kaldor himself has clarified and modified his own position since their enunciation. The basic thrust of the model consists of the following propositions:[1]

i) The faster the rate of growth of the manufacturing sector, the faster will be the rate of growth of Gross Domestic Product (GDP), not simply in a definitional sense in that manufacturing output is a large component of total output, but for fundamental economic reasons connected with induced productivity growth inside and outside the manufacturing sector. This is not a new idea. It is summed up in the maxim that the manufacturing sector of the economy is the "engine of growth."

ii) The faster the rate of growth of manufacturing output, the faster will be the rate of growth of labor productivity in manufacturing owing to static and dynamic economies of scale, or increasing returns in the widest sense. Kaldor, in the spirit of Allyn Young (1928), his early teacher at the L.S.E., conceives of returns

---

The author is Professor of Applied Economics at the University of Kent at Canterbury.

[1] Some of the propositions are not as Kaldor originally stated them, but we shall return to the original argument later.

to scale as macroeconomic phenomena related to the interaction between the elasticity of demand for and supply of manufactured goods. It is this strong and powerful interaction which accounts for the positive relationship between manufacturing output and productivity growth, otherwise known as Verdoorn's Law (1949).

iii) The faster the rate of growth of manufacturing output, the faster the rate of transference of labor from other sectors of the economy where there are either diminishing returns, or where no relationship exists between employment growth and output growth. A reduction in the amount of labor in these sectors will raise productivity growth outside manufacturing. As a result of increasing returns in manufacturing on the one hand and induced productivity growth in nonmanufacturing on the other, we expect that the faster the rate of growth of manufacturing output, the faster the rate of growth of productivity in the economy *as a whole*.

iv) As the scope for transferring labor from diminishing returns activities dries up, or as output comes to depend on employment in all sectors of the economy, the degree of overall productivity growth induced by manufacturing growth is likely to diminish, with the overall growth rate correspondingly reduced.

v) It is in this latter sense that Kaldor believes that countries at a high level of development, with little or no surplus labor in agriculture or nonmanufacturing activities, suffer from a "labor shortage" and will experience a deceleration of growth; not in the sense that manufacturing output is constrained by a shortage of labor, which he suggested in his Inaugural Lecture was the U.K's problem but now regrets and retracts (1978).

vi) The growth of manufacturing output is *not* constrained by labor supply but is fundamentally determined by demand from agriculture in the early stage of development and exports in the later stages. Export demand is the major component of autonomous demand in an open economy which must match the leakage of income into imports. The level of industrial output will adjust to the level of export demand in relation to the propensity to import, through the working of the Harrod trade multiplier:[2] the rate of

---

[2] For an exposition and an elaboration of the Harrod trade multiplier, see Kennedy and Thirlwall (1979) and Thirlwall (1982).

growth of output will approximate to the rate of growth of exports divided by the income elasticity of demand for imports (see Thirlwall, 1979).

vii) A fast rate of growth of exports and output will tend to set up a cumulative process, or virtuous circle of growth, through the link between output growth and productivity growth. The lower costs of production in fast growing countries make it difficult for other (newly industrializing) countries to establish export activities with favorable growth characteristics, except through exceptional industrial enterprise.

This catalogue of propositions is more or less the full Kaldor model of growth rate differences in advanced capitalist countries. Now let us trace its origins from 1966, examine the evidence that he presents at various stages along the way, and consider the barrage of criticism to which the model has been subjected and how Kaldor has reacted to it and subsequently modified his position.

Kaldor's first law: there exists a strong relation between the growth of manufacturing output and the growth of GDP.

Kaldor argues that a fast rate of economic growth (g_{GDP}) is associated with a fast rate of growth of the manufacturing sector of the economy (g_m), which in turn is a characteristic of the transition from "immaturity" to "maturity," where "immaturity" is defined as a situation in which productivity is lower outside industry (particularly in agriculture), so that labor is available for use in industry in relatively unlimited quantities. Kaldor's Inaugural Lecture suggestion was that the U.K., with a comparatively poor growth record, suffered from "premature maturity" in the sense of having reached the stage of roughly equal productivity in all sectors of the economy before attaining a particularly high level in manufacturing industry. Taking a cross section of twelve developed countries[3] over the period 1952-54 to 1963-64, Kaldor found a strong correlation between g_{GDP} and g_m:

(1) $\qquad g_{GDP} = 1.153 + 0.614 \, (g_m) \quad r^2 = 0.959.$
$\qquad\qquad\qquad\quad (0.040)$

---

[3] Japan, Italy, West Germany, Austria, France, Denmark, Netherlands, Belgium, Norway, Canada, U.K., and United States.

Since the regression coefficient is significantly less than unity, the equation also implies that the greater the *excess* of the rate of growth of manufacturing output over the rate of growth of the economy as a whole, the faster the overall growth rate. Setting $g_{GDP} = g_m$ shows that rates of growth above 3 percent are found only in cases where the rate of growth of manufacturing exceeds the overall growth of the economy; that is, where the share of the manufacturing sector in the total economy is increasing. In other words, the high correlation between the two variables is not simply the result of manufacturing output constituting a large proportion of total output. There must also be a positive association between the overall rate of economic growth and the *excess* of the rate of growth of manufacturing output over the rate of growth of nonmanufacturing output (g_{nm}). This is confirmed by Kaldor's data:

(2) $\quad g_{GDP} = 3.351 + 0.954 \, (g_m - g_{nm}) \quad r^2 = 0.562.$
$\qquad\qquad\quad (0.267)$

The contention that the strong correlation between g_{GDP} and g_m does not depend on manufacturing output constituting a large part of total output is also supported by the fact that there is an almost identical relation between the growth of nonmanufacturing output and the growth of manufacturing as in equation (1):

(3) $\quad g_{nm} = 1.142 + 0.550 \, (g_m) \quad r^2 = 0.824.$
$\qquad\qquad\quad (0.080)$

There is no correlation between the rate of growth of GDP and either agricultural output or mining. There is a correlation between the growth of GDP and the growth of services, and the relation is virtually one to one; but Kaldor suggests that the direction of causation is almost certainly from the growth of GDP to service activity rather than the other way round. The demand for most services is derived from the demand for manufacturing output itself. Cripps and Tarling (1973), taking the same twelve countries over the longer period 1951 to 1970, and breaking the data up into four subperiods and pooling, provided support for Kaldor's first law:

(4) $\quad g_{GDP} = 1.295 + 0.603 \, (g_m) \quad r^2 = 0.899.$
$\qquad\qquad\quad (0.031)$

Research by the present author (in collaboration with David

Vines, 1980) on low- and middle-income countries shows the same strong cross-section correlation, and that the faster g_m relative to g_{GDP}, the faster the growth of GDP.

What accounts for the fact that the faster manufacturing output grows relatively to GDP, the faster GDP seems to grow? Since differences in growth rates are largely accounted for by differences in productivity growth, there must be some relationship between the growth of the manufacturing sector and productivity growth in the economy as a whole. This is to be expected for one of two main reasons, or both. The first is that wherever industrial production and employment expand, labor resources are drawn from other sectors which have open or disguised unemployment (that is, where there is no relation between employment and output), so that the labor transference to manufacturing will not cause a diminution in the output of these sectors. In addition, the expansion of industry will automatically generate an increase in the stock of capital employed in industry.

A second reason is the existence of increasing returns, both static and dynamic. Static returns relate to the size and scale of production units and are a characteristic largely of manufacturing where in the process of doubling the linear dimensions of equipment, the surface increases by the square and the volume by the cube. Dynamic economies refer to increasing returns brought about by "induced" technical progress, learning by doing, external economies in production, and so on. Kaldor draws inspiration here from Allyn Young's pioneering paper (1928), with its emphasis on increasing returns as a macroeconomic phenomenon. Because economies of scale result from increased product differentiation, new processes, new subsidiary industries, and so on, it was Young's contention that they cannot be discerned adequately by observing the effects of variations in the size of an *individual* firm or of a *particular* industry. Economies of scale and increasing returns derive from general industrial expansion, which should be seen as an interrelated whole or as an interaction *between* activities.

The empirical relation between productivity growth and output growth in manufacturing industry has come to be known as Verdoorn's Law following Verdoorn's paper (1949) showing such an empirical relation for a cross section of countries in the interwar period. Although the coefficient can be derived from a static Cobb-Douglas production function, it is essentially a dynamic relationship dependent on the rate at which capital is growing relative to labor and the scale parameters, which may include both static and dynamic returns (Thirlwall, 1980). This leads us to Kaldor's second law.

Kaldor's second law: there is a strong positive relation between the rate of growth of productivity in manufacturing industry (p_m) and the growth of manufacturing output (g_m).

Kaldor's test of this relationship gives:

(5) $\quad\quad p_m = 1.035 + 0.484\ (g_m) \quad r^2 = 0.826,$
$\quad\quad\quad\quad\quad\quad (0.070)$

or

(6) $\quad\quad e_m = -1.028 + 0.516\ (g_m) \quad r^2 = 0.844,$
$\quad\quad\quad\quad\quad\quad (0.070)$

where e_m is employment growth in manufacturing. The two equations are two ways of looking at the same relationship since $g_m = p_m + e_m$. Only in the construction industry and in public utilities is a Verdoorn relation also found to exist. The primary sector, agriculture and mining, reveals no such relation. In both agriculture and mining, productivity growth shows a large trend factor independent of the growth of total output, and the regression coefficient is not significantly different from unity using equation (5). Productivity growth has exceeded output growth in every country. In the case of transport and communications, Kaldor finds no correlation between productivity growth and output growth. In commerce, there is a high correlation, but the constant term using equation (5) is *negative*.

Returning to the strong relationship between p_m and g_m, the question has been raised of what is cause and what is effect? Some say the direction of causation could be from fast productivity growth to fast output growth because faster productivity growth causes demand to expand faster through relative price changes. In this view, all productivity growth would be autonomous. But if this were so, argues Kaldor, how can we explain large differences in productivity growth in the same industry over the same period in different countries? The reverse causation argument would also be a denial of the existence of dynamic scale economies and increasing returns. Kaldor would no doubt concede that there is an interaction process at work through cost and price changes, and that a well-determined estimate of the Verdoorn coefficient requires simultaneous equation estimation.[4]

If productivity growth in manufacturing is faster the faster the rate of growth of manufacturing output, and this is one of the explanations of the faster growth of GDP in countries whose share of manufacturing is rising, what determines the growth of manufacturing output? The explanation lies partly in demand factors and partly in supply factors, and both combine to make fast growth a characteristic of an intermediate stage of economic development. Following the arguments of Allyn Young, the more demand is focused on commodities with a large supply response, and the larger the demand response (direct and indirect) induced by increases in production, the higher the growth rate is likely to be. For there to be self-sustaining growth, two conditions must be present: returns must increase, and the demand for commodities must be elastic in the sense that

> a small increase in [their] supply will be attended by an increase in the amounts of other commodities which can be held in exchange for [them]. Under such conditions, an increase in the supply of one commodity *is* an increase in the demand for other commodities and it must be supposed that every increase in demand will evoke an increase in supply. (Young, 1928, p. 534)

The growth process is a complex interaction of supply and demand. The demand for industrial products is very elastic in the intermediate stage of development and continues to be so in maturity. There is no constraint on growth here. But whatever the demand for commodities, growth may be slowed down by supply constraints. There may be a labor constraint and/or a commodity constraint (Kaldor's meaning of a balance-of-payments constraint). Kaldor originally claimed that it is difficult to prove that the balance of payments is the *effective* constraint on the rate of growth for the U.K.: "This would only follow if it could also be shown

---

[4] Kaldor suggests that if the relationship between p_m and g_m is accepted, a country's productivity performance ought to be judged by deviations from the Verdoorn regression line. On this test the U.K. does not fare too badly, and deviations from the line appear to be closely related to investment behavior.

that, with a faster rate of growth of exports, the country could have achieved a higher rate of growth of manufacturing production" (1966, p. 24). Would growth have come up against other supply constraints? It is at this juncture in his two lectures that Kaldor suggested things in the context of the U.K. which created controversy but which he has since retracted. For example, he states, "inelasticity in the supply of labour seems to me the main constraint limiting the growth potential of the U.K. in a way in which it is not true of any other advanced country with the possible exception of Germany in the last few years" (1967, pp. 41-42). The U.K. is almost alone in having reached a stage of "maturity" with no low-productivity sectors outside industry where labor can be tapped.

Kaldor now believes that manufacturing output growth is fundamentally determined by export growth and that employment will respond to higher output growth. The point he makes about a labor surplus outside industry is still relevant, however, because the faster the growth of output determined by (export) demand, the greater the rate of labor transference to manufacturing industry from other sectors of the economy where productivity is lower (or where there is no relation between output growth and employment growth), so that the faster the *overall* rate of productivity growth will be. In this sense the U.K. has been short of labor because of its relatively small agricultural sector. The relationship between the rate of labor transfer to manufacturing and overall productivity growth is a part of Kaldor's third law, which is considered in more detail below.

Since Kaldor retracted his view about the U.K. economy early on in 1968 in reply to some niggling points of criticism made by Wolfe (1968), it is a pity that there should have been subsequent criticism of the model as a whole based on a misunderstanding, which in turn, through the way tests of the model have been conducted, has led some to reject Verdoorn's Law. The trouble seems to have started with the work of Cripps and Tarling (1973), who although writing in 1973, and in close academic contact with Kaldor, continued to interpret him as believing that manufacturing output growth is *dependent* on employment growth (and not the other way round) and so set up the Verdoorn relation with productivity growth in manufacturing as a function of employment growth in manufacturing. They found that their version of the law holds from 1951 to 1965 but seems to break down in the period 1965 to 1970. Rowthorn (1975), with no reference to Kaldor's

(1968) reply to Wolfe, also continued to interpret Kaldor as believing that manufacturing output growth is endogenous and employment growth exogenous and used the same Verdoorn formulation as Cripps and Tarling. Rowthorn claims to show that Kaldor's results, as well as those of Cripps and Tarling, are heavily dependent on the inclusion of Japan in the sample of countries which, because of its deviant position on the scatter diagram, must be regarded as a special case.

Now it is perfectly true, since $g_m = p_m + e_m$, that mathematically speaking there are four different specifications of the Verdoorn relation:

$$p_m = a + b(g_m) \quad 0 < b < 1$$

$$e_m = -a + (1-b)g_m$$

and
$$g_m = \frac{a}{1-b} + \left(\frac{1}{1-b}\right)e_m$$

$$p_m = \frac{a}{1-b} + \left(\frac{b}{1-b}\right)e_m.$$

Only if the equations are exact will the estimates be the same. From an economic and econometric point of view, the specification is not a matter of indifference. Rowthorn criticizes Kaldor for estimating the Verdoorn coefficient "indirectly" using the first two specifications rather than what he considers to be "directly" using the fourth specification. He contends that had Kaldor done so, his estimate of the Verdoorn coefficient would have been much lower. But if output growth is exogenous and employment growth is endogenous, the Cripps-Tarling and Rowthorn specification of the Verdoorn relation is not correct for well-known statistical reasons. Moreover, Kaldor's original results using the correct specification of the Verdoorn relation do *not* depend on the existence of Japan in the sample. The r^2 between p_m and g_m excluding Japan is 0.536 and between e_m and g_m is 0.685. Research by Vaciago (1975) for eighteen European countries over the period 1950-69 supports the existence of the traditional Verdoorn relation:

$$p_m = 1.05 + 0.60(g_m) \quad r^2 = 0.786.$$
$$(0.07)$$

Moreover Verdoorn's Law is *not* (contrary to the popular view) an indispensable element of the complete Kaldor growth model. Even in the absence of increasing returns in manufacturing (which is difficult to believe), the growth of industry would still be the governing factor determining overall output growth as long as resources used by industry represent a *net* addition to the use of resources (a) because they would otherwise have been unused, (b) because of diminishing returns elsewhere, and/or (c) because industry generates its own resources. This leads us on to Kaldor's third law.

Kaldor's third law: The faster the growth of manufacturing output, the faster the rate of labor transference from nonmanufacturing to manufacturing, so that overall productivity growth is positively related to the growth of output and employment in manufacturing and negatively associated with the growth of employment outside manufacturing.

High manufacturing output growth is therefore important for overall productivity growth, and in this sense labor in the U.K. may have been in short supply. Kaldor's first test of this hypothesis (1968) is to regress GDP growth on the rate of increase in employment in manufacturing:

$$g_{GDP} = 2.665 + 1.066 \ e_m \qquad r^2 = 0.828.$$
$$(0.110)$$

The strong correlation is support for the hypothesis unless e_m is closely correlated with total employment growth. There is no relation at all, however, between g_{GDP} and the growth of total employment. These two results can only be reconciled if *overall* productivity growth is positively correlated with employment growth in manufacturing and negatively associated with the growth of employment outside manufacturing (e_{nm}). This is confirmed:

$$g_{GDP} = 2.899 + 0.821 \ e_m - 1.183 \ e_{nm} \qquad r^2 = 0.842.$$
$$(0.169) \qquad (0.367)$$

Cripps and Tarling support the links in Kaldor's third law and the law itself. They find in their sample of countries that the supply of labor from the primary sector (agriculture and mining) is consistently higher in countries with a faster growth of output. Moreover, the association is much stronger than for total employment growth, suggesting that the primary sector is consistently a more important source of labor in fast growing countries and periods. There is also a negative relationship between the growth of output and the absorption of labor by the tertiary sector.

Cripps and Tarling find no relation between the growth of output and employment in the nonmanufacturing sector. The implication is that growth can be accelerated by diverting labor to manufacturing where there is a correlation, and this is a plank in Kaldor's argument.

Cripps and Tarling confirm Kaldor's third law for both the period 1951-65 and the period 1965-70 notwithstanding their finding that the Verdoorn relationship apparently broke down in the latter period (but using an incorrect specification).

1951-65:
$$p_{GDP} = 1.172 + 0.534 \, (g_m) - 0.812 \, e_{nm} \quad r^2 = 0.805.$$
$$\phantom{p_{GDP} = 1.172 + }(0.055) (0.202)$$

1965-70
$$p_{GDP} = 1.153 + 0.642 \, (g_m) - 0.872 \, e_{nm} \quad r^2 = 0.958.$$
$$\phantom{p_{GDP} = 1.153 + }(0.058) (0.125)$$

The importance of manufacturing growth for productivity growth outside the manufacturing sector is strongly confirmed.

The role of demand

The *Economist* newspaper (November 5, 1966), in reviewing Kaldor's Inaugural Lecture, expressed surprise that a Keynesian, and an advocate of export-led growth, should come to the conclusion that the major factor constraining the growth of U.K. manufacturing output growth had been a lack of labor. Their explanation was that Kaldor, being in the Treasury at the time, had to be careful about mentioning balance-of-payments difficulties and such unmentionables as an overvalued currency and export incentives! Another explanation would be that he was providing a theoretical justification for the Selective Employment Tax, which had just been introduced, without at the time realizing that the case for such a tax does not rest solely on the grounds that increasing returns exist in industry whose output growth has been constrained by a shortage of labor. A tax would be fully justified to raise the overall rate of productivity growth if there is no correlation between output growth and employment growth in the service sector. It could also be, of course, that a balance-of-payments constraint on manufacturing output growth is related to labor supply difficulties in certain sectors of the economy.

Subsequent model specifications and results have confirmed the importance of demand factors as determinants of the growth of manufacturing output and that employment growth must be considered endogenous. Cornwall (1976), like Wolfe (1968), casts doubt on whether the statistical evidence on employment growth in different sectors, unemployment and vacancies, and relative wage movements shows that manufacturing output was constrained by a labor shortage. Service employment was rising faster than manufacturing employment in the 1950s and 1960s, and from 1966 to 1981 there was a loss of three million jobs in manufacturing industry. Cornwall sets up an alternative demand-orientated model, in which labor supply is assumed to adjust to demand, in which the determinants of the rate of growth of manufacturing output are a technological gap variable proxied by the reciprocal of a country's level of per capita income, the investment ratio, export growth, and population growth. Differences in European growth rates are readily explicable in terms of these demand determinants. None of this casts doubt, of course, on Kaldor's fundamental contention that the manufacturing sector is the engine of growth, which Cornwall accepts.

Parikh (1978) also confirms, using a simultaneous equation approach, that it seems to be demand that determines output growth and output growth which determines employment growth. In Parikh's simultaneous equation model, employment and output are both endogenous, recognizing that in practice there undoubtedly exists a two-way interaction between output growth and productivity growth. Employment growth is made a function of output growth, the growth of the work force, and investment; and output growth is a function of employment growth and exports. Parikh finds that it is output growth in manufacturing that determines employment growth, and output growth depends primarily on export growth, not on employment growth. He concludes, "it is the rate of growth of industrial output that seems to be constraining the growth in employment, and low growth in manufacturing may be attributed to demand factors." Parikh confirms the view that Kaldor now holds, and for which there is a good deal of other evidence (see Thirlwall, 1979), that the rate of growth of industrial output and GDP is fundamentally determined by the rate of growth of exports in relation to the income elasticity of demand for imports. Through the benefits that faster manufacturing growth then brings, countries become engaged in a cumulative process of relative improvement, with the consequent relative decline of other countries, because fast growing countries are able to sustain their advantage in export activities which gave fast growth in the first place, and slow growing countries find it difficult to break out of the vicious circle working against them.

Kaldor's change of mind on the causes of slow growth of the United Kingdom (if it was a genuine change of mind and not a provocation!) does not undermine the significance of the complete model for an understanding of the growth process in advanced capitalist countries. In many ways, bringing in the foreign sector, the richness of the model is enhanced. Moreover, a breakdown of the Verdoorn relation, if it has broken down, does not undermine the model either. While further testing of the model may be in order, there is already enough evidence, and surely there can be broad agreement, that:

i) manufacturing growth is the engine of GDP growth;
ii) the higher the rate of manufacturing growth, the faster the overall rate of productivity growth;
iii) labor is necessary for growth to take place, but manufacturing output is not constrained by it because there are more fundamental demand constraints which operate long before supply constraints bite;
iv) labor is very adaptable and elastic, and even in mature economies more labor used in manufacturing need not be at the expense of growth elsewhere;
v) the fundamental demand constraint on the growth of output in an open economy is the balance of payments.

REFERENCES

Cornwall, J. "Diffusion, Convergence and Kaldor's Laws." *Economic Journal*, June 1976.

Cripps, T. F., and Tarling, R. J. *Growth in Advanced Capitalist Economies 1950-1970*. Cambridge University Press, 1973.

Kaldor, N. *Causes of the Slow Rate of Economic Growth of the United Kingdom.* Cambridge University Press, 1966.

_____. *Strategic Factors in Economic Development.* Cornell University Press, 1967.

_____. "Productivity and Growth in Manufacturing Industry: A Reply." *Economica*, November 1968.

_____. "Economic Growth and the Verdoorn Law—a Comment on Mr. Rowthorn's Article." *Economic Journal*, December 1975.

_____. *Further Essays on Economic Theory.* Duckworth, 1978.

_____, and Vines, D. "A General Model of Growth and Development" (mimeo), 1980.

Kennedy, C., and Thirlwall, A. P. "Import Penetration, Export Performance and Harrod's Trade Multiplier." *Oxford Economic Papers*, July 1979.

Parikh, A. "Differences in Growth Rates and Kaldor's Laws." *Economica*, February 1978.

Rowthorn, R. "What Remains of Kaldor's Law?" *Economic Journal*, March 1975.

Thirlwall, A. P. "The Balance of Payments Constraint as an Explanation of International Growth Rate Differences." *Banca Nazionale del Lavoro Quarterly Review*, March 1979.

_____. "Rowthorn's Interpretation of Verdoorn's Law." *Economic Journal*, June 1980.

_____, and Vines, D. "The Harrod Trade Multiplier and the Importance of Export Led Growth." *Pakistan Journal of Applied Economics*, 1(1), Summer 1982.

Vaciago, G. "Increasing Returns and Growth in Advanced Economies: A Re-Evaluation." *Oxford Economic Papers*, July 1975.

Verdoorn, P. J. "Fattori che Regolano lo Sviluppo della Produttivita del Lavoro." *L'Industria* (English translation available on request from A. P. Thirlwall), 1949.

Wolfe, T. N. "Productivity and Growth in Manufacturing Industry: Some Reflections on Professor Kaldor's Inaugural Lecture." *Economica*, May 1968.

Young, A. "Increasing Returns and Economic Progress." *Economic Journal*, December 1928.

Part IV
Increasing Returns, Decreasing Returns and Cumulative Causation

[42]

THE CASE FOR REGIONAL POLICIES*

николаs Kaldor

In Britain, as in other countries, we have become acutely aware in recent years of the existence of a 'regional' problem—the problem, that is, of different regions growing at uneven rates; with some regions developing relatively fast and others tending to be left behind. In some ways this problem of fast and slow growing regions has not led to the same kind of inequalities in regional standards of living, in culture or in social structure, in the case of Britain as in some other countries—such as Italy, the United States or France. And in general, the problem of regional inequalities within countries is not nearly so acute as that between the rich and poor countries of the world—with differences in living standards in the ratio of 20:1, or even 50:1, as between the so-called 'advanced' countries and the 'developing' countries. Yet, as investigations by Kuznets and others have shown, the tremendous differences that now divide the rich and poor nations are comparatively recent in origin. They are the cumulative result of persistent differences in growth rates that went on over periods that may appear long in terms of a life-span, but which are relatively short in terms of recorded human history—not more than a few centuries, in fact. Two hundred, or two-hundred-and-fifty years ago, the differences in living standards, or in the 'stage' of both economic and cultural development of different countries, or parts of the globe, were very much smaller than they are today.

The primary question that needs to be considered is what *causes* these differences in 'regional' growth rates—whether the term 'regional' is applied to different countries (or even groups of countries) or different areas within the same country. The two questions are not, of course, identical; but up to a point, I am sure that it would be illuminating to consider them as if they were, and apply the same analytical technique to both.

In some ways an analysis of the strictly 'regional' problem (within a common political area) is more difficult. There is first of all the question of

* The fifth annual Scottish Economic Society Lecture delivered in the University of Aberdeen on February 18th, 1970.

how to define a 'region' within a political area—a problem that does not arise when political boundaries, however arbitrary they may be from an economic or social point of view, are treated as a given fact one need not enquire about. There is in fact, no unique way of defining what constitutes a 'region'—there are innumerable ways; the most that one can say is that some ways of drawing such boundary lines are more sensible than others; and given the fact that this is so, the exact demarcation of a 'region' may not make too much difference to the subsequent analysis.

Another aspect in which the analysis of 'region' within a country is more difficult is in terms of the identification of the fate of an area with the fate of its inhabitants. The mobility of both labour and capital within countries tends to be considerably greater than between countries—even though economists, in their desire for clear-cut assumptions on which to build, tended to over-estimate the one and to under-estimate the other. (There is only an imperfect mobility within countries, and there is also some mobility between them.)

Finally, a region which is part of a 'nation' or a 'country' tends to have common political institutions, a common taxing and spending authority and a common currency—all of which have important implications on the manner in which its external economic relations are conducted.

The Role of 'Resource Endowment'

But subject to these differences, what can we say about the causes of divergent regional growth rates—whether inter-nationally or intra-nationally? If one refers to classical or neo-classical economic theory, the common explanation is in terms of various factors—summed up under the term 'resource endowment'—which are themselves unexplained. Some areas are favoured by climate or geology; by the ability, vitality, ingenuity of their inhabitants, and by their thriftiness, and these innate advantages may be enhanced by good political and social institutions. Beyond suggesting that the right kind of human material is fostered by a temperate climate—in zones which are neither too hot nor too cold—and all of this owes a great deal to historical accidents and to luck, the theories which explain riches or poverty in terms of 'resource endowment' do not really have anything much to offer by way of explanation.

Nevertheless one must agree that they go as far as it is possible to go in explaining that part of economic growth—and until fairly recently this was much the most important part—which consisted of 'land based' economic activities, such as agriculture or mineral exploitation. These are clearly conditioned by climatic and geologic factors—the suitability of soil, rainfall, the availability of minerals, and so on. These provide the natural explanation why some areas are more densely settled than others; and why the comparative advantage in procuring different products (and which settles the nature of their external trading relations) should differ as between one area and another. No sophisticated explanation is needed why it is better

THE CASE FOR REGIONAL POLICIES

for some areas to grow wheat and for others bananas; or why some areas which are lucky in possessing things with a fast-growing demand (such as oil or uranium) are fortunate, from the point of view of their growth-potential, in relation to others which possess minerals with a slow-growing or declining demand—coal, for example. We would all agree that some part of the interregional specialisation and the division of labour can be adequately accounted for by such factors.

It is when we come to comparative advantages in relation to processing activities (as distinct from land-based activities) that this kind of approach is likely to yield question-begging results. The prevailing distribution of real income in the world—the comparative riches or poverty of nations, or regions—is largely to be explained, not by 'natural' factors, but by the unequal incidence of development in industrial activities. The 'advanced', high-income areas are invariably those which possess a highly developed modern industry. In relation to differences in industrial development, explanations in terms of 'resource endowment' do not get us very far. One can, and does say, that industrial production requires a great deal of capital—both in terms of plant and machinery, and of human skills, resulting from education—but in explaining such differences in 'capital endowment' it is difficult to separate cause from effect. It is as sensible—or perhaps more sensible—to say that capital accumulation results from economic development as that it is a cause of development. Anyhow, the two proceed side by side. Accumulation is largely financed out of business profits; the growth of demand in turn is largely responsible for providing both the inducements to invest capital in industry and also the means of financing it.

We cannot therefore say that industries will be located in regions which are 'well endowed' with capital resources for reasons other than industrial development itself. It was not the result of the peculiar thriftiness of the inhabitants of a region, or of a particularly high degree of initial inequality in the distribution of income which 'induced" a high savings-ratio, that some regions became rich while others remained poor. The capital needed for industrialisation was largely provided by the very same individuals who acquired wealth as a result of the process of development, and not prior to it. The great captains of industry, like Henry Ford or Nuffield were not recruited from the wealthy classes—they started as ' small men '.

Nor is there a satisfactory 'location theory' which is capable of explaining the geographic distribution of industrial activities. The only relevant factor which is considered in this connection is that of transport costs. But transport cost advantages can only help to explain location in those particular activities which convert bulky goods—where transport costs are an important element, and where processing itself greatly reduces the weight of the materials processed. If say, two tons of coal and four tons of iron are needed to make a ton of steel, it is better to locate steel plants near the coal mines and the iron ore deposits; and it these are themselves situated at some distance from each other, it is best to locate the steel plants near both places, in proportions determined by the relative weight of the two materials per unit of finished product—i.e., in this example, two-thirds of the plants near the iron ore, and one-third near the coal mines—since this arrangement would alone ensure full utilization of transport capacity in both directions.

But where the effect of processing in reducing bulk is not so important, the location of the processing activity may be a matter of indifference—whether it is near the source of the materials, near the market for the products, or anywhere in between. It is often suggested that such 'footloose' industries tend naturally to develop near the market for their products. But this again is a question-begging proposition. Great urban conurbations are normally large centres of industrial activity—the 'markets' are there where the 'industry' is. The engineering industry in this country is highly concentrated in and around Birmingham—it is also a great 'market' for engineering goods of various kinds. But it does not explain why either of these should be located there, rather than in some other place, say Leeds or Sheffield.

The Principle of 'Cumulative Causation'

To explain why certain regions have become highly industrialised, while others have not we must introduce quite different kinds of considerations—what Mydral (1957) called the principle of 'circular and cumulative causation'. This is nothing else but the existence of increasing returns to scale—using that term in the broadest sense—in processing activities. These are not just the economies of large-scale production, commonly considered, but the cumulative advantages accruing from the growth of industry itself—the development of skill and know-how; the opportunities for easy communication of ideas and experience; the opportunity of ever-increasing differentiation of processes and of specialisation in human activities. As Allyn Young (1928) pointed out in a famous paper, Adam Smith's principle of the 'division of labour' operates through the constant sub-division of industries, the emergence of new kinds of specialized firms, of steadily increasing differentiation —more than through the expansion in the size of the individual plant or the individual firm.

Thus the fact that in all known historical cases the development of manufacturing industries was closely associated with urbanisation must have deep-seated causes which are unlikely to be rendered inoperative by the invention of some new technology or new source of power. Their broad effect is a strong positive association between the growth of productivity and efficiency and the rate of growth in the scale of activities—the so-called Verdoorn Law. One aspect of this is that as communication between different regions becomes more intensified (with improvements in transport and in marketing organisation), the region that is initially more developed industrially may gain from the progressive opening of trade at the expense of the less developed region whose development will be inhibited by it. Whereas in the classical case—which abstracts from increasing returns—the opening of trade between two regions will necessarily be beneficial to both (even though the gains may not be equally divided between them) and specialisation through trade will necessarily serve to reduce the differences in comparative costs in the two areas, in the case of the 'opening of trade' in industrial products the differences in comparative costs may be enlarged, and not reduced, as a result of trade; and the trade may injure one region to the greater benefit of the other. This will be so if one assumes two regions, initially isolated from one another, with each having both an agricultural area and an industrial and market centre; with the size of agricultural production being mainly determined by soil and climate, and the state of technology; and the size of industrial production mainly depending on the demand for industrial products derived from the agricultural sector. When trade is opened up between them, the region with the more developed industry will be able to supply the needs of the agricultural area of the other region on more favourable terms: with the result that the industrial centre of the second region will lose its market, and will tend to be eliminated—without any compensating advantage to the inhabitants of that region in terms of increased agricultural output.

Another aspect of assymetry between 'land-based' and 'processing' activities (which is basically due to economies of large-scale production) is that in industrial production, contractual costs form an important independent element in price-formation; competition is necessarily imperfect; the sellers are price-makers, rather than price-takers. Whereas in agricultural production incomes are derived from prices, in industrial production it is prices that are derived from, or dependent on, contractual incomes (i.e. on the level of wages).

As a result, the 'exchange process'—the nature of the adjustment mechanism in inter-regional trade flows and money flows—operates differently in the two cases. In the case of trade between agricultural regions, the classical theory of the adjustment process is more nearly applicable. The price of agricultural commodities rises or falls automatically with changes in the balance of supply and demand; these price changes in individual markets will automatically tend to maintain the balance in trade flows between areas, both through the income effects and the substitution effects of price changes. Where the goods produced by the different regions are fairly close substitutes to one another, a relatively modest change in price—in the 'terms of trade' —will be sufficient to offset the effects of changes in either supply or demand schedules as may result from crop failures, the uneven incidence of technological improvements, or any other 'exogenous' cause. If the goods produced by the different regions are complements rather than substitutes to each other, the adjustment process may involve far greater changes in the terms of trade of the two areas, and would thus operate mainly through the 'income effects'. But in either case, the very process which secures an equilibrium between the supply and demand in each individual market through the medium of price changes will also ensure balance between sales and purchases of each region.

In the case of industrial activities ('manufactures') the impact effect of exogenous changes in demand will be on production rather than on prices. 'Supply', at any rate long-run supply, is normally in excess of demand —in the sense that producers would be willing to produce more, and to sell more, at the prevailing price (or even at a lower price) in response to an increased flow of orders. In this situation the adjustment process operates in a different manner—through the so-called 'foreign trade multiplier'. Any exogenous change in the demand for the products of a region from outside will set up multiplier effects in terms of local production and employment which in turn will adjust imports to the change in exports; on certain assumptions, this adjustment will alone suffice to keep the trade flows in balance.[1]

Some time ago Hicks (1950, p. 62) coined the phrase 'super-multiplier' to cover the effects of changes of demand on investment, as well as on consumption; and he showed that on certain assumptions, both the rate of growth of induced investment, and the rate of growth of consumption, become attuned to the rate of growth of the autonomous component of demand, so that the growth in an autonomous demand-factor will govern the rate of growth of the economy as a whole.

From the point of view of any particular region, the 'autonomous component of demand' is the demand emanating from *outside* the region; and Hicks's notion of the 'super-multiplier' can be applied so as to express the doctrine of the foreign trade multiplier in a dynamic setting. So expressed, the doctrine asserts that the rate of economic development of a region is fundamentally governed by the rate of growth of its exports. For the growth of exports, via the 'accelerator', will govern the rate of growth of industrial capacity, as well as the rate of growth of consumption; it will also serve to adjust (again under rather severe simplifying assumptions) both the level, and the rate of growth, of imports to that of exports.

The behaviour of exports on the other hand will depend both on an exogenous factor—the rate of growth of world demand for the products of the region; and on an 'endogenous' or quasi-endogenous factor—on the movement of the 'efficiency wages' in the region relative to other producing regions, which will determine whether the region's share in the total (overall) market is increasing or diminishing. The movement of 'efficiency wages' (a phrase coined by Keynes) is the resultant of two elements—the relative movement of money wages and that of productivity. If this relationship (the index of money wages divided by the index of productivity) moves in favour of an area it will gain in 'competitiveness' and *vice versa.*

As regards the movement of money wages the one uncontroversial proposition that one can advance is that given *some* mobility of labour, there is a limit to the differences in the levels of wages prevailing between industrial regions, or between different industries of a region. Indeed, it is a well

---

[1] The necessary assumptions are that all other sources of demand except exports are endogenous, rather than exogenous—i.e., that both Government expenditure and business investment play a passive role, the former being confined by revenue from taxation, and the latter by savings out of business profits.

known fact that whilst the general level of money wages may rise at highly variable rates at different times, the pay differentials between different types of workers, or between workers doing the same job in different areas, are remarkably constant. This may be the result partly of the mobility of labour but also of the strong pressures associated with collective bargaining for the maintenance of traditional comparabilities.[2] But this means that the rates of growth of money wages in different regions will tend to be much the same, even when the rates of growth in employment differ markedly. On the other hand, under the Verdoorn Law, the rates of growth of productivity will be the higher, the higher the rates of growth of output, and differences in the rates of productivity growth will tend to exceed the associated differences in the rates of growth of employment.[3] Hence differences in the rates of productivity growth are not likely to be compensated by equivalent differences in the rates of increase in money wages.

In other words, 'efficiency wages' will tend to fall in regions (and in the particular industries of regions) where productivity rises faster than the average. It is for this reason that relatively fast growing areas tend to acquire a cumulative competitive advantage over a relatively slow growing area; 'efficiency wages' will, in the natural course of events, tend to fall in the former, relatively to the latter—even when they tend to rise in both areas in absolute terms.

It is through this mechanism that the process of 'cumulative causation' works; and both comparative success and comparative failure have self-reinforcing effects in terms of industrial development. Just because the induced changes in wages increases are not sufficient to offset the differences in productivity increases, the comparative costs of production in fast growing areas tend to fall in time relatively to those in slow growing areas; and thereby enhance the competitive advantage of the former at the expense of the latter.

I am sure that this principle of cumulative causation—which explains the unequal regional incidence of industrial development by endogenous factors resulting from the process of historical development itself rather than by exogenous differences in 'resource endowment'—is an essential one for the understanding of the diverse trends of development as between different regions. In reality, the influences and cross-currents resulting from processes of development are far more complex. The intensification of trade resulting from technological improvements in transport or the reduction of artificial barriers (such as tariffs between regions) has important diffusion

[2] It has also been true in an international context that the comparative differences in the rates of growth of money wages in the different industrial countries had been smaller (in the post-war period at any rate) than the differences in the rates of productivity growth in the manufacturing industries of those countries, though the reasons why this has been so are not as yet well understood (cf. e.g. Kaldor (1960), paras. 22-23 and Table I).

[3] Recent empirical analyses of productivity growth in manufacturing industry suggest that a 1 per cent. increase in the growth of output is associated with a 0·6 per cent. increase in productivity and a 0·4 per cent. increase in employment (cf. e.g.: United Nations, 1970).

effects as well as important concentration effects. The increase in production and income in one region will, as such, stimulate the demand for 'complementary' products of other regions; and just as, in terms of microeconomics, falling costs generally lead to oligopoly rather than monopoly, so the principle of cumulative causation leads to the concentration of industrial development in a number of successful regions and not of a single region. These 'successful' regions in turn may hold each other in balance through increasing specialisation between them—some area becomes more prominent in some industries and another area in some other industries.

Actually, in terms of national areas, Kuznets found that different industrialised countries are remarkably similar in industrial structure, at similar stages of industrial development. The tremendous increase in international trade in industrial products between highly industrialised countries since the Second World War was more the reflection of specialisation within industries than that between industries: it was mainly in parts and components and machinery for industrial use. For example, in the case of the motor car industry, whilst most developed countries have a developed and highly competitive motor car industry (and are large net exporters) there has been a huge increase in international trade in motor car components—with some countries supplying some part of a carburetter to everybody, and some other country doing the same for some other part of the engine, or the carburetter.

There are also important dis-economies resulting from excessive rates of growth in industrial activities in particular areas: the growing areas will tend to have fast rates of population growth (mainly as a result of immigration) with the associated environmental problems in housing, public services, congestion, and so on, and these at some stage should serve to offset the technological economies resulting from faster growth. But as is well known, many of these dis-economies are external to the individual producer and may not therefore be adequately reflected in the movement of money costs and prices. A counterpart to this are external economies in the slow growing or declining regions—in terms of unemployment of labour, or an underutilised social infrastructure, which again tend to be external to the firm and hence inadequately reflected in selling costs or prices. There is some presumption therefore for supposing that, if left to market processes alone, tendencies to regional concentration of industrial activities will proceed farther than they would have done if 'private costs' were equal to 'social cost' (in the Pigovian sense) and all economies and dis-economies of production were adequately reflected in the movement of money costs and prices.

REGIONS AND COUNTRIES

It is time now that we consider some of the basic differences in the mode of operation of this principle—i.e. of 'cumulative causation' as between different regions of a single country and as between different political areas.

THE CASE FOR REGIONAL POLICIES

There is, first of all, the fact that the inter-regional mobility of labour is very much greater than the international mobility of labour. As a result differences in regional growth rates cannot cause differences in living standards of the same order as have emerged in the last few centuries between more distant regions, separated by political and cultural barriers. Real earnings no doubt improve faster in the areas of immigration rather than in areas of emigration, but the very fact of easy migration limits the extent to which differences in regional growth rates will be associated with divergent movements in earnings per head. The fact that trade unions are nation-wide and collective bargains in most countries are on a national basis, is a further reason why the movement of real earnings in various regions broadly tends to keep in step.

A second, and even more important fact is that a region which forms part of a political community, with a common scale of public services and a common basis of taxation, automatically gets 'aid' whenever its trading relations with the rest of the country deteriorate. There is an important built-in fiscal stabilizer which arrests the operation of the export-multiplier: since taxes paid to the Central Government vary with the level of local incomes and expenditure, whilst public expenditures do not (indeed they may vary in an offsetting direction through public works, unemployment benefit, etc.), any deterioration in the export-import balance tends to be retarded (and ultimately arrested) by the change in the region's fiscal balance —in the relation between what it contributes to the central Exchequer and what it receives from it.

This 'built-in' fiscal stabiliser—i.e. that a fall in exogenous demand leads to an increase in the public sector deficit, and thereby moderates the effect of the former on employment and incomes—operates of course on the national level as much as on the regional level; and it is one of the main reasons why a fall in exports does not generate a sufficient fall in the level of incomes to maintain equilibrium in the balance of payments through the adjustment in imports. But the important difference is that in the case of the region the change in the local fiscal balance is externally financed; in the case of the nation the balance of payments deficit causes a fall in reserves, or requires 'compensatory finance' from abroad, which is by no means 'automatic'.

This seems to me the main reason why there appears to be no counterpart to the 'balance-of-payments problem' on the regional level. It is often suggested, by the 'monetary school' that the reason why a country with a separate currency gets into balance of payments difficulties, whilst a region never does, is because in the one case the 'local money supply' is reduced in consequence of an excess of imports over exports; in the other case the monetary authorities offset the effects of the adverse balance on current account by 'domestic credit expansion'—by replacing the outflow of money (resulting from the excess of imports) with 'new' money. In my view this way of looking at the problem is putting the cart before the horse. The 'replacement of the money' is simply a facet of the fact that the foreign trade multiplier is arrested in its operation through the induced fiscal deficit —possibly aggravated also by the fall in private saving in relation to private domestic investment (though in practice the latter factor may be quantitatively of less importance, since the foreign-trade multiplier will tend to induce a reduction in local investment, and not only in local savings). But exactly the same thing happens at the regional level—with the outflowing money being (at least partially) replaced by a larger net inflow from the Exchequer, which is a direct consequence of the 'outflow'; but since it happens automatically as part of the natural order of things nobody kicks up a fuss, or even takes notice of it.

In these ways 'regions' are in a more favourable position than 'countries'. On the other hand sovereign political areas can take various measures to offset the effect of an unfavourable trend in their 'efficiency wages' which is not open to a 'region'—i.e. by diverting demand from foreign goods to home goods, through varying forms of protection (tariffs and non-tariff barriers, such as preferences given in public contracts) and occasionally also—though usually only very belatedly, in extremities—through adjustment of the exchange rate.

Of these two instruments for counteracting adverse trends in 'efficiency wages'—protection and devaluation—the latter is undoubtedly greatly superior to the former. Devaluation, as has often been pointed out, is nothing else but a combination of a uniform *ad-valorem* duty on all imports and uniform *ad-valorem* subsidy on exports. The combination of the two allows the adjustment in 'competitiveness' to take place under conditions which give the maximum scope for obtaining the advantages of economies of scale through international specialisation. Protection on the other hand tends to reduce international specialisation, and forces each region to spread its industrial activities over a wider range of activities on a smaller scale, instead of a narrower range on a larger scale. The effects of protection in inhibiting the growth of industrial efficiency is likely to be the greater the smaller the G.N.P. (or rather the gross industrial product) of the protected area. It is no accident that all the prosperous small countries of the world—such as the Scandinavian countries or Switzerland—are (comparatively speaking) 'free traders'. They have modest tariffs, and a very high ratio of trade in manufactures (both exports and imports) to their total output or consumption.

It has sometimes been suggested—not perhaps very seriously—that some of the development areas of the U.K.—such as Scotland or Northern Ireland—would be better off with a separate currency with an adjustable exchange rate vis-à-vis the rest of the U.K. For the reason mentioned earlier, I do not think this would be a suitable remedy. However, we have now introduced a new instrument in the U.K.—R.E.P.—which potentially could give the same advantages as devaluation for counteracting any adverse trend in 'efficiency wages', but with the added advantage that the cost of the consequent deterioration in the terms of trade (the cost of

THE CASE FOR REGIONAL POLICIES

selling exports at lower prices in terms of imports) is not borne by the region, but by the U.K. taxpaying community as a whole.

For this same reason, perhaps, the drawback of R.E.P. as an instrument is that it would be politically very difficult to introduce it on a scale that could make it really effective. The present R.E.P. is equivalent to a 5-6 per cent. reduction in the 'efficiency wages' in the manufacturing sector of the development areas. Since 'value added by regional manufacturing' is no more than a quarter, or perhaps a third, of the total cost of regional export-commodities (the rest consist of goods and services embodied that are mainly produced outside the region) the effect of a 6 per cent. R.E.P. is no more than that of a 2 per cent. devaluation (for the U.K. as a whole). It thus could have only one-fifth of the effect on 'regional competitiveness' which the recent U.K. devaluation had on the U.K.'s competitiveness in relation to the rest of the world.

Development Area policy comprises a host of other measures as well, of which the differential investment grant is the most costly and the most prominent. In my view investment grants as an instrument are less effective for the purpose of countering adverse trends in competitiveness than subsidies on wages (and not only because they stimulate the wrong kind of industries—those that are specially capital intensive) but I would agree that this is an issue that requires closer investigation than it has yet received.

I should like to end by mentioning one other possibility. Given the limitation on the scope of development expenditures by the natural disinclination of the Central Government (or the Parliament at Westminster) to spend huge sums in subsidising particular regions, isn't there a case for supplementing Central Government sources from local sources—through more local fiscal autonomy? For example, if it was found (and agreed) that R.E.P. is an efficacious way of subsidising regional exports (I suppose this is far from agreed at the moment) and that this may have dramatic effects in terms of enhanced regional development in the long run, would it not be in the interest of the regions to supplement the centrally financed R.E.P. by the proceeds, say, of a local sales tax? Perhaps this is a dangerous suggestion since in practice the growth of locally financed subsidies might simply be offset by lesser subsidies from the Centre. It would be less 'dangerous' however, if it was the Central Government which offered to raise the level of such subsidies—R.E.P. or even investment grants—on condition that a proportion of the cost should be raised by local taxation. Clearly, far more could be spent for the benefit of particular areas, if the areas themselves would make a greater, or a more distinct, contribution to the cost of such benefits. But these are thoughts for the distant future; long before they become practical politics we shall be deeply involved in the same kind of issues in connection with our negotiations to enter the Common Market.

Cambridge

References

Hicks, J. R. (1950). *A Contribution to the Theory of the Trade Cycle*. Oxford.

Kaldor, N. Monetary Policy, Economic Stability and Growth, a memorandum submitted to the *Committee on the Working of the Monetary Systems*. Principal Memoranda of Evidence, Vol. 3, pp. 146-153, London, H.M.S.O.

Myrdal, Gunnar (1957). *Economic Theory and Underdeveloped Regions*. London.

United Nations (1970). *Economic Survey for Europe for 1969*. Geneva.

Young, Allyn (1928). Increasing Returns and Economic Progress. *Economic Journal*, December 1928.

[43]

A MODEL OF REGIONAL GROWTH-RATE DIFFERENCES ON KALDORIAN LINES[1]

By R. DIXON and A. P. THIRLWALL

PROFESSOR Kaldor has been a long standing critic of the application of neo-classical modes of thought to the analysis of economic growth and development. In recent years, in particular, he has followed the line of Myrdal [1] in attacking the predictions of neo-classical theory that regional (national) growth-rate differences will tend to narrow with trade and the free mobility of the factors of production. The essence of the argument is that once a region gains a growth advantage it will tend to sustain that advantage through the process of increasing returns that growth itself induces—the so-called Verdoorn effect [2]. The fullest statement of Kaldor's views at the regional level is contained in a lecture to the Scottish Economic Society published in 1970 [3]. Unfortunately, the model he presents is purely verbal and lacks the rigour and precision that one normally associates with Kaldor. The purpose here is to attempt to formalize the model in order to clarify its structure,[2] and to consider such questions as: the role of the Verdoorn effect in contributing to regional growth-rate differences; whether regional growth-rate differences will tend to narrow or diverge through time; and how policies of regional 'devaluation' can raise a region's growth rate.[3]

---

[1] We are grateful to Professor Kaldor, Professor G. Rosenbluth, Professor C. Kennedy, Mr. I. Gordon, and Mr. J. Craven for critical comments and suggestions for improvement on an early draft of the paper.

[2] This would seem to be worth while especially in view of the confusion that already seems to have arisen. For example, one author (Richardson [4], pp. 30–4) represents Kaldor by specifying productivity growth as increasing at an increasing rate with respect to the growth rate, and the efficiency wage decreasing at an increasing rate with respect to the growth rate. This leads to the odd result that a region with a steeper productivity-growth relation will end up with a lower equilibrium growth rate! Furthermore, Richardson's representation of Kaldor's model lacks an explicit export demand function which is the heart of Kaldor's model. The price and income elasticities of demand for a region's exports turn out to be important determinants of its equilibrium growth rate (see later).

[3] Kaldor, it will be remembered, has been credited with the invention of the Regional Employment Premium which since 1967 has given a flat-rate subsidy per unit of labour employed to employers in manufacturing industry in Development Areas. It should be stressed, however, that local 'devaluation' can only raise permanently a region's *growth rate* if the export demand function is additive rather than multiplicative; that is, if the demand function is such that the rate of growth of exports is based on absolute price differences between domestic suppliers and competitors as opposed to the difference in the rate of growth of prices between domestic and competitive suppliers. If the rate of growth of exports is the dependent variable, a multiplicative export demand function is much easier to handle, but, as we shall see, if it is employed, a flat-rate subsidy to labour combined with 'mark up' pricing, cannot raise the equilibrium growth rate permanently. The same is true of the effect of currency devaluation at the national level. For a fuller discussion, see later.

202 REGIONAL GROWTH-RATE DIFFERENCES ON KALDORIAN LINES

The model is difficult to formulate the way Kaldor describes it but we can capture its essence relatively easily and bring out its important features. Kaldor sets up the problem by assuming two regions, initially isolated from one another, each with an agricultural area and an industrial and market centre. Trade is then opened up between the two regions, and Kaldor suggests that the region with the more developed industry will be able to supply the needs of the agricultural area of the other region on more favourable terms with the result that the industrial centre of the second region will lose its market and will tend to be run down without any compensating advantage in the form of increased agricultural output. The way that we can capture the spirit of this idea is to model an individual region's growth rate and then to consider the sources of interregional differences—stable or divergent—in terms of the parameters of the model. For example, in the two-region case a necessary condition for the persistence of stable regional growth rate differences is that the steady-state equilibrium growth rates of the two regions differ. For the growth rates of two regions to diverge a necessary condition is that the growth rate of one of the regions diverges from its own equilibrium rate. It is also a sufficient condition if the growth rate of the other region is stable or diverges from equilibrium in the opposite direction. If Kaldor's arguments are first used to examine equilibrium growth in one region, therefore, the assumptions implicit in the hypothesis that regional *per capita* incomes and/or growth rates may diverge can then be readily seen. This is the approach adopted here in an attempt to formalize the model without violating its spirit. His more complex verbal argument is easily accommodated within the framework outlined. The approach is essentially partial equilibrium in the sense that each region is considered in isolation from all others, and interregional relationships are not considered explicitly. Interregional relationships are considered implicitly, however, since we argue that it is the Verdoorn effect which can sustain high growth in one region once it obtains an initial growth advantage, which then makes it difficult for other regions to compete on equal terms.

In setting up the model we have five specific purposes in mind: First, to make clear the role of the Verdoorn relationship as it affects regional growth-rate differences; secondly, to suggest that while the model in theory can generate divergent or convergent regional growth paths, in practice, given reasonable parameter values for the model, regional growth divergence is not likely, as is sometimes implied by use of such phrases as 'circular cumulative expansion and contraction' and 'vicious spirals',[1] and that the model is best interpreted as predicting constant persistent regional growth-

---

[1] Beckerman [5], in a model of export-led growth which bears many similarities to Kaldor's, and predates it, seems to be suggesting a divergent process at the national level.

rate differences sustained by the Verdoorn effect;[1] thirdly, to bring out the importance of regional structure in determining the equilibrium growth rate, a feature of regional growth which Kaldor does not stress; fourthly, to evaluate wage subsidies as a policy device for reducing persistent regional growth-rate differences; and lastly, for interest, to see how close the model comes to predicting the U.K. growth rate over the post-war years.[2]

The model[3]

The main thrust of Kaldor's argument is Hicks's view [6] that it is the growth of autonomous demand which governs the long-run rate of growth of output. Using the 'super-multiplier' Hicks showed that on certain assumptions both the rate of growth of induced investment and the rate of growth of consumption become attuned to the rate of growth of autonomous demand so that the rate of growth of autonomous demand will govern the rate of growth of the economy as a whole. Kaldor argues that in a regional context the main autonomous demand factor will be demand emanating from outside the region; that is to say, the demand for a region's exports. According to Kaldor, regional growth is fundamentally determined by the growth of demand for exports, to which the rate of growth of investment and consumption adjust. We can therefore write:

$$g_t = \gamma(x_t) \qquad (1)^{4,\,5}$$

where g_t is the rate of growth of output in time t

x_t is the rate of growth of exports in time t

---

[1] Of course, even constant persistent growth-rate differences will be sufficient for regional *per capita* income levels to widen if population growth is the same in each region.

[2] Unfortunately the model is not operational at the regional level in the absence of information on vital parameters and variables.

[3] The basis of the model has also been presented and discussed in the context of regional disparities and regional policy in the E.E.C. (see [13]).

[4] Apart from the theoretical considerations underlying this specification there are a number of practical considerations that make export demand for highly specialized regions (or countries) extremely important. In most industries in a region, local demand is likely to be trivial compared with the optimum production capacity of the industries. The viability of regional enterprise must largely depend on the strength of demand from outside the region. There are also a number of important reasons why export demand may be a more potent growth-inducing force than other elements of demand, especially in open, backward areas—either regions or countries. The first is that exports allow regional specialization which may bring dynamic as well as static gains. Secondly, exports permit imports and imports may be important in developing areas which lack the capacity to produce development goods themselves. Thirdly, if the exchange of information and technical knowledge is linked to trade, exporting facilitates the flow of technical knowledge which can improve the growth rate.

[5] In the short term, autonomous investment (e.g. originating from government) may compensate for poor export performance. As far as the model to be developed is concerned, however, the inclusion of two autonomous demand components leads to complications in deriving the equilibrium and dynamic solutions to the model since the weights attached to the two components will vary with the growth rate. This, coupled with the fact that the export component will ultimately dominate the other component if export growth is faster than autonomous investment growth, has led us, like Kaldor, to ignore investment demand in the model. All investment is induced.

204 REGIONAL GROWTH-RATE DIFFERENCES ON KALDORIAN LINES

and γ is the (constant) elasticity of output growth with respect to export growth (= 1 if exports are a constant proportion of output).

Note that all the growth variables throughout the model are measured in discrete time.

Now let us consider the determinants of export demand and the form of the export demand function. Kaldor is not explicit on this point but seems to be suggesting a multiplicative function such that the rate of growth of a region's exports will be related to the rate of change of 'domestic' and 'foreign' prices and the rate of growth of 'world' demand i.e.

$$X_t = P_{dt}^{\eta} P_{ft}^{\delta} (Z^{\epsilon})_t \tag{2}[1]$$

where X_t is the quantity of exports in time t
P_{dt} is the domestic price in time t
P_{ft} is the competitor's price in time t
Z_t is the level of 'world' income in time t
η is the price elasticity of demand for exports
δ is the cross elasticity of demand for exports
and ϵ is the income elasticity of demand for exports,

which, for discrete changes, gives the approximation[2]

$$x_t = \eta(p_d)_t + \delta(p_f)_t + \epsilon(z)_t \tag{3}$$

where lower case letters represent rates of growth of the variables.

The multiplicative demand function is easy to handle, but, as suggested earlier, it leads to some difficulty if one wishes to interpret Kaldor's model as predicting that wage subsidies can raise *permanently* a lagging region's growth rate. On the other hand, there is no reason why Kaldor should be interpreted in this way; he is (perhaps deliberately) vague on this point. Presumably few people would want to argue that a once-for-all currency devaluation, which is analogous to a continual wage subsidy at the regional level, could raise a nation's growth rate permanently. We return to this point later. Returning to equation (3), the rate of growth of income outside the region (z) and the rate of change of competitors' prices (p_f) are both taken as exogenous to the region. The rate of growth of domestic (export) prices (p_d) can be derived from a mark-up pricing equation of the form:

$$(P_d)_t = (W/R)_t (T)_t \tag{4}[3]$$

---

[1] Alternatively, $X_t = (P_d/P_f)_t^{\eta} Z_t^{\epsilon}$, which is frequently how the function is estimated, which implicitly assumes that $\eta = \delta$. E.g. see Houthakker and Magee [7].

[2] i.e. excluding interaction terms.

[3] Since we specify (in keeping with Kaldor) the mark-up to be on unit labour costs, and not on total *prime* costs (which include raw material costs), any change in imported raw material costs will be included in the last term of equation (5).

where P_{dt} is the domestic price in time t
W_t is the level of money wages in time t
R_t is the average product of labour (in the export sector) in time t
and T_t is $1+\%$ mark-up on unit labour costs in time t.

From equation (4) we can write the approximation

$$(p_d)_t = (w)_t - (r)_t + (\tau)_t \qquad (5)$$

where the lower case letters stand for discrete rates of change of the variables.

The third proposition in Kaldor's model, which is the linchpin of the system, is that the growth of labour productivity is partly dependent on the growth of output itself (Verdoorn's Law), i.e.

$$r_t = f_3(g)_t \qquad f'_3 > 0 \qquad (6)$$

or
$$r_t = r_a + \lambda(g)_t \qquad (7)^1$$

where r_a is the rate of autonomous productivity growth and λ is the Verdoorn coefficient.

Equation (7) provides the link between exports and growth via productivity growth and prices. Combining equations (1), (3), (5), and (7) to obtain an expression for the equilibrium growth rate gives:

$$g_t = \gamma \frac{[\eta(w_t - r_a + \tau_t) + \delta(p_f)_t + \epsilon(z)_t]}{1 + \gamma\eta\lambda}. \qquad (8)$$

Remembering that $\eta < 0$, the growth rate is shown to vary positively with $r_a, z, \epsilon, \delta, p_f,$ and λ, and negatively with w and τ.[2]

Note that the Verdoorn effect is a source of regional growth-rate differences only to the extent that the Verdoorn coefficient (λ) varies between regions or initial differences exist with respect to other parameters and variables in the model such that $0 < \lambda < 1$ serves to exaggerate the effect of the differences. In other words, the dependence of productivity growth on the growth rate *per se* is not sufficient to cause differences in regional growth rates unless the Verdoorn coefficient varies between regions or growth rates would diverge for other reasons anyway.

It is equally clear, however, that it is the Verdoorn relation which makes the model circular and cumulative, and which gives rise to the possibility that once a region obtains a growth advantage, it will keep it. What this

---

[1] Relating productivity growth in the export sector to the rate of growth of total output, as opposed to the rate of growth of exports, is to treat the economy as if it were a single fully integrated firm in which it is impossible to distinguish between production runs for export and production runs for domestic consumption. On the assumption that $g = x$, however, the equilibrium growth rate is unaffected.

[2] The effect of η is ambiguous since it appears in both the numerator and the denominator of the equation. Whether growth varies positively or negatively with the absolute size of η depends on the other variables and parameters. To determine the effect of variations in η numerical analysis would have to be resorted to.

means is that the Verdoorn relationship plays a sustaining role in the regional growth process, and a sustaining role in the persistence of regional growth differences once they have arisen due to initial differences in the other parameters of the model.

Suppose, for example, that a region obtains an advantage in the production of goods with a high income elasticity of demand (ϵ) which causes its growth rate to rise above that of another region. Through the Verdoorn effect, productivity growth will be higher; the rate of change of prices lower (assuming w and τ are the same in both regions), and the rate of growth of exports (and hence the rate of growth of output) higher and so on. Moreover, the fact that the region with the initial advantage will obtain a competitive advantage in the production of goods with a high income elasticity of demand will mean that it will be difficult for other regions to establish the same activities. In models of cumulative causation, this is the essence of the theory of divergence between 'centre' and 'periphery' and between industrial and agricultural regions. This is also the essence of Kaldor's view that the opening up of trade between regions may create growth differences which are sustained or even widened by the process of trade.

Notice that an autonomous shock which raises a region's growth rate is not sufficient for its growth advantage to be maintained through the Verdoorn effect unless the autonomous shock affects favourably the parameters and variables of the model (or is a sustained shock). This consideration is important when we come to consider the role of wage subsidies as a device for affecting the growth rate of a region.

The dependence of the equilibrium growth rate on the parameters of the model, and the sustaining role of the Verdoorn effect, is illustrated in Fig. 1 below. For illustration, but without discussion for the moment, the growth rate is shown converging to its equilibrium rate. The disequilibrium behaviour of the model is considered explicitly in the next section.

The distance of the curves from the origin reflects factors affecting each variable other than the variable specified in the functional relation. Fig. 1 shows clearly the link that the Verdoorn relation provides between exports and growth via productivity and prices, and its sustaining influence. The steeper the slope of the Verdoorn relation (i.e. the higher λ), the higher the equilibrium growth rate will be and the greater the divergence between regional growth rates for given differences between regions in other variables and parameters.

Divergent or convergent growth?

We come now to the second purpose of formalizing Kaldor's model which is to consider under what circumstances there will be a tendency for regional growth rates to diverge. In a two-region model, a necessary condition for divergence is that the growth rate of one of the regions diverges from its equilibrium rate. Whether divergence will take place is essentially an empirical issue depending on the stability conditions of the model in disequilibrium. None of the cumulative causation school, including Kaldor, are clear as to what the stability conditions are in their various models. In order to consider the growth rate in disequilibrium a variety of

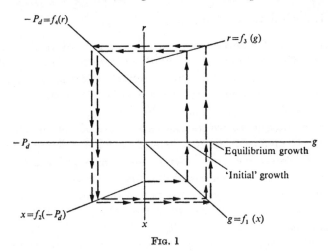

FIG. 1

lag structures could be introduced into the equations which constitute the model. If, for simplicity, we confine ourselves to a first-order system, inspection of the model shows that, since the model is 'circular', a one-period lag in any of the equations gives the same stability conditions, namely that convergence to or divergence from the equilibrium growth rate depends on whether $|\gamma\eta\lambda| \lessgtr 1$, as illustrated in Fig. 1.[1] To consider the growth rate in disequilibrium it would not be unreasonable on economic grounds to specify exports in time t as a lagged function of its determinants. It can take time for exporters and/or foreign buyers to adjust to changes in prices and income. Thus we could write $X_t = (P_d)_{t-1}^{\eta}(P_f)_{t-1}^{\delta}(Z)_{t-1}^{\epsilon}$ giving the approximation:

$$x_t = \eta(p_d)_{t-1} + \delta(p_f)_{t-1} + \epsilon(z)_{t-1} \qquad (9)$$

where the lower case letters are discrete rates of growth as before.

Using equation (9) instead of (3), and combining with (1), (5), and (7),

---

[1] A one-period lag in two of the equations, giving a second order system, yields two real roots $\pm\sqrt{(-\gamma\eta\lambda)}$. The stability conditions are therefore the same as in the first-order system. This is true however many equations are lagged. This fact considerably enhances the generality of our result.

208 REGIONAL GROWTH-RATE DIFFERENCES ON KALDORIAN LINES

and assuming the rate of growth of the exogenous variables to be constant, gives the first order difference equation:

$$g_t = \gamma[\eta(w_{t-1}-r_a+\tau_{t-1})+\delta(p_f)_{t-1}+\epsilon(z)_{t-1}]-\gamma\eta\lambda(g_{t-1}), \qquad (10)$$

the general solution to which is

$$g_t = A(-\gamma\eta\lambda)^t + \frac{\gamma[\eta(w_{t-1}-r_a+\tau_{t-1})+\epsilon(z)_{t-1}+\delta(p_f)_{t-1}]}{1+\gamma\eta\lambda} \qquad (11)$$

where A is the initial condition.

The behaviour of g depends on the value of $\gamma\eta\lambda$. Since $\eta < 0$, $(-\gamma\eta\lambda)$ will be > 0. The condition for cumulative divergence from equilibrium is that $(-\gamma\eta\lambda) > 1$.[1] In our view this is unlikely because: $\gamma = 1$ if exports are a constant proportion of output; the price elasticity of demand for exports (η) rarely exceeds 2, and the Verdoorn coefficient rarely exceeds 0·5.[2] Taking realistic values for the parameters of the model, therefore, the most likely prediction must be one of constant differences in regional growth rates determined by differences in the equilibrium rates; not divergence. Admittedly, our disequilibrium specification is arbitrary but the fact that a one-period lag in any one of the equations gives the same stability conditions, and likewise when more than one equation is lagged, considerably enhances the generality of the result. It also serves some purpose to give a (not unrealistic) specification which suggests on empirical grounds that divergence is not very likely, if only to induce those who adhere to the cumulative causation school to specify more precisely the model they have in mind and to show the conditions under which regional growth rates would diverge through time. In our specification we suggest that diverging regional growth rates would seem to be possible only if the equilibrium rates themselves diverged through time because the determinants of the equilibrium rates were themselves time dependent. For example, the price and income elasticities of demand could change in the course of time as the structure of production changed. This possibility is not pursued further here because of the obvious difficulties it would present for the solution to equation (10).

Regional structure as a determinant of growth

The second term on the right-hand side of equation (11) (i.e. the particular solution to the first-order difference equation) shows that the

[1] Since the equations that constitute the model have omitted higher order terms containing g_t, the stability conditions of the model are necessarily an approximation.

[2] Kaldor has agreed in correspondence that implicit in his argument that regional growth rates may diverge is the assumption that $|\eta\lambda| > 1$ for one region, and argues that he does not regard $|\eta| > 2$ as an unrealistic assumption.

equilibrium growth rate depends on seven main economic parameters and variables that may vary from region to region: η, w, r_a, τ, ϵ, δ, and λ.[1]

If it is assumed that the percentage mark-up on unit labour costs is constant in each region, and that for institutional reasons w is fairly uniform from region to region,[2] we are left with differences in η, δ, r_a, ϵ, and λ as explanations of differences in regional growth rates. The price and income elasticities of demand for regional exports will depend on the nature of the products produced. The rate of autonomous productivity growth, r_a, and the Verdoorn coefficient, λ, will depend on the technical dynamism of productive agents in the region and the extent to which capital accumulation is induced by growth and embodies technical progress. The determinants of r_a and λ are closely related to the determinants of the position and shape of Kaldor's technical progress function [8]. The technical progress function in linear form may be specified as:

$$r = d + \pi(m) \qquad (12)$$

where r is the rate of growth of output per man
           m is the rate of growth of capital per man
and d is the rate of disembodied technical progress.

Now let d and m be functions of the rate of growth of output so that:

$$d = \alpha_1 + \beta_1(g) \qquad (13)$$

and
$$m = \alpha_2 + \beta_2(g). \qquad (14)$$

Substituting (13) and (14) into (12) gives:

$$r = (\alpha_1 + \pi\alpha_2) + (\beta_1 + \pi\beta_2)(g) \qquad (15)$$

hence:
$$r = r_a + \lambda(g)$$

where
$$r_a = (\alpha_1 + \pi\alpha_2)$$

and
$$\lambda = (\beta_1 + \pi\beta_2).$$

The autonomous rate of growth of productivity, r_a, is determined by the autonomous rate of disembodied progress, the autonomous rate of capital accumulation per worker, and the extent to which technical progress is embodied in capital accumulation. The Verdoorn coefficient, λ, is determined by the rate of induced disembodied technical progress, the degree to which capital accumulation is induced by growth and the extent to which technical progress is embodied in capital accumulation. To the extent that the determinants of r_a and λ vary between industries, r_a and λ may also vary between regions depending on the industrial composition of the regions.

[1] Ignoring time subscripts and assuming z and p_f do not differ between regions.
[2] For evidence see [9].

210 REGIONAL GROWTH-RATE DIFFERENCES ON KALDORIAN LINES

From this analysis, it would appear that the message of Kaldor's model is that raising a region's growth rate is fundamentally a question of making regions more 'competitive' and/or altering the industrial structure so that goods are produced with higher income elasticities of demand and higher Verdoorn coefficients attached to them. [1,2]

Regional 'competitiveness'

To make regions more 'competitive' a policy of wage subsidies to manufacturers in lagging growth regions is sometimes advocated, to achieve the same effect regionally as a policy of currency devaluation nationally. The argument needs to be treated with some caution, however. It is easy to show that a wage subsidy in a regional context is equivalent to a devaluation of the currency in a national context, but the argument that wage subsidies can raise a region's growth rate permanently is less convincing. To show the equivalence of wage subsidies and currency devaluation, let the price of domestic exports in terms of the overseas currency equal P_0. Then $P_{ot} = P_{dt} \times$ exchange rate, or:

$$p_{ot} = \theta_t + p_{dt} \tag{16}$$

where p_{ot} is the rate of change of home prices expressed in overseas currency in time t

θ_t is the rate of change in the exchange rate in time t

and p_{dt} is the rate of growth of prices in domestic currency in time t.

Expressing the domestic price in the same units as the overseas currency, equation (3) becomes:

$$x_t = \eta(\theta_t + p_{dt}) + \epsilon(z_t) + \delta(p_{dt}) \tag{17}$$

and the equilibrium growth rate is:

$$g_t = \frac{\gamma[\eta(w_t - r_a + \tau_t + \theta_t) + \epsilon(z_t) + \delta(p_f)_t]}{1 + \gamma\eta\lambda}. \tag{18}$$

Partially differentiating (18) with respect to θ gives:

$$\frac{\partial g}{\partial \theta} = \frac{\gamma\eta}{1+\gamma\eta\lambda}.$$

and with respect to w gives:

$$\frac{\partial g}{\partial w} = \frac{\gamma\eta}{1+\gamma\eta\lambda}.$$

Hence, $$\frac{\partial g}{\partial \theta} = \frac{\partial g}{\partial w}.$$

---

[1] And also higher price elasticities of demand if $\partial g/\partial p_d > 0$.

[2] The Verdoorn effect is also an important determinant of the capacity (or natural) rate of growth, g_n. Let $g_n = r + n$ where r is the rate of growth of productivity and n is the rate of growth of the work-force. But $r = r_a + \lambda g$. Substituting, we have $g_n = r_a + \lambda g + n$. The higher λ, the higher g_n. If $\lambda > 1$ there is no constraint on the growth rate. This is the situation of 'increasing returns for ever'.

But neither devaluation, nor wage subsidies, can have a permanent effect on the *rate of change* of the exchange rate or money wages, only on the *level* of the exchange rate or money wages. The effect of devaluation and wage subsidies on the rate of change of the exchange rate and the rate of change of money wages is once-for-all. Unless the export pricing function, or the export demand function, is additive the effect of devaluation, or the introduction of flat-rate wage subsidies, on the growth rate cannot therefore be permanent.[1] θ and w become zero in the periods after wage subsidies have been introduced and devaluation has taken place.[2] As far as an additive export demand function is concerned, it is not at all clear what demand function would generate the argument that the *rate of growth* of exports is related to the absolute difference between domestic and foreign prices.[3] It seems unfortunate that the success or otherwise of government policies with respect to regional wage subsidies will depend on the (unknown) form of the pricing and export demand functions. The relation between export prices and the growth of output is a subject which seems to be treated far too casually in the theory of trade and growth. We believe that it is much more satisfactory to regard the level of exports as determined by relative prices in a multiplicative demand function than by the absolute difference between domestic and foreign prices in an additive demand function. If this argument is accepted wage subsidies at the regional level are equivalent at the most to an autonomous shock which, as we argued earlier, could only affect the growth rate permanently if the structural parameters of the growth model were thereby affected favourably. If anything, however, policies of 'devaluation' tend to ossify a region's or country's industrial structure, impeding structural change. Export promotion and import substitution properly directed offer a much more hopeful solution to lagging growth caused by unfavourable price and income elasticities of demand for exports and slow autonomous productivity growth. At the regional level, this policy conclusion points to the need to relate regional taxes and subsidies to activities with particular structural characteristics rather than to particular factors of production,

---

[1] However, regional devaluation could have a permanent effect on the percentage level of unemployment (%U). The initial effect of devaluation will be to lower %U. Since %U is the outcome of the difference between the growth of labour demand and supply, and the growth of demand is unaffected by devaluation, the lower level of %U can persist. Moreover, the cheapening of labour relative to capital could induce the use of more labour-intensive techniques. Interpreted as a weapon to combat unemployment, therefore, regional devaluation may have merit. As a means of stimulating regional growth, however, its value is doubtful.

[2] In fact, if money wages are rising through time, a *flat-rate* wage subsidy per man will actually raise the rate of increase in money wage costs after the initial introduction of the subsidy since the percentage effect of the subsidy is smaller in the next period.

[3] Beckerman [5], who has used an additive function in a national context, is not clear on this point.

212 REGIONAL GROWTH-RATE DIFFERENCES ON KALDORIAN LINES

either capital or labour. We believe the income elasticity of demand for exports to be a particularly important parameter at both the national and regional level. Regional policy for stimulating regional growth could usefully direct its attention to identifying activities with a high income elasticity of demand and encouraging these to locate in depressed regions by policies of capital incentives and labour subsidies.

Application of the model

It is hard to apply Kaldor's model at the regional level without being able to identify regional exports and to estimate such crucial parameters as the price and income elasticities of demand for exports, let alone the other parameters of the model. The model is general enough, however, to be applicable to a nation as well as to a region within a nation. Indeed, a similar model to Kaldor's has been developed by Beckerman to account for differences in rates of growth of European countries over the post-war years [5]. It is interesting to see what equilibrium growth rate for the British economy is predicted over the post-war period when equation (11) is applied to the data. We restrict the period of analysis to 1951 to 1966 to avoid the more recent years of high inflation following devaluation of the pound in 1967, and to achieve consistency with the study of Houthakker and Magee [7] which estimates the price and income elasticities of demand for British exports over the period 1951 to 1966. Their estimate of the export demand function, $X = A(P_d/P_f)^\eta Z^\epsilon$, is $X = A(P_d/P_f)^{-1.24} Z^{1.0}$. Since η and δ are not estimated separately, as specified in our model, we shall apply the coefficient on relative prices to the difference between the rate of increase in domestic and foreign prices, implicitly assuming that $\eta = \delta$.[1] Our feeling is, however, that their estimate of the price elasticity is on the low side. Junz and Rhomberg [11] have estimated it at between -1.86 and -2.29, and most forecasting of the British economy takes a somewhat higher figure. As a compromise estimate we take $\eta = -1.5$. The best estimate of the rate of increase in prices of major competitor countries is 2.0 per cent per annum.[2] From the United Nations National Accounts Statistics, G.D.P. growth of Britain's major export customers averaged approximately 4.0 per cent per annum over the period. Domestic wage inflation averaged 6.0 per cent per annum so that, assuming the percentage mark-up on labour costs remained unchanged, $w+\tau = 0.06$. Estimates of the Verdoorn relation for Britain from regional cross-section data gave $r_a = 0.02$ and $\lambda = 0.5$ [12]. Lastly, assuming exports to be a

---

[1] The parameter estimates are those obtained after adjustment of the equation for the presence of serial correlation in the residuals. Before adjustment, $\eta = -0.44$ and $\epsilon = 0.86$.

[2] See index of export prices of manufactured goods for major industrial countries in National Institute of Economic and Social Research, *Economic Review*, Quarterly.

constant proportion of output, $\gamma = 1$. The full list of parameter values used in equation (11) is: $\eta\, (= \delta) = -1\cdot5$; $w+\tau = 0\cdot06$; $r_a = 0\cdot02$; $\epsilon = 1\cdot0$; $z = 0\cdot04$; $\lambda = 0\cdot5$; $\gamma = 1$, and $p_f = 0\cdot02$. Solving for the equilibrium growth rate gives $g = 4\cdot0$ per cent per annum. This is above the actual and natural (capacity) rates of growth experienced over the period 1951 to 1966 of 2·8 and 2·9 per cent per annum, respectively [10]. One reason for the over-prediction of g could be that the estimate of r_a is too high, based as it is on the use of data for manufacturing industry only. Autonomous productivity growth of 1·8 per cent per annum ($r_a = 0\cdot018$) would be consistent with the actual growth rate experienced of 2·8 per cent. This would also be closer to the autonomous rate of productivity growth actually experienced in the economy as a whole if the Verdoorn coefficient for all industry is also 0·5. We conclude that the application of Kaldor's model to the British economy is not inconsistent with the evidence; on the other hand, it should be stressed that the calculation of g is very sensitive to small changes in the parameter values of the model.

Conclusion

Our attempt to formalize Kaldor's model has the pedagogic virtue of bringing into the open the structure of the model and the main determinants of regional growth-rate differences. Whether or not we have done justice to Kaldor and represented his views faithfully, we believe that the model presented captures the main elements of an open economy growth model which has relevance to regions within countries and to open developed and developing countries alike. At the national level, a built-in balance of payments constraint would make the model more realistic.[1] No attention is paid in the present model to the fact that the rate of growth of output may generate a level of imports in excess of exports, necessitating demand contraction. At the regional level, it is difficult to conceive of a balance of payments constraint on growth, except to the extent that there may be a constraint on the regional money supply. There is certainly no requirement that exports and imports must balance to preserve the value of a currency in the foreign exchange market, which may be required at the national level. We have neglected here the consideration of balance of payments constrained growth in order to concentrate on the basic model. To incorporate such a constraint, however, may be a useful addition to the model, especially for application at the national level.

University of Papua, New Guinea
University of Kent at Canterbury

[1] The absence of a balance of payments constraint may be another reason why the model is tending to over-predict the actual U.K. growth experience.

REFERENCES

1. MYRDAL, G., *Economic Theory and Underdeveloped Regions*, Duckworth, 1957.
2. VERDOORN, P. J., 'Fattori che Regolano lo Sviluppo della Produttivita del Lavoro', *L'Industria*, 1949; translation by G. and A. P. Thirlwall available on request.
3. KALDOR, N., 'The Case for Regional Policies', *Scottish Journal of Political Economy*, Nov. 1970.
4. RICHARDSON, H., *Regional Growth Theory*, Macmillan, 1973.
5. BECKERMAN, W., 'Projecting Europe's Growth', *Economic Journal*, Dec. 1962.
6. HICKS, J., *The Trade Cycle*, Oxford University Press, 1950.
7. HOUTHAKKER, H., and MAGEE, S., 'Income and Price Elasticities in World Trade', *The Review of Economics and Statistics*, May 1969.
8. KALDOR, N., 'A Model of Economic Growth', *Economic Journal*, Dec. 1957.
9. THIRLWALL, A. P., 'Regional Phillips Curves', *Bulletin of the Oxford Institute of Economics and Statistics*, Feb. 1970.
10. THIRLWALL, A. P., 'Okun's Law and the Natural Rate of Growth', *Southern Economic Journal*, July 1969.
11. JUNZ, H., and RHOMBERG, R., 'Prices and Export Performance of Industrial Countries 1953–1963', *I.M.F. Staff Papers*, July 1965.
12. DIXON, R., *Studies in the Structure and Growth of the Regions of the U.K.*, unpublished doctoral dissertation, University of Kent, 1973.
13. THIRLWALL, A. P., 'Regional Economic Disparities and Regional Policy in the Common Market', *Urban Studies*, Feb. 1974.

[44]

Excerpt from Michael J. Boskin (ed.), *Economics and Human Welfare: Essays in Honor of Tibor Scitovsky*, 273–91.

Equilibrium Theory and Growth Theory*

Nicholas Kaldor

1. Introduction

My purpose is to explain why I regard prevailing economic theory, as taught in the regular textbooks in most of the universities of the Western World, as thoroughly misleading and pretty useless—in terms of the theory's declared objective of explaining how economic processes work in a decentralized market economy. It is useless for formulating nontrivial predictions concerning the effects of policy measures or other changes.

Section 2 is a brief discussion of what I consider to be the basic assumptions of equilibrium theory. Section 3 is a discussion of what is wrong with these assumptions—why these hypotheses are misleading as a starting

---

* Originally a lecture given in the University of Barcelona, April 1973, and published in Spanish [*Cuadernos de Economia*, Barcelona 2, May–August (1974)].

point for making generalizations about the behavior of the economic system. Finally, Section 4 is a brief outline of the postulates needed for an alternative approach—a "nonequilibrium theory"—which I should like to call a "growth theory," because it would be primarily concerned with the manner of operation of the (both exogenous and endogenous) forces in a market economy making for continuous change and development.

2. The Main Characteristics of Equilibrium Theory

The basic characteristics of existing equilibrium theory are:

(1) It is permeated by a basic dichotomy between "wants" and "resources," "tastes" and "obstacles" or "ends" and "means." (One could equally say, with Bentham, between "pleasure" and "pain.")

(2) It follows from the basic assumption that men have given "wants" or "needs," which in a basic, though not precisely definable, sense are given by man's nature, independently of the social environment and of the social institutions created for satisfying them, that the essence of "economic activities" is regarded as that of allocating "scarce means which have alternative uses" (Robbins, 1932). The price system, the market mechanism, and the legal institutions, property rights, contracts, etc., are regarded as social instruments for "resource allocation." Under *ideal* conditions, individuals, whether in their capacity as producers or consumers, by acting rationally but quite independently of each other—that is to say, by acting so as to maximize something—bring about an "optimum" allocation of resources which secures the highest or maximum satisfaction to each member of society in the specific Pareto sense of no one being capable by any change in his *own* arrangements, i.e., in his own set of decisions concerning production or consumption, of making himself *better off* without making some others, or at least one other person, *worse off*. A's pleasure is maximized subject to B's being given. So everyone is as well off as he could be subject to everyone else's satisfaction being given.

(3) "Wants" are satisfied by the consumption (or destruction) of "goods" (including nonmaterial services). Goods are produced out of labor, natural resources, and goods; i.e., to a large extent, goods are produced out of each other, and only a proportion of goods produced in any year are destined to satisfy wants in that year. The goods which are available at any point of time, or over an interval of time (such as a year) for the purposes of producing goods, together with the labor and natural resources so available, are called "resources."

(4) The essence of equilibrium theory consists of stating, in a comprehensive manner, the properties of such a Pareto equilibrium—having demonstrated that on certain basic "axioms" such an equilibrium can be assumed to exist. The necessary axioms include, first of all, that the supply of resources (the total amount of each kind that is available) is given "exogenously" in some sense—though what the precise meaning of exogeneity is when one tries to clothe the skeleton and think of "resources" as concrete objects as they appear in reality, and not just as mathematical symbols in a system of equations, has never been satisfactorily resolved.

(5) For the purpose of demonstrating the existence of such an "equilibrium," it is also assumed that the productive relationships—the "transformation functions" or "production functions"—are universally *known* and of a *given* number; equally, there are a *known* and *given* number of different goods.

(6) Equally, the distribution of the *ownership* of resources among individuals is given exogenously.

(7) Similarly, the preference functions of each individual are assumed to be given and invariant over time, and invariant also with respect to the preferences of other individuals.

One can draw a distinction between the axioms necessary for a Pareto-optimal resource allocation to exist, and the additional assumptions required for supposing that a *market economy* will tend to function in such a way as to bring about (fully, or with a certain degree of approximation) an equilibrium allocation of resources. In order to show that the market mechanism will function in this way, it is necessary to suppose further that:

(a) transformation functions must be *linear;* there is an absence of increasing returns (or economies of scale), i.e., production is equally efficient, irrespective of the scale of production;

(b) competition must be *perfect*—each individual "transactor" can sell anything or buy anything in unlimited amounts without affecting market prices, and therefore prices are the only type of information required for individual decisions; and

(c) there is *perfect knowledge* of all relevant prices by all "transactors" (or "economic agents");

(d) there is also "perfect foresight" in the sense that over time the experience of individuals serves to *confirm* (and not to contradict or "disappoint") the expectations in the light of which they made their decisions in the past.

The real purpose of all these assumptions is to show that there is at least one set of prices which, *if established in the markets,* would leave everyone content to go on as they are—that it would not be to anyone's interest to revise their decisions (or "plans") concerning their *own* activities in the sphere of production and consumption. But this in itself is not sufficient to show that markets will operate so as to approach an equilibrium of this description from any arbitrarily given starting point. For, if transactions are conducted at nonequilibrium prices, this in itself will alter the conditions of equilibrium—it will come to the same as a change in the distribution in the ownership of resources between different individuals. (It can also affect conduct by creating false anticipations.) Hence, in the pure Walrasian model, it is assumed that the system of equilibrium or market-clearing prices is established *before* any transactions are made, by a process of *"tatônnement,"*[1] which is the same as assuming that the markets *are* in equilibrium, without showing how they got there. Nor has it been demonstrated that this equilibrium is a stable one; i.e., that it would maintain itself in the face of chance disturbances.

Moreover, the whole approach is necessarily "static" in the sense that it assumes that the forces operating in the economy can be characterized in terms of a *unique* point (or a predetermined point) to which any *changing* system converges and at which all forces making for change are exhausted—in other words, to a state in which the various forces hold each other in balance in such a way as to establish an unchanging routine. Once the system attains equilibrium, it remains in it forever.

Now all human societies are in a process of continual change—a change which differs from the continual biological change of ecological systems in nature only in that it is far speedier and takes more spectacular forms. Within the framework of equilibrium theory, there are two ways in which attempts have been made to introduce change into the system while preserving the notion that it is in continuous equilibrium:

(1) The first is the assumption that there are "markets" at which purchases and sales can be made not only for the current period but for *all* future periods as well; decisions then depend on prices in both the current and all the "future" markets; the system is in intertemporal equilibrium when, at the ruling prices, both the "spot" and "future" market supplies and demands are in equilibrium for *all* future periods and not only for the current period. The purpose of this approach is to establish that on certain axioms, such an equilibrium price system for all "commodities" (with

---

[1] The meaning of the French word *"tatônnement"* according to *Petit Larousse* is *procéder avec hesitation.* In Walras, it means a cautious approach to business which enables people to discover the right prices *before* transactions are made.

each "commodity" having a time suffix for the date of its availability) exists. The real world admittedly bears only a very limited resemblance to this model, since apart from some specific commodities for specific periods in the near future, such futures markets do *not* exist.[2]

(2) The other approach is to assume that changes are only due to purely exogenous factors which proceed in time wholly independently (or at least *largely* independently) of economic decisions which depend on prices; and the price system operates so efficiently as to produce an optimal allocation of resources for each period taken separately. In other words, the system is in continuous equilibrium, even though the quantity of available resources and technological knowledge is changing over time—for, in each period, the system produces a Pareto-optimal allocation for the quantity of resources and the knowledge of technology *pertaining to that period*.

The trouble with that approach is that there is nothing in the theory to explain how the system gets into equilibrium and what happens when it is out of equilibrium. The "production frontier" which is supposed to shift at some exogenous rate in time is meaningful only if the system is actually *on* the frontier and not *within* it. For any movement of the system *toward* the frontier increases capital as well as output, and therefore changes at least one of the parameters which define the "frontier."[3]

3. Why Equilibrium Theory Is Wrong

The Walrasian equilibrium theory is a highly developed intellectual system, much refined and elaborated by mathematical economists since World War II—an intellectual experiment, as Kornai (1971) called it. But it does not constitute a scientific hypothesis, like Einstein's theory of relativity or Newton's law of gravitation, in that its basic assumptions are axiomatic and not empirical, and no specific methods have been put forward by which the validity or relevance of its results could be tested. The assumptions make assertions about reality in their implications, but these are not founded on direct observation and, in the opinion of practitioners of the theory at any rate, they cannot be contradicted by observation or experiment.

---

[2] Also it would be a mistake to equate the markets in "futures" in the real world to the "dated" markets of equilibrium theory. The "futures" markets of the real world relate to transactions between hedgers and speculators; they do *not* attempt to match supplies and demands accruing at particular future dates.

[3] This point is further considered on pp. 279–281.

3.1 The Effects of Complementarity

My first criticism of this approach is that it concentrates on subsidiary aspects and not the main aspects of market processes. Equilibrium theory elevates the "principle of substitution" (as Marshall called it) to be the "be-all" and "end-all" of all economic activity—the main explanatory principle of the forces which operate on the economy. "Resources" are limited substitutes (or substitutes at margin) both as regards production and consumption, hence profit maximization and utility maximization are essentially substitution problems—a problem of equating prices to marginal rates of substitution in production and consumption. This is misleading because it ignores the essential complementarity between different kinds of products and different kinds of activities, and the nature of the market impulses which result from this complementarity.

Take, for example, capital and labor. These are essentially complementary to each other; this aspect is far more important than the fact that they are also "substitutes" in some respects—i.e., that enterprises can be induced by relative price changes to use more or less mechanized techniques of production involving greater or lesser amounts of "capital" per worker.

The French Physiocrats and English classical economists were of course conscious of this complementarity; they regarded the role of capital accumulation as one of raising production by increasing the level of employment of the economy (so as to increase the amount of labor that is effectively utilized in production) and not for the purpose of substitution of "capital" for "labor" in relation to labor already employed.

Another example is the interdependence of different kinds of economic activities as is shown in the distinction between the primary, secondary, and tertiary sectors. Industrial (or manufacturing) activities—which are "secondary"—consist of the processing or refinement of crude products which are the output of the so-called "primary" sectors, agriculture and mining. They depend on agriculture also for food which is the consumption-good or wage-good par excellence. Hence, an increased availability of primary products is a necessary precondition for increased industrial output; in the same way, an increase in industrial activity necessarily increases the demand for primary products. The same is true of "tertiary" services: the scale on which they can be provided is dependent on the output of both the primary and secondary sectors.

In equilibrium theory, if the economy is assumed to possess two industries such as manufactured goods A and food products B, the available resources are supposed to be divided between them, depending on consumer preference. The nature of neoclassical general equilibrium in the

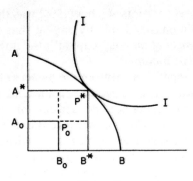

Figure 1

simplest case of two factors and two industries is shown in Fig. 1. The locus of "efficient combinations" is given by the "production frontier" A–B. This assumes that factor supplies X and Y as well as the transformation functions for A and B are given. Ignoring (for the purpose of our argument) the difficulties in the way of representing collective preferences by indifference curves, point P^* can be said to represent the "equilibrium" position at which the two kinds of products are produced in the most preferred ratio, and at which output (A^*, B^*) is at a maximum, given the resource constraints.

But this is a false way of looking at things. The two industries do not make use of the same resources and, insofar as they do, these resources are not, in any meaningful sense, allocated between them.

Labor is common to all activities, but there is always "surplus labor" in agriculture—labor can be withdrawn without any adverse effect on output and normally with a favorable effect. (This can be expressed by saying that normally the marginal product of labor working on the land is zero or negative. The reason is that the density of population living on the land is generally such that output actually produced does not require the *effective* employment of more than a fraction of the labor force available.) There is no such thing as "full employment of labor" except as a short-term phenomenon in a given area (or locality).

Equally, capital cannot be regarded as a *given* quantity which is allocated between the two sectors. On the contrary, each sector generates (or "accumulates") its own capital in the course of its own expansion.

The growth of output and the growth of capital, in the sense of the increase in the stock of goods (or stock of durable goods) serving the purposes of production, are not two different things but merely two different *facets* of the same process; neither is prior to the other nor a precondition of the other. It would be better to say that they are the same thing viewed from two different aspects. Fisher (1906) was the first economist to my knowledge who emphasized this by saying that the stock of goods existing *at a given moment of time* is "capital"; the flow of goods accruing *over a period of time* is "income."

It is true that the competition between the owners of capital to seek the most-profitable activities brings about a certain tendency to equalization in the rate of return; but this is not because capital "flows" between the various sectors in any real sense, but because the rate of accumulation of capital in each particular sector varies positively with the rate of return of that sector, so that sectors with higher rates of profit will expand relatively fast in relation to other sectors and this tends to bring their relative prices, rates of profit, and hence rates of accumulation down, so that the *profile* of the rate of expansion of different sectors tends to approach a structurally determined pattern, determined primarily by technical relationships and also by the income elasticities of demand of consumers. (In reality, at any one time the high rates of profit are made in the so-called "growth industries" resulting from dynamic change.)

But the main point to bear in mind is that under favorable conditions (of which I shall say more later), the expansion of any one sector tends to stimulate (via a demand effect) the expansion of the others; so that production, under favorable conditions, escalates by a kind of chain reaction—each sector receives impulses through market phenomena, and transmits impulses in turn.

The market is thus not primarily an instrument for *allocating* resources. It is primarily an instrument for transmitting impulses to change; it would be truer to say that the market mechanism creates or generates resources than that it allocates them. (There is, of course, also an allocative aspect, but I think this should be regarded as subsidiary and not the primary or most important aspect, and, as Kornai (1971) has recently shown, the markets can perform their allocation functions through a "stock-adjustment" mechanism which is not primarily guided by prices and which is capable of functioning irrespective of prices.)

The implication is that the so-called "equilibrium position" (or the locus of all such positions, such as the "production frontier" shown in Fig. 1) cannot be derived from a study of "data" independently of the actual position in which the economy finds itself at any given time. For, suppose that the initial position of the economy at $t = 0$ is P_0, yielding outputs A_0, B_0. Since these outputs serve as the commodity inputs of the processes of production (and are not use-goods destined for personal consumption), any movement of the system toward optimal allocation necessarily enlarges the quantity of resources available to the economy and therefore changes the position of the production frontier.

Equilibrium Theory and Growth Theory

Since P_0 was a nonoptimal position by definition (i.e., a position at which the marginal rates of substitution of the factors in the two industries were *not* equal), any movement of the system toward "equilibrium"—i.e., to the northeast of P_0—will increase the amount of resources available to at least one of the two industries, if not both. Hence, if P^* was assumed to be the optimum position of annual output when starting from an initial position P_0, it could no longer be the optimal position if one started from any intermediate point such as P_t, with $A_t > A_0$ and $B_t > B_0$ as outputs. This means that the position of the frontier can be defined only if the state of the economy is actually *on* the frontier to start with. Otherwise, one cannot define the frontier except by reference to some *particular* starting point; and any movement of the system toward the frontier from that starting point will necessarily shift the "frontier" itself outward. The optimal output cannot be defined except by reference to the quantity of capital; but the quantity of capital cannot be defined except by reference to output, since output and capital are fundamentally only different ways of looking at the same thing.[4]

Thus the first thing which is wrong with the paradigm of equilibrium theory is thinking of a "given" quantum of resources which are "scarce" and always fully utilized, and which are effectively allocated between different uses. This view permeated the classical school of Ricardo and his followers as well as the neoclassical economists, and it is at the basis of Say's law, *la théorie des debouchès*. The latter is best expressed in Mill's (1848, p. 95) dictum that "there is no over-production; production is not excessive, but merely ill-assorted." If agriculture can employ only a limited number of men (because of the shortage of land), the rest could be employed only in industry and services. If this meant an "overproduction" of industrial goods and services relative to agricultural goods, industrial prices[5] would fall in terms of agricultural prices (agricultural prices

---

[4] Adherents of the neoclassical theory may object that this is no more than a "complication," since under the assumption of homogeneous and linear functions the increase in output associated with an increase of capital will be less than proportionate to the increase in capital, so that after a certain number of steps (or a certain number of time periods) the actual frontier will eventually be reached even if that frontier will by then have become far removed from what it appeared to be at the starting date. But this proposition critically depends on the assumption of linear homogeneity of the production functions which ensured that any increase in capital per man will increase output per man less than proportionately. If one abandons the assumption of linearity and allows for increasing returns, it is no longer true—in which case one could equally hold *either* that the frontier will forever remain an unattainable goal *or* that the distinction between an actual historical situation and the equilibrium situation ceases to have a definite meaning.

[5] The same holds for the prices of services provided by the tertiary sector, but for simplicity we shall neglect the existence of the tertiary sector in this analysis.

will rise in terms of industrial prices, which is the same thing). This will mean a transfer of "real" purchasing power from industry to agriculture, which will go on until the producers in the agricultural sector are able to buy all the goods which industry is capable of producing in excess of industry's own absorption of such goods, whether for purpose of consumption or capital investment. Hence, the price mechanism of competitive markets, which causes a *fall* in the prices of goods in excess supply and a *rise* in prices of goods in excess demand, will always bring about a set of prices at which *all* markets are cleared—to say that demand can never be sufficient to match the potential supply for any or all commodities is the same as saying (according to the Say–Mill view) that the supply would still exceed the demand if the price of any or all commodities fell to zero.

However, this view ignores the peculiar nature of labor, the price of which can never fall to zero—however much the potential supply exceeds the demand in the labor market. Since industrial activities—the processing of crude products of agriculture and mining—invariably require labor, the value added by manufacturing activities cannot fall below a certain minimum (given the productivity of labor in terms of industrial goods), and this minimum sets a limit to the extent to which agricultural prices can rise in terms of industrial prices. But this is the same as saying that in normal circumstances supply cannot equal demand *simultaneously* in both the market for agricultural goods and the market for industrial goods. If the agricultural market is in equilibrium in the sense that the maximum which the sellers are prepared to sell at the prevailing price equals the maximum which the buyers are willing to buy at that price, the industrial market will *not* be in equilibrium in that sense, since the amount actually produced and supplied may be smaller than the amount that would be supplied at the prevailing price, if sufficient demand existed at that price. It is therefore wrong to suggest that the actual output of the economy is determined by the availabilities of resources—capital, labor, and land—which will then be fully utilized irrespective of the structure of demand. If agricultural output is limited by the scarcity of land and not be the availability of labor, and the price of industrial goods in terms of agricultural products is dependent upon the minimum wage which must be paid to labor, then industrial production will be limited by demand and not by the available resources, while the amount of capital available to industry will necessarily vary *pari passu* with the level of industrial production; in other words, capital will also be limited by demand.

This is the intellectual basis of the doctrine of the "foreign trade multiplier," according to which the production of an (industrial) country will be determined by the *external* demand for its products, and will tend to be that multiple of that demand which is represented by the reciprocal of the proportion of *internal* incomes spent on imports. This doctrine asserts the very opposite of Say's law: the level of production will *not* be confined by the availability of capital and labor; on the contrary, the amount of capital accumulated, and the amount of labor effectively employed at any one time, will be the resultant of the growth of external demand over a long series of past periods which permitted the capital accumulation to take place that was required for enabling the amount of labor to be employed and the level of output to be reached which was (or could be) attained in the current period.

Keynes, writing in the middle of the Great Depression of the 1930s, focused his attention on the consequences of the failure to *invest* (due to unfavorable business expectations) in limiting industrial employment *below* industry's attained capacity to provide such employment; and he attributed this failure to excessive saving (or an insufficient propensity to consume) relative to the opportunities for profitable investment. From this came his concentration on liquidity preference and the rate of interest as the basic cause for the failure of Say's law to operate under conditions of low investment opportunities and/or excessive savings, and the importance he attached to the savings/investment multiplier as a short-period determinant of the level of production and employment.

In retrospect, I believe it to have been unfortunate that the very success of Keynes's ideas in connection with the savings/investment multiplier diverted attention from the "foreign trade multiplier" which, over longer periods, is a far more important and basic factor in explaining the growth and rhythm of industrial development. For, over longer periods, Ricardo's presumption that capitalists save only in order to invest, and hence the proportion of profits saved would adapt to changes in the profitability of investment, seems to me more relevant; the limitation of effective demand due to oversaving is a short-run (or cyclical) phenomenon, whereas the rate of growth of "external" demand is a more basic long-run determinant of both the rate of accumulation and the growth of output and employment in the "capitalist" or "industrial" sectors of the world economy.

3.2 Increasing Returns

The second major objection (which in some ways is connected with the first) concerns the assumption of linear-homogeneous production functions, i.e., the neglect of increasing returns to scale. Here again classical economists show an insight and awareness that is lacking in the neoclassical school. Adam Smith, as is well known, attributed primary importance to the proposition that the efficiency of production—i.e., the productivity of labor—depends on the division of labor, and the division of labor in turn depends on the size of the market. He devoted the first three chapters of the *Wealth of Nations* to an exposition of this basic law, and he regarded the existence of this law the most important reason for the existence of a "social economy"—one in which men devote themselves to producing particular things for the market and obtain the commodities they require largely through exchange. Smith's view was that the degree of specialization in particular processes or in particular portions of processes is constantly enlarged through an increase in the size of the market: the processes of production used when 20,000 pins can be sold daily are very different from the processes used when the daily demand was only for a few hundred pins. Hence productivity expands as the market expands, but the increase in productivity resulting from a larger market in turn enlarges the market for other things and by the same token causes productivity to rise in other industries. As Young (1928) said in a famous article:

> Adam Smith's famous theorem amounts to saying that the division of labour depends in large part upon the division of labour. This is more than mere tautology. It means that the counter forces which are continually defeating the forces which make for economic equilibrium are more pervasive and more deeply rooted than we commonly realize" [p. 533].

Young said that with increasing returns "change becomes progressive and propagates itself in a cumulative way [p. 533]."

Indeed, these cumulative forces—which Myrdal (1957) called "the principle of circular and cumulative causation"—largely explain the polarization of the world between the rich and the poor countries that occurred during the last two centuries. Owing to increasing returns, industries tended to be developed in particular growth centers, and in their development they inhibited the growth of industrialization in other areas. The country which became rich and attained high incomes per head was a country which became "well endowed" with capital and in which therefore the capital/labor ratio became very high. But this capital was largely accumulated out of reinvested profits in consequence of increasing demand, and the ability to use so much capital in relation to labor is very largely a reflection of the scale of activities and not of the relative price of capital and of labor. As Young (1928) emphasized, it would be absurd to suppose that it would "pay" to make a hammer just to drive a single nail, or to furnish a factory "with an elaborate equipment of specially constructed jigs, lathes, drills, presses and conveyors to build a hundred automobiles." It was the increase in the size of the market (not the savings or the rate of interest paid on loans) which made it possible to use so much more capital per worker. The best proof of this resides in the fact that while the capital/labor ratio increases dramatically in the course of progress (and varies dramatically in the same period between rich and poor countries), these enormous differences (of the order of 30 : 1 or 50 : 1) in the capital/labor ratio are quite uncorrelated with differences in the capital/output ratio. If production functions were as neoclassical theory supposes—as is assumed, for example, by Samuelson (1967) who emphasized as the central proposition of neoclassical theory that *"capital/ labor up: interest or profit rate down: wage rate up: capital/output up"*—the capital/output ratio would be all the higher the higher the capital/labor ratio.[6]

In fact, the universal experience has been that whether one takes cross-sectional studies, as between different firms in the same industry or of the same industry in different countries, or takes a time-series analysis of the movement of labor productivity and of the capital/labor ratio over time, there is no evidence at all to show that high labor productivity—which is almost invariably associated with a correspondingly high capital/ labor ratio—is associated with any increase in the amount of capital per unit of output. If anything, the contrary appears to be true. The capital/ output ratio in the more advanced countries, such as the United States which has the highest capital/labor ratio and the highest output per man, is *lower* than in countries at a low level of industrial development, such as India.

Neoclassical economists attempted for a time to reconcile these phenomena by introducing the *deus ex machina* of a "Harrod-neutral" technical progress which proceeds at an exogenous rate in time. Since technical progress is incapable of being independently measured, this of course was equivalent to making the whole theory untestable or vacuous. Moreover, technical progress is supposed to proceed at some exogenous rate in time, whereas the phenomena to be explained—the high correlation between the capital/labor ratio and of output per man, and the absence of any correlation between these two factors and the capital/output ratio—applies equally to cross-sectional comparisons of firms and industries and to time comparisons. The observed phenomena are, of course, capable of a much simpler explanation: the existence of increasing returns to scale, which makes it possible to use more and more capital with an increase in the scale of production, without encountering diminishing returns. If the use of more-specialized machinery is economical only with higher levels

---

[6] In fact, it is easy to calculate on the basis of a Cobb–Douglas-type production function that if the capital coefficient of the function is one-third and the labor coefficient two-thirds, doubling the capital/labor ratio would involve the increase the capital/output ratio by one-half.

of output, there is no reason why a rise in labor productivity should be associated with any fall in capital productivity, but with that explanation, the whole neoclassical value theory clearly goes out of the window.

4. An Alternative Approach to Growth Theory

Most abstract economic models postulate a "closed system," but they apply the conclusions reached to open systems, such as national economies, without being fully aware of the inconsistencies involved in this procedure. "Foreign trade" has always been treated as a special branch of the subject; for the general analysis of prices and markets, it was usual to assume a closed economy, defined by given resources, commodities, markets, etc., which are self-contained.

There is no such really closed system except the world economy as a whole, and, to capture the really important aspects of the economic mechanism, one ought to use a paradigm which embodies the significant features of the world economy as a unit as a starting point in the basic theoretical model before tackling the more complicated models required for particular non-self-sufficient "regions" or "countries."

In a first approximation, one should consider the world economy as consisting of two vital sectors: the production of primary goods (food and raw materials) and the production of "secondary" goods (industry—the processing of crude materials into manufactured goods, whether for industrial use or for final consumption).[7]

Primary production is agriculture (including forestry and fisheries) and mining. These are "land-based" activities in the sense that natural resources play a vital part in the ease or difficulty of their performance—e.g., climate, the nature of the soil, and what is beneath the surface in the form of minerals. In some languages, such as German, such activities are referred to as "archproduction" (*Urproduktion*). This conveys the idea that this is the *fond et origine* of all human activities—everything else comes from there; it also conveys the idea that production at any time is governed by the *productivity of the soil*—which is not just a matter of nature but of the state of technology and the amount of capital expended in the past—and not by the productivity of *labor*. For, however essential labor is in all such activities, there is always more labor (and generally much more labor) available than can be *effectively* used on any given area of land. This is because the density of population in any given area is itself a function of the productivity of the soil—the more food is produced, the

---

[7] The tertiary sector—services of all kinds—could be ignored in a first approximation.

more people there will be. Since the output of the soil is a constraint on the labor force, one cannot, at the same time, assume that the labor force is the effective constraint on production—only one of these constraints is likely to "bite" at any one time. And there can be no doubt that with rare exceptions—such as when a region is invaded by new settlers bringing with them a much superior technology capable of producing very much more food per acre of land, as was the case with the first European settlers in America or Oceania—it is the Malthusian constraint which is the critical one, and not the labor constraint. Hence, there is generally disguised unemployment in the rural areas of the world, and economic development essentially consists of tapping these labor reserves. In the course of development, the proportion of population in agriculture diminishes in a dramatic fashion. (In prewar Bulgaria it was 90%; in present day Britain it is less than 3%.)

Secondary production converts crude materials into finished goods in two ways—through direct inputs, such as raw wool or cotton made into clothes, and through the food consumed by industrial labor, which is an "indirect" input.

It is important to emphasize that the potential supply of labor to industry is *unlimited;* since the transfer of labor from the primary to the secondary sector (allowing for international as well as intranational migration) can be limited only by the rate at which such labor can be absorbed or utilized, it cannot be constrained by the size of potential supply. (This is true even when international migration is inhibited, so long as capital and enterprise can move across political frontiers.)

But while the supply of labor to industry is practically unlimited, the price paid for the use of that labor cannot fall below a certain amount in terms of primary goods. For wages must cover a certain minimum means of subsistence, irrespective of the size of excess of the supply of labor over demand. Moreover, it is the peculiarity of industrial labor, in modern days of high organization and even in the ancient days preceding modern industrial capitalism, that the supply price of labor *in terms of food* contains a strong conventional element; wages tend to have a downward rigidity in terms of food prices, around the "attained" or "customary" level, at any rate in free (nonslave) societies, even when that level bears no recognizable relationship to subsistence needs in some biological or calorific sense.

This makes the prices of industrial goods in terms of agricultural products—the terms of trade between industry and agriculture—virtually independent, except in very short periods, of the supply/demand situation in agriculture. (That is to say, agriculture is not likely to obtain *better* prices in terms of industrial goods in times of scarcity. It is less clear that it does not obtain *worse* terms as a result of superabundance, but I believe that over longer periods the latter proposition is likely to be true as well.) Hence, the level of prices of processed goods in terms of foodstuffs is determined by three factors $\bar{w}$, l, π, and given by the formula

$$p = (1 + \pi)\bar{w}l$$

where p is the price of manufactured goods in terms of food, $\bar{w}$ the wage of labor in terms of food, π the share of profits in terms of food, and l the labor requirements per unit of output = 1/(productivity).

There are important asymmetries in the position of these two sectors:

(1) Primary output can be assumed to grow at a certain rate owing to technological progress in landsaving inventions (whether in the form of new crops or new means of planting, new fertilizers, cheapening transport, or the discovery of new substitutes, e.g. synthetics, requiring fewer natural resources). All these have in common is the fact that they are land saving—i.e., they allow more to be extracted from a given natural environment. However, the exploitation of new technology requires capital investment; capital investment is a matter partly of the size of the surplus over the consumption needs of the primary sector, and partly of the terms on which industrial goods can be obtained in exchange for primary products—in other words, on the terms of trade p. Hence, the rate of growth of primary output will be all the greater the more favorable are the terms of trade to agriculture. This is projected by the downward-sloping nature of the $\dot{A}/A$ curve in Fig. 2.

(2) With regard to industry, as was argued earlier, there is a minimum supply price below which no production would be forthcoming; this at the point k where $p = \bar{w}l$. Industrial production can grow only if some part of the output is "ploughed back" in the form of industrial investment. To the

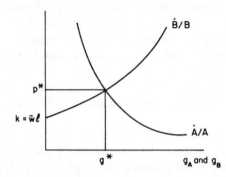

Figure 2 $\dot{A}/A$ is the growth rate of agricultural production, $\dot{B}/B$ the growth rate of industrial production.

extent that this happens, $p > k$, the excess $(p - k)/k$ being equal to the share of output which is "retained" by the sector for the purpose of investment by the sector. In industry, therefore, investment "finances itself" since it generates equivalent profits (excess of p over k) automatically. If, in addition, part of the profits are consumed (profits generate consumption), $p - k$ will be that much larger.

(3) This means that, in the case of *secondary output*, the *supply price* of industry curve $\dot{B}/B$ starting from $k = wl$ will rise in a functional relation to $g_B \equiv \dot{B}/B$ (Fig. 2).

There should exist at any one time a point at which $g = g_A = g_B$ and (abstracting from consumption out of industrial products) $p = (1 + \pi)\bar{w}l = (1 + gv)\bar{w}l$. Whether this point is reached and, if reached, maintained over time, is a complex problem which I cannot enter into here. But *supposing* the system does have a tendency to settle at p and will grow at the rate g, this itself will vary with time, since, owing to economies of large-scale production and laborsaving (as distinct from land-saving) technical progress, $dl_t/dt < 0$, B/B will shift downward with time, hence p_t will be falling with t, and g_t will be rising. With both labor- and land-saving technical progress and a *given* real wage in terms of food (or primary products), economic growth should not only be continuous but would show a tendency to continual *acceleration* (at any rate when exhaustible resources are ignored).

(4) However, there is no *need* for this to happen in this way. Real wages need not be constant at $\bar{w}$; $dw_t/dt > 0$ is quite possible, owing to all kinds of things—monopolistic or oligopolistic price policies by industrial firms, or the pressure exerted through trade unions.

A special case is $dw_t/d_t = -dl_t/d_t$, in which p_t will be constant over time and g_t will be constant $(dg_t/d_t = 0)$. But $dw_t/d_t > -dl_t/d_t$ cannot be excluded either, in which case $dg_t/d_t < 0$: with wages rising faster than productivity in industry, the equilibrium growth rate will tend to diminish.

(5) In any case, we can assume that the rate of expansion of industrial capacity is "induced": the "accelerator principle" governs the rate of capital accumulation in the industrial sector. At any given p_0, the growth of "outside" demand proceeds at the rate g_0 and this induces, by a multiplier/accelerator process, a corresponding rate of capital accumulation and of the growth of output in industry.

(6) Hence on *this* model, industrial growth is dependent on the exogenous components of demand for industry—that part of the demand which comes from "outside" the industrial sector: the growth of its exports (even though this may only amount to a small fraction of the total output or demand—the rest will tend to be resonant with it). Hence *industry* will determine what the terms of trade will be, since p will depend on factors endogenous to the sector; but the growth of purchasing power of the

primary sector (which is the same as its growth of output $\dot{A}/A$) will determine the growth rates of both; and $\dot{A}/A$ is itself a function of p.

All this, of course, is a tremendous oversimplification, deliberately neglecting numerous complicating elements. But the main message to be drawn is that if one assumes that markets function so as to be consistent with expansion—which means that an increase in supply of A will increase the purchasing power of the A sector for B products and vice versa—the rate of growth will ultimately depend on the growth of foodstuffs and basic materials, which is itself dependent on p as shown by some such relationship as the $\dot{A}/A$ curve in Fig. 2.

So, finally, it is the progress of land-saving inventions—including here the continued invention of new substitutes for existing materials and sources of energy—which not only sets the limit to growth, but in the long run governs the rate of growth.

All this is true if we regard world industrial output as a single entity. To analyze the divergent trends in the growth rate of different regions and countries, we must go further and consider the competition between different industrial areas. Owing to the economies of large-scale production and of spatial (geographical) concentration, industrial growth tends to be concentrated in urban areas: the growth of industry and of urbanization are closely related. But any *particular* region may have a rising, constant, or falling share in the total world market for "industrial goods" (including its own "protected" market). In the course of time, new industrial centers emerge and displace, or narrow, the market for the older centers. The fast-growing countries *gain* in competitiveness, for their "efficiency wages" $w_t l_t$ fall in relation to those of areas which grow more slowly—whose market share is diminishing.

In industrial growth, owing to increasing returns, Myrdal's principle of "cumulative and circular causation" operates. Success breeds success; regions or "countries" whose industrial exports increase faster than world net exports have a faster rate of economic growth; this tends to depress the rate of growth of the regions whose share of world trade is diminishing in consequence.

Industrialization is the key factor in economic development. All rich countries with high incomes per capita are industrialized countries. Myrdal's principle explains why rapid growth tends to be concentrated among a relatively small number of "successful" areas, and also, why, within that fortunate group of areas, the relative wealth and standard of living are subject to continuous change—poorer areas with lower efficiency wages overtake areas which were initially richer, but, owing to higher wages in relation to their productivity, are unable to stand up to the competition of others. Both the growing polarization of the world between developed and underdeveloped, or rich and poor countries, and the remarkable shifts in the relative positions of individual "rich" countries are, in my view, to be explained by the same basic principle.

References

Fisher, I. (1906). *The Nature of Capital and Income.* New York: Macmillan.
Kornai, J. (1971). *Anti-Equilibrium.* Amsterdam: North-Holland Publ.
Mill, J. S. (1848). *Principles of Political Economy,* Vol. II. London: John W. Parker.
Myrdal, G. (1957). *Economic Theory and Underdeveloped Regions.* London: Duckworth.
Robbins, L. C. (1932). *An Essay or the Nature and Significance of Economic Science,* p. 12. London: Macmillan.
Samuelson, P. A. (1967). *Economics—An Introductory Analysis,* 7th ed., p. 715. New York: McGraw-Hill.
Young, A. A. (1928). Increasing Returns and Economic Progress. *Economic Journal* (December).

Kings College
Cambridge University
Cambridge, United Kingdom

LIMITS ON GROWTH*

By NICHOLAS KALDOR

I REGARD it as a great privilege to have been asked to give the second of the Special Lectures which the University of Oxford arranged as an annual event in honour of Professor Sir John Hicks. I do so for both personal and professional reasons.

For convenience of exposition, though not on account of its prime importance, I should like to speak of my personal reasons first. Sir John Hicks is one of my oldest friends in England, and I owe him an immense debt for all that he taught me at the time when my knowledge of economics was very rudimentary. He is four years my senior—a difference which is hardly worth a mention now, but was of enormous significance when we were both young and he was a fullly qualified teacher in economics when I was a first year undergraduate. John Hicks first came to the L.S.E. from Oxford as a lecturer in 1926. I arrived a year later, and began as a first-year student reading for an economics degree in October 1927.

I first got to know him when I attended his lectures on Advanced Economic Theory. I remember a great deal of that course since it gave an exposition of the theories of Walras and Pareto and how they compared with the partial equilibrium method of Marshall. After my graduation I was awarded a Research Studentship and I moved into a small unfurnished flat in Bloomsbury which, as it happened, was next door to the one occupied by John Hicks. It did not take long before we saw each other frequently—indeed almost daily, for meals in small Italian restaurants, and talked about economics incessantly. There was at least one occasion when we went on a joint continental holiday. This, in some ways idyllic, arrangement came to a halt (though only temporarily) with my marriage, closely followed by a Rockefeller Fellowship in the United States, while Hicks married a close L.S.E. friend and fellow graduate student, Ursula K. Webb (who died recently) who was the real founder of the *Review of Economic Studies.* When the *Review* first appeared it was treated by the professionals with considerable scorn. Hayek thought it could not last for more than a year. Keynes thought there was no real need for it since, as the editor of the *Economic Journal,* he believed he had never had to turn down an article that was worthy of publication on account of pressure on space. Fifty years later the *Review* is still going strong and nobody would say now that its existence has not been justified.

Though we never shared a university again, and lived in different cities and hence saw each other much less frequently our mutual friendship was never in question—even though the gaps in erudition between us, though they may have narrowed in the course of the years, were never closed. I

---

* The second annual Hicks Lecture, delivered in Oxford on November 28th, 1985.

© Oxford University Press 1986

never had the patience to learn mathematics; Hicks got a first in Maths Mods at Oxford, and taught himself a number of foreign languages sufficiently well to be able to read and enjoy treatises on economics that were not available in English. As a result he was able to cut himself loose from the narrow dogmatism of Robbins and Hayek, and in this I followed him eagerly. He recommended that I should read Wicksell and Myrdal as an antidote to Hayek. But I learnt most from him in connection with his early work on Money and on general equilibrium economics; and I believe I was allowed to read *Value and Capital* almost chapter by chapter as it was written.

Now, coming to the professional reasons, which are far more important, John Hicks is an economist in the great classical tradition: undoubtedly one of the greatest now living, not just in this country but in the Western World. He is a pure economist in the sense that his interest is in developing general economic theory by improving the framework of assumptions whenever the case for such an improvement is established, and in exploring their implications as fully as logical reasoning, aided by mathematics, makes possible. Unlike others, whose interest in economics is more pedestrian, Hicks' main aim is the pursuit of knowledge as such. He is not an advocate of particular economic policies: he allows his readers to make up their minds on such matters—his own views and preferences are on most occasions kept firmly in the background. In this he differs from some other famous economists who developed the subject for the sake of finding better arguments for their preferred policies for improving the performance of the economy.

Hicks of course is also primarily interested in exploring the limits on production and growth but without any preconceived objectives of supporting one particular set of policies as against others. In this respect Hicks is nearer to the grand tradition of the Lausanne School of Walras and Pareto than to that of the English classical economists.

His main virtues are the virtues of the intellectual—they are found in the thoroughness and patience with which he explores the implications of particular assumptions to the last detail—I would almost say, to the "last unsuspected detail". Indeed the feature that impresses me most in reading his works is the scrupulousness with which he pursues the numerous aspects of a problem—aspects the existence of which would not have been suspected by a more impatient and less intellectually thorough economist like myself.

But the most impressive thing about Sir John Hicks is the sheer magnitude, I would indeed say, the incredible magnitude, of his written record. He is the author of three major treatises—*Value and Capital, Capital and Growth,* and *Capital and Time,* any one of which could be regarded as an ample testimony of the concentrated effort of a life-time. But in addition to these three treatises Hicks published a large number of important and famous books on particular topics, beginning with the *Theory of Wages* in 1932, his *Contribution to the Theory of the Trade Cycle* in 1950, the *Theory of Economic History* (which is my personal favourite), and various books on monetary economics down to his most admirable, though difficult, methodological essay on *Casuality in Economics* published in 1979, or 47 years after the appearance of his first book. In between he published at least three books containing papers on monetary theory, and this was followed by three large volumes of Collected Essays on Economic Theory which appeared in the last few years. I cannot say that I have read everything which Hicks has written, though in relation to any other author (with the possible exception of Keynes) my score of having read and studied Hicks is rather a high one, and the more one considers his books the more one marvels how one man could have accomplished all this, and at the same time made such an extensive and continuing study of the works of others, as is evidenced by the broad variety of his references in the footnotes which are adduced to support particular points in the text.

One of Hicks' most engaging qualities and a rare one among academics, is the readiness with which he is prepared to set aside his previous writings if in the light of further thought he sees a problem differently from the way he approached it before. Unlike lesser men, he never feels constrained by his past utterances. As he put it in the Introduction to *Capital and Time*, "it is just as if one were making pictures of a building; though it is the same building, it looks quite different from different angles. As I now realise, I have been walking round my subject, taking different views of it." (No such sentiments could be expressed by an author who writes a treatise entitled *Principles of Economics*.)

As John Hicks argues in his latest book, economics is on the edge of the sciences and also on the edge of history—it is on the borderline of both. The economist, unlike the historian, is primarily concerned with the present, and for the sake of the present, is also concerned with the past—with the historian it is the other way round. More generally I would say that economic theory embodying hypotheses concerning the causal relationship between events should help us to understand the forces which shape historical developments. Ideally one would like to see induction and deduction closely interwoven. This however is not generally possible. The main reason, I think, is that the results derived by deductive reasoning necessarily presuppose a whole framework of assumptions, some of which may be supported by empirical investigations, while others may turn out to be immaterial.

However, the critical assumptions underlying theoretical propositions are not known in advance; hence the applicability of a theory, its explanatory power, can only be properly gauged after the deductive process is completed.

I shall choose as the main theme today Hicks' interpretation of the prolonged post-war boom, and the causes of its breakdown after 1973. It is found in a long essay on "Monetary Experience and the Theory of Money" which first appeared in a volume of essays on *Economic Perspectives* in 1977, though it may have been written sometime before that. The main purpose of Hicks' paper is a review of monetary theories from Hume to Wicksell and to Keynes and to deal with the slow and uninterrupted inflation which characterised the whole of the post-war period but which proceeded at a moderate pace—the so-called "creeping inflation"—of the 1950s and 1960s. It only became more violent (in all industralised countries and not just in Britain) in the mid-seventies. After showing that the long post-war inflation—the *moderate* inflation—was an indispensable prerequisite of fast economic growth and universal full employment (since it made it possible for the slow growing countries to prosper provided that inflation was large enough in the fast growing countries), the maintenance of full employment in the industrial or so-called "secondary" sectors of the world economy (and as Hicks says, it is this sector which Keynes in the *General Theory* mainly had in mind) critically depended on an adequate growth in supplies in the "primary" sector (i.e., in agriculture and mining) which provide the indispensable inputs for the secondary sector. The classical economists were well aware of this; the Law of Diminishing Returns is a consequence of the fact that land is in fixed supply, and "land" (meaning the natural environment) is the critical factor both in the production of food and in the provision of raw materials of all kinds as well as of sources of energy. Hence the basic pessimism of all classical economists concerning the long-term possibilities of economic growth. The accumulation of capital, in the classical view, is a necessary but not a sufficient condition for growth. The growth of production will be less than in proportion to the increase in 'resources' (meaning both capital and labour), it must therefore involve (given the level of wages as determined by the costs of subsistence) a falling rate of profit which is indeed (I am here quoting Ricardo) "checked at repeated intervals by the improvements in machinery, connected with the production of necessaries, as well as by discoveries in the science of agriculture". However, sooner or later the Law of Diminishing Returns must reassert itself. The motive for accumulation (I am quoting Ricardo again) "will diminish with every diminution of profit and will cease altogether when profits are so low as not to afford them [the manufacturers] an adequate compensation for their trouble and for the risks which they must necessarily encounter in employing their capital productively".[1] Sooner or later all avenues will inevitably lead to the long run equilibrium of the Stationary State. And on the way to it it appeared inevitable that a steadily rising proportion of resources should be absorbed in the procurement of food, leaving less available for everything else. This was the main lesson to be derived from the Law of Diminishing Returns.

As is the case with many of the long term predictions of economists, subsequent history not only failed to support the predictions but led quite

---

[1] *Principles*, Sraffa edition, pp. 120 and 122.

universally in the opposite direction. The proportion of resources of the world economy (or the world *trading* economy—as Hicks prefers to regard the real-world equivalent of the economist's motion of a "closed economy") which was required for the primary sector of production has steadily diminished with economic progress—indeed in the views of some it was the steady fall in the proportion of resources required for satisfying primary needs which made possible economic progress and rising living standards in a steadily growing number of countries or areas. The proportion of the annual labour force occupied in agriculture in Britain is estimated to have been around 50 per cent in the 17th century but less than 36 per cent in the early 19th century; 20 per cent by the middle of that century, 8 per cent by 1900 and only 2.5 per cent today. (Even the earliest figure—50%—is much lower than that of other European countries of the period, e.g. France. This indicates that even prior to the Industrial Revolution England was a relatively rich country in Europe, the reasons for which would deserve closer investigation than they have yet received.)

It is true that today home production covers only around 60 per cent of our food requirements (this is a higher figure than that of the early decades of this century). But even so, the proportion of labour and capital resources needed to provide food for the whole of the population is 5 per cent or less—less than one twentieth. This is consistent with the figures for other countries having a modern, commercialised agriculture—for example, in Australia the proportion of the labour force in agriculture is around $6\frac{1}{2}$ per cent, but two thirds of the output is exported, so the proportion required to provide food for the indigenous population is only around 2 per cent. This may be lower, but not much lower, than the figures for Western European countries as well as America, in all of which the agricultural work force fell dramatically since the Second World War. As far as one can tell, this process is by no means at an end.

But this is only the labour-saving measure of technical progress in agriculture, which tells us nothing of the rate of growth of output, and how it compares with the rate of growth of demand for primary products. For that we need another measure of technical progress, looked at from the "land-saving" or "natural resource saving" aspect. It is the latter aspect which is crucial for growth. I define a land-saving innovation as anything which increases the total yield of a given area, whether agricultural or mineral (including sources of energy), though it is impossible to say whether the innovation is the result of new knowledge or merely newly adopted knowledge. The same kind of haziness which Sir John Hicks found in the notion of an industrial production frontier which depended on capital and labour resources, also applies to the production frontier for primary products—we cannot really distinguish movements along the curve from outward shifts of the curve. Anyhow, the real issue is whether the growth of labour productivity in industry and services and the growth of land productivity in agriculture and mining (the latter including oil-extraction)

LIMITS ON GROWTH

are in an *appropriate relationship* to one another (which need not imply proportionality).[2]

As Hicks says, from the early 1970s on "the Keynesian identification of the limit to growth with Full Employment of Labour is called into question".[3] During the Bretton Woods period full employment was the effective barrier but since then, the effective barrier has been different (quoting Hicks) "full employment cannot now be reached since the supplies of primary products that would be needed to support it are not available".[4] As my lecture is mainly intended to cast doubt on this proposition, I think I ought to add that I was just as convinced of this as Hicks was[5]—indeed more convinced, since Hicks went on immediately to qualify his statement by saying that the experience of the early 1970s may have been a temporary one due to "the exceptional expansion of 1972–3 which imposed an exceptional strain". (This resulted, I presume, from the sudden relaxation or disappearance of the balance of payment constraint in a number of countries which followed the abandonment of Bretton Woods.)

Indeed, the year 1973 was unique for its fast economic growth—which was higher in that year in *all* industrial countries than in any previous year or any of the subsequent years. Manufacturing output rose by 9.5 per cent in the U.K. by 10.3 per cent in the seven main industrial countries (including the U.S.) and by 10 per cent in the OECD countries as a whole. These rates were at least 50 per cent higher than the average rate of growth of industrial production in the previous 25 years, and while it can readily be granted that they were not sustainable, given the rate of growth of the output of primary products, the shortage of primary products certainly cannot explain why the rate of growth of industrial production in subsequent years—that is to say, in the years 1973–1984—should have fallen so low—to $1\frac{3}{4}$ per cent a year in the European OECD countries as a group, as against the growth rate of $5\frac{3}{4}$ per cent a year achieved in the previous 25 years. Indeed, in the light of these figures it is in my view impossible to maintain that the Depression of the Seventies (and after), with the reappearance of heavy unemployment in the industrial countries, was a consequence of *supply constraints,* the effects of which would have been aggravated, not alleviated—as many people maintained at the time on both sides of the Atlantic—by the more deliberate use of Keynesian policies acting on effective demand. The most one can say is that uncoordinated measures of expansion by individual countries would have tended to

---

[2] Strict numerical proportionality is not of course what is required, since the income elasticity of consumption demand for foodstuffs is less than unity and that for manufactures and services greater than unity—but the main point made in the text is valid in the sense that there is a "warranted" relationship between them at any particular level of real income.
[3] *Economic Perspectives,* p. 98
[4] *Ibid.* p. 99.
[5] cf., "Inflation and Recession in the World Economy", *Economic Journal,* December 1976, pp. 704–708.

aggravate the imbalances in international trade and payments. Indeed it was the disproportionality between import and export propensities of individual countries under conditions of fully liberalized trade which was the major cause of the well-nigh universal state of recession.

I think it is in this context that Sir John Hicks' distinction between fix-price and flex-price markets is important. The manufacturing sector is the archetypal case of fix-price market—at least in the present century—when manufacturers are almost invariably price-*makers* and quantity-*takers*, and not the other way round. The working of this system is by no means fully clarified. It generally involves some firm, or firms, assuming the role of a price leader which other manufacturers follow—hence from the consumers' point of view, there is not much difference whether he buys from a high cost firm or a low cost firm, the differences in efficiency are reflected, not in a difference in prices (for goods of the *same* quality), but in differences in profits per unit of sale of different producers which, as we know from various kinds of statistics, are very large indeed.

Everybody practices mark-up pricing, but it is the price-leaders' costs and mark-up which determines the permissible, or viable, mark-up of the others. In such markets supply tends to equal demand in the sense that the flow of actual production tends to approximate actual take-up, or consumption, but this is not "market clearing" in the economists' sense, since the actual production of the representative seller is below his optimum production at the prevailing price—below the level of production that would maximise his profits. Differences between demand and supply in this sense are mainly reflected in stock changes; a fall in demand leads to an undesired (or involuntary, as the Keynesian term goes) accumulation of stocks, and *vice versa* if demand exceeds supply. The market operates via changes in quantities rather than in prices; in the relation of actual stocks to desired stocks, which tend to get eliminated through the operation of the stock adjustment principle. In markets of this type uncertainties concerning the future growth of demand mainly affect the degree of utilization of capacity; it pays the manufacturers to maintain capacity in excess of demand and keep the growth of capacity in line with the growth of demand. They are in a position to do this precisely because in the absence of keen price competition their profits will be large enough to finance new investment on a continuing basis. Prices are changed too, but these happen mainly as a result of changes in costs, either of raw materials or of labour, or both.

In flex-price markets, on the other hand, markets operate far more closely to the text book manner; the individual producer has no control over prices and cannot benefit from withholding supplies. Prices *fall* when supply (in this case it is the true supply, which means the *maximum* amount that sellers are prepared to sell at any particular price) exceeds demand and *vice versa*. In these markets short-term stock changes are also important and they can exert an influence both in a price-stabilizing and also a price-destabilizing direction. The stocks are held, not just by producers and

LIMITS ON GROWTH

consumers but mainly by market dealers (intermediaries) who maintain "buffer stocks" to be able to buy or sell to their customers at any time they desire even if the timing of purchases and sales is not perfectly synchronised. They make their money on the "dealers' turn" between their buying and selling prices, which are both varied stimultaneously according as they perceive that their stocks are changing in one direction or another, contrary to the desired norm.

In performing these functions the dealers almost inevitably become speculators as well, who increase stocks on their own initiative when they expect prices to rise, and *vice versa* when they expect prices to fall. While their normal functions as dealers operate in a price-stabilizing direction, their speculative transactions have the opposite effect. As a combined result price movements normally continue until a point is reached when traders feel that prices are abnormally low (or high as the case may be), in which case their policy goes into reverse (they buy in the expectation of a rise, when they consider that prices have fallen "too far", and so on) which creates a turning point, followed by an equally rapid movement of prices in the opposite direction. So commodity prices in unregulated markets behave like a yo-yo, they move up and down by very large amounts, normally within a period of a year or less. Keynes, writing in 1938, calculated that the *average* annual difference between the highest and a lowest price, over a ten-year period, amounted to 67 per cent in the case of four commodities (rubber, cotton, wheat and lead).[6] After 1945 the same kind of fluctuations continued, according to some authorities on an even larger scale, particularly after 1971,[7] and rising and falling prices tended to alternate in two-year periods more often than within a single year. Thus the sharp rise in prices in 1972–73 (by 150 per cent in terms of the index of commodity prices) was followed by a sharp fall of the order of 25 per cent in 1974–75, and a sharp rise in prices in 1976 (by over 40 per cent), followed by a fall in 1977; a rise in 1978–79 of over 30 per cent followed by a sharp fall of 26 per cent in 1980–82, and again by a further 20 per cent in 1984–85.[8]

The working of flex-price markets is thus in fact very inefficient—it is attended by large fluctuations in prices which are not regular enough to be predictable in extent or timing, and which generate risks that act as a drag on production.[9] Hence whenever a stabilization scheme succeeds, it is soon

---

[6] "The Policy of Government Storage of Foodstuffs and Raw Materials", *Economic Journal*, 1938.

[7] According to Prof. Sylos Labini, the variations in raw material prices were three times as large in relation to changes in world industrial production, than before 1971. Cf., Sylos Labini, *On the Instability of Commodity Prices and the Problem of Gold*; cf., also the graph in *Lloyds Bank Review*, July 1983, p. 25.

[8] These figures relate to an index number of 12 commodities—they are not comparable therefore with Keynes' figures which related to a group of four commodities only.

[9] It could be argued that competitive markets would be far less inefficient if dealers carried much larger stocks in relation to turnover as this would enable them to exert a far greater price-stabilising influence as part of their actual business. However, the stocks which they find profitable to carry are themselves related to the profit made on the "dealers' turn" which is itself kept down by competition. Thus the same forces of competition which made intermediation relatively costless are in part responsible also for the large fluctuation of prices.

followed by a rise in production which brings about a large accumulation of stocks (butter mountains or cocoa mountains) which give the impression to consuming countries that they are made to pay too high a price as a result of the price stabilization scheme, whereas the presumption is that *without* price stabilization the effective price paid for commodities over the average of high and low periods would have been considerably more and not less.

If the prices in commodity markets could be stabilized through international commodity price stabilization schemes, as Keynes advocated strongly (though unsuccessfully) during the War, it is highly probable that the long-term rate of growth of output of primary commodities would be sufficiently enhanced to equal or to exceed the requirements arising from any *feasible* rate of growth of industrial output.[10] For while there is no *ultimate* limit to industrial production in a world context, there is a limit to the rate at which output can grow, a limit given by the sequential character of production, as analysed in *Capital and Time*. Just as it takes nine months to produce a baby, and it cannot be done in less, so in a world where it needs steel to make machinery and iron and coal to make steel, and each of these processes takes time, there is a limit to the rate at which additional labour can be absorbed in productive activities.

In agriculture, or in primary production as a whole, the same limitation due to the sequential character of production applies but it need not impose any *narrower* limit provided that adequate stocks are carried to ensure the success of the price-stabilisation scheme. For the real difference between primary production and secondary production (that is to say, between agriculture and mining on the one hand and industrial production on the other hand) resides in the short term elasticities of supply. In industry, on account of the nature of competition and marketing, an increase in demand is likely to call forth an increase in output fairly smoothly without much delay or impediment. In agriculture and mining on the other hand production normally responds to increased demand with some delay, particularly in the case of minerals where increased capacity may require the sinking of new shafts, etc. Over a longer period, on the other hand, there is no reason to suppose that the elasticity of supply of primary products be any less—indeed, historical experience shows the opposite, since the prior requirements for primary products could be satisfied with a *steadily falling proportion* of labour and capital devoted to the primary sector. This is despite the fact that technological progress involves the substitution of primary products for labour—in the form of energy generated by fossil fuels in place of human muscle power—as well as the substitution of manufactured goods (machinery) for labour.[11]

---

[10] As was found with the pre-war "marketing boards" in African countries, the introduction of an assured price gave a very large encouragement to peasant production.

[11] I am ignoring in the context of this lecture the truly long-term problem created by the exhaustion of reserves of non-renewable sources of energy and minerals which agitated some scientists (Meadows and Co. and the Club of Rome) some 15 years ago. The uncertainties surrounding this question are too large to enable worthwhile consideration of this problem. For

(*continued overleaf*)

LIMITS ON GROWTH

The basic requirement of continued economic growth is that the various complementary sectors expand in due relationship with each other—that is to say that general expansion is not held up by "bottlenecks" in key sectors. However, in the course of time, under the influence of technical progress, both of the natural-resource saving and labour-saving kind, the requirements of expansion may become considerably modified. In the manufacturing sector which becomes more important as real incomes rise, there are considerable economies of scale, as a result of which manufacturing activities are subject to a *"polarisation process"*—they are likely to develop in a few successful centres, and their success has an inhibiting effect on similar developments in other areas. The realisation of these economies of scale normally requires also that numerous processes of production which are related to each other are carried out in close geographical proximity.

As a result different regions experience unequal rates of growth of output and of population. The industrial areas experience a growing demand for labour which may involve immigration from other areas once their own surplus labour is exhausted. Technological development in primary production on the other hand, tends to be more labour-saving than land-saving, so that the growth of output may go hand in hand with a falling demand for labour; and though output per head may grow fast in real terms, the level of wages will tend to remain low (and may even be falling)[12] as a result of a growing surplus population. Since labour cost per unit of output is the most important factor in determining selling prices (at any rate under competitive conditions) the low wages prevailing, in terms of *industrial* products, will mean that the terms of trade will move unfavourably to primary producers, which may be the main factor, along with the low coefficient of labour utilisation, for their state of "under-development" characterised by low standards of living.

The important contrast—which I regard as a major factor in the growing inequality of incomes between rich and poor countries—resides in the fact that the benefit of labour saving technical progress in the primary sector tends to get passed on to the consumers in the secondary sector in lower prices, whereas in the industrial sector its benefits are retained *within* the sector through higher wages and profits. (The main reason for this

(*Footnote 10 continued*)
one thing, *known* reserves are no indication of total available reserves, since it becomes totally uneconomic to search for reserves where known reserves exceed 30–40 years current consumption. It must also be borne in mind that technical progress has generally succeeded in circumventing scarcities arising from the shortage or insufficiency of particular commodities (the best known example is Darby's invention of the coking of coal which made iron production independent of timber supplies at a stage when deforestation caused an acute shortage of timber) and there is no reason why this process should come to a halt. (Cf. W. Beckerman, 'Economists, Scientists and Environmental Catastrophe', *Oxford Economic Papers*, November 1972)

[12] Sir Arthur Lewis had shown that the spectacular increase in both labour and land productivity in sugar production over 40 years coincided with a fall in wages in sugar plantations.

difference lies in the differing manner of operation of perfect and imperfect competition.)

Industrial growth leads to both higher real wages and a higher volume of employment, which will mean a higher concentration of the population in urban areas. This may entail cumulative advantages through the spread of knowledge and education with favourable repercussions on progress through the application of scientific knowledge to industry. These go well beyond the economies of large-scale production, though these economies, through their need for geographic concentration, may have been instrumental in creating them. The reverse side of this (of which we have heard much recently) is found when the industrial sector, due to falling market shares in relation to other centres, becomes stagnant and then goes into a decline, causing unemployment which tends to be concentrated in the inner cities of large towns which fall into decay.

In the primary producing regions, by contrast, technical progress involves a combination of rising production and of falling demand for labour, resulting in both open and disguised unemployment, the natural corrective for which is the movement of populations from agricultural to industrial areas. However, actual mobility has never been large enough to even out the differences in the level and the rate of growth of real wages between agriculture and industry—not even within the same country, and much less so when the required movement is across political boundaries.

There is thus no effective tendency to level out the differences between the advanced industrial areas and the surplus-labour agricultural areas; on the contrary, if our analysis is correct, the benefits of technical progress of *both* sectors tend to accrue to the *industrial* sector. This means that the faster the growth of technical knowledge the more the "the terms of trade" will turn against the primary producing areas and the greater will be the inequality between rich and poor countries.

Hence contrary to the view expressed at the beginning, the fall in growth rates and the rise in unemployment levels in the advanced industrial countries after 1973 was not the inevitable consequence of shortages in primary products—the indications are that the supplies of food, raw materials and energy would have proved adequate to the needs of the advanced industrial countries—particularly so if their prices had been kept steady by stabilisation schemes, instead of showing the sharp movements due to changes in short-term market expectations, and if there had not been the rise in prices due to monopolistic restrictions such as the creation of the oil cartel.

Thus the physical limits on growth (as distinct from the actual limits which became increasingly dependent on a complex of policy objectives) have continued to be set by the availabilities of labour in the advanced industrial countries—just as was the case in the first 25 years after the Second World War. If the maintenance of full employment in the industrial countries came under increasing strain it was as a result of accelerated inflationary trends caused by the sharp rise in commodity prices after 1971—which are likely to have been largely speculative in origin, following America's abandonment of the gold standard. (This is shown by the fact that the movement of commodity prices closely followed the movement of the gold price[13] and the repercussions of this on the cost of living and hence on the rate of money-wage increases which aggravated the process.) The reaction, almost universally, was to deal with the problem as if it had been caused by demand inflation, not by cost inflation—in other words, by tightening fiscal and monetary policies (though for reasons that are evident, it is very difficult for any single country to stand out against the prevailing trend—unless it isolates itself by quantitative controls over trade as well as strict control of foreign payments).

For Britain the lower growth rate of the world economy meant an actual fall in industrial production after 1973, the level of which has still not been regained. Despite recent Ministerial claims of five years of uninterrupted growth, current manufacturing output is still 12 per cent below 1973 and 7 per cent below 1979. The counterpart to this was a heavy increase in unemployment, the incidence of which was concentrated in old areas of manufacturing industry, which are often found in the decaying inner city areas of large towns, where prospects of finding alternative employment opportunities are virtually non-existent. Twelve years of industrial decline has thus created *within* Britain the same kind of contrasts between prosperous and depressed areas as exist in the world at large between developed and under-developed countries.

King's College, Cambridge, U.K.

---

[13] Cf. the graph in OECD *Economic Outlook*, December 1973, p. 106.

GROWTH AND THE TERMS OF TRADE: A KALDORIAN TWO SECTOR MODEL (*)

Ferdinando Targetti

University of Trento and Bocconi University

1. INTRODUCTION

Kaldor relies on an induced investment function in his first model of growth (Kaldor 1957(*b*)). He holds that while Keynes' investment function is autonomous, an investment function of a growth model must be induced. In the Corfù Conference (Kaldor 1958) he tried to demonstrate that the only stable equilibrium in the goods market, once the investment is induced, must be a full employment equilibrium.

His idea is that a one sector model of growth cannot have a constraint from the demand size ([1]), and his theory of distribution provides an adjustment of warranted growth rate to the natural one. In this sort of economy a productive capacity constraint does not work, whereas sooner or later a labor supply constraint will arise.

Kaldor potentiated this idea in his inaugural lecture (Kaldor 1966) where it is claimed that the responsibility for the comparatively bad performance of the growth rate in the UK economy can be attributed to the increasing rigidity of the supply of labor from agriculture to the manufacturing sector.

The thesis is partly modified in a subsequent work (Kaldor 1968) in which it is held that—even in a closed economy—if a positive wage differential exists between a progressive sector (manufacture) and a backward

---

(*) I would like to thank, without implicating, Lord Kaldor for the discussion I had with him on the argument of this paper and Mr. Davis Vines who began to work on this subject with prof. Thirlwall several years ago and who made very useful comments on a first version of this paper. I wish also to thank the partecipants to a Seminar I gave on this subject at New York University the 11th of May 1984. I aknowledge the Italian « Ministero della Pubblica Istruzione » which has financed this research (Quota 40%, comitato 13, esercizio 1982/83).

([1]) See G. Harcourt (1965) for a critical comment.

sector (not only agriculture, but also part of the tertiary sector), then the demand for labor, induced by the growth of the advanced sector, will not be constrained by the rigidity of labor supply, because the higher demand for labor of the advanced sector will induce a higher supply of labor from the backward sector. (Furthermore, in an open economy immigration can make the supply of labor elastic to the manufacturing sector.) Zero (or positive) marginal productivity of labor in the backward sector allows, a la Lewis (1954), that a withdrawal of laborers from that sector does not reduce the output of the sector itself.

Having discarded the rigid-labor-supply explanation, the bad performance of the growth rate of some countries has been explained in terms of comparatively low growth of the exogenous component of effective demand, which is export (Kaldor 1971) [2].

Nevertheless, although the argument of the low growth of export could be put forward to explain the different rates of growth pertaining to different countries (or a group of countries) [3], it cannot explain the growth of the world economy as a whole: in this case all imports and exports are cancelled out and the exogenous component of demand will disappear. Then the limit to growth remains to be explained.

Moreover, in a period of stagflation for the world economy, Kaldor's previous models of growth were also weak for two reasons: first because, as we have said, they presupposed full employment, so that the model could rely on an induced investment function; second, because in these models price inflation and price deflation are short-term processes whose job is to accommodate the distribution of income to « finance » capital accumulation brought about by technical progress. Even when price inflation is the outcome of the dynamic wage-profit spiral (Kaldor 1959) it presupposes an excess demand in the goods market (i.e., an « actual » rate of growth exceeding the « warranted » rate).

If full employment is abandoned then two problems emerge. One is the way in which a new investment is financed, if it can not be financed through a price increase due to excess demand in the goods market. This problem is not addressed here. Some suggestions can be found in some

---

[2] In its turn the bad performance of British exports has been initially explained by Kaldor in terms of avervaluation of the sterling pound (Kaldor 1971) and subsequently in terms of the backwardness of British goods exported (Kaldor 1978).

[3] The argument has been developed in Thirlwall (1979). He stated the simple rule according to which the ratio between the income elasticity of the exports of one country and the income elasticity of its imports is a good proxy for the ratio between the rate of growth of that country and the rate of growth of another country of group of countries.

of Kaldor's papers (1966, 1980), where, following A. Wood (1975), a single firm—and by aggregation the whole economy—finances its growth by marking up its costs. (As a consequence, Kaldor's (1956) rejection of Kalechi's theory of distribution, based on the degree of monopoly, should now be partly amended.)

The second problem which emerges is the search for the limits to growth and the search for the reasons why inflation can emerge without excess demand in the goods market.

Thus, in the 1970s a new interpretation of the stagflationist bias of the modern world economy has been worked out by Kaldor (1976). That article was preceded by three articles about growth and equilibrium (Kaldor 1972, 1974, 1974b) which deal more extensively with the theoretical model underlying that interpretation.

One of the main concerns of these articles is to stress the importance of complementary between sectors, which has been forgotten by « neoclassical » models of growth based on substitutability among factors. It is interesting to note that neither modern classical nor neoclassical economists who have dealt with a dual economy, such as A. Lewis (1954) and D.W. Jorgenson (1961, 1969), have pointed out the crucial role of the terms of trade and the balanced growth of an economy with complementary sectors. The « classical » model of accumulation a la Lewis put emphasis on the complementary between two sectors of the economy (industry and agriculture) from the point of view of the distribution of income, but it has missed the link from the demand side (Kaldor 1954). The model, in fact, is unable to show that—in a closed market—the excess of industrial output over the investment in the sector must be sold to the agricultural sector. The terms of trade between the two sectors must play a double role, the first being to extract surplus from agriculture to industry, and the second being to, at the same time, create agricultural income which will be transformed into industrial demand. If it does not work properly, the phenomena of stagnation and inflation (« stagflation ») can emerge.

This paper attempts to bring together Kaldor's ideas about a model of growth for an economy with two complementary sectors.

2. GROWTH AND EQUILIBRIUM EXCHANGE OF THE TWO SECTOR MODEL

Let us suppose that the economy is divided into two sectors producing, for the sake of simplicity, mining and agricultural goods and manu-

— 82 —

factured goods. The hypotheses of the model are as follows: In both sectors a classical-Kaleckian saving function prevails, *i.e.*, workers consume what they earn. Furthermore, as in Marx's reproduction schemes, the manufacturing sector provides investment goods for both sectors and the agricultural sector provides wage-goods for both sectors. Moreover, as in Kalecki (1954) and Sylos-Labini (1972), the system of pricing and the inducement to grow are different in the two sectors.

It follows from these behavioral hypotheses that in the manufacturing sector the price is *made* by marking up the cost of labor, and in the agricultural sector the price is *taken* by the market. In the manufacturing sector the growth could be supposed to be induced by technical progress a la Kaldor (1957*b*). The investment function depends on the demand. The demand to this sector is the demand for investment coming from both sectors. In equilibrium the demand coming from the manufacturing sector to the sector itself is self-perpetuating, *i.e.*, the profit is fully reinvested. However, the demand for investment also comes from the agricultural sector. If this demand falls, the state of confidence of the entrepreneurs of the manufacturing sector is shaken, and as a consequence the profit is not fully invested, so that the equilibrium rate of growth falls. In the agricultural sector, the possibility of growth depends not on the demand but on the income that the sector earns selling goods to the manufacturing sector.

Finally, we deliberately forget the problem of the differences in the capital output ratios of the two sectors and of the change in techniques brought about by the relative price change.

The definitions are as follows: P is total amount of profit; W is total amount of wages; A is agricultural output; M is manufacturing output; I is investment; l is labor per unit of output; w is wage per unit of labor; a and m are suffixes indicating the agricultural and manufacturing sectors; μ is the mark-up; p isthe price of manufactured goods in relation to agricultural goods, *i.e.*, the quantity of A in exchange for a unit of M; g indicates the rate of growth of output; r the rate of profit; v the capital-output ratio; π the share of profit; s_p and s_w the propensities to save out of profit and out of wages. From the distribution side, the system can be written as follows:

$$\begin{cases} A = P_a + W_a \\ M = P_m + W_m \dfrac{1}{p} \end{cases} \qquad (1)$$

where W_a and W_m are the amounts of a and m distributed to workers.

Introducing the hypothesis of saving-investment behavior of the two classes and remembering that investment goods come from the «m» sector and that wage goods come from the «a» sector, the system can be written as:

$$\begin{cases} A = pI_a + W_a \\ M = I_m + wlM\dfrac{1}{p}. \end{cases} \qquad (2)$$

On the hypothesis that $s_p = 1$ and $s_w = 0$ we can express the rate of growth of the two sectors in terms of sectorial share of profit and capital/output ratio:

$$\begin{cases} g_a = \dfrac{\pi_a}{v_a} \\ g_m = \dfrac{\pi_m}{v_m}. \end{cases} \qquad (3)$$

Hence, on the hypothesis of constant capital-output ratio, we can write:

$$\begin{cases} g_a = \dfrac{P_a/A}{pI_a/\Delta A} \\ g_m = \dfrac{P_m/M}{I_m/\Delta M}. \end{cases} \qquad (4)$$

The equilibrium of the exchange will be given by:

$$\begin{cases} P_a = A - W_a = W_m \\ P_m = M - W_m\dfrac{1}{p} = M - wlM\dfrac{1}{p}. \end{cases} \qquad (5)$$

The first equation of system (5) says that the demand of wage goods coming from the manufacturing to the agricultural sector equalizes the profit (and hence the investment) of this sector. The second equation says that profit (and hence the investment) in the manufacturing sector is given by the difference between the output of the sector and the amount of goods that must be transferred from the sector at the equilibrium terms of trade, to the agricultural sector in order to pay manufacturing workers at the prevailing wage rate.

Substituting the equations of system (5) into those of (4) we get:

$$\begin{cases} g_a = \dfrac{P_a/A}{I_a/\Delta A} \cdot \dfrac{1}{p} \\ g_m = \dfrac{M(1- w/p \cdot l)/M}{I_m/\Delta M} \end{cases} \quad (6)$$

If we call $\dfrac{P_a/A}{I_a/\Delta A} = \varepsilon$ and $\dfrac{\Delta M}{I_m} = \eta$ we can write:

$$\begin{cases} g_a = \varepsilon \dfrac{1}{p} \\ g_m = \eta\left(1 - wl \cdot \dfrac{1}{p}\right). \end{cases} \quad (7)$$

Plotting p on vertical and g_a and g_m on horizontal axes, figure 1 represents the two equations of system (7).

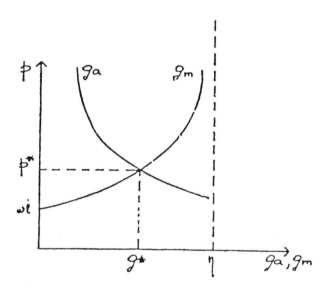

Figure 1

A similar figure is shown in Kaldor (1974).

Given the share of profit in agriculture ($P_a/A = W_m/A$) and the productivity of investment in agriculture ($I_a/\Delta A$), if constant return to scale prevails, the curve g_a is a branch of a hyperbola.

The curve g_m has a positive intercept on the vertical axis at wl value and an asymptote at η value. The latter value indicates the limit beyond which g_m cannot grow—the price limit at which all the output goes to workers and hence g_m in zero.

At $g_a = g_m = g^*$ the equilibrium is a balances equilibrium. Given labor productivity in the two sectors, at g^*, the two sectors can grow without demand or supply constraints. It should be noted that the value of growth in the manufacturing sector requires an investment which must be financed by an amount of profit which leaves a residual quantity of manufactures goods that, at prevailing p^*, is exchange with wage goods in a sufficient quantity to leave the workers satisfied. The equilibrium terms of trade p^* have two tasks: one is to balance the two sectors; the other is to extract surplus from the manufacturing sector to finance the growth of the sector itself. The second equation of system (2) in fact could be transformed in the following way. Multiplying the left and the right side of the equation by p/M, the equation takes the form

$$p = \frac{I_m}{M} p + wl, \qquad (8)$$

which is compatible with the pricing of the sector,

$$p = (1 + \mu) wl, \qquad (9)$$

if

$$I_m = \mu \left(wlM \frac{1}{p} \right) \qquad (10)$$

which follows from the two hypotheses that profit is obtained by marking up the cost of labor and that the profit is fully invested.

Another thing must be noted. The rate of growth of equilibrium g^* is common to both sectors. This depends upon the hypothesis that there is no substitutability. This hypothesis is rather cavalier, above all about the «m» sector. If the «a» sector goods are a technical input, as well as wage is an input, this would mean the absence of technical progress substituting manufacturing input for raw material, which is contrary to the evidence. However, the hypothesis is strong even in our model because it means that the expenditure of workers does not follow the Engel law—i.e., the substitution of manufactured commodities for agricultural commodities as income grows. A caveat follows. The «true» rate of growth of «m» is due to a weighted average of two parts of the «m» sector, one which depends on input «a» and another which does not depend on it. As a consequence, the «true» rate of growth of «m» depends on the speed of the process of substitutability, with which we do not deal here, and on the growth of the «a» sector, on which we focus our attention.

3. CHANGES IN THE PARAMETERS OF THE CURVES AND SOME «LAWS» ON THE TERMS OF TRADE DEDUCED FROM COMPARISONS OF EQUILIBRIA

On the basis of our model we can now study some famous «laws» on the terms of trade by means of changes in parameters in the equations of system (2) and the corresponding shifts of the curves.

3.1. *Classical thesis on rising relative price of agriculture*

The most famous thesis on the long-term dynamics of relative prices is that of West and Ricardo. According to West and Ricardo, the law of long-term diminishing returns in agriculture will lead to a secular rise in the relative price of agriculture. Our system—stated in terms of rate of growth—is not able to properly show this point. The system would have to be stated either in terms of absolute quantities or in a three-dimensional plane in g, p, and time. However, one could imagine (figure 4) a continuous shift to the left of the g_a curve as time goes on. As a conse-

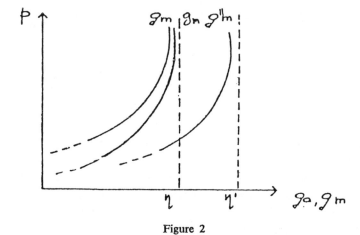

Figure 2

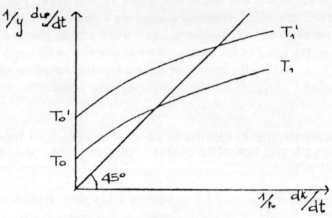

Figure 3

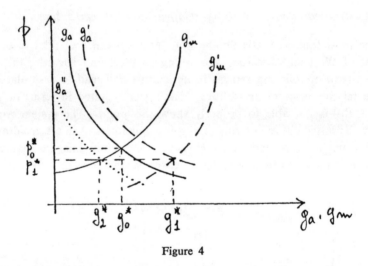

Figure 4

quence, the « pure » Ricardian case—with diminishing returns and no technical progress in agriculture or discovery of new lands and without substitution of agricultural goods with manufacturing—is the limit at which the terms of trade improve in agriculture but the rate of balanced growth falls through time, finally reaching a zero value. In that case, the shift of the g_m curve due to an increase in productivity of labour leads to a further improvement of the terms of trade in agriculture, but does not affect the balanced rate of growth.

We can say that the beliefs of a secular rise in the relative price of agriculture has been shared by all classical and English neoclassical economists—by Smith, Mill and also Marshall ([4]). The most interesting case is the one of A. Smith. In *The Wealth of Nations* ([5]), the Scottish economist deals extensively with the dynamics of prices in the process of development. He distinguished several sectors with different trends in the costs of production: corn constant, products of animals increasing, and manufacturing decreasing. In general Smith thought that productivity in agriculture would have had a lower trend in relation to industry because in the latter the division of labor could be introduced more extensively. This Smithian idea is also captured by the modern Keynesian theory of technical progress. According to Kaldor (1957b), in the industrial sector the rate of growth of productivity of labor is induced by the rate of growth of accumulation (which is the rate of growth of the capital endowment per worker) in a cumulative process upto the equilibrium point at which the two rates of growth balance. That point implies a constant capital output ratio through time. If we deal with the rate of growth of productivity, relative to Kaldor's equilibrium point, we will have a move to the right of the g_m curve with a constant asymptotus η (g'_m on figure 2). However, one can think of a new stream of invention and an upward shift of Kaldor's technical progress function (fig. 3) from $T_0 T_1$ to $T'_0 T'_1$. « This upward shift... will cause (once and for all) a fall in the capital-output ratio ». This leads g_m to shift to g''_m (fig. 2). The terms of trade in the long run goes against the agricultural sectors (increase in p^* in fig. 4) in both cases of Smith's and Ricardo.

3.2. *Modern thesis on falling relative price of agriculture*

After the second World War, the United Nations published two studies (U.N. 1949, 1962) showing a fall between 1876 and 1948 of the terms of trade between primary products and manufacturing in international commerce. Some economists deduced a secular law on the falling relative price of agriculture. The most interesting thesis is the one of Prebish (1950) and Singer (1950). The law of secular fall is based on two assumptions, first, that the income elasticity of manufactured goods is higher than that of agricultural goods, and, second, that agricultural goods are

---

[4] Continental and marginalist economists, by contrast, did not have any thesis on this argument.
[5] A. Smith (1952), Book I, Chapter I and XI. For an enlightening discussion on this Smithian theory see P. Sylos-Labini (1976).

sold in competitive markets, whereas manufactured goods are sold in oligopolistic markets ([6]). They deduced from this law a negative outcome for the development of LDCs. In fact for the LDC's—which export raw materials and import capital goods—a worsening of the terms of trade means a limit to growth ([7]).

We can capture a substantial part of this story by means of our model. Let us suppose that both sectors experience a positive rate of growth of productivity; the relative magnitude is not important. But suppose that while in the agricultutal sector this is translated into a fall of relative price for a given level of rate of growth (*i.e.*, in fig. 5, a shift to the right of the g_a curve), in the manufacturing sector the rate of growth of productivity is absorbed by an equal (or even greater) rate of growth in real wages. That is to say that the g_m curve does not move (or moves to the left g'_m).

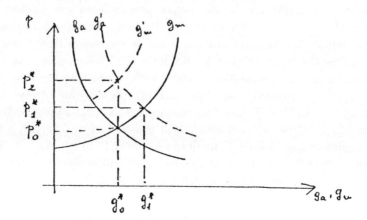

Figure 5

([6]) P. Sylos-Labini (1981) held that in the last century the classical law, and in this century (up to 1971) the opposite law, worked because of the change in market structure. In a later work (Sylos-Labini 1982) he has held that because of the collapse of the international monetary system, which was based on the dollar and a fixed exchange system, speculation on raw materials became much stronger (as raw materials performed the role previously held by the dollar as a store of value). As a consequence, we can see a sharp contrast between the price behavior for raw materials before and after 1971.

([7]) An even more extreme thesis has been held by Marxist theorists such as E. Mandel (1978) and theorists of the « unequal exchange » such as A. Emmanuel (1972) and the late Singer (1975), who held that *all* goods exports by LDCs are subject to falling relative prices, either because of the different characteristics of the labor market in the two economies or because of the monopoly power of technical progress in the more developed countries.

In fact if w and l in the second equation of system (1) move in the opposite way with the same speed they leave $w \cdot l$ unchanged ([8]). The outcome of the shift of the g_a curve entails a higher p^*, (p_1^*), i.e., a fall in the relative price of agriculture.

Note that another aspect of the outcome is a higher g^*, (g_1^*). This is in contrast to the Prebish-Singer view. It is because this model captures only part of their thesis and in particular their first assumption is no taken into account, i.e., that the income elasticity of manufactured goods is higher than that of agricultural goods ([9]).

4. SHIFTS OF THE CURVES AND DISEQUILIBRIA, ABSENCE OF SECULAR LAWS AND STAGFLATION BIAS

The two long-term laws which we have just discussed grasp only part of the reality. Actually some recent empirical investigations ([10]) give a much weaker support to the theory that a long-term tendency in one or another derection of the terms of trade exists. The terms of trade move—above all recently—in an oscillatory process rather than as a trend. Moreover, their cyclical behavior has a stagflationary bias.

The explanation we give is based on the differences in pricing and inducement to growth of the two sectors. The shifts of the curves that we have previously analyzed are suitable to describe a comparative static analysis between two states of equilibrium with different parameters. In reality a shift of one of these curves could entail a shift of the other. This interrelation derives from the different pricing systems and the different inducements to growth of the two sectors (which we have described here in 2).

If we suppose a long-run equality in the rates of growth of wages and productivity in the « m » sector, we can reinvestigate the cases examined in section 3. The previous analysis has shown that a curve shift is followed by a new equilibrium combination of p^*/g^* which does not set in motion a cumulative process of inflation and/or stagnation. In reality, however,

---

([8]) Rather, an « income policy » in the « m » sector would affect the rate of growth of the « a » sector. This is because higher real wages in the « m » sector mean higher profit level in the « a » sector. With constant return to scale and an infinite labor supply in the « a » sector this leads to a higher level of investment, which leads to a higher rate of growth (like an increase in population which leads to a higher natural rate of growth in the Harrod-Domar model).

([9]) As we have noted and will see below, this is a difficulty that our argument faces several times.

([10]) See Spraos (1980) and Ercolani (1983).

changes in the terms of trade, in one or another direction, could lead to these very processes.

4.1. *Lower productivity growth in agriculture and inflation*

Let us first consider the case dealt with in section 3.1 of lower productivity growth of the « a » sector associated with a worsening of the terms of trade for the « m » sector. It should be remembered that in this sector the pricing is based upon a mark-up on costs. If wages in terms of goods remain unchanged and if the mark-up—that is, the decision to grow of the « m » sector—also remains fixed, the change in the terms of trade will push the monetary prices of the « m » sector up in order to restore the previous level of the terms of trade. In other works, in order for p^* to accomplish, even in the new situation, its double task—to equilibrate the exchange between the two sectors and, at the same time, to reflect the pricing of the « m » sector—the curve g_m must shift to the left from g'_m to g''_m until the previous p^*_0 is reached (fig. 6). It should be pointed out that the effect of the return from p^*_1 to the level $p^*_2 = p^*_0$ is obtained through an inflationary process.

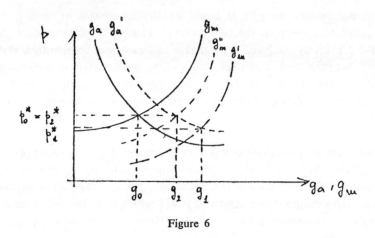

Figure 6

Another thing should be noted on the rate of growth. The balanced rate of growth reached after the inflationary process g^*_2 is lower than the one (g^*_1) that would be reached in the case where terms of trade for agriculture improved. This is because the income earned by investors in the « a » sector is lower under the terms of trade p^*_1 than under p^*_2. That is to say that the « a » sector buys less « m » goods, *i.e.*, it makes less investment, which reduces its own rate of growth (a movement on the left along the g_a curve). As a consequence, the balanced rate of growth is lower. The difference between g_1^* and g_2^* represents a « lost differential rate of growth ». This loss is more detrimental to the « a » sector than to the « m » sector, because the latter can compensate for it by means of the substitution effect (which we addressed at the end of section 2), and the former cannot.

If decreasing returns prevail (one can think of oil fields), the above process leads to more extreme consequences. Decreasing returns shift the g_a curve to the left as time goes on (fig. 7); the relative price of agri-

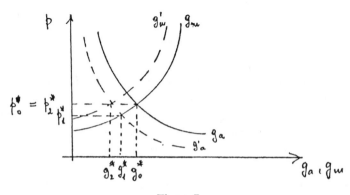

Figure 7

culture rises to p_1^* and the balanced rate of growth falls to g_1^*. However, if the manufacturing sector succeeds through an inflationary process in returning to the previous terms of trade, the final outcome will be a further decrease in the balanced rate of growth (g_2^*).

4.2. *Higher productivity growth in agriculture and deflation*

Let us now consider the « modern » case we have dealt with in 3.2. which can be represented by a right wing shift of the g_a curve to g_a' (fig. 8). The new equilibrium level is at point H. However, in order that the economy can move from the old equilibrium point 0 to the new one H, prices and quantities have to move together. A gentle fall in the relative price of agriculture and a higher demand for « m » goods ([11]), despite

---

([11]) This happens because the overall income of the « a » sector is increases, due to higher demand for « a » goods by « m » workers because of the fall in the price of « a » goods.

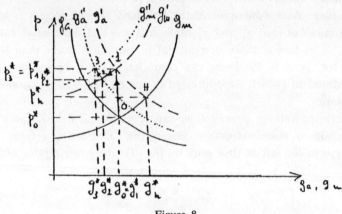

Figure 8

the fall in the price, moves the equilibrium from 0 to H along the g_m curve. But if the excess supply of the « a » sector leads to a sharp fall in the « a » price [12], let us suppose from p_0^* to p_1^* (or whatever p's related to the points between 1 and H), the outcome could be different. The income of the « a » sector falls and it is not raised by a higher demand for the « m » sector, which is sluggish in response to a fall in price of its inputs. The « m » sector is—by contrast—sensitive to a fall in the demand for its goods. The reduced price and income of the « a » sector and the demand from it creates an « effective demand » constraint to the « m » sector. Every point on the left of g_m—even if suboptimal—is feasible for the « m » sector. With the terms of trade that do not clear the market the economy is caught at a point to the left of H.

4.3. *The cycle in terms of trade and the stagflation bias*

We can now put together the analysis we have done on 4.1 and 4.2. Suppose that the process described in the previous subsection has taken place and that the economy is, say, at point 1 (fig. 8). In this case, the excess supply in the « a » sector will lead to reduced productive capacity, in order to obtain a higher price and hence income. This reduction pushed the g_a' curve to the left, for example to g_a''.

The intersection between g_a'' and g_a' is at point 2. The relative price of agriculture has now risen ($p_2 < p_1$). According to the argument put

---

[12] This case has been delt with by Kaldor 1984 in his third lecture.

forward in subsection 4.2 this forces an inflationary process to occur in the « m » sector and pushes the sector to reach the previous terms of trade, even if it is at the expense of its own as well as the overall rate of growth. The new equilibrium position, once the shift from g'_{rh} to g''_m has been considered, is shown by point 3. The path from 0 to 3 describes the oscillatory process of the terms of trade along a declining growth trend.

4.4 Summary and conclusions

In the Introduction we raised the question of the constraints to growth in a closed economy (or in a world economy) which compel the system to run below the level of full capacity. The problem was dealt with along Kaldorian lines by means of a growth model of an economy with two complementary sectors: agriculture and manufacturing. We have found that the constraint is either in decreasing returns in the former sector or in low effective demand in the latter, once the relative price (or the terms of trade) does not work « properly ». It fails to work due to the different pricing systems and inducements to grow in the two sectors.

In section 2 we discussed the equilibrium properties of the model. In section 3 we discussed, in terms of our model, the classical law of the secular fall in relative prices of primary commodities in relation to manufactured goods. In section 4 we argued that if the behaviour of the two sectors is properly specified, it does not lead to any secular fall or rise, but leads, rather, to fluctuations in the terms of trade. These fluctuations when they occur are accompanied by inflation and a falling rate of growth.

One normative conclusion which could be drawn is that if the relative-price system does not work, one has to rely on the quantity-buffer-stock system (Kaldor, Hart, Tinbergen 1963). Going back to 4.2, one can see that, once the potential rate of growth in primary products increases, if a buffer-stock system (national or international) absorbs the excess supply, it prevents price and income of the sector from falling and also prevents a fall in the effective demand in the other sector. The stock will be reduced when demand in the manufacturing sector increases due to the increases in income of the primary product sector created by its selling goods to the buffer-stock institution.

The reduction of agricultural productive capacity in the U.S. throughout the 1960s (which is an example of the process we have dealt with here in 4.3) was one of the factor which led to higher corn prices at the end of the decade (Kaldor 1976). This is generally recognized as one of the main reasons for the subsequent rise in the price of oil. The response of the manufacturing sector to the increase in oil prices has led to a process of inflation in order to restore the previous relative price (terms of trade). This brings about a fall in the balance rate of growth as described in 4.1. While these processes take place the relative price (terms of trade) does not rise or fall steadily, but rather oscillates.

BIBLIOGRAPHY

Emmanuel A. (1972): *Unequal Exchange: a study of imperialism of trade,* Monthly Review Press, New York, 1972.
Ercolani P. (1983): « Prezzi relativi e sviluppo economico: una analisi della evidenza empirica », *Moneta e Credito,* n. 144.
Mandel E. (1978): *Late Capitalism,* Verso Edition, London.
Harcourt G. (1965): « A critique of Mr. Kaldor's model of income distribution and economic growth », *Australian Economic Papers,* June.
Hart A.G., Kaldor N. and Tinberger J. (1966): « The case for an international commodity reserve currency », U.N. Conference on Trade and Development, Geneva.
Jorgensen D.W. (1961): « The development of a dual economy », *Economic Journal,* June.
Jorgensen D.W. (1966): « Testing alternative theories of the development of a dual economy », *Theory and Design of Economic Development,* edited by I. Adelman and E. Thorbecke, Johns Hopkins University Press, Baltimore.
Kalecki M. (1954): *Theory of Economic Dynamics,* Allen & Unwin, London.
Kaldor N. (1954): « Characteristics of economic development », published in *Essays on Economic Stability and Growth,* Duckworth, London, 1960.
Kaldor N. (1956): « Alternative theories of distribution », *Review of Economic Studies,* n. 2.
Kaldor N. (1975a): « Capitalist evolution in the light of Keynesian economics », *Sankya,* May.
Kaldor N. (1957b): « A model of economic growth », *Economic Journal,* December
Kaldor N. (1961): « Capital accumulation and economic growth », Internal Economic Association conferece, Corfù 1958; published in *The Theory of Capital,* edited by F. Lutz, Macmillan, London.
Kaldor N. (1966a): « Marginal productivity and the macroeconomic theory of distribution », *Review of Economic Studies,* n. 4.
Kaldor N. (1966b): *Cause of the Slow Rate of Growth in the United Kingdom,* « Inaugural Lecture » at Cambridge University, Cambridge University Press, Cambridge.
Kaldor N. (1968): « Productivity and growth in manufacturing industry: A reply », *Economica,* November.
Kaldor N. (1971): « Conflicts in national economic objectives », *Conflicts in Policy Objectives,* edited by N. Kaldor, Basil Blackwell, Oxford.
Kaldor N. (1972): « The irrelevance of equilibrium economics », *Economic Journal,* December.
Kaldor N. (1974a): « Equilibrium theory and growth theory », in *Cuadernos de economia,* May-August, republished in *Economics and Human Welfare: Essays in Honor of Tibor Scitowski,* edited by M. Baskin, Academic Press, New York, 1979.
Kaldor N. (1974b): « What is wrong with the economic theory », *Quarterly Journal of Economic,* August.
Kaldor N. (1976): « Inflation and recession in the world economy», *Economic Journal,* December.
Kaldor N. (1978): « The effects of devaluation on trade in manufacture », *Further Essays in Applied Economics,* Duckwrth, London.
Kaldor N. (1980): « Introduction » to the second edition of *Essays on Value and Distribution,* Duckworth, London.

Kaldor N. (1984): « Causes of growth and stagnation in the world economy ». Five « Mattioli Lectures », Bocconi University, Milan, 21-24 May.
Lewis A.W. (1954): « Economic development with unlimited supply of labor », *Manchester School*.
Prebish R. (1950): « The economic development of Latin America and its principal problems », *ECLA*, U.N. Department of Economics Affairs, New York.
Singer H. (1950): « The distribution of gains between investing and borrowing countries », *American Economic Review Papers and Proceedings*, May.
Singer H. (1975): « Dualism revisited: A new approach to the problems od a dual society in developing countries », Paper read at the Glasgow Conference on Dual Economy, September 1969. Published in *The Strategy of International Development*, edited by A. Cairncross and M. Pouri, London.
Smith A.: *The Wealth of Nations*, Encyclopedia Britannica, Chicago 1952.
Spraos J. (1980): « The statistical debate on the net barter terms of trade between primary commodities and manufactures », *Economic Journal*, March.
Sylos-Labini P. (1972): *Sindacati, Inflazione, Produttività*, Laterza, Bari.
Sylos-Labini P. (1976): « Competition the product market », *The Market and the State: Essays in Honor of A. Smith*, edited by T. Wilson and A.S. Skinner, Clarendon Press, Oxford.
Sylos-Labini P. (1981): «Prezzi rigidi, prezzi flessibili, e inflazione», *Moneta e Credito*, Dicembre.
Sylos-Labini P. (1982): « On the instability of raw material prices and the problem of gold », *The Gold Problem: Economic Perspective*, edited by A. Quadrio-Curzio, Oxford University Press, Oxford.
Thirlwall A.P. (1978): « Il vincolo della bilancia dei pagamenti come elemento di spiegazione delle differenze internazionali dei tassi di sviluppo», *Moneta e Credito*, Dicembre.
U.N. Dept. of Econ. Affairs (1949): *Relative Prices of Exports and Imports of Underdeveloped Countries*, Lake Success, New York.
U.N. (1962): *Instability of Export Marker of Under-developed Countries*, New York.
Wood A. (1975): *The Theory of Profit*, Cambridge University Press, Cambridge.

A GENERAL MODEL OF GROWTH AND DEVELOPMENT ON KALDORIAN LINES

By A. P. THIRLWALL*

I. Introduction

ARTHUR LEWIS says in his Presidential Address to the American Economic Association: "the economist's dream would be to have a single theory of growth that took an economy from the lowest level of say $100 per capita, past the dividing line of $2,000 up to the level of Western Europe and beyond. Or to have, since processes may differ at different stages, a set of theories growing out of each other longitudinally, and handing over to each other. Or putting aside what happens after $2,000 is passed, to have at least one good theory for the developing economy from $100 to the dividing line". (Lewis, 1984). Lewis's dream will probably remain as such, but I believe we know enough about the development process to provide the basis for his second best—namely a set of theories growing out of each other longitudinally and handing over to each other. Such a model would give pride of place to agriculture, and its complementarity with industry, in the early stages of development, with export growth taking over in the later stages. There can be little doubt from the empirical evidence (see Kaldor, 1966, 1967 and Sen, 1983) that the pace of long run growth and development is closely associated with the growth of industrial activities. The fundamental question is what determines the growth of industrial output? To anticipate the answer, in an individual country, which starts closed and then trades, agricultural growth is the driving force in the early stage of development and export growth in the later stages. These represent the two fundamental sources of *autonomous* demand for industrial output. Although the model that I shall develop below is abstract in places, and contains many simplifying assumptions, I believe that it contains a number of important insights, and appears to have the potential to explain a wide range of the phenomena we observe in the growth and development process. The complementary growth of agriculture and industry is well documented for individual developing countries, both historically and in the contemporary world economy (see later), and export-led growth receives

---

* The author is grateful to Professor Kaldor and Mr. David Vines for extensive discussions in the early stages of the preparation of the paper, and to Colin Clark, John Craven, Richard Disney, Charles Kennedy, Arthur Lewis and participants in Seminars at various Universities for helpful comments on preliminary drafts of the paper. The inspiration for the paper comes from a two sector (agriculture–industry) model that Kaldor lectured on in Cambridge for many years, hints of which can be found in his Harvard Lecture (1975b); his Presidential Address to the Royal Economic Society (Kaldor, 1976), and in his essay in honour of Tibor Scitovsky (Kaldor, 1979). Kaldor has always presented the model as representing the world economy, but I realized its potential as the basis of a general model of growth and development when listening to his lectures as a visitor in Cambridge in 1979. Two anonymous referees suggested useful amendments to the model and have helped to improve the clarity of expression.

© Oxford University Press 1986

200 MODEL OF GROWTH AND DEVELOPMENT ON KALDORIAN LINES

strong empirical support in many developed and newly industrialising countries (see the work of Balassa, 1980, and some of my own work e.g. Thirlwall 1979, 1982).[1]

Before developing the 'longitudinal' model in the spirit outlined, I should like to mention briefly what I consider to be the major shortcomings of traditional development theories. In a fully neoclassical two sector development model (e.g. Jorgenson, 1969), the answer to the question of "what determines the rate of growth of industrial output" would lie in the allocation or supply of scarce factor endowments, technology and tastes, all exogenously determined. The first objection to this approach is that neither labour nor capital are scarce in the manner envisaged by the model. It is very doubtful, particularly when considered in a growth context, whether less labour on the land means less agricultural output. All the evidence suggests an enormous 'dynamic' surplus of labour, with increasing food production going hand in hand with a declining agricultural workforce. And capital is not "allocated", it is accumulated. There is no way of withdrawing capital from one sector for use in another. Rather the process of industrial production itself generates its own capital (A. Young, 1928; Kaldor, 1979). Secondly, there is no treatment of the complementarity between the output of one sector and the output of the other within the framework of reciprocal demand. There is no recognition that the level of output in agriculture may itself determine the demand for the output of the industrial sector and vice versa, and there is no explicit role for the terms of trade as the mechanism for achieving balance between the supply of and demand for output in both sectors, so that growth is neither supply or demand constrained below its potential.

Lewis's classical model (Lewis, 1954) is an improvement on neo-classical models in that labour is plentiful and capital is accumulated but it is still basically a supply orientated model, with the demand for the output of the industrial sector side-stepped. Lewis's discussion of the relationship between the two sectors focusses only on checks to the expansion of the capitalist surplus, and particularly on how a deterioration in the industrial terms of trade chokes the rate of capital accumulation. There is no recognition of the fact that a worsening terms of trade for industry may be associated with faster industrial growth because of higher rural incomes which accompany a faster growth of agriculture. There is no analysis of trade between the sectors. Johnston and Mellor (1961) recognised this worrying feature of the Lewis model many years ago when they perceptively remarked: "one of the simplifying assumptions of the (Lewis) two sector model is that expansion of the capitalist sector is limited *only* by a shortage of capital. Given this assumption, an increase in rural net cash income is not a stimulus to industrialisation but an obstacle to expansion of the capitalist sector".

---

[1] Irma Adelman (1984) has recently formulated the notion of agricultural-demand-led-industrialisation (ADLI) and finds support in simulation studies.

Johnston and Mellor continue "there is clearly a conflict between emphasis on agriculture's essential contribution to the capital requirement for overall development and emphasis on increased farm purchasing power as a stimulus to industrialisation. Nor is there any easy reconciliation of the conflict".

The challenge of reconciliation has never been taken up in a satisfactory way, not even by Lewis himself who recognised the limitations of his 1954 model in his 1972 essay in honour of Prebisch (Lewis, 1972), where he distinguishes three models: (i) his original classical model with no trade between sectors and no foreign trade; (ii) a second version with a closed economy, but the capitalist (industrial) sector depending on trade with the non-capitalist sector for food and raw materials, and (iii) a third version with an open economy whose industrial sector trades either with the non-capitalist sector or with the outside world. The latter two versions are not well developed and in a sense the model to be developed corresponds to them.[2] There is a resolution of the conflict in Lewis, referred to by Johnston and Mellor, if the complementarity between industry and agriculture is recognised from the outset, and it is remembered that there must be an equilibrium terms of trade that balances the supply of and demand for output in both sectors.

It would be wrong of course to give the impression that economists have not appreciated the need for an integrated model of agriculture and industry with emphasis on the complementary linkages between industry and agriculture, although it would be equally true to say that the importance is still not widely appreciated. In the 25th anniversary issue of the *Manchester School of Economic and Social Studies,* September 1979, celebrating the publication in 1954 of Lewis's original article, none of the papers there come to grips with the fundamental deficiency of the classical and neo-classical approaches to development stressed here; that is, the neglect of complementary demand. Ragnor Nurkse (1962) fully recognised the importance of demand linkages between the agricultural and industrial sectors: "the relation between agriculture and manufacturing industry offers the clearest and simplest case of balance needed for economic growth. In a country where the peasantry is incapable of producing a surplus of food above its own subsistence needs there is little or no incentive for industry to establish itself: there is not a sufficient market for manufactured goods. Conversely, agricultural improvements may be inhibited by a lack of market for farm products if the non-farm sector of the economy is backward or underdeveloped. Each of the two sectors must try to move forward. If one remains passive the other is slowed down". Fei and Ranis (1964), though (neo?) classical in outlook, believe that balanced growth lies at the root of Japanese economic success in the late 19th and early 20th century. They

---

[2] The capitalist-non-capitalist distinction is not wholly synonomous with the division between industry and agriculture, but it is clearly the growth of industry that Lewis is concerned with.

quote Lockwood's (1954) study of Japan: "The growth of primary production was interrelated with industrialisation and urbanisation at every point.... As industry developed, it offered a widening market for the food and raw material surpluses of the countryside.... On the other hand, the increasing productivity of the primary industries created a growing home market for manufactures and services". The World Development Report 1982 shows the very close correspondence between agricultural development and industrial growth: "In the 1970s agricultural growth exceeded 3.5 percent a year in 18 of the 31 countries whose gross domestic product (GDP) growth was above 5 percent a year. During the same period in 15 of the 22 countries with GDP growth below 3 percent a year, agricultural growth was only 2 percent or less. Meanwhile agricultural and GDP growth differed by less than two percentage points in 15 of 20 countries experiencing moderate growth. There have been exceptions, of course, but they prove the rule: fast growth in GDP and sluggish agriculture were evident only in countries with oil or mineral-based economies, such as Algeria, Ecuador, Mexico, Morocco, and Nigeria". (Walters, 1982). The World Development Report 1979 had earlier remarked "a stagnant rural economy with low purchasing power holds back industrial growth in many developing countries".

II. The basic two sector model of agriculture and industry

The significant features of the basic model to be developed are firstly that it formally models the complementarity between industry and agriculture, and secondly it explicitly derives the equilibrium terms of trade, and the consequences of disequilibrium. The basic model to be developed and extended is presented informally in Kaldor (1975b and 1979) who discusses it in the context of the (closed) world economy divided between primary producing countries on the one hand and industrial countries on the other.[3] But clearly the model is equally applicable to an individual dual economy closed to trade. Having presented the basic model, I shall then extend it in various directions by: (i) introducing technical progress in agriculture through a technical progress function; (ii) introducing the possibility of labour supply constraints in industry (in the sense of a higher real wage having to be paid for labour); and (iii) opening up the economy to trade. A number of interesting things can then be seen and done with the model. For example: (i) it can be subjected to autonomous shocks (such as harvest fluctuations), and the attempt by the industrial sector (capitalists) to force the pace of growth; (ii) it can be seen how industrial growth becomes supply or demand constrained if the terms of trade between the two sectors are not in equilibrium; (iii) Prebisch effects can be seen i.e. the institutional mechanisms which may generate a long run tendency for the agricultural terms of trade to deteriorate (Prebisch, 1950); (iv) it can be seen how

---

[3] See Vines (1984) for a formalisation of the model in a 'North–South' context.

through time, the importance of export growth will come to dominate the growth process, and (v) the model is also versatile enough to incorporate the Mydral/Hirschman notion of circular and cumulative causation. Finally, the model helps to explain why some countries have industrialised and developed sooner than others, and points to a number of ways in which the smooth functioning of individual countries (and the world economy) could be enhanced. One of the fundamental conclusions of the closed economy model is that in the long run the growth of industry is fundamentally determined by the growth of land savings innovations in agriculture as an offset to diminishing returns. This contrasts with the standard neoclassical result that the long run steady state growth of industry is determined by the exogenous rate of growth of labour supply in efficiency units, as in the model of Findlay (1980), for example.

Production and expenditure assumptions in agriculture and industry

First of all, let us assume a closed economy with two activities, agriculture and industry. Agriculture produces wage goods, food or 'corn', by means of inputs of labour time, land and capital goods (steel). Industry produces a composite good, say steel, by means of labour and capital goods, that can either be invested or consumed. Industry sells steel to agriculture in exchange for food.

Agriculture

There is a reservoir of surplus labour in agriculture. Disguised unemployment exists, which takes the form of work sharing—a ubiquitous feature of the agricultural sector of most developing countries. The marginal product of labour *time* in such circumstances is not necessarily zero but the marginal product of labour itself may be considered zero if the total number of hours worked on the land remains the same when a unit of labour is absorbed into industry. Thus changes in agricultural output are assumed to be independent of changes in the number of men. In this section the level of technology in agriculture is also held constant. The price of agricultural goods is assumed to be determined competitively in free markets.

Capital is obtained from the industrial sector in exchange for the agricultural surplus or saving. The lower the price of industrial output in terms of agricultural output, the faster will be both the rate of increase in agricultural output and agriculture's purchasing power over industrial goods. This can be shown formally as follows:

Let a proportion of agricultural output be consumed in agriculture itself and a constant proportion (s_a) saved to exchange for industrial goods.[4]

---

[4] A constant savings ratio in agriculture implies that agricultural output and population grow at the same rate. This would be the case if population growth was endogenous in the tradition of Malthus, and is consistent with the observation that the vast mass of people in developing countries are on the edge of subsistence.

204 MODEL OF GROWTH AND DEVELOPMENT ON KALDORIAN LINES

Agricultural saving may be expressed as:

$$S_a = s_a Q_a, \qquad (1)$$

where Q_a is agricultural output and S_a represents the agricultural surplus.[5] The agricultural surplus may be used either for the purchase of investment goods from industry (I_a) or consumption goods (C_{ia}). If p is the price of steel in terms of corn (or the industrial terms of trade), then the total amount of industrial goods obtained by the agricultural sector in exchange for the agricultural surplus is:

$$(I_a + C_{ia}) = S_a/p \qquad (2)$$

Equation (2) is a market clearing equation.

Now the growth of agricultural output may be expressed as the product of the investment ratio in agriculture and the productivity of investment in agriculture (σ).[6]

$$\frac{\Delta Q_a}{Q_a} = \frac{\sigma I_a}{Q_a} \qquad (3)$$

Substituting (1) into (2), and obtaining an expression for I_a for substitution in (3), gives:

$$\frac{\Delta Q_a}{Q_a} = \sigma \left(\frac{S_a}{p} - \frac{C_{ia}}{Q_a} \right) \qquad (4)$$

Equation (4) not only gives the rate of growth of agricultural output but also the rate of growth of purchasing power, or demand, over industrial goods (g_d). The equation traces out a hyperbola showing an inverse relation between the industrial terms of trade and the growth of agricultural demand for industrial goods. The more favourable the industrial terms of trade the lower the rate of growth of demand, and vice versa. The relation is shown in Fig. 1 with the terms of trade between industry and agriculture (p) measured on the vertical axis and growth (g) measured on the horizontal axis. A rise in agricultural productivity will shift the curve outwards, as will a rise in the agricultural savings ratio. Notice that the higher the amount of agricultural saving devoted to industrial consumption, the lower the agricultural growth rate for any given term of trade, and vice versa.

Industry

Industry produces steel by means of inputs of labour and capital, and fixed coefficients of production are assumed. The productivity of labour can

---

[5] The agricultural surplus represents the food left over after all consumption claims have been met by peasants, capitalists and the vast numbers of tertiary workers (including civil servants and the armed forces).

[6] Equation (3) is definitionally true, but does not imply that output depends *only* on capital. σ is the gross productivity of capital, not the net productivity holding other factors constant.

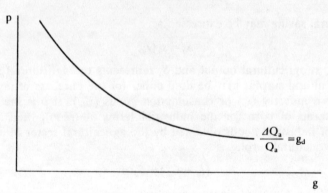

FIG. 1

be improved by technical progress, but for the moment the level of technology is held constant. Because of the existence of surplus labour in agriculture, the supply curve of labour to industry is infinitely elastic at some conventional real wage. The determinants of this real wage are considered later. All steel which is not sold to agriculture for food or consumed by industrial workers is invested. There are assumed to be profitable investment outlets for all saving.[7] The price of industrial goods is assumed to be determined by a markup on unit labour costs.

The consumption of workers in the industrial sector depends on the real wage and the level of output. It is assumed that all wages are consumed either on the consumption of food from agriculture or on industrial goods. Therefore:

$$C_i = pC_{ii} + C_{ai} = kQ_i \qquad (5)$$

where C_i is total consumption in industry; C_{ii} is the consumption of industrial goods in industry and C_{ai} is the consumption of food in industry; Q_i is industrial output and $k = wl$ is the wage bill per unit of steel output. w is the real wage measured in terms of food and l is labour input per unit of steel output (the reciprocal of labour productivity). For a given l, k is determined by the real wage, which for the present is exogenous.

The growth of industrial output can be expressed as the product of the investment ratio in industry and the productivity of investment:

$$\frac{\Delta Q_i}{Q_i} = \frac{\mu I_i}{Q_i}, \qquad (6)[8]$$

where μ is the productivity of investment. Now I_i is equal to the total output

---

[7] In other words, the natural growth rate is assumed to exceed the warranted rate, typical in developing countries. There is no independent investment function of the Keynesian type, but there is a discussion later of what is likely to happen in the model if the industrial sector attempts to 'force' the pace of industrial growth.

[8] Like equation (3), this equation is definitionally true and does not imply that industrial output depends solely on capital accumulation.

206 MODEL OF GROWTH AND DEVELOPMENT ON KALDORIAN LINES

of steel less the steel sold to agriculture and industrial workers:

$$I_i = Q_i - I_a - C_{ia} - C_{ii} \tag{7}$$

and from (2)

$$(I_a + C_{ia}) = S_a/p$$

Since the agricultural surplus is sold to industry for workers' consumption, $S_a = C_{ai} = \alpha k Q_i$, where α is the proportion of the wage bill spent on food (C_{ai}/kQ_i). Therefore $I_a = \alpha k Q_i/p - C_{ia}$. Substituting for I_a in equation (7) and the result into (6) gives:

$$\frac{\Delta Q_i}{Q_i} = \frac{\mu}{Q_i}\left(Q_i - \frac{\alpha k Q_i}{p} - C_{ii}\right) = \mu\left(1 - \frac{C_{ii}}{Q_i}\right) - \frac{\alpha \mu k}{p} \tag{8}$$

Since it is assumed that all industrial wages are consumed, it follows from equation (5) that $\alpha = 1 - pC_{ii}/kQ_i$, so that equation (8) may also be written as:

$$\frac{\Delta Q_i}{Q_i} = \mu - \frac{\mu k}{p} \tag{8a}$$

In other words, the fact that workers consume only a portion of their wages on food, and the rest on industrial goods, makes no difference to the industrial growth rate. The surplus for reinvestment is the same however wages are disposed of. From (8a) the positive non-linear relation between the industrial terms of trade and the growth of industrial output (g_s) is shown in Fig. 2. The curve has an asymptote, μ, and cuts the vertical axis at k, which gives the minumum price of steel (in terms of food) at which no steel is reinvested in industry itself.

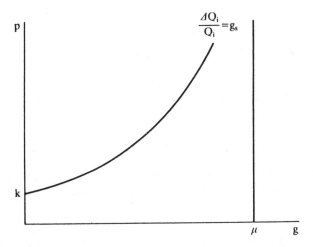

FIG. 2

A rise in the productivity of investment in industry will shift the asymptote, μ, outwards, and an improvement in labour productivity in industry, unmatched by an increase in the real wage, will shift the intercept (k) downwards. In discussing the equilibrium and stability of the model, and in extending it in various directions, it will now be assumed for simplicity that all industrial goods are used for investment. This will simplify the algebra without affecting the insights of the model. It has been shown that the consumption of industrial goods merely serves to lower the agricultural growth curve.

Equilibrium

The stationary equilibrium growth rate (g^*), and the equilibrium terms of trade (p^*), are found where the two curves (from Figs. 1 and 2) cross in Fig. 3. Formally these equilibrium values are found by solving the pair of

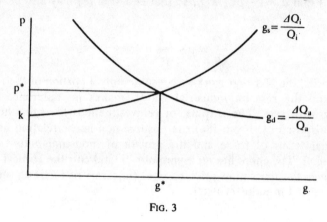

FIG. 3

equations (4)[9] and (8a). This gives:

$$p^* = k + \frac{\sigma s_a}{\mu} \qquad (9)$$

and

$$g^* = \frac{1}{k/\sigma s_a + \dfrac{1}{\mu}} \qquad (10)$$

The equilibrium growth rate will be faster, the higher is the productivity of investment in industry and agriculture, μ and σ; the higher is the

---

[9] Assuming $C_{ia} = 0$. The more agriculture consumes from industry, and the less it invests, the further to the left the g_d curve will lie and the lower the equilibrium terms of trade and growth rate.

208 MODEL OF GROWTH AND DEVELOPMENT ON KALDORIAN LINES

agricultural savings ratio, s_a, and the lower are industrial wage costs per unit of output, k. The terms of trade move in favour of industry and against agriculture, the higher are k, σ and s_a, and the lower is μ.[10]

This equilibrium solution implies that steel output and food output should be in a particular relationship to each other. If food demanded in exchange for steel is kQ_i[11] and food offered (the agricultural surplus) is $s_a Q_a$, then in equilibrium the ratio of steel output to food output must be:

$$\frac{Q_i}{Q_a} = \frac{s_a}{k} \qquad (11)$$

or

$$Q_i = \frac{I_a}{k} \quad \text{(where } I_a = s_a Q_a / p \text{)} \qquad (12)$$

This is the Harrod trade multiplier result that at a given terms of trade ($p = 1$) at which trade is balanced, industrial output is a linear multiple ($1/k$) of the 'export' of industrial goods (to agriculture), where k is the propensity to import (agricultural goods) (see also Thirlwall, 1982).

Stability and the consequences of a disequilibrium terms of trade

Now suppose that equilibrium is disturbed. Is the model stable, and what are the consequences for growth of a disequilibrium terms of trade? Whether the model is stable or not depends on the nature of the adjustment process out of equilibrium. Since the model is set up in terms of growth rates let us relate adjustments of the terms of trade to differences in the growth rates of supply and demand.[12] In this case, the stability of the model out of equilibrium depends on the slopes of the g_d and g_s curves and on the coefficient of adjustment of the terms of trade to divergences between g_d and g_s. The last of these factors is crucial. The adjustment of the terms of

---

[10] It would have been attractive to incorporate in the model an above-unitary income elasticity of demand for industrial goods; and likewise a below-unitary income elasticity of demand for agricultural goods. This has not been done for several reasons. First, it makes no difference to the structure, or basic insights, of the model. Secondly, it would be difficult to have income elasticities of demand different from unity with at the same time holding constant the ratio of food consumption to output in both sectors, as is assumed in the present analysis. Undoubtedly if the income elasticity of demand for industrial goods in the agricultural sector is greater than unity, the sector would partly meet this growing (proportionate) demand by consuming proportionately less food. Thirdly, in the two sector model the income elasticities of demand for industrial and agricultural goods would have to be the reciprocal of each other for there to be a constant terms of trade which balances the growth of demand and supply in the exchange of food for steel. This would be a restriction on the model which would be difficult to swallow empirically. By ignoring the different income elasticities of demand for agricultural and industrial goods, the equilibrium growth rates of the two sectors at the equilibrium terms of trade are constrained to equal each other.

[11] Assuming $C_{ii} = 0$.

[12] The alternative would be to consider adjustments of the terms of trade to differences in the *levels* of supply and demand.

trade will depend on the behaviour of food dealers or merchants.[13] Suppose that equilibrium at p^* in Fig. 3 is disturbed by an autonomous shift in one of the curves giving a new equilibrium terms of trade. There will be stability if food dealers behave in such a way that the terms of trade moves smoothly from p^* to its new equilibrium level. On the other hand, behaviour may be such that the terms of trade overshoot or become cyclical. The stability conditions can be modelled formally:

Let $q = 1/p$ be the price of food in terms of steel; and let ε_1 be the speed of response of prices to a divergence between the growth in demand for steel and the growth in supply of steel ($\varepsilon_1 < 0$). Such a divergence may come about either through a change in k or a change in s_a which causes a change

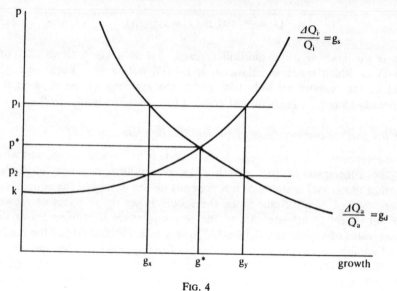

FIG. 4

in k/s_a (a constant k/s_a implying $g_d = g_s$). The diagramatic representation of such shifts is shown in Fig. 4. We have:

$$g_s = \mu[1 - qk] \tag{13}$$

$$g_d = \sigma s_a q \tag{14}$$

$$\Delta q = \varepsilon_1(g_d - g_s) \tag{15}$$

where $\Delta q = q_{t+1} - q_t$.

This gives the first order difference equation:

$$q_{t+1} = [1 + \varepsilon_1(\sigma s_a + \mu k)]q_t - \varepsilon_1 \mu \tag{16}$$

---

[13] Because of differences in the nature of competition between sectors, quantities are assumed to adjust in the industrial sector and prices in the agricultural sector, in response to a disequilibrium between supply and demand.

210 MODEL OF GROWTH AND DEVELOPMENT ON KALDORIAN LINES

The behaviour of the model out of equilibrium depends on the value of $[1 + \varepsilon_1(\sigma s_a + \mu k)]$. Since $\varepsilon_1 < 0$, there will be convergence to equilibrium without cycles if $0 < |\varepsilon_1(\sigma s_a + \mu k)| < 1$.

If $|\varepsilon_1(\sigma s_a + \mu k)| > 1$, the model will generate cycles which will be damped if $1 < |\varepsilon_1(\sigma s_a + \mu k)| < 2$, but not otherwise. If $\varepsilon_1 = 0$, there would be no convergence to equilibrium; if ε_1 exactly equalled the reciprocal of $\sigma s_a + \mu k$, there would be immediate convergence to equilibrium, and if ε_1 was more than twice the reciprocal of $(\sigma s_a + \mu k)$ there would be explosive oscillations. Thus, for a given ε_1, instability results if the responsiveness of supply and demand growth to changes in price is "too great"; or, for given values of this responsiveness, instability results if ε_1 is "too great".

The consequences of a disequilibrium terms of trade are illustrated in Fig. 4. At p_1 the industrial terms of trade are "too high", and at p_2 the industrial terms of trade are "too low".

Suppose there had been an autonomous increase in agricultural productivity (a good harvest) which shifted the agricultural growth curve to $\Delta Q_a/Q_a$ in Fig. 4, but the terms of trade overshoots to p_1. In this case, industry would have the ability or capacity to grow at the rate g_y, but because agricultural prices are "too low", agriculture's growth of demand for industrial goods is constrained to g_x. In these circumstances, the system cannot grow at its equilibrium rate, g^*, but is demand constrained to the lower rate, g_x.

Conversely, suppose there is a bad harvest equivalent to an autonomous decrease in agricultural productivity and the terms of trade overshoots in the opposite direction, below its equilibrium level, to p_2. In this case, the agricultural sector has the capacity to grow and buy industrial goods at the rate g_y, but industry cannot invest enough to grow at that rate, and is constrained in its growth to the rate g_x. As Kaldor (1976) writes "continued and stable economic progress requires the growth of output in these two sectors should be at the required relationship with each other—that is to say, the growth of the saleable output of agriculture and mining should be in line with the growth of demand, which in turn reflects the growth of the secondary (and tertiary) sectors. However, from a technical standpoint there can be no guarantee that the rate of growth of primary production, propelled by land saving innovations, proceeds at the precise rate warranted by growth of production and incomes in the secondary and tertiary sectors. To ensure that it does is the function of the price mechanism, more particularly of relative prices, or the "'terms of trade' between primary commodities and manufactured goods" (p. 704).

The consequence of violent shifts in the terms of trade between industrial and agricultural goods, and of a disequilibrium terms of trade, points to the need for mechanisms and institutions that can contribute to equilibrium and stability both within individual countries (and in the world economy) if growth is to be maximised. Keynes saw the nature of the problem with great clarity in a world context as long ago as 1942, which led to his proposal for a

Commodities Control Scheme (see Moggridge 1980, pp. 113–114): "Assuredly nothing can be more inefficient than the present system under which the price [the terms of trade] is always too high or too low....". Within individual countries, credit to finance merchant stocks, and the pricing policy of Marketing Boards, are of prime importance and must be examined closely. Low (relative) prices for agricultural commodities, which in a classical model are beneficial for industrial growth, may in practice constrain growth if the implied terms of trade mean that there is an excess supply of industrial goods because agriculture lacks the purchasing power to buy them.

III. Credit, forcing the pace of growth, and inflation

In the model so far, capitalists in the industrial sector play a passive role, simply investing the surplus of steel. There are no mechanisms by which manufacturers may invest in excess of this. In practice, finance and credit mechanisms exist which allow capitalists to force the pace of industrial growth if 'animal spirits' move them. Within the structure of the model we can see the processes by which the industrial growth rate may be raised, and the various constraints.

If credit is increased to finance extra capitalist investment, the markup will rise in line with the extra aggregate demand for industrial goods, and the money price of steel will thus be higher. What happens then depends on three major responses. First, is the agricultural sector willing to supply more food at the existing money price? If so, this amounts to 'forced saving' in agriculture to finance the investment; the g_d curve shifts out to validate an upward move along the g_s curve. But the agricultural sector may resist such forced saving by attempting to raise the money price of food. Secondly, are industrial workers content with the same money wage in the face of a rise in the price of food as the demand for food expands? If so, this reduces k and pushes out the g_s curve along the g_d curve. If, however, there is real wage resistance, workers will demand higher money wages restoring k and pushing the g_s curve back to its original position. This is the idea of the inflation barrier familiar from neo-Keynesian growth theory (and structuralist theories of inflation, see Olivera, 1964). Thirdly, are some individual capitalists unable to increase their money expenditures fully in line with the rise in the price of steel? If so, this will dampen the initial increase in investment. Monetary restraint will work in this direction. If, however, all producers and industrial workers are able to defend themselves against rising prices, there is a real danger of explosive inflation (see Cardoso, 1981).

There remains the possibility that the government may 'force' savings to match the increased investment by taxing the workers (shifting out the g_s curve) or the corn producers (shifting out the g_d curve). Even here the tax may be resisted with similar inflationary consequences which dampen or abort the development effort.

IV. Technical progress, growth, and the terms of trade

In this model, demand growth for industrial goods must grow in step with supply growth. A lower price of steel has a positive effect on demand growth for industrial goods and seems to be necessary in order that the rate of industrial growth be higher. This would seem to imply that higher rates of industrial growth must be associated with a worsening of the industrial terms of trade, and would appear to conflict with historical experience which suggests that economies grow faster when the terms of trade move in industry's favour.

The explanation of this apparent contradiction lies in the fact that technical progress in both sectors causes *both* curves to shift about, and more so in agriculture where productivity improvements are not so quickly or automatically matched by increases in agricultural consumption. In industry, where labour productivity improvements tend to be matched by increases in real wages (and often more than matched) the share of wages in industrial output remains fairly stable (or increases) and the g_S curve is therefore relatively stable. Variations in the rate of land saving innovations, however, both embodied and disembodied, will shift the g_d curve outwards by varying degrees, and the growth of industrial output can then increase without any deterioration in the industrial terms of trade. An outward movement of the g_d curve due to an increasing rate of technical progress, and the relative stability (and perhaps leftward shift) of the g_S curve for the reasons mentioned, would account for a secular tendency of the industrial terms of trade to improve relative to agriculture—the so-called Prebisch effect—despite the fact that industrial activities tend to be subject to increasing returns while agriculture is a diminishing returns activity, and despite the fact that technical progress tends to be faster in industry than in agriculture. Spraos (1980) has confirmed the Prebisch thesis for the period 1870 to 1940, and the downward trend (excluding minerals) has continued in the post-war period since 1954 (see Thirlwall and Bergevin, 1985).

Diminishing returns and productivity growth in agriculture: the ultimate long run constraints on growth

In the short run equilibrium of the model, the importance of technical progress in agriculture is clear. If there are diminishing returns to land as a fixed factor of production, successive applications of capital will lower the productivity of investment in agriculture, shifting inwards the g_d curve and lowering the industrial growth rate. In the long run equilibrium of the model it can be shown formally how variations in the pace of industrial growth depend fundamentally on the rate of land saving innovations, and that technical progress in industry affects only the equilibrium terms of trade.

To consider productivity growth in agriculture, assume that output growth in the agricultural sector is a function of the amount of capital accumulated,

the quantity of land and the rate of land saving technical progress. Assume further that land saving technical progress is partly disembodied and partly a function of the rate of capital accumulation itself. Let the production function be:
$$Q_a = T_A K^{\alpha_1} R^{\alpha_2} \tag{17}$$
where K is capital employed in agriculture; R is the quantity of land; T_A is an index of the level of technology in agriculture, α_1 is the elasticity of output with respect to capital and α_2 is the elasticity of output with respect to land. Labour (measured in terms of men) is absent from the production function since it is assumed to be in surplus with zero marginal product. From equation (17)
$$\frac{\Delta Q_a}{Q_a} = \frac{\Delta T_A}{T_A} + \alpha_1 \frac{\Delta K}{K} + \alpha_2 \frac{\Delta R}{R} \tag{18}$$
Now assume a (linear) technical progress function:
$$\frac{\Delta T_A}{T_A} = \beta_0 + \beta_1 \frac{\Delta K}{K} \tag{19}$$
where β_0 is the rate of disembodied land saving inventions, and $\beta_1(\Delta K/K)$ is the rate of technical progress induced by capital accumulation. Substituting (19) into (18) gives:
$$\frac{\Delta Q_a}{Q_a} = \beta_0 + \alpha_2 \frac{\Delta R}{R} + (\alpha_1 + \beta_1) \frac{\Delta K}{K} \tag{20}$$
The steady state growth rate of agricultural output at which the capital-output ratio is constant is:
$$\frac{\Delta Q_a}{Q_a} = \frac{\beta_0 + \alpha_2 \frac{\Delta R}{R}}{1 - \alpha_1 - \beta_1} \tag{21}$$
The implication of this analysis is that for given values of the production parameters, α_1 and α_2; given values for the parameters of the technical progress function, β_0 and β_1, and given the rate of growth of land, the steady state rate of agricultural output growth is a constant independent of the terms of trade. In effect, the g_d curve in Fig. 1 becomes a vertical line emanating from the horizontal axis.

The steady state terms of trade p^* must be that which is necessary to make industry grow in step with agricultural output. From equations (8a) and (21) this is:
$$p^* = \left[\frac{\mu k}{\mu - \left[\frac{\beta_0 + \alpha_2 \frac{\Delta R}{R}}{1 - \alpha_1 - \beta_1} \right]} \right] \tag{22}$$

214 MODEL OF GROWTH AND DEVELOPMENT ON KALDORIAN LINES

The importance of the model for an understanding of the pace and rhythm of industrial growth in a closed economy can now be appreciated. The results suggest that technical progress in agriculture (or the discovery of new land) will relax the ultimate constraints on industrial growth, and only these factors will do so. Technical progress in industry affects the terms of trade (by changing k), but not the long run equilibrium growth rate.

The terms of trade in the long run

It has been shown that diminishing returns in agriculture cause the terms of trade to turn progressively against industry but that this tendency can be offset by the increased availability of land and land saving technical progress. And we know that a rising real wage (by raising k) turns the terms of trade in favour of industry, which may be offset by labour saving technical progress. Long term secular movements in the terms of trade are thus the outcome of the balance of these four forces; these are themselves the outcome of geographical discoveries, invention, and institutional pressures. Clearly, there can be no "iron law" of the industrial terms of trade, either deteriorating (as in Ricardo) or improving (as in Prebisch). What happens depends on the balance of these economic and social forces.

V. Is labour supply a constraint on industrial growth?

It is possible that in certain countries, at certain times, the rate of growth of industry may be constrained by a shortage of labour. Only if labour supply is strictly exogenous and unresponsive to demand can labour supply growth be regarded as a constraint on industrial growth in a direct sense. But this is not the case in the real world (Kaldor 1968, 1975a). In the process of development—at least up until the stage of maturity where the marginal product of labour in different sectors of the economy is roughly equal—there is not likely to be a shortage of labour to the industrial sector, and given the demand it may even be forthcoming at a constant real wage. Employment is then endogenous in the industrial sector at an exogenous wage. In the world economy at large there are ample supplies of labour for use in industry. Even in highly industrialised countries, when they have required labour, they have obtained it—often from other countries with surplus labour. Many countries, such as Germany, Canada, the U.S.A., Australia and France, operated generous immigration policies in the 1950s and 1960s specifically for this purpose. There has also been a big increase in female participation in the labour force in recent years which has partly been a response to the pressure of demand. The informal service sector, too, provides a source of labour for the industrial sector not unlike that provided by agriculture. There are a variety of ways in which the stock of labour can adapt its services to the need for labour if the demand is there, including variations in the number of hours worked. With seventy percent of the labour force still on the land in the developing countries, and with the new electronic revolution in developed countries, a global shortage of labour to produce industrial output seems a remote possibility for many years to come.

To obtain more labour, however, a higher real wage may have to be paid. This means that k and the g_s curve will be higher than otherwise would be the case, thus raising the industrial terms of trade and lowering the rate of growth of industrial output in the short-run equilibrium of the basic model.[14] In this sense labour supply can exert a constraint on industrial growth.

VI. The open economy

Let us now move from the closed economy and think explicitly of the model applying to a particular country which may trade. The importance of trade in this model is not that it may affect growth favourably through raising the overall rate of capital accumulation or improving the productivity of investment, but that export demand becomes another source of autonomous demand for industrial output which, in practice, will come to dominate the growth of demand from agriculture. Trade by itself will not affect the rate of capital accumulation unless a country is allowed to import more than it exports or *both* industry and agriculture are able to buy their inputs cheaper abroad than domestically.[15] If goods are homogenous, however, a more favourable international than domestic terms of trade for agriculture would mean a less favourable international than domestic terms of trade for industry. Only if goods are sufficiently heterogenous, and the mix of inputs into each sector could be altered without affecting productivity, might both the agricultural and industrial sector of a country benefit simultaneously from being able to trade internationally as well as internally.

But, as mentioned above, the real significance of trade is that the rate of growth of export demand for industrial output (g_d^w) will, as development proceeds, become an important source of autonomous demand for industrial goods in addition to the rate of growth of demand emanating from the agricultural sector (g_d). In a steady state the rate of growth of demand for industrial output (g_d^I) will be a weighted average of the two rates of growth, where the weights represent the proportion of autonomous demand accounted for by agriculture and exports respectively: i.e.

$$g_d^I = \theta(g_d) + (1-\theta)g_d^w, \qquad (23)$$

The growth of demand for a country's industrial exports is a function of the

---

[14] However, it does not lower the long-run equilibrium rate of growth given in equation (21), since this is independent of k.

[15] Trade may raise the productivity of investment in industry if the availability of foreign exchange allows a fuller or more efficient use of domestic resources. We are not concerned with this issue here.

216 MODEL OF GROWTH AND DEVELOPMENT ON KALDORIAN LINES

growth of world income and a country's relative competitiveness so that:

$$g_d^w = \varepsilon(g_w) + \psi \dot{p}_d \qquad (24)$$

where g_w is the growth of 'world' income, $\dot{p}_d$ is the rate of change of relative prices measured in a common currency; ε is the income elasticity of demand for exports ($\varepsilon > 0$) and ψ is the price elasticity of demand for exports ($\psi < 0$).

It would be unrealistic, however, to assume a steady state, with the two sources of autonomous demand growing at the same rate through time. In every country's economic history there is a date when export demand for industrial goods grows more rapidly than agricultural demand, and so the ratio of export demand to agricultural demand inevitably grows. This results from a combination of a number of factors. First, the growth in agricultural income and purchasing power will come to lag behind the growth of world income owing to the lower income elasticity of demand for agricultural goods. Second, the income elasticity of demand for industrial goods in the agricultural sector is likely to become less than the income elasticity of demand for the country's goods in world markets as the country begins to acquire the technology to make goods for which the income elasticity of demand in world markets is high.

There is a third reason why export demand may come to dominate. If the income elasticity of demand for imports of the industrial sector is greater than unity then industrial imports will grow more rapidly than industrial output. The rate of growth of industrial exports must be faster than the rate of growth of industrial output as a whole if overall balance of payments equilibrium is a requirement and the deficit in industry cannot be matched by a payments surplus in agriculture. Now if the growth of industrial exports is limited by the growth of demand in world markets[16] then this limit will impose an upper ceiling on the growth of the industrial sector consistent with balance of payments equilibrium. Growth becomes balance of payments constrained, at a rate independent of the rate of growth of demand emanating from the agricultural sector. This is also a significant turning point in a country's economic history, which might occur before the point when the growth of agricultural demand falls below the growth of world demand for industrial exports.

If in the long run, $g_d^w > g_d$, then $\theta \to 0$, and equilibrium industrial growth becomes determined by the growth of demand for exports. Export growth becomes the driving force in the system to which other components of demand adapt.[17] If relative prices in international trade are sticky so that

---

[16] Because ψ is low so that it is not possible to greatly increase industrial exports by continuously cheapening them, or because the price of industrial exports is sticky ($\dot{p}_d \approx 0$) due to oligopolistic market structures.

[17] This is the idea of the Hicks supermultiplier which Kaldor (1970) had in mind in developing his export-led growth model in a regional context.

$\dot{p}_d \to 0$; then equilibrium industrial growth approximates to εg_w, which is the dynamic Harrod trade multiplier result assuming balanced trade, a constant terms of trade, and an income elasticity of demand for imports equal to unity (see Thirlwall, 1979, 1982 and Kennedy and Thirlwall 1979).[18]

If industrial output growth and productivity growth are positively related (through Verdoorn's Law) a process of circular and cumulative causation may set in, which benefits industry relative to agriculture, widening disparities in living standards and income per head. This is the essence of centre-periphery models of growth and development articulated by Prebisch (1950) and Seers (1962) in the international context,[19] and Dixon and Thirlwall (1975) in a regional context (see Thirlwall 1983).

VII Conclusion

In this paper I have attempted to develop a general model of growth and development (on Kaldorian lines) which formally analyses the complementarity between industry and agriculture, in contrast to other models of the development process which either ignore this complementarity or discuss it non-rigorously. The model can be applied to both developing and developed countries, and to closed and open economies. For any individual country in the course of development we expect a healthy agricultural sector to be the driving force behind industrial growth in the early stages, superseded by export growth in the later stages. In this sense the model reinforces the belated recognition of agriculture's importance in the early stages of development, and lends support to export led growth theory in the later stages.

The extension of the basic model provides several interesting and important insights: (i) the joint determination of industry's growth rate and its terms of trade with agriculture, and the consequences of disequilibria in the terms of trade for the growth process in individual countries (and in the world economy); (ii) the conditions under which the pace of industrialisation can be forced; (iii) a rationale for the "Prebisch effect", but a demonstration that there is no "iron law" of the terms of trade; (iv) the importance of land saving innovations in agriculture as an offset to diminishing returns; (v) the consequence of labour shortages and rising real wages for industrial growth, and (vi) the ultimate role of foreign trade and export demand as the fundamental source of autonomous demand for a country's industrial goods.

University of Kent, U.K.

---

[18] If, empirically, the ratio of imports to output in the industrial sector was increasing, the income elasticity of demand for imports would exceed unity, and growth would approximate to $(\varepsilon/\pi)g_w$, where π is the income elasticity of demand for imports.

[19] See also Vines (1980).

218 MODEL OF GROWTH AND DEVELOPMENT ON KALDORIAN LINES

REFERENCES

ADELMAN IRMA, (1984), Beyond Export-led Growth, *World Development*, Sept.
BALASSA, B., (1980), *The Process of Industrial Development and Alternative Development Strategies*, Essays in International Finance, Princeton.
CARDOSO, E., (1981), "Food Supply and Inflation", *Journal of Development Economics*, Vol. 8.
DIXON, R. J., and THIRLWALL, A. P. (1975), A Model of Regional Growth Rate Differences on Kaldorian Lines, *Oxford Economic Papers*, July.
FEI, J. C. H., and RANIS, G., (1964), *Development of the Labour Surplus Economy*, Richard D. Irwin.
FINDLAY, R., (1980), "The terms of trade and equilibrium growth in the world economy", *American Economic Review*, June.
JOHNSTON, B. F., AND MELLOR, J. W., (1961), The Role of Agriculture in Economic Development, *American Economic Review*, September.
JORGENSON, D., (1969), 'The Role of Agriculture in Economic Development: Classical versus Neo-classical Models of Growth' in Wharton, C. R. (ed.), *Subsistence Agriculture and Economic Development*, Chicago, Aldane.
KALDOR, N. (1957), 'A Model of Economic Growth', *Economic Journal*, December.
KALDOR, N. (1966), *Causes of the Slow Rate of Economic Growth of the United Kingdom*, Cambridge University Press.
KALDOR, N. (1967), *Strategic Factors in Economic Development*, Cornell University Press, Ithaca.
KALDOR, N. (1968), 'Productivity and Growth in Manufacturing: A Reply', *Economica*, November.
KALDOR, N. (1970), 'The Case for Regional Policies', *Scottish Journal of Political Economy*, November.
KALDOR, N. (1974), 'International Monetary Reform, A Need for a New Approach', *Bancaria*, March; reprinted in KALDOR, N. (1976), *Further Essays on Applied Economics*, Duckworth.
KALDOR, N. (1975a), Economic Growth and the Verdoorn Law: A Comment on Mr. Rowthorn's Article, *Economic Journal*, December.
KALDOR, N. (1975b), 'What is Wrong with Economic Theory', *Quarterly Journal of Economics*, August.
KALDOR, N. (1976), Inflation and Recession in the World Economy, *Economic Journal*, December.
KALDOR, N. (1979), 'Equilibrium Theory and Growth Theory' in *Economic and Human Welfare*: *Essays in Honour of Tibor Scitovsky*, (ed.), Baskia, M., Academic Press.
KENNEDY, C., and THIRLWALL, A. P. (1979), Import Penetration, Export Performance and Harrod's Trade Multiplier, *Oxford Economic Papers*, July.
LEWIS, W. A. (1954), Economic Development with Unlimited Supplies of Labour, *Manchester School*, May.
LEWIS, W. A. (1972), "Reflections on Unlimited Labour" in L. di Marco (ed.), *International Economics and Development*: *Essays in Honour of Raul Prebisch*, (Academic Press).
LEWIS, W. A. (1984), The State of Development Theory, *American Economic Review*, March.
LOCKWOOD, W. W. (1954), *The Economic Development of Japan*: *Growth and Structural Change 1868–1938*, Princeton University Press.
MOGGRIDGE, D., (1980), *The Collected Writings of J. M. Keynes, Vol. xxvii: Activities 1940–1946 Shaping the Post-War World: Employment and Commodities*, London, Macmillan.
MYRDAL, G. (1957), *Economic Theory and Underdeveloped Regions*, Duckworth.
NURKSE, R. (1962), *Equilibrium and Growth in the World Economy*, Harvard University Press.
OLIVERA, J. (1964), "On structural inflation and Latin American Structuralism", *Oxford Economic Papers*, October.

PREBISCH, R. (1950), *The Economic Development of Latin America and its Principal Problems*, ECLA, U.N. Dept., of Economic Affairs, New York.

SEERS, D. (1962), 'A Model of Comparative Rates of Growth in the World Economy', *Economic Journal*, March.

SEN, A. (1983), Development Economics: Which Way Now, *Economic Journal*, December.

SPRAOS, J. (1980), The Statistical Debate on the Net Barter Terms of Trade Between Primary Products and Manufactures, *Economic Journal*, March.

THIRLWALL, A. P. (1979), The Balance of Payments Constraint as an Explanation of International Growth Rate Differences, *Banca Nazionale del Lavoro Quarterly Review*, March.

THIRLWALL, A. P. (1982), 'The Harrod Trade Multiplier and the Importance of Export-Led Growth, *Pakistan Journal of Applied Economics*, March.

THIRLWALL, A. P. (1983), 'Foreign Trade Elasticities in Centre-Periphery Models of Growth and Development', *Banca Nazionale del Lavoro Quarterly Review*, September.

THIRLWALL, A. P., and BERGEVIN, J. (1985), Trends, Cycles and Asymmetries in the Terms of Trade of Primary Commodities from Developed and Less Developed Countries, *World Development*, July.

VINES, D. (1980), 'Competitiveness, Technical Progress and Balance of Trade Surpluses', *Manchester School*, December.

VINES, D., (1984), A North-South Growth Model along Kaldorian Lines, Dept. of Applied Economics, Cambridge, Mimeo.

WALTERS, H. E. (1982), "Agriculture and Development", *Finance and Development*, September.

YOUNG, A. (1928), Increasing Returns and Economic Progress, *Economic Journal*, December.

Oxford Economic Papers 40 (1988), 463-476

INCREASING RETURNS IN INDUSTRY AND THE ROLE OF AGRICULTURE IN GROWTH

By DAVID CANNING

1. Introduction

THE PROBLEM of increasing demand for food coupled with diminishing returns in agriculture was central to the classical growth theories of Malthus (1966) and Ricardo (1951). This theory predicts that the economy must eventually stagnate, due to agriculture using ever increasing resources with falling productivity. This has not happened in the developed world.

The aim of this paper is to demonstrate that, with increasing returns to scale in the industrial sector, diminishing returns in agriculture need not be a barrier to growth. The growth of the economy may be unlimited, despite ever increasing demand for agricultural produce and in the absence of technical progress, if the increasing returns in the capital goods industries are sufficient to outweigh the diminishing returns to capital in agriculture. The engine of growth is firmly located in the industrial sector; agriculture becomes more productive, but only by the use of ever larger amounts of cheap capital goods.

Neoclassical growth theory, as set out by Meade (1961) and Solow (1970), assumes constant returns to scale and the unlimited reproduction of the factors of production, allowing a steady, positive, rate of growth in the long run. It ignores the presence of a fixed factor (land), but seems compatible with the experience of the developed world in the late 19th and the 20th centuries. Kaldor (1957, 1975, 1979) emphasizes growth of manufacturing output, capital accumulation, and the productivity gains these generate. This leads to a theory of economic development which highlights the transition from agriculture to manufacturing as the key to a high rate of growth.

Thirwall (1986) investigates a model of growth and development along Kaldorian lines. The importance of balanced growth is emphasized; agricultural output must grow at the same rate as industrial output in equilibrium. The results of his model are a return to the classical view; the growth rate is regulated by increases in productivity in agriculture and the cultivation of new lands. This constraint may be relaxed for an individual country by international trade, but taking the world as a whole the agricultural sector must eventually dominate.

A simple model is developed to show that increasing returns in industry, and in particular the production of capital goods, may relax the long run constraint agriculture places on growth. With increasing returns in some sectors, and diminishing returns (due to a fixed factor) in others, balanced equilibrium growth is not possible. Even if each sector's output grows at the same rate the proportion of resources devoted to each sector changes; more

© Oxford University Press 1988

importantly, given each sector uses different factor proportions, growth will change the relative rewards of the different factors of production and, given differential savings rates, the future growth rate.

With increasing returns at the plant level in industry we cannot assume perfect competition; the number of firms must be determined endogenously. Industrial structure is very important; fewer firms will allow greater exploitation of scale economies, but will lead to lack of competition and may result in demand growth being siphoned off into higher prices and profits rather than producing extra output. In order to overcome the problem of food production increasing returns in the capital goods industry must be large enough to overcome the decreasing returns to employing capital in agriculture, but small enough to ensure that there are enough firms in the capital goods industry to prevent monopoly pricing.

Instead of concentrating on aggregate relationships I shall construct a small general equilibrium model of the economy. While this is perhaps more detailed than necessesary it does ensure consistency.

Three time scales are considered. In the short period the supply of each factor, land, labour, and capital, is fixed, and equilibrium is brought about by the price mechanism. This equilibrium will determine a particular level of output for the investment goods industries. These investment goods serve as capital stock for the next period. Given a fixed stock of land and labour the medium period equilibrium is the limit of the sequence of short period equilibria with changing capital stocks. The effect of a changed labour supply on the short and medium run equilibria is then considered; the long period behaviour of the system will depend crucially on whether labour supply increases lead to rising, or falling, real wages.

In the short period a higher supply of labour tends to depress real wages. However, profits on capital tend to rise and the medium period equilibrium will have a larger capital stock. With increasing returns in the capital goods industries the price of capital will become lower (provided there is sufficient competition) than before. The real wage may now be either higher or lower than previously, depending on whether or not the lower cost of farm equipment outweighs the effect of increased demand pressure on the price of food. If increases in the labour supply tend to lower the real wage (measured in corn) in the medium period the economy must, in the long run, tend to a position of subsistence wages which constrain population growth. On the other hand, if a higher labour supply tends to increase the real (corn) wage in the medium period there is no barrier to population growth. The condition separating these two cases will be shown to depend on the returns to scale in the investment goods sector and the degree of substitutability of the factors of production.

The model investigated here assumes market clearing. Keynesian problems of effective demand are ignored. Costabile and Rowthorn (1985) discuss a Malthusian model in which unemployment is possible, even in the long run.

Assuming increasing returns in industry gives the model many features of a Kaldorian framework; in particular, output growth in the industrial sector generates increases in productivity. The study of increasing returns to scale and imperfect competition is becoming common in international trade theory (see Venables (1985)). It seems clear that the application of these techniques to growth theory will produce some insights. While it is unlikely that Kaldor would accept the limitations imposed by a simple, static economies of scale, full employment, model, it may provide a useful starting point for formalising his ideas.

The most striking thing in practice about the early stages of economic growth is the shift of resources from agriculture to the industrial sectors, accompanied by an increased (physical) capital intensity in all sectors. These are two features the present model hopes to incorporate.

2. The model

There are three classes in the economy. Workers own an amount of labour L which they sell in a competitive labour market. They spend all their income on either agricultural goods (corn) or manufactures, attempting in doing so to maximise the utility function

$$U(c_a, c_m) = (c_a - c)^\theta c_m^\epsilon, \quad c_a \geq c, \quad \text{and} \quad \theta, \epsilon > 0, \quad \theta + \epsilon < 1$$

subject to

$$p_a c_a + p_m c_m \leq 1$$

where c_a and c_m are consumption of agricultural goods and manufactured goods respectively and p_a and p_m are their prices. We take the wage as numeraire (this gives more simple equations than using a corn numeraire). c represents subsistence consumption of corn without which the worker cannot survive. The demand for corn per worker is

$$c_a = c + \frac{\theta}{\theta + \epsilon}\left(\frac{1}{p_a} - c\right)$$

Workers buy the subsistence level of food and then divide the rest of their income in fixed proportions between food and manufactures. As workers' incomes measured in corn rise they spend a lower proportion of their income on food.

Landlords rent out their land (of total size F) each period, spending all their rents on agricultural goods. This is a simplifying assumption, but will not help our case; in fact it will tend to emphasize the problem of excessive demand for agricultural produce.

Capitalists sell all their capital at the beginning of the period using the proceeds to buy investment goods at the end of the period. These investment goods then serve as the capital stock of the next period. Capital is completely used up in the process of production. The capitalists merely accumulate capital; they have no other aim.

Entrepreneurs buy the factors of production at the beginning of the period in competitive factor markets. They then use these factors to produce goods for one of the three product markets, agricultural goods, manufactured goods or investment goods. The production functions for each sector are given by

$$Q_a = F^{1-\alpha-\beta} L_a^\alpha K_a^\beta \qquad 0 < \alpha, \beta, \alpha + \beta < 1$$

$$Q_m = \sum_{j=1}^M L_j^\delta K_j^{\gamma-\delta} \qquad 0 < \delta, \gamma - \delta < 1 \leq \gamma$$

$$Q_i = \sum_{j=1}^N L_j^\phi K_j^{\sigma-\phi} \qquad 0 < \phi, \sigma - \phi < 1 \leq \sigma$$

where Q_a, Q_m and Q_i are the total outputs of agricultural goods, manufactured goods and investment goods respectively. Agricultural goods are produced under constant returns to scale with three factors, land, labour and capital. Manufactured goods and investment goods are produced under increasing returns to scale at the plant level. However, there are diminishing returns to each factor. The outputs of each plant are added together to get the industry output.

The following assumption is also made

$$\alpha/(\alpha + \beta) = \delta/\gamma = \phi/\sigma$$

This implies that the optimal capital/labour ratio will be the same in each sector. Factor prices therefore depend on the relative scarcity of each factor and not on the pattern of output. The great advantage of this assumption is that we can now discuss equilibrium at the level of the industry with independent demand and supply schedules. Without this assumption any variation in the output of one industry will change relative factor prices, the incomes of the different classes in society, and the demand schedule for that industry's output.

3. Short period equilibrium

The short period is defined by the period in which all three factors of production are fixed in size. Physical capital is assumed to be used up within the period (100% depreciation) while the output of the capital goods industries is not available for use until the following period. It is assumed that there is free entry for entrepreneurs in all sectors; this keeps their profits at zero. Capitalists merely sell their capital stock to entrepreneurs in a competitive capital market; any short period divergence between the demand price and the long period, or normal, supply price accrues to the capitalists (or landlords) as entrepreneurs bid up the price of capital equipment (or land).

It is assumed that all transactions in the short period take place simultaneously. We can think of the factors of production being sold at the beginning of the period in exchange for future contracts in terms of the output of the productive sectors. This avoids the problem of constructing a wage fund to bridge the gap between hiring factors and the sale of output.

In equilibrium we need to determine the output of each of the three sectors, the price of each output and the three factor prices. Taking the wage as numeraire this leaves eight unknowns to be determined.

(i) Agricultural goods. The demand for agricultural goods come from two sources, workers and landlords. Adding these two demands gives:

$$Q_a = c_a L + (r/p_a)F$$

where r is the rent per unit of land. Given workers demand and our production function this simplifies to

$$Q_a = \frac{1}{\alpha + \beta}\left(c + \frac{\theta}{\theta + \epsilon}\left(\frac{1}{p_a} - c\right)\right)L \qquad (1)$$

since landlords consume a fixed fraction of agricultural output.

We now turn to the supply schedule. Given the price of the inputs (l for labour, r for land and p_k for capital) we can calulate the supply price of agricultural goods.

$$p_a = (r/(1 - \alpha - \beta))^{1-\alpha-\beta}(1/\alpha)^\alpha(p_k/\beta)^\beta \qquad (2)$$

This is the cost of production of agricultural goods, assuming farmers use the cost minimising factor proportions. The level of output does not affect the agricultural supply price directly, it does so only through its effect on factor prices.

(ii) Investment goods. We again start by considering the demand schedule. Expenditure on investment goods is given by

$$Q_i p_i = K p_k \qquad (3)$$

where K is the initial, fixed, stock of capital. Capitalists sell their initial capital, K, in the factor markets and spend the entire proceeds on investment goods. A point to note is that p_k, the price of capital at the beginning of the period, is independent of the level of output, Q_i, of the investment goods industry, because of our assumption of equal capital intensities in all sectors. It follows that the price elasticity with respect to the industry's output is -1, that is, demand for investment goods is fixed in nominal terms. Equation 3 can be thought of as determining the demand price of investment goods, p_i. That is, it determines the price, p_i, which can be charged for any given level of output Q_i.

Consider the supply schedule for investment goods. With increasing returns to scale at the plant level the most efficient form of production in the investment goods sector would be a single plant. However this would lead to monopoly pricing and high profits in this sector. Allowing free entry means that prices and profits will be driven down by competition between a number of firms.

We begin by considering the number of firms in the industry to be fixed at N. Each firm decides on a level of output q_j. Given the aggregate output of the industry the price p_i of investment goods then clears the market. The industry is assumed to be monopolistically competitive and we take the symmetric Cournot equilibrium as our solution concept. Taking the production of the N-1 other firms in the industry as given, each firm can construct a demand curve for its own output. Given this, firm j attempts to maximise its profits

$$\pi_j = p_i q_j - L_j - K_j p_k$$

taking into account the fact that changes in its output q_j will change the industry price p_i.

In general, with a finite number of firms, N, of significant size in the industry, each firm will realise that changing its level of output will increase its demand for the factors of production. This will, in general, change the factor prices it pays (in addition changes in factor prices change the distribution of income and the industry's demand curve). We can either assume firms ignore these effects (that is, they think of themselves as 'small' in the factor markets) or, as in this model, make factor prices independent of the pattern of output.

Putting marginal revenue equal to marginal costs (where the marginal cost of output is calculated on the basis of the use of the cost minimising relative factor proportions derived from the production function) for profit maximisation, we have

$$\frac{dp_i}{dq_j} q_j + p_i = \frac{1}{\sigma} \left(\frac{K_j p_k + L_j}{q_j} \right)$$

Note that for $\sigma > 1$ marginal cost, the right hand side of the equation, is less than average cost, AC, given by total costs divided by total output, $(K_j p_k + L_j)/q_j$. Firms will expand output as long as marginal revenue exceeds marginal cost. For equilibrium to emerge marginal revenue must eventually fall fast enough, due to the lower price associated with higher output, to outweigh the declining marginal cost (due to increasing returns) as output rises.

With only one firm in the industry, the monopoly case, the demand curve faced by firms is given by total industry demand. The total revenue of the monopolist, $Q_i p_i$, is given by $K p_k$ and is independent of the level of output. To maximise profits the monopolist will take this fixed revenue with minimum cost, that is with output as close as possible to zero, exploiting the relatively inelastic demand schedule for investment goods.

With more than one firm each will still realise that the industry price is sensitive to its output. However, as the number of firms, N, increases, each individual firm's impact on industry price declines. In the general case, with N firms, the symmetric equilibrium is characterised by the fact that $e_j = (q_j/p_i) \, dp_i/dp_j$, the elasticity of the industry price with respect to firm j's output, is given by $-1/N$. A one percent increase in total industry output drives the industry price down one percent; a one percent increase in output by a single firm represents a $1/N$ percent increase for industry output, if there are N firms, and has a correspondingly small effect on the industry price. Rewriting the profit maximising condition gives

$$(e_j + 1)p_i = AC/\sigma$$

where AC is average cost of production. In the case of N firms we have $e_j = -1/N$ so

$$\frac{p_i}{AC} = \frac{1}{\sigma}\frac{N}{N-1}$$

For N small price exceeds average cost and firms make positive profits. Given that firms enter the industry as long as profits are positive N will increase until profits fall to zero (ignoring the integer problem) and price equals average cost. The number of firms increases to its equilibrium value $N = \sigma/(\sigma - 1)$.

The number of firms is smaller the greater the returns to scale. The profit maximising equation only holds for $N \geq 2$, that is $\sigma \leq 2$. For $\sigma > 2$ the outcome is a monopoly with low output. Even if σ is less than 2 but still large, so there are very few firms, the problem of cartel behaviour, rather than pure monopolistic competition, may appear. The equation only seems appropriate for N large (σ close to 1). In any case, for σ large the fact that N may not be an integer becomes important. For example, if σ is 1.6, N is approximately 2.7, so an industry with 2 firms gives positive profits while competition between 3 firms would give losses. Approximating N by an integer is less important for small σ. In what follows I shall assume the σ is such that $N = \sigma/(\sigma - 1)$ is an integer.

An important point is that N, the number of firms in the industry with free entry, depends only on the returns to scale; it is independent of the level of demand. Increases in demand lead existing firms to expand rather than new firms to be created. It follows that the industry exhibits the same degree of increasing returns to scale as the plant. With other production functions this is not the case. In general expansion of an industry will involve changes in the number of firms operating as well as the output level of each firm, so that the industry's returns to scale will usually differ from those at the plant level.

We can determine the average cost of production for any level of output Q_i, assuming this output is split between N firms who use cost minimising factor proportions and pay market rates for inputs. This gives us a supply price for each level of output, a price at which firms just cover costs,

$$p_i = (\sigma/(\sigma - \phi))(\phi/(\sigma - \phi))^{-\phi/\sigma} N^{(\sigma-1)/\sigma} p_k^{(\sigma-\phi)/\sigma} Q_i^{(1-\sigma)/\sigma} \qquad (4)$$

The first two terms are constants. The price of investment goods (measured in wage units) is increasing in the cost of capital, but falling as a function of industry output due to increasing returns to scale. As N, the number of firms, rises the average cost of production rises, output being split between more firms, losing scale economies. Putting N equal to the zero profit equilibrium number of firms, equation 4 gives the industry supply price for each level of output.

Putting demand price equal to supply price we can determine the industry equilibrium. The reason for using Marshallian "demand price" and "supply price" concepts, determining price as a function of demand on the one hand and supply on the other, is, of course, the fact that given increasing returns, and declining marginal cost curves for firms, we cannot construct a supply curve in the usual way, finding the level of output firms wish to produce taking the market price as given.

(iii) Manufactured goods. Firms in the manufactured goods market act in exactly the same way as for investment goods. The expenditure on manufactures is given by

$$Q_m p_m = L(1 - cp_a)\epsilon/(\theta + \epsilon) \tag{5}$$

so workers spend a constant fraction of their surplus income (the surplus over agricultural necessities) on manufactures. Again the elasticity of the industry's price with respect to its output is -1. We have $M = \gamma/(\gamma - 1)$ as the number of firms in the industry and

$$p_m = (\gamma/(\gamma - \delta))(\delta/\gamma - \delta))^{-\delta/\gamma} M^{(\gamma-1)/\gamma} p_k^{(\gamma-\delta)/\gamma} Q_m^{(1-\gamma)/\gamma} \tag{6}$$

is the industry supply price.

The manufacturing sector plays no real role in the model. The reason for separating it from the investment goods sector is to isolate any increased scale efficiencies which come from a shift in consumption patterns from food to manufactures. With increasing returns to scale the level of industry disaggregation in the model is important. If we assume that two separate goods are manufactured by one production process an increase in the output of one of the goods will tend to reduce the supply price of the other. If the industrial sector is treated as producing a single good, which can be either consumed or invested, a shift in consumption to manufactures tends to give scale economies to the entire industrial sector which lowers the price of investment goods and complicates our results.

(iv) The factor markets. Given constant returns in agriculture, landlords get their marginal product

$$rF = p_a Q_a (1 - \alpha - \beta). \tag{7}$$

This is not the case in other industries, where, due to increasing returns, the sum of the factors' marginal products exceeds total output. The total income of capitalists is the sum of their sales of capital to the three industries given by

$$p_a K = p_k K_a + p_k K_i + p_k K_m$$
$$= L_a \beta/\alpha + L_i(\sigma - \phi)/\sigma + L_m(\gamma - \delta)/\gamma$$
$$p_k K = L\beta/\alpha \tag{8}$$

since $L = L_a + L_i + L_m$, and the capital/labour ratios are the same in each industry. The relative price of capital and labour depends only on the capital labour ratio.

Equations (1)–(8) allow us to solve for the eight unknowns. It is easy to check that the system satisfies Walras' law, that is

$$p_a Q_a + p_m Q_m + p_i Q_i = rF + p_k K + L$$

so total expenditure equals total factor income. For our purposes it is not necessary to solve the entire system explicitly. Solving for the output of the investment goods industry we have $Q_i = K(p_k/p_i)$. The supply price of investment goods, p_i, depends on the output of that industry and the price p_k of capital as an input. Substituting for p_i and using the capital/labour ratio to substitute for p_k we can find Q_i, the output of the investment goods industry as a function of the start of period stocks of capital and labour:

$$Q_i = HL^\phi K^{\sigma-\phi}$$

where H is a constant depending on the parameters of the model.

4. Equilibrium in the medium period

If there is little capital at the beginning of the period its price will be high, higher than the cost of the output of the capital goods industries at the end of the period, and the capital stock will accumulate. Similarly, if capital is too plentiful its price will be low and capitalists will find replacement capital more expensive than the proceeds of their existing capital, and the capital stock will decline.

Taking the quantities of land and labour as fixed, consider a sequence of short periods in which the capital stock in each is given by the level of output of the investment goods industries in the previous period. That is

$$K_{t+1} = H L^\phi K_t^{\sigma-\phi}$$

Proposition 1. For $K_0 > 0$, K_t converges monotonically to

$$K^* = H^{1/(1+\phi-\sigma)} L^{\phi/(1+\phi-\sigma)}$$

Proof. K^* is obviously the only equilibrium of the system. Suppose $K_t < K^*$ then

$$K_{t+1}/K_t = H L^\phi K_t^{\sigma-\phi-1} = (K^*/K_t)^{1+\phi-\sigma} > 1$$

so $K_{t+1} > K_t$. Further

$$K_{t+1}/K^* = H^{(\phi-\sigma)/(1+\phi-\sigma)} L^{\phi(\phi-\sigma)/(1+\phi-\sigma)} K_t^{\sigma-\phi} = (K_t/K^*)^{\sigma-\phi} < 1$$

so $K_t < K_{t+1} < K^*$. Since $K_{t+1} < K^*$, $K_{t+1} < K_{t+2} < K^*$ and so on. Therefore, if K_0 is less than K^*, K_t is an increasing sequence which is bounded above and hence converges. Its limit must be an equilibrium of the system, and so is K^*.

If K_0 starts above K^* we can show by a similar method that K_t decreases monotonically to K^*.

K^* is the medium period equilibrium capital stock.

The essential point in the argument is $\sigma - \phi < 1$. This is easy to see near the equilibrium point. Linearising the system around the equilibrium, and letting x_t be the deviation from equilibrium, we have the approximation, $x_{t+1} = (\sigma - \phi) x_t$, for x_t small.

5. Changes in the labour force

Consider the long run effect of a once off increase in the labour supply. Will this tend to increase or reduce the price of food measured in wage units? If it tends to increase the price of food then an indefinite increase in population cannot be sustained, the amount of food each worker can afford eventually falling below subsistence. However, if food prices tend to fall as labour supply increases there is no barrier from agriculture to an indefinite growth of population.

Substituting for factor prices in the agricultural price equation (2), and taking the capital stock to be at its medium period equilbrium level, K^*,

$$L^{\alpha-1+(\phi\beta/(1+\phi-\sigma))} = A[cp_a + ((\theta/\theta + \epsilon))(1 - cp_a)]^{1-\alpha-\beta} p_a^{-1}$$

Differentiating through with respect to p_a it is easy to show that

$$\frac{dp_a}{dL} \leq 0 \quad \Leftrightarrow \quad \sigma \geq \sigma^* = 1 + \frac{\phi(1 - \alpha - \beta)}{1 - \alpha}$$

In the medium period an increase in population and labour supply will depress food prices if the returns to scale in the investment goods sector are large enough. The critical value σ^*, the necessary returns to scale, falls as $\alpha + \beta$ rises and land becomes less important in the production function. Additionally reducing ϕ and α, making both the agricultural sector and the investment goods industry itself more capital, as opposed to labour intensive, will tend to decrease the critical value σ^*. The absence of any demand side effects on the critical value σ^* is the result of the special assumption that the capital/labour ratio is the same in each sector. If, for example, the manufactured goods sector is more capital intensive than agriculture a shift in demand from food to manufactures as the economy grows will increase the demand for capital, lowering its price to agriculture, and lowering σ^*.

If $\sigma > \sigma^*$ then in the medium period an increase in population will tend to increase the wage measured in corn. However, there may be a take-off problem. The increased labour supply will initially drive wages down. This is the usual result of adding labour to a world with fixed stock of land and capital. If the real wage falls below the subsistence level population growth will be reversed, perhaps before capital accumulation can enable the economy to provide a higher wage. Only when the profits of capitalists, generated by the higher labour supply and lower real wage, have been reinvested to produce a higher capital stock, exploiting greater scale economies, can the benefical medium term effects of a larger labour force be achieved. If the economy starts with a real wage near subsistence growth may not be possible, population increases being reversed before longer run scale economies occur. However, provided the take-off problem can be overcome, the economy can grow, in terms of population size and real incomes, without bound, despite the fixed supply of land.

If $\sigma < \sigma^*$ any increase in L depresses wages measured in corn. The short run effect of falling real wages with an increased labour supply is mitigated somewhat by scale economies in the medium run. However, these scale economies are insufficient and real wages (measured in terms of corn) are lower even after they have taken effect. Successive increases in the labour supply will lead to ever lower real wages. Eventually population growth must end, with wages at their subsistence level.

The pattern of employment changes during the process of economic growth.

$$\frac{L_a}{L} = \frac{\alpha}{\alpha + \beta} \left(c p_a \frac{\epsilon}{\theta + \epsilon} + \frac{\theta}{\theta + \epsilon} \right)$$

In a dynamic economy capable of long period growth an increase in population will tend to depress agricultural prices and reduce the proportion of the labour force employed in the agricultural sector. Given that the capital/labour ratio is constant across sectors this implies a falling proportion of total resources in agriculture. Growth will be associated with industrialisation, in the sense of an increase in the proportion of total resources employed in the industrial sectors. If the returns to scale in industry are large enough the absolute numbers in agriculture may fall. Growth tends to increase real wages, but reduces the cost of capital, and all sectors become more capital intensive in the long period, reversing the short period effects of the labour supply increase. If land is of different qualities the extensive margin of cultivation may even shift inwards as cultivation becomes more capital intensive.

In a static economy, without sufficient returns to scale in the capital goods industries, increases in population tend to increase the proportion of workers employed in agriculture. The capital stock increases, but the cost of capital does not fall sufficiently. The price of corn in wage units rises, the increased demand resulting in higher production costs (mainly higher rents as land is used more intensively), and its per capita consumption by workers falls.

Only a one-off increase in the labour supply has been considered. To complete the model we really require a growth equation for labour supply, perhaps in terms of the real wage. This complicates the model because we cannot then assume that labour supply remains fixed as the economy tends to its medium run equilibrium. The results set out in this section show that, without sufficient increasing returns in industry, growth in the model, in terms of population, must eventually come to a halt due to lack of agricultural output. In the case where the returns to scale are greater than the critical value, but not so high as to rule out competition, unlimited growth of population, and real incomes, is possible, but depends on the exact specification of any population growth equation, and the initial position of the system.

The possibility of a cycle emerges if capital accumulation is slow relative to population growth. A Kaldorian alternative to a population growth equation would be to fix the real wage (the utility level of workers) and assume an unlimited availability of labour at this wage. In this case employment is determined by the capital stock and σ^* is the dividing line between those economies which grow without bound (in terms of quantities of capital and labour) and those which tend to a stable equilibrium.

6. Conclusion

In an economy with increasing returns in industry, particularly in the capital goods sectors, long period growth can be sustained despite the presence of a fixed factor, and no technical progress, in agricultural production. Growth will be accompanied by a process of industrialisation as the proportion of workers in agriculture falls and the economy becomes more capital intensive (in physical terms).

The conclusion to be drawn about the role of agriculture in industrial development is almost the opposite of that found in Thirlwall (1986):

> 'we expect a healthy agricultural sector to be the driving force behind industrial growth in the early stages'
>
> 'The results suggest that technical progress in agriculture (or the discovery of new land) will relax the ultimate constraints on industrial growth, and only these factors will do so. Technical progress in industry affects the terms of trade (by changing k), but not the long run equilibrium growth rate.'

(k is the wage bill per unit output of industrial—including capital—goods). The analysis presented here suggests that it is exactly by changing k, that is to say by reducing the cost of capital to the agricultural sector, that industry can, by itself, be the driving force behind a sustained process of economic growth. Kaldor (1976) similarly fails to provide a role for cheap capital in overcoming the problem of primary sector production, though since he deals to some extent with exhaustible resources as well as agriculture, and works in an international context, the above analysis does not necessarily apply. Here a closed economy, with no exhaustible resources, has been assumed. In this case, provided there are sufficient returns to scale in the capital goods industries, the constraint on growth is not land but, as in Kaldor (1986), the labour supply. Increases in the labour supply allow the economy to exploit the increasing returns to scale in industry.

Investigations of North–South trade, assuming that one region specializes in primary, the other in industrial, production, have been undertaken in a neoclassical framework by Findlay (1980), and in a Kaldorian framework by Vines (1984). Thirwall (1986) should be considered as a similar study, since in his model the real wage, and rate of profit, may differ between sectors. While the results found here cannot be applied directly to such models, the real wage and rate of profit being equal across sectors, they do suggest that the long run growth rate may be determined in the industrial, and not the agricultural, region.

Putting the present framework in a North–South context by allowing different real wages in different sectors greatly complicates the model. The crucial point in such a model is the assumption made about the mobility of capital. If physical capital can be traded in the same way as other goods, complete equalisation of factor prices between regions takes place very quickly. Cheap capital is available to the poorer region with the smaller capital goods industry (in addition there are scale economies from rationalisation as the capital goods industry becomes more concentrated with one world market). If capital is not physically traded but capitalists can buy capital overseas (there are capital flows in the balance of payments) this will tend to aid poorer countries by speeding up their capital accumulation, foreign capitalists exploiting their low real wage.

Without physical capital flows the picture for less developed countries may be very bleak; they are forced to concentrate in agriculture because the developed countries have a comparative advantage in producing manufactures with their cheap capital and scale economies. If the developed countries have a home agricultural sector this gets more efficient, becoming more mechanised to exploit the cheap capital which is available. The developing countries are then forced to compete with this efficient agricultural sector without the aid of cheap capital, which generally requires a low real wage. This process can become cumulative if the developed country continues to grow and achieve further scale economies. This very bleak picture depends on the developed countries being able to compete in agriculture; it is less so if the underdeveloped countries are the only source of food or raw materials.

It is worth noting that while the capital stock in agriculture may increase as the economy converges to its medium period equilibrium, the value of this capital stock, and its share in the national income, will be constant. This may give rise to an empirical problem in distinguishing between increases in productivity in agriculture and productivity in capital production as a source of growth, if capital is measured in value rather than physical terms. This will be true whatever production functions are assumed, since the mechanism proposed is the falling price of capital goods as they become more plentiful and are produced more efficiently.

While, in a formal sense, agriculture undergoes no technical progress in the model, it does adopt different techniques. Growth in agricultural output requires that farmers shift to more capital intensive methods of production. As Robinson (1952) points out, there is little to distinguish between a change in factor proportions along a production function and shift of the function itself due to technical progress; both require new processes and new techniques to be introduced, and a degree of learning by doing. While this is indeed the case it still seems important, if we wish to trace the causes of economic growth, to distinguish changes in agricultural output brought about by spontaneous changes in farming techniques from those induced by changes in factor prices which originate in the industrial sector.

Pembroke College, Cambridge

REFERENCES

COSTABILE, L. and ROWTHORN, R. (1986) 'Malthus's Theory of Wages and Growth', *Economic Journal*, Vol. 95, pp 418–437.
FINDLAY, R. (1980) 'The Terms of Trade and Equilibrium Growth in the World Economy', *American Economic Review*, vol. 70, pp 291–299.
KALDOR, N. (1957) 'A Model of Economic Growth', *Economic Journal*, Vol. 68, pp 591–624.
KALDOR, N. (1975) 'What is Wrong with Economic Theory', *Quarterly Journal of Economics*, Vol 89, pp 347–357.
KALDOR, N. (1976) 'Inflation and Recession in the World Economy', *Economic Journal*, Vol. 86, pp 703–714.
KALDOR, N. (1979) 'Equilibrium Theory and Growth Theory', in *Economic and Human Welfare: Essays in Honour of Tibor Scitovsky*, M. Baskia editor, Academic Press.
KALDOR, N. (1986) 'Limits on Growth', *Oxford Economic Papers*, Vol. 38, pp 187–198.
MALTHUS, T. R. (1966) *First Essay on Population*. Reprinted by the Royal Economic Society.
MEADE, J. (1961) *A Neo-Classical Theory of Economic Growth*. George Allen and Unwin Ltd. London.
RICARDO, D. (1951) *On the Principles of Political Economy and Taxation*. vol. 1 of *Works and Correspondence of David Ricardo.*, P. Sraffa editor, for the Royal Economic Society, Cambridge University Press.
ROBINSON, J. (1952) 'Notes on the Economics of Technical Progress', in *The Rate of Interest and Other Essays*. Macmillan and Co., London.
SOLOW, R. M. (1970) *Growth Theory: An Exposition*. Oxford University Press. London.
THIRWALL, A. P. (1986) 'A General Model of Growth and Development on Kaldorian Lines', *Oxford Economic Papers*, Vol. 38, pp 199–219
VENABLES, A. J. (1985) 'International Trade, and Industrial Policy and Imperfect Competition: a Survey', *Centre for Economic Policy Research*, London, Discussion Paper No. 74.
VINES, D. (1984) 'A North-South Growth Model Along Kaldorian Lines.' *Centre for Economic Policy Research*, London, Discussion Paper No. 26.

NORTH–SOUTH GROWTH AND THE TERMS OF TRADE: A MODEL ON KALDORIAN LINES*

H. Molana and D. Vines*

This paper develops a North–South model due to Nicholas Kaldor, and uses it to investigate the determination of world growth and the terms of trade.

North–South models began with Ricardo.[1] His main concern was the shortage of agricultural land in the North. Accumulation of capital there, thought Ricardo, would increase the demand for labour by the manufacturing sector, and so agricultural wage-goods would become increasingly scarce. This would induce a rise in the price of agricultural goods and hence put downward pressure on the rate of profit, and on capital accumulation. As a result, the classical stationary state would be reached, believed Ricardo, unless an escape mechanism were found.

North–South trade provided a growth-sustaining escape mechanism by enabling two regions to specialise. Because of its abundance of land, the South had a comparative advantage in producing agricultural goods. The North could, therefore, withdraw capital stock from its own agricultural production and reallocate it into the production of manufactures, and by obtaining wage-goods from the South more cheaply, maintain a higher rate of profit, and sustain capital accumulation.

Modern North–South growth models provide variations on this theme (for surveys see Findlay, 1980 and Currie et al. 1988). For simplicity, they tend to assume complete specialisation: the North produces only industrial goods whilst the South produces only primary commodities. Although in these studies, as proposed by Ricardo, the terms of trade play an important role in influencing the growth rate, the corresponding outcomes are often very different from Ricardo's. Lewis (1954) concludes that continuing technical progress in the South might, in fact, turn the terms of trade towards the North. This is the opposite of Ricardo's original concern. Lewis's conclusion, however, is not based on a complete model. Findlay (1980) and Taylor (1983) formulate complete models where both assume a Lewis type structure for the South. For the North, Findlay has a Solow growth model where scarce labour constrains world growth through rising real wages. By contrast, Taylor has a Keynesian North where world growth can be sustained – by investors' animal spirits – if Northern real wages are flexible downwards (see Lewis, 1972 and Costabile and Rowthorn, 1984).

---

* This paper owes much to memorable conversations which David Vines had with the late Nicholas Kaldor and to Kaldor's Cambridge lectures. Thanks are due to Tom Asimakopoulos, Jitendra Borpujari, Geoff Harcourt, Ravi Kanbur, Arthur Lewis, Steven Marglin, Peter Neary, Ted Sieper, Lance Taylor, Tony Thirlwall and Frank Wilkinson who commented helpfully on an earlier related paper, Vines (1984).

[1] For Ricardo, 'North' was Britain and 'South' meant Portugal and the Baltic

Kaldor (1976, 1979) proposes a more Ricardian alternative. He deliberately assumes surplus labour, available at an exogenous real wage, for the North as well as for the South. (For discussion of such an assumption, see Marglin, 1984.) Consequently, as in Ricardo, the main endogenous influence on Northern capital accumulation is the terms of trade. Kaldor's aim is first to sketch out how the equilibria for world growth and the North–South terms of trade are determined by productivity and thrift in both North and South, and second to show how changes in agricultural productivity in the South influence these equilibria. Thirlwall (1986) presents this basic model for a closed economy, rather than in a North–South context. The present paper also attempts to formalise Kaldor's North–South model, but has three further objectives. First, in contrast with Thirlwall, we allow for some substitution in consumption between primary commodities and industrial goods in the North. This modification turns out to be crucial. In addition, besides treating the case with surplus land in the South (like Findlay, Taylor and Thirlwall), we also examine what happens if land is scarce in the South (i.e. the South has Ricardian diminishing returns). Finally, we formally examine the stability of growth and explore the pattern of adjustment out of equilibrium. It will be shown that technical progress in agricultural production will immiserise the South in the short run, will cause the terms of trade to overshoot its equilibrium, and may cause cycles on the way to equilibrium. It is not even guaranteed that adjustment is stable. To some, this might suggest the need for price stabilisation policies but we shall not investigate welfare consequences in this paper.

The rest of the paper proceeds as follows. Section I outlines the model, Section II analyses the growth process and investigates the behaviour of the terms of trade, and Section III gives a brief conclusion.

I. THE MODEL

Following common practice in North–South models, the world is assumed to consist of two regions, the North and the South, and commodities are classified into two groups; agricultural and manufactured. The North uses labour and capital to produce manufactured goods, which are either sold to the South or re-invested as capital goods, or consumed. The South uses land, labour and capital to produce agricultural goods which are consumed in both regions. In the light of the discussion in the previous section, we assume that, in both regions,

(i) the level of output is supply determined and there is no 'Keynesian' demand failure,
(ii) real wages are fixed exogenously and labour is available in surplus
(iii) all wages are consumed and all profits are invested,

and in the south,

(iv) all rents are consumed too, and finally,
(v) *either*, surplus land exists and the rental rate is exogenous *or*, land is scarce and its growth rate is exogenous

I.1. *The South*

The production function in the South is assumed to be Cobb–Douglas with three factors, $Q_s = \Theta L_s^{(1-\alpha-\beta)} K_s^\alpha Z_s^\beta$, where Q, L, K and Z denote ouput, labour, capital and land respectively, subscript 's' stands for South, Θ, α and β are postive constant parameters and $0 < (\alpha+\beta) < 1$. Labour is assumed to be available in surplus at the given real wage rate w_s, fixed in terms of agricultural goods, and labour utilisation, L_s, is obtained by setting its marginal product equal to the real wage rate, namely

$$L_s = \lambda Q_s, \qquad (1)$$

where $\lambda = (1-\alpha-\beta)/w_s$. Using (1) and lettering

$$\sigma_s = \mu (Z_s/K_s)^\gamma, \qquad (2)$$

where $\gamma = \beta/(\alpha+\beta)$ and $\mu = [\Theta \lambda^{(1-\alpha-\beta)}]^{1/(\alpha+\beta)}$, the production function may be rewritten as

$$Q_s = \sigma_s K_s. \qquad (3)$$

We consider two cases with regard to land availability. On the one hand land may be avilable in surplus at an exogenous rental rate r, fixed in terms of the agricultural goods, and land utilisation is derived by setting its marginal product equal to the rental rate: $Z_s = (\beta/r) Q_s$. This implies a constant output/capital ratio

$$\sigma_s = [\Theta \lambda^{(1-\alpha-\beta)} (\beta/r)^\beta]^{1/\alpha} \qquad (2.1)$$

In this case both labour and land will be used in constant proportions with respect to capital. On the other hand it is possible to assume that land is scarce, with Z_s growing at a constant exogenous rate, and with the rental rate determined by its marginal product, $r = (\beta/Z_s) Q_s$. In this case the output/capital ratio, σ_s, is a variable and is determined by equation (2).

Denoting profits by Π, we have $\Pi_s = Q_s - (w_s L_s + r Z_s)$. After substituting for the term in brackets we obtain

$$\Pi_s = \alpha Q_s. \qquad (4)$$

Both wages and rents are assumed to be entirely consumed where, for simplicity, consumption is restricted to agricultural goods only; and profits are assumed to be entirely used for purchasing manufactured goods produced in the North, which are invested and used in the production process:

$$I_s = p\Pi_s, \qquad (5)$$

where $p(\equiv P_s/P_n)$ is the terms of trade and I denotes investment. Neglecting depreciation, we have $I_s = dK_s/dt\ (\equiv \dot{K}_s)$. Substituting from (5), (4) and (3) into the above yields

$$\dot{K}_s = \alpha \sigma_s p K_s. \qquad (6)$$

This equation describes the growth mechanism in the South.

I.2. *The North*

Production technology in the North is assumed, for simplicity, to be of a fixed coefficient type. Given the assumption of freely available labour supply, we may write the production function as follows[2]

$$Q_n = \sigma_n K_n, \tag{7}$$

$$L_n = lQ_n, \tag{8}$$

where σ_n and l are constant parameters and subscript 'n' corresponds to North.

Northern consumption consists of both manufactured goods and agricultural products and preferences are assumed to be Cobb–Douglas where δ is the proportion of wages spent on manufactured goods. The cost of living index is defined by $\phi = P_n^\delta P_s^{1-\delta}$, and the real wage rate, w_n, is assumed fixed so that money wages are $w_n \phi$. Letting D_n and C_n denote consumption of manufactured and agricultural goods in the North, respectively, and assuming that wages are consumed entirely, we have $P_n D_n = \delta \phi w_n L_n$ and $P_s C_n = (1-\delta) \phi w_n L_n$, or, substituting for ϕ and using the terms of trade definition, we get

$$D_n = \delta \eta Q_n P^{1-\delta} \tag{9}$$

$$C_n = (1-\delta) \eta Q_n P^{-\delta} \tag{10}$$

where $\eta = w_n l$. Since all wages are consumed, profits in the North are given by $\Pi_n = Q_n - (D_n + pC_n)$, or, substituting from (9) and (10)

$$\Pi_n = (1 - \eta p^{1-\delta}) Q_n. \tag{11}$$

Profits are assumed to be entirely invested

$$I_n = \Pi_n \tag{12}$$

and, neglecting depreciation, we have $\dot{K}_n = I_n$. By substituting from (7), (11) and (12) into the above we obtain the growth equation for the North

$$\dot{K}_n = \sigma_n (1 - \eta p^{1-\delta}) K_n. \tag{13}$$

I.3. *Trade Balance, Market Clearing, and the Terms of Trade*

We have assumed, for both the North and the South, that total expenditure equals total income and that there is no accumulation of financial assets (i.e. money, bonds, etc.). Thus in neither the North not the South is there any excess of income over expenditure, and trade balance prevails between the regions at all times. The model contains two markets: agricultural and industrial goods. By Walras' law, we need to write the market clearing condition for only one of the markets. For the former, market clearing requires that the surplus over Southern consumption is purchased by the North. That is,

$$C_n = \Pi_s. \tag{14}$$

---

[2] We emphasise that fixed coefficient technology for the North is merely assumed in order to simplify the analysis. By contrast, flexible technology in the South is necessary when land is assumed to be scarce.

Equation (14) completes the model. We solve for the terms of trade, p, at any instant by substituting (4) and (10) into (14) to obtain[3]

$$p = [(1-\delta)\eta\sigma_n/\alpha\sigma_s]^{1/\delta} k^{1/\delta} \qquad (15)$$

where $k \equiv K_n/K_s$. This equation has a straightforward interpretation. At any moment in time K_n and K_s are predetermined. Low K_s means, *ceteris paribus*, a low agricultural surplus and high K_n implies, *ceteris paribus*, large employment in the North and hence a large demand for the agricultural surplus. This corresponds to the case of a high k and, as equation (15) shows, p must then be high to curtail demand.

II. THE GROWTH PROCESS AND THE BEHAVIOUR OF THE TERMS OF TRADE

In this section we derive the conditions for balanced growth equilibrium, where both regions grow at the same rate,[4] and investigate the implications for the terms of trade. Two cases are considered. First we assume that land is available in surplus. Then we constrain the land availability and let it grow at a constant rate. In each case we examine the adjustment process following an increase in agricultural productivity.

II.1. *Surplus Land*

In this case the rental rate is fixed and the output/capital ratio, σ_s, remains constant and is given by (2.1). From (6) and (13) we have

$$\hat{K}_s = \alpha\sigma_s p, \qquad (6.1)$$

$$\hat{K}_n = \sigma_n(1 - \eta p^{1-\delta}) \qquad (13.1)$$

where '^' denotes the rate of growth of a variable. These imply that relative capital growth, $\hat{k} = \hat{K}_n - \hat{K}_s$, is

$$\hat{k} = \sigma_n - \eta\sigma_n p^{1-\delta} - \alpha\sigma_s p \qquad (16)$$

Equations (15) and (16) can be used to determine the equilibrium values, k^* and p^*, when $\hat{k} = 0$ and balanced growth pevails. Fig. 1 depicts the situation: (15) is drawn in Fig. 1(a) as OP_0, Fig. 1(b) gives graphs of (6.1) and (13.1) which are labelled as KS_0 and KN respectively, and (16) is shown in Fig. 1(c) as kk_0. These show the equilibrium situation (k_0^*, p_0^*) where $\hat{K}_n = \hat{K}_s = \hat{K}^*$. The adjustment process can be explained as follows: a large value of k implies a higher p (see equation (15)) and the latter results in a negative value for $\hat{k}$ (see equation (16)). Thus when k is high it is falling and vice versa, giving rise to

---

[3] We assume that the new market-clearing terms of trade is established immediately and do not study the dynamics of its determination.

[4] Both regions grow at the same rate in equilibrium because we assume (for simplicity) unitary income elasticities of demand for both agricultural and manufactured goods. Such a simplifying assumption is present in the basic Ricardian model, and in Findlay (1980) and Taylor (1983), but not in Lewis (1954). See Canning (1988) for a Kaldorian model with increasing-returns in the industrial sector and an equlibrium in which industrial growth is faster than the growth of primary commodity output.

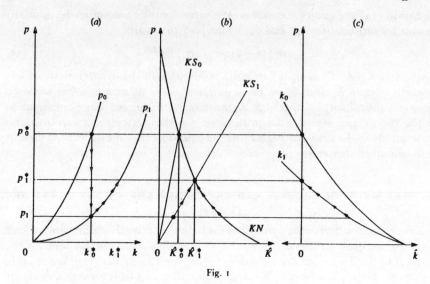

Fig. 1

a stable adjustment process, and the convergence path to an equilibrium is monotonic.

It is now possible to analyse the effect of an increase in capital productivity σ_s in the South. A rise in σ_s can be achieved, as seen from equations (2) and (2.1), by either technical progress (an increase in Θ), or a change in technology (a higher β). The increase in capital productivity will change the terms of trade p. The *final* change, in new balanced growth equilibrium when again $\hat{k} = 0$, can be otained by differentiating equation (16) with respect to σ_s.[5]

$$\partial p/\partial \sigma_s = -(p/\sigma_s)/[1+(1-\delta)\,\eta\sigma_n p^{-\delta}/\sigma_s\alpha]. \qquad (17)$$

As shown in Fig. 1, OP_0 and KS_0 rotate outward to OP_1 and KS_1, and p_0^* falls to p_1^*. This change in p is less than proportionate to the increase in σ_s, i.e. $|(p/\sigma_s)(\partial p/\partial \sigma_s)| < 1$. The reason is obvious from (6.1) and (13.1): if the fall were as much as proportionate then Southern growth would be unaffected by the rise in σ_s whereas Northern growth would rise, contradicting the assumption of growth equilibrium. The *initial* fall in p, at the instant σ_s changes, is larger than the ultimate fall. This can be seen by differentiating (15) with respect σ_s holding k constant,

$$\left.\partial p/\partial \sigma_s\right|_{dk=0} = -p/\delta\sigma_s \qquad (18)$$

[5] This can be obtained by setting the derivative of the right-hand side of (16) with respect to σ_s equal to zero,

$$(1-\delta)\,\eta\sigma_n p^{-\delta}(\partial p/\partial \sigma_s) + \alpha\sigma_s(\partial p/\partial \sigma_s) + \alpha p = 0,$$

which can be rearranged as

$$(\partial p/\partial \sigma_s) = -\alpha p/[\alpha\sigma_s + (1-\delta)\,\eta\sigma_n p^{-\delta}], \text{ giving (17)}.$$

This is a larger impact than that shown in (17), and it is shown as a drop from p_0^* to p_1 in Fig. 1. We see that initially the terms of trade 'overshoot' their full equilibrium. The adjustment process, from p_1 to p_1^*, is shown in Fig. 1 and is stable. During the adjustment process the growth rate of the North exceeds that of the South. We can thus infer that the new ratio of capital stocks, k_1^*, will be larger than its previous level.[6] Also note from Fig. 1 that initially, because p falls so much, growth in the South actually falls, i.e. the increase in σ_s is initially 'immiserising' for the South.[7] Finally, observe that at the new equilibrium there will be a higher rate of growth of capital stocks in both regions,[8] and that the North benefits from a relative increase in the price of manufactured goods.

Our 'overshooting' result is similar to that obtained by Burgstaller (1985). In our model, however, overshooting of the terms of trade occurs because initially the price p must clear the market for agricultural goods, in the absence of other adjustments in the factors underlying supply and demand. But gradually the changes in K_n and K_s, and therefore k, come to bear some of the burden. This is an example of the Samuelson–Le Chatelier principle.

II.2. Fixed Growth of Land

We now turn our attention to the case where the available land is restricted to grow at a fixed rate n, that is

$$\hat{Z}_s = n. \qquad (19)$$

Recall, from equation (2), that in this case σ_s is no longer a constant. Let z denote the land/capital ratio, $z = Z_s/K_s$, so we have

$$\hat{z} = \hat{Z}_s - \hat{K}_s \qquad (20)$$

and from (2)

$$\sigma_s = \mu z^\gamma. \qquad (2.2)$$

Substituting into (6) and (13) we obtain

$$p = [(1-\delta)\,\eta\sigma_n/\alpha\mu]^{1/\delta} z^{-\gamma/\delta} k^{1/\delta}, \qquad (15.1)$$

$$\hat{k} = \sigma_n - \eta\sigma_n p^{1-\delta} - \alpha\mu z^\gamma p, \qquad (16.1)$$

$$\hat{z} = n - (\alpha\mu)\,z^\gamma p. \qquad (21)$$

---

[6] This can be seen by writing equation (15) as $k = [\alpha/(1-\delta)\,\eta\sigma_n]\,\sigma_s p^\delta$, whose derivative with respect to σ_s is

$$\partial k/\partial\sigma_s = k/\sigma_s + (\delta\sigma_s/p)\,\partial p/\partial\sigma_s$$
$$= (k/\sigma_s)[1 + \delta(\sigma_s/p)\,\partial p\partial\sigma_s],$$

which is positive because $(\sigma_s/p)\,\partial p/\partial\sigma_s > -1$, from (17), and $\delta < 1$.

[7] The initial effect on $\hat{K}_s$ is obtained by differentiating (6.1) with respect to σ_s,

$$\partial\hat{K}_s/\partial\sigma_s = \alpha p + \alpha\sigma_s(\partial p/\partial\sigma_s)$$
$$= \alpha p[1 + (\sigma_s/p)(\partial p/\partial\sigma_s)]$$

and substituting from (18) to get $\partial\hat{K}_s/\partial\sigma_s = \alpha p(1 - 1/\delta) < 0$.

[8] This may be verified by substituting (17) instead of (18) into the derivative of (6.1), obtained in footnote (7).

Balanced growth equilibrium is obtained by setting $(\hat{z},\hat{k}) = (0,0)$, and solving the above for z, k and p. This yields

$$z^* = \{(n/\alpha\mu)/[(\sigma_n-n)/\eta\sigma_n]^{1/(\delta-1)}\}^{1/\gamma} \tag{22.1}$$

$$k^* = n/(1-\delta)(\sigma_n-n), \tag{22.2}$$

$$p^* = [(\sigma_n-n)/\eta\sigma_n]^{1/(1-\delta)}, \tag{22.3}$$

$$\hat{K}_s^* = \hat{K}_n^* = \hat{Z}_s = n. \tag{22.4}$$

Thus, the equilibrium growth rate is now constrained by the rate at which new land becomes available. Note also that, apart from the rate of growth of land, only Northern parameters affect the level of p^* (and that $\sigma_n > n$ is required for an equilibrium to exist). The model now has 'fully Ricardian' long-run properties, in the sense that the availability of land in the South constrains the growth of both regions: the terms of trade adjust to make the North grow at this rate. Any tendency of the North to grow faster (caused by, say, a higher δ_n) will be fully thwarted by a worsening of its terms of trade. This model is, in a sense, a polar opposite to that of Findlay (1980) in which the growth of primary commodities adapts to the exogenous rate of growth of the Northern labour force. Burgstaller (1985) also provides a Ricardian model of accumulation.

The dynamic system defined by equations (15.1), (16.1) and (21) is nonlinear. To study disequilibrium dynamics and stability, we first eliminate p and then examine the linear approximation of the system in the neighbourhood of an arbitrary equilibrium $(\bar{z},\bar{k})$. The linear system is

$$\hat{z} = a_1 + b_1 z - c_1 k, \tag{23}$$

$$\hat{k} = a_2 + b_2 z - c_2 k, \tag{24}$$

where a_i, b_i and c_i are constant, and it can be shown that $b_i > 0$, $c_i > 0$ and $(c_1/b_1) > (c_2/b_2)$.[9] These equations are used to construct Fig. 2, where OZ and OK correspond to (23) and (24) for $\hat{z} = 0$ and $\hat{k} = 0$, respectively. OZ is upward sloping since a high value of z depresses the terms of trade p to such an extent that $\hat{K}_s$ falls and $\hat{z}$ rises, unless at the same time k is sufficiently large partly to offset the fall in p. OK is also upward sloping because a higher z depresses the terms of trade p, reduces $\hat{K}_s$ and increases $\hat{K}_n$, unless at the same time k is sufficiently large to raise p and bring $\hat{K}_n$ and $\hat{K}_s$ into equality, as required by $\hat{k} = 0$. Furthermore, OK is flatter than OZ. This follows because, after any increase in z, the rise in k which ensures $\hat{z} = 0$ will leave $\hat{K}_s$ unchanged. But that still involves a lower p and higher $\hat{K}_n$, and so k must be increased and p raised further, to bring $\hat{K}_n$ and $\hat{K}_s$ into equality, as required along OK. Finally, it is clear from (23) and (24) that $\hat{k}$ is negative (positive) below (above) the OK line and that $\hat{z}$ is positive (negative) to the left (right) of the OZ line. The arrows in Fig. 2 show how (k,z) moves towards or away from the equilibrium point E,

---

[9] The linearisation is lengthy and tedious, and has been eliminated because of lack of space. A mathematical appendix can be found in Molana and Vines (1988), available from the authors on request.

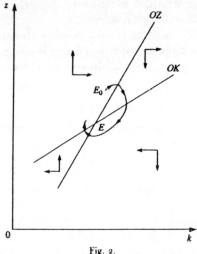

Fig. 2.

where OZ and OK intersect. Adjustment paths may be cyclical or even unstable.

To examine the properties of the model, under the assumption of scarce land, we again consider a departure from equilibrium by increasing the agricultural productivity. This can be achieved by increasing μ in (2.2) and would initially imply a higher value of σ_s, causing effects rather similar to the case considered in the previous subsection. But equations (22.1–22.4) show that the equilibrium level of k and p will now remain unaffected; z^* falls to offset the impact of a change in μ fully. What happens is that, as a result of an increase in μ, extra capital is accumulated in both sectors, but (if the system is stable) eventually their relative size and their growth rates will return to initial levels and production will be relatively more capital intensive in the South. In Fig. 2, the new intersection of OZ and OK will be vertically below the old one.

The immediate short-run effect on p can be obtained by differentiating (15.1), holding other things constant.

$$\partial p/\partial \mu \bigg|_{dk=dz=0} = -(1/\delta)p/\mu. \qquad (25)$$

Thus in the scarce-land case, as in the surplus-land case, the terms of trade would exhibit a sharp fall in response to an increase in South's productivity.[10] However, here p returns all the way to its initial level whilst in the earlier case it only partly did so.

Finally, consider the adjustment process. Suppose that in Fig. 2, point E is the new equilibrium, lying below the original equilibrium point E_0, say. The phase arrows show that the initial fall in p causes $\hat{k}$ to become positive. But it also causes $\hat{z}$ to become positive. Equilibrium at E requires more K_s and a lower z, but $\hat{K}_s$ has fallen. If, for example, the price elasticity of demand for

---

[10] Here, too, the initial effect of the increase in μ is to immiserise the South.

agricultural goods in the north, δ, is too small the initial fall in p and $\hat{K}_s$ may be so severe that agricultural capital accumulation may be unable to keep pace with the growth of land, whose increasing relative abundance will then make p fall even further. Even if the adjustment process is stable, cycles of under and over investment are likely to result (as shown in the Fig.), leading to cycles in the terms of trade.

III. CONCLUSIONS

In this paper we have formalised Kaldor's North–South model. The model assumes surplus labour and fixed real wages in both regions and allows for substitution in consumption between manufactured and agricultural goods in the North. We have analysed the model with both surplus and scarce land in the South. It is shown that in the case of an exogenous disturbance the terms of trade may overshoot its new equilibrium value and/or converge cyclically. The model identifies a low price elasticity of demand for agricultural goods as a potential source of such cycles. It is possible that these cycles may lead to adjustment costs and output losses which we have not considered here. Within its own terms, however, the model supports Kaldor's (1976) conjecture that the price mechanism 'tends to set up perverse cycles in world industrial activity' (p. 713). In order to provide a formal support for Kaldor's conclusion regarding the need for price stabilisation policies one should conduct explicit welfare analysis (See Kanbur and Vines, 1986).

We conclude by noting that our model is rather simple. One could, like Findlay, introduce an exogenous growth of labour and allow real wages to be determined endogenously in the North, or incorporate a flexible choice of technique for the North. It is also possible, although technically more demanding, to introduce 'Keynesian' features by allowing for savings and financial assets which would enable one to examine the balance of payments and debt issues. Marglin (1984) shows how these features could be incorporated within an analysis of the inflationary process in the North.

University of Glasgow

Date of receipt of final typescript: October 1988

REFERENCES

Burgstaller, A. (1985). 'North-South trade and capital flow in a Ricardian model of accumulation.' *Journal of International Economics*, vol. 18, pp. 241–60.
Canning, D. (1988). 'Increasing returns in industry and the role of agriculture in growth'. *Oxford Economic Papers*, forthcoming.
Costabile, L. and Rowthorn, R. (1985). 'Malthus' theory of output and growth.' ECONOMIC JOURNAL, vol. 95, pp. 418–37.
Currie, D., Muscatelli, A. and Vines, D. (1988). 'Introduction.' In *North South Macroeconomic Interactions* (D. Currie, and D. Vines, eds.). Cambridge: Cambridge University Press.
Findlay, R. (1980). 'The terms and trade and equilibrium growth in the world economy.' *American Economic Review*, vol. 70, pp. 291–9.
Kaldor, N. (1976). 'Inflation and recession in the world economy.' ECONOMIC JOURNAL, vol. 86, pp. 703–14.
—— (1979). 'Equilibrium theory and growth theory.' In *Economics and Human Welfare: Essays in Honour of Tibor Skitovsky* (ed. M. Baskia). Academic Press.

Kanbur, S. M. R. and Vines, D. (1986). 'North South interaction and Commodity Control.' *Journal of Development Economics*, vol. 23, pp. 371–87.

Lewis, W. A. (1954). 'Economic development with unlimited supplies of labour.' *Manchester School*, vol. 22, pp. 139–91.

—— (1972). 'Reflections on unlimited labour.' In *International Economics and Development: Essays in Honour of Raol Prebisch* (ed. L. Di Marco). Academic Press.

Marglin, S. (1984). 'Growth, distribution and inflation: a centennial synthesis.' *Cambridge Journal of Economics*, vol. 8, pp. 115–44.

Molana, H. and Vines, D. (1988). 'North–South growth and terms of trade: a model on Kaldorian lines.' Centre for Economic Policy Research Discussion Paper No. 248.

Solow, R. (1956). 'A contribution to the theory of economic growth.' *Quarterly Journal of Economics*, vol. 70, 65–94.

Taylor, L. (1983). *Structuralist Macroeconomics*, New York: Basic Books.

Thirlwall, A. P. (1986). 'A general model of growth and development along Kaldorian lines.' *Oxford Economic Papers*, vol. 38, pp. 199–219.

Vines, D. A. (1984). 'A North–South growth model along Kaldorian lines.' Centre for Economic Policy Research, Discussion Paper No. 26.

A KALDORIAN MODEL OF GROWTH AND DEVELOPMENT REVISITED: A COMMENT ON THIRLWALL

By AMITAVA KRISHNA DUTT*

1. Introduction

THIRLWALL (1986, 1987) has recently developed a formal presentation of Kaldor's (1975, 1979) model of the world economy examining the dynamic interaction between primary and secondary sectors, and thereby contributed to our understanding of Kaldorian growth and development economics. On the basis of his model, Thirlwall has claimed that the Kaldorian model captures the essence of the interaction of the agricultural and industrial sectors *within* dual, less developed economies, that is, the complementarity between outputs of the two sectors within the framework of reciprocal demand, and in particular, the role of the agricultural sector in providing a market for the industrial sector. By so doing, Thirlwall claims that the model is superior to earlier models of agriculture-industry interaction for less developed economies.

The purpose of this paper is to argue that there are problems with Thirlwall's specification of the structure of the Kaldorian model,[1] with its underlying dynamics, and with his claim that the model makes an advance over earlier dual economy models with regard to analysis of the contribution of agriculture to the market for industry. To do so, Section 2 develops the formal Kaldorian model,[2] Section 3 analyzes its underlying dynamics, and Section 4 comments on the role of demand in the model.

2. A Kaldorian model

Consider a closed economy with two sectors, an agricultural and an industrial sector, each producing one good. The agricultural good is a pure consumption good, while the industrial good can be both consumed and invested. Both goods are sold in perfectly competitive goods markets.[3]

In the agricultural sector labour, land and capital are used for production. Labour is in unlimited supply and has zero marginal product so that its level

---

* I am grateful to two anonymous referees of this journal for their perceptive comments and useful suggestions. I would like to thank the participants of a workshop on Dynamic Models at Clare Hall, Cambridge, and Bill Gibson and Michael Landesmann, for their comments.

[1] A similar Kaldorian model has also been developed by Targetti (1985), and many of our criticisms apply to that model as well.

[2] We will develop a model which uses an internally-consistent set of assumptions which produces a model identical to the one developed by Kaldor, and use our version of the model for our critical analysis. This should not be taken to imply that it is not possible to develop models with alternative assumptions which also produce Kaldor's model, but our critical analysis remains valid unless this alternative analysis, which negates our critical discussion, is actually developed.

[3] This may appear to contradict Kaldor (1975, 1979). But see below.

does not affect output. Land is given. Output may increase over time due to land-saving technical change, but this requires capital investment. Assuming strict complementarity between capital and this type of technical change, we have

$$Q_a = a_a K_a \qquad (1)$$

where Q_i denotes output, a_i the capital-output ratio, and K_i the capital stock, all in sector i, and where the subscript a refers to the agricultural sector. Note that the assumption of perfect competition ensures that production fully utilizes capacity. It is assumed that a fixed fraction s_a of total agricultural output is saved, and all agricultural saving is invested within the agricultural sector, so that

$$s_a P_a Q_a = P_n I_a \qquad (2)$$

where P_i denotes (money) price, and I_i investment, in sector i, and the subscript n denotes the industrial sector. Dividing through by K_a, and denoting the rate of growth of capital in agriculture (which, in the absence of depreciation, is I_a/K_a) by g_a, we get

$$g_a = s_a a_a / p \qquad (3)$$

where $p = P_n/P_a$, the industrial terms of trade.

In the industrial sector output is produced with labour and capital using fixed-coefficients technology. The labour-output ratio is b_n and the output-capital ratio is a_n. Perfect competition ensures full capacity utilization, so that

$$Q_n = a_n K_n \qquad (4)$$

Labour, as assumed above, is abundant, and this is formalized by assuming that it is available to the industrial sector at a constant wage in terms of the agricultural good,[4] so that

$$W_n / P_a = \tau \qquad (5)$$

where τ is the fixed level, and W_n is the industrial (money) wage; firms hire all the workers they need at this wage. The workers consume all their income and capitalists, who earn the profits, save a fixed fraction s_n of their income. All saving in the industrial sector is invested in that sector. Our assumptions imply, using equation (5), that

$$P_n I_n = s_n [P_n - (\tau b_n P_a)] Q_n \qquad (6)$$

Dividing through by $P_n K_n$ and using (4) gives the equation for the growth-rate of industrial capital,

$$g_n = s_n [1 - (\tau b_n / p)] a_n \qquad (7)$$

where industrial capital is assumed to be non-depreciating.

[4] Kaldor (1979) took this to be fixed by custom. Following Lewis (1954), we could fix it in terms of average worker (or peasant) income in the agricultural sector, making appropriate assumptions regarding the institutional structure of agriculture.

Regarding consumption spending we assume, for simplicity, that a fixed fraction α of total consumption expenditure is spent on the industrial good, and the rest on the agricultural good.

To examine the determination of the equilibrium growth rate of capital and the terms of trade in the economy, we bring equations (3) and (7) together in the right-hand side of Fig. 1, which is Kaldor's diagram. Equation (3) yields the g_a curve, and equation (7) yields the g_n curve which has a p-intercept of τb_n and a g-asymptote of $s_n a_n$. Defining equilibrium to be a state at which capital (and with fixed output-capital ratios, output) in the two sectors grows at the same rate, equilibrium is seen to be established at the intersection of the g_a and g_n curves and the equilibrium terms of trade and growth rates are, respectively,

$$p^* = (s_a a_a / s_n a_n) + \tau b_n \qquad (8)$$

$$g^* = s_n a_n s_a a_a / (s_a a_a + \tau b_n s_n a_n). \qquad (9)$$

Increases in the parameters s_a and a_a shift the g_a curve to the right and increase g^* and p^*, and increases in s_n and a_n and reductions in τ and b_n shift the g_n curve to right and increase g^* and reduce p^*. Note that the pattern of consumption expenditure, given by α, has no effect at all on the equilibrium values of g and p.

So far the model appears to be the same as Thirlwall's, apart from some minor differences having to do with the fact that he assumes that all industrial saving is invested, and does not make specific assumptions about the agricultural savings rate.[5] The significant difference between our model and Thirlwall's concerns the nature of industrial pricing. While he takes the agricultural market to be competitive, so that the price of the agricultural good varies to clear the market, Thirlwall assumes the industrial market to be non-competitive, and firms set the price as a markup on unit labour costs. Here he follows Kaldor (1975, 1979), who uses Kalecki's (1971) pricing formula,

$$P_n = (1 + z)W_n b_n \qquad (10)$$

where z is the fixed markup rate, determined by the degree of monopoly in industry. Dividing by P_a this implies

$$p = (1 + z)\tau b_n \qquad (11)$$

which is exactly Kaldor's equation in our notation. Instead of making this

---

[5] For example, Thirlwall conducts the analysis in terms of a rate of agricultural surplus instead of a savings rate, and then assumes away the consumption of manufactured goods in the agricultural sector, suggesting that such consumption will shift the g_a curve (our notation) downwards. This analysis is incomplete since it is not explained how this curve can be derived when manufactured goods are consumed in the agricultural sector. Moreover, this analysis conceals an interesting property of the model, that is, that the equilibrium rate of growth of the model depends on the saving rate in agriculture, and not on the marketed surplus rate which depends on both the saving rate and α.

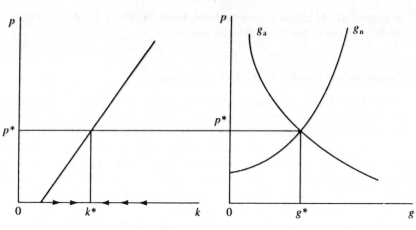

Fig. 1.

price-making assumption, we have assumed price-taking behaviour for both sectors.

We part company with Kaldor and Thirlwall because the markup-pricing assumption is inconsistent with the rest of the model.[6] First, if z, τ and b_n are exogenously fixed, as markup pricing and the rest of the assumptions imply, (11) fixes the terms of trade: thus they are not free to vary, and there is no reason for it to be consistent with the equilibrium level given by (8). Second, Kalecki's (1971) markup-pricing theory assumes that firms adjust quantities and not prices, and this requires that they operate with excess capacity (assuming fixed coefficients as is assumed in all our models).[7] Yet, our model assumes full capacity utilization, which is implicitly assumed also by Thirlwall when he assumes a constant capital-output ratio in industry which is necessary for deriving equation (7) and drawing the g_n curve; it also seems to be implicit in Kaldor's own diagram.[8]

Thirlwall's error does not interfere with his formal model because the markup-pricing assumption plays no part in it. He does not use it in discussing the model, except for mentioning in an unnecessary footnote (p. 209) that quantities (and not prices) are assumed to adjust in the industrial sector. This does not mean, however, that the error is harmless: it will be argued later that

---

[6] Our criticisms also apply to Targetti (1985) who also assumes markup pricing in industry.

[7] Markup-pricing and full-capacity utilization can be made consistent with each other, but only if there is some other mechanism which clears the market. FitzGerald (1990), in his formalization of one of Kalecki's (1972) models, assumes that the government changes the tax rate to clear the industrial market.

[8] Imperfect competition and a variable markup rate are not necessarily inconsistent. For example, the actual market rate can vary to clear the market and the degree of monopoly can set a lower bound to the markup. However, this makes the model formally equivalent to the perfectly competitive model *as long as* the markup is above the minimum set by monopoly power.

it is related to Thirlwall's incorrect emphasis on the role of agriculture in providing a market for the industrial sector.

3. Dynamics and stability in the Kaldorian model

While we have so far defined equilibrium in our Kaldorian model to refer to a state in which the growth-rates of the two sectors are equal, we now turn to a discussion of dynamics behind equilibrium and the question of stability.

This issue is briefly discussed by Thirlwall, who postulates an adjustment equation which makes the discrete-time change in the agricultural terms of trade, $q(=1/p)$, depend linearly on the difference between the sectoral growth rates ($g_n - g_a$, in our notation), and shows that equilibrium will be stable unless the coefficient showing the speed of adjustment is 'too great'. Thirlwall appears to believe that 'quantities are assumed to adjust in the industrial sector and prices in the agricultural sector, in response to a disequilibrium between supply and demand' (p. 209n), but this analysis is not pursued correctly. He argues that for a disequilibrium terms of trade, g_a and g_n are unequal, which implies a gap between the capacity of the industrial sector to grow and the growth warranted by the demand for its product from the agricultural sector, but he fails to point out why these magnitudes should be interpreted as demands and supplies, and why such a gap should lead to price adjustments except for a vague reference to the 'behaviour of food dealers and merchants' (p. 209). Given the competitive market assumption for the agricultural good, the adjustment equation is rather strange, for it implies that if the two sectors grow at the same rate, there will be no change in the terms of trade, even if there is an excess supply and demand in the agricultural market. The alternative Thirlwall suggests in a footnote, 'to consider adjustments of the terms of trade to differences in the *levels* of demand and supply', would seem to be clearly preferable.

To follow this route, however, we need an explicit statement of the characteristics of disequilibrium states, and of the dynamics when the economy is in disequilibrium. We consider two simple and plausible characterizations of such disequilibria and dynamics.

The first distinguishes between the short run in which sectoral levels of capital stock are given and the relative price varies to clear the goods markets, and the long run in which the stocks of capital grow due to investment. Market clearing in agriculture and industry, respectively, imply:

$$Q_a = (1-\alpha)\{[\tau b_n + (1-s_n)(p-\tau b_n')]Q_n + (1-s_a)Q_a\} \tag{12}$$

$$pQ_n = \alpha\{[\tau b_n + (1-s_n)(p-\tau b_n')]Q_n + (1-s_a)Q_a\} + p(I_n + Ia). \tag{13}$$

Equations (2), (6) and (12) imply equation (13), which shows that the clearing of the agricultural market implies the clearing of the industrial one, so that we may confine attention to only the former. We assume that in the short run p responds positively to excess supply in the agricultural market (or excess demand for the industrial good), and formalize this with the equation

$$dp/dt = \Theta\{[\alpha + s_a(1-\alpha)]a_a k - (1-\alpha)[(1-s_n)p + s_n\tau b_n]a_n\} \quad (14)$$

where $\Theta > 0$ is an adjustment coefficient, $k = K_a/K_n$, and the terms within curly brackets is excess supply of agricultural goods divided by K_n. In the short run, given k (with given K_a and K_n), p adjusts according to this equation. Since dp/dt is negatively related to p the adjustment process is stable, so that the economy converges to short-run equilibrium, when $dp/dt = 0$, where

$$p = \{[(\alpha/(1-\alpha)) + s_a]a_a/(1-s_n)a_n\}k - \tau b_n s_n/(1-s_n). \quad (15)$$

This equation can be represented by the line in the left-hand side of Fig. 1. For any k, the short-run equilibrium value of p can be read off from this curve, and the short-run equilibrium values of g_a and g_n can be read off from the g_a and g_n curves.[9] In the long run, k changes according to

$$dk/dt = k(g_a - g_n) \quad (16)$$

which implies, using (3) and (7),

$$dk/dt = k\{(s_a a_a/p) - s_n[1 - (\tau b_n/p)]a_n\} \quad (17)$$

At long-run equilibrium, when $dk/dt = 0$, the expression within curly brackets must vanish, which implies that $g_a = g_n$. This long-run equilibrium is stable, since a rise (fall) in k implies a rise (fall) in p (from equation (15)) which in turn reduces (increases) dk/dt (by equation (17)). The convergence to long-run equilibrium can be shown using Fig. 1: starting from any k above (below) the long-run equilibrium one it can be seen that g_n is greater (less) than g_a, implying that k falls (rises) over time to take the economy to the equilibrium, as shown by the arrows.

The second characterization assumes that p is sticky, but that it adjusts over time.[10] Here p and k are given at a point in time and over time p adjusts according to (14) and k according to (17). The equilibrium for this characterization will be the same as that in the previous one, but the dynamics are different, as shown in Fig. 2. The pp line shows combinations of p and k at which $dp/dt = 0$ and is given by (16). Similarly, the kk line shows combinations of p and k at which $dk/dt = 0$, and is seen from (17) to be given by (8). As illustrated in the figure, the dynamics may be cyclical, but the equilibrium is

---

[9] For meaningful short-run equilibrium with positive rates of accumulation in both sectors we require $p > \tau b_n$ (see equations (3) and (7)). From (15) this can be shown to imply

$$k > \tau b_n a_n/[(\alpha/(1-\alpha)) + s_n]a_a.$$

If this condition is not satisfied, the relative size of the agricultural sector becomes too large to allow market clearing at a relative price sufficient to allow any industrial profits and hence industrial capital accumulation.

[10] There are problems of reconciling fixed prices and excess supplies and demands which we do not go into here, following the fix-price disequilibrium models which assume perfect competition.

A KALDORIAN MODEL REVISITED

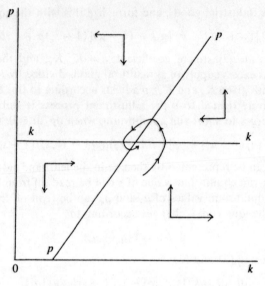

FIG. 2.

necessarily stable, as can be seen by evaluating the Jacobian of the system around the equilibrium, given by

$$\begin{bmatrix} -(1-\alpha)(1-s_n)a_n\Theta & [\alpha + s_a(1-\alpha)]a_a\Theta \\ -(s_a a_a + s_n \tau b_n)/p^2 & 0 \end{bmatrix}$$

which has a negative trace and a positive determinant, which is sufficient for local stability.[11]

Whichever characterization we adopt, for given p, equations (3) and (7) give us growth rates of K_a and K_n, and these can be read off from the right-hand side of Fig. 1. For any given p we find the *actual* rates of growth of the two sectors, and these growth-rates move over time to take the economy to long-run equilibrium.

4. The role of demand

As mentioned above, Thirlwall emphasizes the role of agriculture in providing a market for the industrial good, and claims that the Kaldorian model is superior to Lewis's (1954, 1972) because the latter did not take demand factors into account. He stresses the importance of demand by labelling the Kaldor curves g_d and g_s (our g_a and g_n curves, respectively), stating that the agricultural growth rate curve represents 'the rate of growth of purchasing power, or demand, over industrial goods' (p. 204).

---

[11] If the market for the agricultural does not clear rapidly enough, in practice rationing and/or parallel markets will emerge. We have abstracted from such complications here.

While it is true that in the Kaldorian model the agricultural sectors buys products from the industrial sector, and a higher rate of agricultural growth implies a higher rate of growth of the demand for the industrial good (both for investment and consumption purposes)—and this is shown by the fact that in our model an upward shift in g_a will imply a higher equilibrium rate of growth of the industrial sector—this is true for *any* model in which the two sectors trade with each other. In the Kaldorian model the industrial good is demanded also within that sector, and if it grows more rapidly due to internal reasons (say due an increase in s_n) it will create a market for its own increased output. This is because each sector always (identically) invests its entire saving within the sector, and there is therefore no demand problem in any sector: if they sell their product to the other sector they simply exchange it for an equal value of the product of that sector, the gain in market due to the purchase of its product by the other sector exactly compensating the loss in market due to its purchase of the product of the other sector. Agriculture does not serve as a solution to industry's market problem simply because there *is* no market problem for industry in this model.[12]

Agriculture's contribution to industrialization in this model is from the supply side, through the provision of wage goods and labour to the industrial sector. The wage goods problem arises from the terms of trade: if the industrial terms of trade deteriorates, industry will have to pay a higher product wage, its profits will be squeezed, and accumulaion in industry will be reduced, as shown by equation (7). If the agricultural sector grows faster at a given p (say due to a higher s_a) this will make the industrial sector grow faster in equilibrium, but only because it relaxes the wage-goods constraint, turning the terms of trade towards industry. The labour supply problem arises if τ increases which, as we have seen above, will push the g_n curve to the left and reduce the rate of growth.

This discussion makes it clear that the role of agriculture in this model is similar to its roles in the neoclassical and classical models criticized by Thirlwall. All three models—neoclassical, classical and Kaldorian—assume away demand problems. The neoclassical one (Jorgenson (1961) for example) is different from the others because it assumes that labour is fully employed,

---

[12] The dynamic analysis of Section 3 casts further doubt on Thirlwall's interpretations. In our first characterization there is no sense in which positions out of long-run equilibrium can be called 'demand-constrained', *pace* Thirlwall: the markets clear at any short-run equilibrium. Along a dynamic path when k changes, and given the parameters of the model, if g_n rises over time g_a must fall, which is contrary to what would happen if a higher agricultural growth increased the demand for industrial output and made it grow faster. It is true that a rightward shift in the g_a curve (due to a parametric shift) which increases equilibrium g_a would increase the *equilibrium* growth-rate of the industrial sector, but this must be true in *any* dynamic equilibrium for any model with a balanced growth equilibrium path (as was the case for the Lewis and Jorgenson models as well). While the last two comments apply for our rigid-price model as well, the first does not, since disequilibrium states with excess demand and supply are possible. But, as Fig. 2 makes it clear, there is no one-to-one relation between excess demand or supply for the industrial good, and whether we are above or below the equilibrium p; the direction of excess demand depends on k as well.

A KALDORIAN MODEL REVISITED

but Lewis's and Kaldor's are similar: they both assume that surplus labour exists (so that the wage in industry in terms of the agricultural good is fixed), and that all savings are automatically invested. The only real difference between the two is that the Kaldorian model assumes that there is no intersectoral capital mobility, all savings being invested within the sector of origin, while the Lewis (1954, 1972) model in which the two sectors of a closed economy trade with each other assumes that there is no investment in agriculture where output grows only due to technological change, and the agricultural surplus is invested in the industrial sector.[13] We are thus entitled to call the Kaldorian model a classical one, similar in spirit to the Lewis model.[14]

If demand issues are to be adequately introduced into the Kaldorian framework we need to modify the model of Section 2. In that model we resolved the contradiction between the markup-pricing equation (10) and wage equation (5) by jettisoning the former, but demand issues can be brought in by retaining the markup equation and forsaking (5) instead.[15] This alternative model appears to be closer in spirit to some of Kaldor's other work on the terms of trade and growth, where it is assumed that there is markup pricing in industry, while the agricultural terms of trade are flexible and demand-determined.[16]

Because industry practices markup pricing, it may be assumed that firms adjust output according to demand, so that they have excess capacity; thus we dispense also with the full-capacity assumption given by (4). Maintaining the full-capacity and flex-price assumptions for the agricultural sector, the supply-demand balance equations for the two markets can be written as

$$-[\alpha(1-s_a) + s_a]a_a k/p + (1-\alpha)\{[1+(1-s_n)z]/(1+z)\}u = 0 \quad (18)$$

$$\alpha(1-s_a)a_a k/p - \{1 - \alpha[1+(1-s_n)z]/(1+z)\}u + g_n + g_a k = 0 \quad (19)$$

where $u = Q_n/K_n$, a measure of capacity utilization in the industrial sector. To complete the model we assume that industrial investment depends positively on the rate of capacity utilization in industry,[17] so that, in a simple linear form,

---

[13] Lewis (1954) appears at times to assume away trade between two sectors, but our comments are relevant for his model in which the two sectors produce different products and trade with each other (see pp. 172–3). This corresponds to the second of the three models in Lewis (1972).

[14] See Dutt (1989) for a formal comparison of the alternative models discussed here—as well as others—in terms of a common general framework.

[15] We could actually retain both, determining the terms of trade from (11). In the short run, for given k, we could then determine the level of capacity utilization from the market-clearing equation for the agricultural sector—see equation (18) below. In the long run, with p determined, the sectoral growth rates are determined by (3) and the agricultural market-clearing equation solves for k.

[16] See Kaldor's (1976) analysis of the interaction between the primary producing and industrial sectors of the world economy. It is also consistent with Kalecki's (1971) views of pricing. Other 'closures' are possible, which endogenize the markup in industry but introduce an independent investment function, or which introduce foreign trade. While traces of such alternative models can be found in Kaldor's other work, for the sake of brevity we concentrate on just one model.

[17] This follows Kaldor (1940). It is also customary (see Robinson (1962)) to make the rate of profit an argument of the desired accumulaton function in neo-Keynesian growth models. But since (10) implies tha the rate of profit is given by

$$r_n = [z/(1+z)]u,$$

and since we are assuming z to be given in our analysis, this influence is also being captured by the capacity utilization argument.

$$g_n = \sigma + \delta u \tag{20}$$

with positive parameters, and that agricultural investment depends inversely on the industrial terms of trade so that

$$g_a = \varepsilon/p. \tag{21}$$

The structure of this model is similar to those of the 'structuralist' models of Taylor (1982, 1983), the only major differences having to do with the precise specification of the sectoral investment functions.[18]

In the short run, given the sectoral capital stocks and hence k, we assume that the agricultural and industrial goods markets clear, respectively, through variations in P_a and Q_n, which imply variations in p and u. Substituting (20) and (21) into (18) and (19) we solve for the short-run equilibrium values,

$$u = \delta[\alpha(1 - s_a) + s_a]a_a/\Omega \tag{22}$$

$$p = \Omega k/\{\sigma(1 - \alpha)[1 + (1 - s_n)z]/(1 + z)\} \tag{23}$$

where

$$\Omega = [\alpha(1 - s_a) + s_a]a_a\{s_n[z/(1 + z)] - \delta\}$$
$$+ \{(1 - \alpha)(s_a a_a - \varepsilon)[1 + (1 - s_n)z]/(1 + z)\}$$

Short-run stability requires $\Omega > 0$, which we assume.[19] Observing that the short-run equilibrium value of u is independent of k, and substituting this into (20), we can obtain the g_n curve of Fig. 3.[20] Equation (21) is represented by the g_a curve, and equation (23) by line OA. In the short run, given any k, we can determine p, g_n and g_a. In the long run k moves over time to a balanced-growth path at k^*.

If ε increases equation (22) shows that u will increase: a higher rate of agricultural investment increases the demand for industrial goods for investment purposes and raises industrial output in the short run. Since (20) shows that the g_n curve is pushed up as well, the rate of industrial growth is also increased in the long run. In this model, clearly, faster agricultural growth

---

[18] Taylor (1982) assumes that g_n and g_a are functions of sectoral rates of profit. Taylor (1983) takes g_a to be institutionally fixed and g_n to depend on the gap between industrial and agricultural profit rates. Since with a non-capitalist agriculture the agricultural rate of profit is difficult to define, we have assumed that agricultural investment depends on the terms of trade.

[19] This condition will be satisfied when $s_n z/(1 + z) > \delta$ and $s_a a_a > \varepsilon$. The first of these conditions is the familiar condition that the saving response (to variations in u) in the industrial sector exceeds investment response. The second condition implies that capital always flows out of agriculture; $s_a a_a = \varepsilon$ implies, from (21) that there are no intersectoral capital flows. Capital flows into agriculture are not necessarily destabilizing, since this is a sufficient, and not a necessary condition for stability.

[20] If we substitute for Ω from (24) into (23) we will get an inverse relation between p and u *given* k, and hence an inverse relation between p and g_n from (21). However, since this curve would take k as given it could not be used to examine the dynamic path of the economy. What our horizontal g_n line takes into account is the fact that changes in k and p are proportional and leave unaffected the levels of u and g_n.

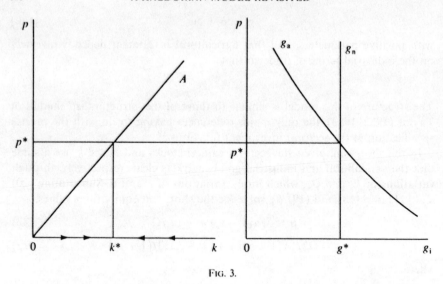

Fig. 3.

increases industrial growth by providing a more rapidly-expanding market for its product.

A comparison of this amended Kaldorian model with the model of Section 2 shows why the latter (and Thirlwall's) does not allow the agricultural sector to play a role in providing a market for the industrial sector. This model differs from the previous ones in two crucial ways. First, it departs from the notion that all saving is identically invested; this is achieved by introducing the independent investment functions. The investment function for the industrial sector implies that the aggregate demand for the industrial good will not identically be equal to its aggregate supply, so that a demand problem for that sector can arise. Second, it allows for intersectoral capital mobility and thereby ensures that the agricultural sector can actually solve the demand problem for the industrial sector by buying from it a different amount than what it sells to it. If we assume away intersectoral capital mobility in the demand-constrained model just discussed and assume $s_a a_a = \varepsilon$, we find, using (18) and (19), that saving equals investment in the industrial sector, or that

$$g_n = s_n[z/(1+z)]u. \tag{24}$$

Equations (20) and (24) then solve for the equilibrium value of u (in both short and long runs), from which it follows that g_n depends only on z, s_n and the investment parameters in the industrial sector. The industrial sector is demand-constrained in the sense that an increase in demand (for instance an increase in σ) will increase the levels of capacity utilization and capital accumulation; but there is still no room for agriculture to solve the market problem for industry: if agricultural income rises (say due to a rise in a_a) the terms of trade will turn against agriculture, but u and g_n will be unchanged. Agricultural expansion does expand industrial demand by raising agricultural income, but since trade is balanced it is exactly offset by a higher demand for agricultural goods by the industrial sector.

5. Conclusion

This paper has developed a consistent, formal Kaldorian model of growth and development, drawing on the work of Thirlwall (1986, 1987). It has also analyzed the disequilibrium dynamics behind the model and demonstrated its dynamic stability, something not adequately done before. This analysis has shown that Kaldorian model is not what Thirlwall—and indeed Kaldor himself—thought it to be, that is, a model of an economy with a fixprice industrial sector and a flexprice agricultural sector, and one which adequately captures the role of the agricultural sector in solving the problem of demand for the industrial sector. Instead, it has shown that the model is similar to that of Lewis which, according to previous interpretations, did not adequately focus on the demand issue.

Though the Kaldorian model does not live up to Thirlwall's expectations, however, we still believe that it is an useful contribution. First, although similar to the Lewis model, it departs from Lewis's static focus on disguised unemployment and develops a dynamic analysis of capital investment and technical change in agriculture which is more relevant for understanding the behaviour of dual economies using industrial capital in agriculture. Second, demand issues can be introduced easily by modifying the model to make it consistent with some of Kaldor's other work. Finally—and this is a direction not pursued in this paper—the model has laid the foundation on which the analysis of several important issues can be based: Canning (1988) demonstrates how the role of increasing returns to scale in dual economies can be analyzed using a Kaldorian model and Dutt (1990) uses the model to analyze the implications of intersectoral capital flows.

University of Notre Dame, Indiana

REFERENCES

CANNING, D. (1988). "Increasing returns in industry and the role of agriculture in growth", *Oxford Economic Papers*, 40, 463–76.
DUTT, A. K. (1989). "Alternative models of agriculture-industry interaction", unpublished, University of Notre Dame.
DUTT, A. K. (1990). "Intersectoral capital mobility in a Kaldorian model of development", unpublished, University of Notre Dame.
FITZGERALD, E. V. K. (1990). "Kalecki on financing development: an approach to the macro-economics of the semi-industrialised economy, *Cambridge Journal of Economics*, 14(2), June, 183–203.
JORGENSON, D. (1961). "The development of a dual economy", *Economic Journal*, 71, 309–34.
KALDOR, N. (1940). "A Model of the Trade Cycle", *Economic Journal*, March.
KALDOR, N. (1975). "What is wrong with economic theory", *Quarterly Journal of Economics*, August.

KALDOR, N. (1976). "Inflation and Recession in the World Economy", *Economic Journal*, 86, December.

KALDOR, N. (1979). "Equilibrium Theory and Growth Theory", in M. J. Boskin (ed.), *Economics and Human Welfare. Essays in Honor of Tibor Scitovsky*, New York, Academic Press.

KALECKI, M. (1971). *Selected Essays on the Dynamics of the Capitalist Economy*, Cambridge, Cambridge University Press.

KALECKI, M. (1972). *Selected Essays on the Economic Growth of the Socialist and Mixed Economy*, Cambridge, Cambridge University Press.

LEWIS, W. A. (1954). "Economic Development with Unlimited Supplies of Labour", *Manchester School of Economics and Social Studies*, 22, 139-91.

LEWIS, W. A. (1972). "Reflections on Unlimited Labour" in L. di Marco (ed.), *International Economics and Development, Essays in Honor of Raul Prebisch*, New York, Academic Press.

ROBINSON, J. (1962). *Essays in the Theory of Economic Growth*, London, Macmillan.

TARGETTI, F. (1985). "Growth and the terms of trade: a Kaldorian two sector model", *Metroeconomica*, February, 79-96.

TAYLOR, L. (1982). "Food Price Inflation, Terms of Trade and Growth", in M. Gersovitz, C. F. Diaz-Alejandro, G. Ranis and M. R. Rosenzweig (eds), *The Theory and Experience of Economic Development*, London, George Allen and Unwin.

TAYLOR, L. (1983). *Structuralist Macroeconomics*, New York, Basic Books.

THIRLWALL, A. P. (1986). "A General Model of Growth and Development on Kaldorian Lines", *Oxford Economic Papers*, 38, 199-219.

A KALDORIAN MODEL OF GROWTH AND DEVELOPMENT REVISITED: A REJOINDER TO DUTT

By A. P. THIRLWALL

THE original purpose of Kaldor's two-sector model of agriculture and industry, which he lectured on in Cambridge for many years but never formalised, was to explain the pace and rhythm of output growth of the industrialised countries in the world economy. He assigned to the terms of trade the crucial role of bringing into balance the growth of demand for industrial output with the growth of potential supply. The two sectors are mutually dependent on each other as a source of supply and demand. As Kaldor (1976) wrote,

> ...continued and stable economic progress requires the growth of output in these two sectors should be at the required relationship with each other—that is to say, the growth of the saleable output of agriculture and mining should be in line with the growth of demand, which in turn reflects the growth of the secondary (and tertiary) sectors. However, from a technical standpoint there can be no guarantee that the rate of growth of primary production, propelled by land saving innovations, proceeds at the precise rate warranted by the growth of production and incomes in the secondary and tertiary sectors. To ensure that it does is the function of the price mechanism, more particularly of relative prices, or the 'terms of trade' between primary commodities and manufactured goods.

The failure of the terms of trade to adjust would lead to sub-optimal growth in the system as a whole. For example, industrial growth would be supply constrained if the terms of trade were too favourable to agriculture, and demand constrained if the terms of trade were too favourable to industry so that the agricultural sector did not have the purchasing power to buy industrial goods.

For those listening to Kaldor's lectures it was clear that what he was saying at the world level had equal applicability to an individual developing economy closed to trade with a large agricultural sector and a nascent industrial sector. It is important to get 'right' the terms of trade between agriculture and industry if the growth of either sector is not to be stifled either from the supply side or the demand side by relative prices being either 'too high' or 'too low'. Classical development theory, as epitomised by the Lewis (1954) model, focuses on the supply side. The lower the price of agricultural (wage) goods relative to industrial goods, the higher the level of industrial profits, the greater the rate of investment and the faster the growth of industrial output is assumed to be. The question of whether industrial output can be sold is side-stepped. Johnston and Mellor (1961) recognised this worrying feature of the Lewis classical model many years ago when they remarked,

> ...one of the simplifying assumptions of the (Lewis) two-sector model is that expansion of the capitalist sector is limited only by a shortage of capital. Given this assumption, an increase in rural net cash income is not a stimulus to industrialisation

but an obstacle to expansion of the capitalist sector...there is clearly a conflict between emphasis on agriculture's essential contribution to the capital requirement for overall development and emphasis on increased farm purchasing power as a stimulus to industrialization. Nor is there any easy reconciliation of the conflict.

It is true, as Dutt points out, that in a later model Lewis (1972) allows trade between the agricultural and industrial sectors, but the two sectors are not formally integrated and the equilibrium terms of trade derived. The beauty of Kaldor's model is that the two sectors are brought together in an equilibrium framework to resolve the conflict referred to by Johnston and Mellor, showing clearly the circumstances under which a rise in the price of agricultural products relative to industrial goods will or will not raise the industrial growth rate. In accordance with the classical model, for example, Lewis remarks that the record of every imperial power in modern Africa was one of impoverishing the agricultural sector so that industry could get its labour input cheap in real terms, but the Kaldor model shows that this will not increase the industrial growth rate unless the terms of trade move in favour of agriculture allowing the industrial goods to be sold. The purpose of my original paper was to lay out the structure of Kaldor's model in equation form, and to examine its properties (see also Targetti (1985)). It is essentially a model of reciprocal demand in which the output level of each sector is a function of the demand coming from the other in relation to its propensity to import. It is in this sense that the output of the industrial sector is determined by demand coming from agriculture.

Dutt's paper makes a valuable contribution to an understanding of the dynamics of Kaldor's model and of its properties if excess capacity is allowed for in the industrial sector, but on the central question of the role of demand, I believe there is a semantic confusion between us. Dutt's major argument seems to be that Kaldor's model is no different from a classical (Lewis-type) model because if in equilibrium one sector clears, the other sector must clear, and therefore the problem of demand does not arise. As Dutt puts it 'agriculture does not serve as a solution to industry's market problem because there is no market problem for industry in this model'. There are two responses. The first is that in none of the Lewis models is an equilibrium explicitly derived. Secondly, I never claimed that agriculture serves as a solution to industry's market problem—rather that in an equilibrium framework, the output of one sector must be seen as a function of the output of the other, and not simply as a function of inputs into the sector. To say that there is not a demand problem for industry in a demand-deficiency sense, does not mean that the level of output is independent of demand. There is a difference between the question of whether any level of output is self-financing (à la Say's Law), and the question of what determines output in the first place. It is true that in Kaldor's model industrial output is self-financing, but it is the demand for investment goods coming from agriculture, in relation to the industrial sector's propensity to import agricultural (wage) goods, that in equilibrium determines the level of industrial output, which is not the same as Lewis's classical model. The result can be shown as follows: at the equilibrium growth rate in Dutt's Fig. 1 (his equation (9) and assuming $s_n = 1$) industrial and agricultural output will be in a particular relationship to each other. If agricultural output (wage goods) demanded in exchange for industrial output is $\tau b_n Q_n$ (where τ is the industrial real wage, b_n is the labour-output ratio in industry, and Q_n is industrial output), and agricultural output offered (agricultural saving) is $s_a Q_a$ (where s_a is the agricultural savings ratio and Q_a is agricultural output), then in equilibrium the ratio of industrial to agricultural output must be: $Q_n/Q_a = s_a/\tau b_n$, or $Q_n = I_a/\tau b_n$ (where $I_a = s_a Q_a p$). In other words, at a given terms of trade ($p = 1$) at which trade is balanced, industrial output is a linear multiple, $1/\tau b_n$, of the export of industrial goods (to agriculture) where τb_n is the propensity of the industrial sector to import (agricultural goods). Interestingly, as I pointed out in the original paper, this is exactly the static Harrod trade multiplier result (but at the sectoral level) that with balanced trade, a constant terms of trade, and exports as the only component of autonomous demand, the national income will equal $Y = X/m$, where X is the level of export demand and m is the marginal propensity to import. Variations in agricultural output leading to variations in the demand for industrial goods will lead to variations in the equilibrium level of industrial output. In fact, the long run property of the model that Kaldor wanted to stress (at least at the world level) is that given diminishing returns to agriculture, the rate of growth of demand for industrial goods will fall leading to a lower growth of industrial output at a given terms of trade unless offset by a positive rate of technical progress or land-saving innovations in agriculture.

Dutt wants to argue that 'we are entitled to call the Kaldorian model a classical one similar in spirit to the Lewis model' because terms of trade changes brought about by shifts in the agricultural output growth curve work only through the supply side. When the agricultural growth curve shifts outwards there is an increase in the demand for investment goods from industry and the improvement in industry's terms of trade allows the industrial sector to grow faster. I do not regard this as a purely supply orientated model in the classical sense. In fact, in this case, demand, in a sense, generates its own supply! In referring to the absence of demand considerations in the classical model, I had in mind the case where there is an autonomous increase in the supply of industrial output through a reduction of real wages or an increase in labour productivity which would shift outwards the g_n curve. The Kaldor model permits the supply to be demanded through movements in the terms of trade.[1]

---

[1] It is crucial to the Kaldor model that the terms of trade are free to vary, but Dutt says that the pricing assumptions of the model do not allow this because the assumption of markup pricing in industry fixes the terms of trade: $p = (1 + z)\tau b_n$, where z is the fixed percentage markup on unit labour costs. I do not understand this. The fact that labour is elastic at a given real wage (τ) does not mean that the real wage is necessarily constant. τ can change if the productivity of labour in agriculture changes and the price of agricultural goods changes. p can also change if b_n changes.

A REJOINDER TO DUTT

If the terms of trade did not adjust (i.e. improve for agriculture) there would be a problem of demand for industry. Indeed, in a classical model it would be theoretically possible for the terms of trade required to equilibriate the supply and demand for agricultural goods to be so low as to violate the minimum set by whatever real wage is demanded in industry. The assumption of a two-sector equivalent of Say's Law brought about by relative price changes would be as invalid as Say's Law in the one sector model which may require an unfeasible rate of interest to balance the supply and demand for savings.

It is apparent that there are different types of demand problems. In the 'open economy' there is the demand problem associated with a (dis)equilibrium terms of trade as I have been discussing above. There are also demand problems associated with not all saving being invested which, I agree, the Kaldor model assumes away, and which Dutt focuses on in his model. In his extension of the model to allow for excess capacity in the industrial sector Dutt ends with the conclusion 'faster agricultural growth increases industrial growth by providing a more rapidly expanding market for its product'—but I would say this is equally true in the model without excess capacity but with demand generating its own supply working through variations in the terms of trade. With excess capacity, clearly terms of trade changes are unnecessary.

In conclusion, I therefore disagree that Kaldor's two-sector model is no different from Lewis's 1954 classical model. Kaldor's is a model of reciprocal demand in which the terms of trade determine demand as well as supply, and in which it can be shown that the equilibrium level of industrial output depends on demand from agriculture (i.e. industrial exports) which must match the leakage of expenditure from industry to agriculture: just as in standard trade theory where the terms of trade are constant, and income adjusts to preserve balance of payments equilibrium.

Keynes College, The University of Kent at Canterbury

REFERENCES

JOHNSTON, B. F. and MELLOR, J. W. (1961). "The Role of Agriculture in Economic Development", *American Economic Review*, September.

KALDOR, N. (1976). "Inflation and Recession in the World Economy", *Economic Journal*, December.

LEWIS, W. A. (1954). "Economic Development with Unlimited Supplies of Labour", *Manchester School*, May.

LEWIS, W. A. (1972). "Reflections on Unlimited Labour" in L. di Marco (ed.), *International Economics and Development: Essays in Honour of Raul Prebisch*, New York, Academic Press.

TARGETTI, F. (1985). Growth and the Terms of Trade: A Kaldorian Two-Sector Model, *Metroeconomica*, February.

Name Index

Allen, R. G. D. 224
Allsop, C. 74
Arrow, K. 266, 273, 287, 337
Atkinson, A. B. 266

Balassa, B. 553
Ball, R. J. 327
Bergevin, J. 565
Beveridge, W. 13, 38
Bharadwaj, V. P. 371
Bowles, S. 62
Brechling, F. W. 242, 322, 327
Brown, M. 337
Brown, P. 224
Burgstaller, A. 593

Callaghan, J. 75
Cannan, E. 4, 179
Chamberlin, E. 7, 243
Champernowne, D. 19, 43
Chatterji, M. 62, 435, 442
Chenery, H. 337, 372
Clark, C. 57
Clark, J. M. 15
Cohen, R. 36
Cole, W. 396
Cornwall, J. 377, 381, 456, 472
Costabile, L. 574, 587
Cripps, T. F. 74, 349, 355, 360, 368, 378, 395, 419, 447, 464
Croome, H. 38
Currie, D. 587

Davidson, P. 76, 81
de Cani, J. 337
Deane, P. 396
Dixon, R. 81, 570
Domar, E. 17, 98, 176, 388
Dutt, A. K. 609, 612

Eatwell, J. 49
Encarnación, J. 197

Fei, J. C. H. 554
Feinstein, C. H. 396
Findlay, R. E. 187, 191, 585, 587
Fisher, I. 510
Ford, H. 479
Friedman, M. 10, 39, 70, 76

Gaitskell, H. 15
Gifford, C. 15
Goldschmidt, C. 29
Gomulka, S. 348, 359, 362, 371, 459
Gordon, D. M. 62
Grubert, H. 187

Hacche, G. 54
Hahn, F. H. 41, 224, 272
Harcourt, G. C. 41
Harrod, R. F. 11, 17, 40, 49, 82, 98, 108, 126, 159, 181, 272
Hart, A. G. 549
Hayek, F. A. von 7, 29, 39, 47, 522
Hicks, J. R. 7, 29, 35, 72, 81, 97, 179, 482, 491, 522, 527
Hill, A. T. P. 410, 451
Hirschleifer, J. 65
Hobson, J. A. 87
Houthakker, H. 500

Johnston, B. F. 553, 611
Johnston, J. 320
Jorgenson, D. W. 536, 553, 665
Junz, H. 500

Kahn, R. 30, 35, 43, 72
Kaldor, J. 28
Kalecki, M. 41, 53, 67, 72, 79, 179, 238, 243, 272, 537, 600
Kanbur, S. N. R. 596
Kennedy, C. 81, 570
Keynes, J. M. 7, 12, 30, 88, 109, 135, 160, 265, 524, 563
Kilpatrick, A. 62
Kindleberger, C. P. 455
King, J. E. 70
Kmenta, J. 395, 399
Knapp, B. 14
Knight, F. 5, 38, 47
Kornai, J. 507
Kregel, J. A. 40, 54
Kubota, K. 241
Kuh, E. 327

Langlois, R. N. 67
Lawson, T. 62
Lerner, A. P. 180
Lewis, A. W. 535, 552, 587, 604, 611, 614

Lie, T. 15
Lockwood, W. W. 553
Luxemburg, R. 179

Madansky, A. 453
Magee, S. 500
Malthus, T. R. 573
Marglin, S. 596
Marshall, A. 4, 109, 286, 323, 508, 543
Marx, K. 10, 28, 39, 134, 176, 245
Matthews, R. C. O. 224
McCallum, B. T. 257
McCombie, J. S. L. 61, 407, 455, 459
McGibbon, J. 410, 451
Meade, J. E. 573
Mellor, J. W. 553, 611
Michl, T. R. 62
Minhas, B. 337
Mirrlees, J. A. 41, 234, 272
Moggridge, D. 564
Molana, H. 42
Moore, B. 77
Muscatelli, A. 587
Myrdal, G. 480, 489, 514, 523

Neild, R. R. 327
Neumann, J. von 29, 35, 38, 43
Nurkse, R. 554
Nuti, M. 239, 241, 246

Olivera, J. 564

Paige, D. 284
Papola, T. S. 371
Parikh, A. 63, 423, 454, 472
Pasinetti, L. L. 35, 43, 245
Prebisch, R. 543, 554, 570

Ranis, G. 554
Reddaway, B. 274
Reder, M. W. 371
Rhomberg, R. 500
Ricardo, D. 31, 42, 179, 543, 573, 587
Robbins, L. C. 4, 29, 35, 504, 523
Robertson, D. H. 20, 268
Robertson, N. 14
Robinson, J. 7, 13, 30, 35, 37, 42, 54, 67, 79, 176, 183, 241, 243, 265, 586
Rothbart, E. 13, 29
Rowthorn, R. E. 60, 357, 362, 373, 388, 392, 395, 400, 409, 422, 446, 468, 573, 587
Rybczynski, T. M. 186

Salter, W. E. G. 42, 288, 322
Samuelson, P. A. 73, 515
Schumpeter, J. A. 87
Scitovsky, T. 29, 38
Seers, D. 570
Sen, A. 552
Singer, H. 543
Smith, A. 48, 66, 286, 458, 543
Solow, R. M. 187, 327, 337, 388, 573
Spence, M. 65
Spraos, J. 565
Sraffa, P. 13, 30, 35, 42, 67, 79
Stiglitz, J. E. 266
Stoneman, P. 429
Sylos-Labini, P. 537

Targetti, F. 42, 612
Tarling, R. J. 74, 349, 355, 360, 368, 378, 395, 419, 447, 464
Taylor, L. 372, 587
Thirlwall, A. P. 39, 42, 58, 64, 70, 268, 466, 473, 553, 564, 570, 573, 584, 588, 598, 602, 609
Thirlwall, G. 58
Tinbergen, J. 388, 394, 549
Trevithick, J. 40

Uri, P. 15

Vaciago, G. 469
Venables, A. J. 575
Verdoorn, J. P. 58, 61, 74, 288, 336, 347, 385, 394, 465
Vines, D. 42, 585, 587, 596

Walker, G. 15
Walters, H. E. 553
Webb, U. K. 522
Weintraub, S. 76
Weisskopf, T. E. 62
Weitzman, M. L. 40, 70
Whale, B. 82
Wickens, M. R. 62, 435, 442
Wicksell, K. 5, 35, 179, 523
Wold, H. O. A. 454
Wolfe, J. N. 329, 334, 371, 468, 472
Wood, A. 536
Worswick, D. 40

Young, A. A. 4, 29, 35, 267, 286, 333, 458, 461, 465, 480, 553

The International Library of Critical Writings in Economics

1. Multinational Corporations
   Mark Casson

2. The Economics of Innovation
   Christopher Freeman

3. Entrepreneurship
   Mark Casson

4. International Investment
   Peter J. Buckley

5. Game Theory in Economics
   Ariel Rubinstein

6. The History of Economic Thought
   Mark Blaug

7. Monetary Theory
   Thomas Mayer

8. Joint Production of Commodities
   Neri Salvadori and Ian Steedman

9. Industrial Organization
   Oliver E. Williamson

10. Growth Theory (Volumes I, II and III)
    R. Becker and E. Burmeister

11. Microeconomics: Theoretical and Applied (Volumes I, II and III)
    Robert E. Kuenne

12. The Economics of Health (Volumes I and II)
    A.J. Culyer

13. Recent Developments in Macroeconomics (Volumes I, II and III)
    Edmund S. Phelps

14. Urban and Regional Economics
    Paul C. Cheshire and Alan W. Evans

15. Modern Public Finance (Volumes I and II)
    A.B. Atkinson

16. Exchange Rate Economics (Volumes I and II)
    Ronald MacDonald and Mark P. Taylor

17. The Economic Value of Education: Studies in the Economics of Education
    Mark Blaug

18. Development Economics (Volumes I, II, III and IV)
    Deepak Lal

19. The New Classical Macroeconomics (Volumes I, II and III)
    Kevin D. Hoover

20. The Economics of the Environment
    Wallace E. Oates

21. Post Keynesian Theory of Growth and Distribution
    Carlo Panico and Neri Salvadori

22. Dynamic Labor Demand and Adjustment Costs
    Giorgio Galeazzi and Daniel S. Hamermesh

23. The Philosophy and Methodology of Economics (Volumes I, II and III)
    Bruce J. Caldwell

24. Public Choice Theory (Volumes I, II and III)
    Charles K. Rowley

25. Evolutionary Economics
    Ulrich Witt

26. Economics and Psychology
    Shlomo Maital and Sharone L. Maital

27. Social Choice Theory (Volumes I, II and III)
    Charles K. Rowley

28. Non-Linear Dynamics in Economic Theory
    Marc Jarsulic

29. Recent Developments in Experimental Economics (Volumes I and II)
    John D. Hey and Graham Loomes

30. Monopoly and Competition Policy (Volumes I and II)
    F.M. Scherer

31. The Economics of Technical Change
    Edwin Mansfield and Elizabeth Mansfield

32. The Economics of Exhaustible Resources
    Geoffrey Heal

33. The Economics of Institutions
    Geoffrey M. Hodgson

34. The Economics of Transport (Volumes I and II)
   Herbert Mohring

35. Implicit Contract Theory
   Sherwin Rosen

36. Foundations of Analytical Marxism (Volumes I and II)
   John E. Roemer

37. The Economics of Product Differentiation (Volumes I and II)
   Jacques-François Thisse and George Norman

38. Economic Growth in Theory and Practice: A Kaldorian Perspective
   John E. King

Future titles will include:

Markets and Socialism
Alec Nove and Ian D. Thatcher

Recent Developments in the Economics of Education
Geraint Johnes and Elchanan Cohn

Economics and Discrimination
William A. Darity, Jr

The Theory of Inflation
Michael Parkin

The Economics of Information
David K. Levine and Steven A. Lippman

Financial Intermediaries
M.K. Lewis

The Political Economy of Privatization and Deregulation
Elizabeth E. Bailey and Janet Rothenberg Pack

Gender and Economics
Jane Humphries

The Economics of Location
Melvin L. Greenhut and George Norman

The Economics of Altruism
Stephano Zamagni

Economics and Biology
Geoffrey M. Hodgson

Fiscal and Monetary Policy
Thomas Mayer and Stephen Sheffrin

General Equilibrium Theory
Gerard Debreu

International Trade
J. Peter Neary

The Foundations of Public Finance
Peter Jackson

Labor Economics
Orley C. Ashenfelter and Kevin F. Hallock

International Finance
Robert Z. Aliber

Welfare Economics
William J. Baumol and Janusz A. Ordover

Agricultural Economics
G.H. Peters

The Theory of the Firm
Mark Casson

The Economics of Inequality and Poverty
A.B. Atkinson

Business Cycle Theory
Finn E. Kydland

The Economics of Housing
John M. Quigley

Population Economics
Julian L. Simon

The Economics of Crime
Isaac Ehrlich

The Economics of Integration
Willem Molle

The Rhetoric of Economics
Donald McCloskey

Ethics and Economics
Amitai Etzioni

Migration
Oded Stark

The Economics of Ageing
John Creedy

Economic Forecasting
Paul Ormerod

Macroeconomics and Imperfect Competition
Jean-Pascal Benassy

The Economics of Training
Robert J. LaLonde

The Economics of Defence
Keith Hartley and Nicholas Hooper

Transaction Cost Economics
Oliver Williamson

Long Wave Theory
Christopher Freeman

Consumer Theory
Kelvin Lancaster

Law and Economics
Judge Richard A. Posner

The Economics of Business Policy
John Kay

International Debt
Graham Bird and P.N. Snowdon

Rent Seeking
Robert D. Tollison

The Role of Money in the Economy
Marco Musella and Carlo Panico

Small Firms and Economic Growth
Zoltan Acs